CYPRESS TREES
IN THE GARDEN

CYPRESS TREES IN THE GARDEN

The Second Generation of
Zen Teaching in North America

Richard Bryan McDaniel

CYPRESS TREES IN THE GARDEN
The Second Generation of Zen Teaching in America
Richard Bryan McDaniel

Text © Richard Bryan McDaniel, 2015
Cover photo of cypress trees © Thomas Quine
www.flickr.com/photos/91994044@N00/6064068908/
Cover photo of Golden Gate Park Buddha © B. Joan McDaniel
Cover photos of bell and meditation hall © Richard B. McDaniel
Author photo © Geoff Gammon

Designed by Karma Yönten Gyatso

Published by
The Sumeru Press Inc.
PO Box 2089, Richmond Hill, ON
Canada L4E 1A3

LIBRARY AND ARCHIVES CANADA CATALOGUING IN PUBLICATION

McDaniel, Richard Bryan, author
    Cypress trees in the garden : The second generation of Zen teaching in America
    / by Richard Bryan McDaniel.

Includes glossary.
Issued in print and electronic formats.
ISBN 978-1-896559-26-1 (pbk.).--ISBN 978-1-896559-27-8 (epub)

    1. Zen Buddhists--United States--Biography. 2. Buddhist monks--United
States--Biography. 3. Zen Buddhism--United States--History. I. Title.

BQ9298.M34 2015   294.3'927092273   C2015-900189-7   C2015-900190-0

 For more information about The Sumeru Press
visit us at *www.sumeru-books.com*

ıy children and grandchildren:
ıvıadeline: Alexa, Katie, & Elizabeth
Jessica: Bryan Michael, Megan, Declan, & Molly
Bryan Keith
Although this may be a path they never follow,
I take comfort in knowing it is there
should they ever have need of it.

Contents

Author's Note

THIS BOOK PRESENTS A SNAPSHOT – A DESCRIPTION OF ZEN TEACHING, PRACtice, and engagement at a particular time. The interviews on which these chapters are based were conducted between March 2013 and September 2014. Even during that short period, significant changes occurred at several of the sites I visited, including the deaths of three of the teachers discussed. Just as this book was being prepared for publication, I received notice that a fourth teacher appeared to be approaching the end of her life; an appeal went out to raise funds for her medical costs because, after a long life dedicated to the Dharma, she did not have adequate insurance to cover the cost of the full-time caregiver she required.

So the book is already a portrait of how things were rather than how they are.

Because I have allowed the individuals interviewed to speak for themselves with as little interference as possible, I have not always defined Zen or Buddhist terms in the course of the narrative as I have done in my previous books. There is, however, a glossary at the end of the book for the benefit of those who might find it useful.

Richard Bryan McDaniel
Fredericton, New Brunswick, Canada
July 2015

A monk asked Zhaozhou,
"What is the significance of Buddhism?"
Zhaozhou replied, "The cypress tree in the garden."

Prologue

THE YOUNG MAN ASSIGNED TO KEEP ME COMPANY DURING DINNER LOOKS more like the football player he had been than the monk he now is. He smashes five hard boiled eggs in a bowl before spreading them on bread and asks me, "What do you want your book to do?"

I was used to people asking what the book was to be about, and I had a stock answer to that question: It would demonstrate the scope of teaching, practice, and social engagement in contemporary North American Zen. But that wasn't what he'd asked me. He asked what I wanted the book *to do*, and that question – like a good koan – startles me into an unexpected answer. "I think I just want to demonstrate that Zen's still a viable spiritual path." The young monk nods his head as if that were a reasonable goal even though there, in the refectory at Zen Mountain Monastery in the summer of 2013, it certainly doesn't seem as if there is any question about Zen's viability.

ZMM, as it's known, is located on the eastern side of the Catskill Mountains about ten miles from the town of Woodstock, where murals of Janis Joplin and Jimmy Hendrix still grace the walls and windows of downtown businesses. The buildings at ZMM preserve a different kind of cultural legacy. The main structure, where we are dining, is a beautiful National Heritage site originally constructed as a Roman Catholic retreat center by Norwegian priests in the 1930s. It is impressive, with vaulted inner stairways and intricate ironwork on the doors and windows. Hinges are individually and elaborately crafted; one portrays a mother robin feeding three young. The inside handle to the door leading to the parking lot is shaped like a grasshopper, which seems appropriate to someone whose interest in Zen had been – at least partially – twigged by the 1970s television show, *Kung Fu*. The zendo is located in what had formerly been the chapel. It accommodates 104 people, and, judging from the numbers at dinner, it will likely be full in the morning.

In addition to residents, like my companion, there are two groups of retreatants at the monastery this evening. One group, just registered, is beginning an art retreat.

The other group is in the middle of a wilderness retreat led by the monastery's abbot, Konrad Ryushin Marchaj. It's listed in the program calendar as "Born As the Earth: Wilderness Skills Training" and is described as an opportunity to learn "basic outdoor skills and engage the teachings of the wild in the context of Zen training." Wilderness camping and zazen. Torrential rains have been falling for the last few days, and, when the abbot came in for our interview earlier, he was soaking wet. As he dried his face with a towel, I asked how the retreat was going. "They are learning about desire," he told me in a deep Polish accent that gave his words a sense of gravity. "The desire to be dry; the desire for a nice hot cup of tea."

Eighteen months after my visit, Abbot Marchaj will be asked to resign his position.

Zen practice, rather than Zen theory, is still less than 100 years old in North America. The first authorized teacher to make his home here was Sokei-an Sasaki who did not begin teaching until 1928. So it is fair to say that Zen is still finding its way on this continent. It is also fair to say that it has not had a smooth take off, and thus my response to my dinner companion's question.

About fifty miles away from ZMM, on the other side of the Catskills, is Dai Bosatsu Zendo Kongo-ji, the first Rinzai monastery to be built outside of Asia and arguably the most significant architectural accomplishment of North American Zen. It's not an easy place to get to. One travels along a narrow county road and then up a gravel lane which was partially eroded by the rain at the time of my visit. I had thought that Zen Mountain Monastery, with its 235 acres, was large, but the front gate of Dai Bosatsu is still two miles from the main buildings. This 1400 acre property includes Beecher Lake – the highest lake in the Catskills – and what is now the guest house had been the hunting lodge of Harriet Beecher Stowe's brother. It is a two-storey L-shaped structure with a steeply sloped roof and is pretty much what one would expect a wealthy 19th century family to have built as a private mountain getaway, although one marvels at the effort it must have taken to construct it here. Across the lake, there is a large bronze Buddha seated on a boulder gazing serenely across the water.

But any sense of wonder at finding the Beecher family's lodge hidden back here is quelled when one notices the monastery building itself. A local architect, Davis Hamerstrom, had traveled to Japan to study Zen architecture in Kyoto and, using imported craftsmen when necessary, had recreated a traditional Japanese temple complete with classic tiled roof, tatami mats on oak floors, and sliding shoji screens (inside storm windows). There are stone lanterns on the grounds, a huge bronze bell

– sounded by a log suspended from chains beside it – and, within, there are antique Asian treasures. The whole is a work of art.

But in spite of its beauty, the monastery is nearly empty. At the time of my visit, there are only a handful of monks, and two of these are from Japan.

Dai Bosatsu is the resident training center for the Zen Studies Society of New York, which, at the time of my visit, is still in disarray after its abbot, Eido Shimano, had been pressured into resigning three years earlier because of sexual interference with female students. Accounts of Shimano's activities had been accumulating for decades. While I was conducting interviews at Zen Centers throughout North America in 2013, the full extent of his behaviour was chronicled by *New York Times* writer Mark Oppenheimer in an e-book entitled *The Zen Predator of the Upper East Side*.[1] But as outrageous as Shimano's behavior was, his activities had been overshadowed by another story Oppenheimer published in the *Times* just a few weeks before I began my tour.

On February 11, 2013, his *Times* article announced that "Zen Buddhists across the country" were "upset and obsessed" by reports of the sexual improprieties of, then, 105 year old Joshu Sasaki in California. Again the abuse had been going on for decades but had been kept secret until Eshu Martin – a former priest in Sasaki's order – released an article on the internet site *Sweeping Zen* entitled "Everybody Knows." It begins with the bald statement that Sasaki

> – has engaged in many forms of inappropriate sexual relationship with those who have come to him as students since his arrival here more than 50 years ago. His career of misconduct has run the gamut from frequent and repeated non-consensual groping of female students during interviews, to sexually coercive after hours "tea" meetings, to affairs and sexual interference in the marriages and relationships of his students.[2]

Although the term Zen specifically refers to a particular school and practice of Buddhism, it has acquired a number of popular connotations in English. It can suggest tranquility, serenity, peace of mind; it can imply obscure wisdom or spiritual accomplishment. There are books on the "Zen" of archery, gardening, golf, and motorcycle maintenance. It has become a marketing term. There is Zen tea, Zen breakfast cereal, Zen perfume, Zen detergent, the "Zen of Zin" zinfandel, a Zen chocolate chip cookie, a Zen underwire bra, and an early electric car called the

Zenn. Jon Stewart had his "Moment of Zen" at the end of each episode of *The Daily Show*.

The classic definition of Zen is summed up in a four line poem attributed to Bodhidharma, the legendary Indian missionary who brought the practice from India to China:

> A special transmission outside the scriptures;
> Not dependent on words or letters;
> By direct pointing to the mind of man,
> Seeing into one's true nature and attaining Buddhahood.

In spite of that lack of dependence on words and letters, there are hundreds of books in English (including three by me) on the topic. Buddhist scholars like Thomas Tweed and Helen Baroni point out that far more people have read about Zen than have spent any time at a Zen Center. They refer to these as "armchair Buddhists" or "night-stand Buddhists." A few may practice on their own without the aid of a teacher; some might even claim to be "Zennists." The number of North Americans, however, who actually profess to be Buddhists, let alone Zen Buddhists, remains miniscule; 0.7 percent of the population in the United States, according to 2007 census data; the figure is slightly higher (1.1 percent) in Canada. But those percentages include all forms of Buddhism including the rapidly growing Tibetan Buddhist sects. The total number of "Zen Buddhists" in North America can probably be described as "statistically inconsequential." And, with the revelation of the misdeeds of people like Sasaki and Shimano, the number appears to be decreasing, leaving – among other things – the elegant halls of Dai Bosatsu empty.

Unfortunately, Sasaki and Shimano are not alone. The short history of Zen in America has been littered with reports of philandering Zen teachers: Richard Baker in San Francisco; Zenson Gifford in Toronto; Genpo Merzel first in Bar Harbor, Maine, and then again in Salt Lake City; Taizan Maezumi in Los Angeles; the Korean Seung Sahn in Providence. Sasaki and Shimano, however, were in a league of their own.

Both had established thriving Zen Centers in the mainland US after fleeing other locations. Shimano came to New York from Hawaii, after Robert Aitken – the abbot of the Honolulu Diamond Sangha – learned that two female Zen students hospitalized with mental health issues had previously been in sexual relationships with him. Sasaki fled Japan after spending a short time in jail because of an investigation into the misappropriation of funds at a temple where he was *fusu*, or business manager. It was also later revealed that he had fathered at least two children for whom he assumed no responsibility.

The sexual improprieties of both were concealed for decades by center members, both male and female, who remained loyal to their teachers. That loyalty was due to the fact that, in spite of their personal behavior, they were both effective Zen teachers and could be kind and supportive friends. Leonard Cohen has frequently been quoted to the effect that his admiration for Sasaki was such that had Sasaki been a Heidelberg physicist, Cohen would have learned German and studied physics. The novelist and naturalist (and former CIA operative), Peter Matthiessen – although he later withdrew as Shimano's student – wrote movingly about Shimano's sensitivity, friendship, and support during the final illness of Matthiessen's wife, Deborah Love.

Like all of us, Sasaki and Shimano had multiple and contradictory elements in their personalities. The problem was that both were viewed by their students not simply as teachers of Zen but as Zen Masters, and Zen Masters are supposed, at least by their disciples, to be beyond such inconsistencies.

"Zen Master" is an unofficial technical term referring to one who has mastered a particular practice. The model is that of master and apprentice. In Japan, there are masters of the tea ceremony, master flower arrangers, and master swordsmen. There can also be master carpenters, master piano tuners, and master electricians. A master carpenter, for example, might train hundreds of perfectly competent carpenters who anyone would be satisfied to have work on their house, but he may only train one or two persons whose skill matches his own and who have the ability and the inclination to train others. Those that reach that level of accomplishment might be named "master" craftsmen in their own right.

Although Zen Masters are usually priests, they do not have to be and, in America, often are not. But they are all teachers. Individuals attending a temple in North America are unlikely to be passive members of a congregation – as in Asian countries where Buddhism is a devotional religion – but are rather students. Serious students seek instructors who can help them achieve specific goals, and they are often willing to put up with disagreeable quirks of the teacher's personality in order to get that training. In Zen, the goal is spiritual awakening – the "Buddhahood" cited in Bodhidharma's poem – which is variously described by the people profiled in this book, but which, in general, is understood to be an awareness of and deep personal experience of one's interconnectedness, the realization that one's fundamental nature is no different from that of all existence.

Several of the Zen teachers I spoke with pointed out that mastering one aspect of life doesn't mean mastery of others. Zen Masters are not necessarily Tea Masters, and they may not even be very good at arranging flowers. One teacher spoke of "silos of development," suggesting that the attainment of spiritual insight does not in itself imply personal or emotional maturity.

Gerry Shishin Wick is one of the students who remained loyal to Taizan Maezumi after it was discovered that he was an alcoholic and had been involved in affairs with some of his female students. During my conversation with him, Shishin pointed out that he had come to Maezumi to learn the Dharma. "If I wanted to learn to play the violin, I'd find the best master I could to teach me to play the violin. Now, if he was mean to his children, that may or may not affect whether I continued to study the violin…. I don't lightly abandon people. If it were my father, I wouldn't abandon him, and Maezumi Roshi was my spiritual father. So I stayed there and helped right the ship."

But then – unlike Sasaki and Shimano – Maezumi acknowledged culpability, expressed remorse, and sought help by going into an alcoholic rehabilitation program.

Both Sasaki and Shimano were effective teachers. They made the Dharma appealing. They inspired people, and they successfully guided students to some degree of awakening. Even some of the women who complained about their behavior expressed gratitude for them as teachers. One of the women who wrote to the Witnessing Council established in response to the "Sasaki Affair" described both the times she had suffered unwanted sexual advances from Sasaki – whom she refers to by his title, Roshi – and her frustration with the "intimidating culture of hierarchy and secrecy" at Sasaki's primary center, Rinzai-ji in Los Angeles. Then she goes on to say:

> I stayed with Roshi because my experience largely was that he was a great and gifted Zen and koan teacher, and I believe I received great benefit from the other sanzen meetings – those unburdened by his sexual interests. I had met with other Roshis and teachers, but I felt he was absolutely the deepest and best teacher.[3]

Others were unable to accept the disconnection between the teaching and the teacher. A poem by a female student, Karen Tasaka who died in 2010, was first circulated privately and then more widely on the internet. It had been written in 1988:

Roshi, you are a sexual abuser
"Come" you say as you pull me from a handshake onto your lap

"Open" you say as you push your hands between my knees, up my thighs
fondle my breasts
rub my genitals
french kiss me

you put my hand on your genitals
stroke your penis
jack you off?
this is sanzen?
...
We came to you with the trust of a student
You were our teacher
You betrayed us
You violated our bodies
You rape our souls

You betrayed our previous student-teacher relationship
You abuse us as women
You emasculate our husbands and boyfriends

Roshi, you are a sexual abuser
Your nuns you make your sexual servants
Your monks and oshos are crippled with denial
Roshi, Sexual Abuser.[4]

In the face of anguish such as that expressed in this poem, talk of "silos of development" seems facile.

Zen practitioners daily chant the Four Vows, promising to save (liberate) "all beings without number," to eliminate "endless blind passions," to pass innumerable Dharma Gates, and to achieve "the great way of Buddha." The most fundamental ethical teaching of Buddhism is *ahimsa*: "Do no injury." And yet the blind passions of Shimano, Sasaki, and other Zen teachers and leaders have caused enormous harm not only to the women in their sanghas but to all practitioners within the wider Zen community throughout North America.

As I sit in the dining hall at Zen Mountain Monastery, it appears that although North American Zen has been wounded, it is still too early to toll its death knell. And perhaps something valuable will come out of all the suffering. Shishin Wick provided me this felicitous analogy: "Due to the difficulties, there is more awareness among American teachers about integrating compassionate living with awakening. I use the example of the development of the lathe. The first lathe was handmade and was crude. But that lathe could be used to make another more accurate lathe which could be used to make an even more precise lathe and so on. Zen and Buddhism will evolve in the US gradually. My prayer is that the original depth of understanding will not be lost."

Unfortunately, Zen leaders continue to fall from grace.

Only three weeks after I had submitted the first draft of this present book to the publisher, I received an e-mail from the head of the order to which ZMM belongs informing me that Ryushin Marchaj had been relieved of his duties as abbot. By Ryushin's own admission, he had been engaged in "an intimate relationship with someone outside our sangha," thus betraying his partner, a member of the order, "breaking our spiritual union vows and ending our marriage." He also admitted that he had been exploring "shamanic traditions and religions" and that his inclusion of elements of these in his presentation of the Dharma "was irresponsible and might have caused some confusion, and may make people have doubt in the dharma."[5]

The lathe still requires – and, doubtless, will continue to require – refinement.

ZMM is more than one man, even if that man is the abbot, and I remain impressed by both the level of commitment I found there as well as the sheer scope of the program. Zen's evolution on these shores is proceeding in ways none of the pioneers who brought it here could have foreseen. And if some of the experiments – such as shamanism – may be questionable, others have proven unexpectedly fruitful, opening up opportunities for practitioners not only here but around the world.

ZMM is a serious residential training center associated with the Mountains and Rivers Zen Order in the same way Dai Bosatsu is associated with the Zen Studies Society. There are thirty-one residents when I visit, ranging in age from 20 to 86, each of whom – like Asian students of previous centuries who were kept waiting at the gate before being allowed inside the temple grounds – had to formally petition for permission to enter. Prospective residents stand at the threshold and recite:

> I come here realizing the question of Life and Death is a vital matter
> I wish to enter the Zen training program of Zen Mountain Monastery
> I understand the rules of this temple and assume full responsibility
>   for maintaining them
> Please, guide me in my practice.

The program is strict. My dinner companion tells me that when he and his girlfriend, another resident, decided to move in together, they were required to leave the community for three years and then do five hundred prostrations in the Buddha Hall before being considered for readmission to the residential program. Later his partner remarks, "It's interesting how his memory softens it. I remember 1000. We did 500 one day and 500 the next day."

In addition to the residents, I am told that there are about 350 formal students who attend at least two week-long retreats (sesshin) a year plus take part in an annual three month ango or practice period. Then there are the casual participants who come for occasional sitting practice, and others who participate in wilderness retreats, or in retreats on calligraphy, archery (kyudo), watercolours, and so on.

In other locations, in addition to guiding people to awakening – the stated goal of Zen practice – Zen teachers have operated hospice programs for AIDS patients, conducted street retreats in which participants live with the homeless, and developed mindful-eating programs as a means of combating obesity. At Dai Bosatsu and the Zen Studies Society of New York, the current abbess is not only rebuilding those communities but is also the principle teacher at a sangha in Syracuse which provides outreach ministries to prison populations and to individuals with mental disabilities resulting from injury or congenital affliction.

It was specifically the unique way that Zen practice in North America is evolving that attracted my attention as I was working on an earlier book about the pioneer teachers in America – *The Third Step East: Zen Masters of America*. So in 2013 and 2014, I undertook a tour, a pilgrimage – an angya – during which I visited Zen Centers from California to Maine, from Quebec down to New Mexico. I interviewed more than 70 teachers and otherwise significant individuals (the doctor operating a Zen-sponsored hospice, the former wife of the founder of ZMM), as well as senior and not-so-senior students, seeking to get a sense of the "scope of teaching, practice, and social engagement" in contemporary North American Zen.

I had only two prepared questions: "What do you say to someone who knocks on the door and asks about the function of Zen?" and "How did you become engaged in practice?" These, I felt, were adequate to begin a conversation which I could then allow to develop freely.

As I look back on this pilgrimage, my first reflection is how enjoyable it was. I was welcomed graciously and had the good fortune to meet warm and generous individuals who responded to my (at times impertinent) questions frankly and with good humor. Almost to a person, they are the type of people one would enjoy spending an afternoon with drinking beer and discussing something other than Zen.

So although it had not been my original intention to write an apologia for Zen, still – as I tell the former football player who willingly spent three years and 1000 prostrations to return to the residential community at ZMM – I have come to hope it will be that as well. In spite of the challenges of the past and present – and, in all probability, those of the future – it is a path which I and others continue to find profoundly rewarding. And it seems to me that the best approach to take in this work is to allow those I met to present themselves in their own words with as little interference as possible. Ultimately, they are the only apologia contemporary North American Zen requires.

CHAPTER ONE

Three Abbots

MYOGEN STEVE STUCKY
ZENKEI BLANCHE HARTMAN
SOJUN MEL WEITSMAN

THE SAN FRANCISCO ZEN CENTER HAS THREE MAJOR PRACTICE FACILITIES. The principal one, simply called City Center, is located on the corner of Page and Laguna Streets not far from the Haight-Asbury district and about a mile and a half due east of Golden Gate Park. The building is a former Jewish girls' residence, and the ironwork on the landings of the fire-escape is graced with Stars of David. There is a sign by the front door which welcomes me, but, when I try to enter, I find the door locked.

A woman is seated on the front steps, speaking on a cell-phone. She appears to be waiting for someone, so I ask if she is Myoki, the assistant to the Central Abbot and my contact person at the Center. She isn't but says that she can find Myoki for me. We ring the bell and are allowed into the foyer. Myoki is fetched and explains that the community is currently in the Buddha Hall for the noon chanting service. She indicates a place where I can wait.

I deliberately chose to begin this series of interviews at the San Francisco Zen Center. It was not the first Zen program in America, but with its establishment Zen in America can be said to have got into full gear. Its practice center at Tassajara Hot Springs in Los Padres National Park was the first Buddhist monastery to be established outside of Asia.[6] SFZC is probably still the largest Zen community in North America and, in terms of holdings, easily the wealthiest.

In the foyer, there is a statue of Kannon, the female Bodhisattva of Compassion. The original Bodhisattva of Compassion in India, Avalokitesvara, was male. His insight into the nature of Emptiness is celebrated in *The Heart Sutra*, still chanted almost daily at Zen Centers worldwide. The figure changed name and gender as it was imported into China and later Japan. Such transformations are inevitable when a system of belief or practice travels from one region to another and is adapted to a new environment.

The foyer is large and dark, with what appear to be business offices on the left as one enters. The Buddha Hall is on the right. There are banners and paintings on the walls depicting Shunryu Suzuki, the founder of SFZC. Windows look out onto a small inner courtyard very prettily laid out. From my seat, I can just see into the Buddha Hall where the chanting service, accompanied by full body prostrations, is taking place.

SFZC considers itself a monastic – although not celibate – community. Monasticism is not a way of life I have ever felt drawn to, but it is one which I find intriguing. Occasionally, I visit a small Trappist monastery 165 kilometers (slightly more than 100 miles) from where I live in Atlantic Canada. There, too, monks gather at noon to chant a service called Sext. But there are only eight, and they are elderly. By contrast, 150 people are currently in residence at SFZC's three practice centers. If guests who come for short periods are included in the count, the total resident population at times exceeds 200. Then there are another 400 individuals not in the residential program but associated with the center, and beyond these a system of affiliate centers. A few of the chanters in the Buddha Hall appear to be in their late sixties or seventies – aging hippies remain the mainstay of North American Zen practice – but others cannot be much older than 25.

When the service ends, I'm introduced to the Central Abbot, Steve Stucky, a big, robust, and healthy-looking man whose shaved head suits him. He has a warm, engaging smile, and the rough hands of someone who has earned a living as a landscaper. Two of the past abbots at SFZC, he informs me, will join us for lunch: Blanche Hartman and Mel Weitsman.

There is a complicated governance structure at SFZC. After the difficulties they had in the 1980s, it was decided that there should be two co-abbots who would serve limited terms. Then, in 2010, a third position – that of Central Abbot – was instituted.

The complexity of the governance structure reflects the complexity of the San Francisco Zen Center's history.

SFZC was established by Shunryu Suzuki, who had been an obscure village priest in Japan with no particular stature. In 1959, he was sent to San Francisco to be the resident minister at Sokoji, the Soto Zen mission which provided for the spiritual and cultural needs of about sixty families of Japanese descent. His duties were much as they had been in Japan, to carry out ritual activities, weddings, funerals, and memorial services. He was expected to chant sutras on behalf of the community and to conduct a weekly Sunday service. Zen may be the meditation sect of Buddhism, but, as far as Suzuki's congregations in Japan and California were concerned, meditation was an activity for monks.

It was young people from the mainstream culture who, inspired by a combination of psychedelic drugs and their reading of Zen popularisers like Alan Watts, first sought out Suzuki as a Zen Master and meditation teacher. Traditional Zen training molds individuals of impressive character, and so, while Suzuki had been a relatively ordinary figure in Japan, he proved to be an extraordinary figure in America.

He let it be known that he meditated every morning in the shrine room at Sokoji, and people from outside the Japanese community began to join him there. As their numbers increased, the congregation at Sokoji objected, and Suzuki moved his meditation students to the building where I am invited to lunch with the Central Abbot and two of his predecessors.

All three abbots are wearing rakusus, the bib-like garment which in some centers signifies ordination, in others that one is a professed Buddhist, and in still others that one has made certain progress in one's training. Variances in something as simple as this is a characteristic of American Zen. Steve Stucky's rakusu is worn over brown robes, Blanche Hartman's over a turtle neck, and Mel Weitsman's under a worn jean jacket. They alternately address or refer to one another by their first names or their Dharma names.

None of these three is Suzuki Roshi's direct heir. He had only one, Richard Baker, whose role at SFZC can be likened to that of Saint Paul within Christianity. In 1971, Baker was ordained abbot in place of Suzuki, who was terminally ill and would die two weeks later. It was a position everyone – including Suzuki – assumed Baker would hold for life. Everyone was wrong.

Suzuki had admired Baker's energy and his ability to get things done; so much so that he had, perhaps, been willing to overlook other aspects of Baker's personality. Michael Downing reported that before giving Baker transmission

> – Suzuki asked Mel Weitsman what he thought. Mel responded with a question. "Do you think he's ready?" And Mel remembers that Suzuki-roshi said, "Sometimes we give it when a person is ready, and sometimes we give it to somebody and hope."[7]

When Baker first came to Zen Center, it had an annual budget of slightly more than $5000. Under his leadership, that grew to more than $4 million. Zen Center real estate holdings were valued at $20 million. They operated a number of businesses including an organic farm, Green Gulch, and what became the premier vegetarian restaurant in San Francisco, Greens. There was also a bakery, a stitchery – which made meditation cushions and mats – a bookstore, and an organic-produce market and corner convenience store.

Such growth is always the result of the combined efforts of many individuals, but Baker had a way of taking personal credit for each aspect of Zen Center's success which left others feeling that their contributions were undervalued. This would be as much a factor in his eventual downfall as the sexual affair with a donor's wife which precipitated it.

Although Baker was married and had children, the affair was not his first. Several women at Zen Center had been the objects of his attention, although he was not as voracious in his appetites as Sasaki and Shimano. In fact, at one point in the early 1980s, he urged the Priests Council at Zen Center to support the Zen Studies Society's efforts to bring Shimano under control. On the other hand, it was noted that he himself appeared to target the more vulnerable women in the community.

The affair, his management techniques, and the opulent lifestyle he affected as abbot all led the center's board to take a step unprecedented in the history of Zen; they dismissed the abbot. Nothing similar had ever occurred before. In the Asian tradition, if students have a problem with their abbot or teacher, they leave and seek another. But in America in 1983, there were not many teachers for students to go to. More to the point, center members had made significant investments of energy and time helping to build Zen Center into what it had become, and they were unwilling to abandon it.

Another Japanese teacher – Dainin Katagiri – acted as interim abbot for a year, after which the board appointed Reb Anderson, Baker's heir, as the new "abbot for life." Baker then remembered that he had not completed his investiture of Anderson and questioned his right to be abbot. The board ignored that bit of pettiness, but the situation became further complicated when Anderson was arrested for waving a gun about in a low-income housing project. He had been robbed of $20 by a man with a knife just outside Zen Center, and his response was to fetch a gun he had found in Golden Gate Park years earlier – under equally bizarre circumstances, taking it from beside a corpse he'd found but did not report – and chase after the thief.

The board chose not to dismiss Anderson, but they did set term limits to the abbot's position and brought in Mel Weitsman to act as co-abbot.

The period between Baker's dismissal and Weitsman's appointment as first co-abbot of Zen Center was one of catharsis. The community was fractured. Those who remained loyal to Baker accused his detractors of engaging in a witch hunt. There were people who felt they had been deceived, that their trust had been betrayed. There were others who just felt wounded by the in-fighting. Many fell away from practice. Others stayed but their hearts were no longer in it. As Weitsman told Michael Downing:

> Zen Center was in decline for at least five years. We had meet-
> ings where people were saying, "Why should we have to obey the
> rules?" It became anarchic. City Center became a kind of hotel on
> Page Street – where people were living there and bad-mouthing
> Zen Center. They had lost their faith in the practice.[8]

Slowly, they rebuilt. But first, operations had to be simplified. Businesses were closed. Properties were sold. New policies and structures were implemented. It was a difficult and complicated process, and one which has been described elsewhere, notably in Downing's *Shoes Outside the Door* which examines Richard Baker's fall from grace in – as Zen doyen James Ford put it – "excruciating detail."

The Richard Baker story and Downing's book are so frequently referenced whenever SFZC is mentioned that, as we settle around a table in the dining hall, I begin by asking the three abbots if they think the book presented a fair portrait of Zen Center.

Blanche Hartman pounces on the question. "No! He said all that anyone wanted to speak about were the difficulties. That wasn't true. That's all *he* wanted to speak about."

Mel Weitsman's response is more measured. "The Downing book may have been fair, but there were some inaccuracies and some over-emphasis on a certain aspect. So it doesn't represent the whole picture. Maybe in that way, when you say fairness, the unfairness may have been in the over-emphasis of one aspect. Which was what Downing was interested in."

I mention another book.

"The thing is," Mel says, "those books were all from the outside. There's nothing from the inside. So in that sense it's unfair because it's someone speaking about Zen Center rather than the main subject speaking about what's really going on."

"So whatever you write will be unfair," Steve Stucky says with a smile that brings crinkles to the corners of his eyes.

"Life is unfair," Mel remarks.

There are probably more ways in which SFZC differs from other Zen centers in America than there are similarities, although some of those differences weren't as extreme in the past. The idea of multiple abbots with limited terms of office, for example, is unique to them. I ask how the abbots are chosen, and Mel explains: "We have an Elders' Group, and they discuss it among themselves. Then they decide on someone and present their recommendation to the board. When the board decides, we light a fire in the fireplace and smoke goes...."

It's only a few days since the election of Pope Francis, and everyone at the table laughs. The three of them are relaxed and at ease. They've all been interviewed before.

Abbots are appointed to a four year term with the option of a three year extension. "See, when Suzuki Roshi was abbot there were no questions," Mel continues. "But the founder is different from succeeding abbots. So the founder doesn't have any term limits, but succeeding abbots like Richard...." He shrugs his shoulders. "He incorporated Zen Center as a corporation sole, which meant that one person has the voting capacity of the whole board, and Richard was also abbot for life because there was no question about it. But after Richard, then Katagiri became abbot for one year, as a kind of interim abbot, then Reb became abbot, and then it became evident that one abbot was not enough, so they asked me to be a co-abbot with Reb."

Mel is being understandably discreet. But it's also true that being in charge of three large and separate training centers was a big responsibility for one person. And the idea of term limits was actually based on a Japanese model.

"We had two models to compare to from Japan," Blanche explains. "The two main temples of Soto Zen. At Sojiji, the abbot for the main training monastery is an abbot for term, and then they go back to their home temple. But at Eiheiji, the abbot is for life, and they've come to the point that they don't appoint someone abbot until they are in their 80s. Although they got a little fooled last time because the abbot lived to be 105. So there were those two models to choose from, and at the time it seemed, 'Well this works for Sojiji, all of those abbots who have been abbots for seven years then went back to a home temple which supports Sojiji.' I was on the committee that worried about this, and we really didn't know what we were doing too much, but we took that model. Looking at how it's all worked out, I'm not so sure it was a great idea."

"Well, it has its good points like everything else," Mel says. "It has its good points, and it has its problems. It keeps a person from being domineering, and it gives senior students the opportunity to be abbot, and that's become a kind of rite of passage."

❊

Mel Weitsman first became interested in Zen when Shunryu Suzuki was still at Sokoji, which was as much a cultural center for the ethnic Japanese community as a temple. "I was an artist working in San Francisco and had a lot of friends, and some of them said, 'You know, there's a Zen temple on Bush Street.' One guy would go there to play Go, and someone else said, 'I practice there.' I didn't know what a Zen priest was, but this fellow told me, 'There's a little Zen priest there, and I practice there. We sit zazen.' So, little by little, I got information. And one day, about 4:00 in the morning, we walked down McAllister Street to Bush Street and went to zazen. That was my introduction." It was 1964.

"Then this little old man came behind me and straightened my posture, and I felt really great. So every once in a while I would go back, and one day I just decided, 'This is it. This is exactly what I've been looking for.' Because I was looking for something, although I didn't know that it was Zen. But it was perfect."

"But when you left," Hartman reminds him, "you went and bowed to that little old man, didn't you?"

"Oh, yes. That was Suzuki Roshi. He was called Revered Suzuki then; he wasn't called Suzuki Roshi. So he was just another priest. I liked him, but I didn't know who he was, what he was really about. So, as I kept going back, I decided that this was what I really wanted to do. And I've been doing it ever since."

When I ask what Suzuki Roshi was like, Mel tells a story. "Every morning we'd do the robe chant, where you put your robe on top of your head after zazen. Of course, nobody had robes then," he chuckles, "and it was all in Japanese. So I asked, 'What's that chant we do in the morning after zazen?' And Katagiri was there, and Katagiri was looking through the drawers for a translation and Suzuki Roshi" – Mel makes a patting motion with his hand – "'Stop,' he said. 'It means love.'" Mel smiles. "'It means love. That's all.'"

In 1967, at Suzuki's request, Mel established the Berkeley Zen Center, which is a center for lay practice and the largest of SFZC's satellite centers. It is where Blanche Hartman began her Zen practice in 1969.

"One day I was at the house of my best friend, and we were just having coffee. She had a headache, and it was so bad she asked me, 'Could you see that?' I said, 'What?' 'That headache.' I said, 'I can't see your headache.' She said, 'It was so bad, I thought you could see it.' The next morning, she went to a doctor and was diagnosed with an inoperable brain tumor. She went into a hospital for radiation treatment, went into a coma, and died. That was all within two or three weeks.

"I was 43, and she was about my age. We both had kids about the same age. And I thought, '*I'm* going to die! Me, personally. It's not just later, when you get old. Oh, my God! How do you live if you know you're going to die? Who knows that?' So I started getting interested in a whole bunch of stuff I had never paid any attention to.

Somebody told me about the Berkeley Zendo, and I went there for zazen instruction. Mel wasn't there that day, but I had zazen instruction on July 3rd, 1969, and I started sitting every day after that. And I would sit there thinking, 'What am I doing? I don't know anybody else who does this. This is weird. What will my friends think?' Finally I said, 'It doesn't matter. There's somebody in there that wants to do it because she gets up at 5:00 every morning to go to the zendo to do it before she goes to work.'

"Suzuki Roshi used to come over to Berkeley to give a talk on Monday mornings, and when I met him, I thought, 'He knows. He knows what I need to know.' I don't know why I felt that, but I definitely felt it. Then I had an experience at a student strike at San Francisco State College where my son was a student. I had an experience of a face-to-face encounter with a riot squad policeman, who I would have said – had anybody asked me – was the opposite of me, but I had an experience of identity. We were just a few feet apart, and we made eye contact, and I had this experience of identity with him. And it was sort of like, 'What was that? Who understands that? What happened? How can a riot squad policeman and me be identical?' But it was clear – no question – that this is the way it is. It was just, 'How can I understand this? Who understands this?' And I thought, Suzuki Roshi looked at me like that. He didn't make a separation."

Blanche succeeded Mel as co-abbot of Zen Center in 1996. She was the first woman to hold that post.

The dual-abbot model continued until 2010, when the abbacy was restructured. The positions of the co-abbots now became Abiding Abbots, one resident at City Center and the other at Green Gulch. With the reorganization, Steve Stucky became the first Central Abbot of Zen Center as a whole.

Although Stucky has a Buddhist name, Myogen, he is generally known as "Abbot Steve." He had achieved near-mythic stature at Zen Center as a result of his role, along with four other monks, in staying behind and protecting the Tassajara practice center during the 2008 Basin Complex Fire.

He grew up in a Mennonite farming family in Kansas and spent his summers working the wheat harvest from Texas north back into his home state. During the Vietnam War, he received a draft deferment as a conscientious objector and did alternative service work with inner city youth in Chicago, where he lived in a commune. It was there that he began a personal investigation into the way in which his mind and memory interfered with what he perceived.

"For me it was an interesting question, what can I actually see clearly? And I began to notice my own thoughts. So I started, just on my own, investigating it.

And then a friend of mine, handed me the book *The Three Pillars of Zen* by Philip Kapleau and said, 'This may be what you're doing.' So I started sitting based on the instructions in it. Then I went and met Kapleau, but I didn't particularly like him, so I kept on going."

I ask why he hadn't particularly liked Kapleau.

"I was raised a Mennonite and a pacifist, and I felt his style was militaristic. That was kind of off-putting to me. And he was also very much oriented towards *getting* something which I wasn't sure I wanted to get that much. I wanted to stop and inquire. That was my own intuitive feeling about it. And then I was travelling around. I was in Cambridge, and I sat with the Cambridge Zen group for a while. And I saw Suzuki Roshi's *Zen Mind, Beginner's Mind* in a bookstore, so I opened it up, and I read a page of it, and – I don't know – this was a pretty interesting person, an interesting mind. But I didn't want to buy any books then because I was travelling light. So I put it back on the shelf. Then I was sitting in New York with Eido Shimano, and one night he announced that Suzuki Roshi had died in San Francisco. That kind of piqued my interest, because I was asking around about what was happening with this San Francisco Zen Center, and someone said, they have an American leading it now. And I thought, 'That should be interesting.' Because I had never felt that Zen was foreign; sitting is something that's available everywhere.

"So I hitch-hiked across the country, and I was one of those people who came to the door, knocked on it. Someone opened it a crack. 'Whadda you want?' And I said, 'I came here to practice Zen.' And they said, 'Well, did you make some arrangements?' And I said, 'No, I just came across the country.' And they said, 'Wait a minute.' And they closed the door!"

Blanche lowers her head between her hands and shakes it. It had been like that in the early days, she admits. "My entire focus when I was abbess was to get people to smile at whoever they opened the door to." But it hadn't always been a safe neighborhood. The reason they currently had a large and heavy donation box in the foyer – and the reason why the door had been locked when I arrived – was that someone had come in and walked off with the smaller one.

Eventually the guest manager came to the door and invited Steve in. "She sat with me in the little alcove, and we talked for a few minutes, then I signed up to be a guest student for a week."

He had no place to stay, so he slept in Golden Gate Park, hiding his sleeping bag in the bushes during the day when he went to the center to meditate.

"I met Richard Baker within a couple of days, and I thought he's kind of an interesting person. So we connected, and I stuck around."

He stayed for eight years and, being the only resident with any serious agricultural experience, was instrumental in the development of Green Gulch Farm. After the disruptions which followed Baker's departure, Steve became a "householder priest." He married, had three children, and worked as a landscape contractor. He maintained his Zen practice, however, and established an affiliate sitting group, the Dharma Eye Zen Center, in San Rafael. He also did the course work for a degree in pastoral counseling at San Francisco Theological Seminary and worked with the Buddhadharma Sangha in San Quentin prison. In 1993, he received Dharma transmission from Mel, and, in 2007, he became a co-abbot with primary responsibility for Green Gulch. Three years later, he was appointed the first Central Abbot of Zen Center.

I ask why the third abbacy was established.

"We have three temples," he explains. "There's a need to coordinate and have some oversight about what happens and the decisions that are made that affect all three temples. So to have someone in a position to take responsibility for those things that affect all three temples allows, at least in theory, a particular temple to have an abbot, or abbess in this case. So we have a Green Gulch abbess, Linda Cutts, and we have a city center abbess, Christina Lehnherr, and I'm in the role of central abbot in coordinating all three. Curiously enough, at our most monastic training center at Tassajara we have chosen to have practice periods that are led in rotation. So we don't have anyone who is abbot of Tassajara, but we take turns leading the practice periods there. So we share leadership in that way."

I ask if the abbot's role is that of an administrator or a teacher.

"That's an on-going balancing act. It's both. Teacher with some administrative responsibilities."

"I think part of the impetus," Blanche adds, "was having someone who was a teacher being more directly involved in the administrative realm because the administrative realm gets so caught up in fund-raising and planning and that sort of stuff that sometimes practice concerns might get lost if we didn't have someone who was practicing as a teacher directly connected with the administrative realm. So it's maintaining a practice focus within the administrative realm. That's what I think the function of this position is. Maybe I'm wrong."

"Thank you," Steve says, giving her one of his world-class smiles.

In all probability, the primary factor determining which Zen Center a newcomer will come to is proximity. But the next factor – and this had especially been the case during the early days of Zen in America – is the desire to work with a specific teacher. Many people, like Steve, who read *The Three Pillars of Zen*, went to Rochester to work with Philip Kapleau. Others went to Minneapolis to work with Dainin Katagiri and to Los Angeles to work with Taizan Maezumi. Large numbers of people came to San Francisco to work with Shunryu Suzuki and, later, Richard Baker. Today, however, if one comes to SFZC there isn't one teacher but many.

"We have over a dozen Dharma-transmitted teachers at Zen Center," Steve tells me.

This is another of SFZC's unique features.

"Usually you only have one teacher," Mel notes. "But we have lots of teachers who are peers. Right? So, to have just this one person perpetually be the teacher, well, what are all these other teachers going to do?"

Personally, Mel has more than twenty Dharma heirs. "A lot of the abbots who have succeeded me have been my students." That includes both Steve and Blanche.

In addition to its three practice centers, SFZC has another ten sitting groups, like the Berkeley Zen Center, spread about the city for non-residential practitioners. Steve explains that these "sometimes meet in peoples' homes, and some of them meet here with one of the practice leaders assigned to them. So that gives people a chance to get to know Zen Center in that way. And now we have a big group for people in recovery from various addictions, mostly alcohol, but others as well. That's an open group that meets every Monday night. There's another group called Young Urban Zen, and they have a separate meeting for people who feel, 'Well, I'm not so sure about coming and getting involved in the formal practice, but I'd like to meet with people from a younger generation who have some interest in Buddhism.'"

In addition to which, there are the people who just come for an occasional lecture. "There are probably twice as many at the lectures as there are at zazen," Blanche tells me. There is also regular, and well-attended, introductory sessions. "I don't know for sure what happens to all those people who have zazen instruction," she remarks. "Every week, twenty or more people have zazen instruction."

There are two major schools within Japanese Zen, Soto and Rinzai. The books which first introduced Zen to North Americans focused on the Rinzai School, which emphasizes the importance of attaining kensho – or awakening – the "something" that Steve Stucky had not been so sure he felt a need to "get" when he met Philip Kapleau. Shunryu Suzuki and other teachers within the Soto tradition, on the other hand, maintained that it was the practice itself that mattered, not seeking anything from it. To sit properly in zazen was sufficient. In *Zen Mind, Beginner's Mind*, Suzuki said:

> The most important thing is to forget all gaining ideas, all dualistic ideas. In other words, just practicing zazen in a certain posture.

Do not think about anything. Just remain on your cushion without expecting anything. Then eventually you will resume your own
true nature. That is to say, your own true nature resumes itself.[9]

"Basically," Mel tells me, "the practice is without promise or without hope.
So you give up all hope. Ye who enter here, give up all hope. But, of course, when
people first come to Zen Center, they want something. So what are we giving them?
What we're giving them is that we're taking everything away eventually."

"Giving them themselves," Steve adds.

"Your whole life is practice," Mel continues. "That's the story of Zen Center. It's
not like you come to practice and then go away and do something else. Practice is
your whole life. And no matter what you're doing, it's practice."

"If you're paying attention," Blanche says.

"Yeah, well, even if you're not paying attention because most of the time you're
not paying attention. You know, within Sangha – community – there is Buddha and
Dharma. And in Dharma – the teaching – there is Buddha and Sangha. And in Buddha, there is Dharma and Sangha. So all three, they're the three legs of the pot. If one
of those legs is missing, then the pot is not complete. So Zen Center is a complete
practice. It has Buddha, Dharma, and Sangha. Each one is a treasure, and they're all
interconnected, and they're all operating interconnectedly all of the time. It's simply
Buddha's practice. If you want something in two words, 'Buddha's practice.' And
this is the other thing about Zen Center, that the beginning is the same as the end."

"All Suzuki Roshi emphasized was beginner's mind," Blanche adds.

"Yeah, beginner's mind. The end of practice is the beginning."

"I think it's always to be interested in, 'What is it?'" Blanche explains. "That's a
lot about what beginner's mind is. 'What is this, I wonder?' To meet everything with
that kind of openness and inquiry, rather than, 'Oh, I know what that is.' Because
everything changes. You might know what it is today, and tomorrow it'll be different. So, stay awake."

"And one other thing," Mel says. "You don't just practice for yourself. This is
the meaning of sangha. You don't practice just for yourself. You lose yourself within
practice."

Social engagement is one way by which one might practice for others. Among other
things, SFZC's vision statement calls upon it "To develop and expand Zen Center's
social outreach program."[10] Their outreach programs serve both the male and female
prison systems in the area. There is the special practice Steve had mentioned designed

for people in recovery, and the Center provides meals for a local homeless shelter. One of their most acclaimed programs had been the Maitri Hospice for people afflicted by HIV/AIDS established in 1987 by Issan Dorsey, one of Richard Baker's Dharma Heirs. It still operates under its own board of directors, as does a second hospice that began at the Page Street center when Blanche was abbot.

"There was a young Chinese woman with a brain tumor who had come to this country," Blanche recounts. "She had been writing to the City of the Ten Thousand Buddhas here in California, which is Chinese Chan Buddhism, wanting to be ordained before she died. But she got here, and she was already quite ill. The tumor was visibly erupting from her forehead. So they wouldn't take her in. So I went to see her in hospital and suggested she could come here and die. That's what happened. That's how room 48 started being a hospice."

I ask about the current relationship between the center and Richard Baker.

"We had a fiftieth anniversary celebration here last year," Steve tells me. "Zen Center was officially organized as an institution in 1962, so in 2012 we had our fiftieth anniversary. I invited him to come. Blanche had invited him here earlier. He came and gave a talk and participated in our ceremonies. I also invited him to come again last fall to visit Tassajara; so we have a pretty good relationship. But it's also true that his memory of things that happened during the time he was here and his opinion about the ethical aspects of it and other peoples' points of view are not all in accord. But I feel that we are in a very respectful relationship."

"Has there been a reconciliation?"

"That may be...." He does not finish his thought.

"Premature," Blanche says after a moment.

"I don't think we're *not* reconciled," Steve points out.

"We're working in that direction," Blanche says.

Later, as she waits outside with me for my taxi to arrive, she expresses regret that Zen Center had not been able to reconcile with Baker. "But," she says sadly, "he couldn't admit that he had done anything wrong. But if you really want to know about Zen Center, you need to speak to him."

Only two of the teachers I sought to interview declined my request. Richard Baker was one of them.[11]

The following October, less than six months after my visit to San Francisco, Myogen Steve Stucky agreed to a three year extension to his term as Central Abbot. Later that same week, he was informed he had stage four pancreatic cancer. A few days after receiving this diagnosis, he gave a public lecture at Green Gulch in which he explained his condition to the sangha. It began with a reflection on a private practice which revealed something of his attitude to both life and Zen:

> For some years I've been doing a practice of waking up with grati-
> tude. First thing, sitting up at the edge of the bed and putting
> my hands together and just saying the word "gratitude." And then
> it's an open question, "For what?" And whatever comes up in my
> experience is that for which I am, I'd say, grateful to have this meet-
> ing. Whatever it is is who I am, and whatever it is is supporting
> me and this life. It's completely beyond judgment or preference. So
> lately I've been grateful to have that practice.[12]

At the time of the talk, he still didn't know long he had to live. The initial esti-
mate was probably less than six months without chemotherapy. With treatment, he
might have twice that much time. The situation, he admitted, was challenging:

> I think of it as a little bit like the Tassajara fire. It's an engagement,
> and there are certain things that I can do to take care of this side,
> and the fire or the cancer will do what it does, and it's a matter of
> paying close attention and keeping attentive and responsive, with
> the thought of being most helpful with what's most immediate.
> And so I'm learning fast, and a lot.

He went on to reflect upon a passage from Dogen:

> "The entire earth is the true human body." The entire earth is the
> true human body. So each human body is also independent and
> simultaneously the entire earth. And sometimes you may really see
> that when you let go of your particular attachment to some small
> identity and realize that the tree is as much a part of me as my
> shoulder. The sky is as much a part of me as my eyelashes. And
> the sound of the ocean is as much a part of me as the sound of my
> own breathing. To actually experience it that way is something that
> shows up in our practice. I think it's not so unusual particularly for
> people who are doing this practice of sitting. I'm very grateful to

have this practice. It sustains me and will continue to sustain me to
the last moment of consciousness.

The talk went on to reflect upon the need to care not just for one's own body but also for the greater body of the Earth of which we are all part.

On November 20, after completing the first of three scheduled rounds of chemotherapy, Abbot Steve announced that he would not continue them. In mid-December he formally stepped down as Central Abbot, and, early on the morning of the last day of 2013, he died.

Zen Center mourned the passing of a gracious, insightful, and inspiring man, and then went about the process – as he had been confident they would – of seeing to his succession. Eijun Linda Cutts, who had been the Abiding Abbot of Green Gulch, became the new Central Abbot. Furyu Nancy Schroeder took over as Abiding Abbot of Green Gulch, and Rinso Ed Sattizahn became Abiding Abbot at City Center.

The San Francisco Zen Center is fortunate that it had a pool of qualified people upon whom they could call in order to ensure that Shunryu Suzuki's legacy continued.

In other Zen communities, however, the issue of succession has been more challenging.

CHAPTER TWO

Three Oshos

MYOKYO JUDITH MCLEAN
SEIJU BOB MAMMOSER
YOSHIN DAVID RADIN

1

THERE ARE MORE THAN TWENTY ZEN CENTERS AFFILIATED WITH JOSHU Sasaki. The majority are in the United States, but there are others in Europe and two in Canada. The center in Montreal, Enpuku-ji, is located on rue Saint-Dominique. I'm told that Leonard Cohen lives down the block. If so, he's an unassuming person. The houses are modest multiplexes in what the Enpuku-ji website describes as an "ethnic neighborhood." Throughout my visit, I hear the voices of children playing outside and dogs barking.

Enpuku-ji is entered through a miniscule side-garden. A small sign on the gate post bears the single word "Zen," an arrow pointing right, and the house number. Zengetsu Myokyo Judith McLean walks up the street just as I pull into the drive. She is a slight woman with close-cropped hair and a charming smile who looks younger than her sixty years. She unlocks a back door, and we enter into a single long, narrow, room. The back end is a small kitchen. The rest of the room is taken up by the zendo, which currently has two rows of five zafus facing one another. At the far end, there is an altar with a graceful statue of Kannon.

The contrast with SFZC couldn't be more stark, but, in fairness, this is a branch and therefore a more just comparison would be with one of their satellite centers, like Mel Weitsman's in Berkeley. Even so, Enpuku-ji is tiny.

We sit at a small kitchen table, and Myokyo offers me tea. I ask how her students address her.

"They call me Myokyo."

"Not 'sensei' or anything like that?"

She ducks her head and shakes it. She has a number of shy mannerisms. She tells me she makes it clear to them that she isn't a teacher. So, presumably, I shouldn't call them students.

"What is your relationship to them then?"

She pauses a moment. "I don't know what there is to teach in Zen. I mean, you talk a little bit about your experience, and you set an example about how you go about doing things. So I resist the word 'teacher' because to teach is very active. There's something to teach, and you teach it. But that's not what happens here. I don't see it like that."

She has a gentle demeanor but, she warns me, has been told that her eyes flash when someone doesn't follow the zendo procedures correctly. "They think I'm angry. I'm not really. I just want to make sure they're doing things properly."

She is an ordained monk and priest, an "osho" in Rinzai-ji terminology.[13] She is also the Buddhist chaplain at McGill University.

Thirty-five years ago, she accompanied a boyfriend to California to attend a sesshin directed by Joshu Sasaki. The boyfriend had to return to Canada on family business. She stayed. After the retreat, she had hoped to remain at the Mount Baldy training center for an extended training period, but Sasaki cancelled it and sent everyone home. She returned to Nelson, British Columbia, where she worked in fabric and paper design, earning just enough to maintain a studio and be able to fly down to do annual sesshin at Mount Baldy.

After three years of this, in 1984, Sasaki suggested she consider taking part in the winter training period. "But I couldn't do that because I'd just borrowed money for supplies for fall and Christmas sales. But the seed was planted for me to go for a training period, and, the next winter, I went." And there she remained. She was ordained a monk and received her Dharma name which means Clear Mirror.

"What is Sasaki Roshi like as a teacher?"

Her answer surprises me. "He was cruel. He was strong. He was…."

I interrupt her. "What do you mean, 'cruel'? Why was that the first thing you said?"

"Oh, because I was talking with a student here yesterday, and, it seems to me, it was a very effective tool for dissolving the ego."

"Can you give me an example?"

"Well, a personal example…." She reflects for a while, then says: "One of my sisters died when I was at Mount Baldy. She was a search and rescue person. Her plane crashed; she died. He didn't say anything about that to me. No consolation or anything, just sent me off to go home to the funeral. Then another sister died. Then my father died. And through all of those deaths, no consolation from him. In a sense, that felt a little bit cruel.

"The strongest teaching he gave me was that he gave me a lot of responsibility." She was made head monk of Rinzai-ji in Los Angeles in 1992 and was there during the Rodney King riots. Sasaki, himself, was away at the time. "That was a lot of responsibility, because we were hemmed in. There were fires all around us and so on. And never any comment about 'job well done' or how bad it was.

"And while I was at Rinzai-ji, there was a very, very difficult older nun. She was an alcoholic. Very difficult. She used to drive people away from the Zen Center. So I was in charge of her there, and I dealt with her in an okay way. Then the Roshi turned the tables on us, and he made her the head monk. And things went kind of crazy. Like really crazy. So that was a cruel situation. And he watched and watched and no comment. He watched to see how I dealt with that. So at the time, that seemed cruel to me. But he's just cutting off any kind of attempt to grandify oneself or to even feel competent. Because we all had something more to learn in the sense of dissolving our self."

"Why did you put up with it?" I ask. "Why did you continue working with him?"

"His methods are very effective. I mean, when your whole world falls apart, then you learn from that. And if that keeps on happening, then you keep on learning. And so if I had someone who was just kind and helped me along a little bit, that wasn't so interesting. So I think it's a very particular kind of character that would study with a teacher like that. I was very stubborn, but there was *never* a doubt in my mind that this was the person I wanted to study with, that I was glad to be studying with. No doubt. Even when it was difficult and I felt he should really give me a break once in a while, still there was no doubt in my mind."

In 1999, she was ordained an osho and given the additional name Zengetsu, Zen Moon. She worked at several centers including the large training center, Bodhi Manda, in the Jemez mountains of New Mexico, as well as at the Albuquerque Zen Center, the largest of the affiliate centers for lay practice. In February of 1995, she returned to Canada.

"Was that at Sasaki Roshi's suggestion, or did you just decide, 'It's time for me to go home'?"

"No," she says with a laugh. "We don't really do that. People who have trained at Mount Baldy just give their life to practice. So no personal decisions like that, usually. What happened was, I was cooking dinner for Roshi one night, and he came up beside me and asked, 'Where do you want your Zen Center to be? Where do you want to start a Zen Center?' And out of my mouth popped, 'Montreal.'"

Leonard Cohen offered a house he owned as a location for the new center. It's the house that Myokyo now uses as her residence. She discovered early on that she had to change the location of the zendo because people knew the building belonged to Cohen and would show up at the door expecting to find him there.

"When I introduce people to the practice sometimes it's a knock on the door, but most of the time it's organized so that people are together in a group, and I begin by asking them why they've come. So that kind of flushes out all the possible reasons they might have or all the possible ways in which they think about Zen. And then I speak to each of those things. And I basically say that Zen is a practice; it's not a lifestyle; it's not a way of thinking. You don't need to believe anything when you start Zen practice. It's a practice. And everyone does the same practice. And through the practice of zazen, peoples' minds become clearer, and we begin to dissolve the mind that separates us from everything else in this world.

"I think most people come to Zen because they want to make themselves better. So they have a goal in mind. And that goal is usually about becoming a different person, becoming a better person. So I'm pretty clear about slashing that idea to bits."

The practice, as she describes it, is very simple. "So following the breath but eventually that kind of tightly following the breath disappears. So just very basic zazen, and that's actually what I've done up to this point. The last thirty-five years, that's the practice I've been doing. Joshu Sasaki Roshi actually discourages us from latching onto any kind of focusing tool, including the breath. So maybe it is shikan taza after a while. You know, just sort of sit."

She does warn new people, "Anything you've read may or may not be something that's going to happen to you. But mostly what's going to happen to you is that you're going to be very uncomfortable sitting in a cross-legged posture, and you're going to really start thinking a lot about your notions of how life should be and what you should be like and how you are. And so you'll begin to question all that in the context of quiet sitting in this upright posture that has the potential for making you very present and very 'in the moment.' So an experience you're not having usually. We're usually way, way far away in our minds.

"I talk about seed thoughts: notions, ideas, feelings, physical sensations, or emotions. As we become conscious of one of these, we decide, first of all, whether we like it or not, or maybe it's neutral. If we don't like it, we stuff it back, way down somewhere back and get rid of it. If we like it or it's just neutral, we just add another thought and that carries on into a story. I reassure everyone that there's no problem with that. Our minds are creative. The creative process is what our minds are for.

The problem is we think that that story is our life. And so in zazen you begin to learn that that's not correct, that our story is not our life. The effort is to observe what comes up and then to simply let it go away before you even begin to discriminate or make a judgement about that thought, to be so clearly present that you can actually observe what comes up in the mind and then let it go by.

"So people can visualize that or understand the words, but then when they go to do it, it's absolutely, absolutely difficult. And then, immediately, they're not present. Right? And so they know that, and I know that, and I say, 'Then you need to keep going back to the present.' You need to physically keep placing yourself here. Most of them probably won't have the…the…. What do you call it? The verve, the desire…the *tenacity* to continue. But, you know, we need to be sparked by something to be tenacious. So I say, 'Probably most of you won't have it.' That's okay, too. You know?"

She's smiling as she speaks. It's clear she doesn't expect the practice to attract large numbers of people, and she's comfortable with that.

After she assures me she's willing to talk about the recent reports in the media, I ask how accurate she believes the allegations are.

"Well, there are any number of different allegations. So it would be hard to say that they were all accurate. Sasaki Roshi has always been very sexual in his training methods. I was aware of that on the eve of my starting practice with him, and it didn't discourage me from starting practice."

"In what way sexual?"

"He wasn't afraid to touch a student in what some might consider a sexual way. Not across the board, though. I was in contact with all of the people that I've sent to sesshin for the last thirty-five years, and, of the six women that replied, none of them actually had been touched sexually by the Roshi in sanzen. And when I say that, he might have touched their breast. So when I say 'sexual' it might be as simple as reaching and touching their breast, and, for some women, that would be sexual abuse. Other women would laugh it off. I think there were different kinds of relationships that Roshi had with his students – both male and female – a whole range of relationships that happened."

I ask about Eshu Martin, whose article on the *Sweeping Zen* website had begun the current news coverage.

She takes a deep breath, almost a sigh, then says that Eshu had only done about "five or six" sesshins before Eshin Godfrey, of the Zen Center of Vancouver, asked Sasaki to ordain him a monk. Sasaki agreed, stipulating, however, that Eshin remain

Martin's teacher or guide. After a while, Eshin – "although it was not appropriate" – gave Martin permission to meet with students individually. "Then Eshu started to present himself as a venerable teacher, and started to build a whole big sangha, but *also* to charge a lot of money for people to start practice and to continue practice. So when this was pointed out to the Osho Council, we looked into it a little bit more carefully. Like, none of us do that. None of us call ourselves 'Venerable.'"

"And he does?"

"Yes, he does. But he wasn't an osho; he didn't have, in our minds, the authority to ordain people, to meet with people individually. That was Eshin's mistake. And certainly to charge the kind of money that he was charging for individual teaching." Some of the fees were for an on-line program.

"It's an interesting concept," I suggest. "On-line Zen instruction."

"He moved to a country place quite a few years ago, and no one wants to go there on a regular daily basis, so that's why he does internet. But we – the Osho Council – wrote to him and asked him to change some things on his website because they weren't correct in terms of him being a Rinzai-ji monk."

"You felt he was claiming something beyond his status?"

"None of Roshi's monks would go anywhere near where he was going. It was just preposterous. So finally it was agreed that we should take back his robes, that he shouldn't be seen as a representative of Rinzai-ji. So some of the oshos went up to meet with his board of directors, and, when we announced that we felt we needed to take back his robes, he announced that he was leaving Rinzai-ji."

Nor, she points out, was Martin the first person to bring up the issue of Sasaki's behavior. "There was another Rinzai-ji osho who was really upset and had opened up a can of worms in 2007." This was Giko David Rubin.

"What was he upset about?"

"About Roshi's sexual activity with women. But what many people don't realize is that there had been many, many of these crises over the years, and we were trying to deal with it. But certainly the Roshi was not stopping."

"Saying that 'we were trying to deal with it' implies you recognized it as problematic."

"It was problematic if people felt they were being harmed. I mean, it wasn't like there were thousands of people feeling they were being harmed. But, yes, we were constantly dealing with it."

I ask if she had any qualms at all about Sasaki Roshi as a teacher.

"No. Absolutely not. I mean, I knew – as I said – on the eve of my starting practice with him that this was going to be part of it. And my involvement with him – my sexual involvement with him – was actually a very, very strong teaching for a long while. And then it became a little bit disruptive to my koan practice, and I just said,

'I can't do this. It's disruptive or too confusing.' And that was the end of it. But it *was* actually a teaching, a strong teaching tool for me personally."

"Doesn't that suggest the teaching pattern for a male student would be different from that for a female student?"

"No. Because I think he would also touch his male students sexually. He would touch their sex organs. I don't know if that's sexual, you know? But he would test their limits the same as he would test women's limits."

I mention the work of Marie Fortune and others who have studied the issue of clergy abuse, appropriate boundaries, and whether it is ever possible to have a reciprocal relationship when one person is in a position of authority over another. Myokyo tells me that she had spent two days the previous week at the Truth and Reconciliation Hearings regarding First Nations children placed in Canada's former Residential School system. "We watched a movie that was very graphic about the kind of abuse that happened. So all of that was very clearly about power structures and the abuses by people in positions of power.

"But," she goes on, "I *gag* – that sounds kind of dramatic – but when I think of Zen Centers putting out ethics statements and who their teachers should have a relationship with or not, all of those things, I think, 'Well, that's just going to be the end of Zen practice.' In Zen practice, we need to go far beyond what we can even conceive of as our limits, need to break through in major ways. There's a good reason why psychologists shouldn't do that, or therapists shouldn't sleep with their patients, and there's good reasons why priests shouldn't rape aboriginal children. But in Zen practice, the whole point is to break out of our limits. So, in my mind, I think it's a disaster if these limits get built into Zen Centers."

"Sasaki Roshi hasn't named an heir, and he's 106 now," I point out. "What happens when he dies?"

"I don't know if it's public knowledge yet; I think it is. But just two weeks ago, he designated an abbot, Eshin Godfrey, and two vice abbots for Rinzai-ji, to oversee the organization. So, he'll step down on July 21st [2013], and those people will come into play. But they're not heirs; they're simply administrative positions. So, no heir. He says he has no heirs."

2

At Myokyo's suggestion, I travel to Albuquerque six months later to meet Seiju Bob Mammoser. As it happens, my visit coincides with the annual October balloon festival. Hundreds of hot air balloons fill the sky as I make my way to the center on

Garfield Avenue. But there is nothing light or airy about Seiju. At the time of our meeting, I have difficulty interpreting his attitude to the interview. At the very least, he seems cautious and reserved. Later, however, I will wonder if he wasn't simply a man under an enormous amount of stress.

Seiju is abbot and founder of the Albuquerque Zen Center, but he had been in Los Angeles when Eshu Martin's article came out. It was Seiju who released a response on behalf of the Rinzai-ji oshos stating that they were "deeply troubled by the allegations of abuse involving some of the students who have practiced at our centers." He announced that in January there would be a meeting

> – for the oshos of our community together with an independent, professional facilitator trained in addressing such matters. We will also invite representatives of the Mt. Baldy Board, the Rinzai-ji Board, as well as members of the ordained sangha to attend. This meeting will be the necessary first step to clarify within our organization what is an extremely difficult and complex issue.[14]

It was also Seiju who spoke on behalf of Rinzai-ji in the *New York Times* article. At that time, he admitted he had been aware of the allegations against Sasaki since the 1980s and reported that there had "been efforts in the past to address this with him. Basically, they haven't been able to go anywhere." He then added:

> What's important and is overlooked is that, besides this aspect, Roshi was a commanding and inspiring figure using Buddhist practice to help thousands find more peace, clarity and happiness in their own lives. It seems to be the kind of thing that, you get the person as a whole, good and bad, just like you marry somebody and you get their strengths and wonderful qualities as well as their weaknesses.[15]

Seiju's involvement with Zen practice began in the early '70s when he came upon a book left on a coffee table. "*Concentration and Meditation* by Christmas Humphreys. An eminently forgettable book. But it made me realize that I was hungry for something, and it got me started." He was 25 years old and was working at a bank in Chicago, a job he gave up in order to travel across the country.

He visited the San Francisco Zen Center briefly. "Stayed for a chanting service in the afternoon and left immediately. Made my way to LA. Stopped at a place called

Cimarron Zen Center at the time. It's called Rinzai-ji now. It was interesting. But it was in Los Angeles, and I grew up in Chicago. I didn't need another big city. They said they had this place up in the mountains. Mount Baldy. So I went there for a week. Liked it. Went back to Chicago. Got my stuff. Went back to Mount Baldy and stayed for five months. For a training period. Seichu. And then – a habit I had – I left."

He describes Sasaki as "an utterly remarkable, unique man." He says Sasaki was "amazing."

"In what way?"

"You meet somebody who inspires you. Motivates you and moves you and demonstrates – in front of you, in his manifestation – exactly what he's talking about. I hadn't really met other teachers. I'd read books. I'd read *Zen Mind, Beginner's Mind*. That was a beautiful book. But he was the first living teacher I'd met. He was sufficient. I didn't have to go see somebody else. I knew what I was dealing with."

But he left when the training period ended. Although the roshi was "amazing," Seiju found "the hierarchy and everything else" unappealing. "It took me a while to understand its value. And until I understood it, I resisted it. And I would leave. I left after that first training period and tried to go back to Chicago. But you can never go back. Which I figured out. And so you have to go forward. So I would go forward, but then I would take off."

His pattern was to go to Mount Baldy during the seichu training periods, then find work elsewhere. "I did migrant farm work for a couple of seasons in the San Joaquin Valley of Central California. And other things, just to make some money. 'Cause I had to pay for this stuff. I didn't have a lot of reserves. They offered me scholarships to stay, and, eventually, I decided to take it. So I stayed there for three and a half years, and along the way I became a monk."

Becoming a monk is the first stage of ordination in the Rinzai-ji school. Monks are placed under the guidance of an osho. This was the relationship between Eshu Martin and Eshin Godfrey which Myokyo had described.

"To be a monk or a nun is basically to live a life where you're learning what you're taking on, and your teacher – whether it's the osho or the roshi – has a significant role in directing that. When you…. *If* you become an osho, then that just means you know what you should do. The Roshi doesn't have to baby-sit you anymore. Or your osho doesn't have to baby-sit you anymore."

"Who takes the initiative?" I ask. "Is it the monk? Or does the osho make some kind of discernment and say, 'Maybe you're ready to take this next step'?"

"I think a most suitable unfolding would be that your osho recognizes it a little ahead of you. Anybody who would come forward and say, 'I think I'm ready' is basically asking to get some real sharp training. Right then. A common problem that you can see in this country is that a lot of people have a sense of themselves as a little further along than they might be. 'I want to teach.' That's dangerous. Very dangerous. Anybody who says that, ask them, 'What is teaching?' And if they don't get up and *do* it, you can walk away. That's pretty simple."

Like Myokyo, Seiju denies being a teacher. "I wouldn't teach you how to sit. I would sit. I would say a few things, and what you understood hopefully you'd do. You know, it's like, am I gonna teach you how to breathe?"

In Seiju's case, it was Sasaki who decided he should be ordained an osho. In 1980, Seiju and a woman he had met at Mount Baldy – Hosen Christiane Ranger – were contemplating marriage. "In Sasaki Roshi's view of the world," Seiju explains, "to get married as a monk, you have to be an osho. So we went through a ceremony. He made all the decisions. I didn't ask to become an osho. It was just one of those things. So we did that, and I became an osho, and I ran this place in Jemez Springs for a while."

The place in Jemez Springs is the Bodhi Manda training center. Seiju remained there for nine years. Then, in 1989, "some people here in Albuquerque wanted to start a group. And they asked me if I would be interested in coming here." He doesn't mention certain other factors – such as the unraveling of his marriage – which contributed to his leaving Bodhi Manda. It was also while he was at Bodhi that Karen Tasaka[16] made her complaint about Sasaki's behavior.

"How did the people in Albuquerque know about you?"

"People would come up to Bodhi for retreats. Roshi would come out to Bodhi, and there would be Spring and Fall training periods and things like that. It was the place. If you practiced Rinzai Zen in New Mexico, you probably went to Bodhi, 'cause it's closer than Los Angeles, and Roshi was out here a fair amount."

The Albuquerque group rented a place, established a practice schedule, and could generally expect between fifteen and twenty people to show up on weekends. The numbers were sparser during the week.

"The level of interest would vary, but it was enough to get started. Then we just went from there. My interest in starting the center here in the city was basically working man's Zen. You had a job. You had a family. You had responsibilities. You wanted to do practice. I wanted something you could do every morning. I wanted something you could do in the evening. So, you could work around your responsibilities and your life, *and* you could do practice."

The membership grew steadily, and, in 1997, they built the center on Garfield.

"What's the community like now?"

"It's a volatile community. It's a dynamic community."

"In what way 'volatile'?"

"Well, you know, there's been some flak over the past year, and that took a toll on this community here. So, a lot of people that would practice here now don't practice here. And I was away for part of that time."

Zenshin Michael Haederle was one of the early members of the Albuquerque Zen Center.

"I was living in Texas, working at a newspaper in Houston, and went through a period of really acute anxiety. I had tried various things, such as psychotherapy, and stumbled across meditation in one of the early mind-body books. It included how-to instructions for meditation. It was the first time in several years that I felt some relief. This spoke powerfully to me. It was telling me something about the value of meditation. And as I started investigating a little more, I became aware that what I was doing was basically derived from Buddhist meditation. I started reading more about that and became particularly interested in Zen. *The Three Pillars of Zen* – which, of course, had that how-to aspect to it – kind of got me started there. Several years after that, we came back to New Mexico, and maybe a year after that, the Albuquerque Zen Center opened. There, for the first time, I got formal instruction."

Seiju might not consider himself a teacher, but he was the person who provided Zenshin his initial instruction, and Zenshin thinks of him as a teacher.

"I have very complicated feelings about Seiju because, more than anyone, he was my primary teacher for 23 years or something like that. To accentuate the positive, he can be a very effective communicator. He's very clear about the core elements of the practice and separating out the wheat from the chaff, the essentials from the superfluous. I owe him a considerable debt of gratitude for that steadfastness on his part. He was good about not indulging the neurosis that was already there. And that provided, eventually, a useful boundary that helped me get clear about what practice was about."

In 1993 and '94, Seiju was called to Rinzai-ji, and Myokyo took over responsibility for the Albuquerque Center. "Until she came here to babysit our sangha, Seiju was the only ordained person I knew. I had only done a few sesshin at that point. Myokyo's funny. She's – relatively speaking – light-hearted, engaged, and engaging. All those things. And it was a very personal quality, so it provided a basis for comparison, sort of a triangulation. You could see what was the Zen part of the individual versus the personality part. Now, after all these years, I can see there are things that are characteristic of people who do Zen practice, irrespective of their individual quirks or personality traits or whatever."

Zenshin became deeply involved with AZC. "I was on the board of the Zen Center for ten years. From about 2001, I did all the newcomers' instruction every Saturday morning. I also edited the newsletter for the better part of twenty years." In 2007, he was ordained a monk by Seiju and, in 2012, was going to be left in charge of the center when Seiju was recalled to Rinzai-ji, but that November Eshu Martin's article was published.

"It's been difficult for a lot of people in the community," Seiju tells me. "It was difficult for me, personally. It was difficult for a lot of people I know. A lot of friends and acquaintances. Long-term practitioners. It's impacted vast amounts of people and unsettled a lot of people. And caused people to doubt the practice. And that's very unfortunate."

As for Eshu, in Seiju's opinion he is clearly one of those people who "have a sense of themselves as a little further along than they might be."

"A lot of people, in taking in all this stuff, have resolved it in their various ways. What I found most difficult is that the propensity to get to a mind of judgement impedes understanding. Once I make a decision – 'That's right; that's wrong; this or that' – then I line up behind my judgement and act. I haven't found a mind of judgement to be particularly helpful for a mind of practice. But the emotional *urge* to get to judgement, because there's a lot of unpleasant stuff that has been talked about – and I can understand that – that would make people unsettled. But I've been on the inside for so long I appreciate the great value that comes from studying with Sasaki Roshi. He's a full-bore person. He completely does what he does. And in the human scope of things, everything becomes a thing. Things are entities. So Sasaki Roshi is a *person*. All right? You're a person. That's a dog. You know? This is a person. That kind of thinking. Very common. Very understandable. Very human. That's not what Buddhism teaches us. Everything is activity. Sometimes I manifest skillful activities. Sometimes I manifest foolish activity. And sometimes I manifest selfish activity. I can be a loving parent, and I can be a terrible co-worker. And I can be both of those and all of those in the same day. And anything else. And in my experience around Sasaki Roshi, he's been a remarkable, deeply committed teacher. Highly intense and highly demanding of his students. And also he can be very intense in these other areas. It's completely consistent with his character, in terms of complete activity. And it seems that, at those times, we weren't dealing with Joshu Sasaki Roshi. We were dealing with Joshu Sasaki, a Japanese man. And he could manifest both of those qualities. People presume that if you're quote 'enlightened' end quote – whatever that means – or 'awake' or anything else, you can't possibly do this other stuff. And I mean, I don't know the answer to that. But it's pretty obvious to me that the one person I've spent time with who seems to come closest to what a lot of people would think of as an 'awake' person has also done these other things. And that, to me, is just skillful activity and unskillful activity. Which, again, we all do in our lives."

Zenshin is a freelance writer and twice interviewed Sasaki, with the aid of an interpreter, for articles in national Buddhist publications. Sasaki's primary translator for twelve years beginning in 1995 had been Giko David Rubin. In 2007, Giko brought the testimony of several female students to the attention of the primarily male Osho Council. This was the "can of worms" Myokyo had referred to. The oshos rushed to the defence of their teacher. "One of them literally advocated beating Giko with a stick. Crazy stuff like that," says Zenshin. But Sasaki apologized to some of the women involved, and Giko, Zenshin, and others believed – or hoped – that the roshi's behavior was now under control.

Then, in late 2009, Giko told Zenshin that Sasaki was accused of molesting another woman. "This after everything else had happened and his supposed apologies. I remember talking about it with my wife and daughter, who was home for Christmas. We had this long conversation. Eventually, I resolved to stop going to sanzen with him, to stop going to sesshin, which I did not announce to anybody at the time. It was just a personal withdrawal of cooperation. It occurred to me at some point that you can't be a teacher if you don't have students."

Then, according to Zenshin, in September 2012, Sasaki asked Seiju to come to Los Angeles in order to be his successor. "My recollection is that when Seiju called me up right after Labor Day 2012, he said Sasaki wanted him to take over as 'abbot.' I remember asking, 'Is this it?' Meaning, 'Is Roshi preparing to hand over the reins?' And Seiju answered, 'Yeah, I think so.'"

The offer, however, was "conditional on Seiju renouncing his abbotship at the Albuquerque Zen Center. He felt Seiju had to cut ties and completely be in LA. So Seiju asked me if I would be willing to serve as *shika*, which means administrator."

Zenshin and his wife – Leslie Linthicum – discussed it. She's also a journalist and, while not a Zen practitioner, is supportive of her husband's practice. Together they decided he would accept the offer, and they would move into the center.

"To make this move, we were preparing to rent out our house and make various adjustments. So we jumped into it, making repairs and all those kinds of things you have to do, and packing things up, and I started reaching out to people at the Zen center, as well as to former members of the Zen center who hadn't been around much, because many had had conflicts with Seiju. I knew that it would be important to have as many hands on deck as possible. And then Eshu Martin's thing in *Sweeping Zen* came out where he says pretty boldly that Sasaki Roshi has been molesting female students."

Confronted with this – as well as with what he considered the inadequate response in the letter Seiju signed on behalf of the Osho Council – Zenshin changed his mind. On December 1, he sent a letter of resignation to Seiju and ten days later sent another letter to the sangha members in which he admitted he had been aware of allegations against Sasaki since Giko's 2007 report.

> Since Giko first raised this issue, several female students have personally confirmed their experiences to me. It has pained me deeply to live with this knowledge, which I did not begin to learn until six months after I had ordained as a Rinzai-ji monk. All of us – Roshi included – took the five fundamental Buddhist precepts: no killing, lying, stealing, misuse of intoxicants or misuse of sexuality. I have struggled to reconcile my vows with my awareness of our teacher's behavior and the knowledge that many of those around him had rationalized it or covered it up. I finally decided two years ago to stop attending sesshin with Roshi, but I did not speak up.
>
> I was not alone. Despite their decades of hard practice, many long-time students seem to put their love for their teacher ahead of the urgent need to acknowledge and respond to the distress of the people who have been harmed. This blind devotion to Roshi has, I feel, actually impaired their ability to fulfill their vows as Buddhist clergy. I now realize that in putting loyalty and discretion above the obligation to speak truthfully, Roshi's oshos and monks (me included) have disserved you, the Rinzai-ji lay sangha. I am very sorry for that.
>
> ...
>
> This is one of the most painful decisions I have ever made. Over the past 23 years this sangha has sustained me in countless ways – it has become my second home. I treasure the many friends I made and am grateful both for Seiju's teaching and for the opportunity I have had to practice with you. It breaks my heart to think I will no longer be able to do that, even as it shames me to know that I have let you down. Leslie and I were looking forward to being able

to serve the sangha in new ways: we're deeply disappointed at how things have turned out.

...

My commitment to serving the dharma has not changed. I continue to sit every day and hope that you will remain committed to deepening your own practice.[17]

Seiju doesn't mention that he had been invited to become abbot of Rinzai-ji. Instead, he tells me he was going to be "the shika, doing day to day business. Roshi was still the abbot." Then Zenshin resigned.

"I had a monk who was going to take over for me when I left here. And in December, when it was announced I was going to be leaving and coming to Los Angeles in January, he decided that he could no longer accept what had happened and everything else. Said, 'I can't be a Rinzai-ji monk anymore.' It made for a very tumultuous time."

Then, before the *New York Times* story was published, two articles appeared in the *Albuquerque Journal*. The first focused on the fact that in the past Sasaki had been accused of molesting women at the Bodhi Manda center in New Mexico. The second article, a week later, was an emotional piece by Zenshin's wife describing the impact the revelations had had on their family. Both stories ran on the front page of the paper.

Seiju tells me that after the articles were published "there was an active movement among some of the people that were trying to take this center out of the Rinzai-ji tradition. Basically be independent. And I resisted that. Roshi had put a lot of energy and money into the place, as well as myself."

I point out that, of course, the stories about Sasaki's behaviour would not have been news to the oshos. Long before Giko's report to the Osho Council, one of Sasaki's most senior students – Gentei Sandy Stewart – had disaffiliated his North Carolina Zen Center from Rinzai-ji in 1992 specifically because "of my objection to the sexual behavior and sexual teaching techniques of the Head Abbot" and "my disapproval of the lack of action by the Head Abbot, board of directors or ordained persons of Rinzai-ji to help those who have suffered on account of this behavior."[18]

"Yeah," Seiju admits in his laconic manner. "It was something that was known about. It was a difficult area to deal with. It's hard to appreciate the influence that Sasaki Roshi exercised over the whole organization because he was extraordinary."

"You keep using the past tense."

"Well, because he doesn't teach like that anymore. I mean, he's debilitated. The amount of lucidity he has during an average day is less than a couple of hours probably. And on some days, he doesn't have that. He's old, and he's weak."

The previous July, as Myokyo had told me he would, Eshin Godfrey from Vancouver went to Rinzai-ji, ostensibly as "designate abbot." By the time of my visit to Seiju, however, Godfrey was being referred to as the "Administrative Abbot." Perhaps that sounded better than "shika."

"Was it your decision to return to Albuquerque?"

Seiju nods his head. "Yeah. I felt I couldn't be effective in Los Angeles. I knew that this community was hurting severely, and I had invested twenty-three years of my life in trying to build this up as a place where people could come and practice."

"Were you able to bring about some kind of reconciliation with the members?"

"Not so many. I mean, you can talk to some people, but I'm not quite sure what 'reconcile' means. It's kind of like some people are really angry, and they're just still really angry. They feel that they've been betrayed in a very deep way, and I understand that. There's no argument with that. No discussion. You feel betrayed. I get that."

"The monk who had been left in charge," I ask, "the one who resigned, is he still engaged in practice?"

"Yeah, I think he has a sitting group."

"But separate from…."

"Yeah, yeah. And there's another group that sits in the city some place. I don't keep track of that very much, but they do something."

Zenshin Haederle maintains a zendo, the North Valley Sitting Group, in a small adobe building – a *casita* – on his property. "We've had about forty people come through the doors. Regularly, it's anywhere from six to ten. And we have day-sits – zazenkai – where we'll have 14 or 15." Mitra Bishop – a Dharma heir of Philip Kapleau now studying with Shodo Harada – has led some of those day sits. Zenshin notes that, compared to Sasaki, Mitra is "180 degrees the other way. A million miles away, and yet she's absolutely the real deal, and a very strong person, and very committed and serious and everything else."

The other group Seiju referred to is the Albuquerque Zero Zen Center hosted by another former Rinzai-ji monk, Myo On Susan Linnell. She's a painter, and her group meets in what had been her studio. "I still paint in there secretly when no one's around," she confides to me, laughing lightly. Myo On also now studies with Shodo Harada. "I really wished that he weren't Japanese or wished he were a woman or something different. But he seemed to be recommended as the Rinzai guy to go to."

<h1 style="text-align:center">3</h1>

Although he is the editor of the book published to celebrate Sasaki's centenary, David Yoshin Radin tells me that he has always kept separate from Rinzai-ji and the Osho Council. "When Roshi said, 'I want to make you an osho,' what I heard was 'a no show.' I thought Roshi was telling me my attendance at trainings had been too infrequent. Then I understood it and told him he was making an osho who was a 'no-show.'" David can remember only one or two Council meetings he has attended. "I've stayed on the east coast and not been involved in a lot of the Rinzai-ji social matters. Just by my choice. I was never fond of those kinds of gatherings. That's all."

There's no signage identifying his Zen Center on the Lieb Road in Spencer, New York, south of Ithaca. One has to know that mailbox 56 marks the drive. A gravel road leads to a cluster of small cabins on one side and, on the other, a large pond with several small wooden bridges leading to islands just large enough for a chair or two. It's a quiet place; bird songs and the calls of frogs – like the snapping of elastic bands – are clear and sharp.

At the back of the property, tucked away in the woods past the cabins, is a small zendo. There is a tea area on one side of a set of shoji screens, then three rows of platforms called tans with seating for fifteen and a few chairs. When the screens come down, three more places can be added to each row. The week after my visit, a sesshin is scheduled which already has twenty-three individuals enrolled; it would be a tight fit.

The dormitories and cabins are not solely for the benefit of the Zen practitioners. They had been built for the participants of the summer Body Mind Restoration Retreats which David's wife, Marcia – or Khadija – developed. Although she, too, studied with Sasaki, her primary path is Sufism, in which she is a Sheikha and a teacher of whirling. The retreats are the Radins' primary income generator and, in effect, support the Zen program, drawing over 300 attendees each summer. According to their web site, the retreats

– are designed to heal and rejuvenate the body and mind. This is not a spa experience; it is a comprehensive program that introduces a way of living that leads to sustainable weight loss and good health. The combination of a living foods diet (organic, vegetarian, raw foods), exercise, colon care, health education classes, yoga, meditation and more allow a deep experience of well being that cannot be found elsewhere.[19]

It is May 2014 when I visit David – he prefers to go by his given name rather than his Dharma name – more than a year since my visit to Myokyo and seven months after my interview with Seiju. A lot has happened in the interim.

Eshin Godfrey resigned as Administrative Abbot of Rinzai-ji in November and returned to Vancouver. On the Vancouver Zen Center's web site, he stated: "There were difficulties in moving on a permanent basis. Visa, health, and marriage among them."[20] In January, Seiju was quoted on the *Sweeping Zen* site to the effect that Sasaki had taken the title "Supreme Abbot" and was "firmly in charge."

But by May, Seiju himself was in conflict with the Osho Council. The issue was the treatment of his former wife, Hosen, who – after being the abbot of Bodhi Manda for twenty-four years – had been defrocked by Sasaki and ordered to turn in her robes. The reason for her dismissal was unclear. On the one hand, she appears to have been accused of overstepping her authority by announcing a seasonal practice period in the autumn of 2013 which she referred to as a kessei. As Zenshin tells me, "Theoretically, you can't have a kessei without a roshi in residence."

But, he adds, there was also a question about her decision to retain control of the archive of video-taped and recorded talks given by Sasaki at Bodhi Manda. When she was asked to turn these over to Rinzai-ji for a project intended to commemorate Sasaki's career, she refused, having been advised by one of her board members – who was an intellectual property lawyer – that the talks given at Bodhi Manda had been "work for hire" and therefore, under copyright law, belong to the center and not to Sasaki or Rinzai-ji.

When Hosen did not immediately comply with Sasaki's demand that she return her robes, a group of eighteen oshos wrote to her on December 13 saying

– we are looking for a very straightforward and sincere response which clearly resolves this impasse, not for a reference to previous statements and a request for more time. We expect you to have entirely moved from Bodhi Manda well before spring kessei, and we are all prepared to help you do this, but we require a clear and unequivocal statement of your commitment. Here is such a statement:

I agree without reservation to comply with Roshi's directives.

I agree without reservation to leave Bodhi Manda and support the transition of Seido to Vice Abbot.

I agree without reservation to move from Bodhi Manda entirely by March 24th, 2014.

I agree without reservation to move from the quarters attached to the Bodhi Manda office, to a dorm room, by February 15th, 2014.

I agree without reservation to compose a letter unconditionally committing to these agreements and will send this letter to Roshi and the 18 of you no later than midnight of December 14th, 2013.

The above statement is the kind of response we are looking for.[21]

The following day, Seiju – in his capacity as a member of the Bodhi Manda board – replied to the authors of this bizarre letter, pointing out that in the late 1980s Sasaki had resigned as abbot of Bodhi Manda, and therefore, under law, the board at Bodhi Manda retained responsibility for the facility and did not recognize Sasaki's authority over them. The reason for Sasaki's resignation, Seiju reminded the others, had been the allegation of sexual misconduct raised by Karen Tasaka. In case any of them failed to remember Ms. Tasaka, who was now dead, he included a portion of the poem she wrote beginning, "Roshi, you are a sexual abuser."

David wants me know that he has chosen to remain at a distance from Rinzai-ji precisely because of circumstances like these.

"But isn't the Ithaca Zen Center associated with Rinzai-ji in some kind of official manner?" I ask.

"It's more a personal temple," he tells me.

"Didn't Sasaki authorize you to set it up?"

"Well, once you're ordained an osho, you're given permission to hang your shingle, so to speak. You have permission to teach. The blessings of your teacher to teach."

"Does that mean you also have the authority, for example, to appoint an heir?"

"Yes. I can ordain up to my level, but I'm more of a lay person. The whole situation here was built by Marcia and myself to serve as a place of practice and other things that go on here. So to be my heir would not be to have this temple. There would be a spiritual heir but not actually a lineage of the temple."

It is an issue to which I will return.

He grew up in New York City and attended Jewish parochial schools, which – as he puts it – "kept me out of bars and brothels but didn't really point much higher." When he was fifteen years old, his father, a rabbi, was afflicted with a very painful terminal cancer. "At school, we had prayers every day, and there are certain intercessional prayers where you're allowed to make requests. And I can recall praying really intensely, 'God, please spare my father. He's a righteous man; he's the head of a congregation; he's a loving father. Why is he going through this? Can't you heal somebody who is righteous?' And I waited for an answer, and the answer that came back to me was, 'You've got to be kidding.' That left me a certain impression about the human relationship to God.

"So that was one strong event in my life. Then I came to Cornell, and I was editor of the student newspaper in my senior year and earned several thousand dollars. I decided to take a year off from school and travel around the world with my earnings. And before I left, I sent in my law school application. I went to California because it was winter. I was going to go the warm way and then come around; so I went west. And then I tripped on acid in Berkeley."

"Your first time?"

"First time. And it was a very strong experience. Very strong." It was a route to Zen that many others followed at the time. Elsewhere in our conversation, David will refer to is as "kick-starting" the practice.

He spent some time in India, experimenting with hashish as a spiritual practice. "But I got really sick because a holy man told me I should drink the water of the Ganges and it would save my life. So I drank it. I lost 45 pounds in three weeks with amoebic dysentery." He returned to the US too ill to attend law school. "And I had been called for the Vietnam draft, but, when they saw me with the dysentery, they just said, 'Good-bye.' So in a certain way, the holy water worked."

He considered entering rabbinical school. "I went to an interview, and they started asking me questions: 'Do you want to be a congregational rabbi? Do you want to be a teaching rabbi? What's your interest?' And I told them that I wanted to meet God in the way that Moses had. Face to face. That was my only interest. They said, 'Well, we can't help you.'" He laughs. "That was the end of rabbinical school. 'That's not what we do.'

"Then I tried going to graduate school in philosophy. Because I had no context for the drug experiences. I was coming out of the blue. I had these experiences of the mind awakening while on drugs, but how do I do that through will? How do I do that through my own intelligence, not through smoking? The drug experience started to deteriorate. And I realized I had to stop. So I took up meditation practice."

"What kind of meditation?"

"Just from books. One was *The Zen Teaching of Huang Po.* One of the teachings in the book was that your mind should be like the sands of the Ganges. If there are diamonds and jewels inside, you're not excited. And if there's terror and horror inside, you're not afraid. Just allow everything to arise. Something like that. And I'd never received a teaching like that. My understanding of religion was a code of law in Judaism, and now here are teachings of how to guide the mind through the deeper states. So I felt drawn to Zen because of the connection to the teaching. I realized, 'There's a path! There are teachings. I just need to find them.' But I was still on my own."

In 1971, he visited Marcia – who at the time was just a friend – in San Francisco. "And there was going to be the first sesshin at the San Francisco Zen Center after Suzuki Roshi had passed away, and so I decided to go to it. And it was *very* different from smoking hashish."

It would be five years before he would try another Zen retreat.

After returning from India, David lived in a hippie commune not far from where he currently resides. "Twelve years without electricity, telephone, and running water," he says, smiling at the memory.

"How did you support yourself?" I ask.

"Oh, chopping wood and carrying water. Literally. Some people had jobs in town, but I was able to get by working on the land pretty much. It was a productive farm, but it couldn't support itself. But we grew a lot of produce and had root cellars and things like that. It was a beautiful scene for a while until sex, drugs, and rock-n-roll blew the place apart."

He still felt the need to find a teacher and eventually returned to India. "I had heard about Swami Muktanada, who was a Hindu yogi. So I decided to go to his ashram. I sold every possession I had at the commune; raised enough money for a one-way ticket to India plus $15. And I thought, 'I'm just going to go to the ashram, and I'm not going to leave.' Got to Bombay. Got to his ashram. And, for some reason, they wouldn't let me in. So I was living in a bus stall across the street from the ashram with no money, no food. It's a long story; I feel silly talking about this stuff."

Of course many who came of age in the late '60s and early '70s could tell similar stories.

"Anyway, I met this guy, Gil. I was out in the street, and I was getting a little bit frantic because I had no money, no anything. 'What am I going to do about this?' And he looked at me and said, 'Don't worry. Behind the thoughts there is no "I".' And it clicked. One of those 'click' moments. So, there it was. The teaching was right in front of me."

Gil might not have been an authorized teacher, but he could – as David puts it – transmit. And with this insight, David's quest shifted in a new direction.

When he managed to return to the US, he became involved in a second commune located by a two-acre pond not far from where the previous commune had been. Eventually, however, it broke down as well. After that, David and his girlfriend, Tessa, bought an old potato chip delivery van and bolted a coal-burning stove to the back floor; its chimney was vented out the roof. Tessa would eventually become his first wife. They went to Saskatoon to visit a friend. "It was the end of November and minus 30."

Through this friend, he met someone else who told him about Joshu Sasaki and suggested he consider going down to Mount Baldy. Tessa's grandmother had just died, and she needed to return home, so David went to Mount Baldy on his own. It was Rohatsu – the December sesshin marking the anniversary of the Buddha's enlightenment – which is generally more demanding than other sesshin. Sittings are longer; discipline is imposed more strictly. David was unprepared for it.

"2:30 a. m. wake up and 11:00 p. m. to sleep. It was outside my usual hours, and the physical pain was unbearable. But there were moments of profound insight that inspired me to just want to keep training with Roshi. So I had an immediate and very powerful bond to Sasaki Roshi as my teacher. His silence and poise were majestic. And his ability to teach that the self – my 'self' – was not identical to my body was direct and powerful. I had never seen anything like that before. Of course I'd studied the teachings, but it's different when you get it live than when you get it from a book. It has the power to break through your own mental states. And that's why all this kafuffle is of no interest to me. I mean, he gave me such a profound gift that everything else is dwarfed."

The "kafuffle" he refers to, of course, is the controversy over Sasaki's behavior.

"How would you explain to someone who's heard these stories why you think Sasaki was such a good teacher?" I ask.

"He was able to transmit the highest wisdom."

"And how did he do that?"

"First, there was a feeling that he was residing in a different residence than I was residing in. I'm an individual seeking the higher wisdom. He seemed to be radiating from the higher wisdom. And through koan training and just his own presence, he could evoke that experience within me. That's what his training and koan work was designed for, for the mind to awaken to its actual nature instead of being constantly in the mind stream. So he could awaken that. He could bring so much presence to the situation that your mind could be quiet and you could see into the emptiness of self."

David felt the power of Sasaki's koan work during that first sesshin. "Roshi didn't train with Mu.[22] He didn't approve of the Japanese koan style. He wanted to do something more direct, what he felt was more appropriate to Americans. So a lot of his koan training was, 'How do you realize the absolute when…boom.' And he would say something, and you would have to manifest – full-body manifestation, not a dialogue intellectually – that you had, indeed, seen the truth of that moment. Which could take place by answering it or just the state of being that arises when that experience takes place.

"I don't want to discuss the experiences because it was a long time ago and all I have is memory. But I do remember, I went out of sanzen during that first retreat, and I was feeling so transformed that, instead of going back to the zendo, I snuck behind his cabin and lay down under a tree so I could enjoy the experience and not be in the pain of zazen. And around five hours later, the monitors came with a full search warrant out for my arrest," he says, laughing.

When he and Tessa returned to New York, "the commune had broken apart, and it wasn't clear what it was going to be. But it happened that the title for the land was in Tessa's name, because she was the only one who had enough money to purchase it, and since we got married shortly after, the land fell into our lap."

In was 1977, and Sasaki was offering annual sesshin at Saint Joseph's Trappist Abbey in Spencer, Massachusetts. David attended one of these, then arranged for Cornell University to sponsor Sasaki's "Seminar on the Sutras" as an accredited course. "Meanwhile, there was a question about what was going to be the status of the old commune, because everybody had left. It was a very strange situation. And so my wife – who was nine months pregnant with our first child – and I went to visit Sasaki, and we offered him the land. 'We're just offering this to you as a gift to make a Zen Center.' He said, 'I can't accept a gift like that, but, if you go back to the land, I'll come and help you establish it as a Zen Center.' Which basically meant he would come and teach. And the baby was born about five days later, and she was named after him. Her name is Joshi."

The former commune was renamed the Beech Hill Pond Meditation Center. Sasaki came the following year to lead the center's first sesshin. Now that he had a family, David didn't feel able to take part in the longer training periods at Mount Baldy, so he went to California only for sesshin and hosted Sasaki's visits to New York. This kept him separate from many of the things that were happening in the larger Rinzai-ji community.

David and Tessa separated in 1980. Four years later, he and Marcia married. They had been best friends for thirteen years before that but had never been involved in a romantic relationship.

"It was *totally platonic*!" Marcia had told me earlier in the day. "I mean, we never kissed. I would have, but he clearly…. Well, you take your lead. You know? The friendship was so precious to me that I in no way wanted to compromise it. So we were best friends." When David finally suggested they explore "a part of our relationship we haven't checked out yet," Marcia's first response was, "'Shit! There goes my best friend!' And then I thought, 'Hmm. Maybe that's what you should be doing with your best friend.'"

The two of them purchased the present site in 1986, around the time that Sasaki made David "a no-show." David seems to have by-passed the process of being a monk under the guidance of a more experienced osho. A small community – including former hippies – started to attend the Zendo on the Lieb Road; another group met at Cornell, in Ithaca. David calls Cornell his "fishing pond."

In the early '90s, Marcia began offering the Body Mind Restoration Retreats. Although David gives talks at these, they are kept separate from the formal zendo activities. There is, however, residue from his old communal perspective in both the design of the retreats and in his approach to Zen.

"I think one of the problems with Zen teaching in America – at least the circles that I've bumped into – is that there's not enough heart in it," he tells me. "There's not enough love in the teaching. The teaching is, 'Do this form; do this; count your breathing; and this and that.' But I think it's so much more important to teach people that they can escape from the misery that their mind is creating, and that, by realizing certain things, it's possible to take care of your mind. People should cultivate tranquillity by practicing kindness. By forgiving people. By not thinking you can undo your pain by hurting people who hurt you. By relaxing in the present moment. Really fundamental kindness ideas that I think are ignored in certain dry Zen places." He smiles and shrugs. "I still have hippie blood."

He remains loyal to Sasaki. "For me, he was a fellow who was a transmitter of the living wisdom. In his personal life, he may have had problems. But it was just something to deal with. Some people flew into emotional drama. Huge emotional drama. And you're not holding the great view when you're caught up in confusion and emotion. You're not holding the space of an osho when you get into emotional drama. Emotional drama means that you're not seeing clearly. 'Oh, there were people who were hurt.' Okay. But it felt to me like it was walking into a tar pit. That's why I didn't want to touch it. I was invited to be on this and that. I didn't feel like my voice would be useful in that environment. I felt like it had so much emotional load to it that I wouldn't have been useful. My way of being was so different from what was happening there."

"You'd said that you had kept yourself at a distance from Rinzai-ji from the beginning."

"That was mostly because I never felt that kind of love-hit in the community. So why would I want to be in a place like that? I had spent twelve years in hippie communes," he says, laughing gently. "And I loved the softness of it; I loved the playfulness of life. I loved the ambitionlessness of it. And then I got into Zen studies, there was silence, but the silence seemed to lack humor. I mean, to me wisdom and love are inseparable. You have a wisdom view that the consciousness – original nature – is holding this as Oneness. It's all interpenetrating Oneness; co-dependent origination. This water in the pond the next day is going into my body. So everything is one beingness without a self. This insight is joyous and relaxing."

"Did Roshi hurt people?"

"I think his actions may have caused some people to have unpleasant emotional experiences. Yes."

"Women?"

"Men too."

"And if one of those women had been someone you were close to – your daughter, for example – would that have affected the way you felt about things?"

"He might have fondled my daughters, but I said to them, 'If that bothers you in the least – this old guy that's been monastically locked up and has a horny side or something like that – and it puts you off, just keep a distance.' But to me, contact with him offered the possibility of contact with very deep spiritual wisdom. He transmitted extremely precious teachings, so I'll always honor him. I didn't want to shut the door to a relationship with him for my children or anyone else because of his conduct.

"When Roshi was coming here to do sesshin, I gave a special orientation and said, 'He has a tendency to caress women's breasts and occasionally pull people in and hug them, feel their bodies, and there doesn't seem to be any way to change that conduct. In sanzen, you're alone with him. But I also tell you that he's a transmitter of great wisdom, and you have to find your comfort zone. And if this is outside your comfort zone, just say no or just don't do sesshin. But I want you to know that.' That was part of every orientation when he was here. You know, you have a fellow who has strange conduct that's not my style, and I couldn't stop him because he just turned a deaf ear. But I still felt his teachings were very precious. That that wasn't his primary activity in life. That was just what happened. He, and we, had to deal with it. So I steered my boat as best I could. I tried to use him for the teachings and not get involved in the social scene I didn't like."

"Sasaki hasn't given inka to anyone," I point out. "So no one is authorized to carry on the type of koan training, for example, that you went through."

"Correct."

"What does that bode for the lineage when he dies? What will happen to the Rinzai-ji line?"

"I don't have any concern about it. It doesn't make a difference to me whether the line continues or not. It's just a question of whether the wisdom continues."

"But in order to continue, doesn't that wisdom need to be entrusted to people who have the responsibility for carrying it forward?"

"I don't think it needs to be carried forward in koans and sanzen. It's possible if your mind is awake, if you're knowing the deeper consciousness and you have some skillful means in order to lead others to that insight, that's the real continuation. The real continuation isn't corporate."

"Well," I argue, "it is corporate in the sense that if there aren't teachers, the practice won't continue."

"That's true, but a teacher doesn't have to have this stamp. The stamp of a teacher is his own mind. The stamp from outside, yeah, it's okay; it makes everything kosher. I know a number of oshos, if they were given inka, for example, I would pay homage to them out of courtesy to my teacher, but I wouldn't have any sense that I'd want to train with them. And there are others who are, I feel, quite ripe, and doing a sesshin with them would be a rewarding experience. Whether it would have the penetration of doing sesshin with Roshi, I don't know."

In a similar way, he is unconcerned about what happens to his own center.

"The way my situation is set up, it doesn't lend itself to an easy transition into a perpetuated thing. So I don't keep that in my mind much. If I had been a renunciate monk who had known this was a corporate thing – by corporate, I mean in the good way; that it existed as an entity without my having it – then that entity would be able to continue itself, perhaps like Daido did at Zen Mountain, where he created a place and could transmit it. But this center is something like a family thing, which I don't think is good or bad. It has its advantages and disadvantages. But if I can transmit the teachings and have some peoples' minds wake up, that would be what I've left. But the physical place here, I don't think is going to work that way.

"You know, I never had any interest in Zen or Buddhism or this or that. I had an interest in the wisdom insight. And that doesn't belong to any name or lineage or tradition or person or anything. It's the true nature of all being. Which I see and I don't see; I see and I don't see."

"So you don't consider yourself a Buddhist?"

"No."

"And if someone were to ask you to define yourself...."

He laughs. "It depends. It would depend on my mood."

"Well," I point out, "you're down as being the abbot of the Ithaca Zen Center."

"Whatever. I don't really care. You know, but if someone says to you something like, 'Behind all those thoughts there is no "I."' And you realize, you see into emptiness, you see the ego-structure is empty of self; it's only thought-created. What religion is that? What religion is a bird singing? What religion is the goose flying around? Making a religion just puts a name on something that has no name. It's a state of being. How can it have a name?"

Earlier in the day, I had spent a couple of hours with Marcia while their dogs chased away the Canada geese seeking to land by the pond.

"Roshi always acknowledged that I was a Sufi teacher and trained me differently than he trained his other students. Which was Roshi's great scope. I'll tell you a funny story. When Roshi ordained me as a nun I asked – because I felt it was important – 'Roshi, what's incumbent on me becoming a nun?' And he looked at me, and he said: 'For you, absolutely nothing.'" She chuckles. "He said it in English. And I said, 'Oh! I'm a "nun-of-the-above."' And David said, 'And I'm finally second-to-nun.' Just to give you insight into our relationship with Roshi. It was very playful and loving and intimate."

For her the matter of succession in the Sufi line is a concern. Talking about the dervish whirling which is an important element in her school of Sufism, she tells me: "I don't know how much longer I'll be able to do this. I have students who have the physical part; now they're ripening their ability to teach what goes along with that. A friend who recently died was the Grand Dame of the Sufi order where I first saw the whirling. She was appointed by the head to be the first teacher. So we're all dying, and it's really important to me to make sure – if I can – that I get everybody ready enough to continue the teaching and practices. In certain ways, Roshi didn't do that."

As with David, her admiration for Sasaki is unwavering.

"There are many fine students whom I respect enormously. But in terms of the criteria for a Sufi it isn't how much you know or how much you've studied; it's really how disappeared you can be into the light. And very few people availed themselves of Roshi's gracious teachings on that level. Their resolve and their dedication and their sincerity have been tremendous, but their actual realization? Perhaps they didn't get that part of Roshi. It's hard to say.

"And so this whole thing about women and all this stuff: I was his inji, his attendant. I helped push the poop out of his body when he was getting older. And he was so appropriate. He was never not appropriate. He met your being. And he was always teaching. Not just in sanzen."

"And yet," I point out, "there were people with whom he was inappropriate."

"There were. And I don't deny that. But all I'm saying is that in thirty years, what I met was this incredible being. I don't even have words to describe what he was, the mirror he was."

4

Zenshin Haederle in Albuquerque has come to believe that Rinzai-ji is not "a Zen Buddhist organization. It's a Zen-flavored cult. And here's why. You talked to Seiju; you talked to Myokyo, and to Yoshin. All three of them said – in varying ways – that Sasaki's the greatest thing since sliced bread. One of the last things Seiju said to me, in fact, was that Sasaki was the greatest Zen Master in the last 500 years or something like that. So stop for a second, okay? What's the basis for comparison? Is there a roshi-meter? None of these people have sat with other teachers. None of them have ever studied in Japan. None of them were encouraged to study in Japan. Their entire view of what Zen is is what Sasaki gave them, what Sasaki has imparted. You've probably heard some of the terminology and so forth Sasaki uses. He's invented his own language. 'Tathagata Zen.' 'Plus and minus.' 'Expansion and contraction.' That, among other things, serves to isolate Rinzai-ji people from everybody else. I can attest from all the years that I was part of it, that there's a tremendous amount of disdain for other teachers and other lineages."

In Montreal, Myokyo admitted that there were probably four oshos – all male – who had ambitions to become Sasaki's successor. "And there was all the jockeying and stuff around that. But the other side of it is that many of us felt that if Roshi named any one of his students as his successor that that would be bad, because it's clear: The tradition is that you must exceed your teacher in understanding in order to be named a successor. And I think for a lot of us, there was no one coming anywhere near that."

Joshu Sasaki died on July 27, 2014, at the age of 107. He had not named a successor.

CHAPTER THREE
Shinge Roko Sherry Chayat

THE STORY OF THE 105 YEAR OLD JAPANESE TEACHER WHO HAD BEEN MOLESTING his female students for more than five decades was the major Zen news item at the beginning of 2013. It was so deliciously salacious even CNN covered it. But Eido Shimano, former abbot of the Zen Studies Society, was in the news as well. It was revealed that he was pursuing a $2 million breach-of-contract suit against the Society for its failure to meet its pension obligations to him. He also claimed that many of the religious and artistic items at the Society's center in New York City – Shobo-ji – and at Dai Bosatsu Zendo were his personal property. He was unable to retrieve these items because the Zen Studies Society had placed a deadbolt lock on the front door at Shobo-ji in order to prevent him from entering without making prior arrangements.

The nearest community to Dai Bosatsu is Livingston Manor, a hamlet of about 1200 people in the region which claims to be the birthplace of fly-fishing in the United States. I came over the mountain from ZMM and stopped at a local diner for lunch. As I paid my bill at the cash register, I asked if they could direct me to the Buddhist monastery. The man behind the counter who had been moderately affable until that point suddenly became less so. "You mean those Japanese?" I supposed I did. "Turn left in front here, drive down past the underpass. You still have another half hour to go after that. Good luck finding it." His tone didn't suggest a genuine concern about my luck.

The woman I came to interview – Shinge Roko Sherry Chayat Roshi – admits, "There's the feeling on some people's part, probably, that we're some sort of elite, exotic, weird sect of some strange religion." Her head is shaved, and she is wearing a samugi, a light brown belted jacket and pants much like a martial arts uniform. The young man who serves us tea also has a shaved head. He is wearing the multi-layered robes of a Zen monk and is on his knees as he places the tray in front of us.

"So there's suspicion on the part of some, I'm sure," Shinge continues. "But I think we've been here long enough that the general community has embraced us.

And we have good interactions with area farmers and shopkeepers, some of whom sell our miso and home-made jams."

Shinge is Eido Shimano's heir and successor as abbot of Shobo-ji and Dai Bosatsu. He retired – under pressure – on December 8, 2010, and she was installed on January 1st. Although she was considered a Shimano loyalist by some, Shinge was the person who ordered the deadbolt installed on the door at Shobo-ji.

From the moment I was met at the door by a young robed monk, I felt challenged by Dai Bosatsu. It did not help that the monk's first words to me were a warning to be careful while walking back to my car because the ticks carried Lyme Disease.

Dai Bosatsu is unquestionably beautiful; architecturally, it is magnificent. But it is also – as the man at the diner had said – Japanese. The monk who greeted me is not, but, when I call to him after he shows me my room, he turns and responds with a sharp, "Hai!" At lunch, a Japanese woman seated opposite me wordlessly demonstrates how to use the three nested jihatsu bowls, precisely where to place the chop sticks, how to unfold the napkin. Nor am I used to having someone kowtow before me after serving tea.

I recognize that to some degree it is a matter of taste. The very elements which make me slightly ill at ease might give others a sense of the authenticity of the practice here, a feeling of being immersed in a tradition with a vibrant cultural and aesthetic – as well as spiritual – heritage. And then, of course, is not part of Zen surrendering what Shinge refers to as "agency," those personal preferences we cling to so tenaciously?

If I am not entirely comfortable with the surroundings, I find Shinge herself charming, witty, and skilled at putting people at ease. The head monastic had told me that Shinge is not what many people expect. "People think of Rinzai Zen as martial and hard and unforgiving and brutal." Shinge Roshi, she tells me, is compassionate, inclusive, and "very feminine."

We begin by chatting about numbers. There are, Shinge tells me, currently eight residents at Dai Bosatsu although two are away because of illness – one with Lyme Disease. Before what she refers to as "the troubles," they had had as many as sixty people at sesshin. The previous May there had been fourteen. A number of women have withdrawn from practice entirely. And then there are those who left with Shimano and continue to study with him elsewhere.

Shinge is an articulate and lucid speaker.

"What the Buddha taught in the Four Noble Truths is something we all know in our own way, but we never really come to see how we can transform our lives accordingly unless we commit to a Zen practice or another spiritual tradition in which meditation is very much a part. There is suffering. Everybody can say, 'Yes. That's true.' The next step for most people is to say, 'It's *their* fault. It's because of such-and-such condition. Such-and-such circumstances. If not for that, I would be fine.' But the Buddha said, 'Look at the cause in your life. When you stop pointing your finger outward, what's really going on?' What is going on in you that is perpetuating suffering, as opposed to merely feeling the perfectly natural ebb-and-flow of pain and gain that everyone experiences? What makes it suffering? What are you thinking right now? How are you interpreting what's happening in your life that makes it suffering? What are you ignorant of in your life? Do you actually think you can make the things that you like stay the same? Do you actually think you can prevent things that you don't like? Does your inner state of dissatisfaction cause you to seek anywhere for any kind of distraction? Anywhere but here?

"Or are you willing to stop, really stop? This is what we do when we sit. We stop. Get off that hamster wheel. For just this breath, can you be present? What happens when you do that? Does your suffering shift? This is what the Buddha taught. Third noble truth: We can enter into samadhi. We can be one with this, as it is. Just this. Just this pain. Not taking it into another anxiety-producing, suffering-producing round, but just be with it. And when we become one with it, it all falls away. This is the experience of zazen. True being. The more we do this, the more we understand the fourth noble truth – the Eightfold Path – how to live.

"Everything the Buddha taught, if we really put our trust in it, we can live our lives very differently. This has a huge impact for each one of us, of course. But, more importantly, we are so interconnected, this has a huge impact on the world, the universe, all beings. So, what is Zen but realizing, for ourselves, the truth of the Four Noble Truths?"

"My father was a soldier in World War Two, and he left, when I was a baby, to be trained and sent overseas. I have one memory that my mother said was when he was on furlough when I was eight months old. We went to visit him before he was shipped overseas. We went down to the army camp – I can't remember where now – in the South somewhere. And my memory is of being very, very high above this enormous vastness of water – my mother told me we had gone to a beach – and of seeing what seemed to be a huge painting, which turns out to have been a billboard.

I was being carried on my father's shoulders. That's the memory that I have, of feeling this exaltation and excitement and sense of wonder, just pure awe. Not too long afterward, he was killed in the Battle of the Bulge.

"My experience of darkness and loss as a very young child is still an acute memory. We moved from the apartment my parents had and in with my grandmother in Brooklyn. My mother went back to teaching school, and I stayed with my grandmother, which was really wonderful. She was a very kind, nurturing woman. But my grandfather had died just before my father, so there was this feeling of mourning. Also the knowledge of the Holocaust was starting to come in. Relatives were talking in hushed tones about people disappearing. Families. My aunts would come over and there were these somber conversations. I didn't know what they were about, but the feeling of tragedy was a constant undercurrent."

"Your family background is Jewish?"

She nods. "My grandmother kept a kosher home. She wasn't particularly religious, but she would light candles on Friday night. We had the rituals. I was fascinated by the candles and lit the tablecloth on fire one Shabbat.

"My mother remarried when I was four, and it was a very dramatic, huge change for me. Even though there was this underlying sense of sadness in my grandmother's house, there was great love. When my mother remarried, my step-father wanted to take us away from what he called 'the ghetto.' So we moved from my grandmother's house to New Mexico.

"He was an extremely difficult man. Right away my grandmother and I felt fear. I remember being in her house before my mother married him, and he came over. I was playing with a friend on the sun-porch, and we were chatting away, and he came out and screamed at us to be quiet. I tried, but I guess we started getting noisy again. So he came out and taped my mouth shut. That was the beginning of what I experienced with him as an ongoing, terrifying violence of one kind or another. Sometimes not physical but emotional.

"We went to New Mexico for a year; then we ended up in New Jersey, and I spent my childhood in a kind of strange mix of disbelief and incomprehension and anger – a sense of deep injustice and grief. I didn't understand what had happened. Why had my whole world changed so radically? I started getting hives all the time. Nobody knew what was wrong, but it was emotional and psychological stress.

"One day, I just sat down under a tree. I was filled with so much turmoil, and I just let it go. I was sitting and my hands were clasped together and I just felt so still, almost as though I had turned into a statue. And at the same time, the feeling of my small bubble of pain completely opened. The entire universe was…. It's very hard to say exactly what happened, what was coming through me. I felt it so strongly, and it was a wonderful blessing.

"I was probably about eight or ten at the time. And then I started doing that regularly. I would sit on a window-seat in my room and do the same thing. I would sit very still. My hands would feel as though they were the size of the Earth. Everything would become very still inside and out, and my sadness would lift, and my small painful existence would open up to the vastness. And I would become the vastness. This was something that I would do from time to time, particularly when I was feeling – oh – just terribly oppressed or confused.

"I was a good student. I loved going to school. Anything to get out of the house. One day in eighth grade we were reading a textbook on various world cultures. I turned to the section we were to read, and it was about Zen Buddhism. There were so many of us baby-boomers – the first of the baby-wave – that they had to cut the cafeteria in two with a sliding door so we'd have a classroom. No windows. So we're in this dark room with one single light in the ceiling. And I'm there, looking at that page, and thinking, 'This is what I've been doing.'"

She sought out books on Zen and found Alan Watts and Jack Kerouac's *The Dharma Bums*. "There wasn't too much back then, at least in the local library. I may have read Durkheim's *Hara* sometime in high school. So I decided I was going to go to a college where I could study Buddhism. But that didn't exist."

Instead, she went to Vassar, and, while there were no courses on Buddhism, "The library had D. T. Suzuki's *Zen Essays* in three volumes and a few other books. I found Nyogen Senzaki's *Zen Flesh, Zen Bones* edited by Paul Reps. That was the second Zen book I bought. The first was *The Way of Zen* by Alan Watts. I just kind of taught myself, continued doing meditation on my own, reading as much as I could.

"Then I went to New York City after graduation and met my first husband, Lou Nordstrom, who was doing a Ph.D. in Western religions and writing a book on Plato at Columbia University. When we decided to get married, I asked him, 'Can we have a Zen wedding?' He was in love and said, 'Okay.'"

They looked up Zen in the phonebook and found that the Zen Studies Society was located six blocks away. They walked over and knocked at the door. "I was wearing my little mini-dress, and Lou's hair was a huge Afro – a blond Afro – he's part Cherokee, part Norwegian. So we probably cut a very un-Zen-like appearance."

Eido Shimano, then known as Tai-san, came to the door, and they explained what they wanted. "'Ooo!' he said. Then, 'Mmm.' Finally, he said, 'Well, come in for tea.' So we did. Had a cup of tea. And I gather he felt our sincerity was such that he would do it."

When they returned to discuss details, Shimano told them, "'You're very fortunate. This is karma. Yasutani Roshi is coming from Japan. He will be here September 2nd, wedding date. He will conduct your wedding.' Okay. Fine. We had our circle of friends. I remember telling them beforehand, 'You cannot get high before this! You have to come straight! This is a Zen temple!' So who knows? But anyway, they were there, and we had a wonderful wedding ceremony that no one could understand.

"So this is what I'd been searching for. I had to get married to find it! I had no idea there was a zendo six blocks away! It was a little apartment with a couple of small rooms. But we went back to sit there that year, and Yasutani Roshi was there, and he was giving lectures, which were in Japanese. We sat outside of the room where he was speaking, because there were so many people, and we were new. Tai-san translated, but it was hard to understand. We just sat there, and had long, long, *long* sittings."

In 1968, they went to France. "I was painting, and I said, 'I really want to go to the South of France.' And Lou said, 'Well, all right. I'll apply for a Fulbright for my Ph.D.' And he got it. He's very smart. And so we went. $1600 for the year. And lived very inexpensively in the South of France. Came back and lived in New York City in an old renovated barn near Poughkeepsie a year later. '69. And I read in the Sunday *Times* architecture section that the Zen Studies Society had purchased and renovated a carriage house on East 67th Street. And the renovation, evidently, had caught the eye of the architecture writer. It was quite beautiful. And I said, 'Lou! Look! Look! This is the same group we were sitting with. Let's go!'"

Nordstrom was not interested at that point, so she went on her own, driving two hours each way. Eventually Nordstrom joined her, and they moved to Rockland County in order to be closer to the center. They became active members and were on the board when the decision was made to purchase the Beecher Lake property. In 1974, just before construction started, they came up for the summer as co-directors.

"Lou was teaching at Marymount College in Tarrytown, and I was working there as publications designer in the PR department, and, when the end of the summer came, we didn't want to leave. So Lou gave up a tenure-track position, and we stayed on. And that year, construction of this building began. We lived with five other people in the original building down the road. It was extremely cold. We had no heat, and it was a really hard winter. We would have to go out in a little pickup truck and throw down shovelfuls of salt and sand so the construction vehicles could keep coming up. And – as you know – the road is not an easy one to come up even when it's in fairly good shape. It was not a good road then.

"It was an exciting time. We were real pioneers. No one knew what this would be like. Eido Roshi had a vision. He was thinking of it as a real break from Japan, a real American Zen that would take root here. We started with great idealism, and, in a way, everything was kind of up for grabs. How we were going to form this community, and how much it would find its shape in the Rinzai container of Japan and China. How much it would find its own shape. It grew organically."

I note that the Japanese cultural flavor is much stronger here than at other places I've visited.

"At this point, yes. At this point, for sure. You really don't even know you're in America when you walk into this building. And that's because Eido Roshi wanted to bring the whole richness of Rinzai Zen to America. But he was always very open with me and others about, 'Now it will be up to you to create an American Rinzai Zen.' He was certainly very cautious about us making a lot of changes right away. I, myself, feel there are changes that I've brought about here, definitely, but I will always uphold the strength and beauty of the Rinzai Zen practice and Japanese aesthetic that we've received. So, it's always a work in progress."

"Eido Roshi is a very dynamic and charismatic person," she tells me. "Our first abbot, Nakagawa Soen Roshi[23] was more interior and outwardly not so interested in matters of form and appearance. He might spill food on his robe, or he would hide his umeboshi plum pits under the furniture; maybe the mice were hungry, you know? Eido Roshi has an exquisite sense of the aesthetic of everything. And in building this monastery, he worked so carefully with the architect on all of it. He's brilliant. They're both – Soen Roshi and Eido Roshi – brilliant men. Well read, accomplished. Eido Roshi is very clear and incisive in his teaching. His teisho, his insights on koan, and his talks on the *Book of Rinzai* are some of the best that I've heard. He can bring something alive that happened – oh! – more than a thousand years ago and really make you feel you're right there. And he's very good in dokusan, bringing a student along to develop keen insight. He's a remarkable teacher. Which makes his flaw all the more tragic."

"Are you comfortable talking about that?"

"Well, it's public knowledge."

"It's pretty public."

"These days, everything is. Yeah." She pauses a moment. "From his perspective, he fell in love. Over and over. He fell in love with his students. And saw their potential and didn't understand how harmful such relationships could be to a student's trust...." There is a much longer pause. "I'm putting this in the most forgiving way."

She is. Love and desire are, of course, very different things.

And, in fact, she had not always been as forgiving. She and Nordstrom left Dai Bosatsu, shortly before it was formally opened in 1976, as an act of solidarity with a number of female students who had openly complained about Shimano's behavior. She didn't return to study with him again until 1990, by which time she had been told his behavior had changed.

"He didn't understand how dangerous, how harmful it can be for a student to have a relationship with her teacher that is sexual in nature when the Dharmic relationship is so precious. It can be very confusing for a student to have that boundary made permeable."

There had been rumors that she had had an affair with Shimano, which she denies, although she said there had been one occasion when Shimano approached her. She admits that, had circumstances been different, she might have been tempted, but the real connection with him had been a deep Dharma relationship.

"Eido Roshi has such power. You feel a tremendous sense of his vitality, even at the age of 80. He walks into a room, and the room changes. So I think for many of the women around him there was a feeling of wanting to be as close as possible. So if he was seductive, for many people it would be confusing; for some it might be enticing. And quite frankly – coming out of the '60s – it was an era of free love. It was a different time. So I think he may have felt it was okay initially, because no one told him otherwise."

There is also the fact that the Japanese have a very different attitude towards sexuality than do North Americans. "As long as you don't talk about it, there's no problem. And, of course, for us, that's just the reverse. If something happens, we need to go on *Oprah*. Talk to everybody. So, it was a terrible collision of cultures and times. I feel bad for all the students who were harmed. I feel bad for him, too. It's just been horrible. I have had to accept this really complex and difficult karma."

She and Nordstrom went to Syracuse after leaving Dai Bosatsu. He had received a one-year appointment at the University there, and they became leaders of a Zen group started a few years earlier by graduate students. After three years, they divorced, but both remained active in the Zen community. Nordstrom moved downstate to study with Bernie Glassman at the Zen Community of New York. Roko – as she was then known – continued to lead the Syracuse sangha, eventually reconfiguring the attic of her university-area home into a zendo.

She had wanted to invite Shimano to Syracuse in 1984 to lead a weekend sesshin, but he was in Japan for the funeral of Soen Nakagawa, so she asked Maurine Stuart, a long-time friend, to lead the retreat instead.

Stuart was one of the women who had stopped studying with Shimano. She did not have transmission, but, on his last trip to the USA, Soen Nakagawa had informally authorized her to teach. In Japan, concern about proper transmission is a serious issue. It may be so for many in the US as well, but the fact is that North American lineages are a mess. Nakagawa had believed the Japanese Zen establishment was festering and had not wanted Dai Bosatsu to be formally associated with it, so even Shimano's status is questioned in Japan.

Roko was ordained by Maurine Stuart in 1985. Five years later, she was invited back to DBZ by the vice-abbot, Junpo Denis Kelly. Before accepting the invitation, she spoke to Shimano frankly about his past affairs and came to believe things were now different.

In 1992, Shimano authorized Roko to teach, and in 1996 she was declared abbot of the Syracuse Zen Center, now called Hoen-ji. Two years later, she became the first American woman to receive transmission in the Rinzai tradition. When Shimano came to Syracuse for the occasion, he discussed with her the possibility of his retirement and his hope that she would succeed him.

"And at that time, I thought, 'Well, he'll live forever. This won't have to be a problem.' In 2005, he wrote the formal letter, put in the Zen Studies Society papers, that I would be his successor as abbot. And nobody knew. It was private."

For ten years after receiving transmission, she continued to work through a process of advanced training with Shimano, which culminated in 2008 when he bestowed the title Roshi on her and gave her the Dharma name Shinge, meaning "Heart/Mind Flowering."

Then in 2010, another student revealed that she had been in an affair with Shimano, and the board and Shinge had to ask for his resignation. The revelation shouldn't have come as a surprise. Two years earlier, the board and senior students discovered a collection of incriminating documents on the internet. A Rinzai priest, Kobutsu Malone, had begun a website entitled the "Shimano Archive." By the time of my visit to Dai Bosatsu, it contained nearly one thousand documents. Malone also maintains the "Sasaki Archive." He may keep these websites up from a desire for transparency and integrity in the Zen community, but – as Shinge notes – there may be a personal motive as well.

"There's a prurient interest in sex in this country that's so bizarre. It's almost like the rubber-neckers around accident scenes. So, I think, this really blew up because of the internet, because someone who had a grudge against Eido Roshi, and, in fact, warned him that he was going to make trouble, did so. And then, of course, once it was all over the internet – you know – that's it forever."

According to Mark Oppenheimer, the grudge was over Malone's ex-wife, who had been in a relationship with Shimano both before and during their marriage. According to Shinge, the grudge was over Shimano's refusal to recognize Malone as an authorized Zen teacher.

"So," she continues, "I was installed as abbot here, January 1. One, one, one-one. 1:00 on the first day of the first month, 2011. And it was a joyous time. And the hope had been that Eido Roshi and I would work together for a time, and he'd teach me various ceremonies that I hadn't done before as abbot."

Instead, she had to ask him not to come to the monastery during sesshin and other occasions when students were present. "As months went by, the board decreed that the best thing was for him not to be on ZSS premises at all, and that if he wanted to teach those students who were still loyal to him, he should do so elsewhere."

"What's the situation now?"

"He has been teaching elsewhere. We were hoping that we could work out an amicable settlement, that he could have a retirement that would be fair, and he would be completely separate from the Zen Studies Society. However, the retirement contract that he had scripted back in the '90s was never funded, so there was no money for it. When he retired in 2010, we started paying him according to that formula knowing there was no way we could keep paying at that level. And we weren't able to work out an amicable solution."

They received legal advice to suspend the pension until something could be resolved. When I last communicated with Shinge, the matter had gone before an arbitration judge who hadn't yet made a ruling regarding the retirement contract.

In spite of everything else, Shinge continues to feel indebted to Shimano as a teacher. "I will always treasure the great Dharma connection I had with my teacher. And I feel grateful to him for helping me to grow in this practice in the way that he did. Whatever the difficulties, they've been – in a way – my greatest koan. One that I'm still working on, that I've not solved. Perhaps I never will."

As abbot, it is now her responsibility to find a way to bring about a sense of reconciliation in the community. She held several sangha gatherings and a "Ceremony of Atonement and Purification" at the end of the Anniversary Sesshin in July. "These have been listening circles where people can speak openly and feel heard."

"You don't think that had been the case in the past?"

"No. People didn't know how to be open. We've held a few of them now. It's been mind-blowing. I've invited people to participate in 'What is our vision? How do we go forward?' It's an exciting time of transition, and we are beginning to feel a real change.

"We have a gem here. It's not just the building. It's not just the land. It's the practice. You know? It's so clear and so given over to really breaking through all the self-deception, all the clutching at what is going on to shore up the ego. We're really working against that. I would say that the teachings here are very strong."

"Can we talk about Dai Bosatsu itself? The Japanese atmosphere here?"

She nods.

"You're not Japanese."

"No. I'm a nice Jewish girl from Brooklyn."

"You talked earlier about the aesthetic. Which I admit is attractive. But this has been the only place I've visited in this journey where I haven't immediately felt at home."

"It's formidable."

"Young western students, in robes, responding 'Hai!' when addressed."

"Yeah. What's going on?"

"Okay. So what is going on?"

She ponders the question a moment before answering. "You know, I spoke about the koan of my teacher. I also have the koan of 'How do I take this responsibility and be true to the gifts and the culture that I've inherited, and yet be true to who I am and who these people are?' It's really not easy to say, 'Well, okay, let's all just be the Americans we are.' Rinzai Zen training is different from the Soto centers we have in this country. It's a different path. And what makes it different? I think there is a very strong emphasis on putting aside one's own comfort. Putting aside agency. Emphasizing ego-killing practice."

"What do you mean by 'agency'?"

"'Agency' means, 'This is what I want to do, and this is how I want to do it.' So saying 'Hai!' is a way of immediately responding, not from personal preferences, but to the moment, to what is being asked. But why not say, 'Yes'? We're here in America. We all speak English. So, these are things that we've inherited, and I'm looking at all of them." She pauses again. "I'm really thinking seriously about the whole mix and what's appropriate and what needs to change to make the place more welcoming, yet not losing the rigor at the same time. Because we should have more people here.

"I don't want this place to be forbidding. I want people who come to feel it's challenging. Yes! Real Rinzai Zen is being taught here. Yes! There's real training. It's authentic. And yet it should not be off-putting. Our practice must be based on Buddha's teachings of love and compassion. How can we do anything here that is not in keeping with that? I don't go for the brutality of the Japanese system at all. I really have done my best to change that. There was a culture of secrecy when I first came.

No one ever knew what was going on. It was a top-down way of approaching training. Someone would whisper something to someone else, and then the next day
something was different. You never knew why. It was also the way some things could
be happening in secret, and no one ever knew. I want to really make it clear – and I
have – that that's gone. That way of dealing with people is gone. I'm not a hierarchical
person by nature. In my place in Syracuse, we do everything by consensus. If I have
an idea, I bring it to my students. We talk it over. We figure out ways of doing it. And
so I have had to go against the dominant paradigm here. In an odd way, I have to be
matriarchal in trying to change the hierarchy." She laughs. "And it's not something
that's wanted by some of the old-timers. They're used to that hierarchy. So…."

This, as she puts it, is her koan. "How can I honor the traditions that I've been
given – literally given. I mean, my taking on the abbotship was handed to me by
transmission. I don't take any of this lightly. I'm very, very committed to honoring
and upholding the best of this tradition. But how can I do it in a way that's not
off-putting to Americans? How can I do it so that people can come here and feel
nurtured and feel inspired?"

In addition to her duties as abbot of the Zen Studies Society, Shinge remains the
abbot of Hoen-ji in Syracuse.

"We have about 75 students. Not all of them come regularly, of course. Some of
them live far away and come only for sesshin. I would say at an average sitting the
numbers might range between twelve and twenty. Sometimes thirty. And for sesshin
between twenty-five and forty."

The Syracuse community is "very involved in engaged Buddhist activities.
We have prison sanghas. We're working on a Hunger Project now. We're bringing
Bhikkhu Bodhi, the founder of Buddhist Global Relief, here in September [2013].
We're putting together a consortium on hunger issues right now. We do a lot with
our community."

I ask what Zen has to offer people in prison.

"They're doing time, right? Perfect place for sitting. It offers them freedom. It
offers them a way of being where they are, and within themselves, feeling free. We
get such beautiful letters from them. They're so deeply grateful to have this practice
offered. And they take part in various Buddhist rituals, like Buddha's Birthday celebrations and Parinirvana ceremonies. It's really very inspiring."

"Do the prison authorities cooperate with all this?"

"It's taken time. You know, we've built it over many, many years. They're very
happy with us. And then we have the Justice Center in the city, the jail. We work with

a lot of women who are there temporarily. They're terrified. They don't understand what's going on. They don't know how their cases are going to go."

"These are people awaiting trial?"

"Mm-hmm. So they are also taught how to meditate and how to find some relief from the anxiety. It's more a conscious stress reduction approach than Zen."

And there is a program called "Home Inc." for people with mental disabilities. "Brain damage from accidents or congenital afflictions of one kind or another. Some of them can't speak. Some of them have difficulty manoeuvring. But this program has been going on now for about five years. They come every week, twice a week, and they love it. They can just sit, and they play the gong, and they chant, and they just love it. I think it's the only place in the world that's offering this for people with mental disabilities. Their counselors bring them every week. Twice a week, to the Zen Center. And one of our members teaches them. I don't think anyone else has reached out to this population. They're treated like lepers in this society. So we do that. And then this Hunger Project I was telling you about is very important, because Syracuse is number one in terms of hunger for cities its size in the country."

"Why is that?"

"Terrible economic losses. All the wonderful mom-and-pop industries gone. Carrier, gone. Allied, gone. Lots of industries, gone. And drugs came in the '80s. It's total dysfunction. The school system, nothing's functioning. And so there are a lot of different poverty programs coming and going. Funding appears, disappears. There are many, many projects to deal with hunger, which can function as separate little fiefdoms. So my idea is – with Bhikkhu Bodhi coming in September and speaking at the university on his Buddhist Global Relief – that we would fashion a local hunger relief program that would bring together all the initiatives. And so we're now forming alliances."

The alliances are made, in part, through an inter-faith community in which she is active. "Syracuse started an inter-religious council many years ago – about thirty years ago – and when I came in 1976, Buddhism was definitely not represented on this council. But over the years, we made some in-roads, and we finally had someone appointed as a representative. You know, it became not only different Christian traditions and Judaism, but eventually" – she whispers in mock-horror – "a Buddhist, eventually" – again in a whisper – "a Muslim. Maybe even a Hindu. So now we really represent the whole city very well, and we work really well together."

The city's population is shrinking. "White-flight started in the '70s and continues. The inner city is mostly a ghetto. Poor blacks. Terrible poverty."

One of her students began an after-school program for inner-city youth. "Because of all the violence. Guns. Gangs. Drugs. Your usual urban thing. So, years ago, I got active in the Inter-Ministerial Alliance which was mostly composed of black ministers, and we started talking with the city and the school system. 'What can we do?' We got involved in a ten-point plan that had been started in Boston. And point eight was how to reduce violence. So I suggested meditation as a way to do that, a way to teach kids to step back from their immediate reactivity. And we ended up with this agency teaching boxing and Zen. Perfect, right? What is the African-American martial art? Right? Oh, people think karate and Zen! No. Boxing! That's what they wanted. Fine. So we've been doing that now for about eight or ten years.

"And the kids come from such dysfunctional homes! The idea of a moment of silence is absolutely foreign. Everyone's always screaming. The TVs are always blaring. The music is blaring. These are kids who are basically raising themselves and their brothers and sisters from different parents. And they are really, really struggling. And so this woman is just beautiful with them. And she's taught them over the years – some of them come back; others are new – how it is to just be aware of your breath and be able to count when you want to punch somebody or shoot somebody. How to be able to just go to your breath and count, 'One…' and feel that space."

The scope of what is taking place at Hoen-ji in Syracuse, at Shobo-ji in New York City, and here at Dai Bosatsu is striking and, I suspect, is a reflection of Shinge's insight and her vision of what American Rinzai Zen is capable of becoming. All of this is still evolving.

A strict practice is maintained at Dai Bosatsu, but it is not unaccommodating. I am still recovering from a broken leg, and, when I go into the zendo that evening to sit with the residents, I find a chair has been provided for me. The head monastic – who has some physical challenges – also uses a chair. I am not able, however, to keep up with the pace of the kinhin line, so I stand in the entry way and watch the procession wind its way along the outer corridor and back inside. As I do so, I reflect that it is a shame there are so few in the zendo this evening. As Shinge Roshi said, this is a gem. It also occurs to me that when some of the Japanese features soften over time – as they will – the temple will be no less impressive as a consequence. Gems shine all the brighter for being polished.

CHAPTER FOUR

Genjo Marinello

GENJO MARINELLO TELLS ME, "ZEN POINTS AT OUR DEEP, TRUE NATURE. Every part of us is true nature, but we don't often tap or touch or dip into the deepest part of our nature which – I think – ultimately blends into what we might call the collective unconscious or capital M 'Mind.' We usually have a very narrow individualist perspective of ourselves and who we are and our place in the universe, and Zen points at an experience or a practice or a training that helps us transcend our ego identity and discover our deeper seamless nature with all beings great and small, animate and inanimate."

In other words, Buddhism posits that ego illusion prevents us from recognizing the inherently non-dualistic nature of reality, as a result of which we fail to understand our interconnectedness with all of being. Zen training strives to overcome that illusion.

Even outside the arena of spiritual practice, there may be sound reasons for attempting to transcend our ego identity, for "breaking through the self-deception, the clutching at what is going on to shore up the ego" of which Shinge Chayat had spoken. None of us, after all, views the world objectively. We all see things from a particular point of view which arises from the information available to us, our personal circumstances, and the impact of a range of external conditioning factors over which we have no control. The differences between the Japanese and North American perspectives in the early days of Zen on this continent, for example, led to confusion and even rancour. But even within cultures, no two people share exactly the same point of view. Consequently, no two people describe things in exactly the same way.

Genjo Marinello is the abbot of Chobo-ji in Seattle. He is a licensed psychotherapist and studied with both Sasaki and Shimano, which gives him a unique perspective on what Shinge referred to as "the troubles." When the Rinzai-ji Osho Council demanded that Eshu Martin return his robes, it was Genjo who accepted and acknowledged Martin's ordination and authorized him to teach.

Genjo traces his own interest in Zen back to a first-year course at Pierce Community College in Los Angeles in 1972. "My freshman English professor was a person by the name of Jim Chambers, and he introduced me and my fellow students to the idea that there was a way to experience or penetrate reality beyond – say – a scientific method, that you could have something called insight or inspiration or intuition, and that you could really tap into some universal truths heuristically by investigating your own internal condition as a microcosm of the universe. And that was an astounding breakthrough, when that idea got across to me. Because I had thought – coming out of high school – that the only way you could possibly examine or understand the universe was through science. And I still think it's absolutely a great way. But when I came to understand that even the scientists were relying on their own inspiration and intuition and insight and then testing it with the scientific method – and that real breakthroughs were coming from insights – I thought, 'Oh, well, what's it take to have insights? How do you cultivate or nurture insights? That seems like what I want to do.' And that brought me around to Zen eventually."

After attending Pierce, he transferred to UCLA where he met a western-born Soto Zen priest named Brian Daizen Victoria. Victoria would later gain some notoriety within the Zen community for his book *Zen at War*, which is an examination of the Japanese Zen establishment's complicity with secular and military authorities during the Second World War.

"He was a student at that time, a graduate student in Oriental Studies at UCLA; I was an undergraduate student in psycho-biology, but I was taking a course in Buddhism. And we had a fellow on the UCLA campus who would come to the grass quad area and would literally stand up on a soap box – he'd carry a soap box and stand up on it – and then would give forth with the most foul-language kind of comedy, tearing apart the administration, the government, religions, just anything and everything. And he would have all us students rolling in the grass. And here was Daizen laughing and rolling around on the ground with the rest of us. And I said, 'That has me intrigued. I have to go up and talk to him.' Because I realized he was a Buddhist priest, and I realized that he was a *Zen* Buddhist priest, and Zen scared me. I knew that I was looking for something to cultivate and invite insight or a deep examination of our idea of a separated identity. I already knew that much; I might not have been able to articulate it as well, but I understood that that was what I was looking for. But Zen scared me because it seemed to play with and also transcend the rational mind. And I was so stuck in the idea that the only way to understand the world was to cling to one's rational mind and discriminating consciousness, that anything that *transcended* the rational mind scared the beegeebees out of me. But that was exactly what I was looking for."

After he and Daizen became friends, Daizen introduced him to a Vietnamese priest, Thich Thien-An, who gave him his first instruction in meditation.

Genjo intended to go into public health, but, after completing his undergraduate degree, he wanted to try something else before returning to school. So he volunteered with VISTA and was sent to Seattle. "It was going to be a transition. I thought I'd do a year or two of VISTA, and I ended up doing three years of VISTA and staying in Seattle and never going on in public health."

He looked for a Zen group to practice with and found the Seattle Zen Center. "It was run by Dr. Glenn Webb who had spent a dozen years in Japan studying Japanese woodblock paintings and pictures and had become quite a scholar in that form and had been introduced to Zen because some of the roshis where he went to go look at the prints told him, 'You won't appreciate them unless you do Zen.' So that's how Dr. Glenn Webb got into Zen."

"Did he accept that that was the case later? That meditation was necessary in order to appreciate the prints?"

"Actually, I think he did. So, he came back to Seattle before I did and started the Seattle Zen Center in the early '70s. I came in the middle '70s – 1976 – and I did my first sesshin with Hirano Osho-san, a Soto Zen priest who came directly from Eihei-ji in the summer of 1977." Genjo had a breakthrough experience on the third day of that sesshin, and his course in life was set.

In a letter Kobutsu Malone included in the Shimano Archives, Glenn Webb wrote:

> Joe [Marinello] and most everybody fell in love with "Hirano Osho" as I suggested they call him. Having a priest with a Japanese face in the group for the first time seems to have been comforting to all participants.

> I must tell you that Hirano displayed some of the unrestrained behavior that Shimano and other "fish out of Japanese waters" do. He was flattered by the attention female students gave him. And I had to insist that he stop touching them inappropriately, reminding him that he was married.[24]

The unrestrained behavior of Zen monks was not limited to the time they spent in the United States.

While studying at Daishu-in in Kyoto, Glenn Webb met Genki Takabayashi who had been expelled from his original temple and was at Daishu-in at the sufferance of the abbot, Soko Morinaga. Takabayashi had been an orphan sent to a temple, Seitai-ji, to be raised as a priest. It was not a way of life he would probably have chosen otherwise, and Webb suspected he

> – grew up somewhat resentful at his fate. Apparently, when he was around 18 his teacher (his adopted father, Gempo Roshi) sent him to the grand priest-training-hall (*sodo*) of Daitoku-ji.
>
> As Morinaga put it to me, on those occasions when he could go out on the town, Genki was a womanizer and pub-crawler. He got one woman from the neighborhood pregnant, she refused to abort the child, and Genki refused to marry her, thereby bringing shame to her family and to the temple. So he was kicked out of Daitoku-ji. As a favor to a friend, Morinaga Roshi took him in. But he made Genki's life hell: when I met him at Daishu-in he was low man on the totem pole, relegated to menial tasks and never allowed to engage in anything important....
>
> He showed no remorse for his sexual misconduct, but he seemed determined to go as far in his training as he could. He was a kind of Zen fundamentalist, regarding his sitting and his adherence to the tiniest detail of Rinzai Daitoku-ji liturgy.

Perhaps remembering how "comforting" a Japanese face had been to the members of his sitting group, and despite the fact that Morinaga was not in favor of it, Webb arranged a visa for Takabayashi and brought him to Seattle.

"I was at the airport when Genki Takabayashi arrived in 1978," Genjo says, "and ended up doing sort of a twenty-year apprenticeship with him as his senior student or most-devoted student."

The following year, the Dalai Lama stopped in Seattle during a North American tour. "He gave a talk at the University of Washington on the Four Noble Truths, and I was sort of blown over by the Dalai Lama and how he handled hecklers who were critical of his association with Tibet and thought that he was somehow a traitor to China. They were protesting on the UW campus, and I just saw him with great aplomb deal with the detractors, and I thought, 'Oh, this guy's really got something.

And I already have a Zen priest here in Seattle.' And after that talk, I went to Genki Takabayashi, and I said, 'All right. Whatever it takes. This is now my path. I'm at a breaking point with VISTA.' I could either go back into medicine – which I thought I would do – or public health with my psycho-biology degree, or I was going to take the path of Buddhism. After the Dalai Lama came, I was bowled over enough that I said, 'All right, I'll go to Japan. I'll do whatever's necessary. I want to become a Zen priest.'"

"How did you support yourself after leaving VISTA?"

"Well, that's quite interesting. I did a little bit of everything. I delivered papers to the paper boys. I worked with other former VISTA volunteers and did retail sales in a toy store, a kite store on the Pike Place Hill Climb here in Seattle. I was already a good kite-flyer, so I was selling kites. Then the Apple II computer had just come out, and we needed an inventory control program and didn't have enough money for a big computer, but we could buy an Apple II. And I wrote a program in basic to track our inventory, and then ended up selling that, and it became a big software company called Satori Software," he says, laughing. "So I made money writing software."

He asked to be ordained, but Takabayashi insisted he wait a year in order to demonstrate the sincerity of his intention. "The Seattle Zen Center was doing four sesshin a year, and I committed to doing all four and to do daily practice." Finally in 1980, at the age of 25, he was ordained an unsui – roughly a postulant – and the following year Takabayashi arranged for him to go to Ryutaku-ji in Japan.

"It was a little teeny temple where Soen Roshi and Eido Shimano Roshi trained, and Genki Takabayashi's Dharma brother, Sochu Suzuki Roshi, was abbot. So that's where I got sent, which was in September of 1981. And I stayed there until February of 1982. So a very brief period. But a winter in a Zen temple in Japan was to be remembered."

"Did it differ at all from what you had expected?"

"Well, I thought people would want to be training there, and, in general, people were training there because that was their lot in life. And they couldn't at all understand that I came there voluntarily to train, because no one would do that. That was incomprehensible, truly incomprehensible. So when I settled on saying that I had been sent there by my teacher, they could understand that. But if I tried to say I wanted to train in Zen, they would just shake their head. 'No. That can't be the reason.' So that was interesting.

"And then, of course, it was a very martial style. I remember one time sweeping a gravel path outdoors with a bamboo broom and whistling a little – just a little bit – and being told, 'No! No, you can't whistle! This is a Zen temple!' And you couldn't do anything right. There was a rule that for six months it didn't matter who told you what to do, when you did it, it was wrong. And if you did it to someone's satisfaction, someone else would come by and un-do it and say, 'No. That was wrong. It has to be done this way.' And whomever was closest to you – because everyone was more senior to you – was correct. So you just had to learn through sort of an ego-annihilation that you could not do anything right. So I thought all that was terribly unnecessary and unkind, but I put up with it."

Eido Shimano's teacher, Soen Nakagawa, had retired to Ryutaku-ji. "He was a recluse at that time, in the abbot's quarters behind the temple. And literally it was like a little hermitage where you would put a tray of food, and then he would slide a little door, take it in, and out would come dirty dishes. Otherwise you never saw him. He never came out of this hermitage. But during sesshin, because my Japanese wasn't so fluent, I would go to a little side room during the teisho time and listen to cassette tapes of Soen Nakagawa Roshi. So I'm sitting in zazen, and I'm listening to a cassette tape of Soen Roshi, and he's so eloquent, and he's so sweet, and he's so poetic, and it's such a treasure. And I just felt honored to be listening to him. And I knew that he was only a few feet away from where I was listening, but, he was such a recluse, I thought I might be in Japan the whole time and never see him. So I'm sitting in this little ante-room, sitting in zazen and listening to his teisho, and in walks this guy in a grubby white kimono, somewhat in tatters. Long white hair and a long white beard. And my mouth drops open. And he sees me, a young American in formal Zen robes, listening to a teisho of his. And he had raided the kitchen. That's what he was doing; he was raiding the kitchen and hoping no one would see him, because it was teisho time and so everyone was in the zendo. So he didn't expect to see me there at all, and he's startled, but he doesn't look startled. He's a roshi. So he just sees me, and my jaw drops open. Of course, I know who I'm looking at. It's not a mystery. And then he just says, 'Gassho!' So I put my hands in gassho, and he walks on by, and that was our first encounter.

"It was around that time that he decided to come out. This must have been November of 1981. And until I left in early February 1982, he was out of his hermitage, which meant he made lots of long-distance phone calls, which aggravated Sochu Roshi to no end, and he was always in the kitchen interfering with the tenzo. But he would have meals with us, and would sometimes sit in the zendo, and it was like the guy walked on air. Usually just in his white kimono, but he got himself a little more kept-up, and he shaved his head. And then I would get to go for walks with him on the temple grounds. He would say, 'Genjo, come walking with me.' His English was fluent. So we would have walks together on the temple grounds."

Genjo admits he came back to Seattle feeling "that I must be some kind of top shit because I got through this boot camp of Zen, and I must know something special. And I had actually had a few breakthroughs there that made Sochu Roshi happy. That's all. It had gone to my head. I must say, I must have been a pill when I came back, and people didn't like me. I was much too 'This is the way it has to be done, and there's no other way to do it. And this is country-bumpkin Zen, and I'm going to straighten this out.' Well, that didn't go over very well. Eventually I calmed down."

When Takabayashi first arrived in Seattle, he was deferential to Webb and modest about his own status. When students called him "roshi," he insisted it was not proper do so. Eventually Webb suggested that since it seemed important to the students, perhaps they should be allowed to. Once Takabayashi accepted the title, he took to the role with vigor. He insisted that the center needed to find dedicated space for a zendo, which he would be in charge of. He announced that the board should make no decisions until he had reviewed them. Webb was then president of the board.

"There was a split between Dr. Webb and Genki Roshi," Genjo tells me. "It's hard to say exactly over what. It was sort of like too many cooks in the kitchen, and they went their separate ways. There were some hard feelings about that in the group, and the group split. It was sort of a schism. I went with Genki Roshi, but I never lost my association with Dr. Glenn Webb and still have it."

In 1990, Joshu Sasaki came to Seattle to lead a sesshin. "We were all thrilled." Takabayashi had been sitting and traveling with Sasaki Roshi for about five years, and Genjo had done several retreats at Bodhi Manda. Genjo was still in his "pill" phase at the time of the Seattle sesshin. "I was being so macho. I was the jikijitsu and was so insistent on my own practice that I sat the whole thing in full-lotus. I sit most sesshin full-lotus today, but then that was a stretch. And I so cut off the circulation in my left leg during that sesshin that today – right now, as I'm talking to you – I can still feel tingling in my left foot."

That same year, Takabayashi decided "to elevate two of his unsui – me and one other – to osho status, but Sochu Roshi dies at that point, and we don't have a connection with the next roshi at Ryutaku-ji, so we just had the ceremony here in the United States without a direct connection to a temple in Japan. So my osho elevation was not sanctioned or stamped by Japan, and that was totally fine with me."

Then Sasaki invited Takabayashi to be the abbot of Rinzai-ji in Los Angeles, presumably so that Sasaki could focus on Mount Baldy. "And Genki Roshi wanted to bring me as his attendant. So we were all going to be inside the Joshu Sasaki Roshi camp there for a while. But Genki Roshi was looking over the center at Rinzai-ji in East LA, and he was hearing gunshots just about all the time. And he was thinking,

'This is not for me. I've got a beautiful family and sangha in Seattle. I'm not moving down to East LA.' And that's when the relationship between Joshu Sasaki and Genki Roshi began to crumble."

I ask if he had heard any concerns expressed about Sasaki's behavior during that period.

"Toward the end of my association, I heard the verse that some woman [Karen Tasaka] had written – that has since become public – that said he'd put a move on her in dokusan, and what was that? She was very wounded by that, and I was shocked. And about the time it was falling apart with Joshu Sasaki, I was feeling like, 'Maybe that's just fine.' Because I didn't want to be in the middle of that."

"What was Sasaki like as a teacher?"

"Lots of strength as a teacher. Very demanding when it came to dokusan. I remember I had once read a book on Zen koans and the way to respond to them, and – boy! – did he pounce on me when I gave something that was from this book! And I certainly learned my lesson, that it had to be genuine insight and your own insight and never read those books! And I appreciated that. I think I really learned something from that. You don't fake it. And so I always felt in dokusan that I was well seen, that his teishos were alive, dynamic, that he was in touch with the collective unconscious or the flow or the Dharma or whatever you want to call it and was a real vessel for that. When he was in sesshin, and when he was giving teisho, and when I was with him in dokusan – which is the only time I knew him – he just seemed spot on."

After his relationship with Sasaki soured, Takabayashi "took up an affiliation with Eido Shimano Roshi because he was trying to keep this connection to Japan through the sanctioned teachers here in the United States. So that's how I ended up jumping from Sochu Roshi to Joshu Sasaki Roshi to Eido Shimano Roshi as sort of my secondary teachers."

In 1997, Takabayashi married one of his students and retired to Montana. Genjo remained at Chobo-ji and was proclaimed abbot in 1999. Twice a year, he would go to Dai Bosatsu to participate in sesshin with Eido Shimano.

I ask whether he considers Takabayashi or Shimano his primary teacher. Takabayashi, he explains, was his "ordination teacher and principle teacher. I wouldn't use primary. I would say primary goes to Eido Shimano."

"What was Eido Shimano like as a teacher?"

"If he thought highly of you, at some point he was really going to tear you down. And you just knew that that was coming. If you were moving up the ranks, there'd be a point where he'd tear you down. And there were two things going on there in hindsight. One, he just wanted to be the top dog. And, two, he wanted to see what you were made of. Both things – I think – were going on, and one of them had a legitimate function, and the other one didn't. One part was narcissistic, and one part of it was, 'Let's push the cub off the cliff and see whether or not it can climb back up.' And that happened to me one time where he used a teisho to really tear me apart in a public forum, which was quite devastating. And I did bounce back. I wrote a letter and said, 'You know, you totally got that wrong. You almost lost me. But I'm not going to lay down that easily. I'll be back for the Dharma and not for you.' And he seemed to respect that."

Shimano had sufficient respect for Genjo that he pressured him to express interest in becoming the next abbot of the Zen Studies Society. "He was pushing me to volunteer to be the next abbot. He wanted me to volunteer. He wanted to hear me say I was willing to do it, that I thought I should do it. And I didn't want to do it. I didn't want to move to New York, and he'd been going through vice-abbots like crazy. I didn't want to be the next vice-abbot he went through even if it did look like he was getting close to the time of retirement.

"But he did put me through a kind of dark night another time where he was pushing me. I really thought it through during a sesshin night, really considered whether that's what the Dharma demanded of me, that I move to New York and pretty much give up my sangha in Seattle. My wife had already told me, 'Good God! If you take a post in New York, I'm not going with you.' So it was going to be the end of my marriage, the end of my career as a psychotherapist, the end of my life as abbot in Seattle. That was a lot to give up! And I remember that night *very* clearly, and I thought to myself, 'Well, he wants me to do it, and I'm not going to do it for him, but if the Dharma requires me to be there, then I would be there.' And that's essentially what I said to him. 'You can have your purple robe back – I don't care about it – but if the Dharma really requires me to be here rather than there, I'll follow the Dharma.' And it took him two years after that, but that's when he made me a Dharma heir. Because I wasn't doing it for him, and he got it. I really didn't care if he made me a Dharma heir at that point, which was a good time to make me a Dharma heir. And I think he was waiting for that. He was waiting for me not to care and also be willing to commit. And that was really transformative for me. I'm grateful to him for pushing me in that way."

In the end, Genjo tells me, his concerns about sexual misconduct led him to disassociate himself from Shimano.

"I think in the cases of both Joshu Sasaki Roshi and Eido Shimano Roshi, they had personality disorders. People with personality disorders can be very brilliant, very talented. They can have deep insight and be really screwed up. And I think they were both narcissistic personalities. I have a license in mental health counselling, and if I were to diagnose them – and I'm licensed to do so – I would say they have personality disorders. Which is really serious. It's kind of a cellular level of arrested development that doesn't keep them from being brilliant, charismatic, intelligent, good teachers in many, many ways, but they're so stuck in their own selves that it's almost like an idiot savant. One area develops and matures broadly, but others are left behind. And I don't think Zen training – in and of itself – was nearly enough to break through a personality disorder."

He does not see a contradiction between their sexual behaviour and their effectiveness as Zen teachers.

"I don't even see it as a disconnect. I just see it as a limited slice of the pie. They are undeveloped in this part of the pie and really developed in this other part of the pie. I think in Zen, it's more likely to find people who have some sort of arrested development that would prevent them from unfolding properly in the karuna realm – the realm of compassion – the three-quarters of the pie that would be open-hearted, do no harm, compassionate. I think the arrested development of Joshu Sasaki Roshi and Eido Shimano Roshi prevented them from opening that big section of the pie. And I think Zen allowed that in the sense that it is focused on starting at wisdom and working out from there. They started at wisdom. Got there. But weren't able to get further because of their personality disorders."

There is a statement on the Chobo-ji website which notes:

> Genjo Osho is very aware of the problems associated with three of his core teachers, Genki Takabayashi Roshi, Eido Shimano Roshi and Joshu Sasaki Roshi concerning their misuse of power to exploit and take advantage of students under their care. He and the Chobo-Ji sangha repudiate and condemn the inappropriate liberties these men have taken with their students.

Genjo is, however, more forgiving of Takabayashi than the others. In a memorial tribute published in the newsletter of the Northwest Dharma Association, Genjo lists three great lessons he learned from Takabayashi. The third and

> – the hardest to accept and perhaps the most important, is that all of us are fully human! That is to say, that though Genki amply demonstrated that we can be and are all vessels of the dharma, we

are also limited, and from time to time stubbornly primitive. There will always be tension between our base instincts and true insight.

When Genki left Japan he abandoned a relationship and a child. He never understood credit or money well, and often found himself in debt. Early on during his time in Seattle we had to warn female participants that there was a good chance he would make a pass at them.

We are all a blend of Buddha and bumpkin; with all the training in the world we will never arrive. In other words, from wherever we are we are always just beginning. I often tell the story of how at least once a year Genki would give a teisho where he would exclaim, "I now just beginning to understand, just now beginning to see."[25]

On the other hand, Genjo is the webmaster for the American Zen Studies Association, and when Eido Shimano gave Dharma transmission to a student – Zenrin Lewis – who had remained loyal to him, Genjo struck that student's temple from the roster of centers listed on the site. His explanation to AZTA members is included in the Shimano archives:

Eido Shimano agrees that a Zen teacher should not be sexual with students; however, this has never stopped him from being a pathological liar and sexual predator of his own sangha. Zenrin accepts that Eido Shimano has done the best he can and supports his continued teaching and actively continues to train with him.

I don't care if Zenrin is a member of AZTA or not, we have no way to say if a member is in good standing or not. Nevertheless, I am in charge of making additions and changes to the AZTA database, and I will not tolerate any longer the use of our database to refer people to a teacher and organization that continues to train with Eido Shimano. So hearing no objection I have deleted his listing from our public database.

If there is a vote to return him to our database, I will not implement it; however, I will resign from this organization and someone else may then restore it.[26]

Not everyone associated with AZTA felt he had the authority to take that step unilaterally, but on January 1, 2014, the public listing of Zen teachers and centers on the website was "temporarily suspended while the organization considers options for restructuring."[27]

I ask if, from his perspective as a psychotherapist as much as a Zen priest, he believes it is ever permissible for a teacher and a student to become involved. "There are," I point out, "certain professions where it's obviously never appropriate; social workers, for example, should never be in a sexual relationship with a client. But it gets a little greyer in other areas. Relationships between university professors and students are frowned upon, but they occur and sometimes even turn into pretty decent marriages. So, is it ever appropriate for a Zen teacher to have a relationship with a student?"

I'm thinking of Genki Takabayashi when I ask the question, but Genjo takes it personally. "Well, first of all, you understand that I'm married to someone who attends the temple."

"I did not know that."

"I mean, she was a long-time member, and we were a couple before she ever came to the temple."

"Okay, so take prior or existing relationships out of consideration. Isn't it possible that a perfectly natural romantic relationship could develop between a student and teacher?"

"Let me put it this way: I used to think of it about the way you were talking about college professors; I thought that Zen teachers were about in that league relative to sexual liaisons with students. And I now think of it as a much higher violation. I think of it more as a psychiatrist or a psychologist and what it would mean if a psychiatrist or a psychologist, who was doing deep therapy with a client, were to cross the sexual boundary. Which is much worse than a college professor and a student. I'm not saying that's a good idea, by the way. But I used to feel Zen teachers were sort of like college professors, and that was my perception. I've moved off that spot. I now think, especially with people who are doing dokusan in the Rinzai tradition, it's very intense work where there's already so much intimacy going on in the crucible of a powerful sesshin. I totally understand the temptation, on both sides, to cross a sexual boundary. But I now think of it as as bad a violation as if a psychiatrist or a psychologist were to cross that boundary. And as a psychologist – or even as a mental health counselor – you're essentially barred for life from ever having a sexual liaison with even a former client. And I think it needs to be at that level."

I had been reminded elsewhere, by some female teachers and practitioners I had spoken to, that the relationships had not always been initiated by the male teacher. "It's been put to me that forming relationships with teachers was one way in which some women felt they could even the playing field. That most centers were male-dominated, and the teacher was often primarily interested in the male students. Students naturally vie with one another for the teacher's attention. This was one way in which the female students had an edge."

"I think that's an actual perception of some women in some centers, and I don't doubt that that's where they were coming from. I still think that if a client or a student comes onto me, it's my responsibility to hold the boundaries for both. Period."

"One thing I came away with from my training in Japan – brief though it was – was believing and seeing that my fellow practitioners then, even though it was their lot in life, were slowly being transformed by the practice. That it worked. That they were becoming more mature, more open-hearted, more insightful as the training went on. All this work had that effect. That made a big impression."

"An element of that training, of course, would be its strictness," I say. "You couldn't whistle while you worked. Was that a factor as well? North American centers appear to be becoming less strict. Is that going to impact their effectiveness?"

"I think so, and this is why – relative to most groups – my style is pretty old fashioned and rigid. It's nothing like Japan. But relative. Because I do think Zen in the west has gotten way too soft. I think that why it works is that it strips away our defences, that the defences that cultivate and coddle our strong ego are worn away. And – especially in the midst of a sesshin – you become so exhausted and vulnerable through the process of doing sit after sit in a very vigorous way that you become malleable and vulnerable and exposed, and your ego defences fall away at the same time as they become very, very active. It's really easy to become angry and upset and stomp around when you're stressed because of the rigor of the practice and the training, but you're also becoming more malleable and more flexible and vulnerable. And that vulnerability and malleability and exposure allows us to get to the deeper levels of our own nature more quickly. I think you get there very quickly if you take shamanic drugs, but then you don't know who you are. So I think this way, you still have a sense of your own identity to some extent, at the same time the process is wearing away the barriers – the artificial barriers – between so-called self and other or between even you and your deeper unconscious. And when those barriers are worn away – literally worn away through the rigors of practice and sesshin – you're bound to have deeper insights. I'm a believer of that."

"And the Japanese forms, such as those maintained at Dai Bosatsu, how important are they?"

"I'm on the side of them being fairly important. I think that if you came to Chobo-ji, you wouldn't have the feeling that you have at Dai Bosatsu, but relative to most Zen Centers in the country, it would feel more Japanese than most. I would say we're in the 90th percentile or something like that. We still eat on benches. We still eat with the nested bowls. We still sit seiza whenever we have tea. There's a pretty Japanese feel to it. I think that's important because in terms of passing on a practice and training that is going to have the strength to bring people to penetrate their own ego defences sufficiently, you need a really strong form. Well, the Japanese have one. It could be any strong form. But the Japanese already have one that's been handed down for centuries. So I'm all for America finding its own strong frame and strong form, but I think it has to be done very slowly in order that the form not collapse. Because I think to have a deep retreat you need that strong form. It's like a pressure cooker, and you don't want people popping out one way or another. You really want to hold the participants in the sesshin in a form that can contain the power that's coming up – both crazy power and awakened power. So since the Japanese already have that, let's borrow it until it slowly morphs into an American form that is as strong. That's what I'm trying to do."

"Thinking back on the centers I've visited, the evolution of an American style seems to be heading in several different directions at once."

"I think it will sort itself out in sort of an evolutionary way. What works will stay, and what doesn't work will fall away. So I'm really not too worried about it. In general, my opinion is that Zen form has become so relaxed that it can't bring people to the depths that I hope Zen practice can bring people to. My sense of probably more than fifty percent of the Zen Centers out there is that the form is not strong enough. And I'm not talking about Japanese or American, but just the form period. So, I think that's going to fall away because it just doesn't bring people to the depth that a strong form can. And I expect there will be the Zen-lite school and the Zen 'More Hard Knocks' school, and there may be two different branches. And there is the danger of it being too stuck culturally in the Japanese or being too culturally marginal or macho. And, no, it doesn't need to be that. We can let that fall away. That's part of the blend of Japanese samurai culture with Zen that can definitely be let go of. But I still think it needs a very strong form in order to bring people past our ego-defences which are *very* strong."

Even the strictest form, however, requires some degree of flexibility.

"Is the sangha at Chobo-ji social?"

"Oh, yes. After zazen every morning, we have an informal social half hour at our local coffee spot. And on Saturday mornings, we have that same kind of coffee-klatch here at the temple. And I would say four pot-lucks a year. One of them we call Toya, which is a day to break all the rules in a Zen temple in Japan. So we have four annual pot-lucks where we hire a babysitter, bring families in, and have a social event. Lots of food. Maybe a Dharma talk. Maybe a council meeting on some subject important to us."

"I did notice you said coffee instead of tea. I suppose in Seattle coffee is sacramental."

"Absolutely. You know, there are people who have tea, but we feel sorry for them."

CHAPTER FIVE

Eshu Martin

IN ALBUQUERQUE, SEIJU TOLD ME: "ESHU MARTIN WAS A POINT OF DISCUSSION in an osho meeting for basically misrepresenting himself. He thought he was a teacher, and he was a monk in training. It goes back to what I was talking about earlier, about certain people feeling that they're good to go, and their osho doesn't think they're good to go. It was a topic of discussion. The oshos sent three oshos to Victoria to talk to Eshu and his board, but I don't think that meeting went well."

Everyone has a point of view.

Eshu lives in Sooke, British Columbia, forty kilometers (25 miles) west of Victoria. Coming into the community, I pass a store advertising malas (Buddhist rosaries) and "singing bowls" – the bowl-shaped gongs used to mark the beginning and end of meditation periods.

The Zenwest Buddhist Society – formerly the Victoria Zen Center – meets in Eshu's house. Alongside the path to the front door, there is a statue of Kannon and a couple of garden gnomes. As I get out of the car, Eshu's wife and two children come from the house on their way out. "I hope it goes well, Dad," the boy, who looks about eleven, calls over his shoulder.

Eshu has just turned 40, which makes him one of the youngest teachers I interview. He is 6'4" and has a shaved head but a well developed auburn beard. We sit at a small table in the dining area next to the kitchen. It's very much a family space. There are colored eggs on the table and Easter decorations on the wall. A central fireplace separates this area from a small zendo that sits twelve; if the dining table and chairs are removed on this side of the fireplace, there's room for another ten meditators. His bedroom, downstairs, has a double mattress on the floor which he takes out into the hall so the room can be used for sanzen.

He has a great laugh which rumbles up from deep within his belly. "What's the purpose of Zen? Oh, man! Well, to be of benefit to all sentient beings and liberation from suffering. Nothing big.... Yeah, I don't know. The purpose of Zen? What was it you asked? The *purpose* of Zen?"

"Its function."

"I don't know if there is a function. For me it's just…." He sits silent for a while, occasionally slapping the table top with his palm. "Living life fully, really. That's what my practice has been about more and more. Fulfilling the capacity of my own life."

"So if somebody comes knocking on your door here and says, 'I hear you're the local Zen guy.' And they asked you what Zen is all about, that's what you'd say to them?"

"It's really rare that someone would come and ask what Zen is. Like a lot of the time, they've done a fair bit of research and now Zen is the favorite flavor of exploration into this great matter of what they think they want. Sometimes it's not what they want. Or sometimes the Zen here is not the Zen that they've found in books. So it depends. Some people want to practice Zen because they heard we do a lot of meditation, and they think meditation is a good thing for stress reduction and all that kind of stuff. Some people come because they realize there's something *more*. Maybe other spiritual paths, other religions, other traditions don't appeal to them for one reason or another. I think there's a lot of western religious burn-out in our culture.

"It's sort of a cliché, maybe, but I suppose Zen really is liberation from suffering. For me, that's a big part of it. It's when you realize not the sort of day-to-day little sufferings but the fundamental dissatisfaction. You sort of" – he snaps fingers – "twig to that in your life, and you say, 'I need to address this.' I've found that Zen is one of the better ways to address it, and so I kind of approach it like that. When, for example, people say, 'I want to relax,' that's always a big concern for me, because meditation is pretty relaxing for a little while. But once the overall noise, the external noise, diminishes, you start to see into the seething mass underneath and" – he's laughing again – "it's not relaxing anymore."

"My sisters say when I was a kid – five or six years old – they asked me what I wanted to do, and I said, 'I want to be a priest.' We weren't raised religious or anything like that, so I don't know that I really knew what I was talking about."

"Where was this?"

"Grew up in Ontario, Whitby and Pickering, Ontario. And when I was in grade three, I asked my parents to transfer me from the public school system into the Catholic school system. And I got…not in trouble so much, but I was sort of considered to be precocious. I remember being asked to leave a classroom once when we had a bishop visit and he'd brought in some of his objects of office. You know, his shepherd's crook and his ring. And I got in a discussion – I think this must have been around grade five or something like this – questioning him about the innate holiness of objects and how that worked. What made an object holy? So I think I was always questioning, but I don't remember being negative about it. I remember being just like, 'How does this work?'

"Then, when I was nine years old, my mother had a stroke, and she was in hospital for a couple of weeks in a coma, and she eventually died. And I had a pretty major crisis, because, during that period when she was in a coma, I was praying assiduously – you know? – and when she died, I was faced with this sort of, 'How can a compassionate, loving God listen to a child pray for his mother and not help?' Right? So I had a religious crisis, and I asked the teachers and the priests and didn't find any satisfaction in their answers. Found them quite pat. Basically, 'When God calls your number, you go.' In retrospect, I suspect there is no satisfactory answer to give to a nine year old child who's lost their mother, but I was really disappointed.

"A lot of this stuff I had no insight into at the time, but, in retrospect, I realize that I was the youngest child, the only boy. They stopped trying after I was born. So they wanted a boy, and I was the golden child. When my mother died, there was sort of an abrupt end to that. My father was working; he was a computer executive, so he was at work, and I was raised by my sister for several years until my father re-married.

"I had very angry teenage years. Vandalism was my crime of choice. And I think fundamentally it was just a lot of pain and grief which I dealt with with drinking and drugs at a pretty early age. By grade eight, I was doing acid and things like that. Breaking things. And then my father remarried when I was thirteen, which...." He laughs softly. "I mean, I'm certainly friends and made peace with my step-mother now, but back then it was sort of I would wake up and the first thing on my mind was how to make this person's life a misery. You know?

"In my later teens, started to get into martial arts because I realized they were more effective, honestly more effective, and more efficient ways of being destructive than just random acts of violence. So got into martial arts. Martial arts led to the *Tao Te Ching*, Eastern philosophy. So I started reading that and going, 'Oh, this stuff makes sense to me.' Then I came across a book called *The Book of Five Rings* by Musashi. Musashi was influenced by a Zen priest named Takuan and so his whole philosophy and strategy is largely influenced by Zen. So you have to have some grasp of what Zen was if you're going to get anything, and in the beginning of the book, in the introduction, in order to sort of encapsulate Zen, there was this parable about these two monks – the older monk and the younger monk – returning to the temple after their begging rounds, and there's been heavy rains, and there's a bridge that's washed out, and on the other side there's this concubine who's distressed, who wants to get across. So the old monk picks her up and carries her across, and the young monk is really upset about it, and, all the way back to the temple, he can't let it go. And at the end, he questions the older monk, saying, you know, *'How did you do that!'* And the old monk says, 'I put her down at the side of the river. Why are you still carrying her?' And for me…I get weepy even now." His eyes are tearing. "Uh…for me, it was like this light went on. Because my anger had come from this real chip on my shoulder that, having been the golden boy, the universe had done this to me or that God had done this thing to me, and my anger at people generally was, 'Don't you realize what a great person I am? Why are you treating me like this?' And what dawned on me when I read this was that it was me. It was me that was picking up this anger and this sense of entitlement and indebtedness every morning. The suffering I was experiencing was not externally imposed upon me; it was like something I was whacking myself with. It was just like a couple of paragraphs, and a bell went and I *wept* and just the whole weight of it hit the floor. And it was at this point, I went, 'Holy shit!'"

"How old were you?"

"It would have been around 1993? So twenty, twenty-one years old. And I was just, 'I gotta check out this Zen stuff. I don't know what that's all about!' So I was living in Pickering where there's no Zen anything. Toronto there is, but it's a couple of hours away. So I went to a bookstore, and there were two books on Zen there. One was Alan Watts' *The Way of Zen* and one was Philip Kapleau's *Three Pillars of Zen*. And I looked through them, and Philip Kapleau's had instructions on how to sit. And that was really what I was looking for, because – just from what I had looked at – basically Zen is about sitting meditation. So you sort of need to figure that one out.

"So I got Kapleau's book and read the instructions and started sitting…um… what? Obsessively? Zealously? I used to sit for several hours in full lotus. I mean, I was a full-blown testosterone wreck. And if you've ever read *The Three Pillars of Zen*, it certainly sort of leans that way. It's really a bombastic read. Given the time that he was studying in Japan, it had to be. But I used to do full lotus for hours and then at one point, it wasn't enough. It was like I was too weak or something."

"What were you doing? Were you following the breath? Were you trying to do Mu?"

"Well, I had started with breath counting, and then it sort of encouraged, 'Find a natural koan.' And I remember, the question I had was, 'What was the fundamental truth of all things?' This was the question I was carrying. And I got this old ski-pole, a bamboo ski-pole, and cut about an eighteen inch section out of it, and I would set it on the floor in front of me. And when I sort of wanted to get up, I would whack myself on the trapezium to sort of goad myself on further. And I have to say – as much as I joke about it now and sort of say, 'Wow! You were really over the top!' – there was some benefit. I think the sitting was really beneficial. And in retrospect, I had some significant insights and openings.

"In a short period of time, the kind of relationships I was making changed. My whole circle of friends changed. I stopped doing drugs. I quit smoking. I met the woman who was to become my wife. I was in theatre at the time; I had done some acting and was going to school for theatre at the time, and Niki and I met. She's a choreographer and dancer. When I met her, she had just gotten off the road with *Up with People*, so she had been traveling all over the world."

Eshu felt a need to leave Ontario, and some people Niki knew in British Colombia invited them to come west. "Sort of, 'You can come and stay with us for a couple of months while you get established in Victoria.' And I thought, 'Oh, west is good. 'Cause west is where the Zen is.' So, we got established fairly quickly, and I was still in martial arts. Martial arts and Zen were going to be my path. So I was in a martial arts store looking through a binder of clubs that were around. And I found this little tiny piece of ripped out lined paper that said 'Victoria Zen Center,' and it had a phone number scrawled on it. So I was like, 'Oh, this is good.'

"I took down the number, and I went and called, and the person who answered said, 'Oh yeah, you come ten minutes early and you get some brief instruction, then we do three periods of sitting meditation.' And they said, 'And you're in luck, because if you come this week, the abbot of the Zen Center of Vancouver is going to be here, and you'll get to meet him.' And I was like, 'Oh, great!' And all the romantic images possible. You know? 'I'm going to meet a nice Zen master, a little Japanese guy.' So I went, and it was in a borrowed space in the local Shambhala Center above some shops downtown. And it was entirely sixty to seventy year-old ladies, mostly English ladies. And I had come west for Zen, and I wanted *Zen!* with a capital Z. And they said, 'Oh, yes, here you go.' And they gave me this little walk through, and I was, 'You people don't know anything about Zen.' And they said, 'Let us introduce you to the abbot.' And I was like, 'Okay, finally.' And out walks Eshin Godfrey, who's this portly English guy, not Japanese. 'Oh, hello'" – in a British accent – "and I'm like, 'Oh, I'm in Hell.'

"So I sat down, and of course – being a real Zen practitioner – cranked my legs into full lotus, and they start the first sit, twenty-five minute sit. No problem. And then this bell rings. And I'm like, 'What's this all about?' And they were starting into kinhin, walking meditation. But because I'd practiced by myself, I'd never really done this. Right? And I had been sitting full lotus, my legs were a little bit shaky, but I was like, 'Like hell all these old ladies are going to stand up and walk and I'm not.' And so I started to stand up and fell directly backwards over this row of cushions, like a redwood tree, not even bending. Completely humiliated. It was great. It was a wonderful thing," he laughs.

"So I got involved in the Victoria Zen Center, and I connected pretty strongly with Eshin at the time. He would come over a couple of times a month to lead a sit here. And in the meantime, he wanted someone to take a stronger leadership role here. So I started reinstituting schedules and promoting longer sits. Started longer sits on Sunday; instituted a monthly one-day intensive. He would come over to lead all these. Then I started to do sesshin with him. They rented a bed-and-breakfast on Galliano Island four times a year, so I'd go and do those. And after I'd done – I don't know – about four or five of those here, I was still wanting more. It still wasn't enough.

"Organizationally, I was really frustrated dealing with these old ladies who seemed to want to keep it a sort of a weekly tea club. Many of them were from a Christian background and there was no Christian contemplative organization in town, so they were sort of like just nesting here really. It was just quiet meditation time together. And that aggravated me."

He shakes his head and smiles. "I was quite a difficult person then. Niki would say, 'I don't know why you kept going, because every time after you came back there would be like this *rant*.' The conversation afterwards would be about *who* was bringing the tea next week, what *kind* of tea it was going to be, whose responsibility the cookies were. And I would just be like: *'GAAAHH!'* You know? And they all had this sort of Zen-itis, I called it; you'd sit in a circle and the idea was that nobody should have an opinion about anything. I used to say, you could say, 'I think we should all start eating babies.' And they would go, 'Well, I am neither for nor against the eating of babies.' You know? And it was just very frustrating. So this sort of bug kept eating away at me."

He told Niki that he needed to enter a monastery and take up a more serious practice. She supported his decision, and Eshin donated flight points so that he could get down to Mount Baldy.

"So in 1997, I went down to study with Joshu Sasaki Roshi for the first time and did a summer seichu there – a summer training period at Mount Baldy – and I loved everything about it. 3:00 a.m. wake up. I mean it was as balls-out-Zen as balls-out-Zen can be. Japanese monks used to come and say, 'They don't train anything like this in Japan anymore. This is crazy!' And I loved it. I loved it all. And I was still writing to Niki and things were nice, but we had kinda said that we didn't know where our roads were going so we'd just follow this for a while."

When the seichu drew to an end, Eshu asked Sasaki about getting a scholarship which would allow him to remain at the monastery. "And Sasaki said, 'No.' He said, '*Monastery* is an English word, and it's not correct. *Training center* is better.' So, he said, people come here when they don't work so well, and they learn how to work. He said, 'You okay. You go back to Victoria. Make Victoria Zen Center.' Which is about the last thing I wanted to do. So my next phone call to Niki was sort of like, 'Heh-heh, guess what?' He said, 'Train with Eshin in Vancouver and come to sesshin as often as you can.' So I came back to Victoria.

"Niki had moved into a L'Arche Community." L'Arche is a residential program for adults with developmental disabilities. "So for a month or two I stayed with a member of the Zen Center that I knew, then I also moved into a L'Arche house, a different one than she was in. So for me, it was a bunch of things going on. One was I needed a place to live. Another was I had burned off some real Catholic angst at the monastery, from my childhood, and so I thought I'm going to try a relationship again in this environment. And I thought, if there's any Christians I can get along with, it will be these people who are living in community with people with disabilities because they're actually doing it, not just talking it. Lived in L'Arche for a year. During which – what? – got briefly back together with Niki; realized we had become totally different people; split up again. She's a very clear person. We had a frank conversation when we started talking about getting back together again."

"Is she a Zen practitioner?"

"Well, that's a good question. She doesn't sit all that often, but I think she's more clear than a lot of people I know. So, we had this very frank conversation where she said, 'We've done the boyfriend-girlfriend thing. We've done the living together thing. If we're getting back together, I want to be clear that we're getting back together to get married. And that's something you need to decide whether or not you want.' And I was still going, 'I want to be a monk, and I don't see these as being consistent.'

"And so I was still doing four sesshin a year with Eshin and going down probably two to three times a year to Mount Baldy. So I was down for sesshin at Mount Baldy and decided to talk to the Roshi about becoming a monk. And he said," – speaking in a Japanese accent – "'Oh, monk. Okay. How 'bout after married?' And I was like, *'What!'* So in the summer of 1998, we got married, and then, in January of 1999, I was ordained at Mount Baldy. Yeah…um…so, what was your question? How did I get involved? There you go. I was pretty involved at this point.

"And I remembered in my teenage years, religion was like evil itself. Religion was the path of stupid people. Period. And I remember being the jikijitsu, the head of the meditation hall at Rinzai-ji in one sesshin. In the morning you sort of do the incense offering and the prostrations and all that stuff. And I remember doing prostrations and I got a glimpse of myself standing in this hall with a big Buddha statue and offering incense to the altar and doing prostrations with my head shaved and in robes, and going, 'You know, if I didn't know better, this looks really religious! How did I get here!'" He laughs.

"But the thing for me was that it worked. Right from the beginning, when I started sitting; it allowed me the space and clarity to actually start changing my life from a place of significant suffering to one where it wasn't so much. It was never an article of faith for me; it was a matter of 'What's the next step? How do I get deeper into this? What's the next thing to do?' And it just led to where, when I looked back, *Whoa! How did I get here!*' So, yeah, that's how I got involved."

He and Niki looked for a house in Victoria. "It was the first time I was renting a place as much for myself and my wife as it was for the Zen Center. The main room of the house was turned into a meditation hall. And people were coming to sit, and the community was starting to grow. And Eshin would come over a couple of times a month, and that was going well. I was getting more experienced in practice, but I was also becoming the main contact person. I was an ordained monk for the community so there was a confusion in the community about who the teacher was here. Who the priest was here. So I had a conversation with Eshin about that and said, 'I think you should maybe come over less. Maybe if you come over once a month instead of twice a month.' And so we did that for a while. Then basically I said, 'I think we should have you come over – I don't know – once a quarter or something like this.' And so there started to be a little bit of distance between us. And there was other stuff going on as well, like finances and things like that."

Because the zendo was in Eshu's home, the board had agreed to pay a portion of his rent, something Eshin disapproved of. "He clearly had issues around money as a whole. I tried to establish what were really clear, financially accountable systems, so there were checks and measures. But it didn't seem to matter to him. It was like, to him, money was dirty."

"And the money came from?"

"Memberships."

"How many members?

"At that time? Oh, gosh – twenty maybe? Maybe! Tiny! Then the distance kind of grew between Eshin and me. I mean, we were still doing a lot of things together. I would go over there for Buddha's Birthday celebrations and things like that. He would come over here occasionally. I would do sesshins with him; I would go over to Vancouver. He started to ask me to do talks at the Zen Center of Vancouver when I would go over there. And then there was a sesshin where something…." He pauses, and when he resumes speaking, he does so slowly and carefully.

"One of the training tools in the Rinzai-ji model seems to be antagonism. The idea is if you can find out where a person's attached, you sort of pick at them there. So that was kind of the way Eshin's relationship with me worked. And then there was a sesshin where I don't know exactly how to explain it except that I kind of saw through it in a very clear way. So what I said to him – and I meant it – was I felt it was like a father and son where the son had come to the place where he needed to leave the father's home and find his own way. And he accepted it. It was during sesshin, and I said, 'I'm going to leave this sesshin tomorrow, because I want you to have time to fill in the hole that I'm going to leave.' I was jikijitsu, so he needed someone. So the next day, he walked me to the gate, and we bowed, and I left. And we agreed. I said, 'I'll go see Sasaki Roshi as soon as possible.'

"And I did go down and see Sasaki Roshi, and, in my first interview, he said, 'No osho your teacher any more. Only Roshi.' So I felt like I'd done the right thing. And things continued to be civil between Eshin and me. He was still the authorizing body in British Colombia. So when people here started to want to do jukai, I said, 'I don't currently have the authorization to do that.' But wanted to do it. So worked with him on a script; had his approval the whole way. I even asked him, 'Maybe you should come and do this.' And he said, 'No. It's fine for you to do it.' And that was also when I got involved with the University of Victoria as chaplain. The Buddhist chaplain that was there – Lama Margaret – was from a Tibetan tradition, and she retired. And I had done some meditation groups and stuff at the university, so had relationships, and she said, 'I think you'd be a great Buddhist chaplain there.' Eshin wrote the letter, on behalf of the organization, and he also registered me with the provincial government to do weddings and things like that. And so in my mind everything was hunky-dory.

"And then I think it was January of 2007 – something like that – he wrote to me and said, 'You're doing everything that an osho does, so I think it's time that we start the process of you becoming an osho, a full priest.'

"Did he have the authority to ordain you or was that something that Sasaki Roshi...."

"Sasaki Roshi. But what was going on, because Sasaki Roshi was getting old then.... Today, April 1st, is his birthday, actually. He's 106 today. And at the time, what was happening was he was the only person able to do it, so he had created this thing called the Osho Council. The idea being that he thought the oshos needed to figure out a way that they were going to govern Rinzai-ji after he died. And they had come up with this process through which the local osho of a monk would sort of sponsor a petition for somebody like me to become an osho. That person would have to get another osho to second that, then the process would go forward. And so Eshin said, 'I would be willing to be your sponsor for this.' And so I said, 'Okay, great.' I was like, 'Wow, this is really cool!' Right?

"So he came. We had a visit. Got pictures of him with the jukai students that I had just done a couple of months before. He saw the new place, 'cause we had just moved out here. And then what? And then I contacted a number of the other oshos that I knew. Kigen Bill Ekeson said, 'Yeah, sure, I'll second you on that. No problem.'"

It had been a few years since he last visited Mount Baldy, and he told Kigen he was considering doing a retreat there. "'This is great,' Kigen said. 'You've been away for a couple of years. I know you've been working up there, but you might want to write a letter to the Osho Council, saying you're coming down.' So that was great. That was in February, something like that, and I was going down for sesshin in July. And I emailed Kigen the letter, and he said, 'I think this is great. I think this will be well-received.' And then three days before I was to leave, I came home and there was a courier-delivered letter that had been put under the door. And it said that I had misrepresented myself as a teacher; I had exceeded authorizations; I was doing things that I shouldn't be doing. Like this whole laundry list that basically said, 'You're so far out of line, like, I don't even know where to start.'"

"And this came from?"

"Mount Baldy, from the Osho Council. And, furthermore, it said, 'You need to apologize for this. You need to do a public repentance ceremony, and, until you're prepared to do that, you should not come to Mount Baldy.' And I was totally flabbergasted. So I contacted Eshin about it, 'cause he was sort of named as 'You need to work with Eshin and Myokyo and Eko [Cheryl Schnabel] – these three oshos – to work this out.' Contacted Eshin, and I was like, 'What the hell is this? What happened?' And Eshin was very strange on the phone. The impression I got was that basically there was a lot of politics going on, that the Osho Council had become kind of a middle-management pissing match. Eshin was a fairly senior teacher, but he was not the head of the Osho Council. The person who wrote this letter to me [Gido Richard Schnabel] was and, as far as I could tell, was really using me as a way to diminish Eshin. Like the reason why I had gotten to where I was and what I was doing was based on Eshin's lack of ability. You know what I mean? So he was very odd. What my suspicion is is that he probably tried to stick up for me and help me to the point where it began to look like it was going to cost him. At which point, he just cut me loose and said some things on the phone that to this day I don't know what to do with.

"One thing in particular, because I was giving talks, I was accused of far exceeding my authority to do that. And I said to him – in a conversation between the two of us, no other witnesses or anything, no reason to lie – I said, 'Eshin, you know, you've asked me to give talks at your center. You've been here when I have given talks at my center. You've asked me to record talks that I've given at my center to send to you for your critique. You shared those with other oshos for their critique. And now you're telling the Osho Council that you never gave me permission or authorization to give talks.' And he said, 'I never gave you permission to give talks.' And I was just…. I didn't know what to do with that.

"So, I had a really great board at the time. The head of our board was a technology executive who was quite successful and knew how to run a board, and I was getting a lot of advice about how to process this effectively as an organization and how to deal with *them* as an organization. And so fundamentally for me it was, 'What does the Osho Council want? If I'm going to make a decision about how to go forward I need to get a list of the sort of things you want from me and decide about whether or not I want to do those things.' So I talked to Eshin and got his list, and I talked to Eko and got her list. And they were two totally different lists on virtually every point. You know, this person said, 'You should not be accepting any kind of money at all, and if you do get money you should be giving it to the osho center that's supervising you.' So I should be giving all that money to Eshin. And that wasn't Eshin telling me that. Eshin was telling me, 'Any money you get should not be going for rent. It should be going into a bank account to save to buy a property.' And so I was sort going like, 'Okay, so your organization doesn't even know what it wants me to do.'

"But the biggest issue was about me exceeding my authority, not having permission to do these thing. And I actually had documented evidence to the contrary, emails, letters from governments and universities that have peoples' signatures on them, that demonstrated that I was very conscientious about what I was doing. And so I was like, 'This is a misunderstanding. All I need to do is give you this stuff, and you can see that I'm not this person you think I am.' So I got all this stuff together and sent it as a package, and said, like, 'I can't apologize for what you're accusing me of, because I didn't do it. So here's the thing.' And basically they swept it off the table and said, 'You're not listening to us. We need you to apologize for this. We need you to shut down your Zen Center.' Basically they wanted me to go back to just having weekly sits. And I thought, 'Oh, this is crazy.'"

He requested a meeting with the Osho Council and was told that his request was inappropriate. Friends from the Rinzai-ji community suggested he talk to Gentei Sandy Stewart, who was then vice abbot of Rinzai-ji and abbot of the North Carolina Zen Center. "So I sent him a couple of letters and said, 'You don't know me from Adam. These are the letters I've been getting. I'm wondering if you would be willing to talk to me about this.' And he said, 'Absolutely.' So I said, 'Great.' So we had this whole conversation. I sent him all of the correspondence. I sent him the timeline and all this kind of stuff, and he said, 'Okay. I'll advocate for you.'

"So he went to some meetings, and they said they were going to have a big meeting in December 2007. So this is sort of a six month process where we're in limbo here. I'm not allowed to go down to Rinzai-ji. They're going to have Rohatsu sesshin – 7th to the 14th – and then they were going to have this meeting afterwards to decide what was going on with Eshu. December 7th, I get a letter saying, 'It's been decided you're no longer a monk; you're no longer a part of Rinzai-ji.' Like, the sesshin hasn't happened, let alone the meeting. The same day the University of Victoria has received a letter saying basically the same thing, 'We don't endorse him as a monk or as a chaplain or anything like that. He's nothing to do with us anymore.' And there's no warning to this or anything. So Gentei contacted me before I actually got the letter and said, 'I just read the letter that was sent to you, and I'm totally flabbergasted by it. I don't know what the hell's going on, let me get through this meeting, and then I'll talk to you.' And then there was just sort of this radio silence, 'cause Gentei goes into sesshin. So after sesshin, I get this phone call from him, and I said, 'How did it go?' And he says, 'Well, I've resigned as vice abbot of Rinzai-ji, and it's been suggested that I return to North Carolina and not come back 'til I don't cause so much conflict. So I think that's going to be a while.' And I was like, 'Oh, my God! This is about me?' He said, 'Actually, no. Your issue wasn't even on the list, because they felt they had decided that before the meeting.' His issue was that he had written a letter about sexual misconduct, put it in writing, submitted it to the Osho Council, said, 'We need to deal with this. We need to address it.' And basically he was totally attacked during that meeting and told that he wanted to see the Roshi go to jail, and he wanted to kill the Roshi and all this kind of stuff. And that it was really his problem, to which he said, 'You know, I think we need to part ways here.' So I said, 'Well, okay, I don't have a place to go. Can I come and practice with you?' And he said, 'Yeah.' So I started going down to North Carolina."

The Victoria board, meanwhile, decided to schedule a vote on whether or not to retain their twenty-five-year affiliation with Rinzai-ji. "And the Osho Council wrote to them, saying, 'We want to come up for that meeting and speak on behalf of Rinzai-ji.' To which the chair of the board said, 'That's inappropriate, because you're not members. This is a membership meeting and a membership decision. However, if you are willing to come up and speak to us, the Board of Directors would be willing to meet with you to discuss this matter.' To which they said, 'We'd be willing to meet with you, but Eshu can't be there.' To which the board said, 'Eshu will be there if you want to come up.' So they said, 'Fine. We'll come up.'

"So Gido, Eko, and Eshin came over to Victoria in full formal robes. And it's kind of irrelevant, but Eko was Eshin's first wife and is Gido's wife. So it was the

three of them that came over. The meeting opens with Gido saying, 'I've been practicing Zen for thirty-five years. How old are you, Eshu?' This is how the meeting
opens. The board chair says, 'We've prepared a power point to share with you what's
been going on here, so you can see and make a more informed decision.' And they're
like, 'We're not here to negotiate. We're here to tell you that Joshu Sasaki's Zen is the
real Zen and if you choose to end your affiliation, Eshu's going to become the next
Zen Master Rama[28] or Jonestown or whatever. It's false dharma.' And this went on
for – I don't know – an hour? The end of the meeting, the oshos go, 'Can we get a
picture with the board?'"

We both laugh.

"It was totally *Alice in Wonderland*. So they left. The board convened a short
meeting, said, 'Are we still going to go through with ending this affiliation?' 'Yes.'
The membership voted unanimously to end the affiliation with Rinzai-ji."

For a while, Eshu went to North Carolina twice a year for sesshin with Gentei. "I
called it, 'Going to Uncle Gentei's farm,' because it's in the south, it's super-friendly
with a kind of laid-back atmosphere. And that's what it felt like. I'd been tossed out
by the family, but old Uncle Gentei would always have me down at the farm."

Then the stories about Eido Roshi in New York started "to come out more and
more, and I was watching that, seeing some familiar inter-relationship stuff. I was
watching Genjo Marinello's response to it, and I was impressed by the way he could
kind of hold both sides. He was able to say, 'Some people think he's a great Zen Master and that none of this can be true and everyone's making too much of it. Some
people think he's a demon, and they want to throw him off the bus. And the reality
is, he has tremendous capacity and insight and terrible behaviour. And how do we
hold these? How do we appropriately address these and call him on it?' And I was
like, 'Oh! This is a very mature way of seeing things.'

"After splitting with Rinzai-ji, I had been in a place of isolation. I'd been cast-out
by Rinzai-ji but not really picked-up by any established lineage. Gentei, sure, but he's
sort of an outcast too and happy to be one. But more than that, I think it was me. It
was my own perspective of being an exile, and no one would have me because I'm this
disobedient Zen guy. Right? And I started to work through this. I wondered, 'Maybe
this is me. Maybe everyone doesn't sterilize their zendo if I walk into it.' So I wrote
letters to Joan Halifax and Chozen Bays and some of the big players and said, 'This is
who I am, and this is what I'm doing, and I want to have relationships, but I've been
kind of hesitant to do that.' And pretty much every one of them wrote back support-
ively. Then I wrote to Genjo and said, 'I really appreciate how you're handling this.'

And he wrote back, and we started a correspondence which really clicked. And I said, 'I'd like to come, do sesshin with you.' And he said, 'That would be great.'

"So I went down last spring, around this time, and did sesshin with him, and it was just like…. It was like starting over again. It was wonderful. Different family feel. I mean all that stuff was cleaned away, and I felt like I'd got back into Zen. For years I'd been dealing with this organizational, familial shit. And it was like, 'Oh! Back to Zen and koan practice!' And, 'Oh, yeah, this is what I got into this for.' Swept just a bunch of old dirt away. And came back and then, 'Oh, like, I'm in a conundrum. I'm very, very grateful to Gentei and all the help he gave me, but this is making me feel alive.' You know? So I had a conversation with Genjo, saying, 'I want to continue with you, but I need to talk to Gentei.' So I had a conversation with Gentei and said, 'This is where I'm at.' And he said, 'Great. You should practice with Genjo.' So I'm committed to go down twice a year to Seattle.

"I did the spring and fall sesshin there last year, and the distance that it gave me on the whole Rinzai-ji thing, I think, was the space that sort of led to me writing the piece in *Sweeping Zen* about Joshu Sasaki Roshi in November, being out of the whole thing and looking back at it. You know, I didn't have any deep direct experience of this stuff going on. I mean, it was going on when I was there, but I was totally oblivious to it. Sesshin is an intense time, and I was primarily concerned with my own experience and surviving it, and I didn't really care or know what was going on."

"There had been rumors for years, for decades."

"Oh sure, rumors for sure. But the rumors I heard were all in the past, and I was born in the '70s. So Roshi came over in the '60s and early '70s, and that was sort of when those stories took place in my mind; that's how they were spoken about. And being a child of the '70s, I had this romantic idea about the '60s and '70s and free love, and so all these stories kind of fit into this consensual-free-love kind of pre-history era that I had no experience with. And it really wasn't till meeting with Gentei, and hearing this was a recent thing and that it wasn't a good thing, that I started to become aware of it. And I had a conversation with Adam Tebbe who maintains the *Sweeping Zen* website, because Genjo had been talking about it to me and said, 'Would you be willing to talk to Mark Oppenheimer of the *New York Times* about this?' And I said, 'I don't have anything. Anything I have is second hand or worse. So I don't really feel like I'm the person to talk about this stuff.' And then Adam Tebbe had this conversation with me, and he said, 'Why do you think that's not enough? How sure are you that this actually went on?' And I said, 'I'm absolutely sure. The people I've heard these things from are completely trustworthy, and I've heard similar stories from so many sources that it would be uncanny for them all to be false.' And I have another friend, Daitetsu Hull, who said, 'Look, you can write it, but all you write is exactly what you know. You can say this is all second hand,

and don't say anything more, don't accuse anybody of anything more. But clearly this is occupying a space in your mind and heart that you need to deal with.' And I said, 'Okay.' And he helped me. Like, I wrote the piece, and it was like, *'RAAA!'* And he specializes in non-violent communication and stuff. So it took us about a week to deflate me out of it and just get down to what needed to be said. And it was published on *Sweeping Zen*, and that's when everything kind of broke loose."

"How do you explain to people that an awakened person, like Sasaki, can behave the way he has?"

"I think that's a great question. It's something Genjo's been talking about and I've been thinking about a lot, and I think there's a significant difference between awakening experiences and mature manifestations. I think you can have a significantly deep awakening experience and still be immature about how that manifests. And I think maturity isn't something that manifests consistently across all spheres of activity. I mean, I think with all these people, if you get into a Zen Center with them – in a sesshin practice environment – I think you would see some very skilled people at what they do. One of my board members met with these oshos when they came up, and he said, 'The image or the metaphor that comes to mind is that they're sort of like weight-lifters, but they only do bench-press.' And I thought that was a really great example. People make the mistake of thinking the awakening experience has this magic effect across all spheres. Many people make that assumption with Shakyamuni Buddha himself; they think that the reason he was able to become such a great leader was that he had had this awakening. And I always say, 'Well, he was raised to be a prince. He had a pre-existing skill-set and maturity in different places, and *then* he had this awakening experience. And it's this combination of maturity and manifestation *with* awakening that really fit the bill in that situation.' And that's what I appreciated about what Genjo was saying about Eido Roshi, 'Yes, very deep in one aspect. And completely unchecked in another, and was never challenged or forced to grow up in that area, and so stays a child.' And when you get that combination, it's very dangerous. And it was cultivated historically when we look at samurai or kamikaze, where you had sort of an infantile consideration of another person's suffering and a loss of self, and you get something very dangerous. And you can cultivate that, if you want to. And I think that's what happens in a place like Rinzai-ji, where the politics are so thick and you have Roshi with all the authority and a complete unwillingness to disseminate that power, and you have a whole crew of people who want to be the next...who want to be the *one*. And any way they can diminish their other brethren is a step up for them. And Sasaki Roshi is a virtuoso at playing those oshos one against another."

"I've had to come to terms with the fact that in several ways much of the cultural format of Mount Baldy and Rinzai-ji is very classic cult. It's different from other Zen in North America and is very classically 'cut you off from your support systems; indoctrinate you into a very specific culture.' Very similar to an abusive family culture, quite frankly. And then keep you there as much as they can.

"One of the things that was most confusing to me when I was going through my problems with Rinzai-ji was, 'Why? Why are they so unwilling to communicate? Why are they so unwilling to look at the evidence that I'm giving them?' And what I think now is that I was a monk who wouldn't do what I was told. And the more I tried to clarify the situation, the more clear it was that I was a monk who wouldn't do what I was told. And in that environment, where you need to keep your mouth shut, that's a dangerous thing. So I think that had something to do with how things went down at Rinzai-ji for me."

"And yet you said that it was a place that worked for you."

"Yeah. Yeah. Because I wasn't in the power structure, my relationship with Sasaki Roshi worked. My relationship with the schedule worked. So, yeah, I definitely benefited. Sasaki Roshi's sanzen and teisho were great; they really did a lot.

"The instruction that really informed me as a human being was: 'Monk after married.' Well, first, 'Go back to Victoria and make Victoria Zen Center' when that was really not what I wanted to do – I wanted to be a real monk on a mountain and all that stuff – coming back and having to sort out relationships with people that I didn't necessarily agree with or an organization that had to get its shit together. 'Monk after married,' being married, making relationship in an awakened, compassionate way. Having children.

"That was the next big fight. Niki and I had a huge fight about that. 'No, no, the Zen Center is my family, and the members are my children.' And her saying, 'Why do you think we got married if not to have children?' And going down and listening to Joshu Sasaki say, 'I don't know why I see so many of you young men come down here and get sore knees and sore backs just so you can understand the teaching of compassion when all you need to do is have children. And immediately seeing your eyes in your children's eyes, you will know self-as-other.' And after a week of this, I'm like, 'I guess I gotta have kids.' Right? 'Cause I remember very clearly, I was unbearable as a monk.

"I had a member who was here early on, maybe 1999, 2000, who came back around 2007, 2008, and he was talking to another member who asked, 'What was Eshu like back then?' And he said, 'I refer to those as Eshu's Zen-Nazi days.' And I remember very clearly watching my son, as a baby, on his stomach, trying to roll over, and sort of feeling this agitation, like, 'Oh, my God, just roll over!' And then having this sudden realization that that's the way I was with the people in the Zen Center. That my attitude was, like, if you couldn't handle this, if it was too tough for you, then you were too weak for Zen, and you should probably do something else. And realized that that would be like looking at this child and saying, 'You might as well give up on walking, 'cause you can't even roll over. Forget about it!' And realizing that maybe a better path would be to nurture and be patient with that child, support that child, and they would get there by themselves. Right?

"So, for me, the awakenings, the value of them is to sort of shake you out of the fixed perspective that you have, and the challenge of practice – Hakuin talks about it – is that it's the post-kensho practice that's most valuable. It's like, 'How do you apply it?'"

Six months after this conversation, on September 28, 2013, in a ceremony held in the Interfaith Chapel at the University of Victoria, Genjo Marinello reaffirmed Eshu as an osho and a Zenji – a Dharma teacher – in the Hakuin Rinzai Zen tradition.

CHAPTER SIX

Shodo Harada and Enso House

1

MITRA BISHOP TOLD ME, "I WAS TRAVELING WITH HARADA SHODO ROSHI many years ago. And one of Richard Baker's students asked Harada Roshi how such things – Baker's affairs with his students – could happen. Roshi's response was, 'They didn't spend a long enough time in the monastery.' Meaning their training was not sufficient. And I think that's the key. It's not enough to have had a kensho, or even two or three; there is what Torei Enji, Hakuin's premier disciple and Dharma heir, called The Long Maturation. Kensho allows us to see a bit more clearly, but then we have to work with what we become aware of in our own behavior and bring it into line with that clear seeing. Kensho isn't anywhere near complete until we have integrated it into our daily life so that everything we do or say or think accords with what we've realized. Kensho has to manifest in our daily life to be of any value whatsoever."

Taigen Shodo Harada Roshi is the abbot of the Rinzai temple, Sogenji, in Okayama. He also maintains a number of affiliate temples outside of Japan. In the US, Tahoma Sogenji is located on Whidbey Island in Washington state. Harada is known as a "teacher of teachers." Several American Zen teachers, such as Mitra, study with him.

Jan Chozen Bays, one of Taizan Maezumi's heirs, is another of his students. "I think it's very important that all teachers have a teacher," Chozen told me. "You're never finished with this work. And the idea that, 'Oh, yeah, I'm finished now that I'm a teacher' is ridiculous to me. There's always work to be done."

Chozen had not been interested in working with another teacher after she left Maezumi's Center in Los Angeles. She even fell away from practice for a time. But her husband, Hogen Bays, who had also left the Zen Center of Los Angeles, "wanted to look around for a teacher, and he had a friend – Wes Borden – who had begun studying with Harada Roshi. And when Hogen contacted him, Wes said, 'This guy is the authentic thing.' And so Hogen went to a few sesshin with him. And I said,

'Look, I've had enough of Japanese teachers, thank you very much, for one lifetime.'
But then Hogen convinced me to go. And I was teaching more, so I knew that I
needed a teacher. So I went, and the very first sanzen with him, I just burst into tears
and wept because I realized, 'Oh, he's picked up the work just exactly where I left it
off with Maezumi Roshi and is carrying it on.' With barely a word-spoken. It was
just like, whammo! Okay! Let's go!"

"What is he like?"

"Well, he's the old school. I mean, I've never met anybody who lives so much
in the present moment. I know he knows who I am, but I don't think he thinks
one thought about me unless I'm right in front of him. Whereas Maezumi Roshi
was very aware of who his students were, what their occupations were, and so on.
Maezumi Roshi was much more socially engaged in that way. Harada Roshi is not.
It's just what's in front of him; that's what he works with. And he's psychic. I mean,
that's the best word we have for it. When your mind is entirely clear, you receive
impressions from everybody else's minds. So one of the frustrating things about
beginning to work with him is you go in with something to say, and he says it to
you. And you go, 'Now wait a minute! I'm supposed to say that. Me first! Don't you
say it!' So, yeah, it takes you a while to adjust to that. You have to go in completely
fresh. There can't be anything from the past one minute that you take in there. It has
to be exactly this right now. Which is very interesting."

Another Zen teacher, Dosho Port, wrote:

> I found Shodo Harada Roshi had the strongest presence of
> no-one-being-present that I had ever felt. After I gave him the
> highlights of my spiritual résumé – what practices I'd done with
> whom, what insights I'd had and how they had impacted daily
> life – I asked him for practice instructions. He gave me a koan that
> doesn't belong to any system, saying that he wanted to work with
> me outside of categories. "I know a little about the Daiun Harada
> Roshi approach," I said, "but what specific suggestions for working
> with this do you recommend?"
>
> "Zen practice," he said, "is not something particular."[29]

Shodo Harada Roshi was born in Nara, Japan, the year before the attack on Pearl
Harbor and grew up during the war years with all the attendant privations, challenges, and sorrows of that time. Although his father was a temple priest, young

Harada had no particular interest in Buddhism until he happened to notice Mumon Yamada Roshi, the abbot of Shofukuji, on a bus. It was during the American occupation, when Japan's national esteem was in tatters and many young people blamed not only their rulers but also traditional institutions, such as Buddhism, for their current plight. Harada and Yamada didn't speak, but the younger man was deeply impressed by the monk's demeanor. The memory of that chance encounter stayed with him, and, after completing university, he entered Shofukuji where he received the Dharma name, Shodo – "True Way."

After three years in the monastery, kensho still eluded him, so he left to live as a hermit in the mountains of the Hiroshima and Shimane Prefectures, dedicating himself to full-time practice and vowing not to return to Shofukuji until he had attained awakening. One day a group of hikers came upon him and, discovering he was a monk, expressed admiration. They lamented that their own family and work responsibilities gave them little opportunity for practice.

Harada later wrote that it was as if

> – all of my burdens had dropped off and everything was awakened within. I realized right then the mistake I'd been making and immediately went back to the monastery. That day on the mountain I realized that there was no self to be bothered! I had been crushing myself and making myself miserable worrying about the problem of realizing enlightenment, when in fact it was found in the living of every single day! Everything would come to me even if I did nothing and ceased worrying about my own little problems. Not to isolate myself up on a mountain, closed off from everyone, turning them all away and worrying about my own small state of mind, but to go and be what every day brought to me – that was my practice and the expression of my enlightenment! Ever since I realized that, my whole life has been completely different. I know there is no problem for myself, because there is no one there to feel that there is a problem.[30]

He recognized that going to the mountain to seek personal enlightenment was essentially selfish. He now realized that awakening to the greater Self had to be for the benefit of others. He returned to Shofukuji and stayed there for the next twenty years.

Shofukuji was one of the Japanese centers which welcomed western students, and an American, Priscilla Storandt, came each morning to join the monks in zazen. She was in Japan to study pottery and slowly became involved in Zen as well. Her time at Shofukuji overlapped Harada's term as head monk, and they became friends.

In 1983, the elderly abbot of nearby Sogenji didn't have a student suitable to assume responsibility for that temple and asked Yamada to recommend someone. Yamada chose Harada. Storandt followed Harada to Sogenji and was ordained a nun, taking the Dharma name Daichi (Great Wisdom). She is generally known by the familiar form of her name, Chisan.

Harada continued to welcome foreign students, and Chisan encouraged his desire to offer retreats in the United States and Europe. At her recommendation, the first US sesshin was held in 1989 at a non-sectarian Buddhist retreat center called Cloud Mountain in southwest Washington state.

In his instructions to beginning students, Shodo Harada explains:

> Each of us is different. We have different hopes and plans, and different, unknowable states of mind. Although these things cannot be measured they are very real, giving each of us our own individuality. Through zazen we are each able to return to our own individuality. Through zazen we are each able to return to our particular essence, to become completely who we are. This return to the quiet place within us, this letting go of all external distractions to return to our original inner space – this is zazen.[31]

The function of Zen, he goes on, is to return to Original Mind, the mind that is "common to everyone and not just me as an individual." This Original Mind, like the mind of a newborn or a mirror, "reflects everything exactly as it is...without judgments, views, or expectation."[32] The ideas, plans, aspirations, fears, and anxieties which generally preoccupy consciousness are nothing more than "shadows that obscure our awareness."[33] Through zazen, one lets go of all thoughts "so that we might return to the mind from which all of our consciousness and awareness comes forth."[34]

> When we realize this mirror-like mind and perceive things exactly as they are, we respond quite naturally to what is in front of us without adding extra layers of opinion and judgment. We act appropriately, with no need to stop and wonder what might be the best way to deal with a particular situation. When we're able to respond spontaneously in this way then we no longer worry about our actions, congratulating ourselves when we're effective

and blaming ourselves when we fail. We no longer have any lingering thoughts about the small self and how it performed. Whether we're praised or insulted it ends with that, even if we've been made a complete fool of. When it's gone, it's just gone. This is our original and natural state of mind.

When we don't cling to fixed ideas about things we can move and respond naturally and freely. This may seem difficult, but even the idea that it's difficult is nothing but a shadow.[35]

2

Although it is called a monastery, Tahoma Sogenji turns out to be more of a hermitage. Shodo Harada is the official abbot but comes only a few days a year to lead retreats. The remainder of the time, the site is under the care of Dairin (Great Neighbor) Larrick who – along with Chisan – is identified as an assistant abbot. Chisan travels with Shodo Harada and acts as his translator, so Dairin (or Rinsan) is the sole occupant of the center during my visit.

Rinsan, who is 60 now, spent his 20s at an ashram in Hawaii studying Kundalini yoga. He acquired an interested in Buddhism in his 30s when he was in Albuquerque and became involved with the Zen Center there. "The main, over-riding teacher there is Sasaki Roshi, and his student, who was running it, is this guy, Seiju, who is probably still down there. And he got me really interested in sitting Zen. I never met Sasaki Roshi. But I was travelling around at that time, and I came up to Seattle and fell in with a group that was affiliated with Harada Roshi and heard about Sogenji in Japan. At that point, I was seriously thinking about going someplace for a year to sit and to find out where that would lead. So I went to Sogenji and met Harada Roshi."

It was 1992, and Rinsan was then in his 40s.

"I went to Japan for two years in the beginning and studied with him and came back and had a job in Seattle and bought a house. And then in 2002, I cashed it in and went back, got ordained, and have been working with him ever since. I've been here, at Tahoma, for the last three years as the head monk." There are, of course, no other monks at the moment, and Rinsan says nothing about being co-abbot.

"Do you remember the first time you met Shodo Harada Roshi?"

"My first meeting was here in Seattle. He was coming here, at that time, two times a year and giving o-sesshin down in a facility by the name of Cloud Mountain." Some Rinzai schools distinguish between o-sesshin, which is always seven days, and other sesshin which may be for shorter periods. "I went and did my first o-sesshin with him there and was very impressed with him as a teacher and as a person. At that time, he invited me to come to Sogenji, but I waited one year and did another o-sesshin with him here. Kept sitting here with his students. And then, like I say, I went to Sogenji. They ask for a one-year commitment. Now I think maybe it's more, because he's getting older. Chisan, who's the personnel director there, really asks people to make an open-ended commitment if they want to work with Harada Roshi in Japan. But at that time, it was a one year commitment."

"Do you need to be able to speak Japanese?"

"Sogenji is intended for westerners, and so the main language is English. Mostly it is European people there. There's always between twenty and thirty students in residence, men and women, but it's not a casual thing. You can't just go there for an o-sesshin, generally speaking, unless you have some extenuating circumstance. So I made the year commitment. I stayed for a year, then I stayed for one more year, and, like I say, I've been working with him ever since."

I ask Rinsan to describe Harada Roshi, and he hesitates. "I wish you could meet him. Have you ever met Roshi?"

"I haven't."

"Because it's a little bit like trying to write a travelogue without going someplace, depending on second-hand information about some place. You know?"

"Sure, but I'm never going to meet Shunryu Suzuki or Philip Kapleau either."

"Yeah. But a lot of Harada Roshi's teaching is in his presence. It is in the way he moves, the way he talks, the way he interacts."

I play him the recording of what Chozen had said about it feeling almost as if Harada were psychic. "Is that similar to your experience?" I ask.

"Completely. Exactly, I mean that's exactly right, and that's why it's really difficult to give somebody an impression through a story of Harada Roshi, because of this presence, this thing that he is. He's like a mirror, and he just reflects back at you who you are. And that's the essence of his teachings. So much so that the stories around him or what he does are kind of incidental. I spent ten years in Japan with him, most of it in a very close way. I was his attendant, and I would drive him around, most of the time in utter silence. In a very comfortable silence – you know? – but in a very intimate way, so that after three days of this, everything had dropped away, and you're just with this guy going from place to place. And that's really the essence, for me, of Roshi: his clarity, his simplicity. He's very childlike."

"How did Sogenji in Japan come to focus on Western students?"

"When he was still at Shofukuji, Harada Roshi had been thinking about going to Italy and doing something there. And also he had interests in coming to Seattle back in '82. Connected with Chisan to come here and establish something. But

Yamada Mumon Roshi asked him, at that point, to take over Sogenji monastery and do whatever he wanted with it, but that he stay in Japan and do that. So, Harada Roshi – the story goes – thought, 'Okay, let's make it a place for westerners here in Japan, and then we can branch off after that. We can establish it here. Figure out how to do it, and then go to these different countries.' So now he has this place, a place like this in Germany, and a place in India. And he goes once or twice or three times a year to each to lead o-sesshin."

Once Harada began leading sesshin in Washington, a sangha began to develop. The One Drop Zendo Association was established with affiliate groups in Seattle, Los Angeles, and Port Townsend. There are similar associations in Germany, India, Poland, Sicily, Denmark, and Latvia.

"Who would have thought there was a Latvian Zen community," I say.

"Yeah, they're on fire. They're really serious. Great sangha."

For a while, Shodo Harada held sesshin at various rented or borrowed locations. "We moved all around, and the sangha, at a certain point, thought, 'We should establish our own place.' Just because it was such a hassle that every time he comes we're in somebody else's facility. We have to try and figure it out. It would take two or three days of the sesshin to figure out how to work it."

Once the decision was taken to establish a permanent center, Harada told his American students that it should, if possible, be in the mountains, the traditional setting for Asian Zen centers. "So they were looking a lot over on the Cascade side closer to the mountains. But some of his students living on Whidbey Island invited him to come here. South Whidbey is a little community of…um…progressive thinkers, however you want to put that. He felt such a warm welcoming by these people in this community that he was open to the idea of getting land here and then this space became known to him. And he came out and looked at it and the quietness and the distance. He didn't want to be close to the city. He wanted people to come out into nature. And this really fit that bill. 'Tahoma' is the name of Tacoma – Mount Ranier – in the local native American language."

The official name of the monastery is Tahomasan Sogenji. The suffix "san" refers to a mountain, and, on a clear day, one can just see Mount Ranier from a ridge which is a twenty minute walk through the woods from the main site. Coincidentally, "ta" signifies "a large amount" in Japanese, and "ho" is Dharma. Tahomasan Sogenji is still very much a work in progress. My visit coincides with a meeting Rinsan has with a local architect who is there to discuss latrine construction. The long-term goal is to establish a residential training center, similar to Sasaki's Mount Baldy.

"Was the hospice here when you first came here or did it come later?" I ask.

"The hospice came a couple of years later. The building was already there. We were using that building, actually – before these buildings were built – for o-sesshin.

It was up for sale; there's twenty acres there. It was a horse farm. And one of Harada Roshi's students saw the land, had some money, and wanted to establish a family trust, and so bought the land, with the house on it, and basically gave it to Harada Roshi, saying, 'Do whatever you want with this.'"

What Harada Roshi wanted to do with it was establish a hospice.

"Is it directly connected to the monastery?"

"It's one unit. It's very directly related. But it's non-Buddhist. It really serves the Whidbey community in a secular way. So it's wide open, although they really are connected at the hip."

The student who donated the hospice property is David Trowbridge.

"About twenty years ago I decided I wanted to live on this island at some time," his wife, Cynthia, tells me, "and I know that David always needs a few years to catch onto my ideas. But it happened when he retired that he knew he wanted to go back to his Zen practice, and he found a group in Seattle. Then we learned that the group in Seattle was associated with Tahoma Monastery. So David began coming to the work days at Tahoma Monastery and weekend sits, and I became peripherally acquainted with this monastery. Then he, too, became convinced that we would like to live on Whidbey Island.

"I had been the primary mover in working with the realtor and that sort of thing. And the realtor said, 'Well, I know a place that doesn't meet your needs, but it's right next to the monastery.' So one weekend when David was leaving, he stopped at the place just down the road from the monastery. And he looked around, and the caretaker came out. And the caretaker happened to be a man he'd been sitting next to in sesshin a couple of weeks previously. And so he showed David all around. And they went to the back of the property, to the pond. And while he was at the pond, David realized that, no, this definitely wasn't our home – the house didn't have the feeling of our home – but it was something that could belong to the community. So David came home, and he was very excited. 'Come see this land. I don't know what it's for, but I think we should buy it for the community.' He was speaking of the larger community of Whidbey. And all of this, the intuitiveness and impulsiveness of David, was totally out of character. He's a scientist by nature and profession and not one to give intuition much credence."

3

Rinsan leads me along a moss-laden path through the woods. It is about a quarter mile to the hospice, which is called Enso House, after the free-form calligraphy circle common in Zen art. In the entry way, there is a large enso done by Harada, who is considered a master calligrapher in Japan.

"In Zen, calligraphy has always been an expression of your state of mind," Rin-san remarks. "So one of Roshi's main calligraphies is the enso, this one stroke circle. In old China, Zen masters traditionally worked with that."

Enso House is what drew me here even though I knew Shodo Harada would not be in residence.

An important shift has taken place in Zen training since the pioneers – men like Shunryu Suzuki and Taizan Maezumi – brought the practice to America from Japan. Much of that early Zen training had been based on monastic models. As Shishin Wick, one of Maezumi students, told me, his teacher was really "only interested in those people who were going to carry on his Dharma," those who would work to become teachers themselves. From that perspective, it is natural for Zen to be considered essentially a monastic practice focussed on the development of prajna or wisdom. This is what Shodo Harada was seeking during his time in the mountains. More recently, however, there has been more concern expressed about the application of Zen training beyond the monastery walls. How can Zen practice benefit those who continue to live "in the world"? The focus, in this case, is on karuna or compassion.

This shift of focus was one of the things had I noticed about Shinge Chayat's approach to training, particularly in Syracuse. Many people, she told me, "will train here and then go into the world and do wonderful work with hospice or some hospital situations or prisons. We encourage that. Do your training. Really purify your heart. Shed all of the ways in which you've deluded yourself, and really look at everything clearly. Solidify your intention, deepen your commitment, and then you will be such a force for good."

Ever since the San Francisco Zen Center established Maitri, hospice care has been a path associated with the practice.

The director of Enso House is Dr. Ann Cutcher. She doesn't answer questions quickly or lightly. When I ask if she is a Zen practitioner, there is a fairly long pause before she speaks, and then she says, "Uh...I don't know."

"Had you been?"

Again a pause before she speaks. "Um...a couple of things. I wouldn't be here at Enso House if the monastery weren't here also. And I wouldn't be here if I hadn't discovered meditation as a very profoundly important part of my life."

As we talk about how she became involved in hospice care, I grow accustomed to her habit of reflecting for a moment before answering a question. "I've always been drawn to death and dying for some inexplicable reason. In my professional life as an internist in an intensive care unit, and in an emergency room, and in chronic care, I just naturally seemed to be the person in our group who was most interested in taking care of the patients who were at the end of their life, who were in hospice. So I can't explain it as anything more than a natural inclination. It's really hard to do this if you don't have that. It's either a natural inclination or not. I don't think you can teach it. And I don't think you know whether you have it until you've experienced it."

Later I learn more about Ann's story from a book David Trowbridge wrote on the history of Enso House.

As a young woman in the early '70s, she had gone to Japan to study pottery. Shortly after she arrived, she read an article by Chisan describing her own experiences as an American pottery apprentice in Japan. The two became friends, and, after a while, Ann started accompanying Chisan to early morning zazen at Shofukuji. Trowbridge quotes Chisan's memories of those days:

> Neither of us had much money. She [Ann] would spend her little money each day going to the public bath and eating raw instant Ramen noodles. I would spend my little bit of money walking to the best German pastry shop and buying their cheapest pastry, which is their little rum stick. She was the ascetic, and I just happened to be the one in the Zen temple. But I was the one who was pigging out on German bakery food. She was the one eating raw Ramen. She was the true Zen person. She didn't need to train with [Mumon] Yamada Roshi, but I did.[36]

After five years in Japan, Ann returned to the United States, completed medical school, and began practicing medicine in Arizona. Not long after, a series of traumas followed one another. Her husband was so debilitated by a series of heart attacks that they needed to hire a live-in caregiver. The marriage failed. Then her mother died from breast cancer. Ann felt she was at a turning point in her life. She took leave from her practice and volunteered with Catholic Medical Missions which sent her to southern India. The conditions there turned out to be even harsher than she had imagined they would be.

"I was terrified. I was scared. The chaos was overwhelming. I was sure there was a catastrophe just waiting to happen." To get to work, she had to walk over a river of excrement – she feared that when it rained, she might slip into it. Typhoid and cholera were rampant, and there were practically no medical supplies. Ann found herself suturing wounds while using no anesthesia at all.[37]

Before leaving India, she visited Calcutta and volunteered briefly with Mother Teresa and the Missionaries of Charity who ministered to the dying of that city. The impact of that experience was such that, when she returned to medical practice in Tucson, Ann volunteered as medical director on a couple of hospice boards.

Then Chisan phoned one day and described what they were hoping to do on Whidbey Island.

"How long have you been here?" I ask.

"Since 2002. I took a sabbatical for a year to help get it organized and thought that's what it would take to get it organized. And at the end of the year, the house was still empty, and there was nothing happening. And I ended up staying, and that was basically because of the inspiration of our first guest."

Later Cynthia tells me that Chisan's call came at a time when Ann was at another turning point in her life. "So she said, 'I'll give it six months.' And she was helping us get through all the paperwork and some of the remodeling stuff that needed to happen. And at the end of six months, we cautiously said, 'Are you staying?' And she said, 'Well, it needs another six months to get everything done.' And she never left, and we never asked her again."

Ann tells me: "This property, which is twenty acres of land essentially adjacent to the monastery property, was on the market for a number of years, and it was actually used as the zendo for several sesshin before the Tahoma buildings were built. Then it was bought by a senior student of Harada Roshi and offered to him to use for whatever he wanted to use it for. And he apparently knew, without much thought, that he wanted it to be a home for people who didn't have a home to die in. And so it's a gift, essentially, to Harada Roshi, and it's Harada Roshi's vision that this should be an end-of-life care home – a safe haven essentially – as a way to give back to this community which has supported Tahoma and helped it grow and become, and as a way for his meditation students to take their practice off the cushion and apply it in life."

Rinsan and I join Ann, and two young Zen students currently working at Enso House, for lunch. Myoo is a nurse from Germany who has been at Enso House off and on for ten years. Peter Torma, from Hungary, has only been here a few weeks. I ask how they see Enso House connecting to their Zen practice.

"It's actually to bring a little bit of the training outside of the monastery," Peter tells me. "This is what the Roshi says. What we do in the training, the mindfulness and meditation – which is actually the same thing – we try to do with the patient and just be there for the moment, just to see what is happening for the moment, what is happening inside of us in that moment and with somebody who is in a big distress, from every point of view – physical, emotional – and not to be overwhelmed by our own fears about that but just to be in the moment and watch inside and outside."

"I don't know exactly what the Roshi would say," Myoo adds, "but for me it is practically every day life; every moment is kind of a Zen training. It doesn't matter where you are. It doesn't matter what you do. This is part of your training. And for me this is partly because I can be so close to the monastery. It's very simple. We just take care of one guest at a time. So it stays very simple in some ways. And also it shows you, I think, in everybody's life that death and birth are two of the most important parts. And this is a good way for me to see the dying part, which you can maybe see giving birth to something new."

About fifteen of Harada's students have worked here at one time or another. I ask how they are chosen. "Do they volunteer to come here, or does the Roshi say, 'You know what? I think it'd be a good idea for you to go to Whidbey Island.'"

"It can be both," Ann says. "It can be either. But I don't think anybody would ever come here who says 'no.' Everyone who comes has had to say 'yes.'"

"Saying 'yes' in theory and saying 'yes' in practice might be different things, though."

"Mm-hmm. And the people who have difficulties are the people who've said 'yes' and realized they really didn't want to say 'yes.'"

"Or they said 'yes' to get out of the monastery," Rinsan remarks, "and when they get here it's like, that's not exactly where they wanted to go."

"The brochure describes this as care-giver training," I say. "So is there the hope that the training students receive here is something they will make use of somewhere else?"

"I don't know that I would say 'hope,'" Ann tells me. "I can just say that it has happened naturally for five of the fifteen, two of whom have gone on to get RNs, and that's neat. It's expanded their lives in a way. But it really doesn't matter to me if people do any part of this when they leave."

"And also one of the volunteers," Myoo says, "her father-in-law died, and she said it helped her stay with her father-in-law really close and helped the process of his dying. So you don't need maybe to be a professional afterwards. You just get a good chance of care-giving, and this can help you in your future life in whatever you do."

They explain that the people who come as "guests" to Enso House are those who have nowhere else to go. If it is possible for people to remain in their homes and receive the necessary care there, that is preferable. "Most people want to die in their own bed surrounded by their own people, their own smells and sights," Ann says.

Rinsan notes, "Tahoma Sogenji, for me, is the really alive part of this whole operation. It has been supported by the local community in a huge way. Most people on the island I've talked to know about Enso House, but they don't know about Tahoma. This is the part, so far, that has blossomed. The monastery part is still in incubation until a good Zen Master is in residence here to really open it up. This training, this care-giving, this opportunity to serve the community in this way is one unit with the monastery. We work closely together. Especially when there's not a guest here, Myoo and Peter and whoever come over there and work, and then, when there is a guest, their energy is more focused over here."

"And you've worked here too?"

"Yeah, yeah. I've worked with this current guest. And Peter's going to be leaving at the end of this week, I think, and I'll jump back in at that point. And I was a six month person here. I did the training and everything. Came from Sogenji and was six months here as a care-giver."

"What did you learn from that experience?"

"I think it really stretched me in a lot of different ways. I had never done anything like that before, hands-on care-giving with people in this kind of a situation. Never been around death at all. One of the most challenging things is taking care of the guest's family. That was really challenging for me. But I did learn, in a very simple Zen way, the impermanence of the situation. It really struck me, being in that room when somebody's dying, taking their last breath. You really get that. You really understand that on a completely different level. But also in the sense of just being there for somebody in a wide open way. Whatever happens. Whatever is needing to happen. Without judgement or preconceived notions; just being there in a very simple way."

As lunch progresses, Rinsan asks Ann to tell me the story of "the old rock-n-roller. That really captured for me the scope of what can happen here when somebody requests something. You move in whatever direction you need to make it happen."

Once more, she takes a moment before speaking. "There are a couple of different things that…. Maybe I'm going to mash a few things together to try and…."

"See where you go," Rinsan finishes for her.

"Yeah, see what happens. One of the things that has been so interesting to me was demonstrated with the very first guest who was here, and I've never forgotten it. He was a man who lived as a hermit, essentially, on a beach in a shack which he'd put together with materials that he'd found. And he was, at the end of his life, being taken care of, essentially, by a circle of strangers who had to walk to his home in order to get there. There was no road. And he had no electricity and no plumbing. His electricity was a big extension cord, but he had no plumbing. And the one friend who was trying to coordinate his care at the end of his life was desperate. The rains were coming; it was September. The friend was leaving town for a couple of weeks; he couldn't keep this circle together. And he'd heard about Enso House. I don't know really quite how. And we weren't ready to accept anybody. We didn't have any insurance; we weren't ready. And it happened at the same time as the sesshin was taking place at Tahoma, and the Roshi was here. This friend came to me in a desperate state, and I went and met the man in his cabin and came back and told the Roshi about it and said, 'We need to do this.' And there was really no hesitation with the whole board even though everyone was exposed because there was no insurance. Anyway, this man was brought here, and he was mute. He didn't speak. I don't know if he didn't speak because he had an organic problem; I don't know if he'd had a stroke. He was suffering from lung cancer. But he was completely quiet, and he had these absolutely alert and awake blue eyes. He could see what was happening. And when he got here, he closed his eyes, and he didn't open them for a couple of days. And he didn't say anything. And I would be in the room with him feeling that he was furious about having been brought out of his space and put in a…" – she struggles to find an appropriate analogy – "…a Holiday Inn! And it was really distressing to me, because I felt this so strongly. And then Chisan came over and sat with him for half an hour and came out of the room and said, 'He's so grateful. He's just so appreciative.'

"And what it made me see is that all this – this whole experience – is projection essentially. That really not knowing what is happening is the basis of everything that happens here, and a projection of our own interior life. So that's one thing I find helpful for me personally, to be reminded of that, that I am creating my own interpretation, and I try to make sure I see that all the time so that I can stay open to what's really happening.

"That's one thing. Another thing was this guy Rinsan was talking about. He was a fairly young man who was really adamantly opposed to his dying. It was just *not* gonna happen. And it was happening. And he was angry, and he was aggressive, and he was sure of himself in that this was not going to happen to him. But he was too physically weak and on too many incredibly powerful analgesics to safely move around the house. And yet he was still determined to do that. And I was concerned all the time that this man was going to fall. Once, he was wheeled in a chair across this room, and he suddenly stood up and went to walk into the dining room. And as he stood up, the wheelchair went out from behind him, and I pushed it under him and said, 'You can't do that!' And he got really mad at me. I pushed him into the dining room, and I said, 'You just can't do that. You're going to fall. It's too scary.' And he said, 'No! *You* are the one who needs to calm down and cool off.'" The people around the table laugh. "He said, '*You* need to cool off!'" She pauses, then adds, "True," and the laughter continues.

"Why was he dying?"

"He had colon cancer, and he had an obstruction of his bowel. He was here for five weeks probably, and not able to eat without incredible pain that required doubling the amount of intravenous narcotic that he was getting continuously. And in spite of that, he was determined to eat. And that was another really difficult thing, to watch him roll himself into the kitchen and open the refrigerator knowing that once he swallowed something, we would have to dial up his narcotic and deal with excruciating discomfort.

"And he was a rock-n-roll bassist who had played with a lot of people on the island over his life as a musician, and he really wanted to gather all the musicians he'd played with together. And they all showed up, some of them on motorcycles, and they brought a cooler of beer, and they set up a whole trap set and two mics for singers, and – you know – mics for the guitars and amplifiers. And we moved everything around, and there was like Led Zeppelin music coming from this dining room. He was too weak to play himself. He couldn't hold his instrument. But he had a chair pulled up, and he sat in the chair, and someone gave him his bass, and the room got totally quiet, and he plucked off this song, and sang, 'Knock, Knock, Knockin' on Heaven's Door.' And everybody just like melted. That was pretty amazing."

"How old was he?"

"He was in his fifties. A young man. Yeah. Younger than me."

"For me," Cynthia says, "Enso House has always had to do with letting go. From the very beginning it has been a lesson in letting go. A lesson in letting go for us in ownership. Although the deed is in the name of the foundation – the family foundation that we established – we feel no ownership of Enso House or ownership around decisions made about what happens there. So it was a profound lesson in letting go, letting go of that need for control, for holding. You know? The land was purchased just before our oldest child's last year of high school, and so it was very much letting go and seeing that what needed to be created could be created. It was sort of a lesson, too, in letting a child go out into the world and really begin to build their life on their own. It also worked that way with our other two children. Letting go is an incredibly rich experience. So that was at the roots of Enso House for me, and that's been part of it, I think, ever since. Letting go of preconceptions of what Enso House needed to be, because it needs to be something different for everyone who walks in through the door. It is an incredibly amazing place."

CHAPTER SEVEN

Three Sanbo Zen Teachers

SISTER ELAINE MACINNES
PATRICK GALLAGHER
HENRY SHUKMAN

1

SHUNRYU SUZUKI AND HIS HEIRS ARE IN THE SOTO TRADITION. SASAKI, SHIMANO, and Shodo Harada are all in the Rinzai tradition. There is a third school, which, while relatively small in Japan, has had a significant impact on the development of American Zen. This is the Sanbo Kyodan (the Fellowship of the Three Treasures), which in 2014 changed its name to Sanbo Zen (Three Treasures Zen).

It was founded by Hakuun Yasutani in 1954 to preserve the teaching of his master, Daiun Sogaku Harada, a Soto priest who was also an advocate of koan study and of the importance of kensho. Sanbo Zen blends Soto and Rinzai elements; much of the structure is Soto, but the way in which koans are used is derived, with some modification, from Rinzai Zen. Several of the pioneers who established Zen in North America – including Robert Aitken, Philip Kapleau, Taizan Maezumi, and Eido Shimano – studied with Yasutani, and Kapleau's book, *The Three Pillars of Zen*, largely consists of Yasutani's lectures and responses to students.[38]

Yasutani's principal heir was Koun Yamada, whose kensho experience is the first recounted in the "Enlightenment" section of *The Three Pillars of Zen*. Like Yasutani, Yamada was committed to working with lay and western students, one of the earliest of whom was a Roman Catholic nun from Canada.

When I meet her, Sister Elaine MacInnes is in her 90s and lives at a home in Toronto for retired members of her order, Our Lady's Missionaries (OLM). I had a difficult time arranging the meeting and did so finally through the agency of one of her students, Patrick Gallagher, who arrives at the house by bicycle just as I pull up in my car.

Catholicism, like Buddhism, has a long and rich contemplative tradition, although it now seems to be fading. "I don't know anybody in the Catholic Church who can teach what I call contemplative prayer," Sister Elaine tells me. So she turned to Zen practice. She was not the only Catholic to do so.

Thomas Merton had been interested in Zen and corresponded with D. T. Suzuki, although he ultimately decided it was not a suitable route for the West. Hugo Enomiya-Lassalle, a Jesuit friend and mentor to Sister Elaine, was given authorization to teach Zen by Koun Yamada, as was Ruben Habito, another Jesuit. Father Patrick Hawk, a Redemptorist, was one of Robert Aitken's heirs; Father Robert Kennedy was a student of Yamada and an heir of Bernie Glassman, and one of Kennedy's heirs is the Trappist, Kevin Hunt. Still, it remains an open question how exclusively "Buddhist" Zen practice needs to be.

Sister Elaine tells me that Koun Yamada never expected her to become a Buddhist. Rather, he told her that Zen would help her be a better Catholic and a better nun. Zen, she explains, "cleans out the garbage." It cuts through the stuff that piles up in one's mind, and it brings one to a state of silence which

> – gives our whole being freedom to "do its thing," so to speak. I have heard more than one Zen Master articulate the process as "giving over" to the Source of the power which animates all of life. We are thus released from the dictates of an imperious ego.[39]

At one level, what she is describing is similar to the way in which musicians – especially when improvising – allow music to flow through them without interference, or the way an athlete can respond at an instinctual level unimpeded by conscious thought. Sister Elaine, who is a violinist, writes of a performance she gave of a piece by Brahms after which her Zen teacher noted: "'You have finally got yourself out of the way.' He didn't mean it particularly as a compliment. For him it was a fact. The way things should be."[40]

She tells the story of the Salt Doll which discovers its identity by allowing itself to dissolve in the ocean. It's an Asian story, but the insight it conveys – called "mystic" – is not unique to that continent. It is essentially the same perception one is called to in the 46th Psalm: "Be still and know that I am God."

In *Zen Contemplation: A Bridge of Living Water*, Sister Elaine wrote:

Yamada Roshi…used to tell his disciples in Japan that every human being is born to be a mystic. One day at Wormwood Scrubs Prison in London, England, after a particularly good first meditation with 24 lifers, we all just sat there in a peaceful kind of silence, not wanting to disturb that place which had brought us together. Eventually I spoke and dared to quote that statement I had heard my teacher say any number of times, that everybody is born to be a mystic. Two or three of the lifers nodded in assent, and there wasn't a snicker of disbelief in the group. Each in his own way seemed to know what I was talking about.[41]

Elaine MacInnes was born in Moncton, New Brunswick, in 1924. Her mother was a musician and took care that her children learned to play as well. Elaine was trained on violin. During the Second World War, a number of training fields were established around Moncton for British pilots. The MacInnes household provided as much hospitality as they were able. It would have been welcome. Photographs of Elaine from the period show a very pretty blonde who appears to have natural poise. Both she and an older sister formed attachments to young Englishmen who later died in action.

She graduated with a degree in music from Mount Allison University and, in 1944, did further studies at Julliard, after which she performed for a while in the string section of the Calgary Symphony and taught violin at the Mount Royal College Conservatory. Her entry into religious life was cautious. It was not, at first, a natural fit. She turned 30 shortly after completing her postulancy, which meant she was older than most of the novices and perhaps more set in her ways. She found the routine tedious, and the pre-Vatican II habit was constricting and uncomfortable. After the Vatican II reforms came into effect, she took pleasure in cutting up the stiff linen cloth of her headpiece and burning it.

Although she felt drawn to contemplative prayer, she could find no clear directives about how to go about it until she came upon a copy of *One with Jesus* by a Belgian Jesuit, Paul de Jaegher.

De Jaegher tells his own story about his desire as a priest to become intimate with God. Intimacy demands two, and he seemed to find his humanity getting in the way. He does not say how it happened, but suddenly he came to realize that it was not only intimacy God wanted of him, but rather identification through experience. I see now it was the leap from relationship to experiential knowing. Henceforth he took the Pauline phrase literally. He developed a spirituality based on the text "I live now not I, but Christ lives within me." (Galatians 2:20)

...

The Jesuit did not give specific directions on how he practised this spirituality, but his book is full of encouragement. I tried a few experiments on my own, but they all went through the thinking process, which I soon discovered was creating an objective twosome. I did, however, have my own inspired insight, that the secret or core of that teaching lay in the two words "not I."[42]

In spite of the challenges, she persisted in convent training and, after taking final vows in 1961, was sent to Japan. She felt an immediate respect for the culture and immersed herself in it. During her time in Japan, she studied flower arrangement (ikebana), calligraphy (shodo), and the tea ceremony (kado). She taught music to children and says, with pride, that – in spite of being a missionary – she converted no one.

She first encountered Buddhist spiritual practice when a friend introduced her to the Tendai monk, Somon Horisawa. After serving them tea, he turned to Sister Elaine and inquired, "How do you pray?" When she asked what he meant, he said, "For example, what about your body position?" "I hastily assured him that body position is not important in prayer, and he heartily disagreed. 'Body position is *very* important in prayer.'"[43]

Her introduction to Zen came a little later. She was studying Japanese music terminology at the Jesuit University in Hiroshima and there met Father Hugo Enomiya-Lassalle, who hosted a small Zen sitting group. "As far as I can remember," she tells me, "that's the first time I heard anything about Zen. And I'm so glad I heard about it from him. The rest of my time in Japan, I met so many people who admired Lassalle. I was reading everything on spirituality then, because that was my first mission abroad. And I liked what I read about Zen, but it was when I got all of this from Father Lassalle that I had a deep inner conviction that this is okay, that this is the legitimate stuff."

When she asked him to teach her, he demurred, saying he wasn't qualified. "And I thought, 'Well, gracious! What's this? Here he is, a Jesuit priest, and he says he's not qualified!' And he said, 'I'll find somebody to teach you.' And I said – and I'm not sure why I said this – I said, 'I think I'd rather go to a Buddhist nun than a Buddhist priest to learn my Zen.' The nuns fascinated me. I was on a bus one time, and I was seated next to this funny-dressed person. She leaned over to me and said, in perfect English, 'I know who you are.' And I said, 'Oh, do you! Who am I?' And she said, 'You're a Catholic nun.' And I said, 'Yes. But, I must say, I don't know who you are.' She said, 'I'm a Buddhist nun.' I was just charmed with her."

Lassalle arranged for her to attend a temple for women, Enkoji. "I went there and met the old roshi. At first she wasn't too keen on me. She looked at me. She had almost no English. Well, my Japanese wasn't too bad, but it was pretty primary." The roshi recited the opening words of the Lord's Prayer in Japanese, then told Sister Elaine: "'If you think your father is in heaven, if you think that is God, there's no place for you in Zen.' And I thought she had made quite a jump, so I said, 'There's some things you're going to have to trust me for.' And I don't know whether she liked that or not.

"They were an ascetic group, and it was terribly difficult. They said, 'Well, you'll have to come and make this sesshin, and we'll get someone to give you your orientation at that.' The rising bell for the nuns at that time was 3:00 a.m., and you had to be in the zendo, all dressed, and doing zazen at 3:05. And it was really tough going. And I didn't have the opportunity for a real dokusan, because we had no translator, and the roshi was still pretty convinced that there wasn't much hope for me because of my Christianity and my sense of God. I think I probably thought at that time that her conception of what I thought of God was wrong. I sensed that. But I had limited Japanese, and the fact is that you can't speak very much to most teachers. I never had interviews with her. I'd go in for dokusan, and she might say something. She might not. She might ask me to say something. And then I'd leave. The dokusan was less than a minute. Which was fine. Sometimes dokusans are like that. But I must have got nourishment from somewhere because I kept going back. To the end, I never got very far with her, but she kept me at this thing."

Then she attended a retreat under Father Lassalle's direction in Hiroshima. "And I had some kind of a little experience. And he said, 'Well, I don't know enough about that experience. I've got to get you with a real teacher.' So he took me to Yamada Roshi on the way home from the retreat."

Unlike the abbess at Enkoji, Yamada welcomed Christians. He was also pleased to learn that Sister Elaine was a musician, because musicians – he said – tended to be less "head bound." He agreed to take her on as a disciple, and, during her second sesshin with him, she came to kensho. She made arrangements with her order to move to Kamakura in order to be nearer Yamada.

"He never pretended to understand Christianity or just what we meant by 'God.' But he was very positive. He said, 'I don't understand it, but the church has gone on for centuries.' And he said, 'Zen belongs in the Church.' I said, 'What do you mean?' He said, 'Well, we're losing it in Japan. It's falling apart. Buddhism is failing terribly. Buddhism has failed my family,' he said. 'Not me. But my children.'"

Yamada Roshi, she tells me, expressed the hope that Zen might eventually become a "stream" within Catholicism.

In 1976, the OLM closed its missions in Japan, and Sister Elaine was sent to the Philippines, although she made regular trips back to Japan to continue her koan work with Yamada. She was posted to Leyte, an impoverished and tuberculosis-ridden region in the Visayas group of islands. It was a tense period in Philippine history. The Marcos regime had established martial law in response to the rise of the New People's Army.

When I met with him in Rhode Island, James Ford told me, "I've got a Sister Elaine anecdote. I sat down with her once, and I said, 'I've heard from three different sources that when you were in the Philippines, in an area where it's perpetual civil war, that a battle crossed over whatever the facility was you were running, and the army was driven back by the guerillas, and a government soldier was wounded, and you hid him in the basement. After he got sent away, a few days later, the battle turned and it went the other way, and you hid a wounded guerilla.' I said, 'Is this true?' And she said, 'Well, what else should I have done?'"

He paused a while, then added, "Sent a shiver down my back!"

One of her duties in Leyte had been to operate a piggery. When she was authorized as a Zen teacher by Yamada, the superior of her order remarked, "Well, if she's a roshi now, I suppose we should make better use of her than having her raise pigs." So she was brought to Manila, where, with the encouragement of the Filipino theologian, Catalino Arevalo, she opened her first zendo.

> By November, we had about 30 sitters and a chapel in which to sit, so we organized a formal installation of the Manila Zen Center on November 21, 1976. Father Arevalo spoke at the mass, and his opening words were: "Today is the Feast of Christ the King. Every particle of creation is filled with the beauty of Christ, the love of Christ, the truth of Christ, and the goodness of Christ." I

couldn't help but think most Buddhists would feel at home with that statement.[44]

Government forces in Manila were suspicious of the Church because many priests and nuns supported the rebel cause. "The vast majority of people who came to me in the Philippines were anti-Marcos," she admits. "And I had to be careful where I went because I didn't want to be put in prison too."

One of the rebel leaders, Horatio "Boy" Morales, and nine other political prisoners were being held at the Bago Bantay detention centre where they were regularly subjected to intensive interrogation and torture. One of his visitors brought Morales a pamphlet published by the Manila Zen Center, and he asked Sister Elaine to visit him. It was a dangerous request to accept, but Sister Elaine did so without considering it anything particularly remarkable.

"The authorities allowed you to visit him?"

"Yes, although some of the guards were nasty, of course. I was told more than once, 'We know what you're coming in here for. You've got full access to Boy Morales, and now you've got time alone with him, too. You're not fooling any of us.'"

She worked with the other detainees as well. "All of them, except one man, who looked very much like you and wrote psychology books. And he said, 'Sister, I've got nothing against you or Zen or anything. I'm just not for that kind of thing.'"

Gradually, the other prisoners were released, until Morales, alone, remained in the Detention Center.

"He sat many hours a day," Sister Elaine tells me. "At least four hours a day. So, that's going to work, eh? But he had a lot to get over; his torture had gone on and on." He achieved kensho and was halfway through the Sanbo Kyodan koan curriculum when the revolution finally ousted Marcos.

After Morales was released, he was asked how he had survived his time in detention, and he credited Sister Elaine and Zen practice.

"Oh, yes," she laughs. "I got phone calls from all over the world because the revolution itself was worldwide news, and he was the last person left in that particular prison. And he gave me full credit for going in. He said what a risk it was for me to go in given the prevailing conditions at the time. 'Because we were the bad guys in prison,' he said."

One of the phone calls came from Ann Wetherall of the Prison Phoenix Trust in England. "She was a judge's daughter born in India when he was on circuit there, and then back in England living in Oxford. Quite an accent! And very sincere. Lovely person. Not well. She'd been having cancer bouts for some time when I met her."

Ann was looking for someone to continue the work of the Trust when her disease would eventually prevent her from doing so. "The Prison Phoenix Trust was a staff of two people who wrote letters to inmates and that's all they did. They didn't go into prisons. Ann asked me if I would go to England, and I was on my way to a meeting in Europe – you know how they have these international Zen meetings – so I went via England to visit her. And she told me about her cancer and about her group." Sister Elaine explained that she had no interest in letter writing, and there the matter rested for a while.

After Ann died, the board contacted Sister Elaine again, and she told them she would be willing to go into the prisons and teach the inmates how to meditate. It had not been their original mandate, but they agreed to support her if she were willing to make the effort. The first prison they worked in was "a therapeutic prison just outside of Oxford. And the warden was Tim Newell who is a Quaker. And we became very good friends. Most of the prisoners had been in for some years and were in therapy."

Newell appreciated her work, and gradually she was able to establish a network of volunteers who taught yoga and basic meditation practice in eighty-six prisons throughout Britain.

After she retired from the Phoenix Trust, she returned to Canada, where she was made an Officer of the Order of Canada in 2001 in recognition of her humanitarian work. Ironically, when she tried to duplicate the work she had done for the British prison system in Canada, she ran into resistance.

"I suspect because the people I was talking to didn't appreciate meditation and didn't know what it could do for human beings," she suggests.

Patrick Gallagher adds, "One of the problems in the early days was that it didn't fit into the slot that they were used to. It wasn't a chaplaincy. It wasn't a specifically religious thing. It didn't fit. So they didn't know what to do with it. I think that your Order of Canada helped. You'd been honored by the country, so you weren't" – he searches a moment for the proper word – "flakey."

We all laugh.

2

"Almost everybody's story is interesting when you ask, 'How did you get involved in this?'" Patrick tells me. We retire to a small café near the OLM house after my interview with Sister Elaine. "I had been interested in Zen in university. I majored in religious studies, so you have to do a little bit of everything. And I was attracted to it. I read some Thomas Merton. I found Zen quite intriguing and appealing. But I graduated, got on with my life and so on. But I'd always known about it.

"Then a friend of mine called me one night, and we were just chatting about this-that-and-the-other, and he said, 'By the way…' – this is what I thought he said – 'I'm going to a talk by a Catholic nun who is also a Zen Master.' And I said, 'That sounds interesting. I'd like to come.' And he said, 'I'll check.' And then the conversation went on, and I thought, 'What do you have to check? Don't you just go and listen?' But by then we were in another part of the conversation. So about a week or two later, I got a call from a woman I didn't know saying, 'I'm calling on behalf of Sister Elaine MacInnes, and she'd like to meet with you.' And I remember thinking, 'Wow! She vets her audience! She must be nervous about the Vatican or something!' So I said, 'Fine.' And she gave me some different options and took the time that worked for me. And I went along to the meeting. I knocked on the door, and this older nun opened the door, and I remember thinking as I went there, 'Well, if it's crazy, it will just be an experience.' We went in and started talking, and I realized in about two minutes that we weren't talking about the public talk that she was giving, but she was vetting me to see if I would be a suitable candidate for a zendo that she was establishing. And I thought, 'What the heck! I'll go with it.' So we had this very interesting conversation about spiritual life and prayer life and these sorts of things. And she said, 'Well, why don't you come along? We're having our first meeting in….' Whatever it was. I can't remember. I biked home and thought, 'I'll give it a shot.' And that's how we met. It was kind of by accident.

"That first meeting was held in the public library basement. And I didn't know the first thing about it. She said, 'Well, we'll start off in chairs, facing the wall. And it's going to be eleven minutes. Don't move and try and keep your mind still.' I thought, 'Oh, my God! That's impossible! Eleven minutes! How can I possibly do that for eleven minutes?' It was an eternity, and I sat there thinking, 'I can't move. I'd be so embarrassed. But this is so hard!'"

"The friend who told you he was going to the talk, did he continue?"

"No. No, he came to the first group, but he didn't continue. I did. Isn't that funny?"

"I guess that's what they call karma."

"Yeah. That's right."

Sister Elaine's priority when returning to Toronto had been to establish a zendo, which now goes by the unassuming name of A Toronto Zendo of Sanbo Zen. "It's 'a' not 'the' since we don't claim exclusivity even here in Toronto," Patrick explains. It was only after the zendo took root that she spoke to the members about the prison ministry, which in Canada is known as Freeing the Human Spirit.

"I never felt called to it," Patrick tells me. "So I didn't participate. I think some people did out of loyalty to Sister Elaine at first. Then it was established as a kind of an outreach, although it's quite independent now. There are people who are part of the prison work who aren't part of the zendo, and over the years there are people who joined the zendo who aren't particularly involved in the prison work."

While it does not have the national scope of the Phoenix Trust in England, Freeing the Human Spirit is currently active in fifteen penal institutions throughout Southern Ontario. As it turns out, the prison ministry grew more rapidly than the zendo did.

"It seemed for a long time there were six or seven of us. And then more people started to come. They'd hear about it, or they'd hear about her. If she ever did a radio interview, we'd usually get a couple of phone calls. It's grown steadily since then. On any given Tuesday, we might get between fifteen and twenty/twenty-one people – depending on the weather and the time of year – who come for two hours. We get more who come for a zazenkai or a sesshin."

The sittings are held in the parish hall of Holy Rosary Church, which by coincidence – and only by coincidence Patrick assures me – happens to be the parish he attends. "But it's not associated with the church at all, and it never has been."

For larger activities, such as sesshin, they make use of facilities provided by Scarborough Missions. "They have this large space they rent out to various groups, and we're one of them. They're very small, Spartan rooms. Shared bathrooms. And a large room that we transform into a zendo."

"Is Sister Elaine the presiding teacher at sesshin?"

"Almost never Sister Elaine. We have a presiding teacher, whose name is Brian Chisholm, and unfortunately Brian got transferred – for work reasons – to the States. So he lives in North Carolina. He comes up for every sesshin and every zazenkai, and those are once a month. But on the Tuesdays between, Sister Elaine often comes. Not always. And I always come. And she offers dokusan to some of the senior students, and then other people can come and see me. I'm the assistant teacher."

A few months after our initial conversation, Patrick was promoted to full teacher status, and I arranged a follow-up interview. I had assumed that he had been appointed to his new position by Sister Elaine, but – he informs me – that's not how the Sanbo Zen tradition operates. All teachers need to be approved by the abbot in Japan, who is currently Koun Yamada's son, Ryoun Yamada Roshi. "Likewise, assistant teachers are approved by the abbot," Patrick tells me. "So you can't just set yourself up if you want to be part of the Sanbo Kyodan."

"Does that mean you had to go to Japan?"

"Well, no, because once a year, every year, there is a *kenshukai*, which is a kind of teacher-training sesshin that's led by the abbot, and it takes place in different places. Used to be one year in Asia, one year in Europe. And now there's more North Americans, so that's probably going to change. You have to be invited to go to that. And it's usually after that that the abbot will say, 'Well, so-and-so is a teacher, so-and-so is an assistant teacher.' This year it's going to be in France." Patrick has been attending the kenshukai since 2009. "You have to be recommended by your teacher and then you're invited, and not everybody can go all the time, because we're all lay-people."

There are four ranks within the order. Besides Assistant Teachers and Teachers, there are people identified as Associate Zen Masters and Full Zen Masters. Brian Chisholm is an Associate Zen Master. Sister Elaine is a Full Zen Master.

I ask Patrick how being a "Teacher" differs from being an "Assistant Teacher."

"I've been authorized to work with koan people and Assistant Teachers do not. And I'm authorized to teach independently. In fact, in the Toronto group – which is a fairly large group – we have this unusual situation where the person who began it, Sister Elaine, is still around and comes and sits with us when she can, offering dokusan to a few people when she's up to it. And we have the other teacher, Brian Chisholm."

Chisholm remains associated with A Toronto Zendo of Sanbo Zen even though Patrick is now a full teacher. "Here's how he and I have talked about it – we were just talking about this the other day, in fact – and he said he's the visiting teacher, and I'm the resident teacher."

"And Sister Elaine is the founding teacher?"

"That's a good title. We've never called her that, but, yes, that's a good title."

Sister Elaine has written that when people tell her they are both Buddhist and Christian, she understands what they mean, but she then refers to the Dalai Lama who once said that to make such a claim was equivalent to trying to put a yak's head on a sheep's body. Buddhism and Christianity are not merely matters of loyalty or respect; they are systems of belief based on specific philosophical premises and asserting particular standards of behavior. In that sense, they are not the same and, in many ways, are not even similar.

For Sister Elaine and others like her, the issue appears to be whether Zen as a practice, a discipline, can be utilized outside a Buddhist context in the way that yoga, for example, is now practiced outside a Hindu context. The core of Zen is kensho, which is not a belief but an encounter and an experience attainable by people of whatever – or no – faith affiliation.

Sister Elaine obviously admires Buddhism. She points out, however, that while one might admire Catholicism, one cannot claim to be Catholic until one has, either as a child or an adult, passed through the sacramental process of becoming a member of the church.

"You mentioned that you were active in your parish," I say to Patrick.

"Not in a major way, but yes."

"In some of the places I've visited, they would say that you can't separate Zen from Buddhism. If you're not Buddhist, you can't really practice Zen."

"Right."

"It's pretty clear Sister Elaine doesn't feel that way."

Patrick chuckles. "Correct."

"I take it you don't feel that way either."

"I don't. To me, Zen is a spiritual discipline. It's an access. As Sister was saying, it's a way of contemplation. And that's non-sectarian. It's non-denominational. So I think, for me, it makes me more of who I am. Part of me is Catholic, as part of me is a father, a husband, a Canadian citizen. So it enriches all of those things. Doesn't contradict any of them."

"So what does Zen do? What's its purpose?"

"Well, there's different ways you could say it. To wake up. To see who you are. To see things as they are."

"Would you say those are three different ways of saying the same thing?"

"I would if you pushed me. Yep."

"How are they different?"

"I think if you wake up and see yourself for who you are, then you see the world the way it is. They are three ways of saying the same thing, but however you choose to say it – whichever iteration you would choose – would depend upon who you were speaking to."

Of course, as Sister Elaine stressed, Zen is ultimately not something one thinks about. It is something one does.

"The only way you're going to find out how to do this is to do it," Patrick says. "There's no trick. There's no secret. You just have to get down on the cushion. That's it."

It is also his experience that Zen is not "a young person's game." During the early days of North American Zen, it had been youth who crowded into places like the San Francisco Zen Center and Dai Bosatsu. Today, however, Zen seems – "this is just my own private opinion" – to appeal to people who have "had a little bit of experience of life, who have suffered somewhat. When you're up against it, when the resources you have are not enough, or if the answers you have don't satisfy, then you might look elsewhere. And I think it's unusual for a young person to have that experience."

3

"I don't really believe that Zen can be divorced from Buddhism," Henry Shukman tells me. "I think there was a time in the early 20th century – with the influence of D. T. Suzuki particularly – where you could talk about Zen without having to consider it Buddhist, that Zen was kind of an aesthetic, spiritual principle that popped up all over the place, like R. H. Blyth writing about Zen in English literature."

Henry has only recently been recruited as the resident teacher at the Mountain Cloud Zen Center on the outskirts of Santa Fe. I ask him how his students address him.

"Henry."

"Not Sensei or something more formal?"

"Technically, they could call me 'roshi' actually. I'm an associate Zen master, just since the other day. I got an upgrade."

The president of his board, Michael Waldron, is with us. "Zen Master Junior Grade," he jokes.

"I've got One Dan or whatever they call it in karate," Henry laughs. He'd received his upgrade during the same kenshukai at which Patrick Gallagher was declared a full teacher; Brian Chisolm also was authorized as an Associate Zen Master at that time.

"It's been a real surprise, I can tell you!" He was born in Oxford, where his father was a professor, and still has what Sister Elaine might call "quite an accent." He pronounces "been" as "bean" rather than "bin"; "can't" comes out something like "cahn't."

Santa Fe city ordinances require that all buildings, even private homes, adhere to a handful of local styles. The Mountain Cloud Zen Center on Old Santa Fe Trail is in Pueblo style, thick adobe walls, softly rounded corners, and projecting viga rafters. It was built by Philip Kapleau and a handful of volunteers in the mid-1980s. Kapleau had not enjoyed the winters in Rochester and hoped the New Mexico climate would be more congenial. The building is small but appealing. The zendo, just inside the front door, seats twenty-two on a raised tan, although the group sometimes spreads onto the floor at its weekly sits.

"A group of students of Kapleau Roshi came out here to Santa Fe in the late '70s with the intention of founding a large Zen training center, which he thought was going to be his next big venture. And they found it extremely hard to do. Two or three possible places came up, and they couldn't get permission, and things just dragged on and on with going to the county, going to the city. You know? And it didn't work out. Then this piece of land was gifted to them. So they built this, and by the time that happened they'd been here quite a number of years. Five or six years or something."

Kapleau had hoped to retire in Santa Fe, but that didn't work out, and he returned to Rochester. A group of twelve volunteers who had accompanied him west, however, remained behind. One of these was Mitra Bishop.

"For a couple of years we had a van," she told me, "and would carpool back and forth to Rochester for sesshin. And Roshi Kapleau came out more than once and gave sesshin at Bodhi Manda, Joshu Sasaki's place in New Mexico.

"We got jobs. Some of the guys had done a lot of work in repair and maintenance at the Rochester Zen Center so they had construction skills, and they turned it into contracting businesses, building houses for sale. I worked, initially, free-lancing doing graphic design work, then I ended up working for Barkmann Engineering, designing heating-cooling systems for buildings. Some people went to work for the state."

In 1989, she returned to Rochester and shortly after left for Japan. The group in Santa Fe was becoming smaller. "When I left, they were going through very serious difficulties and continued to do so for some time. Teacher after teacher after teacher came and eventually decided, 'To heck with it,' and left. Kapleau Roshi stopped going there; Bodhin Kjolhede stopped going there; Danan Henry[45] stopped going there. And then the group started renting it out to different groups to be able to maintain the place. A Vipassana group came in, and even they split up. There was a lot of friction in the earlier years. Then Father Patrick Hawk came, right when I came back from living in Japan. He just died recently. After he had been coming to Santa Fe for a short while, he was diagnosed with prostate cancer. It's amazing, but he lived fifteen or sixteen years with it, teaching all the time except for an initial six month leave of absence when he asked Joan Sutherland to come and teach in his place. She was a brand-new teacher, John Tarrant's successor before Tarrant and Aitken Roshi separated. She came, and that stirred the pot too. And so, again, it was challenging – or continued to be challenging – and it wasn't really until Henry Shukman came that things became smooth."

By then, the regular sitting community consisted of only a few people, including Will Brennan and his wife, Lucie.

"Will invited me to come here and join the very last remnants of the original Kapleau group that had built the center," Henry tells me, "which was basically he and Lucie and maybe two or three other people. And they were sitting here regularly on Wednesday nights and had never stopped for twenty-eight years."

"How did Will Brennan know you?"

"Through my teacher, Joan Rieck Roshi." Joan Rieck is a Sanbo Zen teacher in Albuquerque.

"Zen practice was set up originally for one purpose only, which is to help people with their suffering," Henry explains. "So, am I an exception to that? Not really. I mean, it's a pragmatic practice. It has a practical intention."

"So that's the function? To help people deal with suffering?"

"To help us to suffer less."

"Not to deal with suffering?"

"No. To suffer less."

"And how did you come to it?"

"Well, I had an experience when I was nineteen years old that fell on me out of the blue that resolved everything for me, answered everything, and I didn't know what it was. And for ten years I suffered rather a lot, actually, trying to address it and not knowing how to. You know, I went to church, I...."

I interrupt him: "What was the experience?"

"Well, it was a run-of-the mill experience of oneness," he says with a chuckle. "I was watching the sunlight on the ocean. I had actually just finished writing my first book, and I was very happy. And I was watching the sunlight on the ocean, far from home – I'd been working abroad – and all of a sudden the sunlight on the ocean.... Well, I was trying to figure out if the sea was very, very dark or very, very bright. It seemed to be so dark where the light was not, and so dazzlingly bright where the light was. And it was shifting about. So was it black? Was it white? I just couldn't work it out. And all of a sudden, it simply wasn't outside. It was impossible to say that – you know – there it was and here I was watching it. There just was no separation whatsoever. And in that moment, I was flooded with this sense of love. And the love seemed to be absolutely everywhere. And possibly because of my background as a half-Jewish guy in England – where there's still a certain amount of latent anti-Semitism, actually, even when I was growing up in the '70s – I think one of my issues had been, 'Did I belong?' Or, 'Where did I belong?' And, at that moment, I realized that I belonged beyond belonging. I was made of the same fabric as the whole of creation! There was absolutely no difference. And it was totally, over-whelmingly marvelous. I felt like I'd been taken over – claimed – by a greater love that included everything. But I had no idea what it was. You know? I was stone-cold sober, and I didn't know what to do next."

"Where were you when this took place?

"Ecuador."

"Okay. So how did you come to be in Ecuador?"

"Well, I had gone to Argentina to work, through a colleague of my dad's at his college in Oxford. My dad – you know – thought it would be kind of hale and hearty for his renegade adolescent son to do a bit of manual labor, and through this colleague he was able to organize work for a friend and myself on a ranch in Argentina. We earned some money, and, after a while, when we'd got enough money together, we put on our backpacks and hitchhiked from the end of the farm drive. We went north into Bolivia and traveled right across the Altiplano. That was what I had written about in this book." The book was *Sons of the Moon* and would be published by Scribner's a few years later.

The experience on the beach in Ecuador left him "with a sense of its having been by far the most important thing. So what should I do now? Go back and molder in a library? Which is, in fact, what I did do, in rainy England. Which was all very well, but it wasn't addressing something far more important. But I just didn't know how to begin to think about how to address that."

"Did you immediately recognize it as a religious experience?"

"Not at all. See, I didn't have any religion. I actually thought it was some kind of *literary* experience. I thought, 'Obviously it means I must be a writer,' or something like that, because I'd just finished writing my first book. In fact, it was only ten years later that I found my way to Zen…. I mean, how do these things happen?"

He had published two books by then and was in New Mexico to research a book on D. H. Lawrence. "New Mexico is the only place Lawrence ever owned a home. While I was here, I quickly met some nice people, one of whom was a Zen student – Natalie Goldberg – actually a student of Katagiri's. And one evening we were sitting on her porch downtown, and she was reading a passage of Dogen to me, who I'd never heard of till that day. It was totally bewildering, but I couldn't forget it. It was just one sentence about mountains walking. It's a famous passage, actually, in the 'Mountains and Rivers Sutra.'"

"'The east mountains walk on water'?" Michael suggests.

"Exactly!"

"The east mountains are walking, the west mountains float on water. Something like that."

"Yes. And it just sort of stuck with me, this piece of nonsense, like Edward Lear or something – you know – just making up words. But the next day, I was making tea in the morning when it suddenly hit me. 'He's talking about what I experienced when I was nineteen.' I don't know how I put it together, but it was obvious that the only possible explanation, the only way that what he was saying could truly make sense from the authentic perspective of a human being, was in that experience. There was that degree of what to the everyday logical mind was nonsensical yet it was totally logical, with a logic of its own. It made full sense. I knew, right away, that I had to get trained in Zen. So that day, I asked my friend, 'How do I get trained in Zen?' And she called up a priest, actually a guy who studied for many years with Richard Baker and moved to Crestone with him, a very loyal follower of his, called Robert Winsome, who died, sadly, rather young – in his mid-40's. And I will always be grateful both to my friend, Natalie, who read the Dogen to me, and to Robert Winsome for offering my first training in zazen. We sat together in the little temple on Cerro Gordo, here in Santa Fe."

"So he showed you the posture, how to follow the breath? That type of thing?"

"Yeah. Counting the breath, and I took to it. It immediately felt right. Then I went and sat at various monasteries, particularly Zen Mountain Monastery in New York State. But, actually, it took me a long time to find the right person to be my teacher. I probably wasn't ready even though I was in love with zazen."

"How did you find the right person?"

"I suppose I didn't give up. I kept going to different centers, and I sat and sat and sat for years. Did a lot of retreats. Sometimes the same place repeatedly, sometimes with other people. I sat with Eido Shimano in New York, and at a place in England called Throssel Hole Abbey, which is an offshoot of Mount Shasta, Jiyu Kennett's place in Northern California. I went to Thich Nhat Hanh's place in France. A lot of places. So maybe I just wasn't ready, or maybe they just weren't right for me."

Then he met John Gaynor in Oxford, who had been a student of both Sister Elaine and Ryoun Yamada. "There was something about the naturalness in that zendo by comparison with other places where I'd been. For a start, there were zero power issues. There was so little to exercise power over. People showed up for two or three hours once a week. It was a lay center. There wasn't any money. It was just a little house. You know? Of course we sat in what we have to regard as Japanese form, because we're sitting on zabutons and zafus, and we're bowing and lighting incense. But it was a very plain place, with a plain altar. Much more importantly, it was very natural. It didn't feel as if anybody was adopting or affecting – you know – manners or protocols that weren't natural to them. And I *had* felt that, frankly, in other places where the Japanese forms, I felt, weren't natural. They'd be wearing robes and zoris or whatever, and you could tell they were kind of enjoying dressing up. Well, okay, that's fine. But nevertheless, why? Why bother? I mean, I knew, from that experience I'd had when nineteen, that it was indiscriminate. You didn't have to be wearing a robe or using chopsticks. I wanted the training but in as natural a way as possible. And they seemed to have that.

"The core of the training in that line – which I'm now part of – is koan study. And the lineage was steered into its forms by Harada Sogaku Roshi and Yasutani Hakuun Roshi, who were looking to revitalize the importance of the experience of awakening in Zen, which they both felt had become sidelined in much of Soto Zen as then practiced in Japan. No doubt that may be an over-simplification. Anyway, I liked the way they centralized koan study. Some people in our line do shikan taza, often later on in practice, but on the whole many of us at least sit with the koan Mu. And yet there isn't a great deal of ritual. We follow a simple protocol. I like it. It's crisp and clean and a little bit informal compared to other more ritualistic forms of practice. Of course we all need to find where it's going to resonate for us and feel congenial. That's how it is for me. So how did this happen? How does it happen that people find their teacher? I don't really know. You know, they say when the student is ready they will find a teacher. The teacher will be there."

"How long did you stay with Gaynor?"

"Well, I'm actually still with him. I still sit with him. That's another thing that I liked, that he too still had his teacher, whom he was seeing regularly. I believe that is a significant difference from other places I'd been, where the teachers had been cut loose – or had cut themselves loose – and were sort of meteors floating around on their own, without any real backup, let alone any people they were answerable to. This may be one of the most important problems in contemporary American Zen, the breaking-away of teachers from their own teachers. No doubt people can get into situations where it may seem they have no choice. And their teacher may die, of course. But the cost to the very young Dharma in this country of some teachers having rather recklessly broken from theirs may be immeasurable. When I found John, one reason it felt so much better with him was precisely that true sense of lineage, which, for me, means an on-going relationship; it doesn't just mean a picture of an ancestor on a wall. He, to this day, is not really anything other than a student even though he's a marvelous teacher. But he hasn't been my only teacher.

"I was working on a new book for a publisher, and it took me back here. And fortunately John had a Dharma aunt – in other words, a teacher in the same lineage – Joan Rieck Roshi, who lives down in Albuquerque. Very quiet. Very modest. Very clear. Very deep. A marvelous teacher. John sort of passed me onto her when I came here, and I continued my koan study with her and would see him whenever I was able to. She has a quiet little zendo in Albuquerque called the Todd Street Zendo. Most of her teaching life, actually, has taken place in Europe, even though she's from Wisconsin. And for a while, she led a group in Portland, Oregon, and a group in Dallas when Ruben Habito was away. I think she was there for a couple of years. So she has been somewhat active in America, but much more so in Germany, Switzerland, Italy."

"And how did you get from Albuquerque to Santa Fe?"

"Well, there's a guy I wish you could meet named Will Brennan who brought me here. He's a friend and a sometime-student of Joan Rieck."

Henry had been authorized as a full teacher by Ryoun Yamada by the time Brennan extended the invitation for him to come to the Mountain Cloud Center.

"Let's back up a bit," I suggest. "How did you become a teacher?"

"Oh, well," Henry laughs, "it was all down to my teachers. My teachers said that they wanted me to teach. And I didn't feel particularly comfortable about it, actually. But one of my teachers said to me, 'It's not like there's some institute you can go to. You learn this on the job.' That was John. Well – you know – I'm so grateful to him. If he wants me to do this, and Joan also wants me to and so does Yamada Roshi…. In our line, you see, you go to the abbot. You have to get approved by the abbot. I think one of the reasons quite a few American Zen Centers that derive from Sanbo Zen are no longer part of it may be the business of appointing teachers. They don't like it. Because in Sanbo Zen teachers are expected to bring senior students they'd like to see become teachers to the abbot to be checked out. You have to go to Japan and meet him. You have to go and do retreats with him. And he decides. It may take a while."

This structure, Henry believes, is also one of the reasons the Sanbo Zen tradition has been able to avoid the difficulties which have arisen elsewhere. "Sanbo Zen, to my knowledge, has only had one scandal, and even then it was rather a quiet and brief one. Why haven't we had more? I think if you're an isolated entity – I'm shooting from the hip a bit here – but if you *are* an isolated entity as a teacher, you're going to need to draw some sense of support towards yourself. And maybe you'll be inclined to do that by getting a sense of power – you know – by exerting your authority in more areas than just the Dharma. You allow it to spread beyond the confines of the dokusan room and the teisho cushion. On the other hand, if you have close Dharma brothers and sisters and a Dharma mother or father with whom you have some regular contact and toward whom you have a sense of responsibility, you don't need that so much. You already have the support. You're not an isolated entity. And you can keep your own practice pure. I mean, I've noticed it in myself. It's been the first big lesson for me as a teacher, that I can forget that I'm a student. I've noticed it happen to me at times. It stops feeling right. And then I remember: 'Oh! I'm still a student. I'm still working on my training. I never want to not be a student.' And if I'm not a student, I can't help actually. The more I am a student, the more I can receive the Dharma and the more I can – hopefully – pass it on. I mean, everyone's finding it themselves; it's just a matter of helping everything open up so that we're all more open to receiving it. But if I'm not a student, it's sad. It doesn't feel good. It's yucky."

I return to what he had said about feeling comfortable with John Gaynor, in part, because of the lack of overt Japanese ritual, which leads to questions about the degree to which Zen needs to be Japanese or even Buddhist.

"Is this a Buddhist Center?" I ask. "I mean, in addition to being a Zen Center?"

It is in reply to this question that he tells me, "I don't really believe that Zen can be divorced from Buddhism."

When I suggest that Sister Elaine's center in Toronto is not a Buddhist center, he replies: "I don't think she was trying to hybridize Christianity with Zen. I know a number of Christians who practice Zen. But as a teacher, I'm pretty sure that she just taught Zen. She happened to be a Roman Catholic and found no conflict."

Earlier he had noted that there were different types of Zen depending upon the use the individual practitioner made of the discipline. It's the list that Yasutani had enumerated in his opening lectures as recorded in *The Three Pillars of Zen*. One of these types Henry describes as "Zen outside Zen, people doing some form of meditation not within the context of a Zen Buddhist framework. Such as Christian contemplation."

"And what would they get out of that?"

"Well, I think what they got out of it would be determined by the framework in which they're doing it. So I suppose if it were a Christian, they'd be hoping to get closer to God or something like that."

"If I were a member here, would I be introduced to Buddhist teachings in addition to the physical and mental practice of meditation?"

"Yeah, that's an interesting question." He pauses, then continues: "Zen, of course – generally speaking – doesn't go into, say, the Abhidharma or the traditional Buddhist teachings very thoroughly. It does here and there. And you can tell in the koans that Buddhist teaching was clearly the major background at the time. And I suspect that different masters relied on Buddhist doctrine to greater and lesser extents – the Four Noble Truths, the Five Desires, the Three Characteristics of Existence, and so on. I use very elementary Buddhist teaching. I guess I only know elementary Buddhist teaching. I've been right through Zen training without being exposed to more, except to the extent that I wanted to be."

"So could a student here practice not necessarily Zen *Buddhism* but rather what Sister Elaine would simply call Zen?"

"I wear a rakusu, which officially means I'm a Buddhist, and a number of us do. But many don't. And there's no need to formally be a Buddhist here. But maybe the definition isn't only a formal one, if you see what I mean. I mean, maybe you can consider yourself ..." – he sighs – "...Buddhist in the sense you.... What's the word? Ascribe? Is that the word? No. Where you take on Buddhist...."

"You can acknowledge the value of the teachings," Michael suggests, "in a kind of moral, spiritual realm without necessarily ascribing to the deism of Buddha."

"Yeah!"

"Well," I say, "I don't think most Buddhists would look upon the Buddha as a deity, but there is a code of conduct. Do you, for example, teach the precepts?"

"Well, yeah we do when we do jukai," Henry admits.

"So jukai, They're taking the precepts. They're becoming Buddhists."

"Yeah, but you know, we do that late on. You don't have to. Maybe that's a little strange in our line, but we actually study the precepts rather deeply at the end of our koan study. That means a lot of people don't get to it. With Joan Rieck we did do precept study for everybody, which I think was a healthy and a good thing to do. It's one of the things on my list that we're going to do here, actually."

I remain unclear whether he believes that what Sister Elaine is doing amounts to a "Zen outside Zen." We continue the discussion by email after my visit, and he writes:

On the one hand, Zen Buddhism is clearly a kind of blend of Taoism with Buddhism, as has often been said. Perhaps some Confucianism gets in there too. So very many of our koans include the word Buddha. I just think that to separate Zen from its Buddhist roots and context makes no real sense. On the other hand, from a quite different point of view, of course Buddhism and Zen Buddhism aren't – in a sense – really those things at all. They are simply means to study the fact of being a human being, of having a human body and mind. They are forms within which to go rather deeply into the existential questions: What is life? What is death? Who am I? Why am I here? What should I be doing, granted that I am here?

Yamada Koun says that all religions – ideally – meet in a "common plaza," a shared ground where the individual identity has been seen through and we come to rest in the clarity and emptiness of our true nature. So naturally, no one could claim to have an exclusive monopoly on that.

Yamada Roshi had also expressed the hope that Zen would eventually become a "stream" within Catholicism, although Sister Elaine admitted she did not expect to see that happen within her lifetime.

"So Will Brennan invites you here, and there are about three people left in the community."

"Yeah," he says, happily. "And it's great."

"More than three people now?"

"Oh, yeah, well it starts to grow. I think, actually, I personally have something like thirty formal students here or maybe more. And there's more people beyond that who are pretty regular attendees."

As the time set aside for the interview draws to a close, people are gathering for the evening sit. In its new incarnation, Mountain Cloud is still a young sangha but a sangha with signs of vigor. The zendo will be full this evening, and the people appear to range in age from mid-twenties to late-sixties.

The bell marking the first round of sitting tolls deeply as I make my way outside to admire the grounds and surrounding mountains. This is desert, of course, and I have always appreciated the beauty of such landscapes. The early Christian ascetics known as the Desert Fathers went into the desolate regions of Egypt to dedicate their lives to contemplation and reflection because there is something conducive to that practice in environments such as this. I feel that Philip Kapleau had chosen well in coming here.

CHAPTER EIGHT

John Tarrant

I DID NOT JOIN THE MEDITATORS AT MOUNTAIN CLOUD DURING THEIR EVENING sit because I was recovering from a broken leg and was unable to sit in any of the traditional zazen postures. Elsewhere – at Dai Bosatsu for example – I had made use of a chair, but that hadn't felt right in the Santa Fe zendo with its raised tan.

I went through three surgeries – each to implant a stronger bar down the middle of the bone – before the leg was finally declared healed. The book I took with me to the hospital for the first surgery was one that had been sitting on my shelf for some time but I had not gotten around to reading: John Tarrant's *The Light Inside the Dark*. When, at last, I did open it, I enjoyed it so much that I brought it with me for the next two surgeries as well.

It is a study of the interplay of Spirit and Soul in human life. Spirit, in Tarrant's terminology, is what connects us to the Source from which all of Being comes – call it the Void, Dao, or God. Soul is what links us to and relishes the world of time and the particulars of both enjoyment and the inevitability of suffering. It is a distinction I first encountered many years earlier in Lin Yutang's translation of the opening poem of what I still think of as the *Tao Te Ching*:

> Oftentimes, one strips oneself of passion
> In order to see the Secret of Life;
> Oftentimes, one regards with passion,
> In order to see its manifest forms.[46]

Zen is generally considered a spiritual activity, but Tarrant stresses the importance of both Spirit and Soul. Spirit without Soul can become cold, ascetic, and subject to that sudden upsurge of the denied elements which Jung called the Shadow. That, in turn, can result in "a fall into appetites swollen because so long suppressed – this is why we find scandals in the lives of so many religious figures."[47] Conversely, Soul without Spirit may become base and prone to despair.

It was as much the book's style as its content that made it a satisfying recovery room companion. The author is obviously intelligent and well-read, and he has a poet's facility with language and imagery which makes reading his work slowly enjoyable. As I prepared for my trip to the west coast, I brought my copy of *The Light Inside the Dark* in the hope of having it autographed.

Some writers, when met, prove be very different from their literary personas. John Tarrant, however, turns out to be much as I had imagined he would be. He's Australian – his ancestors "transported in chains to the desolation of Botany Bay"[48] – and his accent would cause me occasional difficulty when I worked on the transcript of the interview although it was a pleasure at the time. There was the same irreverent sense of humor I found in the book. He grinned mischievously throughout the interview, and his frequent chuckles easily burst into a chest-heaving belly laugh.

He is the first of Robert Aitken's heirs, which places him very early in the process of the transference of Zen to the West.

Aitken has been called the first patriarch – he preferred the gender-neutral term "ancestor" – of American Zen. He first learned of Zen while a non-combatant prisoner of war in Japan during the Second World War. A guard loaned him a copy of R. H. Blyth's *Zen in English Literature and Oriental Classics*. Coincidentally, Blyth was not far away in a camp for civilian prisoners where, in spite of his Japanese wife, he was detained as an "enemy alien." In 1944, Aitken and Blyth met when the prison camps in the area were consolidated.

After the war, Aitken began Zen practice in the US, under the direction of Nyogen Senzaki[49] and with a number of teachers in Japan, including Soen Nakagawa and Hakuun Yasutani. Eventually Aitken and his second wife, Anne, established the Diamond Sangha in Honolulu which met in their home near the university campus. As the group expanded, Soen Nakagawa sent a young monk, then known as Tai-san Shimano, to Hawaii to assist them.

When the Aitkens were in their fifties, they purchased a former hotel on the island of Maui as a potential retirement property. Maui had become a popular destination for hippies, enough of whom were sufficiently serious about Zen practice that Aitken and his wife transformed their home into the Maui Zendo, which became an official practice center of the Sanbo Kyodan School.

arts tradition there. But also it was Vietnam time, so there was a lot of tension between the generations."

Australia was heavily invested in Vietnam, and John was drafted. "I was skilful enough and academically well connected enough that I could have never gone, but I was feeling really bad about it. First of all, I just started investigating the war, and I thought, 'I don't know, probably we should be there.' Then I talked to South-East Asian scholars who happened to be at the University of Tasmania, and then the war looked worse and worse to me. I didn't want to go to war, but, if I had to go to war, I didn't want to go for the wrong thing."

The Quakers offered to help young men in his position. "They said, we'll lie for you, and we'll say you're a conscientious objector, but I said I'm really not. But I got annoyed with the authorities, so I resisted the draft. I was the first person to publically resist the draft in my state. And although it didn't turn out to be a big thing, I didn't know that at the time. You know, the worst they would do is beat you up and throw you in jail for a couple of years. It wasn't the end of the world. But I made some public statements and went underground for a few years."

He went to work in "an antique copper smelter" in Tasmania. "It was called the Mount Lyell Mining and Railway Company. It was a mine that was primitive still. It had forklifts and an electric blast furnace, but then some stuff was done with pick-axes. It was great," he says, laughing. "It was a refuge for people who for one reason or another wanted to drop off the ends of the Earth.

"Nobody thought you wanted to go to the mines; those guys in the mines would die to get out of the mines and go to Vietnam. So I could do jobs where no one cared about your draft status. So I had closed off all my options. I mean I clearly wasn't going off to Oxford and become a professor the way people thought I should or be a doctor at home. Those options were closed. I'm interested in the way the decisions we make when we're quite young, quite carelessly in a way – to say, 'Just fuck 'em. They're killing my friends, and they're killing Vietnamese who have nothing to do with me' – how those decisions shaped my life in various ways. Being underground led me to be much more inward than I might have been otherwise. So I became much more interested in the mind."

In between shifts at the mine, he wrote.

"I would work a bit and write, work a bit and write. Mostly poetry in those days. I was also trying short fiction; I was trying to learn how to approach reality with words. In a way, it was more a Zen thing than trying to make literature."

After four years, there was a change of government, "And we pulled out. Australia was more friendly to the opposition to the war in Vietnam than America, because there were these legendary World War Two veterans who were opposed to it – Labor guys."

❀

He became a lobbyist for Aboriginal land rights, an issue Judith Wright had been concerned about, and he discovered that the Aborigines "had some sense of what I was looking for. The people that I liked and connected with didn't have the sense of alienation from the world that I had or the sense that their minds were out of control; so they had a discipline, an aptitude for attention that, for them, was just a cultural thing. It wasn't any big deal to them that they had that, but it was interesting to me."

Then he heard that a couple of Tibetan teachers were coming to Brisbane. "I didn't know what they were doing, but I immediately knew I wanted to sign up. So I signed up for it, sight unseen, a one month long silent retreat."

The Tibetans were Lamas Yeshe and Zopa, who had been working with western students in Darjeeling since the mid-60s and were now, in the mid-70s, offering retreats elsewhere, including Australia.

I remark that a month-long silent retreat seems a tough introduction to practice.

"Oh, it was all right, you know. I'd gone out a lot into the wilderness alone, so that wasn't a hard thing for me. Being silent wasn't hard. Taking a month out of my life – well, I wasn't on a career path or anything, so that was fine."

Yeshe and Zopa, as he puts it, were experimenting with Western students. "They were giving us Deity Yoga. You usually give people a lot of training before you do that, have them do a thousand prostrations, things like that. But they just dropped us in the pool. One of the things I realized from that was that turning the donkey just a little towards the barn was a good thing. It's like that with poetry too, learning to write. I didn't have to be good at writing, I just had to turn myself towards it. I'd come off shift in the mines and just write some poetry, and I knew it wasn't any good, but I knew I was learning how to communicate or to listen to the world better. Meditation was like that too. I wasn't very good at it, but I thought it would teach me how to do it if I just started hanging around with it."

During the retreat, he came upon a book of Chinese poetry and koans. "I got interested in the old Chinese poets. There was a spaciousness in their work that allowed the universe to come through to them. They weren't imposing their mind on the world. There were ideas I could find in the English poets, but the Chinese had something different. There was an extra spaciousness, a receptivity. David Hinton wrote about it quite movingly in a recent book called *Hunger Mountain*. Through translating Chinese poetry he began to understand what it was like to be inside their minds, and it changed his idea of nature, his idea of himself, and what a 'self' was. That was what I was looking for. I was very interested in putting more space in all that and listening to things.

"I came out of the Tibetan retreat interested in koans, interested in koans as poems, poems as koans, that sort of thing. So I got interested in Zen. Met a few people. There were a couple of other people sitting meditation together. They knew something about Zen, and we held a couple of little Zen events. They were militant, fascist sorts of things that converts do, screaming at each other. There are like six people in the meditation hall, all screaming," he says laughing. "But I was willing to be tolerant of that because I could tell there was a genuine project in Zen. I knew it was pretty clumsily manifested, but that didn't worry me.

"So we wrote to a bunch of people. Nobody wrote back. Then somebody told us about Robert Aitken who was in Hawaii and not really an official Zen teacher at that stage. I think some Japanese teacher who liked Hawaii told us we should write to him. And Bob wrote back. An excellent reason to go there. He was this real beatnik, bohemian kind of character who was very pissed off with authority all the time – with everybody, really, especially society. But he'd done this interesting thing of marrying an heiress who was very gracious and floaty with flowing clothes and the ability to drift through smiling who was full of warmth and generosity and feeling, and so she made the whole scene work emotionally." This was Aitken's second wife, Anne Hopkins.

"Anne always liked the bad kids, like the gay coke-head. She liked the young guys that nobody approved of. She had that feel for streety life. And Bob had done this great thing, where he and Anne had taken over an old hotel in Maui. They claimed it had been a geisha house. I never knew if that was true or not; it was one of those rumors that was so good that you didn't want to investigate it. It was an early proto-hippie beatnik thing, clearly modeled on Stephen Gaskin's Farm. By the time I got there, it was an up and running functioning zendo, which was about '78, and it was holding maybe four seven-day sesshin a year. There was a schedule, and if you were willing to get up early in the morning and meditate for an hour and do some work in the morning, you could have the afternoon off and go do whatever you wanted to do.

"But I had this lunatic idea. I wanted to get enlightened. I didn't want to go see the sights of Hawaii. I felt like I'd done all that already. I was 28 or something, and I felt like I had come a long way to do something. I didn't really want to socialize that much, but there were interesting people there. William Merwin the poet was there, and he would turn up at every sesshin at that stage. Or Larry Ferlinghetti would come through and bang on the door, or Paul Reps would give a talk. So it was kind of fun. Everyone wanted to come to Hawaii in those days, and they all came through the Maui Zendo. John Stevens came to show us aikido and read from his translations. Anyway, the connection that was most significant for me was that Steven Mitchell was there. He had been with Seung Sahn for a time and had had the usual falling out everyone has with their teacher, and he had come to be a personal secretary for Bob for a while. He was beginning to work on his Rilke translations at that stage, and I buddied up with him. I liked to sit a lot, and so we'd sit all night and things like that. At sesshin, people would go to bed, and we'd keep sitting. We just liked sitting a lot."

"Why?"

"Why? A misunderstanding about reality, I suppose. We heard it might help," he laughs. "I could tell that something was shifting in my mind, and I could tell my mind needed a lot of shifting. Emotionally, I was not in a great place."

"In one of your books, you describe Maui as being like a cargo cult."

"Well it was. We had a great Japanese temple bell, a big bell that you banged at 4:30 in the morning, and everyone would run about wearing robes, homemade faux monastic Japanese robes. People would say things like 'Hai!' when you said things to them. And they'd bow and gassho and do full prostrations when you went in to see the teacher. He wasn't called 'Roshi' till later, but still there was all this stuff going on. I treated it like cultural white-noise, because I came out of an aggressively secular culture in Australia that wasn't particularly spiritual or religious. So it was more about the arts of the psyche or the arts of the mind than a religious matter for me. I really wasn't touchy-feely or a stoner or all the things everybody was on Maui, but in a way that was fine. Because the kindness I had been given was that they made available a vessel in which some cooking could happen. People were learning and trying to grow up. Some smart people came through sometimes. And it was like a cargo cult. The idea was like if you could just clear some land in the jungle and make some plywood airplanes, the other airplanes will be attracted."

"Follow the forms...."

"Follow the forms and no doubt you'll become a true Zen Master. And I knew that couldn't be it, but the meditation was changing something in my mind. I had dreams that indicated that. So I was just grateful for the opportunity. As in any community, there was a lot of wrestling around about the direction of the community and whether there should be more peanut butter or less peanut butter or if it was *ethical* to eat this or that. Pretty much I tried to stay out of that and just meditate. There were a few Australians there, and we were more practical. I mean there were holes in the roof, and people were arguing about peanut butter! We said we'll mow the lawns and fix the roof – kind of fun projects like that. So yeah, I got interested in that, and, for me, I did feel like it was what I came for. And then I did step through a door in a retreat."

But it was not during a retreat on Maui. His first opening happened while participating in a sesshin on Long Island with the Korean Zen teacher, Seung Sahn. "Seung Sahn got something that Aitken didn't get. Clearly Seung Sahn had had these big weird experiences and in a certain way was operating out of them. In those days, you could visit him, and he was very amiable and loud and Korean. One of my Korean friends said, 'Oh we're the Italians of Asia.' He was like that: spicy food and laughing, poking people and hitting them. I had gone for just a long weekend, a four-day retreat. Everything started to open up for me, and I realized it was all okay. I started to walk through the door, and I started being able to answer Seung Sahn's questions. He had very set questions that provided an operational definition of opening up, which some koan schools do. You know, he'd come in and ask 'What's your name?' 'John.' 'Oh, John. Where'd you come from?' 'Oh, Hawaii, Australia.' And then he'd ask, 'But, what's your name?' And you just knew if you said, 'Well, it's John' – that it wasn't a hearing problem, but he was asking for some other presentation of reality. And I enjoyed playing with him. In that moment, I just started yelling at him. You could tell he had this stick raised and by the time it hit you, you'd better have an answer for him or you'd be out of the room, so I started yelling at him. And I could tell that I was inside something that he understood because then he said, 'Don't break the glass!' Like other people had gotten very excited like that and had broken his glass, and it was very funny.

"So he gave me some koans, and I could answer him with a response that wasn't linear and explanatory. I didn't know then, but he had a system: so many gates you go through and things like that. But I decided not to travel with him. I don't know why. I just intuitively went back to Bob Aitken who had a very careful approach. Bob had the idea that there's a right answer for the koans, and you've got to poke at it to get it. He had written down very carefully his teachers' questions and responses. And he also had thought about the koans somewhat. Seung Sahn didn't give the impression that he thought about them. It was just his tradition. He was in it, and he knew where he was in it. So he was an interesting person, but he wasn't interesting to talk about the tradition with because he just *was* it, if you see what I mean. And Bob was, in his own way, trying to understand, get the meta level consciousness going. And certainly I was. And he had these elaborate notes that he had got from the old dragons like Harada but mostly Yasutani and Yamada whom he had studied with, who were his main teachers. He was modest about his own sense of being in the tradition. Like anybody he would revise his history, but he didn't make great claims for himself. He just felt like he was a pilgrim, and Koun Yamada Roshi had decided he should teach."

"What was he like?"

"Well he really was the opposite of Seung Sahn. Seung Sahn was always laughing and in your face about everything, and Bob was extremely diffident – except when he was angry – extremely diffident and shy and modest about things. And so he was the opposite of what you would expect. He would cough, and his voice was soft, and he was completely unable to speak in public without a script, the opposite, again, of guys like Seung Sahn. Seung Sahn could have a thousand people in the audience, and he would stride up and down and poke at the audience and tease them. And Bob would be reading" – speaking in a slow, somber tone – "'*Mumonkan*, case one. The dog has Buddha nature.' But in a way it was great. I mean, why not? Every kind of dog has Buddha nature. Seung Sahn and Bob Aitken and all.

"I remember one time Yamada came, and everybody would be really anxious when Yamada was coming because this guy was from Japan and had a famous big enlightenment experience. We were all on best behavior, sitting there, and nobody's moving in the zendo. It's all formal Japanese style, and Yamada's coming in, and somebody hands Bob the incense, and he's going to carry it reverently to Yamada. And he turns and treads on his robe, and he trips. And he goes wind-milling down the zendo in front of Yamada, and he yells, 'SHIT!' Really loudly. And it's one of those great moments because you could see that Yamada just didn't care one way or the other. Yamada's like, 'Oh, somebody's wind-milling down the zendo.' And it was touching, because we were all trying way too hard. You know, the cargo cult quality. But Yamada was very sweet, saying, 'You know Zen is dying in Japan; you must revive it in America.' Which we didn't believe because we were in a cargo cult."

"How did you become a teacher?"

"That's a good Bob story. The good thing about Bob was that he really did provide a place where anybody could come, and he was very gracious about these stoned, crazed kids who were unkempt and half crazy or had some project. And there were reasonably literate people there as well to talk to, so it was a cool scene for that period of time. Later on in the '80s, that wave just disappeared. But this was the first wave of Zen, with really interesting characters around. And Bob and Anne just spent their money and created this thing for you, and you didn't have to pay anything to be there; you just had to work to keep the scene going. The other students would tell you the Australians would make you work if you were wacky enough to be there with them. But Maui at that stage was a kind of scene that was dying a bit because there wasn't anything there. It was a place that was gradually being taken over by drug growers and rock stars; it wasn't a culture that would hold a big zendo.

"So we went to Honolulu, and I was involved in running the house there for a while, but then I needed a job, and I started training in psychology. And the zendo would wax and wane depending on who was picking a fight with Dad today, and we just tried to get along and hold it together – sit there. You know, zendos were like that. That's one of the secret things about zendos, that they're halfway houses.

I think Catholic monasteries were and are like that. That's a part of the spiritual archetype, offering people sanctuary or refuge.

"So, anyway, we were holding a retreat – I think it was '83 – and it must have been winter, so it's probably January or February, and it was really wet, and Bob had weak lungs from the prison camp where he had been with R. H. Blyth. His voice would disappear, and he'd start coughing, and he clearly seemed to be sick. I was head of training at that particular sesshin as I usually was, basically because I was willing to turn up and I had finished koan study. I didn't feel I was especially important in the scene, but I would turn up and show the flag. So I went to him and said, 'You know, you're pretty sick.' 'No, I'm fine.' So I went over to talk to Anne, 'You know, I think he's sick. Do you want to gang up on him?' So we had one of those sincere talks which go, 'I don't think your judgment's quite good right now, and you might have a fever, and we'd rather have you shut down the sesshin and be alive than finish it and die' – that sort of thing. One of those earnest conversations one has with somebody who's not listening. But he thought about it, and Anne talked to him and said, 'I think he's right, Roshi.' She called him Roshi by then too. And I said, 'Well, you don't have to do anything about it until interviews this afternoon. So get some rest and let me know. But I can send everybody home, or you can go home, and we can just sit and not have any teaching, and the world won't end.' So he said, 'I'll think about it.' And then he staggered over to the meditation hall and asked me, 'Could I see you?' And so I went over to his quarters, and he said, 'Would you hold dokusan this afternoon?' And I said, 'Okay.' And he said, 'Do you have any questions?' And I said, 'No.' And he said, 'Okay, I'm going home.' And he came in and announced that I would be doing this, to everyone's shock and horror. And so I did it, and that's how I started teaching.

"And I wasn't somebody who had that in his sights. It's hard to be in a system and not want to rise in it; there's a lot of ambition in all spiritual communities. But my way of dealing with that in myself is by trying to be very introverted about, 'What are koans all about?' And I was studying psychology. 'Well, what are the Western maps of what's going on?' So I was all obsessed with that and not trying to be important in the zendo. I wasn't on the board or things like that. And then I said, 'Yes,' which surprised me. But I did. If Bob hadn't been sick, I may have given it more thought and said 'No.' But I said 'Yes,' and I started teaching."

I ask if there had been a formal ceremony.

He says not, but then mentions another ceremony Aitken had done "when you passed your first koan, which in those days was always Mu. There were all these elaborate checking questions that you'd have to answer according to the Hakuin system, and then he'd have a ceremony. This is something that I think Daiun Harada had started. And he'd announce it. You'd walk around, and you'd offer incense and bow to the zendo and walk around and everybody would gassho. It was really a pretty simple ceremony but extremely irritating when the person who had had kensho was annoying to the community. And some people loved it and felt very encouraged, and, of course, often the person who had had this experience was some stoner-girl who had just entered the zendo but had a wide open mind. The really earnest citizens would be stuck forever, and so Bob really didn't want to do that ceremony. He just quietly stopped doing it, and then at one stage Yamada asked him whether he was doing it still. And Bob said, 'No, no, I stopped doing that.' And Yamada said, 'You must start doing it again.' So Bob would wait and wait until the last possible moment. I know I was far into my koan study before he did it for me. Another Australian and I were the last couple of people to do it, and then Bob just quietly dropped it, and it ceased to be."

"Albert Low[50] describes something similar happening in Rochester when he was studying with Philip Kapleau. The people who resolved Mu were awarded a rakusu, and the next morning they would show up wearing them, while other people groaned, 'Oh, Christ! Not *her*!'"

"Well, it was a good thing in a way. The good thing was, 'Why not her? Oh, what I've been judging as merit is probably unrelated to anything.' You know? And so I like that aspect of it actually, the democracy of that system. It could be the sort of person that serious students would look down on but who actually had a wonderfully wide open mind and was much more creative and a bit more spiritual than the rest of us, because we were so earnest and puritan about it all. That's the joke."

"I started doing a Ph.D. in San Francisco at one of those free-standing little universities for psychology and human systems and business. So I was travelling there, and I met a girl and decided I wanted a child. And I decided the west coast was a much more lively place than Honolulu intellectually. Everything seemed to be happening on the west coast; this was the mid-80s. Bob never forgave me, actually. He was hurt when I left. I had no idea he would be so invested in me not leaving."

"He saw you as an heir apparent?"

"Yeah, yeah. He had asked me to stay, take over the zendo.[51] I was just somebody he was quite close to, and I think he felt very bitter about it, actually. But it was the right thing for me to do. I didn't want to run the zendo; it was very hard to innovate there. I just knew if you grow up in a system and try to innovate, it's not going to work, and you have to go someplace new. I knew I wanted to innovate, and I knew if I stayed there Bob wouldn't want me to. So I wanted to come to the west coast, and I did."

John had completed most of the work for his Ph.D. by then. "I just came to California and wrote it up. The school had really smart people who didn't mind teaching a few graduate students. They had some interest in education and mentoring, but they didn't really want to be professors because they were too busy doing something else. Rachel Remen, who teaches at UCSF in the medical school, for example, was teaching mind-body things. Or Stan Krippner who was very interested in shamanism and psychokinetics and the weird powers of the mind and such and research around that. And there was a philosopher called Jay Ogilvy from the Stanford Research Institute. An interesting guy on my committee was Bela Banathy who was Hungarian and who'd helped design the Open University in London and was very interested in learning systems. So I started to see koans as a designed learning system for a discovery process. And I thought, enlightenment is whatever it is, but there's some kind of a before-and-after state that is being marketed here.

"And then I interviewed people who Bob said had had some kind of kensho experience. He used the more modest term than satori, with kensho meaning 'see your true nature' rather than satori which was like – you know – you glow in the dark. But I had had an experience which for me was a profound alteration of how I had seen things, but it wasn't what – when I'd set off – I'd imagined enlightenment would be. I found it had changed some things in me; in other matters, I was just as clueless as I'd ever been. So I was very interested in questions like, 'Do people have different kinds of enlightenment? Are some less clueless about this but more clueless about that?'

"So I decided to start interviewing people, and I discovered that everybody was pretty clueless about lots of things. People had had what they assessed as fairly small shifts. And Bob had said that about Yamada; he'd said that Yamada just pulled a string and coached him through the checking questions and then said, 'Well, that's enlightenment.' And so when I interviewed people, I didn't really have a way to explore all of that. I just wanted to get out of my Ph.D., so I wrote it up at face value.

"But there's a whole other project to be done. There are social expectations. Cognitive dissonance is going on where if my teacher says I have enlightenment then I have to change my experience to match that. And that's very much a part of the whole Harada-Yasutani school, I think. Not to say that in a hostile way but just to say that one can't help that sort of thing happening. It's just human to do that, and in fact humans are always revising their biographies. If it happened this morning, it's already biography. And so I was interested in that, and so I wrote that up and I tried to find analogies.

"I didn't go too far into it because I found something real was going on, but it wasn't what people said it was. I didn't know what it was. I tried to find analogies in western science like catastrophe theory in math and Prigogine's chemical theories. If a system is energetically disordered and you make it more disordered then, instead of disintegrating, some systems will switch to a higher level of complexity and order. I was trying to find models for what, in neuroscience, you think of as a new organization at a higher level, a jump. I always saw koans as a kind of way of transforming our experience of the world and our way of moving in the world. And secondarily, they appeared in a religious vehicle, a boat perhaps. You could have ceremonies if you wanted, or incense or whatever, and meditate. Meditation was an interesting method, not necessarily crucial, but helpful to me.

"Really, for me, it was the koans. So I looked about obsessively for years: 'Let's stop teaching mindfulness; let's start teaching koans.' Google calls this 'A and B testing.' You try one method, and then you try another method, and you observe the results. So I did that with koans. Let's try looking at koans this way, and let's not try demanding a Hakuin answer from people; let's try having people just go with the koan and explore anything that comes to them around the koan."

When he moved to California in 1986, the way he taught Zen at first followed fairly traditional models. "I didn't really try to develop a scene. It built just by word of mouth, and we eventually evolved. We did everything in black robes at first; we did everything with bowing until we stopped doing that. And I realized that, for me, the Japanese forms weren't the essential level of the experiment."

"But you maintained the forms for a while."

"Yeah, and gradually my generation, or even the earlier generation of people, gradually started thinking, 'Well, do I really need to hold my mouth this way and be Japanese?'"

Slowly he loosened the structures and discovered that little was lost in doing so.

"One of your colleagues told me a story of you giving a teisho while bouncing a child on your lap," I tell him.

"Well, I had a baby, and I realized that if meditation in action is it, it's going to be with kids too. I thought that was a crucial part of life if we were going to bring Zen into the modern world. Zen was, I thought, quite hostile to kids. Students of my generation would tell me these horrifying stories about, 'I decided to give up my child so that I could do the Dharma,' and things like that. And I thought, 'Oh, Jesus, I don't think so. I don't think that's got to be a gate for the Dharma.' If you cared about transformation, what would be wrong with having kids in the middle of that? That seemed to me very much a forest-monk samadhi model. One advantage of my having done so much solitary meditation was that I wasn't impressed by claims of credentials."

Once he began to think of koans as a form of designed learning system, his attitude towards them changed.

"One of the things I noticed was that people saw koans as something difficult and probably old-fashioned. I remember meeting people from the Maezumi school and others who were very much going off into mindfulness. And I'd worked with mindfulness and knew it. I'd worked with it in medical schools. I understood it pretty well and had seen the research, and I was sure that koans welcomed the imagination and the grittiness of life in a way that mindfulness didn't. And koans allowed for enlightenment.

"The other thing was that a teacher would just give people a koan – which was what happened to Robert Aitken and why he struggled so much and never really became confident of his own understanding – and they would have no context for it, so they would just feel wrong all the time. Some people were good at dancing or whatever, very intuitive, would make it through that koan system anyway. I happened to be one of those. My work with aborigines made me understand that everything happens within a culture. There's no such thing as a koan outside of the culture or meditation outside a culture. There might be such a thing as enlightenment. It might be a real claim, but the way it's being claimed might be a misunderstanding. So I wanted to transcend that. I felt that something real had happened to me. I had no doubt that there was a real gate that you walked through. Meeting Seung Sahn and later working with Aitken and Yamada, something really opened up for me that changed my life. I had these doubts about life and what is it for and its meaning and that just disappeared overnight. And there was great joy. That sort of thing. But then there were other matters that I just really had no clue about and had to work out and just walk through and suffer and make my own mistakes.

"So the notion that one wouldn't make mistakes was absurd. It would imply that one wouldn't learn. But the notion that one could have a transformation seemed real. And so I was thinking about, 'Is it causable? If so, what causes it? Was it just catalyzable?' In my dissertation I said I think there's a catalyst, but it really isn't caused. Not really a novel idea. But then I started thinking, 'Well, koans seem to have a power of their own.' In the old system, you teach beginners concentration and things to believe, and then eventually, after you've made them feel terrified and inadequate, you give them a koan. But instead, I tried giving koans to beginners. I said, 'This is a really cool thing. It comes out of a poetic tradition, and it will change your life. Here. Try it.' And the koans would blow peoples' minds open, and their lives and everything would start to change. You know? 'Wow, I've been fighting with my mother for twenty years, and now I've stopped fighting' – whatever it is. I thought there was an analogy in the Jungian psychological world; *The Light Inside the Dark* is about that analogy. If you really want to understand a dream, you can drag it up into the light, into the day-world – Freud's thing about a snake is a penis or a coat is your father's protection – or you can go down into the dream world and meet the dreams there. And with koans, I thought to train people to just let the koan take them down into some deeper place where their usual mind isn't operating. The usual thought process is operating like a hamster on a treadmill, but, with the koan, that isn't happening. Or if it is going on, it's not being believed or identified with.

"Any good koan will take people into the depths. In fact, all the great old koan conversations were conversations in that realm. They weren't meant to be mysterious. They were just the best shot the teachers had at showing how it really is. You know, 'every day is a good day' as the koan goes. They meant, 'That's how it feels to me.' There was also a lot of deconstruction; there was a lot of taking apart your view of things. Zhaozhou would be the deconstruction guy. Yunmen offers deconstruction too, but his attitude is more like, 'I'll drop in some image that will start undermining your view of the world.' There's the deconstruction, and then the view that came to you wasn't pre-ordered or a believable thing, or sequenced the way you expected. It was what was appearing for you when you stopped shielding yourself with your stories and showed how you could move in the world. So it was more an event than a thing."

"James Hillman said this great thing about American culture. He lived in Switzerland. He was Jewish by origin, and he said, 'You know, it doesn't matter what your culture is, if you're in Europe or America you've somehow got Protestant ideas about things, that in some fundamental way, success in the world means you're blessed, means God likes you.' So I got interested in, 'What are the core notions we're operating out of?' So if I wear black robes here, it's really different from wearing black robes in Japan. Here it's weird. In Japan it isn't weird. It's a little antique and fussy and a little bit aristocratic and elitist, but it's not weird. Here it's the opposite of those things. It's almost wacky and reveals a failure to be conservative or elitist. So, in the same way, I thought if these koans have some power that can cross culture – and I thought that they did, because they worked for me – what would that power be and how would we know? And so I came to this idea, I'll just experiment with people because they want to do it, and it feels like it helps them. And I'll notice: is it helping them? Are they happier? Are they more creative? Are they reasonably effective in their lives? Do they have a deeper meeting with the real?

"I think if you drop a koan into your psyche, there's enough in common with all psyches that it works. Like tracking your dreams. But the way we'll interact with it will be different from the way an old Chinese person interacted with it, and the consequences are fitting for our culture. There are no koans about kids, but for me being able to interact with my daughter was huge, a huge consequence of koans. And the Chinese discovery about being open to and interacting with the world is a sub-category of that.

"I also noticed with people, they could go through the traditional Japanese training – you know – and answer all the koan questions correctly and be miserably unhappy and kind of narrow, not innovative in any way, shape, or form. In other words, they had taken the whole system and made it reproducible by turning it into a right-answer system rather than an opening your heart or opening the mind system. Zen is full of stories about Elder Somebody who has been around for fifty years and done all the right things and still doesn't have a clue."

The students who were comfortable with this new approach to koan work formed the nucleus of what is now the Pacific Zen Institute, although its associate centers are not limited to the west coast. There is even one in London, Ontario.

"So let's say I hear about the Pacific Zen Institute and hear that you're doing a course and show up at the door. What happens? Does someone teach me how to meditate?"

"Somebody might," he says. But if John is the one running the show, the format would be for people to sit in a circle, usually in chairs. "I've noticed that when you put out chairs and zafus, increasingly people sit in chairs. Young people sit in chairs usually, unless they've done a lot of yoga and like sitting on the zafu. I like sitting on a zafu, but I don't care. Then I'll tell them, 'If you're a veteran, don't listen to me.' Then I'd just talk everyone through the first meditation. Like, 'Here's a koan, here's what you do with it. Have a good time.'"

"Okay, so talk me through it."

"Okay, meditation starts with noticing what you're noticing. Maybe it would help to notice your body if you're that sort of person. Then I'll give them a koan. Let's give them Linji. 'When something appears, don't believe it. Whatever confronts you, shine your light on it. Have confidence in the light that is always shining inside you.' So, that would be one of Linji's clear advice, deconstructive koans. Whatever appears, don't believe it. So I'll just put that into the room. A classic beginner's instruction would be: This is a story. Any part of it that sticks to you, trust that. Don't take it up to the top floor of the grain elevator and find a shelf with a label on it to put it on. Move it into your body; let it sink down; just start keeping company with it. And most of all, don't assess how you're doing. Don't think you're doing well or badly or what you should be doing. Don't think it should be calm; don't think it should be anything. Don't think, 'Meditation's not working; I'm not calm' – that sort of thing. Where koans are going is somewhere deeper. You're not going to a known state of mind. You're opening your capacity to navigate your states of mind. It's outside particular states of mind. I want people to do that.

"Afterwards I'll ask you, 'What did you notice while you were with that koan?' And if you're smart, you'll tell me. You'll tell me the problems you had, and I'll start tinkering with it, and you'll start tinkering with it. And then you'll come back, and you'll try it again, and you'll realize, 'Oh, my mind can do something when it's trusted to organize itself without me fussing, without me telling it what to do. And the organization it does is superior to the organization I would think up for it.' And that would be creativity. Right? So koans are the creative life as it's happening now."

What of the people who are looking for more traditional Zen training?

"Sure, I can guide you through that, but I notice you just can't sit still. So what are you doing to your mind? Maybe you're not meditating; maybe you're just flogging yourself. So let's not work at grasping enlightenment. Right? Although I think that's what that old system is encouraging. That's why people have such a hard time getting awake, because they're too busy assessing their condition and forcing themselves."

"So you dismiss what's been called the samurai approach to Zen training?"

"Here's what I can say: We can stand up to anybody in terms of macho. People need to take risks, but they may be internal risks rather than involving the exo-skeleton. I have a more mammalian approach. The question is, 'What should we risk?' If you step through the gate with a koan, you might be happy, you might not have to disapprove of yourself, judge yourself, second-guess yourself. If you are judging yourself and criticizing yourself, you're also doing that to other people, and you're not much fun to be around. Under those circumstances, Zen centers become half-way houses, and people think they're doing it wrong all the time.

"For me Zen is a more blessed path than that and more embracing. With Zen koans, the big thing is empathy and that loving feeling that happens when the world we have made up really does get destroyed. Then there's an incredibly warm experience of meeting and appreciating others."

"Compassion. Karuna."

"Yeah, that's what I was saying. But I'd say it's closer than that. It's more like, 'Oh, I am! I can feel I am. I am you!'

"I'll tell you a story my daughter told me. A friend – a Zydeco singer from Louisiana who she had been very close to – died. He had that Louisiana habit of just dropping by with food, and, if you weren't here, he'd just open the door and wait for you. I used to keep chardonnay in the fridge because he liked it, and he'd just open the fridge. And my daughter would often be home and she'd sit down, and he'd pour himself a glass of wine, and they'd talk to each other till I came home. So she was close to him, and it was a big deal when he died. So that's when she really started meditating. She had to go away to New York to do a high school program, and there she began to sit with koans. Later on, she said, 'Well, I tried all these things.' She was really mad at her boyfriend, and she said, 'So I tried every kind of meditation. I went through the manual.' Like the loving-kindness, the this or that, the breathing, and then she said, 'Oh, all right, I'll just have to try a koan.' So she did the story about the person being chased by a mountain lion, and there's nowhere to go, so they slide over a cliff. And there's a vine, and they're hanging onto the vine. They look down below, and there's a grizzly bear. Then a white mouse and a black mouse come out and start nibbling at the vine. But there's a strawberry nearby, and they reach over and eat it, and how sweet it tastes!

"So she said, 'I just started sitting with that, and it was all right. I didn't have a problem with my boyfriend anymore.' But she said, 'Mindfulness didn't help.' So there is a story-quality to koans. There's a mythopoeic quality in the psyche that likes and gets opened by that."

Before I leave, John does sign my copy of *The Light Inside the Dark*. He also he gives me several cards printed by the Pacific Zen Institute. On one side, there is art work by people associated with the institute; on the other, there is commentary. One is a calligraphy of the characters for "Moon on the Water." On the reverse, it reads: "OK. Here is one koan method for happiness in all its simplicity. Just find a relationship with the koan. You don't have to get ready or settle yourself down. You just start living inside your own life and let the koan keep you company like a good dog or a friend. The koan doesn't go anywhere else or ever leave you…. You can keep company with a koan without assessing, criticizing or judging yourself. The koan doesn't find fault. And even if you do criticize yourself, don't criticize that. Compassion finds an entry. This is important."

CHAPTER NINE
Joan Sutherland

JOAN SUTHERLAND IS THE FOUNDER OF THE AWAKENED LIFE COMMUNITY BASED in Santa Fe, New Mexico, and the Open Source network of communities throughout the Western United States. She is also listed as a "Senior Teacher Emerita" of the Pacific Zen Institute. She was the student with whom John Tarrant worked most closely in the task of re-imagining koan practice.

Her house is on the Cerro Gordo Road just a short distance from the temple operated by the Maha Bodhi Society where Robert Winsome first introduced Henry Shukman to zazen. It's about a ten minute walk – fifteen for me using a cane – but the caretaker is away, and it's locked. We do, however, hear the hollow knock of a han being struck at the Upaya Zen Temple only a few yards away. The resident teacher at Upaya is Joan Halifax, an heir of both Bernie Glassman and Seung Sahn.

"Do people ever get the two of you confused?" I ask.

"All the time," she admits. And, of course, there is also Joan Rieck in Albuquerque.

We return to her place along a different route. This area had once been agricultural land, and her house had previously been a barn. The outside wall is fieldstone, and Joan shows me where she had to mortar it in order to keep the "critters" out. The interior has been transformed into a lovely living space with smooth white walls and exposed rafters. Because of the building's previous use, the ceiling is higher than expected and there is still a former hayloft window in its peak.

An altar to Guanyin – the Chinese incarnation of Kannon – is in one corner of the room, with an unlit stick of incense in a bowl. A large calligraphy of the word "Buddha" graces a wall. There are several other Buddhist touches as well as a large votive painting of the archangel Santo Miguel. "We live here," she explains. "We have to pay attention to the local deities."

I ask if she's a Buddhist, and she responds without hesitation. "No."

She is, however, an authorized Chan teacher, a roshi, and a priest, even though these may not be how she identifies herself. She describes herself simply as a "teacher in the koan tradition." John Tarrant told me, "Joan has a complicated relationship with traditional Zen types. They don't have the right box to put her in and tend to exclude her. Zen is still a bit like the start-up world with regard to women. It's okay to be a woman if you are old and not too feminine and take care not to be original."

It strikes me that, other than Sister Elaine MacInnes, Joan is the only female teacher I'd interviewed to have long hair. Not all of the other women had shaved their heads, but they seldom had hair much longer than a military buzz-cut. She also has dimples when she smiles. Perhaps these things shouldn't matter, but one can't help noticing them.

"Is what you do really Zen?" I ask.

"That's a good question, and one I ask myself all the time. It depends upon what you mean by Zen. Before the recorder went on, you were talking about a kind of spectrum from conservative to – what should we say? – innovative. I would put myself at the innovative end with a big caveat, which is that the innovation is based on my understanding of the deepest layers of the tradition. So – this is a long way to answer your question – I studied Chinese and Japanese. I have a Master's in East Asian Languages. I read the texts in the original. I'm immersed in them. And it is out of my understanding of those very, very old roots that something new is developing. So I don't feel at all like I'm a break with the tradition. I feel like we're trying to find how that original spirit is best expressed in our 21st Century North American communities. So, to that extent I do want to claim a deep connection to that tradition, which I would call Chan rather than Zen. The thing that makes answering your question complicated is that I am not part of the way we've inherited Zen in a particular form from Japan. I choose – quite deliberately – not to be part of that mainstream. So does that mean I'm Zen or not Zen? I don't know."

"I met with Henry Shukman yesterday who expressed the opinion that one can't separate Zen from Buddhism. Would you disagree with that?"

She tells me she has trouble with black and white answers.

"Chan is the way the Dharma flowered originally in China, but, when the Dharma came to China, it met very old, very established, very beautiful traditions which were already in place. And so what happened in China was different from what happened in India. Early Indian Buddhism was focused a lot on getting off the Wheel of Samsara, of getting out of a painful life. And when the Dharma came to China, that was a problem the Chinese didn't know they had. They weren't looking to get out. And I think the shift to something that was trying to get deeper into life and have a more intimate relationship with life is a really, really big change."

❁

It's natural for students to speak with enthusiasm about their teachers. The Sasaki students I interviewed, for example, tended to use superlatives whenever they spoke of him. But there seems to be a special affection in the way Joan's students talk about her. Tenney Nathanson, who leads the Desert Rain Zen Center in Tucson, told me that "she has an incredible kind of luminosity about her. There's something that kind of shines from her."

Sarah Bender, who teaches in Colorado Springs, stressed the importance Joan puts on collegiality. "Her emphasis is on the warmth and generosity with which we offer this practice to each other, with which we hold this form in order to support each other's awakening. I know that may sound like, 'Well, duh! That's what everybody's doing.' But sometimes that can be felt as a rigid holding of sacred space separate from everything else which can make a pretty bumpy ride when you get home. But in her community, it's felt to be very much integral to the whole proposition of practicing in a community of generosity. It's a difference of emphasis, perhaps, but it's felt."

"You are aware," I mentioned to Sarah, "that there are those who look at what she and John Tarrant are doing as diminishing the koan tradition."

"I do know that, and it simply is not my experience. I do think a person could try to do what Joan is doing and, not understanding it, end up with something not as powerful. But that is not the case for Joan's teaching. On the contrary, she goes to the root of the tradition and brings forth new growth from that root. She has an unbelievable love, respect, and affinity for the teachings of the ancestors."

That respect for the teachings of the ancestors is something apparent throughout our conversation, and I realize, that in addition to being an attentive, compassionate, generous (and possibly luminous) teacher, she is also a scholar. It's easy to overlook that, however, because she doesn't speak like one. Instead she speaks with a depth of passion unusual in Zen circles.

"I'm just in awe of the beauty of this tradition," she tells me, her voice choking slightly, "and it will make me cry because it always does. My desire is to convey what I can of that or create a field in which other people can experience it for themselves. So, I'm just in love. You know? And what I do comes out of that being in love with the tradition and being in love with what happens when we can share it amongst ourselves. I'm also concerned, because I feel like it's hanging by a very slender thread in the west. So I feel a sense of urgency."

"What is the function of Chan?"

"Awakening. Without question."

"And that means?"

"Awakening is a process. It's not a sudden event, which is why I use 'awakening' rather than 'enlightenment' which, I think, is a word obscured behind a cloud of projection. So 'awakening' is a process that happens over the course of our whole lives, and if I had to define it really simply it would be by using one of the Chinese synonyms for enlightenment, which is 'becoming intimate.' So it's a matter of becoming intimate with the world. The practice is a lot about clearing away what gets in the way of our intimacy with the world. That is the powerful deconstructive quality of the koan tradition. And when the clearing away has been done, and we stand on the bare ground, we've made ourselves fetchable by something else."

"*Fetch*-able," I repeat, unsure I heard her correctly.

"Fetchable. Able to be fetched by – you know – the whole of the universe. And so it becomes a kind of return from a feeling of exile to a feeling of being deeply at home. And there are moments where that 'being fetched' is very powerful, and those we would call 'opening moments.' And then there's all the deconstructive work that leads up to that, and there's all the integrative work that comes after such moments. And that whole process is the process of awakening. And I have this crazy notion that the whole universe is involved in a kind of large project of awakening, and really what the koans are about is allowing us to join most freely and most helpfully in that large process of the awakening of the universe."

"So the starting point for someone who comes to study with you might be a feeling that they're not intimate with or are deracinated in some way from Being?"

"I've seen people come in through two main doors, although obviously people have idiosyncratic reasons for doing it, too. One is the one you're describing. The problem of suffering. The other is people who have had experiences of openings that have been separate in their lives – that thing that happened that was so powerful – and they want to make it something that's really alive in their lives all the time."

"When I was about thirteen, I was living in Southern California on the west side of Los Angeles, and I could take a bus in one of two directions. One was to the ocean where I would go surfing, and the other was either to the big bookstore right outside of UCLA or the museum downtown. Hence that was sort of my life, defined by the bus lines. And one day I was in the big bookstore outside of UCLA, and I found the *Daodejing*, and, with a kind of thirteen year-old's arrogance, I thought, 'Someone understands! Someone sees the world as I see it!.' So when I got to college, which wasn't too long after that, they said, 'What do you want to major in?' And without even thinking about it, I realized I wanted to learn the languages so that I could read

Daoism in the original, because I had an intuition that that would be important. So that's how I got involved in language studies. And I'd also been doing my own kind of spiritual stuff, meditating."

"How did you find out about meditation? Or was that just part of growing up in Southern California?"

"When I was in high school, one of the only games in town was the Vedanta Society. You could go there and learn to meditate and read their books and stuff like that. And that's how I got into it. And then when I was at university – at UCLA – I had a professor, Professor Ashikaga Ensho, who asked me if I wanted to do a seminar with him, and I said, 'Of course.' And I showed up, and I was the only person there. So it was a one-on-one situation, and we were translating *The Gateless Gateway*, one of the koan collections, together. And it was really a transformative experience, and I began to understand – as he was teaching me – that he wasn't correcting my vocabulary or my grammar, but he was really giving me the Mind behind the koans, and it clicked. I understood that there was this really vast, beautiful tradition and that there was a practice attached to it. And so then I began wandering through Zen and a little bit through Tibetan practice, but I was a..." – she laughs – "...I was a failed Zen student until I found the koans."

Her first exposure to Zen had been through one of Shunryu Suzuki's students, Jakusho Kwong, in the Soto tradition.

"In what way a failed student?" I ask.

"Mine was an unrequited love."

She graduated with a degree in East Asian Languages only to discover there was little she could do with it. "My one job offer was from the CIA. Which I declined. And – oh – I kind of held it for a couple of decades, actually, not really knowing why I'd done that study. I went off and did other things."

Unrequited or not, she continued to practice with Kwong, and, when he suggested she formally become a Buddhist, she did so. "I thought if my teacher invited me, I needed to show up. As I recall, I think we were his first precepts' group. So this friend of mine and I were sewing our rakusu cases together, and it was at the beginning of the AIDS crisis when it was still called Gay-Related Immune Deficiency and stuff like that. And he, as a gay man and therapist, was doing this amazing, brave work where he was going to the prisons and talking with people, because people who were HIV-positive in prisons were being beaten up and murdered by the other prisoners because they were afraid of them. We were talking about that among this group of people as we were sewing, and I was told later that other people became upset about our conversation and said it was wrong to have a conversation about such negative things while we were preparing to take refuge. And I thought, 'I'm not gonna last long here.' That was really sad, because the first moment I walked into that beautiful zendo I felt that I'd found refuge.

"Anyway, several years later my friend did, in fact, die, and I went to his funeral, and the roshi who was conducting the funeral was John Tarrant. And for the first time in a while, I thought, 'Huh! There's something there. There's something that I can really feel.'"

She began to study with Tarrant and rediscovered the koan tradition Professor Ashikaga had introduced her to, and, as she put it, "I knew I was doomed."

"What was John like when you met him?"

"He was wild. He was brilliant. I knew he knew something. He was different than any other Zen person I'd ever seen. I think two things: He was so rooted – he *is* so rooted – in being a person of the west, and the Zen that he teaches and the writing that he does comes completely out of a western perspective that has digested the Dharma from the east, and I really appreciated that. And then when we began to do koans together, it was a very rich relationship.

"The way we thought of koans and eventually the way we would teach koans began to change. We had a sense that the translations we were using had gone through a lot of generations and weren't maybe as connected to the originals as they might be. And I said, 'Oh, I can figure that out.' And so we started – actually I think when I was still a student – to relook at the originals of the koans. Each koan tradition has a collection of Miscellaneous Koans which is particular to them, separate from the classical collections. And I think the first project we really worked on was revising the Miscellaneous, to make it more reflective of the way we were looking at koans."

"When I interviewed John, he told me he came to think of koans as a kind of 'designed learning system for a discovery process' which leads to awakening or kensho. Does that make sense to you?"

"I think what that captures that's important to me is the intentionality of the koans. I think koans have their own life, have their own fate. Over the centuries, there have been cycles of tremendous vitality in the koan tradition, and then it got institutionalized and went dormant, only to be revived again by someone like Dahui in China or like Hakuin in Japan. But the koans always survived! And so my image for that is of a giant dragon coiled at the bottom of the Pacific Ocean, and the dragon is dreaming the koans all the time, and every once in a while she kind of stirs in her sleep. And there are some of us who are listening for dragon murmurings, and, when we hear them, we try to interpret them. That's the poetic way of saying it."

She began teaching in 1996 and received inka from John Tarrant two years later. For a while, her approach was fairly conventional. "When you become a teacher you receive a list of koans and their answers, and the traditional way of teaching is that a student must find *that* answer for each koan before going onto the next. And what was beginning to happen was students were bringing in answers that often had that traditional understanding but included much more of their lives and their experiences. And John and I kind of looked at each other and said, 'The koans are trying to jump out of the box. Is it our job to stuff them back into the box and make everybody do it the way we were taught? Or should we pay attention to what's happening?' And that took about eight milliseconds to figure out."

Inevitably, the way in which they viewed Zen practice began to modify. "The heart of the sesshin event is incredibly powerful, but we inherited it from Japan in a very formal way. I learned that way, and, in the beginning, I taught that way, but my feeling was that we were serving the forms, always trying to get them right. And I wanted to get to a situation where the forms were serving us and serving the awakening of the participants. So again John and I collaborated on looking at the forms we'd received. What was really important to keep because it was powerful or beautiful? Being beautiful was enough if it engaged people's souls and encouraged awakening. On the other hand, what really didn't matter anymore? What was culture rather than Dharma? What was Japanese culture rather than Dharma? Fundamentally, what was the spirit of things? When we redid the liturgy, for example, we asked with each chant, 'Why is this chant in the liturgy? What purpose does it serve? Is it the best thing to serve that purpose?' And so we were always trying to get to the underneath and then, from there, to find out how that original intention might best be served now. And in that process, things changed a lot."

She now offers two kinds of retreat. "One is a meditation retreat which is based on the old sesshin model. There's silence and a kind of simplicity and fasting from experience and all that. That's still present. But many of the formal aspects have simplified or changed or dropped away. And then I teach another kind of retreat, a koan retreat, which has a lot more alternation between silence and conversation."

I ask how the transformation of the retreats had come about.

She reflects for a moment before responding. "There were two things I noticed. One was what seemed to be happening out of my control entirely – how great is that? – the koans and what students were doing with them. The other was that if I looked at it empirically, I didn't always think that the results I was seeing in students indicated that the method was quite right. I was seeing a lot of unhappiness, a lot of psychological difficulty, a lot of turmoil and conflict within the larger sangha. Now, I'm not speaking so much about my students, but in the larger group, a long time ago. I thought, 'There's something off with the method if this is the result.' So those were the two questions that arose.

"And then I just began watching and listening and trying to understand. And I listened in two directions. One was toward the ancestors, and with them I would include the koans. What are they saying? What do they seem to want? How can I more deeply understand what their...um...dark gift to us is?" She laughs. "So that's one direction of listening. And the other direction was what's happening in the sangha, what's happening with students and people's practice? And then I took a vow of silence. I said, 'I will not speak of this beyond my own students for ten years because I don't know anything yet. I need to discern and understand.' And so I did. I just kept quiet about it and really listened hard for ten years. And then I started blabbing."

"What did you mean when you said that the results you saw in the students suggested the method wasn't quite right?"

"One of the great gifts of my early life as a teacher was that I was immediately sent to a lot of different places. I went around California and to Tucson and here to Santa Fe and up to Colorado. So I saw a lot of different people in different circumstances, and I saw a lot of people who came from different traditions. And what I saw was a lot of partial openings. I saw people had gotten a certain amount of insight, but it hadn't quite gone all the way through. And I came to see that as a potentially devastating experience. A partial opening can be a terrible thing because the first part of the experience is a kind of winter where meanings drop away, and it gets very big and still. But if you don't go all the way through to spring, to a return of all the things of the world in their radiance, that's a bleak place to stay.

"So that was my early experience, and then later I came to feel that the way the koans were often being used, in my opinion, didn't allow students to harness the potential of the koans to be integrated into their lives, to illuminate their lives, to help them work with things. That when you had this sequence of koans with a sequence of answers, it was something you could compartmentalize and not really let into your life and let it shake your life up like crazy. And so what you had was people going through this compartmentalized process almost like a curriculum, but it most often wasn't transforming their lives or resolving their doubts."

But in the early days, many students were less interested in integration than they were in achievement.

Joan has the ability to express things in memorable ways. "There's this very American thing that people want transformation without having to change."

It is a view which was reinforced by books that portray awakening as a lightning-bolt experience rather than a process.

"I think what attracted people to that model of kensho was the hope that you can transform without actually having to do the hard work of living your life. And – you know – you put someone under enough physical and psychic stress, and you do sometimes produce a kensho experience. But it doesn't mean very much because it's what happens after that – when you integrate it into your life – that stuff really happens."

I ask what occurred during her ten year period of silence.

"I began to feel I could, at least in some respects, understand what the potential of the koan tradition might be, and that I might even create circumstances in terms of practice situations in which that potential might start to play itself out. So I guess there was a kind of a confidence that came from that. I knew just enough to set a field and then watch what happened in the field."

"Why specifically koans?" I wonder. "What makes them different? Why couldn't you do the same thing with religious texts, the sutras, or even poetry?"

"Well, koans do include religious texts and poetry, as well as popular songs and folk stories and pretty much everything else. It's just that the koans often subvert their ordinary meanings, because the koans are focused not so much on conveying content as on the potential of anything to wake us up. They've been used for centuries. And a koan is not just a bunch of words on a page; it's the field of everything that happens when you take up a koan. When a group takes up a koan, the koan field gets that big. And then if you include the generations of people who have worked on the koan in the past, the field gets very, very large. We include some contemporary poems or excerpts of poems now in our Miscellaneous Koans, and I think it may very well be that those poems can become like that over generations. But I think there's that aspect of time and the field that are really important to the koans."

"But everything comes out of a particular cultural matrix," I argue. "As you said, koans drew material from Tang dynasty folklore, poetry, and so on. So the weight of the past that you're talking about is cultural and a very different culture from that of people living here in Santa Fe today with its own very distinct heritage. Doesn't that become an impediment?"

"It can become an impediment, but I don't think it has to. And if you hold onto a sense of being in the middle of a process rather than being at the end of a process, you recognize that you're just doing in your generation what people have been doing for generations prior and will do – we hope – for generations to come. So we're just a moment in a large process. And absolutely where we live, what the stories of this place are, the spirits of this place, all of that is incredibly important. And part of our job is to include each generation – in each place – in the tradition.

"I think it's like art in any of these cultural matrices that you're talking about; art coming out of any particular cultural matrix will sometimes transcend it. I mean, we're still looking at Vermeer, and we're still looking at the cave paintings at Lascaux because there's something that transcends Cro-Magnon life or 17th century Dutch culture."

"There is, but we also probably look at them differently from the way people who originally saw those paintings looked at them."

"And that might be part of their power, that we have to figure out our relationship to them. And when we have a relationship that's different, we enlarge – actually – the original art. I'll give you an example with Vermeer. I have this sense that Vermeer was painting at the end of the Thirty-Years War in order to evoke a feeling of peace in his viewers, so that people could remember what peace was like and rebuild the culture. And I was very touched to hear that when the Yugoslav War Crimes trials were going on, the chief judge – who was receiving this terrible, deadly diet every day, of atrocity – would go at lunch time to a nearby museum and sit with the Vermeers. And what he brought to and took from the paintings was different than what somebody in Vermeer's time would have, but no less real. And so suddenly the possibility of a Vermeer painting becomes larger."

She and John Tarrant came to realize that a demystification process was needed in order to reduce the barriers between students and the koans. One element was simply, whenever possible, to avoid foreign terms. Some terms remained because there was no appropriate English equivalent; *Dharma* and *Dao* are examples. But instead of calling the face-to-face meetings with students "sanzen," they called it "work in the room," which was the translation of an original Chinese term. When dealing with the first koan of the *Gateless Gateway*, they used "no" instead of "mu."[52]

"And it makes a huge difference," Joan tells me. "Let's use 'No' instead of 'Mu' so we have the same experience a Japanese-speaking person would have with 'Mu.' See what happens. 'No' became incredibly powerful in quite unexpected ways. So we said, 'Okay, that's good. We'll hold onto that.' And then instead of looking for the student to 'answer' the koan, I would say 'respond to.' So we've moved from 'answer' to 'respond to.' And allowing people to understand that their response to the koan is everything that happens while they're keeping company with that koan. Not just the moment when they're in 'work in the room'. And so asking them, 'What's it been like keeping company with this koan? What have you noticed in your life? What's happening in your dreams?' So that was a huge difference. Rather than having this encounter where you come in, 'What's your koan?' 'It's X.' 'What's your answer?' 'It's Y.' 'No.' It becomes, 'What's it like?' Which is a very Chinese way of asking the question. And listening for that and helping someone – if they need the help – find a response that has the flavor of the traditional response as well."

"And how did students react to that?"

"They loved it…. Well, some people who had already been part of the traditional way of doing it didn't. Some people can be conservative about things like that, and they felt a kind of anxiety that something was going to be asked of them that they hadn't signed up for. In the early days, some folks had become comfortable with the compartmentalized kind of process where you learn the tricks, and you have eight different responses, and you just bring one out. You know? So there were some people who disagreed and fell away. Left. But other people had become dissatisfied with that kind of practice and wanted to go deeper. And as time goes on, people who come to it fresh have expressed that it's made a profound difference in their lives."

"I can't say that my other teachers ever asked me to exclude my life," Sarah Bender told me, "but when I started to work with Joan, there was a way in which any kind of separation between a formal response to a koan or sort of an expected response to a koan and my life was unnecessary. And it was not at all that she was taking a psychological approach. I wouldn't call it that at all. I would just say that there was no longer any barrier there at all. And the *creativity* of response to koans was given its full play. So not very long after starting to work with Joan, I had a dream in which I was with a woman in a room, and we each had a knitting needle, and we were tossing a ball of yarn, back and forth, catching it on our knitting needles. And there was that quality to my work with Joan. We were playing with yarns."

We talk for a while about the mechanics of her teaching, the differences and similarities with what takes place in more traditional centers. "Work in the room" sessions, for example, tend to be longer and therefore not as frequent. And there are what she calls "Koan Salons" in which a group looks "at a koan together, usually over the course of a few weeks. Although the salons have been open, it's weighted heavily toward people who have been doing the practice for a while because that affects the nature of the conversation. But there are always a few people who are artists, say, who love it because it relates somehow to their art, and I think it's really valuable to have that mix."

"How do you decide which elements to retain and which not?"

"Do they serve the awakening of the participants? If they do, great. If they don't, don't need 'em. But also then we watch. And there have been some things that dropped away and then came back. And after the initial paring down, there were other things that left later. We're always watching it.

"Awakened Life is a fairly new community," she points out. "I only moved to Santa Fe seven years ago, in 2007. So when the first core-group of people sat down to decide, 'What are we going to do here? What is this going to be?' one of the first decisions we made is that we wanted to create a culture rather than an institution. And that was based on the idea that there are many institutions of Zen in this country already, and that's not where we wanted to put our energy because, of course, that pulls energy in a particular direction. Energy and resources. We really wanted to create a culture. And so a lot of the kinds of questions about what stays and what goes also has to do with 'What do we want to be part of our culture?' And the culture is how people live the tradition as householders together in this time and place."

The Awakened Life membership, she tells me, has a strong sense of community. "There's some stuff that kind of defaults to me, but there's a whole lot of stuff that's based on consensus and organic growth. What's happening in peoples' lives? What's happening in peoples' practice? What would serve their practice best now? Let's add this kind of retreat. Let's not do that anymore. Let's try this. You know, it's always changing in relationship to what's happening in peoples' lives."

This is the sense of what Sarah Bender had called "collegiality," community members supporting one another rather than focusing solely on their own progress within the tradition. "They're unbelievably supportive of one another," Joan marvels. "The surest sign of that to me is that they get together outside of the official programs and just meet, and they talk, and they do koans together, and they sit together, and go on camping trips together where they sit together. And there's this whole very intense network among the core people who are really engaged in each other's lives like that."

Nothing the Pacific Zen Institute or Awakened Life does provokes the ire of other teachers as much as the idea of koan discussion groups. John Tarrant, however, had suggested it was actually a very traditional approach. "The Chinese used to sit around and discuss koans," he told me. "That's what the *Book of Serenity* and the *Blue Cliff*

are about. People would sit around and talk about koans in a kind of salon. They didn't have the Japanese way that was secret and held closely to the chest."

"Today, of course, it's expected that students won't talk about their koan practice," I noted.

"Yeah, and that's just nonsense," he said with a chuckle. "We're westerners. We talk about everything. You want us to lie about it? Of course we're going to talk about koans. I have an intelligent apologia for that, which is that our ancestors were Europeans at universities in places like Padua and Milan, where people were discussing absurd things such as Christian theology. But the notion of inquiring into reality led them to anatomy and cosmology, chemistry, all these things that we've inherited. You can give people all the Japanese answers to the koans, and it won't help them at all. Right? But if they get it, they'll still get it."

"Individual koan study continues to be a cornerstone of our practice," Joan tells me. "But something even people doing one-on-one work will say over and over again about the koan salon is that there's something that happens when you have, say, between fifteen and twenty people in a room all responding to a koan in their own way. And you hear things you couldn't possibly have imagined yourself. So it's incredibly enriching of each person's individual experience. What's also bubbled up from the ground is that people started to get together in small groups, maybe just two or three people, when someone was having a problem in their life or a psychological difficulty, and they would take up a koan together to directly address something that was happening in someone's life. And they call them Life and Practice Conversations. That's very new; it's only been happening the last, maybe, couple of years. And that might end up being a great contribution they're making to the practice."

"What is the role of the teacher?" I ask.

"They bring three things. First, they bring the tradition with them, which more and more the participants won't have a relationship with themselves."

"Because we're too distant from it?"

"Because we're getting distant from it, and because now a different kind of person is attracted to the way we're teaching, some of whom don't have a lot of Zen experience. So the first thing a teacher brings would be immersion in the tradition, the perspective that provides, and the ability to communicate that in a helpful way. The second would be — one would hope, if you've hung your shingle out as a teacher — that you've had a certain kind of experience that's going to affect how you see things. You bring that perspective, which will be different from other people's until it's not. Until there are other people who have that same perspective. And a third is that I think of my job with people with whom I work individually as holding their awakening until they can hold it themselves. I can see their enlightenment, and I can hold that possibility…can hold that actuality for them and reflect it back until they're aware of it themselves."

"If you were training someone you think might have the potential of becoming a teacher someday, would you expect them to have the same depth of background you have?"

"I don't think that's possible anymore. Because in our lay line, I don't see people able to dedicate their whole lives to this anymore. Everybody I've made a teacher is something else as well, like a professor of English at the University of Arizona or whatever. This is something they love and do, but it's not the only thing they do."

We come back to the issue a little later.

"People don't want to become teachers nearly as much as they used to," she says. "The Santa Fe community actually asked me not to make any teachers here. Which in a way is great. Because it used to be a sesshin was rank with competition and jealousy and all of that because so many people wanted to be on a teacher track. There's something glorious about nobody caring about that!"

"You describe Awakened Life as a lay tradition. So no one becomes a monk or a priest?"

"We aren't monastic, and you only become a priest if you're made a roshi. But you don't identify primarily as a priest."

"So you are a priest."

"Yep. But I identify as a householder."

"And would your potential heir be a priest?"

"Well, senseis don't have to be priests. Roshis become priests when they're made a roshi."

"Automatically?"

"Yeah."

"But senseis can fulfill traditional priestly roles, perform wedding services, things like that?"

"Yes."

"Is there a minimum amount of familiarity with Buddhism necessary? Should they know the Four Noble Truths? What the klesas are? Skhandas? That type of thing?"

"For a teacher? Absolutely."

"Can they do that and still be actively engaged in another faith tradition?"

"Yes."

I am still thinking of my conversations with the Sanbo Zen teachers, and, when I mention Sister Elaine, Joan remarks with a laugh, "I don't think being a

Roman Catholic religious is any more…um…disqualifying than being a Professor of English."

As the conversation draws to a close, I motion to the altar in the corner of the room and remark, "I have to assume, from the Guanyin – and there's another outside – that the compassion component is as important as the wisdom component in your teaching."

"I believe wisdom is made up of insight *and* compassion. I was talking to someone recently about being a teacher and about that 'You numbskulls! You idiots!' kind of East Asian Zen thing. Right? And I said, 'You can't do that with westerners.' You just can't, because our psyches and our cultures are different. And I've come to see that part of my job as a teacher is to let someone know that they're really loved so that they can relax and can let go of all of the, 'How am I doing? What's she thinking of me? Am I getting this right? Am I winning?' That whole ghost world can drop away because there's a field of love and of acceptance. And then we can take great risks together."

"At a retreat we were asking questions during one of the evening sessions," Tenney Nathanson, the Professor of English, recalls, "and someone asked how she would define awakening, and she just said, 'Attentiveness and compassion.' And the person was kind of scandalized and said, 'That's it?!' Joan said, 'Yeah, that's it.'"

A single meeting with a teacher for a few hours is insufficient to get a full sense of their approach to practice and teaching. Consequently, I met with certain of the people I interviewed more than once, conducted follow-up interviews by Skype with others, and maintained – at times lengthy – e-mail correspondence with others. In a letter sent to me nine months after my visit to Santa Fe, Joan Sutherland further clarified her vision of the work in which she is engaged:

> For me, the koan tradition carries something very old and very pre-
> cious, which is not identical with mainstream Buddhism or even
> mainstream Zen, drawing as it does on ancient springs expressed
> in China as Taoism and shamanism. Mostly this is an underground

river, bubbling up and refreshing the surface, with its orthodoxies and institutions, from time to time. It's meant to remain a counter-current, never to become an orthodoxy itself, so that it can preserve our connections to what has largely gone underground in the great empires of the world: the moral claim of the natural world upon us, an appreciation of women's voices, inquiry countering funda-mentalism and annihilating certainty, etc. While the koan tradition is capable of aboveground corruption (see World War II in Japan), there has always persisted underground this tendency, this memory, this life force that many of us value and long to strengthen in our lives now. I believe the koan tradition is one quite beautiful way to do that.

What does that look like in practice? An example would be includ-ing endarkenment as well as enlightenment in how we see awak-ening. By endarkenment I mean two things: first, a deepened understanding that there is an unknowable mystery at the center of things – what the Taoists called the Great Mysterious, what Shitou Xiqian was referring to when he spoke of branches of light stream-ing from the dark, and, maybe, what astrophysicists mean by dark energy. What is it like, as a consequence of embracing that central mystery, to be profoundly comfortable with not knowing (Chan monastics used to greet each other by saying, "I am not certain"); to value what can be learned only in the dark ("In the dark, darken further," advises the *Daodejing*); to lean back with trust against a mystery that the poet Hanshan called "a tree older than the forest it stands in"?

And second, if that's the face of endarkenment turned toward eter-nity, the other face, turned toward the world, is the realm of the bodhisattva vow, of our willingness for our hearts to get broken and stay broken, and then to meet with our individual hearts the great broken heart of the world. That is – perhaps, we'll see – a potential of the koan tradition that our innovation has unleashed.

In May 2014, Joan retired from active teaching citing health issues. Since then, she has focused her attention on a project called *Cloud Dragon: The Joan Sutherland*

Dharma Works which was established to provide her teaching, writing, and translation work as wide a circulation as possible. Her heirs, like Sarah Bender and Tenney Nathanson, continue her approach to koan work with students.

CHAPTER TEN

James Ford

ALTHOUGH THEY BOTH RECOGNIZE JOHN TARRANT AS THEIR PRIMARY TEACHER, James Ford seems as different from Joan Sutherland as Providence, Rhode Island, is from Santa Fe. The state license plate declares Rhode Island to be the "Ocean State," but, even with GPS instructions, my wife, Joan, and I are unable to find the waterfront. This forms our first – doubtless inaccurate – impression of the city. One can be just as easily misled upon meeting James.

As well as being the founder of Boundless Way Zen, James is a Unitarian minister currently assigned to the First Unitarian Church located – as if one were caught up in a modern-dress enactment of *The Pilgrim's Progress* – on the corner of Benefit and Benevolent Streets in the city of Providence. It turns out he is not the first but the third professed Buddhist to hold this post. It is clear I don't know much about Unitarianism.

It is a beautiful spring day in Providence; bright yellow forsythia bushes are rife; a street fair of artists and artisans have turned several blocks of Benefit Street into a pedestrian mall. James arrives in the church parking lot just as Joan and I are getting out of our car. He is in shorts, sandals, and a Hawaiian shirt. A small beard and glasses with large round lenses gives him a professorial look. He does not, however, have the professorial manner, and one suspects he might be an effective but fairly conventional minister.

He is clearly proud of this building – called a Meeting House – which had been the First Congregational Church of Providence before becoming the First Unitarian Church of Providence, and he takes us on a tour. It is a pleasant structure constructed along traditional lines, brightly illuminated by natural light coming through tall double-lancet windows. The supporting columns of the nave have elaborately carved capitals, and from the domed ceiling there hangs a large, three tiered candelabra. James obligingly poses for a photograph behind the lectern of a ship's prow pulpit raised high above the congregation.

The interview takes place in his office in the Parish House, an administrative building connected to the Meeting House by an atrium. His ministerial robes hang on the back of the office door. There is a votive candle to the Virgin of Guadalupe under a Mexican papier-mâché rainbow on one shelf, a framed rendition of the *Heart Sutra* in Kanji over another set of shelves, a New Mexican horned cow skull, and a statue of an ape contemplating Darwin's skull.

The first impression one gets is that James is a little fussy and old-fashioned. My opening question provokes him to exclaim, "Heaven's-t'-Betsy," an expression I don't think I've actually heard spoken outside of John Wayne-era westerns. Once we have spent some time together and relaxed in one another's company, he is less formal. When I mention the difficulty Joan and I had locating the waterfront, he explains the difference between New York City "where streets are laid out in a neatly ordered numbered and lettered grid so one can find one's way around" and Providence and Boston, where the guiding principle behind the way in which streets are laid out seems to be "Fuck you."

It's hard not to like him.

One way in which he is very similar to Joan Sutherland is in his concern for this tradition and his hope that it will be more than – as he puts it – a "historical blip." He has given serious consideration to the structures which need to be developed in order to ensure the continuance of teaching and practice in America and is both well-reasoned and passionate when discussing the topic.

It is my question about the function of Zen that elicits the "Heaven's-t'-Betsy!" response, which is then followed by a slight pause. "I think it's to heal the heart."

"How does it do that?"

"Well, we have a technology of the spirit: Sit down. Shut up. And pay attention." He is a witty and charming conversationalist; he would make an excellent dinner guest. "And for those of us like me who are not real good at sitting down, shutting up, and paying attention, there are koans."

"Fair enough. What's the function of Unitarianism?"

"We-ell, I think it's the cure of the human heart."

"And how does it do it?"

"It's an interesting approach which, by a peculiar evolution, more resembles Daoism than anything else. A little dash of Confucianism thrown in. It does it by an appreciation of our complete connection to the natural world, and it manifests in ethics and social engagement. So, it's not Buddhism, but it's easy for a Buddhist to be part of it."

"Is it a Christian denomination?"

He has been asked the question before.

"The way I say that is: It shifted somewhere between the end of the 19th century and the early decades of the 20th century from being a liberal Christian denomination to being a liberal denomination with Christians. What you just saw is a typical New England Protestant Congregational Meeting House. On Sunday, the structure of the service is deeply Protestant. But we're not driven by the Scriptures.

"The principle I think that Unitarian Universalism works on is that there is no creed – we're radically anti-creedal – but there is a recognizable style. If one has a very adamant theism, a particular belief that if you don't toe the line something bad is going to happen, then you're not going to be happy going in with the crowd. We do have something called Principles and Purposes. They are incorporated in the Preamble of the By-laws of the Association. They're not a creed, in that one need not affirm them in order to become a member, but they are a good faith attempt at describing the current positions of Unitarian Universalism. There's seven of them; three are relevant. Two taken together, I think, are a theological statement. One asserts the preciousness of the individual. Another, the seventh, is an assertion of radical interdependence. And I'd say if you took those things together – the individual is precious but only exists within context – you've got, I think, the heart of the theological project. And then there's something called the fourth principle which calls for free and responsible search for meaning. You can come and just be, but generally the invitation is to some kind of engagement."

"Were you involved with Unitarians before you became involved with Zen or did Zen come first?"

"Zen first. Yeah, for me, after I left the monastery...."

"Okay, let's back up. Monastery?"

He was brought up in a fundamentalist Christian family. "Mainly in California. We moved a great deal. My daddy was a ne'er-do-well, and my small joke is that I didn't realize people could move during the day until I was grown up." The family anchor was his maternal grandmother, Bolene Bernard, "who was a spirit-filled woman and a Baptist deaconess, and we went to churches where the spirit led her. My childhood was great. Adolescence wasn't so great. I think I worked my way into atheism at about 16.

"The rational stance is agnosticism. Atheism, at least in contemporary use, is an emotional stance. And so for me it was a kind of engagement; I was constantly on a quest. And my first realization that religion didn't have to be the really narrow Christianity of my childhood was when I discovered Vedanta through Aldous Huxley and then, through him, Christopher Isherwood who wrote those really lucid books about Vedanta. *Ramakrishna and His Disciples* was, I think, the first. And then I read primary texts."

"This was while you were still in high school?"

"Yeah. I was 17, something in that area. And I was stirred up enough that I actually went to the Vedanta Society in Berkeley for one service. But it was a little too much like a Protestant church. I've thought about it in retrospect. At the time, I thought, 'Gee, it's all these old ladies.' And then I realized they were mainly about my age now, 65, if not a little younger. They would have been fascinating people who were in their sixties in the '60s. You know? They came of age in the teens and '20s, which was a very fascinating period of spiritual turmoil. What would have led them into Vedanta must have been fascinating. But I turned away, and it was good because I think I would have run into problems with the purity part of Hinduism and Vedanta.

"But this was the San Francisco Bay Area, and there were a lot of things to find. My well-worn line is that after I realized psychedelics were unlikely to save the world, somebody said, you've got to check out Shunryu Suzuki. And the shortest version for this is I took instruction at the San Francisco Zen Center in zazen."

I had found the story of his first day at the San Francisco Zen Center recounted elsewhere and had included it in my chapter on Dainin Katagiri in *The Third Step East*. "They had this program. You went in. Got a little talk. Then got formal instruction in how to do zazen. It was given by Claude Dalenberg. Then off to a formal interview, and my first formal interview was with Dainin Katagiri – 'Sensei' in those days – and, if I recall the conversation correctly, he said, 'How long have you been sitting?' And I said, 'Five minutes?' He said, 'Good. Keep that mind.' And, yeah, that's good advice."

He did not stay at SFZC long. "I was young and foolish, and they seemed to be too big an institution. And I'd got it in my head that ordaining would solve all my problems, and they actually had requirements, so...."

"What problems were you seeking to resolve?"

"Oh, I was an existential wreck. I loved Camus. A little Sartre. So, I was worried about meaninglessness. I'm pretty sure death was part of this deal. Yeah. I was on a quest for truth."

There was something about Buddhism, however, which led him to believe that if there were an answer to his problems, it might be found there. "Then Jiyu Kennett blew into town. Actually, I've been trying to reconstruct her history recently. There's this whole hagiography machine around her at Shasta[53], but it's pretty much my belief that she had a charter to start a school in London and had swung by San Francisco because it was the first successful outreach to the gaijin."

Peggy Kennett was an Englishwoman who had joined a Theravada group in London in the 1950s, then went on to study Soto Zen at Sojiji, where she received the Dharma name, Jiyu. She developed a unique teaching style peculiarly influenced by High Church Anglicanism. "You can say many things about Jiyu Kennett," James tells me. "Some really good. And among those was she was real smart. She arrives in San Francisco. She thinks about London. She decides she's going to set up her business in California. She moved into a flat on Potrero Hill, and I was her first student. Now Josh Baran claims he was her first student, but he arrived there on a Thursday, and I was there on a Wednesday."

James began sitting regularly with Kennett, and, when she had to return to London for a while, he was invited to move into the flat on Potrero until her return, "with the proviso that I marry my girlfriend. Which I've never forgiven Jiyu for. We got married, and it caused sadness for both of us. But I moved in, and I was a residential practitioner from that point on."

Kennett returned from England with sixteen disciples in tow, so larger accommodations were found in Oakland. James was ordained an unsui, after which the group relocated again, this time to Mount Shasta, where Kennett established Shasta Abbey.

"I received transmission up in Mount Shasta."

"How old were you?" I ask.

"Oh, I did the math a while back. Twenty? I can't remember now. Twenty-one or twenty-two. Yeah. A child. And part of the problem was, I did have some experiences. She was a big kensho person. A little floaty about what that precisely meant. Her official teacher was Chisan Koho, and he was one of the Soto people who had done some extensive koan training. Though as I cast my memory back onto those days, I don't think she had a real grasp of koan work. But she worked with it a little bit, and she was definitely interested in experiences. And I had experiences. But it was very cultish, and eventually the dime dropped even for me, and I left. I wasn't with her three full years.

"So, there I was, casting about. What am I going to do next? I thought I was done with Zen. I liked the sitting. I continued sitting for a while, though it gradually fell away. And I looked around. So I went to the local Episcopal Church. I danced with New Age Sufis. You know. Cast about."

While studying with Jiyu Kennett, James had met Samuel Lewis, the founder of the Sufi Ruhaniat International, and, after leaving Shasta, he lived for a while at the Sufi residential community in San Francisco. It was there that he met his present wife, Jan. "We were always a bit fish out of water. Jan was pretty political, and I was vastly more prajna than bhakti. But I consider that time a valuable part in my life, mostly because of Jan, but also I developed a genuine sympathy for the more ecstatic aspect of spirituality.

"Then I found the Unitarian Church. It was a great home. It had all the community stuff. It was light on spiritual practice, but it had good community and a way to act in the world and a social-conscience thing that resonated deeply with my view of the world.

"Very soon after that, I resumed sitting. I started a little sitting group just because I knew I wasn't going to sit by myself. And a few people started coming. There was a fellow who joined – Jim Wilson – who had been a monk with Seung Sahn, and he was a very senior student. He was being groomed for transition." Wilson was then living in San Francisco and was looking for a place to sit. "The Koreans do a form of koan work, and I was deeply intrigued because I'd read about it but hadn't actually encountered it in a way that seemed to be done by someone who knew what they were doing. So I badgered him even though he said he wasn't authorized to teach. I threatened him. I said, 'Well, you want a place to sit, don't you?' And we worked with koans for a little bit. I still recall he broke off half of the 'All things return to the One. What does the One return to?' I can vividly recall sitting in the room with him. I had a little bookstore, and he was looking out the window; looking at the books. But I knew the answer. You know? And then we launched into it. We ran. We did that for…I can't honestly say. Maybe a year, until he decided he didn't want to do it anymore. It was beyond what he felt he might be useful for.

"By then, I'd closed the bookstore I had been operating; had started going back to school and was working at another bookstore. And I decided I had to have a teacher. I checked out the local Soto guy on the hill, but there was no juice. And so I wrote this long letter to Robert Aitken. And the day I mailed it, this guy walks into the bookstore with a woman, and he says, 'Do you have anything unusual in Orientalia?' And I said, 'Ha! We have a Lafcadio Herne ghost story with hand-colored plates.' He said, 'Let me see it.' We went over, unlocked the cabinet. He said, 'How much is it?' I said, 'It's a hundred bucks.' And this is twenty-five years ago. And he says, 'I'll take it.' I said, 'Oh! For yourself?' 'No,' he said. 'For a gift.' 'Who's the gift for?' (As you can tell, I'm a pushy personality.) 'For my teacher.' 'Teacher of what?' He said, 'Zen.' And it turns out, his name is John Tarrant, and he's a student of Robert Aitken, and he's just come over to finish his doctorate."

James and John met a couple of times after this initial encounter. James was still testing the waters. "He's a year younger than me. And then Seung Sahn was running a Yong Maeng Jong Jin, which is what they call a sesshin. Although it's kind of cool because apparently it translates roughly as 'Intrepid Sitting.' But colloquially, 'To leap like a tiger while sitting.' And it was great. I mean, I had a great connection with Seung Sahn. I liked him. We rolled through a couple of koan. But they served kimchi for breakfast. I mean, I like kimchi – don't get me wrong."

"Which is?"

"Oh, kimchi is pickled cabbage. And it's usually some degree of spicy. It's the national side dish of Korea. You have it with breakfast, lunch, and dinner. But for me it was symbolic of the fact that too many of the students there were speaking in broken English. You know, a guy with a Ph.D. in literature was speaking this broken Korean-English. It was that kind of guru worship which just wasn't working for me. So I went back after the retreat and gave John the box of incense.[54] Yeah. That was twenty-five years ago."

"What was he like when you first met him?"

"Young. Arrogant. Brilliant. And of the mix, brilliant was the most obvious. The others were not far behind. To this day – having met many people – I'd say the most interesting mind of all the Zen teachers I've ever met. Absolutely *brilliant* command of the koan literature. And an absolute anarchist. He's just absolutely uninterested in the institutional issues or social norms. I think these days he's found his niche because almost all his students now are artists, poets, writers, or people with that kind of mind set. I think he's found the perfect niche in what the current PZI is."

Tarrant had told me that he had been teaching more traditionally when he met James. James tells me they worked together for almost twenty years. "For the first seven, eight years with him, we worked very closely. Then I graduated seminary."

"So you're doing both of these at the same time?"

"Yeah. They're both concerned with the matter of the heart. How do we actually live? And for me, they both filled holes in the other. So Zen as John presented it – pretty much Zen as we find it in the west – it's like going to a gym. You know? You go. You do your Zen thing, and then you take your shower and go home. And the consequences in life are not particularly well explored. It's the shadow of the monastic inheritance. You go. You hear a talk. You do koans or whatever. And then that's kind of it. And for me, Unitarians offered the other part of the picture without having a competing spiritual practice at the time. So for me…you know…. People call me a Zen Unitarian. People say all kinds of unkind things about me," he chuckles.

"Is that an unkind thing to say?"

"I don't mind it. But I consider myself a pretty mainline Buddhist of a rationalist sort."

"You suggested that Unitarians might be a little light on spiritual practice. Is that where Buddhism complements it?"

"Right. And then how to move into community. How to live with other people. And how to act in the world. Unitarians – you know – thick ethic. Great ethic. And it's an ethic grounded in a natural world, in how we are as we are. Very compassionate and open hearted."

In 1991, James was called to his first congregation, in "the suburbs of Milwaukee, and from that point on, I started just coming out for retreats. So I did four sesshin a year, I think. And then we looked for ways to communicate. We did some phone work. We tried writing letters."

"This was all before email and Skype?"

"Yeah. I finished koan work before those became an option."

"What was Milwaukee like?"

"Well, you know, Unitarians are very similar across the board. Although, you get to places like Milwaukee and there are a substantial number of people who've lived in Wisconsin their entire lives. It was kind of interesting, but I didn't like the snow. Now, my wife, Jan, says I'd seen snow before, but I claim I never saw snow fall out of the sky until I went to Milwaukee. And, I mean, it was *beautiful*, but I had no anticipation that it would be quiet. Loved the view. But the next day, it didn't go away. We've lived in New England now for – I don't know – thirteen years, and maybe a dozen times it's dipped below zero. Whereas in Milwaukee the thought occurred to me, 'Oh my God! My eyeballs could freeze!'"

Although James was an ordained Soto priest and had received transmission from Jiyu Kennett, he told Tarrant he would not begin teaching until John authorized him to. When James went to Milwaukee, John gave him permission to start a group and give talks.

Four years later, he transferred to Tempe, Arizona. "The church was actually a foundation of the first Unitarian Church of Phoenix to serve the academic community, and from that point on I've served academic churches."

"This is an academic church, here in Providence?"

"You bet. There is no university in the state of Rhode Island that we don't have tenured faculty from. It's just part of our lot. There are more Ph.D.s, and M.D.s than you could shake a stick at. It's fun. I mean, it's the way my mind works. So I'm their people, and they're my people. And that's great. And somewhere along the line, John authorized me to teach.

"It's a system that kind of spins out of Robert Aitken, so there was this kind of short-tether teaching permission, where I could do koan work and such but I couldn't give transmission. But he gave me the title 'sensei' and a kotsu, and I started teaching from that point somewhere in the mid-'90s."

I ask how his Zen teaching fits in with his Unitarian ministry.

"My sanghas have always been housed in the church, and there's a tension if people didn't like me. The first allegation is 'conflict of interest.' And it took me a while, but by the time I came here – which is a lot of years later – I'm fully transmitted; I have books written. They wanted me, in part, because I was a Buddhist."

"Do you have people who are both members of the congregation and Zen students?"

"Yeah, there's always an overlap. So this is my fourth church. And each one, I've started a sitting group. I've started seven or eight sitting groups over my life. And at the beginning, they're nearly all members of the church. Our group here, I would say, is a quarter or a third, probably, members of the church. And that's a big range, from people who've actually been in leadership to people who occasionally attend services. I would say in Boundless Way, there's definitely a Unitarian influence, but we're not the majority. The large majority of people don't have anything to do with Unitarianism directly."

"How did Boundless Way come about?"

"So, when I left Arizona, I asked John what to do with the group there. Because, especially then, when I leave, I have to really not be connected to anything to do with that parish. It's part of the professional, ethical guidelines. And John was in a position where – at that moment – he took it on personally. So it became his group. And I think when I left there, I pretty much ceased seeing myself as working in the Pacific Zen Institute, which is how his organization had evolved. When we were in Arizona, John split from the Diamond Sangha. I would have gone with them, but actually I was an apprentice teacher at that point in the Diamond Sangha, and the bastards never even asked me. They just eliminated me along with him," he says, laughing.

"But you also separated from PZI?"

"Yeah, it was just stylistically…I'm more conservative. I wanted to do more something related to my priestly origins." He means within the Soto tradition; Unitarians do not have priests. "I started having a lot of friends in the Soto tradition and wanted to see where that would fit. And it was totally uninteresting to John. And then by the time we're here, it's just way far away."

By the time he came to New England, he was working independently, leading his own sesshin, and accumulating students. He was also "acutely aware of how pretty much all American Zen lineages collapse after their founder is gone. I'm not sure, but I think it's a structural flaw in the transmission. In Japan, transmission came as part of a larger package with accountability and institutions. Zen came west with some practices and Dharma transmission, and I think that's just not enough."

Zen transmission in Asia takes place within a cultural and institutional context that does not yet exist in North America, where the majority of Zen practitioners – and even a sizeable number of Zen teachers – are lay.

"Lay people as leaders are a phenomenon of the Dharma in the West. Really interesting. But I also think – speaking narrowly, just of Zen transmission – that a cluster of practices and Dharma transmission are not enough. It doesn't sustain itself. The Dharma transmission itself – when it's pulled out of this larger context – is cultish and very individualistic. So, if you give Dharma transmission to somebody, in fifteen minutes they're going to break away and do their own thing. At least that appears to be what we've witnessed in the west so far. There are attempts at corrrectives that are emerging."

James is involved with both the American Zen Teachers Association (AZTA) and Soto Zen Buddhist Association (SZBA). AZTA, he tells me, is essentially a "support group. They don't even want to call themselves a professional organization." He estimates its membership probably includes 80 percent of the teachers in North America. But then, as he puts it, "there's this whole question of who's a Zen teacher? It's more than who authorizes them. The great struggle in the AZTA is it doesn't want to be a credentialing body," he is speaking slowly and with some care, "*but* they have to have a standard for membership. And they're cross-tradition. So there's nobody who's a teacher in the AZTA who would be qualified to be a teacher in every other group. Their expectations are so different. I've come to believe there are quasi-objective things we can hold onto. Some kind of general acknowledgement of an authorization with an intent to be an independent teacher. And probably somewhere between three and five hundred days of retreat – you know – for either sesshin or whatever. There are increasing numbers of people who do not fulfill that second category who have the first category." There are people, he admits, who have membership in AZTA but whose qualifications as teachers he doubts.

"With Boundless Way, we're attempting to be a prototype of an organization that can outlast the teachers."

The critical step in the creation of Boundless Way was the involvement of two other teachers, Melissa Blacker and David Rynick. They're married but are authorized to teach in different traditions.

Melissa is James's heir.

"Without David and Melissa, it would just be the James Show. Me and my heirs. But David's there. And with David, there's a great eye, and there's great heart. But he's not in my line. He's George Bowman's heir. And George is his own bit of weirdness, a Seung Sahn Dharma successor who spent more years sitting retreats with Joshu Sasaki than he did with Seung Sahn. So we're working on how we can create something that we can all be part of. And it's involved a lot of bowing on all of our parts. I think David has had to bow a little bit more because the form, the style, the presentation is following the Japanese model. And we have the institutional framework to reference. So there's some things we agreed to. The ordination model we use is the Japanese Soto thing that comes through Jiyu Kennett, though we're open to having a Soto priest from another line joining us, and that would be utterly fine. We've agreed to use the Japanese style of documentation, based upon the Soto *san matsu* documents, but for David, in the lineage part of the documents, he uses his own lineage. We've talked with the SZBA Executive Director, and their current view is that as long as they're *san matsu* documents, they don't care who's the line in it. They will accept that as part of the transmission. So I ordained David a priest, but he's a Dharma heir of George. But he can ordain priests that can be accepted into the SZBA. And then our struggle will be, if they ever change their mind, because they're trying to turn into a denomination, and they're going to have standards.

"My commitment is to David and Boundless Way. My primary commitment is to Boundless Way. I don't think it'll fall, but those are the tensions that happen. I think the fact that we pay attention to the institution is going to be our saving grace. The primary project is awakening, and we know that. But we also know if we want this to last and serve other generations, something more than what has been going on has to happen."

"You think an official structure has to be established?"

"And there are costs to that. We may not be as shamanic as other groups, but I think we're going to have fewer sex scandals too."

The fourth – and most recent – teacher within Boundless Way is Josh Barton, who, like Melissa, is James's heir. James is acknowledged as the Founding Abbot but tries not to pull rank. David – who is not his heir – is the current abbot of Boundless Way, which is a concrete way of demonstrating their openness to multiple lineages. "And we invite others to join us, though there needs to be simpatico."

"There are different models across the country," I note. "In San Francisco, they said that one comes there not necessarily to work with a specific teacher but to become part of a community. But in most other centers, when I show up at the door, what I'm going to end up doing is working with a specific, individual teacher."

"With us, we do have a specific teacher's relationship. One person signs the documents, but we expect people to interview with all of the Boundless Way teachers. And we want people – especially as their practice matures – to do retreats outside of our community. We don't exclude any teacher, but we may share opinions. In fact, I will definitely share opinions about other teachers. Not with a 'don't go,' but with a 'Watch out for the hands' or whatever."

And while there are teachers who will only accept their own students for sesshin, James tells me that Boundless Way has "fairly good entree to the larger communities."

James has given a lot of consideration to the challenges facing North American Zen.

"I think for us to succeed, for us not to simply fragment into meaninglessness with bunches of people with titles and no juice, I think there need to be some institutional structures. There needs to be some large obligations that take us out of repeating these little cult things. And I've got some hope for the SZBA in that regard. There's ten times as many Soto people as Rinzai people, and most of the Harada-Yasutani people can fit into Soto very easily. So I'm hoping there'll be something there."

"Are you picturing some kind of central authority or an oversight body?"

"It's so hard to say what's going to be the expectations. I think we need a couple of things. I think we need a mutually agreed-upon code of ethics we can buy into and that's enforceable."

"I spoke recently with one of Joshu Sasaki's oshos – a woman – who felt strongly that it was inappropriate for Zen centers to issue ethics statements."

"Yeah, and they're working with it, aren't they?"

I admit that it's a point of view I had difficulty understanding. "I suppose it's that whole 'there is no one who kills, no one who is killed' thing," I say, thinking aloud.

James is unwilling to accept that kind of casuistry.

"Well, if you live in the Absolute. That's the problem. You get these cultish elements where it's all about Emptiness. 'There are no ethics.' But I don't live in the Empty Realm. I live in a realm that has emptiness and phenomena. There are three bodies of the Buddha. Emptiness, Dharmakaya, is one of them, and we've got to have that insight. There's no Zen without a true and deep penetration of the matter of Emptiness. But there's also no Zen without a true and deep penetration of the matter of the Nirmanakaya, the world manifest in time and space. We live in a world of cause and effect and consequence. And to have Zen absent that is…. Well, there's an old Japanese saying: 'Vision without action is a fantasy. Action without vision is a nightmare.' Zen without precepts is cults and damaged people."

"And, of course, there are also all those 'endless blind passions' we've vowed to do something about," I say.

"Fucking-A. You know? Right."

As I said, first impressions can be misleading.

"We need a balance," he continues. "And so, yeah, we might lose some shamans. And we're probably better off for it."

Without some form of shared principles and fundamental guidelines, James fears "there's a real good chance that we'll simply attenuate into an historical blip. Many American sanghas are aging. I think there's going to be a big die-off. But it won't be a complete die-off." His heir, Josh Bartok – like Eshu Martin – is in his early 40s. "So, there are these forty-something teachers, and I've got others who are coming close to *denkai*. And when I was out in San Francisco, I was surprised at how many twenty-somethings, thirty-somethings were there.

"But the fact is some sanghas are old, and they will disappear. And there'll be a fresh start. I think they'll be more conscious about ethical concerns. The other thing is our teachers. Mainly they're just meditation teachers. They know nothing else. They don't know Buddhism. They don't have pastoral skills. They're meditation teachers. We need people who are more balanced. We need priests. We need people who do something vaguely like seminary. It doesn't need to be seminary, but they need to be educated, they need to have practices, and they need to be supported in some manner. I don't know if it will all happen. There are an awful lot of moving parts."

Then there is the matter of competition between lineages. "People have got to accept each other's lineage. We've got to stop pretending there's only one true way."

"Well, it's not just lineages," I point out. "It's teachers. I'm Rinzai. You're Rinzai. But my teacher's the right teacher, and your guy, I'm not too sure about."

"And we've got to get past that. We've just got to bow to each other a little bit more."

I review the points he's made. "So first, you believe there need to be ethical guidelines which can be ratified and enforced."

"Right. There needs to be some kind of common agreement and some sort of mutual accountability. There also needs to be some sort of commonly accepted standards of training for teachers. Generally that fits within the priestly model. And it isn't just meditation. I mean, you need to have meditation – absolutely, that's the heart – but in addition, you need to be educated; you need to actually know the difference between Theravada and Mahayana Buddhism; you need to have some sense of the history. You don't need to be a scholar, but you need to know a little bit more than teachers often do.

"And the third thing, I think, is there needs to be some new way of envisioning how to support teachers."

"Is there not a fourth element as well?" I ask. "Some means of determining the legitimacy of authorization?"

"Oh, yeah. Absolutely. I just assumed that. But you're right, because our transmissions are all over the map."

"There are at least two different formulae. You've got the Rinzai – and I suppose Sanbo Kyodan – formula which is based on attainment, and then you've got the Soto formula where if you stick around three or four years, you'll get transmission."

"Well, in the West, it's ten to twenty. But, you're right, Soto has a problem around awakening and how important that moment is. It's a problem."

"That's at least four things we've listed. So where does the central authority come from? Who defines these ethical guidelines or sets the criteria for teachers?"

"Well, I don't know. I'm part of a project. We're an experiment. What we do, we write down, and we throw it up on the web. And if we change it, people will know we changed it. We can't pretend that it was always the new way."

"Are you getting any cooperation with this experiment?"

"Outside Boundless Way? I think it's on the table. We're all talking." He grins a little wickedly. "I think after the great die-off something will emerge. You know, I write on the subject. I'm hoping it won't all disappear into the ether, and that other people are thinking about it. So I believe a chastened Zen institution may emerge.

"The fascinating thing about Soto is that it really is a system that's more than the personalities. An unawakened teacher can produce an awakened student. And it's fascinating. I think a non-awakened person can use the curriculum and have awakened students. It's such a lovely system. And, you know, the student's more important than the teacher in that regard."

He believes certain lineages show more vitality than others. "I've got some hope for the Kapleau people, Bodhin Kjolhede and Sunyana Graef and that gang. They're a little harsh, but there's something real there and juicy. And I think the Soto crowd – although they desperately need koans – they don't have a lot of prajna, but they've got everything else. But we're all a little weak in compassion, and I think we would do well to look at the Unitarian Church for that. Unitarianism has a great potential of being helpful to Zen as it tries to move past these first two generations."

"Has anyone other than you made the link between Unitarianism and Zen?"

"No. I'm it for now. There is another Unitarian minister who, I think, will be named a Sanbo Kyodan teacher in a couple of years But that's it. But most Zen groups in North America started in the basement of a Unitarian church," he adds.

❀

Some months after this interview, James announced his coming retirement from the Unitarian ministry in 2015. He and his wife intend to return to California, where he hopes to establish a new Boundless Way group in Long Beach. He has also resigned from the membership committee of the AZTA, which he served on for twelve years, in order to take up a position on the board of trustees of the SZBA.

CHAPTER ELEVEN

Three Boundless Way Teachers

MELISSA MYOZEN BLACKER
DAVID DAE AN RYNICK
JOSH BARTOK

1

I DON'T BELIEVE IN FATE. I DON'T EVEN HAVE MUCH CONFIDENCE IN THE CONCEPT of karma, except to recognize that we're the product of our choices as well as of our environment and experience. Occasionally, however, one encounters something that just seems to have been meant to be.

The Boundless Way Temple in Worcester is on Pleasant Street which is also the junction between highways 9 and 122. Even if there were not a banner on the fence (erected by the Steadfast Fence Company), one could hardly miss the place because of the five foot tall Buddha out front.

"The statue! Oh! It's so cool!" Melissa Blacker tells me, breathlessly.

One immediately notices Melissa's energy, exuberance, and apparent boundless enthusiasm for just about everything. "We were at this restaurant," Dosho Port told me, trying to convey his impression of her. "And she was like" – affectionately imitating her voice – "'Oh, these crêpes are so good! You guys, these crêpes! They're the best crêpes!' Then, like, 'Arugula! Look! Arugula! Ohhh!' You're just so impressed with how delighted she is with everything."

"The statue! Oh! It's so cool! So, we bought this building – David and I bought this building – three and a half years ago, and we knew that we'd have to sell it to the sangha at some point, but the sangha didn't have the resources, and we did. We were actually really lucky. We took a chance. It's worked out great, and now this year the Leadership Council of the Temple – which is an affiliate of Boundless Way Zen – has started a capital campaign to purchase the temple from David and me. But, when we moved here, the outside was quite the disaster of fallen limbs, weeds everywhere.

And we had to build that handicap ramp that you saw. And so while we were building the ramp – we had some volunteers building it – in the middle of it were all these weeds, and David was weeding it with some people one day, and they were about to cut this thing, and he said, 'No, no, no, no. It's a flowering cherry tree. I think it's a flowering cherry tree.' And they cleared the weeds away, and there was this little cherry tree. And it was just beautiful, and it was contained within the ramp. Hadn't been planned. Right in the middle of where the ramp was. And you didn't see it.

"And meanwhile we had to do all these improvements to the building, including install a sprinkler system in case of fire. So the guy who was cutting through the pavement to divert water from the city into the temple came up to David one day and said, 'You guys need a Buddha statue?' And" – laughing – "we have a lot of Buddha statues, thank you very much. And, 'No, this is an out-door one.' Well, we have an out-door one about a foot and a half tall. 'No, no. This is a really big one.' A friend of his had ordered it for a customer who wanted it for his garden. A Buddha to sit out in his garden. And when it arrived it was that *huge* statue which was – like – way bigger than he needed for his garden. I think it was a hairdresser, a Vietnamese hairdresser in town, wanted it. And there are two other temples in town; they're ethnically Vietnamese. We're the only convert temple. And the guy had offered it to both the Vietnamese temples. One was hosting this giant jade Buddha that was travelling all over the country, and so they couldn't do it. The other one had just paved their driveway. They couldn't do it. So we were number three. And David went down to the yard where it was being stored, this rejected Buddha statue nobody wanted, and it was surrounded – I have a photo on my computer somewhere – by statues of Mickey Mouse and naked Venuses on couches, and it was just sitting there. And so he took a photograph of it and showed it to James Ford and me, and we said, 'We should buy it!' And he said, 'No, no. It's really big.' And James said, 'It's going to get smaller with the years.' So now it seems like a normal size to me. They sold it to us wholesale, 'cause they just wanted to make back the money, so it wasn't very much money. And we asked everyone in the sangha to contribute to it. Got way more money than we needed for it. Bought it. It came here on a flat-bed truck. We had this whole ceremony when we placed it there. Then David did some research and found this local quarry that made these little white stones. So we asked the guy, 'Would you pick them up for us?' So he picked up a truckload of them and gave them to us. We didn't have to pay for them! So it sort of was this amazing thing. It looks like we designed it to be there. But the cherry tree and the Buddha and the handicap ramp were all chance occurrences that just came together!"

Some things, it seems, are just meant to be.

It strikes me that it might also just be meant for Melissa to be here. The students I speak to stress the welcoming atmosphere at the temple, something I notice almost upon arrival. David Rynick and Melissa Blacker are a delightful couple, and one naturally wants to spend time with them.

"I was raised in a secular household, so I never had any religious training," she tells me. "In fact, my parents were very suspicious of religion."

She was nine years old in the early '60s when she had an experience she now recognizes as a spontaneous kensho. "But I was just a little kid. I had no idea. There was no framework for it. So, I was a smart little girl, and I decided I wanted to study what had happened to me.

"I was at a summer camp, and we were camping on the beach at Martha's Vineyard, a beautiful island off the coast of Massachusetts. And on this island, this particular beach faced east. And I got up out of my tent and went, spontaneously, to sit on the beach in what I now recognize as Zen posture. I was sitting there, little folded legs and just very, very still – and I'd never sat still like that before – and watched the sun come up. And it was as if there were this incredible sense of the aliveness of the world. I saw the individual motes of light come up and then the sun, and I was *utterly* transformed by it and was so excited. And, being a kid, the first thought I had was, 'This must be what grown-ups know. This is, like, the great secret of being a grown-up.' So I was very excited to see my mother the next day. I got on the ferry, and she picked me up, and I said, 'Mommy, Mommy, I saw the sun come up!' But, you know, code for, 'I get it now!' And she was a very loving mother, and she said, 'Oh, that's so nice, honey. Sunrises are beautiful.' And I totally knew she didn't know what I was talking about."

Earlier Melissa had told me, "What Zen does in the world is it finds a way to talk about an experience which is very hard to talk about, 'cause whenever we put words to it, it divides it up. And it's this experience of a reality that's beyond what I like to call 'consensual reality.' It's the real, true perception – not an idea – of everything being one fabric, of everything being this one thing that's multi-faceted and is continually alive and going on."

After trying to talk to her mother about her experience, however, she felt the need to keep it secret, doubting that others would understand.

"I would say, for the next ten years – I was just entering being a teenager – I studied and read and asked questions, and I got interested in Buddhism and Hinduism and yoga through reading; I started practicing yoga through books. I almost became a Transcendental Meditation practitioner because I was trying everything. But I didn't because of a weird karmic circumstance where I was going to a workshop and the friend I was going with had a crisis, and we ended up spending the whole day in a subway station while she cried. I think I must have been about fourteen."

"You were headed off to a TM workshop at fourteen?"

"Yeah, I know, but I wanted to find the answer. I was looking for somebody who'd explain it to me. And when I was in my first year at Wesleyan University, one of my professors offered a course called Emptiness, which was a freshman seminar. There were only twelve people in it. He was a very wild and crazy guy. He actually became a friend of my husband's later. And he taught us how to meditate, taught us about Daoism, Buddhism, and Zen. He had lived in Japan briefly. And I read this stuff and I thought, 'Whoa! This makes sense!'"

But it would still be another eight or nine years before she took up serious practice. "So now we're talking around 1980. So I had met David. I was fresh out of college, looking for a job. Anthropology and music major. I was playing piano for dance classes at Wesleyan University and teaching voice and piano. And he was the co-coordinator of a food coop in Middletown, Connecticut, which is where Wesleyan is. And his other co-coordinator had left to go to India – which is what people did back then – and I applied for that job. I was hired by a committee, but we always joke that he hired me. We started working together and fell in love over the organic rice bins."

David and a friend, Randy Huntsberry, had formed a dance troupe, for which she became the accompanist. Huntsberry, coincidentally, was the professor who had offered the seminar on Emptiness. "Our group was called Sonomama, which means, in Japanese, 'just as it is.' And it was an improvisational company, mostly dance with some music. And David was a potter, and I was a musician, and we were trying to make our living running the food coop. Then, a friend of ours told us about his Zen teacher who was giving a talk, and we went to hear him, and both of us were like, 'Wow!'"

The teacher was Richard Clarke, who had studied with Philip Kapleau and then had established himself as a teacher even though Kapleau had not authorized him to do so. "Everyone else in the world of Zen says that he didn't have official transmission. So he was very isolated, but he was the only Zen teacher I knew. And he said, 'Go out and meet other Zen teachers.' But he was the guy. So both David and I studied with him. And then it came to be that he had those really terrible ethical boundaries that so many of those people did around then."

David left Clarke first and later studied with George Bowman of the Korean Kwan Um School, but Melissa – in spite of the unwanted attention Clarke paid her – stayed for a while. "Because I was really loyal to him, but then…like, the ethical stuff just went over the top, and I had to leave. So, I was a Zen orphan at that point. That's what James Ford called me when he met me. So, I'd been a Zen student for twenty years, and Richard had said, 'You're my Dharma heir….' It was an awful period for me, because I just loved Zen practice."

In the course of her Zen studies, she also met Jon Kabat-Zinn who was experimenting with mindfulness meditation in a stress reduction clinic he ran at the University of Massachusetts in Worcester. "We had moved here for a job that David had running a school. And I had also vowed to get my graduate degree in grief counselling. So we had both gone from being artists and musicians and – you know – kind of hippies in the '60s and '70s to professional people in the '80s. We'd turned into yuppies. It was kind of interesting. So I was a psychotherapist, and David was a headmaster of a school, and we started a new life here in Worcester, and I met Jon Kabat-Zinn and asked him for a job and ended up working for him and working at the Center for Mindfulness for the next twenty years. So my professional life was as a teacher of meditation and a trainer of teachers of meditation in the mindfulness community. Meanwhile I was also studying Zen with Richard Clarke, and then I met James.

"This is sort of a sweet story. He had just moved to the area from the west somewhere." She laughs. "He had come from the west like Bodhidharma. He came to be the minister at the Newton Unitarian Church, and we were members of the local Worcester Unitarian Church – David and I – because we wanted something for our daughter, some spiritual basis for her." She pauses for a long while and then continues, speaking slowly and reflectively. "And I had left Richard. I was his senior student. But I made a big declaration to the whole sangha that I was leaving. I was bereft. It was a horrible time. And yet we were functioning as teachers, although neither of us had received transmission to teach. Both George and Richard had said, 'Go ahead, start a group.' So we had been running a sitting group, a meditation group in Worcester since we first got here, and ran it out of our home and had a group at the church. So the associate minister at the church had met James at a conference for Unitarian ministers and had bragged to him, 'We have a Zen group at our church.' And James immediately asked, 'What's their lineage?' You know, the kind of questions you would ask. And our minister didn't know, so he came up to me one day in the dining hall and told me this story, and I just started to cry. It was just one of those moments. 'I used to have a teacher, now I don't.' So I said, 'Why don't you give me his email address. I'll tell him myself.'

"So, I wrote James: 'Reverend Tom Schade said blah blah blah.' And he immediately wrote back and said, 'Let's meet!' So we actually tried to meet a couple of times, and he kept standing me up. That's my recollection," she says with a laugh.

"*He* kept standing you up?"

"Yeah. And this turned out to be a thing he does. He just takes on too much. He makes me look like somebody with nothing to do, and I'm really busy. But he's just constantly busy. So we finally met. He came to our old house. We lived up the street in a nice house with our daughter. And he came and visited, and we just liked each other immediately. And after he interviewed me, I said I'd like dokusan. And he said, 'Sure.' And I had completed – in big quotation marks – koan practice with my first teacher. Which meant that I'd gone through the koans the Kapleau school uses. And he said to me, 'Why aren't you already a teacher? This is crazy.' And I said, 'Because, you know....' And then he did some investigation and found out the gossip about Richard. And I asked him if he'd take me on as a student. He said, 'Sure. You're going to be an advanced student.' I said, 'No. I want to start from scratch.' Because I was so traumatized from leaving my first teacher. So I just started the koan curriculum from the beginning.

"I worked with James all the way to the end. And just *loved* working with him. It was a completely different vibe. He's so friendly and so warm. And there had been a lot of rigidity in my original training – you know, from the Kapleau style – and in his training (which was from John Tarrant and Robert Aitken's line), the form's not so tight. So I loved that. I loved the freedom of it. And there were a lot of people who had been refugees from my old teacher who came to study with me even though I wasn't an official teacher, and I absorbed James's style of just meeting people with friendliness. And they loved it. They just loved it. And I loved it. I saw that people my first teacher had completely ignored – because they didn't fit some very narrow frame – were people of the Way. And I loved seeing that in everybody. So James realized that at a certain point I had his mind, and he decided to give me Dharma transmission."

James wanted to authorize her in both the Aitken-Tarrant lineage and the Soto tradition in which he had been ordained by Jiyu Kennett. "But to give me Jiyu Kennett's transmission, I had to ordain as a priest. So, I had *no* desire to be a priest, especially not a Soto priest. But I did it, because he was my teacher. And during the ceremony itself, it was really transformative for me. So I ordained as an unsui priest, and then – we did this in stages, and that's how we give transmission now to our students – I became a senior priest, a shuso. And then he gave me what's called *denkai denbo*, which is the first of two stages of transmission. So I received transmission both in the Soto tradition and in John Tarrant's line. And then, at a certain point, he gave me *inka shomei*, which in our tradition is a capper to denkai denbo, so that I can be called 'roshi.' We don't use those titles much in our school. Everyone calls me Melissa. And they call him James, and they call David, David.

"So James and I started teaching together. He had me start teaching before he gave me transmission. And David and I had been teaching together because we'd been running the Worcester group since 1991. And at a certain point we decided to throw in our lot together, the three of us. It was great for me, 'cause I had a certain way of teaching with David and a certain way of teaching with James. And that's created an interesting thing. I think one of the hallmarks of Boundless Way is that we honor these three transmissions. So David had then received transmission from his teacher, George Bowman, in the Korean Rinzai lineage. And we've incorporated elements from all three, the John Tarrant-Robert Aitken-Harada-Yasutani line, Jiyu Kennett's line, and Seung Sahn's line. Our liturgy is mixed together, all three. And then James gave transmission, recently, to another student, Josh Bartok, who's in Cambridge. And he had studied at Zen Mountain Monastery, so he brought in a lot of that style. So we try to honor all these different strains.

"All of these are different ways of pointing. We teach our students shikan taza – just the standard Soto practice – *and* koan practice. If you plot it on a bell curve, I think we have a couple of students who just do koan practice, and a couple that just do shikan taza, but the majority do some combination of both. They rest in shikan taza and mostly work with koans in dokusan. But sometimes they'll sit with them, if we give them instructions to. And people will also see us in dokusan. We have our private individual students, but we encourage our students to do dokusan with the other three teachers. And we have senior students, some of whom have permission to give interviews. So a student in Boundless Way Zen could see twelve different people for interviews in a month. And the onus – the responsibility – of practice is on the part of the student rather than teachers. So it's very student-oriented. And, of course, people do what we call shoken; they take individual vows with one teacher."

John Tarrant had written – in the book I kept returning to after each of my leg surgeries – that the spiritual path leads to "an experience of enlightenment or awakening, the veils that obscure our view are lifted and our oneness with God and the universe is revealed."[55] In some cases, however, that experience initiates entry onto the path, is its beginning rather than its culmination: Melissa watching the sun rise; Henry Shukman's experience on the coast of Ecuador; Shinge Chayat's discovery of stillness as a child. Joan Sutherland had noted that people came to practice "through two main doors." One was the problem of suffering, and the other was the spontaneous experience of awakening that the individual then wants to integrate in their life "make it something that's really alive in their lives at the time."

"For me," Melissa says, "Zen is really a path to joy. My whole life is about meeting suffering. Like my father died when I was fifteen, and I had a lot of terrible things happen to me off and on throughout the years. Not that terrible, but – still – difficult stuff. So I could have gone down that route. I was depressed. I was anxious. But this little core, this kernel of delight has always been the guiding light I keep orienting towards. Like, I know there's something beyond all this."

"Wonder, awe, gratitude, reverence," I say, offering her a personal formula I had come to through my own practice.

"Yes! Yeah! Wonder, awe, gratitude and reverence. I love it! When everything drops away, that's what's revealed!"

Which is by no means a denial of the reality of suffering.

"We've been talking about this recently," she tells me. "You know, since the first noble truth is the truth of suffering, there's sometimes the feeling that it's sequential; you have to suffer; then you have to see the truth of suffering, and then blah, blah, blah. But another way of looking at it is that suffering exists, and suffering itself – the truth of it – is ennobling. It is a noble truth of suffering. And suffering never goes away. But there is a way to live with it in a more spacious manner. And so we don't turn away from suffering. I think suffering and joy are like two sides of the same coin. But you can get stuck. You can also get stuck in joy, which could be a problem."

The house on Pleasant Street is also Melissa and David's home. Even after the Temple purchased the building and grounds a few months after my first visit, they continue to live there "as resident teachers." The zendo is on the right as one enters. There is a fireplace with a cluster of toys in the middle of the room; a Beanie-Buddha sits on the mantelpiece with a smaller Buddha in his lap. "That was a fridge-magnet, and the magnet fell off," Melissa explains. "So he needed a home."

The atmosphere does not lack formality. I sit with the group one evening, and protocols are rigorously adhered to. But there is still a home-like atmosphere.

Katherine Foo, a student at Clark University, was staying in residence during one of my later visits.

"It feels very welcoming here," she tells me. "The space in which Melissa communicates teachings – to me – is in all realms of living here, in a way that feels very welcoming. For example, you probably know that they use the interview as a way of teaching. It's not only around koans. And so I hadn't gone to the last two, because I had no question to ask. And this morning, Melissa made a point to check in with me before our day started after sitting, saying, 'You know, we say that it's optional, but really you should come.' And I asked whether I should come if I didn't have a question, telling her that after one of the Dharma talks and in an interview I had last week, I just had no more questions. Something shattered, and I was in a different place. And Melissa said, 'It's really important that you know that you can lean into us. That those interviews are a chance to find grounding and support in us, in the teachers.' She followed this by encouraging me to lean into the Sangha as well. And I felt there was something characteristic in that exchange about the way that Melissa teaches. She's very emotionally intelligent, and I think she sensed that I was withdrawing in my practice and that this can be my style or my tendency. And she wanted to be really clear and upfront that, 'This is how we practice, and we want you to know that we're here for you.' So there's a certain kind of power or strength in that, a directness. But also this warmth. So, for me, that teaching communicated a strong teacher-student relationship, but it wasn't only about the teacher-student relationship, but also the student-sangha relationship."

2

"David was a preacher's kid," Melissa tells me, "and grew up in an entirely different household than the one I did."

"My dad had a very visceral faith," David says. "He believed that God is someone we can know in our daily life. Not someone who sits in judgement, but someone we can engage with. So I'd always been interested in that. And in college – Wesleyan University – I did some study in religion, took a course called 'Understandings of Jesus' taught by a Marxist Christian who presented a different kind of Jesus than my dad taught. And that sort of expanded my thinking about what this revolutionary message might be. Then I took LSD. And in the trip I had this incredible experience of non-duality and knew for myself – without a doubt – that I'd never been separate; I'd always been connected. This was my junior year in college."

He pauses a moment, then backs up to explain that before university he had spent his senior high school year as an exchange student in Nagasaki where he had "heard about Zen, and it seemed like quite a ridiculous thing to do, to sit still and get whacked by sticks." He did, however, study judo while in Japan. "And we meditated before every practice. So I asked my teacher, 'What are we supposed to think about?' And he said, 'Nothing.' And it didn't make any sense to me.

"Anyway I was quite successful at Wesleyan. I was in the university senate and a resident advisor and co-captain of the wrestling team. But I was more unhappy than I had ever been before in my whole life. And I was incredibly disillusioned, because I had done everything I was supposed to do, and it didn't do anything for me. So it was a very difficult period of feeling this success – everything that I'd imagined, a brand name college and recognized and the president and I were on a first name basis – but I was very unhappy, very separate. So I took LSD this one time, and it really blew my mind. And actually part of the trip was a Christian metaphor. I had this image of being crucified and dying, and it was like twenty-four hours long, and, when it was over, I was grateful to be alive. I thought, 'This could have gone many different ways.' I never took LSD again.

"So I had this incredible experience and for several weeks after that people would just come into my dorm room – they just wanted to hang around – and I would see how beautiful they were. I would see that everything is fine. And they knew that I saw that. And so I tried to talk about this experience and went to the

Protestant chaplain who had *no* clue about what I was talking about. The Jesuit priest had read about this, but he didn't know either. So something had happened, but nobody could help me. And what happened then, over several months, is that the immediacy of the experience wore off. But it was very much about God and moving toward God.

"So that summer, I went out west and hitch-hiked and went up in the Beartooth Mountains in Montana by myself, figuring God was there. But I was just bored and didn't know how to deal with my mind and didn't find anything there. I really wanted to be holy, but, after about six months, I realized I was just on another ego-trip. I was there about ten days, up in the mountains, and then I came out, and I was hitch-hiking on a road going both directions, 'cause I didn't really care where I was to go. And I got picked up by two brothers, twins. One was an outdoor mountaineer, and the other was living in this Vedanta monastery in Upper Michigan. I ended up going back with the guy to the Hindu monastery, which was an orchard farm, and lived there for a week. I almost decided to stay, but I ended up going back for my senior year at school. It just got too confusing, and I decided the spiritual path wasn't for me."

Back at Wesleyan, he reassessed what he was doing in college. "I had always thought that education was finding out what the teacher wanted and giving it to her. So I did very well in school. And I read people well. So you give it to them, and they say, 'Oh, you're really smart.' Well after the LSD experience, I said, 'Oh, it has something to do with *me*.'

"I was the prodigy of the sociology department, but I realized suddenly that these people spent their lives studying life 'out there,' and I didn't want to spend my life studying other peoples' lives. So my senior year in college I started dancing, and I started doing pottery. And those two things – dancing and making a pot you could drink out of after writing papers that had very little meaning to me – were *incredibly* satisfying. I had money left over from scholarships, so I continued dancing, and I joined an improvisational dance company. I was a member for ten years and also started making pots and worked in the food co-op for a while." Where he and Melissa fell in love over the organic rice bins.

"Can we go back to that unhappiness you were talking about, before you set off for the Beartooth Mountains?" I ask. "Unhappy about what exactly?"

"A feeling of isolation and a feeling that everybody else wanted to be me except me. I was likeable, had a nice personality and all this. I think partly since my dad was a minister, I grew up really tuning into other people. When I tell women about that, they really resonate. I learned to get by by pleasing other people. And I did really well. I got a lot of what I wanted. But I had no clue what was inside me. I spent all of my time listening outside. So my senior year, the pottery and the dance and even the courses were much more, 'What do I want?' And I'm glad it didn't happen till my senior year in college, because it's much harder to get work in when you don't feel you have to. I was like, 'I don't have to turn this in for you to approve me.' Then the unhappiness shifted; it was more of a longing for that experience of oneness that I had and lost. But at some point I gave up the spiritual search and took a job at the food coop. Decided I'm not going to be a minister. I'm not going to go to seminary."

"Had that been expected?"

"That was an option. Although my father said, 'If there's anything you can do except seminary, you should do it.' He was disillusioned with the ministry and eventually left it to be a therapist because he felt he could continue God's work more effectively there."

"How did your family react when you went from being the sociology prodigy to being a potter?"

He pauses a moment before answering. "They were happy I was alive. My mother's brother killed himself when I was ten days old. And on my acid trip, I told them, I actually had a moment of deciding whether to live or to die and realized that it didn't make any difference, that life had happened in its fullness and length. So, they were terrified. 'What's happened to our son, and what's he gonna do?' But they were incredibly supportive when I spent a year dancing and making pots. They couldn't have been more supportive. Which is really extraordinary. They are really amazing human beings. And I was supporting myself; I was being responsible. I didn't spend much money; didn't need much money."

Then he and Melissa attended the talk by Richard Clarke. "I knew he knew this experience of non-duality, that he had been there. And he said, 'This is a place human beings can go.' And it was so vivid. I had never met anybody who talked like that. And he said, 'There's a way to move toward that, and it's to sit still.' And the Zen idea that it's already here – that there's not some other place we're trying to go or some other place we're trying to be – made it clear to me that this was the path. But I hated sitting still! It was like, you know, some people talk about, 'Oh, the first time, it was so wonderful!' I was like, 'Oh fuck! I'm gonna die!' My mind was going crazy! But I knew it was the path, and so I started sitting two minutes a day, because that's all I could tolerate. I figured if I tried half an hour a day, I wouldn't last a week. So, I said, 'I'm going to do this.' Two minutes a day. I'd set my little timer, and I'd be just about jumping out of my skin."

When I wrote to John requesting an interview, I included a list of the other Zen teachers I had arranged to speak with. In his reply, he warned me: "We are not a similar animal (we are doing a rather different project) to the other creatures you are talking to." I had been aware of that, but I was also aware that at one time he had been "similar" and that, as a result, two very different streams of teaching and practice in America are now traced back to him.

"I got interested through poetry," he tells me, "but I was also interested in the whole problem of having a mind, and having it work not that well. It seemed there were intrinsic product errors in the mind. My mind was often doing things that I hadn't given it permission to do."

We meet at his house in Santa Rosa, California, and begin our conversation outside. There is a Tibetan mask on one of the porch posts and, on the table by which we sit, a wooden Buddha – given to him by Robert Aitken – now missing one hand. But the ambient noises outdoors prove to be too intrusive for the recording, and we move to his office, which is a large, untidy room with art work and papers strewn about. It is not the pristine and austere work space one might associate with a Zen teacher, but it suits him. He sits in a wood and leather chair which creaks every time he shifts his weight; the creaking would be a greater challenge than his accent when I worked on the transcript.

"I lived with an Australian poet. It was one of those random things. A friend of mine happened to be the daughter of someone who had a place in Australian culture something similar to the place of Robert Frost in American culture." The poet was Judith Wright. "She had a big house in the country, lots of books and time. Her husband had recently died, and so she didn't mind having a young person about to dig in the garden and to have a glass of wine with at night and sit and talk to. So I had a lot of access to the world of poetry when I was quite young. But like many people at that time, I didn't fit my culture very well.

"The way I think of it now is that whatever Zen is pointing to is different from primeval Buddhism in that there is this sense of learning dance moves, of listening to music playing. It's different from finding the right technique or the right explanations. There is a doorway you can walk through, and when you walk through that door, life's more fun, more vivid, more empathic. So I'd had experiences like that, and I think they're natural. But for one reason or another those experiences of the rightness of the world had then become extremely unavailable. So I set off looking for them. That's the story I tell myself about Zen."

He had grown up in Tasmania, which he describes as being like the "back side of the moon. There weren't many people there. But it was an interesting place full of people who had run away from all over the world, and there was an underground

From the first, David tells me, Melissa was ready to try a retreat, but he doubted he would be able to sit still for a whole day. Mental turmoil was his primary challenge, but the physical challenges weren't negligible. "The first day retreat I did, my knees were really hurting. So I went in to see Richard, and he said, 'So I notice that you seem to be quite emotional, and – you know – tears coming up.' And I said, 'Yeah, my knees are hurting so bad!' And he looked at me, and he said, 'Why don't you sit in a chair?' So that was my first great Zen advice. You know? 'Why don't you sit in a chair?'"

He and Melissa began a regular practice with Clarke. "Every week, we'd go sit with him, and we did a number of retreats. The retreats were *incredibly* difficult for me, but I'm also an incredibly stubborn guy, a former athlete. I was a wrestler in college. So there was an athletic part to it – you know – 'I'm not gonna stop.' And also some urgency, and a clear sense that this is the hardest thing I've ever done, but even at that time I couldn't imagine anything more worthwhile."

Clarke's focus – like Kapleau's – was on attaining kensho. "And that fit into what I wanted. So my first ten years were pretty much chasing enlightenment."

Then Clarke began to show undue attention to certain of his female students, including Melissa.

"So that became somewhat of an issue for me.... No. Not somewhat of an issue. It was like, 'What are you doing?' And at that point he said, 'I'm sorry.' But he also said, 'You're making it up. It's not a big deal.' So when he confessed to the whole group, I didn't really believe him. And at that point I stepped back from him. But Melissa said, 'I really want to continue with this guy because there's something here.' So we set up some boundaries where it seemed okay. It seemed important for her to do that.

"That was the late '80s, I think. Something like that. And for a couple of years I was on my own."

In 1989, he was working at the Hammonasset School in Madison, Connecticut. "I taught pottery, photography, outdoor education. So I was a part-time art teacher, and the school was in crisis, and I ended up getting appointed to the board of trustees as the faculty rep."

The school was in financial trouble, and the board wanted to close it. But David helped a group of parents "raise a quarter of a million dollars in one week, because it was an amazing school. And I became interim head and then was appointed head with the idea of leading the school into the future. But the line was so sharply down it was impossible to turn it around. So I got to preside over the death of a school. My first great leadership assignment was doing that. But as part of that I got involved in the National Association of Independent Schools and through it met a psychologist who was working with George Bowman."

Bowman had transmission from Seung Sahn in the Korean Zen tradition and was operating the Cambridge Buddhist Association. "I started sitting some retreats with him, and I also started seeing him in sort of a Zen therapy kind of thing."

"What is that?"

David sighs then says with a laugh, "I think it's when you pay a Zen teacher to spend more time with you than you can get in dokusan. Uh…George was trying to make something up, figure out a way to support himself. So it would be me talking with him about my life as practice. But one of the things George has been big on is the *Genjokoan*.[56] So our real problem is not any old case of the Chinese masters, but our real problem is *us*. How do we work with our own lives?"

"Were you finding it any easier to sit by the time you met Bowman?"

"Somewhat. Although I vividly remember one of my early retreats with George, and, toward the end, he said, 'So noticing that we've settled down, and that we're all in this deep place….' And I'm like" – whispering – "'I'm not!' But I could sit really still. I don't think I have any natural bent for sitting still, but I see it as incredibly important and somehow I've learned from it. I don't know how, but I've been tempered or forged or ground up or whatever it is and so have a real faith in it.

"Slowly, over the '90s, it got better. But George was surprised when early on I said, 'You know, it's like taking my medicine.' I was pretty committed and faithful. *And* there were also times of great brightness and ease, but they wouldn't last. And that was incredibly upsetting, and I always thought I was doing it wrong. One of the things George has always been clear about is the opening and closing. Early on, he said to me, 'You know, sometimes I'm on top of the mountain and life is so beautiful and precious. And the next morning I wake up crumpled at the bottom of the cliff, and I think I've done something wrong. But it's not true.' So more and more it became apparent that sometimes we're clear, and sometimes we're confused. And this is not a problem to be overcome. This is called being human. So how do we live in this world where, even if we touch what is most precious, we can't hold onto it, and the more we try to hold onto it, the more we suffer. So that's the Zen that I know.

"So getting more at home with that. Now when I'm on retreat, and I feel the confusion coming, I don't always have to panic. Because before you got some clarity, got your Mu going or got your Who,[57] you could feel some wobble in it, and you could panic. And then you try harder, and you panic more. So now it's more" – in a singsong voice – "'Okay. So now the energy is dissipating. So now I am the dull-Buddha.' Or – you know – 'Now I am the sad and lonely Buddha.' And I am so grateful to George for this very clear teaching of present moment as the true way. And especially these moments that are habitual and we know are not it. The teaching is that everything is Buddha nature. It's already here. And there are times when I would bet my right arm that that's not true. They couldn't mean this place! But those difficult times are the entry places. You know? So that's much more part of my experience now."

Bowman bestowed inka on David in 2007 and final transmission in 2012. David explains, however, that he does not have a Kwan Um transmission because Bowman had disaffiliated himself from the school by then.

"When I was studying with George, he wasn't teaching the Kwan Um koan system because he had gone to study with Joshu Sasaki for the last thirty years. So my basic practice with George is shikan taza but with a kind of Rinzai flavor, looking at the present moment as a koan. So here it is and how do we manifest it? So not simply a spacious sitting but a real penetrating into this moment. But I have worked much less with koans than Melissa and James, who come from the Soto lineage. So it's an interesting flip-flop."

David also did two week-long retreats with Joshu Sasaki.

"He was extraordinary. You know, he works with very simple koans, and you meet him four times a day, whether you want to or not. The dokusan can last thirty seconds; two or three minutes is a long time. He doesn't speak English very well. And the first week I was there, I was really disoriented, but about the third day I settled in. So I went into my meeting with him and bowed, and he said, 'Oh! You've arrived.' You know? He knew. He could see, and I felt incredibly met. He wasn't interested in talking about how I felt or what was going on for me in the zendo. Wanted me to answer this impossible koan. Had absolute faith that I could answer it. I had absolute faith I could not answer it. And so I was there in this sesshin getting wrong answer after wrong answer, four times a day. But I decided the last night, 'Whatever it takes. Stay up and do it.' And so we're in a ceremony late one morning, and then everybody starts talking, and I said, 'What's happening?' And they said, 'The retreat's over.' I had missed the last night! It was quite wonderful! So I was an utter failure, and that was fine.

"I know that he's been incredibly immoral and damaged people and not been accountable to anybody, but he was an incredible, loving presence in a wordless way. Actually he said to me at one point, 'The essence of Buddhism is to love everything and not to struggle.' I talked to George about that, and George said, 'You know, he was reflecting *you*.' Because certainly this is my understanding, but I feel touched by him and met by him in some deep and wordless way."

When the Hammonasset School closed, David and Melissa moved to Worcester, where "I got a job as a headmaster of a gap-year program here in Worcester. It was for students mostly between high school and college where they would come from all over the country and live in apartments we owned here in Worcester. They'd begin with three weeks of Outward Bound then do a series of three full-time internships based on whatever they were interested in. This idea of learning from our life had been so powerful for me that I thought it would be great to do this. And we also worked with low-income kids in the public schools. It was a very Buddhist view of education in some ways; it's about uncovering and finding out what people love and telling them to do it."

David was with the school from 1991 to 2003, after which he left to pursue a career as a "Life and Leadership Coach."

"I work with people to help them clarify what they really love and to bring it into their lives. So I work with leaders, some in the for-profit world. Work with a lot of clergy. And work with creative people, teachers, and people in higher education. People who want to make a change in their life or take their business to the next level. And the model is that I don't know what anybody else should do, but I have a great faith that we all have some calling or something that we love. And that when we walk in the direction of what we love, we're most effective and we're most fulfilled.

"I work with people who are religious leaders, and we talk about God, if 'God' is the word they use. I'm quite comfortable as long as we know we're talking about some mystery that we can't know. I do a lot of work with the Episcopal House of Bishops. They have a coaching program where they have veteran bishops coaching new bishops. Peer coaching. And so for the last six years, every time the House of Bishops in the United States gets together, I go and do a training for a day about how to coach and coaching as trusting that the Spirit is already at work and trusting the radical competence of this new person. So moving away from, 'Well, I'm the old guy, and let me tell you how to do it,' to a much more spiritual basis. And so they know I'm a Zen person, but I talk about God and occasionally Christ and about a Spirit."

"So in Boundless Way," I note, "you have a Unitarian Minister, a Life Coach, at least two distinct Zen traditions. And somehow all of this works out?"

"Yeah, and I think it's one of the most powerful things about how we teach. Usually when there's one teacher, you think, 'Oh, this is what it looks like!' So Seung Sahn people start talking with Korean accents. Right? But when Melissa gives a Dharma talk, she's Melissa. When I talk, I'm David. And James is James, and we haven't made any effort to sound like each other. And the thing that excites me most about our sangha is that when our senior students give talks, they sound like themselves. They don't sound like me or Melissa or someone else. So, there's variety, but there's also this common thread, and, when we do retreats together, that feels incredibly important. It's incredibly rich."

I ask if it ever happens that a student expresses a desire to work with a specific teacher.

"We do get some people who have heard about James and want to work with him or Melissa or some me, and we say, 'This is how we play.' You don't have to go to dokusan with all of us, but I think once people do, they appreciate it because it's like they get reflected in a slightly different way. The common thing for us is an appreciation of what's in the room. So for me it's Buddha after Buddha coming into the room, and each one teaches me. I work with koans now too, but the approach is not – you know – you have to get my right answer or I'm sending you out of the room. It's what's alive; it's appreciating whatever appears in the room."

"What does Boundless Way mean?"

He laughs. "Well, my first answer is it's a come-on. 'Cause it's not boundless. There actually are some bounds." He reflects for a moment. "You know, I think it refers to a kind of expansive view. Yeah. I mean – as I say – I don't think it's true, but there is some aspect of it that I think the name does reflect. Some kind of Spirit. That this is not about being sectarian. I guess that's one of my biggest hopes, that we don't become 'Zen Buddhists,' that there is something here that's more important than the language we use or even the tradition we have. This is an amazing container for that, and people get it. You know? You can feel it when you walk into the building. You can feel it when you come on retreat. So maybe the Boundless Way is this thread that is not Zen, is not Christian, it's human life.

"The relationship between the four of us is the essential center of this organization. And how we treat each other and our willingness to be honest and to deal with difficulties as they come up is essential. Because in one way this is an incredibly robust organization, and in another way it – like everything else – is incredibly fragile. Because all four of us have permission to go off and be *the* man, and we continually have to come up against each other and be human together.

"People are often surprised when they come here. They say, 'You guys laugh a lot.' We say, 'Yes.' And I think it's so essential. This work is so important, and it can get so heavy and overwhelming as we all get a taste of it. But if we're not laughing, I think we're heading down the wrong path."

3

Josh Bartok's Greater Boston Zen Center is situated, along with Harvard and MIT, in Cambridge. It is a large, open space on the second storey of an old commercial building. There are three calligraphies by Shodo Harada in the entryway and an original set of the Ten Ox-Herding Pictures (the Zen equivalent of the Stations of the Cross) running along one wall. Josh admits he admires the aesthetics of Japanese Zen. In the sitting area, thirty-five zabutons and zafus are placed evenly on the floor; more, he informs me, can be added if needed.

What one first notes about Josh is his relative youth; he turned 43 just a few days before I meet him. "I'm youngish for a Zen teacher," he admits. Although we are both on straight-back chairs, he sits cross-legged. He speaks with a great deal of emotion and makes large gestures with his hands. His voice has power, and I suspect his Dharma talks are dynamic. There's also something a bit boyish about his manner. What I am most struck by, however, is his candor.

He grew up in a secular Jewish family in Northern Virginia. "Celebrated the holidays; ate the food. Never feel as Jewish as I do in front of a whole bunch of Jewish food." His parents were divorced, and he lived with his father, a psychiatrist. In his second year at Vassar College, he took a course on Buddhism which included a field trip to Zen Mountain Monastery. He found the experience intriguing enough to spend a month at the monastery the following summer. "And then I forgot about it."

His major was Cognitive Science. "It's an inter-disciplinary field of study, involving neural science, computer science, philosophy, linguistics, and psychology. I took a seminar on consciousness, and, by the end of the seminar, I could give you a systems-level explanation of consciousness; I could talk about computational models of consciousness and neurological disorders of consciousness. But I realized there were two questions I couldn't answer. One was: 'What the heck is this thing we call consciousness anyhow?' As a field, we couldn't actually arrive at a robust definition of what it was we were talking about when we used that word. Kind of like not being able to find the Self even after exhaustive search. That was one thing. The second question it couldn't answer was, 'Why does it hurt so much to be me?' That course clarified for me that that was the real question I was trying to answer."

"What were you hurting from?"

"A number of things. I was an angst-ridden adolescent and kid, and, by the end of college, I was emotionally struggling. I'd been in a major car accident at the end of my sophomore year, had a substantial concussion and subsequent brain injury that impacted my ability to do my work, to process and retain information. I was struggling with relationships, with imagining the future. At the time, I was sure was I going to go to MIT to do a Ph.D. in cognitive science. I think I even had my application filled out, but it never made it to the mailbox.

"There's a lake at Vassar, Sunset Lake, and I remember looking out over it as I was angsting away inside my head – it was someplace I went when I was stressed and overwhelmed – and I was looking at some ducks." He speaks slowly and with emphasis. "And these ducks were *just being ducks!* And I was so struck with the apparent ease and naturalness of that activity for them, the kind of *duckness* of their being ducks. At the same time I was struck by how hard, how excruciating it was for me to be me. Fortunately I had had enough exposure to Zen at that point that I was vaguely able to conclude, 'I think this may have something to do with how I use my mind.' So in that moment, I decided to *not* do what I had been sure I was going to do, namely go to grad school."

Instead, immediately after graduation, he went back to Zen Mountain Monastery where he lived for the next year and a half.

Josh has mixed feelings about his time at ZMM and about Daido Loori.

"I'm profoundly grateful to Daido and his militaristic approach at ZMM. He had what I'm going to call a closed-handed, withholding style. Everything about his teaching and the way the monastery functioned, implicitly and explicitly, conveyed a message that there is something *you haven't gotten.* 'I have something you don't' is the implicit message. Even his way of saying, 'I have nothing you don't have' also conveyed, 'I have something you don't.' And that was so important to me. It was motivating and attention-grabbing. I don't think my teacher, James Ford, would have been able to reach me at that age, as a 20 year old know-everything, angsted-out and wanting something to grab on to. So I really needed that; it was helpful to me."

On the other hand: "During a mondo – a kind of semi-casual semi-formal Zen dialogue thing – Daido was talking about his approach to Zen teaching, koans and dokusan and such. And he said, 'The student points to the relative; the teacher points to the absolute. The student points to the absolute; the teacher points to the relative. The student points to both; the teacher points to neither. The student points to neither; the teacher points to both.' 'That,' he said in summary, 'is Zen teaching.' I raised my hand and asked, 'How is that not just being an asshole?'"

"And he said?" I ask, laughing.

"You know, that's where the memory ends."

One of the things he found lacking at ZMM was a supportive sangha.

"All of the monastics at the time I was there were in relationships with each other. And that took place in the context of the Zen Mountain Monastery rule that you can't start a relationship while living there. And yet, from Daido on down, all of the monastics were partnered. And it was excruciating for me. The monastic schedule was hard, but that was fine. The thing that became too painful for me was the period off schedule – hosan, free time – when the community evaporated. The monastics paired up with their partners and went off, and I was left behind.

"There wasn't any support. There wasn't, really, a sangha. It was like a work-week sangha. And in struggling with all of this, I reached a really black depression. I was struggling with my longing for intimacy, for relationship, and those kinds of things. And I talked to one of the senior monks there, and he said, 'Well, you know, just turn it off. Like a faucet.' I remember his faucet-turning gesture. Like that! And that was so profoundly unhelpful, so invalidating, so almost anti-human that I reached a kind of a suicidal level of depression. There's a little cemetery up the hill, and there's one memorial for somebody who I knew nothing about aside from his name and the dates of his life which made it clear he was in his young 20s when he died. And I was certain he was a suicide. I have no knowledge of that, but that's something I felt. And I would often spend time – a lot of time – in front of that grave.

"And I reached a place where I decided, 'That's it. I'm going to kill myself.' I had a plan. I was going to swallow silver-polish or something like that. I had no one to talk to. Just the unfollowable advice to 'just turn it off like a faucet.' During doku-san, when you got in, you were lucky to get a sentence out before you got rung out. Sometimes Daido seemed halfway to his bell as you were making your first bow to him. So that was not a context for feelings. But then somehow my depression broke into a kind of almost manic clarity. And I realized, 'You know what? I'm just going to *leave*.' So I told the head monk that, and he said, 'You renewed a year commit-ment. You can't leave.' I said, 'I understand. I'm leaving.' And he said, 'Okay, well, you should tell Daido.' I did. I don't actually have a memory of that conversation, but I do remember the head monk then saying, 'Okay, so, pack your car and be out of here in three hours.'"

He spent a few days in Woodstock, then drove to Boston. "I had been the editor of the *Mountain Record* while I was at ZMM, and I really enjoyed that stuff. I talked with a friend who was writing some poetry, and I really enjoyed talking with her about that and the refining of the words, so I got it in my head that I wanted to be an editor, and I wanted to be an editor of Buddhist stuff." Three major Buddhist pub-lishers – Shambhala, Tuttle, and Wisdom – were all located in Boston at the time.

"I got a tiny amount of freelance stuff from Shambhala and Wisdom, and some manuscript reviewing for Tuttle. But it didn't really take hold. I couldn't make it work. And I eventually gave up on trying to be an editor." He sits for a moment reflecting, then says, "When the manic 'I can do anything' experience left, I got really depressed again. I was really hit hard by my lack of supports."

I ask if he is bi-polar, and he doesn't answer immediately. When he does, he speaks very precisely.

"So, the answer to that is complicated. I do meet the criteria, or I have met the criteria, for major depression and major manic episodes. But I've never had a manic episode aside from when on very high doses of steroids for Crohn's disease and this single episode induced by – I think – the stress and strain and invalidation at Zen Mountain Monastery. So not classic or syndromal in any sense. I've never been on lithium. I have been on other mood stabilizers, when I have to take steroids, but I'm not now and haven't been on them for a long time. However, I have been on anti-depressants, which are helpful to me in a way not exactly in keeping with the syndromes of bipolar disorder."

He pauses again, and I tell him we don't need to continue the subject if he'd rather not.

"No, I'm fine discussing it, but I am ambivalent about whether I would want to see it in print. On the one hand, I think it's really useful for people to be able to see Zen teachers as coming from specific and painful kinds of paths and histories. It's just that I didn't wake up today *planning* on telling this story. But I'm happy to continue."

After the manic energy which preceded his decision to move to Boston faded, he once again felt suicidal. He considered hanging himself but couldn't go through with it. He tried turning to alcohol for a while. "But I really didn't like alcohol, didn't like being drunk," he says laughing. "So the path of substance abuse through alcohol didn't really seem like it was going to work for me either. I punched through a window in my apartment just because I understood that that was something that people sometimes do, and I thought it might somehow help. It didn't really help much, and now I had a broken window and a cut hand."

Throughout this period, he had been seeing a psycho-pharmacologist who had given him a prescription for Ativan. One day he took seven pills, "Which is totally not at all in the ballpark of enough to actually kill a person, and, left to my own devices, I would have woken up the next day maybe, well-rested or hung-over or something. But I'd been talking to my dad every day, and he was expecting me to call, and when I didn't and he couldn't reach me, he accurately guessed what had happened. So he called an ambulance for me, and I woke up to EMTs knocking at my apartment door."

His father arranged for him to be admitted to Harvard's McLean Hospital where Josh remained an in-patient for ten days, including his 23rd birthday. "So there I was at McLean, and I realized I was with people who were *really* sick, people who had profound problems. And part of what had always been hard for me existentially was taking responsibility for my life. And now I realized I had reached a place, a circumstance, in which I had successfully abdicated responsibility for my life. I was now in a place where I *didn't* have to take any responsibility for anything, I could just be *sick,* and the hospital would take care of everything. I could just be like these people. But now that I had it, I could see I didn't want that. And I started to get a certain amount of my shit together."

His personal experiences led him to work in human services. "I started out working in behavior management in a skilled-nursing facility that worked with people with brain injuries and violent behavioral sequelae. So I was restraining and checking on people. Then I moved up to doing cognitive therapy with brain-injured people as a behavior specialist. After that I worked in a special needs school as the assistant clinical director."

At the same time, he had a side job reading Tarot Cards. "I originally started doing it for free, but it turns out you can't get any customers if you do it for free. People are so certain that they're going to get what they paid for that it communicated it wasn't that valuable. So I started charging for it and did that for a substantial period of time. I wouldn't read the future. What I would tell people was that I would read the *present.* The way Tarot works is very interesting. It's a really beautifully encoded system of human wisdom. Once you learn the cards and the heart of them, any set of cards you draw for anybody, if skillfully read, will have something useful to say regardless of whether anything else is going on at the time. And this started to relate to my sitting because part of what I would do is just pay attention and listen to people, including listening to myself and the things that arose in my mind that ordinarily I would dismiss because I couldn't quite account for what those things were doing there. So in that way, it was kind of a Dharma practice for me and arose out of meditation practice."

He was also sending his resumé around and received an offer from Tuttle to be an in-house editor on a freelance basis. "So finally, after seven years in Boston, I got back to why I moved here." He worked on a number of Buddhist books. He was sitting on his own but also traveled to Oregon a few times to attend sesshin with Chozen Bays and spend time with her community.

From Tuttle, he moved to Wisdom Publications. "And one of my colleagues at Wisdom would ask me about Zen a lot, and I would tell him about my experiences and share my understanding with him and was very clear, 'Zen teachers are a specific thing, and I'm not one of those. I'm just a guy talking to you.' But we started sitting together, originally in a cubicle that was empty in the morning. Then we shared a space in Davis Square, near the Wisdom offices, with another sangha, I think it was the Friends of the Western Buddhist Order. So we rented space from them for a tiny amount of money per month and started a sitting group that was unaffiliated with anything. We made a website and invited other folks to come sit with us, and although he and I both provided beginning instruction in zazen, we were very clear that we weren't Zen teachers. And people came. It was a small group of good folks."

"Over the course of the next couple of years, part of my work at Wisdom was acquisitions scouting, trying to find interesting authors or new teachers. So I would monitor lists of current Zen teachers and write to some of them." One of these potential new authors was James Ford. Josh wrote to him care of an address in Arizona.

"Then I got a call from him at my desk at Wisdom, and he said, 'So, how did you find out about me?' And I explained that I'm always monitoring to see if anybody new comes to town, and I'm also doing acquisitions scouting. And he said, 'So when you were looking for people around here, you found me?' I was, like, 'No, I wrote to you in Arizona.' And he said, 'Oh, no, it got forwarded to me. I live right here in Newton now.'"

They met, and Josh's sitting group eventually aligned itself with the group James had established at the First Unitarian Society of Newton. "But I had James on sort of an extended probation because he was *so* not like my image of what a Zen teacher is. Part of why Daido worked for me as a first teacher – and also part of his shadow – is that he did seem to be exactly like what you think a Zen teacher *should* be like, cigarette-smoking excepted. But James was *nothing* like that. So in my mind, I was looking askance at him for a couple months, maybe even years. 'Does this guy have anything going on at all?' It just wasn't clear to me at first, but over time it became clear he did. And it also became clear that he had an astonishingly generous and good heart. He was just such an excellent example of a good person, of a mensch."

An example of his generosity was the way he reached out to Melissa around this time, as a result of which the sitting group she and David hosted in Worcester came to join together with James' Unitarian group to form Boundless Way Zen.

"I will take credit for coming up with that name. It sprung from something that James said to me. I was stressing about something about myself or my practice or something, and James looked at me, and he said, 'Josh, the Way is wide and forgiving.' And that kind of became the seed for something. 'Wide Way' didn't sound right, more like a plus-size men's store. But the Zen way is actually beyond wide. It's boundless. So that's how we got there.

"And James sees part of what he's doing in the world as finding Dharma orphans and helping them. I was one those. I was intensely committed to the Dharma and had been doing Dharma stuff in different kinds of contexts since I was 20-something.

So I was among his Dharma orphans, as was Melissa, and now he's adopted others as well."

Twelve years after beginning work with James, Josh was authorized as a teacher in his own right.

I ask if he still suffers from depression.

"So, I don't suffer from incapacitating depression; I still suffer from depressed moods and anxiety. But these have been great Dharma teachers for me." He pauses a moment before continuing. "I started taking anti-depressants and many of them were excruciatingly not good for me, and one was really helpful. But even once I found the one that was helpful, I fought against the idea of taking it. It felt like a moral or spiritual failing or a deficit of will-power or something. So I resisted the fact that I needed that. And I did – functionally – a whole bunch of on-off-on trials in which I would stop taking the medication, and, reliably within two months, I would be back in Hell. Then I would take it again, and it would resolve back into the regular difficulties of life. But then I'd need to prove it to myself again after a period of time. And I did this enough times to convince myself that it seems – for whatever reason – I need this. Now this doesn't mean that my mood doesn't go down or that I don't have struggles. The image I have is that we all have our mountain we need to climb, and part of what depression – or a biological disposition to depression – can do is put you in a pit at the base of that mountain. And what medications can do, at their best, is get you up to level ground where *all* you have to do is climb your mountain as opposed to having to struggle your way out of a pit or out of quicksand over and over and over again.

"So, again, I wouldn't say that I have bi-polar disorder, but my moods do cycle up and down. And this has been an enormous teacher for me. I have enormous practice with both high moods and low moods which have helped me see that these subtle mental formations are moods and emotions. They still come, but I'm able to recognize, 'Oh, this is just fear. It's just anxiety. This is that depression thing that happens to me.' So there are times when I get anxious and overwhelmed, and I will occasionally take my sleeping bag into the darkened bathroom and just huddle in the dry bathtub with the covers over my head for a little while, but, kind of rapidly, I arrive at, 'Okay. Good enough now.' And I go back about my business."

"There are people who would question whether one can practice Zen while on medications," I point out.

"And so what would that even mean, if it were true? If you are on meds, you're fucked? The Dharma doesn't apply to you? Sorry, but you're screwed? I mean, what is that? So the reason I'm comfortable talking about this is that it needs to be said. There needs to be something that is a possibility for the rest of us, even and especially those of us who struggle. I love the Dharma so much, and for thirteen years at Wisdom I spent my time with my head in peoples' Dharma minds and Dharma words and Dharma books. And the Dharma has transformed my life and has made my life make sense. It has helped me be a good person and a good partner, and it has helped me do stuff that scares me. It has helped me do stuff that I care about. It has helped me do stuff that matters in the world. It's helped me make a difference in the lives of other people. What would it even mean if the Dharma were somehow closed to me because I have what seems to be a kind of biological disposition for getting incapacitated by depression?

"And, moreover, the Dharma completely failed to end my depression. So partly what it's done for me is help me find liberation *amid* suffering rather than liberation *from* it. And that is much more robust, so much more useful, so much more reliable. My moods have taught me something really important about the Dharma too: to see that the Dharma cannot be about some content of mind or some content of consciousness and not some other content of mind and not some other content of consciousness. Contents of consciousness are only ever going to be contents of consciousness, and the Dharma is much bigger than that. The nature of my mind necessitated that I really clarify this for myself. Medications don't begin to do your spiritual work for you. You still have to do it, and you still have to make use of Dharma tools. And in my case what the medications have enabled me to do is to do that."

"Almost everybody comes to Zen – in a certain sense – for the wrong reasons. Many of us come to Zen because we want to feel calm or we want to relax or we want to have thicker and stronger and more indestructible armor to protect us from the slings and arrows of being human and living a life amid other humans. And what I call one of the Great Bait-and-Switches of Zen is that rather than getting more and thicker armor, what we come to see is that we don't actually need the crappy, fallible armor that we have been so desperately clinging to. We can let go of even that armor. And this doesn't mean that we don't feel pain; in fact, it means we *more fully* feel it. And we can let these things into our hearts, into our lives and be undestroyed by them. This is the significance of the title of James's book, *If You Are Lucky, Your Heart Will Break*. That pain – that difficulty, that weeping, that suffering of the world – that's the good stuff. That's what it's about. And so this is a path about being more fully human. In addition to everything else, the Dharma is a really sophisticated way of looking at the human mind and the world and the nature of suffering, and it just makes a lot of sense to me. Walking the Zen path is hard; and it's painful; and it's slow; and it's not what most people want, especially when there are other things that say, 'Hey! We will totally reduce your stress! Hey! If you meditate, you will get these abilities! Learn how to stop thoughts!' Or, 'You don't even need to meditate! You can just use this little device that you put on your finger; or you can just listen to these sounds; or you can just take this dietary supplement!'

"Part of what I love about the Dharma is that it just *makes sense*. I often say, 'It's not true because it's the Dharma; it's the Dharma because it's true.' It's what's there when you actually carefully look."

Compared with what John Tarrant and Joan Sutherland are doing, Boundless Way Zen appears traditional – perhaps even staid – but it has carried out its own experiments. Josh has a facility with analogies and compares the current scope of North American Zen to "the Cambrian explosion when it was as if nature was trying out all these different body types for creatures and whole bunches didn't work, didn't last, but some of them did. And this is what's going on now. There's a whole lot of mutations going on; some of them will prove adaptive and sustainable. Many of them will not."

The collective model of Boundless Way Zen, for instance, has resulted in what he calls a "progressive apprenticeship model to teaching."

"One of the things that can happen with Zen is it becomes binary, in that you're either a teacher and completely beyond reproach, or you're not and should really just shut up. But we have several levels that we invite people to step forth into Dharma teaching in various ways and contexts."

He admits that it can be challenging for students to have four teachers, "each of us from a different perspective, with a different personal view and karma and all that."

But the benefits outweigh the challenges. "In a certain way, if you only have one teacher then it's hard to differentiate your teacher's view from the Dharma itself. And teachers – certain kinds of teachers – tend to play into that thing. One of the shadows of Zen is the tendency to minimize that our own view has any impact on the expressions of the Dharma or to say that it somehow shouldn't. So to the extent that you only have one teacher, it becomes hard to differentiate their view from the Dharma itself. But when you have multiple teachers, it becomes like one of those Venn Diagrams. There are these overlapping circles, and there is a portion of it that thoroughly overlaps, and there's also big portions of it that don't overlap. I think that really serves students by doing two things. One, it clarifies that there's stuff in one's teaching that is personal, that is related to personal karma. There's personal styles and expression, and that that isn't the Dharma itself necessarily. So, it was easy when studying with a charismatic teacher like Daido to subtly mistake, 'I really want to clarify the Dharma for myself' for 'I want to be like John Loori,' and to think that being like him is somehow the goal, to think that the Zen path meant being like your teacher when, in fact, it means being like yourself.

"The second benefit of the over-lapping and non-over-lapping qualities of our teaching – and we encourage students to use all of us teachers – is that you can't be exactly like your teachers, because they aren't exactly like each other. So that sets up a fruitful dissonance which almost requires students to find the heart of the Dharma for themselves, find what their Dharma expression is, find what resonates with their heart, find what they can verify, and find how they want to use it. Because there are these multiple examples of what a Dharma life is, and it's not possible to be like even one, but especially not to be like more than one."

Josh admits that from one perspective it doesn't matter if traditional Zen survives but then quickly adds, "However, I love Zen so much; I love the tools of Zen and the forms of Zen; I love the texts of Zen. And this tradition as it currently exists has been extremely helpful to me. And I, pedagogically, see how much the tools of the tradition help me to teach and what a loss it would be for that tradition to disappear! It doesn't mean the truth of the Dharma would or even could be lost. But anybody being able to wield *these* tools skillfully, *that* could be lost. And then we'd have to find other tools. But, right now, we have some adequate tools that still need refining."

A sense of lineage is important to him.

"But we don't derive legitimacy from that alone. The thing is, Dogen and Hakuin, they were great teachers who skillfully taught something that's important. And we see ourselves as having learned this important thing, and we're also teaching it. And we fully acknowledge that there are many places where the lineage charts are totally made up. So I have a lineage scroll that shows me going back in direct lineage to the Buddha which is completely fictional in a really important way. And also – in addition to being not true – it's totally true."

"That in some way, shape, or form there has been this continuity of teaching."

"Right. It's not nothing. The Dharma is a specific thing. It's the Dharma."

"And," I suggest, "as it evolves in the United States, it will necessarily differ from Asian Zen."

"So there's this Cambrian explosion of Dharma forms. And some of them are going to survive and some of them aren't. And just like species, even though they have a common ancestor, this one doesn't recognize that one as a mate anymore.

They are different species. And that will happen with the Dharma too. And that's okay."

CHAPTER TWELVE

Bernie Glassman

T HAT ALL THINGS ARE SUBJECT TO CHANGE IS SO EVIDENT IT ONLY WARRANTS
being considered a basic tenet of Buddhism because of the human tendency
to ignore the fact or to seek to prevent it. Zen teachers, of course, are as
subject to change as anyone or anything else.

In 1971, Bernie Glassman was the Chief Administrator of Taizan Maezumi's
Zen Center of Los Angeles. At the same time, he was also an aeronautical engineer
at McDonnell-Douglas. By 1979, he had left engineering and was in New York City
where he surrendered his jacket and tie for a shaved head and the formal robes of a
transmitted Zen teacher, complete with attendants to position those robes correctly
when he took his seat in the zendo. A little later, he doffed the robes for overalls and
drove a delivery truck distributing baked goods to upscale dining establishments in
the city. When I meet him at his home in Montague, Massachusetts, he's casually
dressed in a blue patterned shirt and loose white slacks with suspenders that he occasionally adjusts as we speak. He's bearded and wears his long grey hair tied back in a
pony tail. Toward the end of the interview, he takes a clown's nose from his pocket
and puts it on.

I begin by asking if he is still teaching.

"It depends on how you define teaching. Not in a formal way. I have many
Dharma successors. If someone wants to study, I will refer him to them. But I
organize these Bearing Witness retreats. If somebody says they want to learn about
Bearing Witness or about the tenets of the Zen Peacemakers, I say, 'Well, come to a
Bearing Witness retreat.' Other than that, I do some workshops – very few – at some
of the places that are run by Dharma successors of mine. About five of those. Then
a couple I do with my wife, Eve, in places where it's beautiful, and we can combine
it with vacation. And I volunteer in different parts of the world, and maybe that's

my biggest teaching. So some people go with me but mostly just the fact I'm doing that – I think – is a statement."

He was born in 1939 in the Brighton Beach area of Brooklyn, a low income, immigrant neighborhood – "So I've always felt comfortable in poor areas" – the fifth child and only son of parents who had come to the United States from Eastern Europe.

"My mother died when I was eight. She had three sisters in the States. The rest of the family died in Poland."

"During the war? They were Holocaust victims?"

He nods his head. "Right at the beginning. And her sisters in the States were all in the Communist Party. My father wasn't really socially involved, but he had three sisters, and *they* were all in the Communist Party. I was brought up in that kind of environment. My cousin was the head of the Communist Youth Movement."

He was an inquisitive child and took to disassembling and reassembling small appliances, radios, and television sets. This innate curiosity led him to study engineering. "The school at that time was called – maybe it still is – Polytechnic Institute of Brooklyn. It merged with NYU. Had a very good mathematical department. I was focusing on aerodynamics, but when I graduated I went into interplanetary work. There's no air," he says, chuckling, "so we were much more concerned with dynamics. I oversaw the development of manuals for trajectories to go to Mars, manned missions to Mars. It was that kind of work. But in 1958 when I was a junior, in an English class one of the books we had to read was *The Religions of Man* by Huston Smith. And there was one page on Zen, and it really caught me. So I read everything in English on Zen.

"After I graduated, I was sitting in a pizza place with a friend – he was in my graduating class, also an aeronautical engineer – and he said, 'What do you want to do with your life?' And I said, 'Well, there's three things I want to do. I want to live in a Zen monastery.' So this is 1960. 'I want to live on a kibbutz in Israel. And I want to live in the Bowery, in the streets of New York.' And now I've done all three.

"So I hired into Douglas – it's now McDonnell Douglas – and in '62 I left. I quit, and I went to Israel to explore living there. I would have been drafted if I had just left McDonnell-Douglas, so I wound up getting a teaching assistantship at the Israel Technion in Haifa. I was there a year."

"What led you to the kibbutz?"

"My early readings. Around Bar Mitzvah time, somewhere between twelve and fourteen, I did this major exploration of – not religion so much – but I called it 'reasons for and against the existence of God.' So I read through lots of literature, and I got very interested in the kibbutz movement. This one kibbutz observed Shabbat as a day of silence, and they did a lot of meditation, and those ideas were totally in line with everything I was reading. But Israel was too chauvinistic for me. Like everybody had a chip on their shoulder, and 'This will never happen to us again.' And 'We're not going to be servants to anyone.' That was my experience at any rate. So I decided not to stay."

He had, however, met the woman who became his first wife – Helen Silverberg – on the ship going over. Back in the United States, he sent out his resumé to appropriate corporations, and, once again, McDonnell-Douglas made the best offer, so he returned to them. He and Helen married and settled in Santa Monica. It was the early '60s, and there was a lot of interest in Zen and related issues among young people. Bernie became involved with a group of similarly minded individuals who read Philip Kapleau's *The Three Pillars of Zen* and tried to follow the zazen instructions it provided. They even paid a visit to the ethnic Japanese temple in LA, where Bernie first met the man who would later become his teacher, Taizan Maezumi.

Hakuyu Taizan Maezumi had been raised and trained in the Soto tradition of his father, who was a temple priest. Later he received transmission in the Rinzai and Sanbo Kyodan lineages as well. The Soto-shu, the central authority of the Soto school in Japan which would send Shunryu Suzuki to San Francisco in 1959, sent Maezumi to Los Angeles three years earlier. It was his first official posting; he was 25 years old at the time.

"He was a young monk working in the temple in Little Tokyo in LA," Bernie continues, "and I started to sit there. But then I left because there was really no English there. So I created my own zendo in my garage, and I did it myself. And then I think it was around 1966, I saw there was going to be a workshop led by Yasutani Roshi. So I went to that workshop, and this young monk was the translator. I realized, 'Wow! He speaks English.' I recognized he had been in this Temple in Little Tokyo, but now he had his own place. He had just opened it, and I joined him. So from '66, I was totally with him, going every day, and I became his right-hand man."

Bernie passed the koan Mu during a sesshin presided over by one of Maezumi's teachers, Koryu Osaka. Later and deeper openings – what he calls, using Hakuin's terminology, dai-kenshos – were yet to come. But Maezumi was confident now that he had a student who would be able carry on his teaching, and, when he returned to Japan to complete his own koan work, he left Bernie in charge of the LA Center. On his return, Maezumi ordained Bernie and gave him the Dharma name Tetsugen, meaning "to penetrate subtleties."

Later that year, when he was sent to Japan, Bernie accomplished the second goal he had set himself after graduation. When he returned, he was – by his own admission – a "fanatic." He and Helen moved into the ZCLA residential program with their two children.

His dai-kensho occurred in 1976.

"As far as I'm concerned, the function of Zen is to help people experience the interconnectedness of life. The oneness of life. So there have been many upayas throughout the years of how to do that, and it's not strictly relegated to Zen. So Zen – as you know – means 'meditation.' And that's been a major upaya. But even in Zen, all kinds of techniques and tricks have been used to help people have that experience. In '76, I had an experience which changed my venue of teaching from the zendo – the meditation hall or the temple – to society. I had an experience of what I call the 'Hungry Ghosts' – which is a term in Buddhism – but an experience of the thirsts and the hungers of everything around. And simultaneously I experienced it as myself, as that these were all aspects of myself. And a vow came up to try to satisfy those hungers. Those were hungers for food. Hungers for power. Hungers for love. Hungers for greed, status, acknowledgement. All kinds of hungers. So my work really moved into whole different spheres."

He's collapsing time. Before he became deeply engaged in alternative upayas, his original approach to teaching had been more traditional. When he was interviewed by Helen Tworkov in the mid-1980s, he told her that for a long while

> I followed a standard textbook way of passing *mu* which doesn't happen all that often. And in a way I got trapped by that. It took me a few years to realize that it doesn't happen that way all the time. I was naïve and thought that 'I' worked really hard. So I thought all you had to do in the zendo was push a person really hard and that 'it' would happen. And, also, I felt that it was extremely important for some kind of opening to occur. In this I was influenced by Yasutani Roshi. I felt that openings were critical and that you really had to push. And I saw a lot of effect from doing that. I saw that by pushing people in certain ways you really could get them to let go and they really did have some kind of experience. So there was reinforcement for this style. Then, over the years, I began to see the shallowness and decided that it was not the best way of doing things. It's very dramatic and you gain a lot of power and everyone's having these far-out experiences, but over the long run my own sense was that it wasn't where Zen practice was at.[58]

Maezumi operated ZCLA along traditional lines, and Bernie couldn't change that. But as chief administrator it was his responsibility to find ways to financially support the center, and what he could do was look for ways which also responded to the needs of the largely poor and Hispanic neighborhood in which they were located. With the help of Dr. Jan Chozen Soule (now Bays), for example, he established a medical clinic.

"Tetsugen was Roshi's first successor," Chozen told me. "The first serious student, resident student, who moved with his family into the Zen Center, and he had a model which involved establishing businesses which would help support the center. So we had Zen Landscaping, Zen Painting, Zen Carpentry, publishing – which brought Daido Loori in – and the clinic.

"Tetsugen's idea was to take peoples' talents and use them in the Dharma setting in the Zen Center. So he said, 'Oh great. When you come, you can set up a clinic.' So we started a clinic which was, at first, just to serve the people at the center and then the neighborhood. So a poverty clinic, and I was used to working with poor patients and Hispanic patients, so that was fine. Then somebody came who was a nurse; so we had a nurse at the center. And we gradually added people." They acquired a nurse-practitioner – "a new idea at the time" – and a second physician, as well as specialists in chiropracy, acupuncture, naturopathy, and homeopathy. "So we had this combination of Western and alternative medicine which was very unique at that time, and people from wealthy areas, Hollywood and Rodeo Drive, would come to the clinic. So we had this weird situation where we had Sikhs and people with Gucci bags and very, very poor Hispanic patients, all together in the same waiting room."

In Bernie's mind, it was all Zen practice.

"Where the zendo was in LA was a poor area," he tells me. "So I started that clinic. And I founded a number of businesses. Already my thinking was moving that way, but still my main interest was helping people to become One. And I was starting with a standard kind of enlightenment experience. But my definition of 'enlightenment' kept shifting.

"The enlightenment experience is an awakening to the interconnectedness of life, but it keeps deepening. So at first it's really awakening to the oneness of oneself. And then of the family. And then of the group. And then of the society. And then of the world. Then of the universe. Almost any Zen workshop I'm in, I'll start by defining what I mean by enlightenment – the experience of the interconnectedness of life – and I'll quote Kobo Daishi who's the founder of the Japanese tantric sect, Shingon, and he said that you can tell the depth of a person's enlightenment by how they serve others. And I've sort of drifted into that."

In December 1979, Maezumi asked Bernie to establish a center in New York. "For me, a very key thing was that over and over he said to me that I should take whatever I can from him – in terms of Zen – and then spit out what I think won't work in this country. He said, 'I'm not an American. I'm Japanese. And I can't present the American Zen. You've got to do that.' That was key. And when I went to start the Zen community in New York, he said, 'I'm gonna stay away for a year so you won't be influenced by me or want to do things that please me. You're on your own.' That's very rare. 'Cause most Zen teachers I've met want their students to replicate them. And he made that very clear that that was not the point."

I ask if there had been a community associated with Maezumi in New York before Bernie went there.

"It's sort of interesting, the whole phenomena, because in '78 I went on a trip around the country basically to talk to parents of students that were at the Zen Center of Los Angeles. There was a lot of disharmony, and a lot of parents were afraid their kids were in a cult. So I decided to go around and talk with them and show them pictures and talk about what's going on. At that time, my intention was to remain in LA and help that get bigger and bigger and do my things there. But to help fund the trip, I would give talks at colleges or different places, and in New York I was on a radio show, an NPR kind of radio show. The show was called 'In the Spirit' run by a guy named Lex Hixon. It was a three hour show, in which we talked for an hour and a half, and then an hour and a half questions from the audience. And before he opened the mic to the call-ins, he said, 'Wouldn't it be nice if Sensei' – they were calling me Sensei at that time – 'moved back to New York. Everybody who wants that to happen, come to my house next week.' And we did a workshop there. And then I did some retreats in New York, and so there was already a fairly large group wanting me to come back and start something."

A suitable house for what was to be called the Zen Community of New York was found in Riverdale; two months later, however, the twenty-six room Greyston Manor was put up for sale by Columbia University. Maezumi was impressed by the structure, which had been designed by the architect of Saint Patrick's Cathedral. It had a hefty price tag, and the board was anxious; Maezumi, however, assured them Bernie would be able to find the necessary funds.

"From what I've heard," I tell him, "you had a pretty traditional style when you started teaching."

"Yeah. Maezumi said to me, 'I don't want anybody to be able to criticize you.' Of course it's impossible. So he trained me very well. I did two koan systems: the one that comes through Yasutani Roshi, but then he had another teacher, Koryu Roshi. And both of them were in different lines through Hakuin. So I did two different koan systems. And I was trained very well in terms of the whole Soto liturgy and their stuff. And I was maintaining all of that."

He had not been in New York long, however, before he looked for a way to shift the focus of practice from the zendo to society.

"I've heard a few people saying, 'What's Bernie going to do next?' You know? So, I'm an unknown, which is what I like. I'm motivated by, 'How do you help people experience the oneness of life.' What are the ways? At first, it was all zendo-oriented. Now the venue shifts from the zendo to society. So what are the upayas in society?"

Zazen remained the core practice. "We had a very heavy zazen schedule. Very heavy sesshin schedule. And then I added other elements. In 1980, I started to emphasize the five Buddha families. That's done more in Tibetan practice. There's the mandala – the circle of life – and it's normally broken into five energies. They're called Buddha energies. And one is spirituality. That's the center of the mandala. And one is ratna, which I translate as the 'livelihood' family. One is karma, which I've translated as 'social action' family. One is padma, which I translate as 'relation-ship,' the world of relationships. And one is vajra, which is the world of steady train-ing. And so when you see Tibetan mandalas, they're full of all these images – these are creatures within the five families – and they do a lot of studies in that way.

"Well, I picked up the five Buddha families originally from Trungpa Rinpoche,[59] but then I read a lot about them. So even before I came to New York, I had a meeting with the people who were going to be on my board in '79, and I said, 'We're going to develop our community in the light of the five Buddha families.' The meditation retreats were in the spiritual family – in the middle. But it also meant we were going to do things in terms of livelihood, in terms of social action, in terms of relationship. And that's what I did. I started to develop techniques within those fields. We de-veloped strong meditation practice and training practice first. Some of the people who were closest to me wanted me to get immediately into social action. I said, 'No. First it's the meditation and training. And after that I want to develop work in the ratna – the livelihood world – 'cause that's where the resources come from. And *then* it's social action.'"

"So, you started by grounding them in practice and then moved from there into livelihood," I recap.

"Yes. Except that I would say 'grounding them in meditation.' 'Cause I use 'prac-tice' for the whole thing. I'm constantly having to correct people, 'cause people will say, 'Well, first you practice, then you do social action.' I say, 'No! Social engagement

Buddhism is *a* major practice. Zazen is *a* major practice.' For me, the word 'practice' means to get rid of the subject-object relationship, so that can be done in anything. You can wash dishes as a practice. That's pretty common Zen too. Bring water, that whole kind of work. But people would look at me and say, 'I can see where chopping firewood, that's a practice, or cutting a carrot a certain way, that's a practice. But working with homeless? How can that be a practice?' I mean, for me, I was constantly contradicting this. To do things in your life, whatever you're doing in your life and doing it in a way which decreases the subject-object relationship – in other words whatever helps you experience the interconnectedness of life – that's practice."

His first Livelihood enterprise in New York was the Greyston Bakery. "All the staff were Zen students. We had about thirty people living in this mansion, and their training was also on the floor of the bakery."

"Why a bakery?

"Well, this was all pretty well thought out. So I wanted to get into a business, and I also knew that I wanted to use it as a basis for our social action work. So we spent about nine months deciding what to do. And I had certain principles. It had to be something where we would be able to hire folks who had no experience. I wanted it to be large, to have an effect. I had different criterion, and we explored different businesses. It had to be something where we could get the funding to start it up. So, Baker Roshi in San Francisco – I was friendly with him – agreed that I could send six people to his bakery, the Tassajara Bakery, to train. He already had a very successful bakery. Not in the light of what I wanted to do, but it was very successful. And it met the different criteria in the best way."

Eventually, the Greyston Bakery was providing delicacies to restaurants like Sardi's and the Russian Tea Room as well as to hotel and museum coffee shops. But, like most start-ups, it took a while to turn a profit. Once it did, Bernie expanded the nature of the project.

"And then when we were in the black – this is a couple of years later – I said to the folks, 'It's time to open this up now.' I said, 'I'd like to hire local folk. Are you willing to train? To take somebody on as an apprentice and train?' And everybody voted yes. So we opened it up to folks in the neighborhood."

The neighborhood was Yonkers.

"We lived in Riverdale, which is very, very expensive. A very wealthy area. Riverdale is part of the Bronx, so it's part of New York City. North of Riverdale is the city of Yonkers which is part of Westchester County. It's the poorest part of Westchester County. And it's fairly large. The population is about 200,000, and it's pretty large in area. Right north of it is Scarsdale. Right east of it is Bronxville where Sarah Lawrence College is. So it's surrounded by wealth. And parts of it are...I wouldn't call wealthy but are well-to-do. But the southern part is extremely poor. At that time, Westchester County was one of the wealthiest counties in the US but it had the highest *per capita* of homeless in the country. So it was perfect for me in terms of doing the work I wanted to do in that I felt that what we did there could serve as a model, 'cause it would stand out."

"When you say homeless, is this a street population? Shelter population?"

"Mostly shelter. At that time, the biggest percentage of homeless in Yonkers were single-parent families. Mostly women, but there were some men. So that was the largest percentage. And the families were being warehoused in motels. So there were shelters. There was some temporary housing. And a lot of hotels. And the hotels were horrible, drug-ridden places."

The situation of the people Greyston sought to assist was complicated, and it needed to be addressed – as Bernie puts it – holistically. In order to take part in employment training, clients needed childcare. "The only childcare that existed in the area was if you were on welfare. If you got a job, you lost your childcare, and then you lost your job. So we handled childcare. I wanted to hire some homeless people, so we took the kids into the bakery, which was illegal. We didn't have a separate nursery."

Even that was inadequate, because, he explains, "the homeless folks would be moved from place to place."

Westchester County paid for families to stay in hotels which were, at times, long distances from where the children went to school. So the county instituted a taxi program to transport the children. "They had to go to school in their home of origin, these were mostly like an hour taxi cab ride from the schools. The taxi cab would show up with five kids. Dropped the kids off. Even in the winter. The first kid he'd drop off would stand in the cold for maybe an hour before the school would open."

But on weekends, the hotels sometimes evicted families because it was more profitable to rent the rooms by the hour to prostitutes and their clients. "So on Fridays, the mother didn't know if they'd be at the same motel that night. So they would tend not to send the kids to school. And then they could lose the kids to foster care, because they would be deemed as irresponsible. So that was the scene. And to bring homeless people to start working, it was too unstable. So we had to wait until we got around to the housing which took two more years."

Today – although Bernie is no longer directly involved with it – Greyston continues to provide training and employment to the community of Yonkers; it is also involved in housing, childcare, after-school programs, and other social supports, including a community garden.

In 1991, Bernie accomplished his third goal. He held the first Street Retreat in which participants spent a week living with the homeless. "I didn't allow people to bring money. I did insist on people begging. We slept and ate at different places so that people would get an experience of different venues. In New York, I did not sleep in shelters. I never wanted to take a bed from anybody who needed a bed. So we slept in the streets, on trains, bus terminals. Different venues.

"Fifteen to twenty people would be average. We would meet, and I would give the initial orientation for the retreat. And then I'd break us into packs of three. And there's a pack leader, somebody that's got experience being on the streets. We'd sleep together. And we'd gather together usually twice but at least once a day to do what's called 'council,' sit in a circle and discuss what's happening to us. I liked to do it twice a day, but it didn't always work. Things would happen in the streets.

"We ask that for a week before you come you don't shower and you don't shave. That's about the only preparation we ask. Because our first tenet is 'not knowing.' Come completely open. No fixed ideas. What's much more important to me – but impossible – is to ask you to let go of any ideas of what it might be like. But everybody comes with some ideas of what it's going to be like.

"I did an orientation the first day. We'd gather somewhere. But my orientation was pretty damn simple. Don't take off your shoes and leave them so somebody can steal them. If you're going to go on your own – everybody was in a pack of three – but if you want to go on your own, you can do that, but you got to make sure that your pack leader knows that you are going to do that and where you're going to be. And, as I said, we sleep together in trains, in bus terminals. Wherever. But in those indoor places, we were getting kicked out all the time. Police would come and move us along. We'd have to catch the next train, stuff like that, but, during the evening, you can't go on your own. That's a rule.

"The other rule is always tell the truth when somebody asks. You don't have to volunteer but tell the truth. And to mix with people. So I encouraged people to tell people, 'This is my first time I'm here.' You know, everywhere we've lived, Eve and I, we start off on a street retreat. So we lived for a while in Santa Barbara. We went into the streets, where homeless people live, met people, and I said, 'We just came here.' And it's true. We'd just moved here. 'We just came here. Where's a good place to eat? Where's a good place to sleep?' You know? If they were to say, 'Why are you doing it?' We'd say, 'Well, I actually have a home, but I like to experience living on the streets in the neighborhood where I am.'"

"How do people respond when you tell them that?

"Always positive. Been doing it twenty years. Never had negative."

"And how do more traditional Zen students respond to all this?"

"You know what I'd tell a traditional Zen student? Or anybody? Anybody. How're you filling your time? Being here now. When you're on the streets," he says, chuckling, "there's nothing to plan. You're not thinking about your business. I mean, you are the first half day you're there or whatever. But after a while, all you're worried about is, 'I gotta pee. Where am I gonna pee? I'm hungry. Where am I gonna get food?' I call it a 'plunge.' My Bearing Witness retreats, generally they start off with 'plunges.' It's a way of getting you to deal just with what's coming up."

One of the hardest lessons participants learn is how people avoid seeing them when they're on the street.

"There's this actress, Ellen Burstyn. She's about eighty now. Anyway, she came on the streets with me. We'd been friends, and she was involved in the formation of Zen Peacemakers; it was called Peacemakers Community at that time. But she came on a street retreat maybe fifteen years ago. It was in New York, lower Manhattan, Bowery area. And there's a café, and she went up to these women sitting outside, drinking coffee or whatever, and she asked for some money. And a woman gave her a dollar. She starts across the street, and she was very happy she got this dollar. And then she started to cry, and she thought, 'Why am I crying?' And she realized the woman that gave her the dollar did it like this." He turns his face away. "The woman couldn't look at her. She had never felt that in her life. That story's in her autobiography. And recently I heard her give a talk somewhere. This was fifteen years ago, and she still talks about that.

"Now I started a form of soup kitchen which came out of my initial experience of being on the streets twenty-two years ago. At Greyston, we didn't do shelter work or soup kitchen work. But what I experienced on the streets twenty-two years ago was, at the soup kitchen, there were people who were wonderful, and they loved us, and they gave us food, but there was no dignity. We could feel that they felt a little superior to us, felt they were in a better class than us. So I wanted to start a soup kitchen where you couldn't tell who was homeless and who was wealthy. The servers could be homeless, they could be wealthy. I wanted a place that had music and that was a place kids could feel good to come to and could play. Most soup kitchens I've been to, mothers are afraid to bring their kids. But dignity was a key thing. And there's nobody that's been on these street retreats that afterwards is able to look past a homeless person, to not see them and say, 'Hi, how are you? What's your name?' Money was never the issue. It was dignity and love and acknowledgement. You know? That whole thing of 'you don't see me' is much more important than 'you didn't give me any money.'"

Bernie developed the Zen Peacemaker Order in 1994 as a way for practitioners to become engaged in social justice issues. Gradually it developed into an interfaith network known as the Peacemaker Community which emphasized the integration of spiritual practice and social action through three tenets: 1) Not knowing, 2) Bearing witness, 3) Loving action. By 1996, he had left Greyston to focus on this new program and the Bearing Witness retreats he facilitated in locations such as Auschwitz.

When I ask about Bearing Witness, he begins by explaining the first tenet, "Not knowing."

"I created these plunges as a way of helping you experience 'not knowing,' bringing you into a situation where your rational mind can't fathom it. The experience of 'not knowing' is hopefully to not be attached to your ideas. Have lots of ideas, that's fine. Have lots of knowledge, that's fine. But to not be attached. And not thinking that this idea or this process is going to take care of the situation. Go in completely 'not knowing.' And the plunge is helping you to do that because it's bringing you to a place where your mind, your ideas don't work. Your mind doesn't know how to rationalize this, and that's sort of an instantaneous sensation.

"'Bearing witness' – to me – means to stay in that situation. So it takes time. So it's not enough for me to say, 'Go into the streets and meet with a homeless person.' You have to live there to be in that. And if we create the environment right, then people will experience 'bearing witness.' Being in that state of non-duality. So it's getting you into a state of non-duality.

"Auschwitz, same thing. I do an annual retreat at Auschwitz. In any of the Bearing Witness retreats, there's no teaching. What I'm doing is setting an environment. So the environment at Auschwitz is I bring in as many different kinds of people as possible because the Auschwitz retreat – for me – is around diversity and the 'other.' It's an icon for a place that killed everybody who was an 'other.' In our daily life, the main way we deal with the 'other' is to ignore them. We don't invite them to dinner. We won't listen to them on TV. You know? We don't read those books. I mean, we all have our own club that we feel comfortable in. Everyone else is the 'other.' So Auschwitz was an extreme case where you kill everybody who's not an Aryan. It's a place where you kill the gays. You kill handicapped. You kill the gypsies. You kill the Jews. You kill Catholics. You kill Polish intellectuals. Because they all didn't fit Hitler's club model. But – you know – we did lynchings of blacks. We do bashing of gays. So, it's a common thing. So Auschwitz, for me, is an icon.

"So in our retreats, we have representatives from different groups. We always have gypsies. We have survivors. We have the children of survivors. We have children and grandchildren of SS people that ran the camps. And over the years, it's got to be known, so it's changed a bit. Now, for example, we have also Israelis and Palestinians. We have people from Rwanda there, and we're going to do a 'Bearing Witness' retreat in Rwanda next year."

The first Rwanda Bearing Witness retreat took place the following April – 2014 – during Holy Week. Genjo Marinello was one of sixty participants.

"The absolute bottom worst moment I had was being in a schoolroom adjacent to a Catholic church where a huge massacre happened," he tells me. "In this room, essentially for pre-schoolers, Tutsi children were brought. Everyone was hoping there would be some protection from the Catholic Church, and, in earlier pogroms of the Tutsis, they had been protected if they got to a church. But in this case, it was just another killing field. It was pointed out to us that the blood stains on the brick wall of this particular classroom was where the children had been killed by having their heads bashed against the wall. And their compatriots had to watch this, and then it would happen to them. That was the low point."

Genjo met Bernie around the time the situation at the Zen Studies Society was unravelling. He was visiting Joan Halifax in Santa Fe when Bernie happened to be hosting an event there.

"I was attracted to his efforts to bring Zen out of the zendo. At least from where I'd come from – from all the controversy in New York – it felt almost claustrophobic inside the Zen circle, and he had done something to bring Zen out of its box, what he calls 'out of the clubhouse.' And I liked that, so I decided to go with him on the next Auschwitz retreat."

Genjo took part in two Auschwitz retreats. In the mornings, participants sat in meditation on the railroad platforms where the cattle cars had brought Jews to the camp and the first discernment had been made deciding who would be sent directly to the gas chambers and who would be reserved for slave labor. At noon, a truck came and provided the meditators a bowl of thin soup and a piece of hard bread. At the end of the day, they held the Councils.

"It comes out of the Ojai Foundation, their way of bearing witness through council. It's very old and ancient, going back to indigenous cultures sitting in a circle around a fire. It is a way of hearing and listening deeply and spontaneously to each other without cross-talk as a way to communicate, share, and heal."

But it is not always easy.

"The first time I went, there were two or three Palestinians, and then three or four Palestinians the second time. So you had Jews and Palestinians in the same room doing Councils around genocide and people being kept in camps behind barbed wire. In a situation like that, there are going to be sparks."

2014 was the twentieth anniversary of the genocide in Rwanda, during which, in a one-hundred-day period between April and July of 1994, as many as one million Rwandans, primarily members of the Tutsi community, were systematically slaughtered by Hutu extremists. The dead amounted to nearly a fifth of the nation's people and almost three-quarters of the Tutsi population.

The Bearing Witness retreat took place at Murambi. "Murambi was perhaps the most horrific period in the hundred days of the genocide," Genjo tells me. "50,000 people were gathered from around the region and were told they would be offered protection at this site, but all 50,000 were killed in the course of one day, in fact in the course of seven hours. So that's 7000 people killed an hour. And we sat at that spot. We went down to that memorial; we sat – literally – on the mass grave. We saw a number of bodies, preserved in lime, in postures of prayer and fright. We visited the pits where the mass graves had been dug and covered over, even covered over by the French and made a volleyball court or something like that in order to try to hide the massacre. All sixty of us went and sat zazen on the mass grave there."

Half the retreat participants came from outside the country; the other half were Rwandans. "There were both Hutus and Tutsis, but no one would tell you who they are. You might be able to guess – from circumstances or from how tall they are – which grouping they had been labelled, but they won't tell you anymore. You ask them, and they say, 'I'm Rwandan.'

"We had a perpetrator who had been through the reconciliation process in the country and had done some prison time, and he had met with survivors and had dedicated his life to a life of amends, trying to get out from under his own guilt and remorse. And we had the child of a woman whose family had practically been eliminated in the genocide. And as much as we had taught everybody about how to do Council, this woman said, 'You know, I've never been this close to a perpetrator telling me about how he killed dozens of people.' Then she broke into tears. Two women left the circle with her, and she didn't come back. She couldn't be in the same circle with a perpetrator."

Does it matter whether this is Zen or not?

"I think they've done a very good job of bringing Zen out of the box and translating it into a modern idiom that is more easy to grasp, or get your head around, than ancient Chinese koans," Genjo says. "I've spent thirty years trying to understand that stuff and feel as though I got a lot out of it, but Bernie really has brought it out of the box. I know exactly where his three tenets of 'not knowing, bearing witness, loving action' derive from in Buddhism, but there's nothing Buddhist in these tenets *per se*. And I think it's brilliant to bring it out in that way and to put it to some practical use.

"There's something about being present at a place where genocide has happened and just sitting there and absorbing it. It seems to help those who are bearing witness, and it also seems to help the culture heal.

"We stayed in a church conference center that was on a hill above Murambi, and we would walk down through the village – just a rutted dirt road – and they would see these sixty people who were an even mix of Rwandans and internationals. You could tell that some of them were curious. Some of them were astounded. Some of them were skeptical. But most were happy and honored that we were there to bear witness. We didn't just visit the site. It was clear that we went there, stayed all day, then went back. Through this little village up and down to get there. And the message we got from them was, 'Thank you for coming and being a witness to this horror even twenty years later. We appreciate you honoring the dead.' And that was pretty moving."

Before I leave Montague, there is still the matter of the clown's nose.

"In 1997," Bernie tells me, "I decided that it was time for my wife at that time – she's passed away; her name was Jishu; she was the co-founder of the Zen Peacemakers – it was time for her to take over the Zen Community of New York, and I was not going to be formally involved in teaching any more. But what I wanted to do was go around to my Dharma successors that had places and make sure that they weren't being too arrogant or thinking they knew too much. And the best way to do that would be to pop-up unexpected as a clown and disrupt what was going on. So I went to a friend of mine, Wavy-Gravy, and told him what I wanted to do and how do I get trained? And he assigned a trainer to me, Mr. Yoo-hoo. So Yoo-hoo and I did a lot of workshops on 'Clowning Your Zen.' Now, 'clown' is not the best word. In Native American, its Coyote. In Europe it's the *nar*, which we translate as jester. He can say things to the king that nobody else can say.

"So that was my idea. And then it turned out that the guy who was training me was a coordinator for Clowns Without Borders – *Payasos sin Fronteras* – and they work in refugee camps around the world. So I've been with him in refugee camps in places like Chiapas. And I found that to Bear Witness in a refugee camp is fantastic. Because you go there, you don't know the culture at all. And you don't know what the refugees have been through. So you *have* to be in a place of 'not-knowing.' You can't assume that anything you know is going to be funny, and you got to bear witness to the kids, 'cause you're doing things. And part of our training is how do you present something very lightly and then make it heavier, whether it's anger or love or hate or whatever. And that's what you've got to do. Do something very lively. See whether a smile appears or fear appears. And back away if it's fear, and if it's a smile, make it heavier. And then bear witness to the mothers. Are they feeling comfortable? And eventually to the fathers. Usually the kids are up front. Mothers are a little further back, and we've been in places where mothers never saw their kids smile. So I carry my nose with me everywhere I go," he says taking it out of his pocket, "and I'm always ready to make sure that if a situation seems too heavy or too 'knowing'" – he puts the nose on – "I'll put my nose on and shake it up. It's another upaya," he says, laughing.

CHAPTER THIRTEEN

John Daido Loori

ETWEEN SCHEDULED INTERVIEWS, THE PROGRAM COORDINATOR AT ZEN
Mountain Monastery takes me on a tour of the grounds in her car. In addition to the heritage building where my dinner companion had asked me
what I wanted the book to do and the recently built administration building next to
it, there are cabins for residents, a Japanese tea house, solar panels spread in a field,
and other structures. There are people all about, engaged in the maintenance which
the site requires. It's an extensive operation.

We approach a roughly fashioned wooden structure open in back. Through
the opening, I can see a large carved block. There is a huge mala – the 108-bead
Asian rosary – encircling the opening. When we come around the front, the block is
revealed to be a bas relief Buddha. This is the monastery's graveyard shrine. Opposite
it, a stupa commemorates Taizan Maezumi as ZMM's first abbot and John Daido
Loori as the second.

Graves are marked, Japanese style, with simple upright wooden planks. Mounds
of stones and small personal items are placed near the markers by mourners. One
grave has a statue of the Virgin Mary, who, I have come to recognize, is often seen
as a Western equivalent of Kannon. John Daido Loori's marker identifies him as the
founder of the Mountains and Rivers Order. There is an American flag at its base,
signifying that he was a veteran.

James Ford had discussed the need for "commonly accepted standards of training" for Zen teachers. "We need people who do something vaguely like seminary. It
doesn't need to be seminary, but," he said, Zen teachers "need to be educated." It was
an issue to which Daido Loori had also given considerable thought. Most Americans
enter Zen training, he noted, without knowing anything about Buddhism.

> One of the problems we face with Zen in America is that it has no
> continuity of tradition or standards. The Zen that arrived in this
> country has come from several places and cultures: from China,

Vietnam, Japan, Korea. It was been taught by scores of teachers, and out of this evolved a real mixture of what is called Zen training. Today the training is very different as you go from center to center. There are no agreed upon guidelines of practice, no standards of transmission. There are a number of authentic lineages and a large group of unsanctioned teachers. The distinction between monks and lay practitioners has almost completely dissolved, to the point that at most centers the idea of a Zen monk has become just that – only an idea. Lay practitioners are practicing and living precisely the same as the monks. Why call one group "monks" and the other group "lay students" when there is virtually no difference between them?

...

In most instances, the thrust of what Zen in America was and continues to be is zazen and the teacher-student relationship, which is the basis of the mind-to-mind transmission, common to both the Rinzai and Soto Schools. Not a lot of attention is given to other aspects of practice, particularly to the area of moral and ethical teachings, the Precepts. People "take the Precepts," but how much real training goes on in living the Precepts? Are the Precepts actually read, understood, engaged, lived? Are they a spiritual status symbol or the very substance of this life? There seems to be a real danger of stylizing and diluting this ageless practice to fit our fleeting fancies, to remain relatively comfortable, and miss the opportunity to realize our true nature.[60]

ZMM is not a seminary, but it has more potential to serve as one than any of the other places I visit. The scope of training here is broad. Loori developed what he called Eight Gates, which are enumerated in a pamphlet the Program Coordinator gives me: 1) zazen, 2) the student-teacher relationship, 3) liturgy, 4) art practice, 5) body practice, 6) Buddhist studies, 7) work practice, 8) right action. "Grounded within a rigorous monastic matrix," the pamphlet states, "the Eight Gates training emphasizes practice, realization, and actualization of our true nature."

One of the residents explains the Eight Gates this way: "The matrix here, the eight gates, are eight different fingers pointing to the moon. They're opportunities for people of different dispositions to find entry. So you have artists who immediately recognize the possibility of finding the Dharma in the creative act. And then you have others who resonate with the academic study. But all of us do all of it to different degrees."

Most of the gates are self-evident, but there are surprises. I ask what body practice is.

"Body practice can be lots of different things for different folk," the resident tells me. "But in your first year you don't have a choice. You're either doing yoga or you're out on the field doing Ultimate Frisbee. In silence! And you're paying attention to throwing it well and catching it well and positioning yourself well on the field."

The walls of the new admin building are graced with Daido's photographs. The subjects seem abstract until, when viewed more carefully, they're revealed to be close-ups of natural phenomena – the grain in rock or wood, the tracery of veins in a leaf. Daido had a love of photography going back to his boyhood, when he had occasionally turned the family bathroom into a darkroom.

This building houses the monastery offices, a lecture hall, and multi-purpose rooms. The Program Coordinator arranged for me to use one of the latter to conduct interviews. On my second day at ZMM, I spend an afternoon with Joan Yushin Derrick who is the monastery's Japanese Tea Instructor. She was also Daido's second wife and remained with him as a student after their marriage dissolved. She had been with him longer than anyone else here.

We begin by talking about Daido's time in the Navy. "He enlisted at the age of 16 using his brother's birth certificate, who passed away when he was still a little boy," Yushin tells me. The brother had been born two years prior to John. "So, John's whole life he had two social security numbers. It made me crazy. He'd say, 'My real birthday is June 14, but my other birthday is February 22nd.' And I was like, 'No. You were only born on one day.' It was a regular argument. He enlisted to get away from the step-father – his father died when he was 8 or 9 – and it was either that or hurt his step-father. He was emotionally and physically and verbally abused by the step-father."

"Do you know what rank he rose to?"

"Oh, gosh! I don't know. That was the first wife, Nancy. I know that he was in a lot of trouble in the navy because he was very politically-oriented, always bucking authority. And I know he was in the brig a lot," she adds with a laugh. "When he got out, Nancy encouraged him – even though he hadn't graduated high school – to get a college education, get a job in big corporate businesses. And he did."

"What kind of big corporate business?"

"He was a chemist for International Flavors and Fragrances. Head of a big department. Research. He invented the lime flavor for jell-o! I know! It was so funny! And he hated the job. He'd been there for too, too long. So divorcing the first wife, meeting me, almost the same week. That's another story."

He gave up the corporate world to study photography with Minor White. In addition to being an internationally respected photographer, White was a teacher in the Gurdjieff tradition.[61] He offered retreats in which photography was presented as a spiritual art. Students meditated in the morning before beginning their day. Although White was not a Zen teacher, he gave koan assignments to his students, instructing them to find visual rather than verbal responses. John Loori was assigned the koan which asks, "What is your original face? Your face before your parents were born?"

While engaged on this assignment, Loori set up a shot by a tree. Light filtered down through the leaves and branches. There were indistinct sounds in the distance, perhaps flowing water. He had a deep experience of silence. Eventually he noticed that the sun had set and several hours had gone by. The experience passed, but, afterwards, he sought ways to recapture it. In 1974, he saw a poster for a lecture series organized by Chogyam Trungpa at Harvard University. He and Joan attended it, and he was particularly impressed by one of the conference participants, Eido Shimano.

"John was extremely enamored with him and his talk and everything about it. The whole umbrella. The next day off, he went to the bookstore and the library, ravenous to find out more about Zen. I thought, 'Okay.' I'd lived at Ananda Ashram in Monroe, New York and had been around a lot of different gurus. So meeting a Zen Buddhist monk wasn't a big thrill for me. It was the content of his lecture that Daido was impressed with. We found out where the monastery was, and we went there together a couple of times. We'd had a baby in 1972, so it was a little difficult, and two teenage boys from his first marriage were living with us. I was pretty home-bound for a good part of that time, but John would go once a week. Then we heard there was a Buddhist festival that Eido Roshi was going to appear at with other Zen teachers. We got a baby-sitter and went for the weekend, and we heard about Mae-zumi Roshi and this Los Angeles place."

It was at this festival that Yushin discovered her own calling.

"The monks and the Zen teachers, half the time I didn't know what they were talking about. I was a hippie girl living in a yoga ashram. I wasn't totally interested, but following the husband is part of what I did. But one afternoon I saw on the schedule that there was a Japanese tea ceremony demonstration in an auditorium, and I begged off and said, 'I'm going to see that. You go and do what you're going to do with the Zen guys.' I didn't know anything about the tea ceremony at all."

She arrived at the presentation early and fell asleep waiting for it to begin.

"Then I heard the commotion of people coming in and people behind me and around me. So I kind of sat up, pretending I wasn't asleep. And on the stage.... It had been as empty as this table. Now there was this magnificent set-design of a tea-house with flowers and calligraphy and people in kimonos. And it was so magical! I was just enamored with the set before they even started! And Hisashi Yamada Sensei was, at the time, the director of this Japanese tea ceremony school in the upper eastside of New York City. He came out to the microphone and introduced himself, and he was such an elegant, beautiful man. He had black hair. He had a black robe with a beautiful belt and a purple sash or something. And he didn't look like the Zen Buddhist monks, but there was that Japanese elegance about him. I just fell in love. I was totally enamored. I wanted to learn more about this. So as they were tearing down the set, I stayed in my seat until they were almost ready to leave. Then I went up onto the stage and asked him where I could learn how to do this. And he laughed at me and said, 'I knew you would come eventually!' He was so cute! Gave me his business card, and I started tea ceremony lessons."

In 1976, the Looris learned that Maezumi would be giving a summer course at Trungpa's Naropa Institute in Colorado. John applied for and got a position at the institute teaching mindful photography. "Which then put us right in the same arena with Maezumi Roshi, Tetsugen Glassman Roshi, and Dennis Genpo Merzel Roshi.[62] The three of them were staying in an apartment house for the teachers. And we had the apartment next door. I mean, it was written in the stars. The universe gave him what he needed, and off we went. We brought our child with us, and I did a little day-care program. I was a kindergarten teacher so it was easy for me to be with children.

"So, at that point, getting to know Maezumi and following him around when he wasn't teaching photography or doing all the political nonsense that was going on with Trungpa Rinpoche – oh, boy! – it was a wild and crazy summer. 1976. By the end of that period of time, he and Maezumi were totally connected, and Maezumi asked him if we could come to Los Angeles to live. He was enlarging the community. At the time, there were only about twenty people living in a couple of different houses on Normandy and Wilshire. John was given that opportunity in August or September, and Christmas Eve we packed and drove to Los Angeles. Which was another insane thing. In the middle of a blizzard, moving out of a house way up the mountain. But we got to Los Angeles, and we were given one room in a house with the Glassmans, Tetsugen and his wife, Helen, and their two children. We were given one room on the third floor. Supposedly very temporary, because they were completing an apartment for us to live in. Well, that took nine months."

"Daido was busy with starting the publication center for the Center and associating intimately with Maezumi Roshi. I was busy trying to survive on the third floor in this one little room with a four year old child and getting a pre-school set up and all that stuff."

There were twenty-seven people in the residential program at ZCLA when the Looris arrived. By the time they left, there were 200.

"And they all lived within one square city block. All of the homes, all of the high-rise apartments, garden apartments, they were all eventually purchased by ZCLA. And we eventually moved out of that house and had our own apartment, but it was almost a year later. I was completely crazy. Completely crazy! I thought Maezumi Roshi was completely crazy. I thought the teachers, everybody there were completely crazy. It was so hot! In Los Angeles, after moving from a mountain top in December to Los Angeles! It was so hot and the energy there was hot. And our son was not well. He was ill all the time. With allergies, with colds, sore throats, with temperatures, and it wasn't too long after we moved there that he was diagnosed with a malignant brain tumor. So that was my priority. And also Daido – I don't want to slight that – we were hand in hand with everything that needed to be done for our son. He's now forty and lives right downstairs in a house that I own, and he's completely well. We had a rough time with the tumor, the surgery, the radiation, and the therapy and the recovery was rough for a couple of years. It stunted his growth, and he had hair-loss, and some eye difficulty. But he's a strong survivor. He has been living, basically, in the Zen community ever since he was two. His name is Asian." She laughs. "When he was born, I wanted to name him things like Oak or Sequoia. You know? Anything unusual. And Daido wanted to name him traditional Italian names like Giovanni or Biblical names."

"I hadn't realized Loori was an Italian name."

"Yes. His father changed his name before Daido was born. Very Italian. We spoke Italian, both our families. I'm from Naples and Rome; his family more from the south of Italy. But very, very Italian and traditional. I mean, he was always singing Italian songs, and he was always pinching cheeks and being an Italian guy. And he definitely wanted more of an Italian name for our son. But the one thing we did agree on was we had a love for the Orient. So we tossed the coins of the I Ching. And what came up was 'The Cauldron,' a nurturing pot in the fireplace that made the soup to nourish the family. So we thought that was cool. So Cauldron was good for me. I liked that. Let's call him Cauldron Loori. And Daido goes, 'Uh…I'm not sure that's the right one.' And when he was first born, he had a blood disorder, and he was in the hospital a week after I left. And I was coming back and forth all day and every day. He was laying in this little incubator. He had long black hair. He was yellow because he had jaundice. And his hands were just beautifully laying on his chest with long fingers. He looked like a little Chinese sage. So Daido and I looked at each other and went, 'Asian!' It just came to us. The child told us his name is what happened, and we were happy with that."

"Daido threw himself full force into monkdom and was moving along quickly in koan study and the procedures that were needed to become a monk and then a teacher. He was just driven. It was meant to be. You know? He was kind of like Don Quixote. He had this dream, and he was definitely going to fulfill it.

"Meanwhile, behind the zendo doors were other stories. He was doing really wonderfully well with Maezumi Roshi, and Maezumi Roshi was an incredibly unusual man once I got to know him. And I don't want to defend all the terrible things that went on there at the time. There was alcoholism. There was womanizing. There was so much craziness around the brilliance. And some of Maezumi Roshi's talks were brilliant! And inspiring. So I became one of his students in 1977 because I wanted to know what he knew. I don't know if I ever found out, and I'm still wanting to know," she laughs.

"So there was a lot of craziness going on at that place. There was an amazing amount of drinking. It was always started by the roshi, and all of us just jumped right in. We figured, you're sitting hard in sesshin, and it's a tortuous week, let's party when it's over. Which was crazy. And when Daido realized that it was crazy, he stopped and told Maezumi Roshi, 'I'm not going to be doing this drinking.' He said, 'I think there has to be another way. I feel I've got joriki during sesshin and all of the energy from the retreat, and then I throw it away six hours later. That's crazy.'

"That's when he started to elevate in my eyes. He started to look like one of our fine teachers out of that place. And our marriage changed at that point. He became my teacher. He became my son's healer. We walked hand-in-hand with that. But as far as the marriage, it was a totally different energy. You know, when I married him, I thought we were going to have a little white house with a picket fence. We were going to grow a little garden. We were going to go to the movies. Boy, was I shocked and surprised when none of that was going to happen. And my son's health and well-being was more of a priority to me than anything else. So being a student was part time. Being the wife was part time. Being the healer and mother – and I learned a lot about healing during that time – was the priority.

"When we were asked to come back to New York, I didn't want to leave California. I was really annoyed. I wanted a separation. I wanted to stay there. My son had a wonderful group of healers there. I loved California. I loved being on the beach. I did not want to come back to New York. But Maezumi convinced me. I resisted, and I cried, and I begged, and I threatened, and it didn't make a damn bit of difference. Maezumi sat there like stone. He just listened to me till I spent myself out with the handkerchiefs, and he goes, 'It will be wonderful, Yushin. You will do good job, Yushin. Will you help him?' He always had a habit of, 'Will you help him? Will you really help him?' And like an idiot, I'm sitting there" – in an exasperated voice – "'Okay.' And off we went. I flew back with my son, and they drove – again – late December, in a blizzard, not in Los Angeles, but it was as they got closer to New York.

"There were people in Riverdale who wanted to start a Zen community. And Bernie Tetsugen Glassman was the teacher who was sent to do that with Daido at his side, as a partnership. And Maezumi Roshi really thought that that would happen. It lasted about ten minutes. They were two totally different people. Totally different teachers."

Although Daido and Yushin were still married, they lived separately, and Yushin wasn't comfortable in Riverdale.

"It was a huge undertaking, and the people who gave the money for this place – Greyston Mansion – to get started, the donors in Riverdale, were very, very wealthy. And the house that they gave us to live in was in a very exclusive neighborhood. I mean, I was embarrassed to go outside in jeans. It was beautiful and wonderful, but we were uncomfortable there. And my son started first grade at PS 132 with fifty kids in the Bronx, and that was another crazy situation. I was fearing for my life just walking him to the school."

The residents of Riverdale sent their children to private schools. Yushin had to walk her son to the nearest public school which was a good distance away.

Meanwhile, it was becoming clear that Daido and Glassman had very different views about Zen practice. According to Ryushin Marchaj, Bernie Glassman's

> – mixture of Judaism, Christianity, Buddhism, and social action
> put Daido off. Almost immediately he started exerting pressure on
> Tetsugen to let him begin an affiliate group upstate, a place solely
> dedicated to residential programs in Zen and the arts. Tetsugen
> agreed but asked Daido to wait a year, remaining in the city to
> assist him with developing the center in Yonkers.[63]

As it turned out, Daido and Glassman went their separate ways before the year was up.

"By Spring, John realized he couldn't stay in Riverdale and that he needed to find his own place. He didn't exactly have it as an agenda, but we have a friend who lives here in Mount Tremper who was one of the students in the photography class many years ago. And his name is Neil, and he invited us up for a weekend because he wanted to show John this place. 'Oh, you're just going to flip out. It's perfect!' They'd been communicating every once in a while. We drove up. John, Neil, Asian, and myself came here. It was a crisp Spring day; the sun was shining. The gate was closed, and we parked outside the gate and walked in. And I saw John go pale. I saw him actually unable to breathe, he was so impressed and excited. He just kind of held onto the wall there, and he said, 'What is this place?' So Neil told him.

"The story is it was built around the turn of the century out of wood and then burned down and then they rebuilt it with stone, quarried here on the mountain, and the oak trees that they lumber. It was Norwegian priests. The property was inherited by this Norwegian priest, and he came here to build himself a church. And he built a big church. And he had Norwegian carpenters and helpers and other priests do this, as well as the neighborhood community and the mountain trades-men and craftsmen. So when they rebuilt it in – I think the sign says it was com-pleted in 1926 – this is what it looked like. But when we saw it, it had gone through many, many different owners. After the Norwegian priest had passed on, everything kind of fell apart. For a while it was run by a bunch of nuns, who thought it would make a nice nunnery. That was difficult. After the nuns fell apart, somebody told us that there were Russians who came in and wanted to take it over and yadda yadda yadda. And eventually it was just boarded up and left to die.

"However Harold Harr and his wife and their twelve children and the Lutheran community from Long Island were looking for someplace to have a children's camp in the summer. And that was – I guess – the late '60s maybe? And all of them would come up from Long Island and run a children's camp for under-privileged children out of New York City. So each summer, they would have a couple of hundred kids here. There was a swimming pool right underneath this building. We tore it up and built this building over it. And all the windows were broken. There was bubblegum stuck on everything.

"So the day that we came, Harold was sitting here on the grass, on the hill, looking at the building. He had come by himself, and it's early March, and he's looking at the building, and he's thinking, 'I just can't do this another year.' He was worn out. His kids were older. He and his wife had been chief cook, camp directors, yadda yadda. You know? And it's 200 acres! So he was just sitting here, starting to figure out what he had to do. Lots of developers wanted to buy it. The Lutheran Church that he'd been associated with thought it would be a huge benefit if they sold it and got rid of it and didn't have to deal with it anymore. And Daido comes walking up the drive, very slowly, with Neil and our son, Asian, behind him, and he sees this man, and he just walks straight towards him. And Harold stands up, and they shake hands. They both sit down on the grass; they start talking. And Neil had to go someplace. Asian and I went down to the river, and we fiddled around. It was freezing cold, but we walked all around. Kept checking to see if they were still there. A few hours later, when Neil came back, John was standing here, shaking hands with Harold Harr. So Harold goes back down, gets in his car, and John comes back to Neil and says, 'I think I just bought this place.' He was sparkling! He was thrilled. He had twenty-five cents in his pocket.

"So on the drive home, I go, 'What are you thinking? Who do you think is gonna clean that big old house?' I was again, like, crazed! I could not believe that he wanted to move into that place! Well, when we got back, the first thing he had to do was discuss it with Bernie Roshi and Maezumi Roshi. They got in a three-way phone conversation, Maezumi in California, Bernie and John in Riverdale. And Maezumi said, 'If that's what you really want to do. You know, Bernie needs you.' He tried to keep them together. But they both knew that it was the best thing to do. So we proceeded to beg for funds from people who might be interested in forming a Zen/Arts community."

Daido was able to borrow $10,000 from friends to put a down payment on the property. The immensity of the project he had undertaken was daunting, and there were times he questioned himself. But one morning he was in a coffee shop in Woodstock browsing through a copy of the local newspaper and came upon a review of a book called *Mountain Spirit*. The headline included a passage from Dogen which Daido had copied into his own journal just before leaving Los Angeles: "These mountains and rivers of the present are the manifestation of the way of the ancient Buddhas." As Yushin said, it seemed to be written in the stars.

"So that was the idea from the start?" I ask. "To focus on both Zen and the arts?"

"Absolutely. And that was a challenge in itself. I remember Bernie Glassman introduced us to Lex Hixon, who had a radio show, WBAI, in Greenwich Village. Lex has passed on, of course, but I think the show is still on the air. It was very New Age, and Lex was this elegant tall, blonde man who wore white robes from studying with a teacher – Sufi, maybe – in India or somewhere, and Lex was so happy that we had contacted him to see if we could get on the radio to put an appeal out – just to put feelers out – to see how many people would be interested. Lex agreed to a Sunday morning at 9:00, and I was sitting by the one telephone in the house with the number that they had given out. I was to answer the phone and take names and phone numbers and addresses to send people information. It was just to get some idea how many people might be listening and how many people might be interested. All I said was, 'Hello?' I did that 125 times. That's how many people called during that one hour show. And by that time I was writing on every scrap of paper and upside down and all around. And I'd thought I was going to get maybe two phone-calls.

"125 people were very interested, and Daido being who he was – brilliant in that way – immediately decided the name was going to be the Zen Arts Center. He had a logo. He had information printed up, and we mailed it all out. And we decided that sometime early summer we would have a meeting here for the weekend. About a hundred people showed up."

Yushin was concerned about the practicalities of housing that many participants. "There were beds, but they had bed-bugs. Everything was a mess. Basically it was, 'Bring your own bedding and provide your own space. You can have a tent or you can sleep on the floor. Whatever.'"

She and Daido arrived a couple of days before the retreat was to begin and found a motorcycle club camping on the hill. "Daido walked up, and the leader sort of surfaced and came to him, and they talked, and he told them what we were about to do in two days. And he said, 'You know, this property is also part of the campgrounds across the road.' Which is right on the river. He asked them if they would like to camp there. It meant that they had to move everything, and some of them didn't want to move. So the ones with the children stayed, and everybody else moved across the road.

"We proceeded with these people finding their way here, parking everywhere. God knows where they came from. They were hippies. They were military. They were in robes. They were anything and everything. All interested in the Zen Arts Center. In the meantime, a photography group had contacted Daido and wanted to associate here. It was out of Millerton and was called Aperion. They were accredited with some other photography school, and Peter Schlesinger was the head of that. He was a photographer that Daido had met through Minor White, and he wanted to be able to come and live here with us and become students of Zen and have photography a big part of the center. At first Daido thought that was a good idea. It lasted about twenty minutes. Peter and his students also came that weekend. Maybe ten of them.

"And Peter and Daido sat up at the head – where the altar is – they sat up at the head of the room, sitting cross-legged. We brought blankets and things. There were wooden pews along the wall that the Lutherans used when they did church services. So my son and I sat in the wooden pew at the top corner. And all these other people were coming in, and we thought they were going to sit in zazen, like we did in Los Angeles, like we did in Riverdale whenever there was a meeting. But these people weren't trained. They weren't interested. They could care less, or they didn't know how to do it. We have a photograph, and it's hysterical. They are lying down, sitting up, sitting together, wrapped in blankets, spread out, a hundred of them in every different way. It looked so chaotic and crazy. And I'm sitting on the bench, and I'm going, 'Oh, my God! These people are crazy. This is another crazy scheme.' I had no idea how he was going to do it. But he was driven, and – as you see – it happened.

"But Peter and Daido were sort of like a two-headed dragon. They were both Geminis to start with, and they were both very creative, and they both had definite ideas of what they wanted to do here. Peter wanted it to be photography classes, workshops, programs, free-thinking. He wanted to encourage musicians and artists to come, which, in the end, is what we do here anyway. Peter wanted programs to happen very late at night and wasn't interested in the early morning meditation."

Daido had a different vision. "He was a very organized person from the Navy and Zen training and from probably before that. He wrote out a schedule. Dawn: you wake up, then zazen. Breakfast. Work practice. Lunch. Nap or rest period. Work practice. Dinner. Meditation. That was the schedule, and that's how it's been for 34 years. And he was not giving in on that. Peter, on the other hand, had concerts out here on the grass. People drinking, smoking, doing all the things that people did at that time, going home at 2:00 in the morning. And those of us who were going to be sitting…well, there would be like three of us in the zendo in the morning.

"The break, when it came, was not a good one. The break in Riverdale with Bernie was easy. They had a party for us. They gave us gifts. We said goodbye. We had big to-dos, dinner parties. Maezumi came from Los Angeles. Bernie came from Riverdale. And it was a very amicable split. The split with Peter Schlesinger and the Aperion Photograph School was not. Some of the students that came with him wanted to stay here. They wanted to study with Daido; they wanted to study Zen. Not too many, a handful. But that wasn't good for Peter. He was very embarrassed. He was angry. He had put a lot of time, effort, money, and energy into it, and he didn't like the way this was coming down."

After the photography group left, Daido set about establishing a more formal training center. "We got a new sign: Zen Mountain Monastery. Then the serious students started to come. People like Shugen – Geoffrey Arnold – who's head of the order now and Ryushin – Konrad Marchaj – and Bonnie Myotai Treace." These three would become Daido's only heirs.

Despite marital difficulties, Yushin and Daido retained a good working relationship. "I was teaching the tea ceremony, raising our son, and doing whatever needed to be done. I was the cook, the ino – the one who starts the chanting – I was the monitor; I was in the front office; I was on the phones. It was very busy. We lived in that little white house over there. It's called the Jizo House and is presently the monastery store. We had one phone in the front office and an extension in the house. For the whole first year, that's all we could afford, one telephone with an extension. So I was in the office. Whoever called, if they wanted to talk to John, I would run over to the house and say, 'You've got a phone call.' He'd pick up over there; I'd run back to the office. This was during the day when my son was at school. I was always in the office or the kitchen. I lost 50 pounds because I was constantly running! After a while we developed a flag system. He was very organized. I would put the flag up. If he was looking out the window, he'd see he had a phone call. It was a hoot.

"I don't know how…. The universe gave us everything we needed. It was amazing. Time went on, and people came. Wonderful people who were very devoted and very interested and very committed to the practice. And things started to happen. We had two Japanese monks who Maezumi Roshi sent from Japan – Dosho Sawakawa and Seido Suzuki – and they did all of the instruments that you see. They got them from Japan, and they made the bases out of trees that they would find in the woods. They helped with everything – the kitchen – and they organized everything. It was beautiful. I loved them. It was only one year, and I really cried when they left because they were a tremendous help. They are both now heads of temples in Japan.

"Eventually we had people who wanted to live as residents. So they had to really renovate the rooms to make them liveable because they were all in disarray. They were a mess. And then we started this tradition where the abbot and the two attendants go to every single room of the building offering incense. If there's someone living in a room, there's a little altar just like the one behind me that is set up and the abbot will…. Well, at the time he was not the abbot. He was a sensei. He was the head of this place. Maezumi Roshi was the acting abbot until Daido had the ordinations done through the Soto school in Japan to become the abbot. Anyway, we would go into these rooms. I was carrying the incense box. Someone else was carrying the bell. And he would see each room and how people lived. And he would lean over and say, 'You need to take down that Rolling Stones poster.' Or, 'He needs a closet.' Or whatever. That also was from the Navy. When the ship is being inspected, everybody's standing at attention. There were these poor students standing by the door, waiting to see what they needed to change in their rooms. Eventually we ran out of space and started to work on the cabins and A-frames. So people would have really pleasant places to live. And it just grew and grew and grew."

The training program which evolved at ZMM was inevitably a reflection of Daido's personality and background. People who described him to me uniformly recognized his brilliance, but they also occasionally suggested he wasn't always an easy person to work with.

The young monk who had been my dinner companion, tells me, "I'd been reading about the monastery, and I'd seen the web-site, and decided, 'I'm going to do this. I don't know why. I don't know what, but I'm going do it.' And I remember reading about the Ox-Herding pictures, 'cause Daido in his book has a section about the Ox-Herding pictures and a commentary on each stage. And in stage six, Daido says, 'Stage six is like you get to the point of no return.' And I remember thinking to myself, 'Okay, I'll go there for a year, and I'll get to that point and won't go any further. I don't want to go past the point of no return. I'll just get right up to that edge, and then I'll come back and play football again, and life will go on, and I'll have some sort of special powers and so on.' So I came for a year. I didn't know what I was getting myself into at all," he says, pronouncing each word distinctly. "I remember going through the interview processes and stuff on the phone, and the guy on the phone saying, 'You know, we've had Navy SEALs come here, and they couldn't do this. Why do you think you can do this?' I told him, 'Well, if I treat it the way I treated playing football, I'll be fine.' And I remember him just laughing at me on the other end of the phone. He just laughed at me!"

"What was Daido like?"

He considers the question a moment before answering. "Daido was from a different era. He was in the Navy, like, in the '40s. You know? They just had a different salt about them. 'God damn it!'" He mimics in a harsh, deep voice, pounding the table with his fist. "'God damn it!' Kind of like that. You know? When he died, there was a lot of process about the ways he hurt people."

"Hurt people how?"

"I think he hurt people with his anger. He hurt people with this chauvinistic old school mentality, that sense of being a guy who grew up in a male-dominated world. That's where he came from. It's old school like you'd see in that show *Mad Men*. You call women 'Dames' or 'Dolls' whatever. I mean, I didn't perceive him that way, but I'm not a woman."

"Daido was incredibly intense," a practitioner at Toni Packer's Springwater Center told me. "Incredibly compassionate. But you never knew which it was going to be. He looked like the janitor walking around. If someone who didn't know better saw him, they would say, 'Who's that old janitor?' Then he'd put his robes on and come into the zendo, and you know?

"He was the most interesting teacher I've ever met by far. And I've met a lot. He didn't ever come across as, 'I'm a Zen priest. I'm a Zen Master.' Totally the opposite. You know, he could play that role. And when he did it, he did it. But I'm an ex-football coach. I like strong masculine energy. So I was attracted to his energy and the way he did things. Old Navy man. Straight to the point. No bullshit. I liked that. Tough as nails, yet incredibly compassionate."

"If you were having a beer with friends and telling stories, what story would you tell about Daido?"

"I think one of the funniest ones was, I was taking the compost out. And there was about two and a half feet of snow. And the compost is full, so I have a big garbage can, and I'm struggling along. Daido pulls up in his jeep and just looks at me from a distance. He watches me struggle for fifteen minutes. Finally get it all done. I'm walking back towards him, and I'm thinking, he's going to say, 'Wow! Andy, that's hard work, isn't it?' Or, 'Good job.' So I come up to the jeep, and he said, 'Jesus Christ, Andy! Where the Hell did you learn to empty compost? You're doin' it all wrong!' Classic Daido.

"And then the other one I'll never forget is I had face-to-face with him once, and we were talking about some pretty intense stuff. And towards the end, he goes deep into thought, and I think he's going to say something profound. Finally he goes, 'Jesus, Andy! Can't they get you a robe that fits?'"

The young woman who had been my first contact at ZMM told me: "By the time I arrived, I think Daido had entered sort of his grandfatherly phase. He reminded me of my two grandfathers put together. He had a very unique way that he kind of inhabited his body. When I think about him, I think of him kind of sprawling in a chair, chewing gum, and sort of gesturing with these giant hands. You know? Just the way he was in his body. He could be so gentle and soft. He could be ferocious. But he was never mean to me. I saw him be ferocious with other people, and I'd think, 'Oh, my God!' And stories I heard from the early years! I would have never made it. Having somebody yell at me like that! But to me he was always accessible. And I always felt really seen by him. I felt totally seen by him."

She had been 26 years old and living in New York City when the twin towers came down on September 11th.

"I had just started a new job working in the corporate world. I remember being just so completely freaked out and realizing for the first time – non-intellectually –

that I was going to die. It could happen today. And what was I doing with my life? Was I happy? I didn't even know what 'happy' would mean. So I didn't recognize any spiritual questions, I was just really freaked out. And so I started a process. I changed my career and my partner and I moved a bunch of times, read a bunch of books, and went to churches, and was just looking and looking and looking. I didn't really know that much about Buddhism, but I went to a Sunday morning program at the temple in Brooklyn. And Shugen Sensei gave the talk. And I was just like, 'Oh, my God! There's a religion that's based around answering my questions. That's so fantastic!' And I resonated immediately with zazen. There was something about sitting down and being quiet. And several months after that, I met Daido for the first time. He had come down to the temple, and I talked to him briefly on Sunday in my typical way," – speaking in a sing-song tone – "'I just started practicing. What should I do now?' And he was like, 'Have you done a Zen training weekend?' And I said, 'No.' And he's like, 'You should do that.' So I came up here in May of 2005 for my Zen training weekend, and I walked into the dining hall, and it was just like, 'Oh, shit! This is it! But how am I going to do this?'"

"What's it like to live in community here?"

She laughs gently, then surprises me. "Uh…it's lonely. I've never experienced loneliness the way I have here. And I thought I was going to avoid that feeling by living in a community. But actually I feel very lonely here sometimes. And it's so challenging."

She reflects a moment, then says, "Maybe 'lonely' isn't the exact right word. I feel my fundamental aloneness as a person, my fundamental condition. It feels true. It doesn't feel good all the time, but it feels true. Just like nobody can get me out of the corner that I put myself in, or nobody can let go of a thought for me. Ultimately, I really am alone in this. And I think the community functions, in a way, to drive you crazy. So that you really have to work with yourself."

"What do you mean by that?"

She grins and leans forward to whisper, "I mean there are people here who drive me nuts! They get on my nerves endlessly." She's laughing. "And I'm sure I serve that function for multiple people in this community. But we're all here working on it. We all have this one thing in common. There's a lot of space here for people to just be themselves. And I think if you stay long enough, you realize, 'I'm not going to change these people to be the way I'd like them to be.' Do you know what I mean?

"There are times when I look around, and here we are in these grey polyester robes eating fruit salad with chop sticks, and I just think, 'What are we doing? This is insane!' And yet! Here we all are! So, yeah, living in community is super challenging, and sometimes I really hate it. But that's just a feeling that I have because I still have some expectation that it shouldn't be this way. But it is this way. I mean, it's great too.

I have a couple of friends among the residents, though not as many as a person would think. Most people here are not my friend; they're more like my family. The crazy family that you choose to live with. But that's what makes it a practice gold-mine. I mean, if you're up against it all the time, especially if you want to wake up, that's a huge benefit."

"What do you mean by that? Waking up? What does that mean to you?"

"If you want to be unconditionally free regardless of the circumstances you find yourself in. That's what it means to me. I'm super not into the whole enlightenment experience thing. I think it's important to have insight as you continue in your practice. But I'm so not interested in kensho or enlightenment. To me, if a person can dis-identify with a thought, that's enlightenment. Can you pick up a napkin that's dropped on the floor? Can you help this person that you actually don't like? To me, that's enlightenment. So I think for me personally, when I use certain terms it's different from how other people may use them. So what I mean by the 'benefit of living in community' is, I really want to be free in my final moment of life, as I'm dying. And this is really good training for that, because the day is filled with 'I don't want to do that.' Or like Bartleby the Scrivener, 'I'd rather not.' You know? All day long. And so I feel like I'm training for my death in a way. And I mean that sort of joyfully." She laughs. "It's not the Death March to Bataan, even though I kind of make it sound like that."

"Daido was married four times," Yushin tells me. "I was number two. I'm still around though. I don't know. Can't get rid of me too easily. Number three was Bonnie Myotai Treace. She had been a writer, a teacher of writing at a college in Florida and was very serious. It was about the time I decided I wanted to move into the French Inn next door. I needed to get off the campus a little bit," she chuckles. "We separated. I moved in next door. Bonnie entered, and they became teacher-student-friend and from there to teacher-student-Dharma successor. Then she needed a place to teach that was not here, and he decided that something in the city might be good. 'Why don't you look around?' And she did and found this magnificent building. And she got loans from the bank, and she got a community together and started teaching there."

This was the Zen Center of New York, located in Brooklyn, which is still maintained by the Mountains and Rivers Order.

"Wife number four, Rachel, came onto the scene about seven years before Daido died," Yushin tells me. "She was not a Zen student. She met him at a gallery opening. They had photography in common. She's a cinematographer, a very fine photographer, and an artist as well – a lot of different medias, watercolor, oils. But photography was the connection for them. She wanted to know more about his work. He wanted to know more about her work, and they started to meet for coffee. She didn't come into the monastery as a student. She was not at all interested in Zen Buddhism or meditation. But they had a keen connection and fell in love – I suppose – through the eyes of their cameras. So she moved into the abbacy and lived there for a number of years, maybe three or four – not too many – three or four.

"I was always around. We had the child, and the child grew up, got married. Now we have a grandchild, he's eleven. So all of us were friendly, very connected, always seeing each other. And I was still a student here at the monastery. When the transformation happened from husband to teacher and I moved off campus, that's when I seriously started to study with him as a teacher and went into dokusan more than ever before. More than with Maezumi. But anyway, Rachael moved in. They became a couple. She wasn't around too much. She had her own life, taught art to people who lived in Harlem. She had a special class that she did there. She was always working on a movie, or she was working on an exhibit of some kind.

"Then one day he calls me up, and he goes, 'Yushin, do you remember where our divorce papers are?' And this was like twenty years before. I said, 'Oh, my God. No. Maybe I can get a copy for you.' He needed it to marry Rachael. He wanted to marry Rachael.

"After he was diagnosed with lung cancer, the monks did everything they could, running this place when he was not well or going to treatment. I brought Italian food over there all the time; whatever Italian dish I was making, I would bring it over to him. And our son was always coming and going. And we saw the changes happening; he started to get frail and fragile. And he wanted to marry Rachael, and we needed to get all the paperwork in order before he could do that, so that she would have authorization for him at the hospital. The monks couldn't always do it. I couldn't do it. Our son wasn't always available to go to the hospital if he had an episode or a seizure or something. So they got married real quick, and it was a beautiful thing. Ryushin married them, and the photograph is beautiful, and the community was happy about it."

John Daido Loori died on October 9, 2009, at the age of 78.

"Rachael comes around at Thanksgiving and at Christmas time, and I know where she lives. I call her and email occasionally. But she didn't have anything to do with Zen. So she's living in Woodstock, and she's the widow, at this point. So…I…I still miss him. Daily." She doesn't need to say so; I can hear it in her voice. "He was the biggest part of my life. I followed the man around for over forty years. First he was my friend, then he was my lover, then he was my husband, then he was the father of my child, then he was my teacher. And once that happened, you don't let go of that. I didn't divorce him as my teacher."

CHAPTER FOURTEEN

Jan Chozen Bays

J
AMES FORD TOLD ME, "I CALL CHOZEN BAY'S SANGHA THE CHILDREN'S CRUSADE."
He was speaking in jest, but it's not an inaccurate description.

In the dining area of Great Vow Zen Monastery I listen to several students discuss their teacher. Most of them, but not all, are in their early twenties; one only turned 20 a few days earlier. Although they are all monastery residents, their manner of speaking and the things that interest them are much the same as their contemporaries'.

"This one time I was standing out on the front sidewalk with another resident," a young monk tells me, "and we were talking about video games or something like that, this kind of magical thinking and how that relates to practice. And as we were standing there talking, Chozen walks by shaking a maraca and singing to herself; she's like 'La-la-la-la-la.' And I'm like, 'Hey, Chozen, did you ever meet any masters with supernatural powers?' And she stops and says, 'Maybe,' and then just goes on shaking her maraca and singing to herself."

By this point in my visit, I don't even give a second thought to the mention of a maraca.

The recently-turned 20 year old informs me, "All long-term residents have to go square-dancing at least once."

"It's part of the deal?" I ask. "You come here, you go square dancing?"

"Yeah. And then I went once and loved it so much that I come back every week."

"Not in monastic garb, though?"

"No, I have a square-dancing outfit." When the others laugh, he quickly points out, "So do they."

The laughter is collegial. They are comfortable together and supportive of one another. It is an attractive community.

"She has a freezer full of dead animals," someone else tells me.

The sole female in the group, who is only slightly older than the young man who goes square dancing, says: "Yeah, I've only been here for three months, so there's not too much contact with Chozen, but I had heard these stories, that she collects dead animals and preserves them, and stories of her taking a big cleaver and, you know, cutting the chest bone? And I didn't really believe it, but then the second week I was here, we passed around a dead bird at breakfast! – which we do a formal oryoki-style breakfast, a silent ceremony and then we have a reading period after that. We'll usually read science articles or some kind of up-to-date thing to kind of keep in contact with the world. And so for reading period that morning, we passed around a dead bird that she had found the other day.

"And then a week later, we all were given little plates, and they passed around these tubes, and they were full of these hibernating bees Chozen has been cultivating. They're not honey bees, but they're bees that will help to repopulate the bee population. And we took them out of their little cones and put them on the table and sorted out the ones that had survived and were going to thrive and the ones who'd had it. So we've been keeping them in the fridge for the past month, till it gets warm enough for them to actually come out and survive. And I found that really surprising, that a Zen teacher was doing that kind of thing at breakfast. But I really appreciate that. She's so interested in so many different things, about bees, about plants, and about animals, medicine, meditation, Zen. She's willing to share all that with us."

Chozen Roshi and her husband, Laren Hogen Bays, are co-abbots of Great Vow Zen Monastery located in a former elementary school in Clatskanie, Oregon, a self-proclaimed Christian township of 1700 persons. The name of the monastery refers to the vow of Jizo Bodhisattva, who swore to work for the benefit of all beings until even the "hells were empty." His image – often in the form of a child monk – is prominent on the grounds. At the back of the monastery property, a set of moss-covered stone steps leads to a garden of Jizos in a large wooded area. Jizo is the protector of women and children, so is a natural choice for a Zen teacher who is a pediatrician.

"I was born on the day that Nagasaki was bombed," Chozen tells me. "My parents were pacifists in World War II. They were living in Chicago. My dad was at the University of Chicago. And they were happy that I was born but very sad about the bombing. So I always knew that I was born on that day, and I had planned on my 60th birthday to take 60 Jizos to offer in Nagasaki. But then people heard about the project and got interested. So we had people send in Jizos from all around the world, every state in the United States. And we ended up taking those Jizos – about 40,000 – to Japan."

Many of the figures in the garden are adorned with caps or scarves; some have toys laid at their base. The garden is a place where parents can leave figures in memory of lost pregnancies, or on behalf of children who are ill or have died, children who are struggling with any manner of physical or psychological challenge. It is a quiet and beautiful place.

"My first husband was a Jewish academic at U of C San Diego, and we had two children at that time, and I was trying to learn some of the Jewish rituals so they could be included in their heritage from his side. I was learning the *Barukh atah Adonai* which you say on Friday night for Shabbat. He was only culturally Jewish; he wasn't religiously Jewish. And then he got interested in Zen because he was a new professor and was having tension headaches and pre-ulcer symptoms. And one of his graduate students said, 'Oh, there's this other professor over at San Diego State, and he said Zen actually helped him a lot. Maybe you'd like to learn that.' The fellow's name was Richard Etheridge. So my husband went over to Richard's house and learned to do zazen. I went along, but I was an intern at University Hospital at the time and working 70 hour weeks, so I fell asleep under the coffee table while he was learning to do zazen, because in medical training you learn to sleep whenever you can.

"Then he began sitting every day. Every morning he would get up and sit, and I was impressed with his dedication and the changes that meditation brought in him. So the next thing that happened, in 1973 we went on sabbatical to Australia, and it was the first time in my life that I wasn't fully occupied with school, because I'd gone to elementary school, high school, medical school, internship, residency, and then suddenly I had this year off. I would say that it was the first time I suffered in my life, because conditions were very different in Australia. To wash clothes, for example – and I had a child in diapers – you had to fill up a washing machine with water, plug it in and it would agitate, then you had to drain it and then put your clothes through a wringer to get the soap suds out. Then you filled it again and put the clothes back in and plugged it in, and it agitated for a while and then you put them through the roller and hung them out to dry and then ironed them, because they were all wrinkled. And the house had mold on the ceiling. I was just frustrated. I felt like, 'All this busy-work, what is it for?' Because I'd just finished my internship, and I'd been doing very dedicated work at a county hospital.

"So I began to sit. I read *Three Pillars of Zen*, because it was the only book of instruction at the time. So when I would get my baby down to nap, I would sit during that time. And that was an experience of a duck to water. Before I had tried sitting and hadn't been so interested. In the group we had gone to in San Diego, you sat facing the wall and then you did this weird chant, and then everybody was like tea and silence. Then everybody got up and left; nobody said a word to each other.

And I was raised in a Protestant church where there was a lot of fellowship. But here there was no fellowship aspect; so I just thought Zen was weird. But my experience was very different when I sat in Australia. Like a duck to water. I said, 'Oh, I know this from long, long ago.' It reminded me of how, when I was young, I used to spend Saturdays in the forest. We lived in a rural area in upstate New York outside of Albany. And I would get up early and just go out into the forest or meadows and streams and climb a tree and sit up in the tree for hours. Reading. Just being. Or I would sit by a pond and watch the dragonflies and just be. So it seemed very familiar, that experience of just being and not doing, and I really took to it. I loved it.

"Then when we came back from Australia, I started sitting with a little group in San Diego. And that group was interesting because a lot of teachers came out of it. Joko Beck was kind of 'Mother Zen' for that group."

Charlotte Joko Beck had studied with Taizan Maezumi at the same time as Bernie Glassman and Daido Loori, and Joko encouraged Chozen and her husband to go to Los Angeles to meet Maezumi. "So we began commuting up to LA, which is about a two hour drive from San Diego. I did my first retreat there, a weekend retreat. Really enjoyed it. Then I did a seven day retreat, and after that I was hooked."

"Maezumi Roshi had a very playful quality. He would be very serious and very ferocious in the sanzen room but he also had a very playful quality, and he was always learning. He loved to learn. He actually learned English and spoke it quite well, which a lot of other teachers from Japan didn't. One day I went over and his little daughter – who was a year-and-a-half I think – was frustrated and was pulling at her hair. And he said to her, 'Michi, don't be so neurotic.' And I said, 'Roshi, where did you learn the word *neurotic?*' He just looked at me and beamed; he was so proud of himself. He was very accurate in his language. I helped him with some translations of Dogen Zenji, and he wanted to know all the nuances of the English words that could be used to translate Japanese words so that he could pick the right nuances. He was very careful of his language, very precise. And that was really fun.

"He was also funny when he got drunk, which was unfortunate because then people would encourage him to get drunk, because another side came out. He would do this imitation geisha which was really very funny. But he would also tell you the truth. The Japanese don't usually tell you the truth because they don't want people to lose face. For example, if Maezumi Roshi had something he wanted to tell me that was difficult, he would tell one of my Dharma brothers, and then they were expected to come tell me, because then I wouldn't lose face by being confronted by Maezumi Roshi directly. And vice versa. He would tell me something that I had to tell them.

That's the way it's done in Japan. So it took a while to learn that. But when he was drunk, he would be very honest. In Japan, if you're drunk, you can be forthright, and it's all forgiven the next day. So you could tell your boss — because everybody goes out drinking after work; that's standard in Japan — so you could say something rude to your boss and the next morning it would be totally forgiven. It's the one time that that very tightly contained society can let go. It's an alcoholic nation essentially. So, when he was drinking, he would tell you what he thought of you. And you wanted to hear that, and you didn't want to hear that. But the temptation was very strong to hear that. So people would drink with him, or sit with him when he was drinking, just to find that out. I don't drink, so I wasn't particularly interested in that.

"He was also very astute. So one Saturday a month, we would have beginners come, and we would do a whole day with them, including lunch, where we would do the eating instructions. And I had just finished with the morning instruction for them, and I was coming up the walkway and met Maezumi Roshi, who said, 'Oh, how was it?' And I said, 'Oh, it was just great. They were so eager and so enthusiastic.' And he looked at me, and he said, 'Oh. A room full of people just like you.' Which was true," she admits with a laugh. "But he would catch you at something — you know — catch your mind being a little off, just a little off.

"Generally, he was very grandmotherly and kind to me, I think because he knew just a little reprimand would go a long way with me. I liked that. But once I did complain to him. There was a woman at ZCLA who was deeply troubled and had a terrible past. She was an older woman. And she asked for work where she didn't have to be with people. She couldn't bear to be with people. So they set her to weeding the grounds which she was happy to do. She liked to be with plants; it was soothing for her. But just outside of our house at the Zen Center, I had just planted a lot of flowers, little, tiny flowers, seedlings and so on. And I came out, and she had torn them all out. I went to Roshi to complain. He looked at me, very severely, and he said, 'Chozen, I don't want to hear you ever say anything like that again. You have no idea what her life has been like. Your life has been very fortunate.' And that's all he had to say, and it was like a knife to the heart. I just had to shift my whole idea of who she was. And he knew who she was; he knew her suffering."

"After I left LA, I read a lot of books about religious groups and how they got into trouble, just to figure out how we got into trouble and get some perspective. And an account that resonated with me was Poona, when Rajneesh[64] was at his height in Poona, and, in one of the books about that, this woman said, 'We felt like we could do anything. We could accomplish anything.' So, Rajneesh could say to them, 'Tomorrow we're going to have a big celebration, and we need decorations.' And they would stay up all night, and they would make flower-garlands and papier-mâché elephants and so on. They just had this feeling of 'we can accomplish anything.' Very high energy. That's what it was like at ZCLA. There was just that feeling of 'together we can accomplish everything. We can all get enlightened together, and, whatever's needed along the way, we can accomplish that.'

"The weird thing about it – and this is part of how Zen got established in North America – is that we took the Hippie Commune and combined it with a Zen Monastery. And, of course, that has its problems, and our teachers were trying to figure that out."

"How aware were you of what was going on elsewhere, in San Francisco, for example?"

"We were very separate. My explanation is that we were doing something weird, in terms of how our families looked at it, and so to self-justify what we were doing, dropping out of careers…. I mean, I dropped out of a tenure-track position at the university; my husband was a tenured professor, and we just dropped out and went to the Zen Center. So, to justify that to ourselves, we had to believe we were doing absolutely the right thing, and that we had the best teacher in the world. And so we were like little enclaves at first, and it took another generation to disperse that. So we knew there was a San Francisco Zen Center, but Suzuki Roshi wasn't the best teacher. And we knew there was Katagiri Roshi. But our teacher was the best. Our center was the best.

"There was a conference I had to lecture at in San Francisco, and I arranged to stay at the Zen Center, and it was an eye-opener. 'Oh, here's this whole community of nice people, and they practice well and Baker Roshi.' In retrospect, it was right before everything fell apart. That same year, Baker Roshi came to ZCLA. And Roshi and Genpo and Tetsugen and all the guys happened to be gone, and it was just us girls running the Zen Center. And I remember sitting down with him, with a couple of other women, and we had this very down to earth conversation in which he said the most interesting thing. Talking about the empire he had built and that we had built, he said something like, 'You know, everything is impermanent, and it may all come crashing down one day.' Well, in retrospect, he had left the San Francisco Zen Center and everything was coming crashing down. We didn't know that, but he said it with such poignancy and emotional depth that I realized, 'Something's wrong here. He's not happy.'"

"The first time I read about enlightenment, I understood what it was. I had that feeling of, 'Oh, yeah, I know this. It's definitely possible to accomplish this. It's just hidden from me by a thin veil. I know exactly what it is.' I was raised in a liberal Christian context, but I was never quite comfortable. I always felt I had to translate everything that was being said; that God wasn't a guy up in the sky. But in Zen, I didn't feel like I had to translate. I felt like, 'Oh, they're speaking my language about the way the world is.' So it just seemed natural and comfortable. And I wanted to become enlightened. I thought it was definitely possible and wanted it to happen. So I was willing to do whatever that required. And I loved koans. I passed Mu very early on and then just started chomping through the koan curriculum. It was like dessert. It was like a meal and dessert all combined. I just loved koans.

"I had family obligations, so I couldn't sit in the evening; I had to help the kids with their homework and so on. And then, because I was a physician, I was constantly getting called out. In retrospect, I think that was an advantage, because I had to put every minute of my time in the zendo to good use. I couldn't day-dream. Because I was constantly getting beeped out. Or I would go into dokusan and work on a koan, and, as I was about to leave, Roshi would say, 'Oh, by the way, you know, so-and-so who just came in has a sore throat. Would you go see them?' So, forget silent sesshin. I just had to go in and out, in and out, in and out. So the time on the cushion was very precious."

"So we had this very strange mix of hippie-commune and monastery, and not a terribly clear understanding of our own psychology. I think there is some spiritual-by-passing that often happens in Zen. Dick Baker's an example; there are lots of examples. So what happened with me was that I fell in love with Roshi. In retrospect, after doing a lot of study and reading, I would say I fell in love with the Dharma through Roshi, as embodied by Roshi. In a way, what you're falling in love with isn't the Dharma in that person but your own potential. So, it's like a mirror. You're falling in love with your own potential to become what this person embodies for you, or your version of it. Then you want to become more and more intimate with it, but because our human understanding of intimacy is so limited and involves sexuality, you think, 'Oh, this must be sexual. That's a way to become more intimate.' But I think both Roshi and I realized that as soon as our relationship became sexual, this was a mistake. It was a mistaken use of that energy. So we backed out and re-established a teaching relationship, but a very loving teaching relationship. I think we loved each other for a long time. Maybe from the first encounter; I don't know."

It was a little more complicated than she makes it sound. Her affair with Maezumi affected both of their marriages. Chozen and her husband divorced. She entered into a relationship with Hogen, who was the naturopath at the medical clinic, and they left the center. Reeling from everything that had happened, she stopped practicing Zen a while, even though by this time she had received Dharma Transmission.

"After I left the Zen Center, I thought about all of us. I thought, if this is enlightened behavior, I'm not interested in it. But I need to investigate it. You know, I'm a physician, so I like to say, 'Okay, here's the condition. I need to learn about it. Learn how to diagnose it early and intervene.' So I read books about the Hare Krishna community and how it had gone awry. The EST community and how it's gone awry. And Synanon and how it went awry. And the Rajneesh Community and how it had gone awry, which was very relevant because he came here to Oregon from India. Bought a bunch of land. Ran into all kinds of problems with authorities. Tried to take over a whole town. Brought in bus-loads of homeless people to stack the voting rolls. Poisoned people. I mean it's unbelievable what happened here in Oregon. And so when we moved to Oregon, the whole state was still smarting from that experience. They're still distrustful of cults.

"So I read about all of those to see what went wrong, and I developed a list of signs of when things are starting to go wrong." Not all of the elements were pertinent to ZCLA, but several were.

"First, the community starts to idolize the teacher and imitate the teacher in all aspects of life. So if the teacher had affairs – and Maezumi Roshi had affairs – then there's a looseness around affairs. Or if the teacher's an alcoholic – in Japan, they call it 'Wisdom Water' – there's this looseness around alcohol. If the teacher divorces, then divorce becomes okay and so on. So there's an idolization, putting the teacher on a pedestal and imitating his behaviour.

"Then there's going to the teacher with questions about all aspects of your life, and the teacher trying to respond to that. The teacher begins to have too much power over your life. So people would go to Roshi and say, 'I'm thinking of changing jobs. What do you think?' Or, 'I'm thinking of getting into a relationship. What do you think?' And he would try his best to answer because he wanted to be helpful. But that's not helpful. Then you have what one of my Dharma sisters called 'too numinous a presence' in the person's life. You have say over too many aspects of their life, rather than just being their spiritual teacher. That can lead to problems.

"Then the next step is usually the belief that we are in the know and it is in the outside world where the problem is. And we're not going to go into the outside world because it's too problematic. So it becomes isolated. There's the inside and the outside, and we're the inside, and we're the best, and we know.

"The next is when the ends justify the means. So the Rajneesh community – and so did the Hare Krishnas – had what they called 'sacred prostitutes.' They would send women out to New York or Tokyo to prostitute and bring money back to the community. So any aspect of 'the ends justifies the means' is the beginning of a downward slide. We didn't have that at ZCLA, but one aspect I saw that made me uncomfortable was that people who were living in voluntary poverty at the Zen Center would go on welfare. And then they would have welfare medical coverage, so they could come to the clinic and we could bill welfare. But these were people who could work, young, strong people, intelligent people. So it was kind of living off the dole in an inappropriate way.

"Then paranoia can take over, and people begin to get armed, which never happened at any of the Zen Centers that I know. But when people get armed and then start plotting against the enemy – and even within the group there's enemy factions and retribution and so on – then you're really in bad trouble. So the Rajneesh people got armed with AK-47s and poisoned people with salmonella."

Maezumi's alcoholism and sexual affairs were revealed at about the same time as Richard Baker's fall from grace in San Francisco. But, unlike Baker, when Maezumi was confronted about his behaviour, he took steps to deal with it.

"Someone who had been his attendant and was in recovery themselves confronted Roshi and said, 'You're an alcoholic, and you need treatment.' And for some reason, Roshi said, 'Yes.'"

"It was that easy?"

"It was the right time. I guess it was the right constellation. I mean, Roshi had already gotten in trouble because he'd had an affair with me, then he had an affair with another woman; his wife had left him. So there was enough ruckus in the community that it was time for a turning point. And he admitted right away that he had a problem and went into residential treatment."

Coincidentally, while all of this was playing out, a film crew arrived.

"A woman from Dartmouth who I think was working on her Ph.D. had come to Zen Center and said, 'I'd like to do a film on the Center.' We'd forgot that she was coming. So in the middle of this ruckus of Roshi leaving to go into residential treatment for alcoholism and the whole community's in an uproar and things are coming out that had never come out before, and we're having meeting after meeting – it was just so sad and such pain and grief coming out – the film crew arrives from Dartmouth!" There is enough distance from the events now that she can laugh at the memory. "And everybody's instinct is, 'Get out of here! We're suffering too much.'

But Roshi said, 'No. This is Zen too. Everything is Zen. This is Zen. Let them come in and film.' So there's this remarkable film where she sits with Roshi, and he says, 'I guess I'm an alcoholic, and I need to do my work.' Very humble. Very straightforward. And then she talks to various people in the community about their reaction to all this. And because Tetsugen was already gone, Daido was already gone – they'd moved east – Genpo went down to be part of the family constellation at the recovery center in San Diego, I'm left holding the bag; so there's an interview with me too about the whole thing.

"So Roshi went to San Diego and stayed there for a month in treatment. And he joined AA, and I think he was a very loyal member of AA for a number of years after that. But the community was in turmoil. Then we had an alcohol intervention for the whole community. So a group came in and did an intervention like they usually do with a family. But there were, like, almost a hundred people there. And it was stunning to all of us, to me, too, because I grew up in a family that doesn't drink, and I don't drink. What stunned me were that the words people spoke on the film were the same words we had spoken in the community all the time. 'Well, he can't be an alcoholic because he doesn't drink during sesshin and so on.' And so to hear a disease – the words of a disease – spoken, as we had spoken them, that was stunning to me. And it was clear we were an enabling community. We were a huge alcoholic family."

In 1984, Chozen and her new husband, Hogen, relocated to Portland. I ask how she chose that city.

"Well, I think several reasons. My sister lived in Oregon for a long time, and I think there was a feeling of gathering back to family, back to a sense of support from family. She lives in Eugene and teaches at U of O. And I wanted to get the kids out of LA and into a more healthy environment. LA was not a healthy environment for them. There was a lot of bullying in school, and they went backwards academically. So that was a motive. I felt like the family had, to a certain extent, been neglected while we were at the Zen Center because we were so focused on getting enlightened. And I had divorced, too, so there was that trauma to the kids. And so I felt I needed to gather the family together and be closer to other family members.

"And then this thing of, 'Wow! If that's enlightened behavior, I don't want anything of it.' So I reacted against practice for several years. I didn't sit at all. Got a job. 'Cause I had to support the kids now that I was divorced and left the Zen Center. Worked back in medicine again, including academic medicine. Just hunkered down and took care of family and lived an ordinary life. And I was intrigued by the realization that 'Wow! There's a lot of ordinary people out there who never studied Zen who are pretty wonderful people.' Then I sort of dragged my new husband through exploring different religious traditions. Just like, 'I've only done Zen for so many years now. I'm so immersed in it I have no perspective.' So we went to a Christian church; we went to a Hindu ashram; we went to an old-fashioned spiritualist group that still existed here that channeled spirits. And we went to a couple of other religious groups, but none of them were satisfying. So gradually we began sitting again."

"Just together at home?"

"Yeah. Uh-huh. Then there was a sitting group in Portland associated with ZCLA, and the teacher of it moved to Mexico City. So the group was without a leader, and they asked would I be willing to lead the group. So the way I would say it is, I built up the practice again step by step. I sat and sat, and 'Oh, yeah, I can see how sitting is helpful.' I had to learn everything afresh. 'Yeah. Sitting is helpful and I can understand now.' Then they wanted services, would we lead the services? So, I did some services. Then they wanted to know would I do a talk once a month? I did a talk once a month. It was only by request. I didn't move forward at all myself. Then would I do interviews? I started doing interviews. And each time, I was saying, 'Is this valuable? And on what basis does it need to be founded on?'

"And then they started meeting in our house. So we had a living room which was pretty much devoted to sitting. It was cleaned out and had cushions, and the group came and sat once a week. That committed us. We had to be ready for the group and welcome the group. And then they started asking for things. They asked for a weekend retreat. And then people asked to have jukai. So Maezumi Roshi came up and helped me with that first jukai ceremony, getting the papers ready and everything, and doing the ceremony. So that was nice. And it just gradually built back up as it seemed appropriate and was requested. Then I became the leader of a group up here."

Once the Zen Community of Oregon was established, Chozen and Hogen began thinking about developing a monastic community. "We decided we wanted to be able to train people to succeed us; I call it the prime directive in Zen, which is 'do not let this die out.' And Maezumi Roshi used to say, 'It's fine to have lay lineages, but no lay lineages have survived.' So, we felt like we wanted to train people to do what we're doing so that when we die it's passed on. And we felt we needed a monastic setting to do that."

Their first training center was located on Larch Mountain in the Colombia Gorge. When that property was declared part of a federal protective area, they searched for another location. They learned that the school district in Clatskanie had been reconfigured and that the Quincy-Mayger Elementary School, with its surrounding grounds, was for sale. And the school district was eager to find a buyer. "Our board president at the time was a real estate lawyer, and he negotiated a deal so that we could buy it with a long-term mortgage at 1¼ percent interest, which at the time was unbelievable, 'cause interest rates were – I don't know – eight or ten per cent. So we essentially got it for free, with monthly payments."

The people of Clatskanie still remembered the Rajneesh Community and were not immediately welcoming. To try to assuage anxiety, the monastery invited the community to a gathering in order to introduce themselves. "We expected about fifty people to come because this is a community of about 1700 people. And we had tea and we had cookies and we had name tags and we had little tables to sit and chat. But when I came in, everybody was lined up. Nobody would wear name tags, and they were afraid to drink the tea, afraid that it was poisoned Kool-Aid. They wouldn't eat the cookies. All lined up in chairs. 200 people."

Chozen had been working at the hospital the night of the meet-and-greet, so she arrived late. "And when I walked in, this woman was saying, 'I would not speak unless my husband had given me permission to speak. And he has given me permission to speak. And I just want to say: What's wrong with all you Christians out there? Can't you feel the hand of darkness? Can't you feel the aura of Satan? These people are here to steal the souls of our children!' I thought, 'Wow! Have we made a mistake!' But then I could see some people rolling their eyes as if, 'There she goes again.' And I thought, 'Okay, they don't all believe this.'"

It was a gradual process. Slowly they overcame suspicions and became active in the wider community. "Country people are really wonderful. Unsophisticated in one way, but very sophisticated in another way. They look at a person and what a person does to judge the person. This is what we've found. So, the first time we went to the donut shop in town, the whole place went silent as we walked in. Then they saw we ordered donuts, and we ordered coffee, and we sat and we chatted and ate. And, 'Oh, these Buddhists eat donuts, drink coffee. All right.' So, they just watch, and if you're a good, decent human being, that's what you're judged on. The rest is kind of irrelevant."

Hogen joined the Kiwanis Club, and Mrs. Bays – as she is known to the children – teaches marimba in local schools.

"Marimba started when we were at our other site. We had a party – a holiday party – and we invited neighbors. And some neighbors came and brought two marimbas and played them. And it was so enchanting; it was such happy music. And there's a cottage-industry in Oregon building marimbas. So I bought a marimba from this neighbor, and I engaged his thirteen year old daughter to teach me to play it, because she was very good. So, she taught me, and I really liked it, and then our first long-term resident came – and she had a musical background – and I taught her to play. And then, there was something going on in the school district where they got a new music teacher, and he learned that we did this. And he said, 'Would you come and teach the fourth graders marimba?' So he selected out a group, and we taught them marimba. That got us teaching kids. Then I just started. Anybody who came and lived with us for a while at Larch Mountain, I taught them marimba. It was part of the training because it teaches people to pay attention. And it teaches people to get over the obstacle of fear. So many people think, 'I can't play music. I'm not musical.' But if you get them started, they start having fun, and it gets them over that thing of 'I can't do this.' And they have to pay attention. One young fellow who had a crazy mind said, 'The only time my mind is quiet is when I play marimba, because I have to concentrate so hard.' It teaches them to listen to everybody else. Once they've got their part, they have to open up their minds to everybody else and play in harmony with them. And, most importantly, it teaches people that you can change your state of mind instantly. So, if people come to rehearsal and they're in a bad mood, within five minutes of playing, they're happy, happy, happy. So it's a lesson that our states of mind are very impermanent. And there are tools to change our states of mind. There are some difficult ones like alcohol and drugs, but there are some very felicitous ones, like playing music. So, if you learn it with music, you can learn it in other ways, you can use other tools of practice, metta-practice and so on, to change your state of mind. So we just have tons of fun, and we do concerts, little mini-concerts, on Sundays. We did one for the Kiwanis Club.

"So because we'd taught in this other school district, we asked the music teacher here, 'Would you like us to teach marimba here?' And he said, 'Oh, yes, please.' Because they'd lost their elementary school music teacher. It's a very poor district and for seven years they had no music education in the school at all except what each classroom teacher would do. So we started an after-school marimba program for fourth graders. In fifth grade they go to band, so it helped them develop the skills to go to band. So he likes that. Then, when it was clear no music teacher was going to be hired for the elementary school, we just happened to have a retired music teacher move into the community who practices with us half-time, lives with us half-time and lives in town the other half of the time. So she began helping us. Then she developed a music program for K through 4. So she goes into the classroom with some of our young people and teaches a basic music module. Which takes the pressure off the teachers to have to do that. And now we have another retired music teacher who's joined her. So we do both this module of basic music instruction, K through 4, and our after-school marimba program. And what's fun about it with the kids is seeing them grow. 'Oh, I can play!' And people appreciate it. It's better than the violin which sounds terrible for years; the marimba sounds great right away. And then they get to go to the retirement home in town and play concerts there. They get very excited about going out and doing little concerts."

I ask where square dancing fits in.

"My parents were square dancers, so I learned when I was a teenager and always enjoyed it. My boyfriends square danced when I was young. Then, long gap, no dancing. But then Hogen and I were immersed in our careers. I was doing child abuse work full-time; he was working with criminals full time. He worked at the state penitentiary and with criminals after discharge, violent criminals and sex offenders. So we did two sides of the same issue. It was stressful work, and I said, 'We need to get exercise, and we need to do something that's really fun.' So I convinced him to take square dancing lessons, and he loved it. So for several years we did square dancing on a fairly regular basis, usually on weekends. And you just lose track of time when you're square dancing. You have to be in the moment. It's a meditation for body and mind, because if your mind wanders, you don't hear the call and you break down the square. So it's good for body and mind. So when the Larch Mountain program got active and then we moved here, we didn't do it for fifteen years. But recently I said, 'You know, our bodies are degenerating. We've done this for umpteen years. We're just totally immersed in Zen. We have to do something else. Let's go square dancing again.' And he was reluctant at first, but now he loves it! He turns into this happy, happy person five minutes after we get in the door. He's just like Mr. Sociable. So it's given us a different life and a different group of friends. They don't care if we're Zen teachers. 'Can you dance?' is all it is."

"Petticoated skirts and all of that?"

"I have them, although fortunately these days you wear more like prairie skirts so you don't have to look like a cupcake. And he has pearl button shirts and a bolo tie, which my son made for him. And now we've got some of the young people here square dancing."

"Which they probably didn't expect they'd be doing."

"No, they didn't. They'll tell you, 'You never know what you're going to get dragged into at Great Vow Monastery.' So – this is another part we haven't talked about – we do a whole nature module. Every morning at formal breakfast, oryoki breakfast, I teach them about nature. Because they don't know diddley about the world around them. And so we started out the with the plants in our environment, teaching them about the various plants and their medicinal uses and so on, edible plants. Then we graduated to microscopic work. I mean, if you look at nettles, which we have around here, under the microscope, they have little hypodermic needles which have acid in them that break off and inject acid into your skin. It's beautiful to see under a microscope. The whole world opens up. And then birds and animals. I bring in road kill, and we dissect road kill. Which they'll also go like, 'Ehhww!' But they're so fascinated, because then they get to see what a liver looks like, what a heart looks like, and what lungs look like. They've never seen that, most of them. They have no idea.

"So part of it is just general education about how to live a life as a human being. A lot of them feel, 'If I buy something and it breaks, I can't fix it.' So we teach them basic repairs. We teach them how to sew. We teach them how to cook. Many of them come here not having a clue how to cook. Haven't even boiled water. Just put stuff in the microwave. So we get them exercising; we get them square dancing; we get them playing marimba. We help them flesh out. And they have to live in family. A lot of them come from very dysfunctional families. If they didn't come from a dysfunctional family, they were bullied. Intelligent, wonderful kids, but they just need some re-parenting. So consciously we're re-parenting a lot of these young people."

"Do you still practice medicine?"

"Only a few hours a week. Mostly lecturing. I don't see patients because for the last 26 years I've specialized in child abuse only, evaluating children for child abuse cases. And when you see a child for child abuse, often you have to go to court, and that could be years later. So I quit seeing patients about two years ago because I needed to wind down my court obligations. So I do mostly lecturing and training now in child abuse, specifically. I train all the new Department of Human Services workers, the state and social service workers. Every eight weeks I go in and do a training for them."

"You also work with victims of clergy abuse."

"Yes, well, when I was investigating, I became very interested in clergy abuse and the dynamics of clergy abuse. My husband and I took a training from Marie Fortune from the 'Faith Trust Institute' down in the Graduate Theological faculty in Berkeley. We were the first Buddhists to do that. And at first it was a little weird, because they were all Christians or Jews who were taking it, but once you changed the terminology a little bit, it was exactly the same dynamics, the same realization that, 'Wow! Alcoholism! It's the same no matter who, what country, what person, what organization, what family.' The same with clergy abuse; it's the same. Catholic. Protestant. Jewish. Buddhist."

"Would you describe what happened in San Francisco and Los Angeles as clergy abuse?"

"Yes, I would. I realized that especially when I began teaching on my own and saw people come in and just open up like little flowers, just reveal themselves like little flowers, I thought – and I was working in child abuse at the time – I thought, 'If you did anything to harm this person, took advantage of them for your own gain in any way, that's child abuse.' I understood it in that context. And so we have a sacred duty – Marie calls it a sacred trust – to honor this person and never ever take advantage of them financially or sexually or misuse power or whatever our own needs are. And we have to know our own needs and know how to get them met without using somebody else."

She was a member of the "Witnessing Counsel" that interviewed people after the Sasaki situation became public. They published a report which, according to Myokyo, displeased many of Sasaki's oshos. Still, Chozen recognizes Sasaki's strengths.

"Just about everybody says he's a wonderful Zen teacher. Very potent Zen teacher. Even a number of the women who were abused by him and left still say so. Most of them, not all of them.

"Working with Marie Fortune has helped me understand this better, her very careful analysis of who has power in a situation, what's misuse of power, and so on, and what is it in the clergy situation, what are healthy boundaries. Because, see, boundaries are seen as problematic in Zen because it's just your ego that sets up these boundaries between you and others. So we want to tear down boundaries. But she says there are some boundaries – like white lines down the middle of the road – that are very important to maintain. So she has a method for helping people understand clergy dynamics and clergy misconduct. Another thing that helped was Ken Wilbur's talks about lines of development. He says that all human beings have many lines of development. So there's the line of development that's the financial line: Can you balance your chequebook? And there's the line of development which might be athletic. And a line of development that might be music and arts: Can you carry a tune, can you design your own music and so on? There might be a line which is social interactive: So are you comfortable with people and can you interact socially with people? Then there's a line of development we might call the 'spiritual line of development.' And just because your spiritual line of development is developed and you can be a potent inducer of spiritual experiences in people and really speak to their spiritual heart and catalyze them into spiritual practice doesn't mean you can balance chequebooks or won't embezzle funds, doesn't mean you can sing on key; it doesn't mean you're a good athlete and so on. So we used to have this magical expectation, I think, that if you got enlightened, all those lines of development would be taken care of, including the ethical line of development. We thought it would just be clear that whatever you did it would be a manifestation of enlightened behavior. We were wrong."

"The envelope for all the activity here is Zen and what helps people within Zen. Because what happens when you become ordained is that all of the talents and skills that you developed from your own personal interests or your own strategies to survive then become the property of the Dharma and will be used by the Dharma. So if you're a businessman like Tetsugen is, you become a Zen businessman.

"So I had practiced mindful eating essentially since my second or third sesshin. Just paying deliberate attention to all aspects of eating. So the movement of the hand. What your tongue does in your mouth. The tastes, the flavors, the sounds. And not just in your mouth, but as you're swallowing it. Being aware of changes in your abdomen and changes in yourself. And the heart, the emotions around eating; that's what I call the Heart Hunger. Then what the mind says about eating. Which is a problem when people are dieting; their mind just interferes with their natural enjoyment of food.

"Then as a pediatrician, I became worried about the obesity epidemic among children. And adults, too, but I started seeing it in the children I was seeing. Obese by age three. Diabetes just rampant among children now, which we never had before. So I saw this issue in pediatrics and said, 'What do we do to solve it?' First I looked at what we had done medically, which is all unsatisfactory. Dieting never works, and it sets people up for eating disorders, especially children if you can get them to diet. Attacking fat, liposuction, and so on, doesn't work. Attack the digestive system, which is what we do now, so we have this by-pass surgery. And I thought, 'Our intestines are innocent; they're just trying to do their work. You can't get in there and rearrange them and think this is going to be beneficial. And surely they wouldn't do that with children.' But they are doing it with adolescents and pre-adolescents now, rearranging their intestinal anatomy! It's unbelievable. They detach your small intestine and by-pass a whole bunch of the absorptive surface and then reattach you down later. So you don't absorb; you get malabsorption and malnutrition. And you have to take a whole lot of supplements because the food is just passing through, unabsorbed. And they also have banding procedures and stapling procedures where they make your stomach smaller. They have a whole bunch of procedures. But the intestine is innocent; it's just trying to do its job. It's terrible the way we think we're going to cure the problem. The problem is in the heart-mind and in our ignorance of what's going on in our body. We've become totally neurotic about eating.

"So I looked at these unsatisfactory solutions – very unsatisfactory for children – and said, 'We need something that's inexpensive (the surgery is $20,000 or $30,000). Inexpensive. Can be learned easily. Can then be practiced. Parents can pass it onto their children. Has positive side effects rather than negative side effects.' And I thought, 'Oh! Mindful eating!' We have this 2500 year old tradition, and I love practicing it and teaching it to people. So in the book, *Mindful Eating*, my Zen life and my medical life came together. And it caught on. It sells well. It's been translated into eight languages.

"I'm going to Belgium to do a workshop. I do them in conjunction with a woman who's an expert in mindfulness-based stress reduction. We teach a five day workshop for professionals on mindful eating. It's called Mindful Eating Conscious Living. So, did I think I would be doing this as a Zen teacher? No. But it's needed. It helps people relieve suffering. It introduces them to meditation. And some go on to meditation and Zen practice."

"Is mindful eating a spiritual practice?"

"Definitely. I mean, spiritual practice is about intimacy, if nothing else. We're born into separation, and that's the source of our suffering. This idea of self and other is the source of our suffering, and all of these things that we do – drinking, gambling, pornography – all of the addictive things in our life are based on wanting to get back to Oneness. So we can teach people to be one with what they're eating. That's the most intimate thing, where you take another being into your body literally, literally intermingle with your body. So we talk about sex as the ultimate in intimacy, but actually eating is the most intimate thing we do, three, four, five, six times a day. So to be conscious and present to it is a Dharma gate into the experience of Oneness. People have mystical experiences when they do mindful eating if they're doing it well.

"There's an exercise called 'Look Deeply into Your Food.' So if you look into the life of a raisin and play it backwards. I ask people to look at how many people's or beings' life-energy flowed toward you in this raisin which is in your hand. And I say, 'Invite those people to the table. Thank them by eating mindfully.' So here you are at the interface. There's all of that, and then, within us, there are more living organisms than there are our own cells. So there are others inside us, more DNA from other beings than there are our own cells. So, I help people understand, 'You're feeding a universe of beings – not an apartment building, not a city – a universe of beings, 10-to-the-16th beings are being fed by what you eat. So recognize that you're nourishing them, that you're giving them a gift.' So it's a spiritual practice to help people understand where they are in this continuum of life. Some of them get it, some of them don't. But for most people, it's like a big, 'Ah ha!'"

CHAPTER FIFTEEN
Gerry Shishin Wick

Z EN CENTERS FREQUENTLY HAVE AN AUSTERE ELEGANCE. THE COLORS TEND
to be muted, shades of beige and brown predominating; often the only wall
decorations are black ink calligraphy scrolls. The riotous colors of Great
Mountain Zen Center at Maitreya Abbey, on the other hand, seem more suited
to Hinduism or Tibetan Buddhism. Hand drawn signs, statuary, a koi pond, and
Tibetan prayer flags identify the site. The house is painted in bright colors: green,
yellow, red. There is an invocation by the outside entrance to the Zendo: "Enlightened ones of the universe, Bodhisattvas, Protectors of the Dharma, together with
planets, stars, and all sentient ones. We open our hearts to transform the five poisons
of ignorance, attachment, pride, envy and anger. May healing love and peace prevail
throughout the whole Earth and entire universe. Maha prajna paramita."

Maitreya Abbey is located in Berthoud, Colorado, fifty miles north of Denver.
The surrounding countryside is farmland and horse ranches. Shishin ("Lion Heart")
Wick has a couple of horses as well as goats and chickens. "Fresh eggs every day,"
he tells me. The Abbey is his home, and, although he has been in Berthoud for four
years – and has been a transmitted teacher since 1990 – the first traditional Zen
sesshin to be held here only took place a month before my visit.

The original Great Mountain Zen Center is located in Lafayette, Colorado,
twelve miles outside Boulder. Shishin had been the President and Spiritual Leader of
that center for thirteen years. By his own admission, the mode of practice there had
been very different from what now takes place at Maitreya Abbey.

If Jizo is the prevailing devotional figure at Chozen's Great Vow Monastery,
Kannon – or Guanyin – is the prevailing figure here. Shishin is a large man with a
black beard and a deep voice, so the distinctly feminine ambiance here is a little surprising. There are numerous statues, banners, and even pastel paintings of Kannon.
Her statue, twice the height of the seated Buddha beside it, dominates the altar in
the zendo. There is a shrine to the Virgin Mary on the grounds as well, a green, yellow, and red scarf tied around her neck. The statue of the Archangel Gabriel beside

her wears a similar scarf. These figures, Shishin tells me, reflect the interest that his wife – Shinko, or "Body of Light" – has in rediscovering the feminine side of Buddhism. The paintings are her work, as is the outdoor signage. Although I hear her footsteps in the house from time to time during the interview, she doesn't join us, and I will leave feeling that I may have got only half the story of this place.

Since it's called an abbey, I ask Shishin if he's the abbot. "Is that the title you use?"

No, he tells me. Shinko is the abbess.

"And you are?"

"The consort," he laughs. When I persist, he concedes that I can think of him as the "Spiritual Director."

We are seated in an open area off the kitchen beside a corridor with rooms for retreatants. There are Kannon murals by Shinko on the walls of those rooms. In the corner where we're seated, there is a large banner of the Bodhisattva and, opposite it, a Tibetan Blue Tara, another female devotional figure.

Shishin repeats the question I put to him: "What's the function of Zen?" He has a soft voice and pauses a moment before continuing. "Well, you know, I think if you'd asked me that question at different points in my career, you'd get different answers. And I guess we're going to take a time-slice right now. I think the function of Zen is to disseminate the essential teachings of the Buddha in a form that can be digested by a non-Buddhist public."

"By a non-Buddhist public?"

He nods. "In order," he goes on, speaking slowly and carefully, "in order, to build a strong enough base of interest in meditation and in Zen Buddhism from which we might find some people who are willing to go deep into it so that they have realizations which preserve the original intent of the teachings in order to carry them forward. So, how's that for a mouthful?"

"I mean, if you'd've asked me forty years ago, I would have said, 'To realize one's essential nature or to realize No Self and impermanence and all that.' But now I think it's more important that more people get exposed to it. And I don't think everybody's going to have a deep, abiding understanding of it, but as long as there's a few people...." He shrugs. "I just don't think there's that many Sixth Patriarchs or Hakuins or Dogens out there. You know?

"I have very high standards in Zen that I inherited from my teacher, Maezumi Roshi, and I've seen people who have studied with me, who I never would have given Dharma transmission to, who have gone to other teachers and gotten Dharma transmission. And at first I thought, 'What the hell?' And then I realized it was actually a good thing for more people to be in a position where they're sharing the teachings, were teaching people how to meditate and disseminating it. And I completely reversed my position on that. In fact, I have a student in Taos who I'm encouraging to develop a meditation-teacher program, kind of like yoga teachers are proliferating all over the country. And I have a feeling that the more people who meditate the better it will be even if it's half-baked."

"Is there a difference between Zen meditation and other forms of meditation?"

"Well, I think it's the tradition. I mean, I haven't done other forms of meditation as a student – I've primarily done Zen meditation – but the ultimate purpose of Zen meditation is to resolve this Great Matter, to reveal one's true nature, to see into the ultimate Dharma, to experience No Self, to experience impermanence, experience the Emptiness. A lot of meditations are just about mindfulness-training, being aware of what you're feeling, what you're doing. And they don't emphasize this awakening experience which is the core of Zen. But, like I said, I think – from what I just talked about proliferating meditation – there's not a lot of difference if you're just learning.

"You know, I was always under the assumption that the more people meditated the better it would be. I used to think, 'Boy! I sure wish the presidents of the United States would take up meditation and all of the leaders of congress.' Well, one of them did. His name is Mark Sanford. He was the governor of South Carolina, and he was caught having a long distance affair with a woman in South America. He told all his staff he was going to hike the Appalachian Trail, and he used government funds to carry on this extra-marital affair. Then he got caught. Anyway, he was forced to resign as Governor, and, the next three years, he started meditating – I'm not clear what kind of meditation he did – in order, I think, to deal with the loss of his prestige and his position and this sort of thing. But then he made a political comeback, running as a Republican in South Carolina against a woman who was actually the sister of Steven Colbert. And he won! You know? After three years of meditation. But his politics are still as conservative and self-centered and seem to be devoid of compassion like so many of the current Republican politicians seem to be. So I thought, 'Hey, this guy meditated for three years, and he didn't learn anything. He learned to be a better competitive politician.'

"And then I started seeing how meditation is being used for people in business to be more competitive, not necessarily to have a more humane, compassionate working place but in order to learn to stay focused so they can drive their competitors out of business more effectively, so they can get beyond being controlled by feelings and so forth and do these things without even having a twinge of conscience. Students do meditation to become better students, and lawyers do meditation to be better advocates for their clients, and so on. And this is really a perversion of the original intent of the practice.

"Then I read about a study at Northeastern University where some psychologists were trying to look at the connection between meditation and compassion. Now certainly as I was trained, I learned that having clear insight was pretty worthless unless it translates into this kind of being in the world that is the way of compassion. That's a natural function of wisdom. But in these other arenas, the techniques were being perverted.

"Anyway, in the Northeastern University study, the way they set up the experiment was they told students that if they came to this program, they'd teach them how to meditate in order to improve their grades and their study habits. So the students came, and they told half of them that they were selected for the program but that it was full and that the other half would have to wait for the next session. They kept tabs on both groups. So for eight weeks – I don't know how intensive it was – but they taught these people how to meditate. It was mostly mindfulness meditation, I think. And they brought them in for interviews after the eight weeks, one by one. Both groups. Ostensibly the group that was put on the waiting list, they were to be interviewed for a continuing program. So in the waiting room there were three chairs, and two of them were occupied by actors, and, when the person came in, they had to take the third chair. Then a fourth person came in on crutches, had a cast on a leg, bandages, was leaning against the wall moaning. You know? It's another actor. So what they were really studying was what the person would do, because the other two who were sitting in chairs were busy texting and looking at their i-phones and were totally ignoring this person. What they found was that those who meditated, about half of them – about 50 percent – got up and tried to tend to the other person and give them their seat. Those who didn't meditate, only 15 percent did.

"I don't know how big the sample was. I think they had somewhere around fifty people in each group; something like that. Now you can draw certain conclusions, but what I found encouraging was that, maybe in spite of themselves, by meditating people showed more compassion. So, it renewed my faith that meditation should be taught as broadly as possible. I think that as many people as get exposed and encouraged to be good people and to practice, the better."

I ask about the Kannon figures, and he explains that his wife, Shinko, believes the feminine aspect in Zen has largely been overlooked. Her early training had taken place at Philip Kapleau's Rochester Zen Center, famed for its "boot-camp" approach to practice. Shishin and Shinko are consciously trying to establish a different atmosphere here.

"We're a lot more gentle. I mean, Shinko was just talking about sitting at Rochester and how the windows were wide open in the winter, and guys had frost in their beards. People had frozen boogers running down their noses, but, if you moved to wipe it, you were shouted at. And they used the kyosaku freely. When we use the kyosaku, we never hit people unless they ask for it, and they can ask for a shoulder rub instead of being hit by the kyosaku. That's just a small thing. We expect people to be on time and to be quiet and to sit as still as they can, but we don't yell at people if they squirm. I think it's just as powerful as the other way."

The training at the Zen Center of Los Angeles, where Shishin trained, was not quite as strict as at Rochester, but it was still dominated by the type of masculine energy common to the pioneers who brought Zen to North America. At one time, that style of training appealed to a lot of people – both men and women – but Shishin doesn't believe it does as much any longer.

"In general, I don't think there's the same kind of commitment that I had or Chozen had or some of the other people you may have talked to had. Because we were ordained, and I don't know what the future of ordination is in this country. Everybody in our center's a lay person. They work and have their own families."

"Could they be ordained if they wanted?"

"Sure. I've ordained three novices, and they all left. But what I wanted to say is, lay people have their own lives, and you can't expect them to put as much energy into a Zen Center as we used to. Like in my case, I quit my job and devoted full time to it."

"It seemed to be part of the culture then, didn't it?" I say. "The '60s; psychedelic drugs; the drive to become enlightened. So the people who come now, what drives them?"

He shrugs. "Well, they're not happy. And they've tried all kinds of things, and this is one thing they're either trying along their path or as a last resort. They want to have peace of mind."

"But there are options. They could take up TM, go to a Shambhala Center, take a mindfulness seminar. Why choose Zen? After all, it has a reputation for being a little tougher than the others."

"Some people like the discipline, like the form. They like the container. I think everybody has different personalities, and, when you find certain things, you relate to them. I mean, maybe you searched around yourself and found that Zen spoke to you more than other practices."

I ask how he first became involved in Zen.

"Well, you already put your finger on it. I was a graduate student in physics at the University of California in Berkeley in the '60s." He pauses a moment before going on. "You know, people ask me this question a lot, and I have an answer. But I think any answer to that question is kind of a rationalization or justification after the fact. If you really think about it, who knows?

"I initially went into physics because I was interested in how things worked – what ultimate reality was – and along the way, I got a Ph.D. in physics. But I realized at some point in my graduate career that it was interesting, but I wasn't going to find any ultimate answers. Although physics advances, it's more like a toroid or a spiral. There's never any closure. So – you know – Berkeley in the '60s, I was exposed to a lot of things. And experiences with psychedelic drugs for me were always very positive and very religious, which is hard to believe, because I was raised Jewish, and I never found it very inspiring and didn't have any religion."

"Did your family practice Judaism?"

"Oh, yeah. I mean, they weren't orthodox, but every Friday evening we had a Sabbath meal, and my mother celebrated all of the holidays. Decorated the house. I call my mother a social Jew rather than a religious Jew. My father was more a religious Jew. He was raised very orthodox. But, still, it didn't speak to me. I didn't find any inspiration in any of the teachers or rabbis that I encountered in my youth. But then psychedelics showed me that what I assumed was reality was very ethereal, very tenuous. The experiences were elevating. And I suppose I was reading things. Around that time, *The Three Pillars of Zen* was first published. I think it was around '65, I got the hardback copy of it and read some of the enlightenment experiences, and said, 'Wow! This is all available without drugs!' So I went over and sat with Suzuki Roshi on Bush Street in San Francisco. I never really became involved there, but I sat there, and I listened to his talks.

"After I got my Ph.D., I had a post-doctoral fellowship in England. And I looked around for some way to continue my practice over there; mostly there were Hindus, a lot of Indian immigrants. So I went to satsangs, and it just didn't resonate with me. But then in '69, the Buddhist Society of London invited Sochu Suzuki to come there. He was Soen Nakagawa's senior disciple. He's an older brother of Eido Shimano Roshi, and he was the abbot of Ryutakuji at the time. He came to London, where I was living, and I went to the Buddhist Society and sat with him. Christmas Humphreys had invited him, but Sochu didn't like the Buddhist Society. It was more of a philosophical discussion group than a practice center. So he encouraged some of us interested in practicing to set up an independent Zen Center. Which a number of us did. It was a small group. He stayed there for over a year and taught us how to meditate. We did sesshins. And then he left. Went back to Japan. We kept it going. And then he sent Katsuki Sekida there, because he had written a couple of books that were popular."

"Which tell you exactly how many cubic millimetres of air to inhale."

Shishin laughs. "Right! He was a funny, funny little guy. But he was there for about six months, then Sochu Roshi came back, and about that time I had finished what I was doing there in England and was coming back to the States."

"What was the focus of your post-doctoral work?"

"I was working on nuclear physics at the Atomic Energy Research Establishment outside of London. I was a science writer and journalist. I did that for three years for the New Scientist magazine. Then I got a job as an oceanographer in La Jolla."

He notices my facial expression and says, "What's the transition? Well, the physics of the ocean. The guy who hired me liked my breadth of interest, 'cause I was a science writer and was interested in a lot of things. But on the way back, Sochu Roshi was coming to New York from London to help Eido Roshi with a sesshin, and he invited me to come. So I went and sat for a week sesshin. I sat right next to a woman named Sherry Nordstrom, who's now Shinge Chayat Roshi. I noticed you talked to her. And it might have been her first sesshin. We sat right next to each other.

"There's a funny story about that. It was a difficult sesshin for me, because, when we sat in London, we were all beginners, and Sochu was pretty lenient with us. But I decided in New York I wasn't going to move – it took a long time for my body to get used to zazen; I was very athletic – so I said I wasn't going to move. But I had tremendous pain. And so after the sesshin was over, I had this guy on the left side of me, and Sherry on the right side. So I went to this guy, and I thanked him for sitting next to me, and he said, 'Boy was I pissed at you!' I said, 'Really? Why?' 'Oh,' he said, 'you were breathing so hard, I started calling you Froggy.' 'Gee,' I said, 'I'm really sorry.' 'Ah, it's okay. I got used to it.' I said, 'Gee, I better go apologize to Sherry.' And I went to her, and I said, 'I'm sorry if I made so much noise – you know – so grating that I disturbed your practice.' She said, 'What? You were like the Rock of Gibraltar. You were an inspiration!' So then I realized, it had nothing to do with me! I was going to introduce them, and I was going to say, 'Sherry, this is Froggy; Froggy, I'd like you to meet the Rock of Gibraltar.'

"But I sat that sesshin with Eido Roshi, and then I asked him, 'I'm going to San Diego. Who would you recommend there?' And he knew a guy named Ray Jordan, and Ray Jordan was a student of Nyogen Senzaki's, and he was a professor of religious studies at San Diego State University. So I looked him up when I got to San Diego, to sit there, and Joko Beck was sitting with that group. So I got to know her, and she said that she was studying with Maezumi Roshi in LA and invited me to go to a sesshin, which I did in 1972. Then I started to sit with Maezumi Roshi, and

I had a heart connection with him – sat with him for 23 years, until he died – and became a successor of his."

"Do you have a favorite Maezumi Roshi story?"

"Well, a couple of things, but I'll tell you the first thing that comes to mind. He had asked me in the '80s to go down to Mexico and help set up a Zen Center in Mexico City because there were a lot of Mexicans who were coming up to LA to sit, and they wanted him to go down there. I used to go down there probably three or four months out of the year. And one time we'd set up a sesshin in an empty house that one of the members had built who was an architect. Maezumi Roshi came, and, while we were in sesshin, the neighbor's dog ran out into the street and got run over by a car and killed. And Maezumi Roshi said to me that we were responsible. I said, 'Really? How are we responsible?' And he said, 'Well, this was an empty house, then suddenly there were people here chanting and lighting incense, walking around. The dog's routine got distracted; it got frightened and went out in the street. So we need to give that dog a proper funeral.' Well, you know, the main thing for me was not necessarily the funeral but that he said, 'We're always responsible.' And for me that was a real teaching. 'We're always responsible.'"

Shishin got a position on the faculty at the University of California, San Diego, teaching Oceanography. San Diego is two hours south of Los Angeles, and Shishin made the trip as often as he could.

"When I first went to the Zen Center in '72, it was fairly small but very vibrant. Once I learned about it, I went to every single sesshin; every holiday I had, I went to sesshin."

After six years of commuting, he gave up his faculty position, took ordination, and moved into the Zen Center. Chozen had described ZCLA as a combination of hippie commune and Zen monastery. Shishin tells me that by the time he moved into residency, the commune aspect had subsided. "It was more of a monastic community. There were a lot of people who were ordained. Maezumi Roshi didn't have people jump through a lot of hoops to have jukai or to be ordained. He told the story of the Buddha who ordained a drunkard who came into his camp, and the guy got up in the morning and noticed his head was shaved and that he was wearing robes, and he ran away in horror. So some of the Buddha's disciples asked, 'Why did you do that?' And he said, 'Well, you know, just having shaved his head and putting on the robes he got the merit.'"

When Shishin came into residence, Bernie Glassman was the head disciple. "I think the growth of the place was primarily due to him, the businesses, the purchases of property. He was very serious. Very focused. When I first met him, he was still studying. He wasn't a teacher. He was just evolving into the things that he did later. He wasn't very approachable at the beginning, but now I love him. We're good friends." Shishin would later serve on the Board of the Directors of Glassman's Zen Peacemakers.

"How did things change for you after you became a resident?"

"Well, that was my life. I was totally devoted. I left the academic career, was a resident for eight years, and that was my life. I sat twice a day every day; during angos, three times a day. I went to all the sesshins. When I got to be a senior student, I was going to Mexico or I would lead retreats or help lead retreats with Maezumi Roshi in various places. Sometimes I'd do two week-long sesshins a month. I mean, whether I was in sesshin or not in sesshin, my life seemed to be the same. And I was always an administrator at the Zen Center."

There was a lot to administrate. The property holdings were not as extensive as those of the San Francisco Zen Center, but they were substantial and included seven houses as well as four apartment buildings. At its peak there were 120 residents. In 1983 – the year Maezumi went into rehab – Glassman and Loori were in New York; Chozen would soon leave for Oregon; Shishin, however, remained in Los Angeles as the center's chief administrator.

Shishin agrees that Maezumi's students probably enabled his drinking.

"When I first got there – you know – it was pretty exciting spending time with him. He'd always invite me to come to his apartment. You said it was a hippie commune, but I was one of the few people that came there who was mature. A Ph.D. university professor." He laughs softly. "But I was still a hippie. Or at least had very liberal thoughts and attitudes. But he'd invite me to drink with him. And I remember one time it triggered something, and I just started crying; something that was a great release for me. And he said, 'That's what I've been waiting for.' So, we used to think – and I heard a lot of people, like Chozen, say it – that when he was drunk was when he was ruthlessly honest as a teacher. But then I saw him doing things when he was drunk that I thought were pretty immature, and I just decided I no longer needed to be around that. Even though I lived there and was close to him, I decided when he was drinking I just didn't want to be around him. He was an alcoholic, but so were most of the Japanese teachers that came to this country. I think that in Japan the culture is so tightly defined – your role in the culture is so tightly defined – that you can only let loose when you're drunk, and they excuse that. You know? It's a cultural thing. I read something that Aitken Roshi wrote that said, 'In our country, we would say someone was an alcoholic. In Japan, they would say, "He likes sake."'

"But we did intervene, and Chozen was there at the time. He went to the Betty Ford Clinic. I don't think it had a lot of impact on him except for a couple of things. One: he never drank in public after that. And, two, he was very contrite about the damage he caused to the sangha and particularly about his relationship with Chozen, who was a Dharma successor. He just felt it caused problems."

The community fractured. A number of members left. Without their contributions, the financial situation deteriorated, and Shishin had to oversee the selloff of several properties.

"Why did I stay? Because I'm very loyal. And I learned in his dokusan room, and he was a real master. And that's what I came to do, to learn the Dharma. If I wanted to learn to play the violin, I'd find the best master I could to teach me to play the violin. Now, if he was mean to his children, that may or may not affect whether I continued to study the violin. But he did – ostensibly – modify his behavior. And there weren't as many issues with women. And I don't lightly abandon people. If it were my father, I wouldn't abandon him, and he was my spiritual father. So I stayed there and helped right the ship, and I was very frank with him. If I thought he was doing something inappropriate, I'd tell him. And he was responsive. I got in a big fight with him one time, and he actually apologized. I can't imagine Kapleau doing that. I think if anybody said anything against Kapleau, they were thrown out."

"Maezumi Roshi wanted to give me Dharma transmission almost immediately after he came back from the Betty Ford Clinic. That was probably about '84. And I told him that I didn't think that the atmosphere was right. I didn't want to receive Dharma transmission with everything still in flux and turmoil and when things hadn't really settled down. But I told him I would do certain things to help right the ship. I'd finished my formal study with him by then. I had – from an earlier marriage – two sons who were entering puberty, who were in San Diego. I told him I wanted to go be near my sons while they were growing up, and I told him I was going to leave the center. But I told him there were certain things I was going to do. There were law suits, and I said I would take care of all that and other things that were going on. And I did that, then I left. I made sure that things were stable at the time, and there were senior students who stayed there who were still studying with him.

"But I also used to come back; he used to ask me to come back regularly and help him with sesshin, which I did, both in LA and at the Zen Mountain Center, as we called it then. It's now called Yokoji, up near Idyllwild. And so I continued to support him, even though when I left I got a job as a computer programmer in San Diego."

"A little loss of stature since your days as a University Professor."

"Well, yeah, but also it was easier in a certain sense. It afforded a living for me. And I had a sitting group in my home. And after that he gave Dharma transmission to Daido. Then there were other people who were coming up, and he had this Japanese hierarchical thing and didn't want other people to have Dharma transmission out of order. Daido was out of order, but Daido had his own place and was successful, and he was older than I was. So finally in 1990, I agreed. Things had settled down, and I continued to go back until he died in '95. When he gave Dharma transmission to his other successors, I assisted him in the ceremonies. I was the senior one in the area because Bernie had gone, Genpo had gone, Chozen had gone. Daido was still on the East Coast, and Joko was the only other one, but she had severed ties."

"So you have a small sitting group, are working as a programmer, come back to Los Angeles from time to time. What brought about the transition to teaching?"

"Well, there were some people living in Boulder that had studied at the Zen Center of LA, and they invited me to come and do sesshins. This was before Maezumi Roshi died, probably around twenty years ago, back in '93/'94. I came here and led three or four sesshins a year."

At this time, he was Director of Electronic Publishing for Merriam-Webster, a position he held until he retired in 2007. Since he was working from home, he was able to move to Colorado in 1996. "I had plenty of time to develop and run a Dharma Center and work for them as well. And I managed to write a couple of books, too."

When he arrived in Boulder, he brought together a number of small sittings groups. "I rallied some people around me. And they continued to grow. We managed to buy a place in Lafayette, which is east of Boulder. Thirteen years we were there; we had quite a run. It was very vibrant at one time, but then people started losing their fire. And that's when I kind of modified my view."

"How big was the community?"

"In Boulder we probably had almost a hundred members or people participating. And then when we moved to Lafayette, we lost a lot of them because people weren't willing to drive the twelve miles from Boulder to Lafayette. And also people in Boulder have the view that there's no spirituality outside of Boulder," he adds with a laugh. "But then we moved out here to Berthoud and even fewer people come. But Shinko and I made a very deliberate decision that this is primarily going to be a retreat center.

It's not going to be a residential Zen Center. We have a regular daily sitting schedule. If people want to come, that's fine. If we get two people or three people, that's fine. You know, we'll sit, and people will join us. If ten people come, twenty. Fine. But what we're mostly focusing on is retreats."

For the first four years that he and Shinko were here, the retreats weren't traditional Zen sesshin but had been based on a book they had published called *The Great Heart Way*, "which is how to deal with emotions and feelings in the context of Zen meditation."

Shinko also led art retreats, "Painting from the Unknown."

Shinko's birth name is Ilia Perez. She was born in Puerto Rico and grew up in Spain. Later, she moved to Florida where she met Philip Kapleau.

"It turned out she and her ex-husband were just a few blocks from where Kapleau was when he was in retirement," Shishin explains. "And she used be like family with them. She could go there and sit in his house. But when Kapleau got very ill, his senior students wouldn't let her in. They put a barrier around him. But one of his successors, Danan Henry, had the Denver Zen Center, and he invited them to come study with him. So she studied with him for a while. That didn't work out. And then she went to study with Pat Hawk. He's a successor of Aitken's; he's a Catholic priest in Amarillo, Texas. She studied with him for a while, then they had a serious disagreement which had to do with her getting in touch with her feminine aspect. And then she heard that I'd moved here, and she started studying with me. She was a very senior student. Anyway, we fell in love. It was a little messy." He laughs, and I suspect there is story here that I am not going to get the details of.

"You credited her with the physical appearance of this place, the art work, the feminine aspect. Was that part of a shared vision you had for this place?"

"Yeah, well, I was mostly running the place in Lafayette, and she was staffing this place. That was the way I'd set it up. But honestly there was a lot of backlash, particularly – almost exclusively – between macho men and the way she was teaching Zen. And it made it very uncomfortable for her to be at the Zen Center, so we left."

"She's an authorized teacher?"

"Yeah. She's my successor, although her basic training was in the Kapleau line and the Diamond Sangha."

"How is what you do here different from what you'd been doing in Lafayette or in Los Angeles?"

"Some of the services we do are more heart-centered. I'd say there is more heart. I'd say in the Zen Center of LA it was more hara; here it's more heart. You know, when I first started teaching – this is even before I was a sensei, when I was an assistant teacher of Maezumi Roshi – I had been told, actually from reading *The Three Pillars of Zen*, that you don't bring personal issues into the dokusan room. It's all about bringing your koan or your practice. And I never did. I never brought personal issues. When I started teaching, all students brought in was their stuff. So I realized that's what's important in people's lives, and I had to think about how to work with it. And that's how *The Great Heart Way* arose. I would say that's one of the main differences, that we have trained ourselves to be more capable to deal with students around their feelings and their emotions. But not buying into stories! We don't go into stories. You know? It's more like just staying in touch with what's going on. And our book is a kind of a manual on how to do it."

The Zen community with which he had been associated in Lafayette and Boulder is now – as he puts it – in diaspora.

"I had about ten students in Lafayette who supported the center and put a lot of energy into it. Two of the women got married, had kids, and left. Two of the men have health issues. One of them very serious. One of the women was on meds and took a real bad nosedive. Another guy, I don't know what happened to him. He fell in love with a younger woman, got very possessive about her, and took her out of the center."

Shinko is his only Dharma heir, although another student has been declared a "Dharma Holder." "He's just turned 50; been studying with me for twenty years. He's been a Dharma Holder for a couple of years, and he'll get Dharma Transmission probably in the next couple of years. I'm having him do more independent teaching. We have a satellite group in South Dakota, in Rapid City. We used to go up there, Shinko used to go up there, and do sesshins. Now I'm sending him on his own. And he has sitting groups in Boulder; he lives in Boulder, and I'm having him take on students there."

Shishin admits he does not, personally, have the support needed to maintain the Lafayette group. "It just happened. You know? All at once. Serendipity. So it was meant. We were meant to put our energy here. So we're building up a sangha here."

"I was just at a meeting that was put on by the Shambhala Sun Foundation. 'What is the future of the Dharma in the west?' And there were people who thought that the texts have to be translated, there has to be a monastic tradition, all those things, otherwise it's going to die out. I just think it's going to evolve into something different. I believe more and more people are drawn to it. And I think when there's enough people, then there will be a foundation of support in order to allow people who are real evolved teachers to spread the teachings. I mean, all of the centers that you've visited are pretty small."

"Well, there are some fairly big ones. San Francisco. Zen Mountain."

"But what's big? It doesn't mean a thousand members; it means a hundred members. There's an evangelical church in Lafayette that has 20,000 members. They bought a whole shopping center. It's growing, but...." He shrugs, then asks: "Out of all the students who went through the harsh winter of Zen, how many of them are really – I use the word guardedly – enlightened masters?"

"But there were people for whom that was never the issue, and yet whose lives were enriched through practice."

"Well, that's what I'm saying is whether they sleep two and a half hours a night or six hours a night they're still going to be enriched and validated in their lives. And I think that whether it was harsh or samuraiesque or whether it's getting softer and more accommodating, the people who are going to rise to the top are going to do it."

It is just – as he said earlier – that he doubts there are very many Hakuins or Dogens out there. If, however, the teaching is spread broadly enough, then there is a greater possibility that it will attract people who will "go deep into it so that they have realizations which preserve the original intent of the teachings."

Perhaps meditation training should be treated as other forms of pedagogy. Children are taught a range of subjects, including mathematics, music, geography, and physical education even though only a minority of them will ever excel as mathematicians, musicians, or athletes. It is only by offering these programs as broadly as possible, however, that the future leaders in those fields are introduced to them.

As I get into my car to return to Denver, I pause a moment to consider the large blue sign propped up against a tree. The wording is free-style, stars separating each word from the next: "So * you * should * think * of * all * this * fleeting * world * a * star * at * dawn * a * bubble * in * a * stream * a * flash * of * lightning * in * a * summer * cloud * a * flickering * lamp * a * phantom * and * a * dream."

It is not a sentiment everyone would see the value of, but the point, surely, is that by having it there the few who have the capacity to see its value will have an opportunity to reflect upon it.

CHAPTER SIXTEEN

Two Catholic Priests

FR. ROBERT KENNEDY, SJ
FR. KEVIN HUNT, OCSO

1

FATHER ROBERT KENNEDY IS A JESUIT PRIEST AND PROFESSOR EMERITUS OF Theology at St. Peter's University in Jersey City. He is also the teacher at the Morning Star Zendo, where he is addressed as Kennedy Roshi. He is quick to correct me when I refer to him as a Catholic Zen Teacher. Rather, he says, he is a Zen Teacher who happens to be Catholic. "The phrase 'Catholic Zen' can imply we are mixing Zen and Catholicism into something new. Kevin and I strive to practice Zen as it is taught by our Zen teachers, but Catholics can pay attention too."

One day in the early '70s – when the Catholic Church was still adjusting to the sweeping changes brought about by the Second Vatican Council – Father Kennedy was listening to the radio while driving and happened upon a talk about Zen.

"The speaker was Alan Watts, and he said, 'Have you noticed that nature is never symmetrical. Or rarely symmetrical. It's more like sand thrown in the wind.' I don't know why that statement hit me with the strength that it did, but I remember that I had to stop the car and think about this extraordinary moment. I forget the purpose of the talk and everything else about it except for that one statement. Which is the way, I think, that we learn sometimes. It's like striking a match. Sometimes it lights, and sometimes it doesn't. But that made me stop and begin to sit. Now why I began to sit, why that question in my mind made me sit is another thing I cannot answer. I'd lived in Japan for many years and had no interest in Zen or Buddhism at all. My interest had been elsewhere."

"So you were familiar with Japanese culture?"

"Yes, I was. I was there for almost eight years. I was studying Japanese and teaching in a Jesuit high school in Kobe and doing theology in Japan. I was ordained in

Japan in 1965. And then I returned to the states for graduate studies, and I finished that in 1970. And it was shortly after that I had this experience."

"Without any instruction, how did you begin?"

"I took a blanket off my bed. I folded it and put it down on the floor, and I started sitting. I can't really be more specific than that. Of course I started reading about Zen. I felt it was a way to go. There was something in my spirit that said I had to stop doing theology and turn to experience. Turn away from theory and learn from my own doing. Because Zen isn't a thinking thing. It's 'let's do it.' And I realized I had to do it finally.

"It was, as Catholics say, a great grace, a great gift. Although at the time I didn't know it, I was filled with a lot of confusion. Of course, this was after the Second Vatican Council when there was a great deal of confusion in the church and some experimentation, and I was part of that generation. So I sat for a few years by myself, and then I knew I had to have a teacher. I had a sabbatical in 1976. I went back to Japan, this time not as a teacher but as a pilgrim. And the Jesuits there helped me by introducing me to Yamada Roshi of Kamakura."

This was Koun Yamada who had expressed to Elaine MacInnes the hope that Zen might become a "stream" within the Catholic Church.

"I remember the first time he walked into the zendo before I met him personally. I was sitting in the back, up against the back wall. I remember vividly the way he walked in to light the incense and to begin the day of sitting. Again, I cannot explain it. The very sight of him walking into the zendo was life changing. Why? I cannot explain. He was younger than I am now, but he seemed old then. He was 68, and stocky, a heavy-set man. But gentle. He was a gentleman. And educated. He knew English and German, and, of course, he kept urging us to learn Japanese and for me to improve my Japanese. And he was gracious and welcoming which was tremendous in itself. He drew many foreigners to him. He was open to foreigners, open to Christians, open to Catholic priests and nuns, and we came to him in great numbers. There must have been a dozen priests and a dozen nuns who were actively sitting.

"I remember him saying, 'I'm not trying to make you a Buddhist. I want to empty you in imitation of your Lord, Jesus Christ.' And that was a wonderful, liberating experience. He swept away, in a sense, all talk about Buddhism. And this was something Maezumi – his Dharma brother – also shared in California. I remember Maezumi shouting to a student once, 'Stop talking about Buddhism! Go into the zendo and sit!' And, in a more gentle way, that is what Yamada Roshi wanted us to do. He opened his home to us; he opened the zendo to us. And truly our faith did not matter. What mattered was our capacity to pay attention. As he said, 'Some foreigners come to Japan, and their will power is strong. Some come and their will power is not so strong.' It was interesting. He focused on will power, on our ability to concentrate. He never asked about what faith we had."

Kennedy spent the spring semester of 1976 in Japan, after which he returned to the United States. "Yamada Roshi recommended I go to Maezumi, his Dharma brother, in California, and that's what I did. And I finished my sabbatical year by sitting in Los Angeles.

"Maezumi Roshi was considerably younger than Yamada Roshi, maybe 25 years younger than Yamada Roshi, and a different person entirely. He was a great teacher, just a different personality. He used the stick a lot. Yamada never did. But Maezumi believed in it. And it worked too. It really gave you energy. The purpose of the stick was to give you energy not to encourage thoughts. And he was not afraid to use it. And he was running – with Glassman Sensei really – almost a hotel with many students who were living right there in ZCLA. So I became part of that world. I wasn't living there, though. The Jesuits have a high school in Los Angeles, and I lived there. And I'd walk every morning, about 4:00 in the morning, down to Normandie Street where Maezumi Roshi had his Zen complex.

"Maezumi Roshi made it very clear that we should make Zen American. We should not imitate the Japanese. And it is not necessary to do so. I think the Japanese can't really be imitated anyway. They're a completely unique civilization. A wonderful civilization. But it's not our job to imitate them. Our job is to find a Zen that is open to American culture, American life. It is not necessary to wear Japanese robes in order to see your own nature. And it's not helpful finally. You're just creating something artificial in a practice that imitates the Japanese. Now some Zen people will disagree with this. But I would just say that Maezumi was clear that we were to do what he could not do, which was to make Zen American. And as soon as Maezumi died, Glassman, for example, said he became himself, not only Maezumi's student but his own man as an American interested in social issues in a way that, perhaps, Maezumi was not."

After his sabbatical year, Kennedy returned to New York where he was on faculty at St. Peter's College. "That's where the Jesuits assigned me. I was teaching theology and Japanese language to beginners in the business program. And when I returned to New York it was to teach full time, and at that time I was without a teacher. I went back summers to sit with Maezumi. But it was around 1980 when Glassman came to New York and set up shop as a Zen teacher there that I became his student. He became my teacher.

"He had a doctorate in mathematics from UCLA, but then he met Maezumi and gave himself completely to Zen. He said it was not easy for him. He made a sesshin before becoming a monk where he realized, 'This is my life.' But he also felt it was his vocation to work for what he called 'the hungry ghosts,' people – not just Buddhists but of all faiths – who needed help in their lives. They are the ones that he wanted to work with. And therefore there's a great social emphasis in Glassman's work. I think it came from his Jewish socialism and concern for social issues. He said a lot of people like Zen because they like to sit in a zendo where it's nice and quiet and peaceful and has a certain artistic flavor. The last time I saw him, a few weeks ago, he said to me, 'Some people like Zen clubs, where they can sit together with like-minded people, where they can be quiet together.' But he brought us out on the street, where we lived with the poor. We were without money. Just begging for money to get a cup of coffee when we needed it. And we were to experience what it's like to have nothing and to live with these disenfranchised people. And that was his main goal as a Zen teacher. To be with the poor and to work with them. He gave us that orientation."

Kennedy studied with Bernie Glassman for eleven years. "And they were wonderful years. Glassman moved around a bit. He started out in northern New York, up in the Bronx. We were given a nice home there for a zendo, but we couldn't afford to stay there, so we moved to a poorer section in Yonkers. And then we moved to a convent that we were able to buy. They were very interesting years. And, again, I didn't live there. I had my own Jesuit life. But I saw him at least once a week and attended many of the sesshins that he ran. I did the koans every week. He was very gracious to me. He always had time for me and encouraged me."

"He was open to non-Buddhists undertaking Zen practice?"

"Oh, absolutely! They all were; every Zen teacher I had – Yamada Roshi, Maezumi Roshi, Glassman Roshi – they were all very open. They knew who I was, what I was, and what I wanted."

"And how did your order feel about this?"

"The Jesuits encouraged me. They support interreligious work. Jesuits have a long history in Japan and a long history of working with Buddhists. I think in the beginning, it started out with some argument and confrontation, but that was quickly resolved and turned into respect and appreciation and cooperation."

"And the broader church?"

"Well, when you talk about the Vatican, remember there are at least twenty-six major divisions in the Vatican, and they don't speak with one voice. The past two popes – John Paul II and Pope Benedict – certainly encouraged interreligious work.

They recognized that this was essential to our Catholic faith, and we had to be open to others. Now that doesn't mean that every priest in the church is equally open to it. But what the Church itself wants and what they constantly urge is interfaith cooperation, that we understand the other, that we appreciate the otherness of them. Not just where they agree with us, but to appreciate their truth that is not necessarily our truth. And finally we were urged – certainly by the Jesuits – to practice with them, to practice their truth, to walk in their shoes. Otherwise we cannot really know them. So that's what I've followed. That's not to say that all bishops are happy with this work, but the teaching of the church is consistent in that this is what should be done. And the Society is deeply involved in this. If I had not been a Jesuit, if I had not been in Japan, I probably would never have thought of Buddhism in my life. So I owe it to the Jesuits and to the church because they introduced me to Buddhism and urged me to pursue these ties, or encouraged me to pursue them."

In 1991, Glassman made Kennedy a Zen teacher.

"I first thought I would just sit quietly by myself. I thought it was a good idea, after you become a teacher, to sit quietly for about ten years," he says laughing. "Ripen a bit, you know. But actually I couldn't sit quietly because Glassman gave me a student right away. Someone he had worked with as a teacher, and he gave her to me to finish the work, and see her through, and make her a teacher. And that was Sister Janet Richardson who's now in retirement in Florida and who is a great Zen teacher herself. Then a few people that I knew came and sat with me. And finally they convinced me that my one bedroom apartment was not suitable for a zendo, and one thing led to another, and we rented this apartment in the same building and turned it into a zendo.

This is the Morning Star Zendo.

"Right now it is an apartment owned by St. Peter's University in Jersey City, and we rent it. It's just a one bedroom apartment, but it suits us quite nicely. We have a kitchen, a little dining area, a place for a zendo, and a room for private instruction for students. No one lives there. We gather and do our Zen work there. We can sit a dozen comfortably, but on Saturday morning, when there's a big crowd, there's as many as twenty-five people there. That's crowded; it's not ideal."

His early students were largely people he knew who had followed his interest in Zen.

"The ones that came originally were all Catholic. Now a few are not. I just made a Buddhist a teacher. The Buddhists were so good to me; the Zen community was so good to me; I'm happy to be generous with them. But most of them had some connection with the Catholic faith."

"I think the first time I had heard of you," I tell him, "was in an article I read probably ten years ago." It was 2005. "You had given transmission to a Trappist Monk. And in the article, the reporter asked the monk what exactly a Trappist Zen teacher did. If I remember his answer correctly, it was something like, 'I don't know, but I guess I'm going to find out.'"

"Yes. That was Father Kevin Hunt."

"Did he find out?"

"Yes. Perhaps it was not what he really wanted or had hoped for. But, yes, the Jesuits supported that transmission fully. I have a letter from the Jesuit General at the time, Father Kolvenbach, approving of my own work and approving of my making a Trappist monk a Zen teacher. Kevin Hunt was capable. He was insightful. And he deserved it. So I reached out to him and the Trappist community, and I made him a Zen teacher."

"What is the function of Zen?"

"Well, all these questions could be answered in multiple ways. I'll just do the best I can with this. Zen is a practical way of doing Buddhism. It was put together by the Chinese around the 6th Century. As Buddhism came from India, it was rather academic. And the Chinese were practical. 'How do you do this? How do you put this into life?' And that was the beginning of Zen with Bodhidharma and the Chinese Patriarchs. The great work of Zen was done by the Chinese between the 600s and the 1200s. That would roughly be the Golden Age of Zen. 'How do you practically do this?' So that was the question. And that was how Zen was formulated."

"And its function today?"

"The same as it was yesterday, to live an enlightened life of service."

"If it's a way of 'doing' Buddhism, then what function does it serve – or potentially serve – within the Catholic Church?"

"Well, first of all, the practice of zazen is not necessarily confined to Buddhism or to any faith. There's a wonderful teaching in Buddhism that Buddhism must leave Buddhism itself in order to enter the field of blessings. Buddhism recognizes that the truth of Buddhism is not simply Buddhist. It is human, and it is for all people. We are grateful to Buddhism for developing Zen, bringing it about, answering some of the questions of, 'How do you do this?' But it is not confined to Buddhism. Now some Buddhists might disagree with this; they might say, 'No. Zen can only be done in Buddhism.' But this is not what Yamada Roshi taught me. And I think this is the truth of it. Anyone can sit quietly and breathe and pay attention and stop thinking and grow."

"Sister Elaine MacInnes, another student of Yamada Roshi, makes a distinction between Zen as a Buddhist sect and Zen as a practice which might have the capacity – in her words – to reinvigorate contemplative prayer in Catholic Spirituality. So she would distinguish between 'Zen' and 'Zen Buddhism.' Is that a distinction you'd be comfortable with?"

"Oh, yes. In other words, Zen can be practiced – as it almost always is – within a Buddhist framework. There are Zen Monasteries that are certainly Buddhist but dedicated to Zen practice as opposed to other forms of Buddhism. So, in that way, Zen can be seen as part of Buddhism, but it can also be seen as a practice that is open to anyone. Yamada Roshi made that very clear, that he was not trying to make me a Buddhist but to empty me, as he said, in imitation of my Lord, Jesus Christ, who emptied himself. He was quite clear. And many Catholic priests and nuns and Catholic lay people went to Yamada Roshi because he was open to us. He did not demand that we become Buddhist in that sense.

"Now, Yamada Roshi said to us – and to me personally – that he could believe in God, but he said that he could not believe that God would make a dualistic world. Well, there's no reason that Christians have to believe that God has made a dualistic world. He said, 'What Christians believe about God is that He transcends human experience, so Zen has nothing to say about that. Zen should not say Yes or No with regard to the existence of God, because the Semitic religions – the Jews, the Christians, the Muslims – believe God transcends human experience. It is a different order of being entirely about which Zen should not say anything.' I remember Glassman Roshi also said that he was a Jewish atheist, and then gradually he realized, 'I can't say Yes or No to this question. There's nothing in my Zen teaching or training that would have me say Yes or No to the existence of God, as Jews and Christians understand God, someone who transcends human experience.' Zen Buddhism is about human experience. They might question the legitimacy of faith in general, but if someone holds it, they would have nothing to say, they should have nothing to say about it."

We come back to the issue of social engagement in contemporary Zen, in particular Bernie Glassman's efforts to take Zen out of the monastery and bring it onto the street.

"Glassman wanted to develop the compassionate side of Zen. He said, 'It's not just about obtaining a private wisdom that you can polish for the rest of your life.' It was that you can be of service to people, and that's why he took us out on the street. Now, Kevin Hunt, as a Trappist monk, is not able to do that. But Zen is expressed according to the circumstances of your life. And he teaches many people who could go out on the street and work there. There are many ways of enfleshing Zen, according to your ability, circumstances, and so on. There's no one way of doing this.

"There's a great teaching in Zen – I think it's in *The Book of Serenity* – that says you liberate people according to type. That means according to their ability, according their capacity to receive the vast Zen Dharma. And you don't force them all into one mold. Glassman's approach was more social than mine is, for example. I don't spend much time on the street, although I remember – with gratitude – the time I had with Glassman. Each one does it according to his own circumstances. There's no one way."

2

"I have a twin brother, and he retires to Florida," Kevin Hunt tells me. "And he's a golfer. So he and his wife buy a place on the golf course. And they're down there, and he goes looking for a threesome that wants to fill out to a foursome. And one of the men is a retired Methodist minister, and my brother mentions that he has a brother who's a priest. And the guy says to him, 'Oh, there's another man in this complex who's got a brother who's a priest.' Gives my brother his name. My brother calls him. They meet and have a game of golf together; they're talking. And so this other guy says to my brother, 'Well, you know, my brother's not only a priest, but he's a funny kind of priest. He's a Jesuit.' My brother says to him, 'Well, if you think that's bad, I've got a brother who's a Trappist monk.' 'Well, my brother the Jesuit is even weirder because he's all involved in Zen Buddhism!' And my brother says to him, 'Well, my brother's just as weird as that because he's also involved in Zen Buddhism.' So it's Bob Kennedy's brother, Bill, and my brother, Ken, who are together."

Kevin's frequent chuckles suit him, as do his Trappist robes. He has the right build and wears them well. He looks the part and is wholly at ease in it. He is a member of the monastic community at Saint Joseph's Abbey in Spencer, Massachusetts, but we meet at the nearby St. Mary's Abbey for Trappistines in Wrentham where he is currently serving as chaplain. At the beginning of our conversation, he tells me there are 63 monks at St. Joseph's, ranging in age from 28 to 98, and 45 women at St. Mary's within a similar age range.

"So you still have young men seeking to enter the order," I remark.

"They're starting to come back. We had a dearth at a certain time, but they're beginning to come in now. Historically, there was a huge influx of men after the

Second World War when, I think, many of the men who had been in the military began to question what is life about. I entered in 1953. I was 20 at the time. But I was kind of funny, because I knew what I wanted to be when I was 13 years old, and it was just finding out where I could live it that took the time."

I mention that the Trappist community located in the francophone region of my home province in Canada has only a few very elderly monks remaining.

"That's something that all the French-Canadian monasteries have experienced," he admits. "The monastery that was at Oka had that problem. They had this huge monastery and a very small community. So they sold the monastery to the provincial government for a school and moved to a new monastery. I think a lot of it was due to the changes in the church before, during, and after Vatican II. I also think that a great many of the vocations after the Second World War entered because they saw the horrors of the war, and that wasn't enough to carry them all the way through. And so many of them left at that time. But I think here in the United States, you are getting a revival in our communities. All of the monasteries are experiencing it. They're not experiencing it in large numbers; they're experiencing it in small numbers. And I think part of the reason for that is in the last thirty years or so they have introduced a rather more stringent system of admitting people into the community. When I think of what they go through now, I never would have survived it." He chuckles. "You know, they have to go through psychological evaluations. They come to the monastery usually over the period of two years or so for three months now and three months later and things like that. When I entered, it was, 'Does he have a strong back? Can he work?'"

There are currently eleven male Cistercian communities in the US plus another six communities for women. And although Kevin expects that one or two of the abbeys may close and their monks relocate to other communities, Catholic monasticism, it appears, is not as moribund as I'd assumed. "It is in the throes of a certain readjustment," he tells me. "I'm 80 years old, so I doubt whether I'll see how it finally works out. But the rigidity we had in the pre-Vatican II monasteries doesn't exist anymore. That rigidity carried a lot of people along just because you had no alternative. Now the communities are much more flexible and are becoming much more – what I would call – lay-oriented than clerical-oriented."

I ask what he means by that.

"Not all Trappists become ordained. And part of it is that the ideal of many of the young people coming in is not to go onto ordination but simply to live as a monk. The rules of the Order have changed significantly. When I entered, for example, you had two classes. You had the lay brothers, and you had the choir religious, and all of the choir religious automatically became priests. Nowadays, that's not true. Usually what it is now, you're told when you enter you have to enter willing never to be ordained. Hmm? And then, later on, after a number of years, if you feel the attraction, you petition the abbot and the community to go on for ordination. And that's usually – I would say – ten or fifteen years after you've entered."

"So at 13 years old, you knew you wanted to be a monk?"

"Well, I knew I wanted to be somebody who lived a life of prayer and meditation."

"I can't remember exactly what I was concerned with at 13, but it probably wasn't prayer and meditation."

"Yeah. I don't know. It's always something I've been attracted to. And I grew up in New York City, and I was at a regular New York City high school. I was not the pious type. But when I was 14 years old, I was working in a local public library. And I can remember going to *The Catholic Encyclopedia* and looking up 'Prayer.' And one of the things they mentioned was the word 'contemplation' and explained that a little bit. And I thought, 'Gee, that's what I would like to be.' Then I went to 'Contemplative Religious Orders,' and it mentioned the different contemplative orders at that time, and it said at the end of it that the only contemplative order now in the United States are the Trappists or the Cistercians. So that was the first time that I had ever heard of them. And then when I was 15 or 16, I talked my parents into letting me go down to Gethsemani for a retreat."

The Abbey of Our Lady of Gethsemani in Kentucky was Thomas Merton's monastery. It is also the oldest Trappist community in the United States.

"I went down there and spent a week and, of course, was very attracted and all the rest of that. And I can remember coming back and saying to my family that I wanted to be a Trappist. And they looked at me, and they said, 'You're doing nothing except going to school until you're 20 years old.'"

When he was nineteen, a year earlier than his parents had insisted upon, he heard about Our Lady of the Valley monastery in Rhode Island and wrote to them. But it recently had been destroyed by a fire, and construction had begun on the new monastery at Spencer. "In the Cistercians, or the Trappists, we really fall in love with a particular monastery. It's not like the Jesuits who are in a Province; we're called to a specific place. In fact, one of the great accolades that they used to give to the early Cistercians was, 'He was a lover of the place and the brethren.' So in 1951, just before they started the construction of Spencer, I went up there. And I said this is where I want to be.'

"My parents were never happy about it. It took me years to find out why. Both my parents grew up in Ireland; they were born in the 1890s. And at that time in

Ireland, the Cistercians was the place people went who couldn't make it in the seminary. And that was their view of what a Trappist was. And, I'm sad to say, my father died with that idea. My mother didn't. That's a funny story. I was coming up for my final vows, and my mother hated the idea that I would be making my final vows. She kept complaining to my sisters, 'Oh, I wish he wouldn't do that! I wish he wouldn't do that.' And they were having what used to be called a Mission at the local parish. And so my sisters said to her, 'Go talk to the priest that's giving the mission and see what he says.' So she went over there, and he was a Franciscan, and she told him, 'My son is making his final vows as a Trappist.' And before she could say anything else, he said to her, 'Madame, your salvation is assured!' After that, she was happy as could be.

"I entered as a lay brother. I was a nice kid out of New York City and had probably never lifted anything very heavy in my life. And when I went in, they immediately gave you a shaved head, and the first thing they did was put me in a ditch with a pick and shovel. And I can remember the first night after the day's work, my head was so burnt I must have looked like a tomato. So I did lay brother's work at the novitiate. As I said, I entered at the end of the construction, so there were still a lot of ditches to be dug. Our monastery's made out of field stone. I worked on picking up stone and house cleaning and washing toilets. The usual things."

"Very Zen-like, isn't it?" I note, and we both laugh.

"Joshu Sasaki Roshi was the first Zen master to visit our monastery," Kevin tells me. "And he got there, and, at the end of a couple of days, he said, 'Except for the color of the clothes, I could be in my own monastery in Japan.' Hmm? Monasticism, I think – no matter what culture or religion it is – it's pretty much all the same."

"I was never the pious type. Nor was I very devotional. I can remember the vocational director when I was entering said to me, 'Well, do you go to mass every day?' And I said, 'No.' And he said, 'You don't go to mass every day?' And I said, 'Look, I've got to be on the subway train at 7:30 every morning. How the Hell am I going to get to mass?' And I was never attracted to devotions. Hmm? And so one of the great difficulties I had when I entered the novitiate was that everything was devotional. We'd have a novena to the Little Flower, and we'd do this, and we'd do that, and all of this stuff. I went to my novice master at one point, and I was very lucky because he was a very experienced and wise old man. Old! Just a kid compared to where I am today. But anyway, I was telling him, 'I just can't do this devotional stuff anymore.' And he said to me, 'Don't worry about it.' We talked a little bit more, and he said, 'One thing you've got to be aware of, and that is: prayer and meditation always become more simple.' And so that was it."

Kevin was still a lay brother and laborer when the order sent him to Argentina to help with the construction of a new monastery there.

"And I had a certain curiosity as to other traditions of meditation and prayer and stuff like that. For example, one of the great helps I had in my early experience of prayer was a little book called *The Way of the Pilgrim* which you've probably heard of. The recitation of that short Jesus Prayer[65] over and over and over again. Hmm? And that became my preferred way of meditation. I still do it fifty-some years later. But I had a curiosity about other traditions. Of course the Jesus Prayer came from the Orthodox tradition. And I did a little reading in Hinduism and a little bit in Buddhism. And then I was sent down to Argentina, and I wasn't there too, too long, and there was a man who visited the monastery. A group of us were talking about the forms of meditation and stuff like that, and he said, 'Have you ever read anything on Zen?' And I said I'd read Thomas Merton's things. I wasn't too impressed by them. He said, 'I've got a book in Spanish that you might be interested in.' I said, 'Oh, yeah?' I was interested in all the traditions of meditation. So he gave me this book, Eugen Herrigel's *Zen in the Art of Archery*. Originally written in German, translated into English, and from English to Spanish, a very poor Spanish translation.

"So, anyway, I'm reading this book, and I'm interested in it. And it tells about how to sit in meditation. It was the first time I really paid any attention to the physical aspect of it. And, of course, one of the great problems that I experienced up to shortly before that time was that our custom had been that you couldn't sit down in church. You either had to stand or kneel. And so when they gave us permission to sit in church, of course, I think the most common practice was what we used to call 'nodding at the angels.'" He mimes falling asleep. "And that was my greatest difficulty. I could fall asleep at a drop of a pin. You know, you had a full day's labor, especially in Argentina where your hardest labor would be when you had your shortest sleep period. So, anyway, as I read this thing, two things impressed me. One was the way they sat. And I read it couple of times, and I said, 'If I try sitting like that, my legs are going to be so painful I won't be able to sleep.' I never achieved full lotus, but I tried to do it a number of times. The other thing that impressed me was that he gave a koan, and that koan really struck me. The koan was, 'What face did you have before you were born?' So I said, 'Gee, I wonder what face I had before I was born. What face did I have? I should keep that in the back of my mind.' Hmm? And so for six or seven years, I got several blankets together – or course, I didn't have cushions or anything – folded them up, sat on them, and for those six or seven years that's what I did."

He passed through his late twenties and early thirties during this period.

"So I did that for about seven years, and, of course, I was very – what the term they use is – 'singular' because I was the only one doing that. And in the tradition of the Trappists at the time, to be 'singular' was not a good thing. But one thing that our tradition has always had and that was we've always had great liberty of spirit to follow our way of prayer. The local superiors thought I was crazy, and they said, 'We don't want you sitting cross-legged in our chapel.' So I said, 'Okay. I'll find another place to do it.' And we had a small infirmary, and our infirmaries always have a little chapel in them. And at that time I was the infirmarian, so I was able to arrange things the way I wanted up there. So there I am, sitting on the blankets. As I said, probably six or seven years passed. And I had no teacher. I didn't know what I was doing right, what I was doing wrong, or anything else. And nothing was happening."

He was not, as he puts it, "blatant" about his practice. "The time for meditation came, I just quietly went up to this little chapel to do my meditation." He was also attending the prescribed hours for prayer. Trappists gather together seven times a day, once for mass and six times to chant the antiphonal liturgical hours.

"So what happened was, people would say to me, 'What are you doing that for? Why are you doing that?' You know, not in a condemnatory way. I told them this is what I'm attracted to. 'Well, is it doing anything for you?' 'No.' So – you know – 'What good is it then?' 'Well, I just feel I want to keep going this way.' Yeah, but, 'You're not with the community.' That was the great singularity thing.

"So I'm up in this little chapel one morning, and I'm thinking to myself, 'Well, you've worked hard at this, Hunt. And you've given it time; you've given it effort. And people haven't bothered you too much about it. They think you're crazy, but they think I'm crazy on a lot of points, so that's all right.' So then I said to myself, 'Okay, I give up.' Now, I'm sitting cross-legged. And I stood up." He pauses. "And, in the motion of standing up, I saw the face I had before I was born." He pauses a little longer. "I hadn't the slightest idea what it was. Hmm? All I knew was that something had happened. So I continued for a couple more years, and then I returned to Spencer."

That was 1969, and the abbot at St. Joseph's then was Thomas Keating, a noted advocate for Christian meditation. When Kevin asked permission to attend a weekend sesshin at the New York Zendo with Eido Shimano, Keating readily granted it.

"So I go down to New York with my sleeping bag, and they bring me in and they say, 'This is the zendo.' They don't tell me anything else. 'This is where you're going to sit. Why don't you try sitting?' Well, it's about 4:00 in the afternoon. And so I put myself in the sitting posture. No one else is in there. I didn't realize that the first sitting was at 7:00, and they were 45 minute sittings. So I sit there from 4:00 until almost 8:00. Not moving or anything. Yeah. Intelligent, I'm not. And I never got in to see Eido Roshi, even though he was giving daisan at the time. So that experience left me with a big question mark whether I would ever meet a teacher or anything like that."

A number of years later, he was travelling in Pennsylvania with another monk. "And he says to me, 'You know, I have a friend who's a nun, who's the superior of a boarding school near Princeton. Would it be alright if we stopped off and said hello to her?' 'Sure. Why not?' We pull up to this boarding school. It's the summer. And we get out, and she meets us, and we're talking. And she said, 'There's something unusual going on here.' And I said, 'What's that?' And she said, 'We're having a Zen sesshin here.' And I said, 'Oh, wonderful.' And she said, 'Yes, and it's being given by a Japanese Zen master. Would you like to meet him?' So I immediately said, 'Yes.' So about fifteen minutes later this little Japanese monk comes out, dressed in traditional robes and everything. And he has his assistant with him. And it was Joshu Sasaki Roshi. So we introduced ourselves, and he finally realized that we were Catholic monks. And he was very surprised because he had thought that Catholic monks only existed in Europe, and he was actually planning to go to Europe to see what a Catholic monastery was like. So I said to him, 'Well, why don't you come up and visit my monastery. It's in Massachusetts.' 'How far away?' 'Oh, a six hour drive.' 'When?' So I said, 'When can you make it?' So he talked with his assistant, and he said" – imitating Sasaki's accent – "'I come at such-and-such a date.' So I come back to Spencer, and I say to the abbot, 'On such-and-such a date, we're being visited by a Japanese Zen master.' And there was a certain consternation, but he said, 'Okay, we'll do that.' And so Joshu Sasaki Roshi came up. And we had him in choir, and he had a room in the monastery itself. So he participated; he ate in our dining room. He gave a couple of talks to the community.

"There was quite a lot of interest in what he said. Basically he spoke of his experience in meditation and the Zen way of doing meditation. And you know, as I said earlier, a novice master had once said to me, 'If there's any rule in prayer it is that it will always become more simple. Less verbal.' And so he addressed that aspect, that in Zen there's no talking. That to speak a word in Zen is already a betrayal. And that was something that we could identify with because we had a rule of silence, and silence is very, very important in our practice. And he loved it, so somebody said to him something about coming back sometime and giving a weekend sesshin. And so he said, 'Yes. I come back next year.'

"Now he had spoken about koan practice and how it was used. And he said: 'I give a koan. To everybody. Same koan to everybody.' And he had noticed when we start our chanting, we make the sign of the cross. And he said: 'Hmm. Hmm. Good practice. Oh, that's a good practice. That's a good practice.' His English was not very good. So he said: 'Koan. Mmm.' He leaned over to me, 'What do you call that, brother?' I said, 'That's the sign of the cross.' 'Ah! Sign cross. Mmm. Good practice.

Strong practice. Mmm. Koan: How do you realize God sign cross? Meditate on that until I come back.' So I did."

Sasaki returned to St. Joseph's regularly for the next ten years. Not all the monks attended these retreats, but there were regularly between 25 and 30 participants. And, over time, people from outside the monastic community joined them. "One of the things that he insisted on," Kevin tells me, "was, 'I'm not here to make you Zen Buddhist monks. I'm here to make you Zen Christian monks.' Hmm?"

By this time, the Trappist order no longer distinguished between choir and lay, and, in 1979, Kevin was ordained a priest. During the abbacy of Thomas Keating, he was also given the opportunity to take part in a number of three-month training periods at Mount Baldy, which he valued even though the environment was very different from that of his abbey.

"Now by this time I'm in my early 40s. And I grew up in New York City, and I'm not easily scandalizeable. I went to high school in Harlem; people smoking pot and shooting up and things like that. I knew this by the time I was 14 years old, and the street-walkers and all of this. But I was surprised at the sexual activity that went on during a training period, but it was the '70s and anything and everything goes. Nobody ever tried anything with me," he adds, wryly. "I don't know particularly why. But I did say something to Sasaki Roshi, and he more or less said, 'I don't know how to control it.'"

He is aware of the stories that have since circulated about Sasaki's own sexual activity. "But I went to him strictly as a teacher, and he treated me strictly as a student. I think he had great respect for the fact that I was a monk. Mount Baldy was very, very strict. And they had a number of Catholic religious that tried it; few of them ever survived more than a week. And I was there and actually probably thriving. You know, the monastic schedule was...." He raises his hands, "I've done this for years. What else is there?"

In 1981, Thomas Keating resigned his abbacy. The new, more conservative abbot, chose not to continue Sasaki's visits, and Kevin was no longer free to go to California. The new abbot, did, however, give him permission to attend a couple of training periods with Seung Sahn in Rhode Island. Still, Kevin did not have a teacher and realized he needed to find one.

"Spencer had been fairly deeply involved in the interreligious dialogue from the time Thomas Keating was the abbot. For example, we were one of the sponsors for the first interreligious dialogue between monastics which took place in Barre, Massachusetts. And when the Insight Meditation Center opened in Barre, they would often ask us to come up and talk about Christian meditation and how it related to Buddhism. So that was going on. Then in the early '90s, I was on the board of directors of Interreligious Dialogue, and I was participating in that. And one of the other monks mentioned to me that there was a Jesuit who did Zen practice who was going to be at the Barre Center for Buddhist Studies. It was Lent, and he was going to give a conference on the Passion and Meditation. The Barre Center for Buddhist Studies and the Insight Meditation Center were right next to each other, and they're only about fifteen miles from Spencer. So several of us went up, and who was it but Bob Kennedy! So we were dressed in our robes and everything, and he was delighted to see us. And we're chatting afterwards, and he mentioned that he had been invited to our monastery in Snowmass, Colorado, to give a five day sesshin. So I asked my superior at the time if I could go to it, and one of the other monks asked to go to it. And he agreed for the two of us to go out to Snowmass. Well, I've always loved Snowmass. I helped to build the place for a couple of months, before I was sent down to Argentina. I'm very good with a sledge hammer and a pick and shovel."

At the end of the retreat, he approached Kennedy and asked to be accepted as a student. Over the next few years, he attended various sesshin Kennedy directed both in the Northeast and elsewhere. "And finally, I would say around 2001 or 2002, I told my abbot I had reached a point in my Zen practice where I thought I had to do an intensive period of koan practice, and I couldn't do that by seeing Bob two or three times a year. So I asked if I could go down and spend a year or so with him in his Jesuit community in Jersey City. And I spent two years there.

"I found Bob to be a very, very good teacher. He is reasonably strict about the practice and the handing-on of the tradition. He's a theologian, so he can talk about things on a theological level. But he doesn't get his Catholic theology and Catholic spirituality that involved with his Zen practice. He expects you to get what Zen's gonna teach you. And he'll help you integrate it in your tradition but not at the expense of watering down your Zen practice.

"One of the difficulties that we Catholics – especially we Catholic monastics and religious – have is that a lot of our training is very theological, very philosophical. And I can remember going into Joshu Sasaki once, and he asked, 'How you manifest God signing cross?' And I started this discussion about the Passion, the theological significance. And he said, 'Too much thinking! Too much thinking!' One time I went in, and I started something like that, and he just went like...." He mimes picking his nose and flicking it on the ground. "And Kennedy was somewhat the same. 'Now, this is your Zen practice. Don't start looking for explanations. If you want to, we can do that on another level, but that's going to be on another level.' And, as I say, he's pretty strict on the practice itself. You sit, you sit, you sit. You sit, you sit, you sit, you sit. He's also very, very compassionate. He was tough on the practice, how you did it. But when it was the right time to be lenient, he was lenient. He'd cut you some slack. But very strict on no intellectual answers. That's one of the harder things to teach Westerners. 'In your practice, I want you to demonstrate! Show me!' Hmm? Bob is very strict on that, and that is the best way to do it."

I mention the 2005 article I had seen. "You were asked what exactly a Trappist Zen teacher did, and you were reported to say that you didn't know yet, but that you guessed you'd find out. Did you?"

"Yeah, I'm finding out. I'm finding out."

"It's a work in progress?"

"It's a work in progress."

I had assumed that most of the students who worked with him would also be members of religious orders, but that's not the case. "I have one group, the Day Star Sangha, that comes here once a month, and we use the retreat facility that we have across the road. And there's another group, the Transfiguration Zendo, that meets once a month in South Bury, Connecticut. And once in a while, if I have an opportunity, I'll go out and give a weekend sesshin here or there.

"What I find is that the vast majority of the people who come are in their late 40s and older, and they've reached the level that they're going to reach in life. They've finished raising their kids and all the challenges of that. And they've reached whatever level they're going to be at in their careers, their work, and things like that, and now, 'I've done it. What was this whole thing for?'"

"Are most of them Catholic?"

"Mostly Catholics, but some non-Catholic people, even some people who consider themselves Buddhists. One or two Catholic religious."

I ask if any of the brothers in Spencer or any of the sisters here in Wrentham practice with him, and he shakes his head.

"So you're still singular," I remark.

"Mm-hmm. I haven't learned anything."

"If a younger monk came to you and asked what Zen was all about, how would you answer him?"

"What Zen…." he starts, then pauses a moment. "The Western Christian tradition of prayer has become extremely rational and intellectualized, focussed more on concepts than anything else. So there was always a certain tendency in the Western church to focus on ideas and concepts. But as my novice master said, 'Prayer always becomes simple.' Hmm? So how do we focus on that simplicity? That we didn't have; we had lost that. And basically what Zen is is that simplifier.

"St. John of the Cross made this little drawing of the ascent of Mount Carmel. It shows a mountain, and there are three roads. One that goes up the center, and two that go around the mountain. And the one up the center, in small writing on each side he's got the word N-A-D-A – nada. And as you go up the mountain, the lettering gets bigger and bigger, and finally at the end – at the top of the mountain – in the biggest letters is the word NADA! Nothing. Nothing. Nothing. We never developed a system or a methodology to go into the Nada. Now, people get into it, but they go into it with a great deal of work and misunderstanding and confusion. That's what *The Cloud of Unknowing* is about; that's what John of the Cross is about and St. Teresa and even the Little Flower.

"There was a book on St. Teresa of Avila. The title was something she'd said when she was a child. Somebody asked her what she wanted in life, and she said, 'I want to see God.' That's all I've ever wanted to do. And Zen has provided the best way for me to do it."

CHAPTER SEVENTEEN

Bodhin Kjolhede

THERE IS A BUMPER STICKER ON BODHIN KJOLHEDE ROSHI'S CAR THAT READS: "Ask me about my vow of silence." We are driving to the Rochester Zen Center's retreat house, located at Chapin Mill, forty minutes from the city. Bodhin's hair is short, but not shaved off, and he is dressed in a navy blue short-sleeve shirt with a banded collar and matching slacks. The Asian priest traveling with us is similarly dressed. "As part of the process of adapting Zen to the west, my teacher – Roshi Kapleau – and I didn't feel inclined to maintain the Japanese samugi," he explains. "We chose something more western, but we also wanted a way to distinguish those who were ordained. So we came up with this." Unlike a samugi, it is something one could wear on the street without appearing too foreign or exotic.

The conversation during the drive is largely casual, but I leave the recorder on. "There has been a recent increase in interest in our introductory workshops, our training programs, and our sesshin, all three," he mentions.

"That's intriguing. Interest in workshops has gone up?"

"Yeah. We have to turn people away. We have to cut it off at fifty."

"What age groups show up?"

"It's all over the place, but there are definitely more people in their 20s and 30s than there were five years ago. It used to be mostly baby-boomers, maybe two-thirds baby-boomers. The baby-boomers are still coming, but now there are fewer of them. And there are a lot more younger people."

"Any idea why this current increase in interest?"

"I have hypotheses, but mostly it's just speculation. I mean, there are those who say, 'Well, it's so hard for young people to get jobs that they don't lose much by coming.'" We both laugh. "But I think it's something more intangible, something deeper happening, some greater interest in the spiritual."

"Probably different factors than in the '60s, though, when drugs – for example – were a big reason people got involved."

"They were for me."

"Yeah," I admit. "When people ask how I got interested in Zen, my short answer is always, 'Mescaline.'"

He looks over at me with a grin and says, "Me too! Mescaline was my drug of choice. It completely changed my view of reality. I was a beer-drinking fraternity guy until my first mescaline trip, and then I just saw the world in a whole different way."

Well, both of our stories are a little more complicated than that, and, as it turns out, his is more dramatic than mine.

We are driving to Chapin Mill because Bodhin is presiding over the marriage of two Zen Center members there. While the wedding proceeds, I spend about two hours relaxing in the sun. It's a lovely 135 acre rural location. This is where all the Rochester sesshin now take place. The building consists of four lengthy corridors surrounding an inner courtyard where the wedding is being celebrated. The zendo is light and airy and easily seats sixty-four participants. One of the staff tells me that they can house up to seventy people here. The site is occasionally rented to other groups ("Of like mind," as Bodhin points out).

Philip Kapleau's grave is located here, just out of sight of the main building. It is marked by the grindstone from the original mill. To pass the time, I do Tai-Chi – which is good for my healing leg – beside it.

Kapleau remains a controversial figure in some circles. The Sanbo Zen people still point out that he had not finished his koan training and therefore is not recognized in Japan as an authorized teacher. When the annual conference of the American Zen Teacher's Association was hosted at Chapin Mill in 2003, James Ford admitted he had reservations about attending. Ford explained that Kapleau, who was 90 at the time of the conference

> – had broken from his teacher Yasutani Roshi many years before. He took to calling himself Roshi and was known in subsequent years to make seemingly self-serving disparaging remarks about other teachers. He also, it seemed to me, gratuitously challenged the technical veracity of the transmission of the lineage from which he had broken – which was the lineage in which I also practiced. But he was also the editor of *Three Pillars of Zen*, a monumentally important book. I cannot express how important that single book was in my life; and this has been true for so many others who've taken up the Zen way. So, in the end I went to see him.

Philip Kapleau was living in a small two-room apartment at the center. His Parkinson's was so advanced he could do little more than sit in his recliner and hold hands with each of us who'd made that trip. About ten teachers – Dharma successors in the Soto, Rinzai, Harada-Yasutani, and Korean Chogye traditions – had made the pilgrimage. There was little option, if we wanted to shake Kapleau's hand, but to kneel in front of him and take the initiative. It had clearly not been set up to require such a supplicative posture, but that was inevitably what was called for.

I found tears welling up from deep inside me – not just for his physical condition, but for gratitude. This crusty old man was a true founder and absolutely one of the most important figures in bringing the Zen way West. For all his flaws, he was a great man and one of the most important people in my life. I happily knelt, took his hands in mine, and thanked him. I remain grateful for that opportunity.[66]

After completing the Tai-Chi form, I lay a stone on his grave and am equally grateful to have had the opportunity to do so.

Rochester, particularly in the days of Philip Kapleau, was infamous for its samurai approach to training, so when I arrived at the center earlier in the day, I was not expecting a particularly warm reception. It is, however, a place I had been looking forward to visiting; historically, it is one of the most important in all of North America. If I am taking the pulse of contemporary American Zen, this is one place where I am confident I will get a sense of how robust or not the tradition is.

The center consists of two adjacent houses linked by a passageway in what appears to be a moderately wealthy residential neighborhood. The grounds and structures are impressive and maybe a little daunting. I am early for my 9:00 appointment with Roshi Kjolhede and am told I can wait on a sofa in the foyer outside the administrative offices. I have been informed that it is a Center, not a monastery, and that the people I see scurrying about are not monks. Both men and women are barefoot and have close-cropped, but not shaved, heads. As they bustle about carrying out their duties, I'm reminded of what someone had written about the San Francisco Zen Center in the days before Blanche Hartman became abbess: "Well, they're not unfriendly."

But if there is a certain stiffness among the students (or perhaps they are just focused on carrying out their responsibilities), Bodhin Kjolhede is relaxed, humorous, and easy to talk to. He is Philip Kapleau's principal heir and remains unabashedly loyal to his teacher. Unlike Kapleau, he did complete koan training, working with teachers in the Soto lineage to which Ford belongs. As a consequence, he was offered transmission in that lineage, which he declined. In a talk transcribed on the Zen Center website, he explained:

> Since I never worked extensively with any Soto teacher, such certification would, I believe, be a mere formality, and contrary to the spirit of Zen's 'mind-to-mind transmission.' Roshi Kapleau's seal – and now my twenty years of teaching experience – is more than enough for me.[67]

"I was raised with no religion at all," Bodhin tells me. "I never went to church in my life."

"Where were you raised?"

"Rochester, Michigan, believe it or not. A northern suburb of Detroit. So no religious upbringing at all, and by the time I reached adolescence I pretty much considered myself an atheist. But I was gripped by an existential questioning of what this is all for. I think it's common for adolescents to have that. For me, every time I looked up at the sky at night – the stars – I had this one question just barrel into my mind: What is the purpose of life? So that was sort of percolating there, but I still had no use for religion. Then two of my five sisters started reading Asian religions, Asian philosophy, and they came here – to the Zen Center – before me, and they were enthralled with what Zen offered. I wasn't there yet, but they encouraged me to read *The Three Pillars of Zen*."

"What year would this have been?"

"1970."

"And you said five sisters?"

"Yeah."

"No brothers?"

"No brothers."

"Lucky you."

"There are two kinds of people. There are those when they hear that say, 'You poor boy!' And the others who say, 'You must have been spoiled rotten.' It was the latter. With a little of the former mixed in."

This is another conversation in which there is a lot of humor, and Bodhin turns out to be one of those people who remind me of Linji's "True man of no rank." Almost inevitably, Zen training – if one persists in it – forms people of strong character. I suspect, at least in part, that it is because these are individuals who know themselves deeply and have nothing to prove to anyone else.

"But, yeah, my sisters came here before me, and I only got to about page four of *The Three Pillars of Zen*. It just didn't speak to me. Looking back on it, I know what it was. I had just not reached the point of critical mass of suffering. I was not really suffering yet. And then fate intervened. I was arrested as I was coming into the United States from Canada with some peyote buttons."

"Whoa! You were bringing peyote from Canada into the US?"

He had been in California after graduating college. "And while I was out there, I bought some peyote from a Native American. And I confused drug experiences – psychedelic drug experiences – with Zen, so I wanted my sisters to try it. But I didn't know if peyote was available in this part of the country, so I hitchhiked across the United States bringing it with me. And it turned out that by the time I got to New York state, I was weary of hitch-hiking, and I decided to skip my sisters and get home."

He thought the quickest route would be to hitchhike through Canada, so he crossed the Peace Bridge between Buffalo and Fort Erie, Ontario, on foot. When he reached Canadian customs, his backpack was searched. Then he was told to empty his pockets. "That was one of the memorable experiences of my life. I had the peyote buttons in my pocket with a whole lot of other stuff, Swiss army knife and all kinds of things. But what I did was, I pulled out all this stuff from one pocket – the clean pocket – laid it out on the desk, and then, as I was reaching for my other pocket, I relied on a diversionary tactic." He asked for instructions about how to proceed to Michigan. The border agent explained that it he couldn't hitchhike through Canada and would have to find another way. The conversation, however, distracted the agent sufficiently that Bodhin wasn't asked to empty the other pocket. "So I'm invulnerable right? I'm invincible."

He spent the night in a clover-leaf on the highway on the American side and was eventually offered a lift from "a guy who was kind of lost." He was also heading to Michigan, and Bodhin convinced him they should proceed through Canada.

"So we went through Canada. We got into Canada all right. And then we got to the Windsor Tunnel. What I didn't know was that he had a pistol in his glove compartment. We get to customs, and, on a hunch, they decided to search his car. They find the gun. So then first they searched him; then they searched the car. A thorough search of the car. They were done with the car. I could have taken the peyote and put it anywhere on the car; they were done with the car. But I didn't know they had any interest in me.

"Then they said, 'Now you.' They took me into an empty house trailer, and they strip searched me, shirt, trousers, undershirt. Then they said, 'Okay. Now your briefs.' And that was when the jig was up. They jumped up, took the plastic bag, and ran away. And as I was sitting there, the remaining custom's official sat there with his arms crossed and said, 'You just ruined your life. You stupid kid, you just ruined your life.'

"Anyway, they came with police and handcuffed me and took me to the Detroit city jail. I landed in the ninth floor. They called it the bullpen. This was a Saturday night. There were eleven other prisoners. Just a holding cell. I learned later that night that two of my cellmates were convicted murderers. And there was every kind of criminal, including a heroin addict who was going cold turkey. He was screaming and vomiting all night. It was a night in hell, but I wasn't hurt. I'd worry a lot more if it happened today, but I wasn't hurt at all. But it was a hellish, hellish, screaming, horrible night.

"Anyway, I looked out the window. Saturday night turned into Sunday morning. I'm looking out the window down at the passers-by on the street. And there's something about that flag – American flag – nothing patriotic but seeing the way it was flapping in the breeze against the blue sky. The freedom of it. The absolute freedom of the flag and these passers-by. I remember thinking, 'All right, they can keep walking; they can turn left; they can turn right; they can go that way, this way. And here I am, boxed in this cell.' And the real killer was realizing that I was a criminal. I'd done my share of binge drinking and pot and hashish, marijuana, mescaline and acid, and everything. But I had this notion in my mind. I thought of myself as a clean, suburban, successful kid. I'd been president of my class almost every year and Honor Society and all that stuff. So until that night, in that cell, I had had this self-identity of a very privileged, successful, well-liked guy. And suddenly I couldn't deny that I was a criminal. I mean, what is identity? But I had committed a crime, and that was really something.

"And I think what helped me with my sentencing was when they took my statement, I just said, 'I did it.' And the guy said, 'Okay, hold on now. You're entitled to legal representation.' I said, 'What? You found peyote buttons on me. I did it.' Anyway I had a cousin who came down the next morning, and I got out on bail. Then the sentencing was also a very memorable experience, because I thought I might go to prison. So I stood before the judge who looked pretty much like you. White hair. High up on the bench. I felt my knees shaking. And I told the judge that I had read these books by Carlos Castaneda and I wanted to experiment. And he said – this is verbatim; these words are etched in my brain – he said, 'Well, son, you made a mistake, and I think you know it. So tell you what I'm going to do. $100 court costs. A year's probation. And if you behave yourself during that year, you can come back to the court, and the court will expunge it from your record.' An extremely light sentence. Extremely light. I think probably because they could see that I wasn't a hardened criminal, and I had confessed to everything. I wasn't trying to lawyer up or anything.

"In any case – and this is where it gets good – during that year, my lottery number for the draft came up. I had already applied for conscientious objector status, and they had rejected it because there was no history of church attendance or anything. So my only recourse to going to Vietnam, at the time, was to go to Canada, and I hadn't ruled that out. I mean, I wasn't sure that I was willing – or ready – to go to Canada because I was very attached to my family, and in those days, go to Canada, that's it! Forever. Anyway, so during that time, my draft number came up, and because I was a convicted felon – the conviction was possession of hallucinogenic drugs – I had a permanent deferment!"

"It was that easy?"

We're both laughing, and he's nodding his head vigorously. "You know the story? I bet you know the story. The Chinese story about the lost horse? 'Who's to say?'"

The story is about a poor farmer whose horse runs away, and, when the neighbors commiserate with him, he says "Good luck, bad luck. Who's to say?" Then the horse returns, bringing several wild horses with it, and the neighbors congratulate the farmer. Again, he remarks, "Good luck, bad luck. Who's to say?" Then his only son fractures his leg trying to break the wild horses. The neighbors return to offer their sympathies. After that, the army comes through the village conscripting all the able-bodied young men but leaves the farmer's son alone.

"There it is. Before the sentencing, I thought it was the worst day of my life, and, in a way, it was. Of course. Then my number came up during the year of probation. And I went back; they expunged the conviction, but the deferment was permanent. They're not tracking what happens with probation and all that kind of stuff. And I had had a little skirmish before all this, in college, where I was convicted of a misdemeanor, possession of stolen property. I was with a bunch of guys and we'd picked up a parking sign – it wasn't me; I want you to know that – someone had picked up a parking sign. We were drunk, and the police threw us in jail for the night. And in Michigan there's a law that after a year, with a misdemeanor, you could have that expunged. So I got them both expunged! But I had my permanent deferment.

"So, as a result of that horrible night, when I picked up *The Three Pillars* again, then it spoke to me. It was clear as day. I needed to do something. I needed to change my life. So during that year's probation – 1970-71 – I was working as a psychiatric attendant at the University of Michigan Hospital, and, as soon as my probation was up, I came here."

"How old were you?"

"I was 22. And I knew when I came here, this is what I wanted to do."

"Do you remember what it was like when you first knocked on the door?"

"Well, actually, before I moved here from Ann Arbor – during that year's probation – I came to an introductory workshop. Then, and still, that's the gateway; you come for an introductory workshop. So when I came that weekend, one of my sisters showed me around the center and everything, and it was at the workshop where the penny really dropped. Meeting Roshi Kapleau had a profound effect on me. There was no question but that he had this sense of spiritual authority that comes out of realization. He was sharp, clear, grounded, and yet serene, energetic. Everything. At the end of the workshop, my sister wanted to introduce me, and, just by way of making conversation, he said, 'So, do you have any questions?' And I said, 'No.' There were no questions left. That was it." Bodhin claps his hands. "Just like that. But I still had to go back and finish my probation.

"Then when I moved here, I wanted to come right into residential training. In those days, you could come for a training program of four weeks or five weeks, and I did that. But at that time I think we were one of only a very few Zen centers in the United States, and we were being flooded with people from all over the country because there weren't many options. So we were overrun with people, and I couldn't start in residential training immediately. I was living with one of my sisters, in her cellar with the centipedes and spiders. But then I worked my way up to where they put me on staff here, and I never left."

"Really? Literally?"

"Literally. I mean, I lived here for fifteen years, and then – when I was 43 – I got married, and now I live with my wife in the city."

"But you've been a professional Zen person all this time?"

"Yeah! I've never done anything since. I have never worked for money elsewhere since 1971."

"That has to be unique."

"I think it is fairly, and I can honestly say I never had one day in these, whatever it is – 42 years – never had one day that I've wanted to do anything else. I just feel immensely blessed."

"I've spoken with a number of your Dharma brothers and sisters, people who were here at the same time you were training, and they frequently talk about the atmosphere in those days. I'm sure you're familiar with the terms people use: boot camp Zen, samurai Zen. Sunyana Graef wrote about an incident where the two of you collided in a dokusan rush, and people actually ran over you instead of helping you up. What was the intent of that very macho atmosphere?"

"I can't say what the purpose was. It was just the way it was. I think it a lot of it was…." He pauses, then sighs. "Roshi Kapleau had spent thirteen years in Japan, and I think when he came here he felt most comfortable with sort of a Japanese martial energy kind of training and, naturally, just continued it here. And for those of us for whom it worked, it worked. Partially because we were so young. When I came to Zen Center, almost everyone was in their early twenties. And it wasn't until quite a few years later that I came to feel, when I took over the center, that that kind of martial energy samurai thing, boot camp thing, was something we needed to let go of."

"You don't maintain that atmosphere?"

"No. I mean, I guess it's all relative. I guess you could align Zen Centers on a continuum, and we may be more toward the rigorous side than a lot of centers. For example, in the zendo we don't allow moving during a formal round of sitting, and I learned, at one of our American Zen Teachers' Association meetings, that a lot of centers are not that strict. They let people move if they need to. We still use what, I gather, is more of the kyosaku than most centers do. But I think we are a lot kinder and gentler than we used to be. Seriously.

"I think the big thing for me was when I went to Japan I trained for three months with Tangen Roshi who had been a mentor, interpreter, friend to Roshi Kapleau. When Roshi Kapleau went to Japan, he spoke no Japanese. In fact, he didn't even know that sitting was required at the monasteries. He went there thinking – in his own words – that he might get satori through some kind of process of osmosis by sipping sake with a master. So it was a rude shock to him when he got there and found out there was this thing called sitting. But when he went to Hoshin-ji, this Tangen Roshi – just a young monk – knew a little bit of English and took him under his care and helped him out. So when I went back many years later, I could see that the atmosphere had changed. Tangen Roshi was the Dharma heir of Harada Roshi, who had had this fierce samurai style at his monastery, but Tangen Roshi didn't have that, didn't use the stick that much. And someone said to Tangen Roshi, 'This doesn't match what I read in *The Three Pillars of Zen*. This is much less martial than I read.' And Tangen Roshi said, 'When Harada Roshi died, Hoshinji fell apart. And that's when I realized the limits of discipline from the outside.'

"So that sort of gave me permission to just ease up a little bit and not try to beat people into kensho. Also the sangha here, meanwhile, had grown a lot older. Though I still think a majority of our members are baby-boomers."

"Really? The people I saw working here this morning obviously aren't."

"That's right. But we have something like 500 members. Maybe half are boomers. I know in our sesshins – which are still not a cake walk – you look down the aisle, and there are a lot of grey hairs. But now, in recent years, we've definitely had an influx of more young people. So maybe it's tipped."

In spite of the strict rules pertaining to sesshin, Bodhin has continued the process begun by Kapleau to adapt Zen to the west. The navy blue shirts and slacks are one example. On the other hand, Bodhin admits that he tends "to be conservative as a teacher. And by that I mean, in the original sense, I tend to want to conserve the tradition. When I first came here, I had some reservations about bowing and doing prostrations and even chanting. I was too proud to think I had any need for that. But I came to find that somehow it works. I still would say that I don't have the strongest devotional personality. But I teach it and I do it – the chanting and the bowing and everything else – because somehow it works. I believe it works."

"Still, the atmosphere here seems less formal than some of the monastic centers I've visited."

"I think it's fair to say that this is one of the distinctions that Roshi Kapleau – as compared to his peers from Japan – was very adamant about, that we have to Americanize Zen. And Americans are – as you know – much more informal than the Japanese. So we try to keep things taut, in terms of the training, but not with those elegant, elaborate, Japanese rituals. So, for example, I've heard that there are other Zen Centers where the teacher, to start off the morning zazen, will go through the zendo and people will all do this deep bow. That strikes me as inappropriate. Not to go off on this, but what I'm constantly aware of – maybe even a little more than Roshi Kapleau was – is how much of Zen from Asia is conditioned by the Confucian ethos of hierarchy and all. And I'm trying to find a balance between not throwing that out completely, because there's a place for it, for hierarchy – I'm not going to apologize for hierarchy – but not over-doing it."

"So dokusan, for example, do students bow or do they prostrate?"

"They do one prostration. And it wouldn't take much for me to eliminate that. But I think it's good to start it off that way. In Japan, when I was training, I'd do three prostrations when I came in and three when I left. But so far, I think just one coming in, one total, is all right."

It is because of his commitment to conserving the practice as he has received it that Bodhin is cautious about how he involves his students in social action.

"We have a program where our members will go into soup kitchens. And there's a whole kind of blossoming – in the last two years – of different ways of engaging with the wider world outside the walls of the Zen Center. For example, I'm trying to give some leadership in the whole spectre of global warming. In fact, just last night we had a meeting where we were talking about how we might have a demonstration to the public of the spirit of Zen the way that we did about thirty years ago. Someone at the Minnesota Zen Center organized what we called a three day Zazen Vigil in New York City. This was on the occasion of some big demonstrations, public protests in New York regarding the proposed deployment of Cruise Missiles in Europe. And so one enterprising guy came up with the idea of inviting Zen Centers to convene across from the United Nations in a place called the Peace Park and to just sit for three days. That had quite a strong effect on me. I thought it was really powerful, something I could get behind more than waving protest signs and marching. So I'm trying to get something like that going regarding climate change. As things stand now, there are about ten of us on the committee, and we're going to invite other Zen Centers to join us in Washington or someplace as part of a bigger, wider demonstration about climate change. But first we'll cut our teeth on a smaller thing in Rochester where we're going to try to cooperate with people like the Sierra Club.

"We're really just getting into this area of social engagement. And – as you know probably – the danger of it is if you become too one-sidedly engaged – socially or politically – then you run the risk of losing the real root of Zen practice."

"There's a big sign out front," I say. "'Zen Center.'"

"Yeah."

"So suppose a kid from the neighborhood – somebody like you described yourself, 'gripped by existential questioning' – comes to the door, and they're not ready to come to a workshop or anything like that yet. But they're curious, and they ask you what this place is all about. What is the function of Zen? What do you tell them?"

"The function," he says, then pauses a moment. "The function of Zen is to enable us to become fully present in everything we do. And in that way, to live out of what's real rather than out of our thoughts. So it's a method. I mean, that's one way of saying it, a very kind of limited way. There are so many ways of talking about Zen. It's a method of meditation – not just sitting meditation but moving meditation – a method by which we can learn to become fully present and aware and responsive.

"I love this word 'responsiveness.' When people sometimes ask, 'Well, what's our responsibility in Zen?' It's to respond to what needs to be done, to what's called for, and that always means out of the present. So that's kind of the short answer I would give."

"How does it do that?"

"How does it do that?" Another pause, and he chuckles. "Well, through the sitting and moving meditation, we learn how unreal our thoughts are and how unnecessary it is to be dwelling on our thoughts. We see the unreality of them; we see, in a very real sense, they're just dust in the mind. I always distinguish – as my teacher did – between these random, irrelevant thoughts and actual thinking. Thinking is something we would never want to abandon. We have this wonderful human endowment, the human intellect, and there are plenty of times we need to problem solve or, in other ways, think through problems. But so much of the time, we're just more awash in thoughts of the future, thoughts of the past, and that is what, I think, is so binding, and so easily perpetuates human neurosis. It's ruminating and fretting about the future and dwelling on the past and so forth. So my teacher, Roshi Kapleau, used to distinguish between thinking – which is a useful thing – and a word he made up, 'thoughting.' Just being pitched around by the thoughts in our minds."

"Okay. So what has all that got to do with koans?"

"Yeah. I think one of the functions of koans is that they reveal what is beyond words and concepts. That's a very simple way to understand koan training. It is a way to access what is beyond what can be apprehended through our senses and our intellect. That there is this other realm that we can access and live out of, respond out of, which is beyond words and concepts."

"You'd said that the entry point for new people is still a workshop. Do you conduct it?"

"Always. I feel they need to see the main teacher in operation."

"What happens in a workshop?"

"I spend the first hour or so just talking about basic principles of Zen, Zen doctrine, Zen and Buddhist both but with more of an emphasis on Zen. I go a little lightly on Buddhism for the introductory workshop because my main thing is to get them sitting, to get them meditating. I don't want Buddhism to get in the way of that, but I also find that Buddhist teaching is profound and unbelievably wonderful, so I sprinkle in a little about Buddhist doctrine, the life of the Buddha, those kinds of things. And then the rest of the day is very practical. The workshop is about seven hours long, and, except for that first hour, it's mostly the 'how to.'"

"And what percent of the people who attend a workshop come back?"

"Well, they're invited to come the next day, and I would say maybe twenty percent do. Then a lot of people will come and sit once or twice or three times in the subsequent weeks and then disappear."

There are seven workshops a year, with an average of fifty participants in each. "So about 350 new people a year," I calculate. "And you said your membership's somewhere around 500 people. So there's a lot of people interested enough to come to a workshop, and yet they don't go any further."

"Not with us."

"I suppose they might go somewhere else but you'd be the biggest show in town."

"Or on their own. Sitting on their own at home."

He further estimates that of the 500 or so members of the Zen Center less than a quarter take part in sesshin. Relatively speaking, even at one of the premier centers in America, the numbers remain small.

"Every time I see – in a popular magazine like *Time* – a pie chart of religions in the United States," Bodhin reflects, "they don't even mention Buddhism. I mean, they have a little sliver that would say 'other' and that would include us."

"And yet," I muse, "there is a lot of talk about Zen. Jon Stewart's 'moment of Zen' at the end of *The Daily Show*, books on the Zen of golf, those little sandboxes you can buy that are supposed to be Zen gardens. So the culture has adopted Zen as a concept associated with calmness, meditation…."

"Serenity. Centeredness."

"All of these things. The concept of Zen seems to have positive overtones, even if the way the word's used doesn't have a whole lot to do with actual Zen practice."

"Yeah. It's a marketing device."

"So what is it about Zen – as an adjective – that appeals to Americans?"

"I think the word is so elusive that people in marketing and advertising can throw it up there, and it will draw a certain kind of interest. It's so inscrutable, it's a kind of Rorschach thing. Most people don't know what Zen is, but there's a snowballing effect where, because it shows up in these different contexts as consistently being serene and calm and kind of zany and wild, then that itself is self-perpetuating."

It was a point I would have explored further with him, but just then a staff member comes to tell us it's time to leave for Chapin Mill.

There is a story that shortly after Bodhin entered the residency program at Rochester, he was told to fix a broken door. So that no one would come through carelessly while he was doing it, he put up a sign: "Open door gingerly; someone working on other side."

"Is it true," I ask during the return trip to Rochester, "that one of the reasons you became Philip Kapleau's attendant is that you knew how to use a semi-colon?"

He laughs and nods his head, keeping his eyes on the road. "Yes."

"So that story's true."

"It is. I mean, it wasn't the only factor, but that's when he first started noticing me."

"I take it that Bodhin is not your birth name."

"No. It's Peter. Bodhin is the name I received when I was ordained."

"And it means?"

"Well, it's just from the word Bodhi, and we put an N on the end because, at the time I thought it made it sound a little less foreign."

"Okay. Earlier, you said you weren't a monk, but you use a Buddhist name."

"Mm-hmm."

"Wear semi-clerical garb."

"Mm-hmm."

"Kind of a shaved head. Which could be a fashion statement."

He laughs and nods again.

"You don't work outside the center. So how is this not being a monk?"

"Yeah. Glad you asked that. Because I want to preserve the original weight of the meaning of 'monk' in the Buddhist tradition, which is taking vows of life-long celibacy and homelessness. So basically renouncing the family. And I feel quite strongly that the word 'monk' or 'monastery' should not be used unless it refers to those who have taken vows of lifelong celibacy. I suspect that places that call themselves monasteries where vows of lifelong celibacy and homelessness are not required are doing so as a kind of marketing device, to create the sense of greater authenticity. But I think it's a disservice to the true Buddhist monks to blur that distinction. So even for ordained people like myself, we have always used the word 'priest' for lack of a better term."

"Do you identify yourself as a cleric?"

"Yeah, I think in the conventional sense of the word."

"You just conducted a wedding. So you have that legal authority."

"Yeah."

There are, it turns out, five priests at the center.

I ask, "What do priests do after they've been trained?"

"They just keep training," again, with a laugh.

"Well, if you were training in Asia you'd probably eventually be appointed to care for a temple. Is that a long-range goal for your priests?"

"Not a goal," he says. "Thirty years ago, when the Zen Center had, like – phew! – ten affiliate centers, then…."

"You don't any longer?"

"No. We have one affiliate center now because all of the others are now under the directorship of an authorized teacher. So when I started, I was in charge of affiliate centers in Sweden, Mexico, Germany – I don't know – a couple of other places. Now in each of those places – New Zealand, too – one of my disciples has reached the point where I thought they could be authorized to teach as independent centers. So they're sister centers still to us, but they're on their own."

The point, of course, is that those centers exist and are viable. The numbers are small, and the membership is largely drawn from a narrow segment of the population, but there is vitality. This brings us back to the hypothesis and speculation Bodhin had spoken of earlier.

"There's a fascinating book called *Generations* co-authored by William Strauss and Neil Howe. It's quite an impressive marshalling of data showing that there are basically four generational types since the sixteen hundreds that repeat themselves in the same sequence, and each of the four generational types has a subset. So what we call the 'baby-boomers' were part of a larger group they call the Idealist Generation. And with the Idealist Generation, religion and education are the big interests. A previous iteration of the Idealists were the Transcendentalists."

The other three generational types are called Reactive, Civic, and Adaptive. The Idealist Generation follows the Adaptive in the sequence. In Strauss and Howe's analysis, the Baby Boomer generation was Idealist; Generation X was Reactive; the Millennial Generations was Civic; the current generation (Generation Z, or what Strauss and Howe call the Homeland Generation) is Adaptive. Therefore, if the sequence holds true – Bodhin points out – the coming generation would, once again, be Idealist, which might explain the growing interest in their workshops, training sessions, and sesshin.

Back at Arnold Park, while Bodhin poses for a photograph in front of the center, a line of Zen students come down the street picking up litter. "Are these your guys?" I ask.

"Takuhatsu," he tells me.

In Japan, takuhatsu is the traditional activity of begging. Bodhin explains that Kapleau had sought an equivalent that would not "appear too foreign, something that fit in with our own culture. He came up with this idea of picking up trash in the neighborhood. Disciplined, in silence, eyes mostly down. And we've continued that. What it has in common, I suppose, with traditional takuhatsu in Japan is that we're demonstrating, bringing into public the demonstration of Zen principles of concentration and – kind of – 'no self.' But there's this added element of service that isn't there in Japan."

The "element of service" is one of the things that differentiates American Zen from its Asian predecessors. There are other elements which do that as well.

CHAPTER EIGHTEEN
Sunyana Graef

THE VERMONT ZEN CENTER IS LOCATED IN SHELBURNE, A SMALL, ARTISTI-cally-inclined community outside Burlington. I notice the Peace Pole at the foot of the Center's drive before I sees the official sign set in a small flower bed. The sign bears the calligraphy signature – or kao – of the 17th century Japanese Zen Master, Butcho-Kokushi: three vertical strokes rising from a single horizontal stroke. This glyph was on the cover and title page of *The Three Pillars of Zen* when it was first released and has been associated with the Kapleau lineage ever since. A similar sign hangs over the entry way to the Rochester Zen Center.

I am struck by the care with which the Vermont Center has been designed and maintained. The grounds cover some 72 acres and are lovingly tended. It happens that my visit takes place in May when the magnolia trees are in full bloom, their bases littered with large white petals. The rhododendron is in flower, along with many colorful bedding plants. Sunyana Graef Roshi informs me that when the house was purchased it was in the middle of an alfalfa field and there was only a single tree, a pine which now towers over the property. The sangha celebrated its 25th anniversary in 2013, and a spruce they planted when they first took over the property is now almost as high as the pine. Several cedars and the other trees, plants, bushes, and flower beds have all been added during the last two and a half decades.

Inside the building, careful craftsmanship is equally apparent. The original house has had several extensions and is now able to accommodate sixty people comfortably during sesshin. The woodwork and the lighting have been designed and constructed thoughtfully. Polished hardwood floors run throughout the building. The first room one enters is a living room, with stuffed furniture and a big fireplace. "When I was looking for a place for a Zen Center," Sunyana tells me, "one of my chief requirements was not a zendo but a living room. What I was looking for was a place where people would have to walk through the living room to get to the zendo. The reason for that is simply that I wanted a sangha to form. And this is where sangha is formed. Not when you're sitting in silence but when you come together in a social environment. So that's why I loved this place. You come in, and you have to walk through the living room. And people would sit here and chat and get to know each other."

Although she tells me that – even after all these years – she finds it difficult to speak in front of groups, she is an accomplished and often dramatic speaker. She stresses her points in various ways, sometimes with a sharp tone, sometimes whispering, sometimes slowing down and pronouncing each word distinctly and separately.

"I would say the function of Zen is to help people be alive. Truly alive. It helps people see who and what they are. Of course, you can practice Zen on many different levels. Right? But if you're practicing Zen on the deepest level, it enables you to see through all of your habit patterns, your ego delusions, your greed, your anger, your ignorance, and get to that point where you truly see. And once you see who and what you are, your life changes and so does everyone else's life, because you touch the world. You're not separate from the world."

"How did I first become involved?" she asks, repeating my question.

"Was there something that came before Zen?"

"Despair. Anguish. Suffering. Pain. Misery. You know. Life." But she says it smiling and chuckling softly. "I had led a very happy life, actually. I had a nice family, a good family, a loving home. But there was always something in me. I can remember being a child, a very young child maybe five years old, thinking, 'Why am I me? Why aren't I that girl in the concentration camp? What made me have this body and this mind?' I was very young, and I always had those kinds of feelings. I was born in '48, so it was after the Second World War."

"Where?"

"In Boston. And naturally I heard a lot about the Holocaust. My family was Jewish. Even though we weren't directly affected by it – we didn't have any close relatives in Europe – but you couldn't help but be affected by it. And so I was always aware of tremendous suffering. And, for whatever reason, I grew up with this heaviness of heart and sense of loss and pain and anxiety. It was the '60s, so I wasn't alone there. Probably 90 percent of the people my age had this to one degree or another. And so there was this searching that happened within me.

"When I was about twelve years old or so, I decided I was going to become a rabbi. And so – and this was a very important thing that happened – I told my rabbi that I had made up my mind that that was what I was going to do, and he just laughed. He looked at me with this kind of scornful look and said, 'Ssshhh! You can't be a rabbi! You're a girl!' And I didn't understand what that had to do with anything.

I had three brothers; they're not interested in religion. You mean to say, they can become rabbis, and I can't because of my sex? And so something just kind of flipped there. I said, 'This is wrong. Any religion which excludes women just because they're women, there's something wrong about that.'" She reflects a moment. "I said I was twelve, but I could have been younger. That's when I began searching – searching for something – searching for a way or path that didn't exclude me because of my sex."

Her introduction to Zen came in 1969, when a professor at Bard, where she attended college, suggested she take part in a sesshin.

"No introductory workshop, no …" I start.

"None of that. Nada. Nothing. He said, 'Yeah, I'll take you there.' So he drove me up to Rochester, and I went to a seven day sesshin. It was the most excruciating experience I'd ever had in my life, and I was sure I would never again attend anything like that or practice or do anything. But I was changed, forever changed. And that was that. I went to one more semester and then moved to Rochester and didn't leave for eighteen years."

"What was that like?"

"What was that like?" She laughs, spreading her hands as she shrugs. "I have no idea what that was like. All struggling with your ego and struggling with your desires. How twenty year olds struggle with everything. Well, at least I did. And I have a very strong egotistical personality and just was not very accepting. But at the same time, I was absolutely determined that I had to live a different life."

In the late '60s and early '70s, the Rochester Zen Center was not yet very forward thinking about gender roles. "The women did women's jobs, and the men did men's jobs. So the women were the cooks, the cleaners, the receptionists. The men attended the meetings and made all the decisions. But at least I could practice. At least the roshi didn't say, 'Oh, you're inferior because you're a woman.'"

The first sitting in the morning was scheduled for 6:00. "But it was an extremely competitive atmosphere back then. You wanted to prove you were the Zen student of the world. So, if the sitting started at 6:00, you had to be in the zendo by 5:00. You gotta be the first one in the zendo; you gotta be the first one in the dokusan line. And I bought into that completely.

"Roshi Kapleau had spent thirteen years in Japan, and the interesting thing about him is that when he was at Harada Roshi's monastery, it was very strict, very samurai. The stick, the shouts, the blows; that whole style of Zen. And he didn't penetrate his koan when he was there. Finally, he went to Yasutani Roshi's monastery, where the monitor was a little old lady. It was very small, very lay oriented, completely different atmosphere, and it was there that he had his break-through. When he came to the US, what style did he bring? Harada Roshi's style! The stick was used fiercely. It was used – I think – inappropriately. So, it was a pressure-cooker; it was incredibly intense. Women, myself included, often stopped menstruating for months and months at a time. You were just pushing constantly."

She tells me the story of colliding with Bodhin in the dokusan line. "It was fierce. Sometimes people would be bleeding. Broken toes. Cuts, bruises. Bodhin and I once collided, coming out the door. I can't remember who ended up on top. I think he ended up on top of me, helped to pick me up, and I" – she says, laughing – "I just ran. People were jumping over us. It was insane! But that was encouraged in a sort of way. I mean, there was an enormous amount of energy that went with those sesshins with that many young people with all their repressed sexual energy and everything else that was being poured into practice. It wasn't…it wasn't entirely healthy," she admits.

"It was just too much. I don't think that it was a good way to practice for most people. Because it pushed people to a point in their practice artificially. That's my objection to the stick. Roshi Kapleau was once hit all night long with a stick. And he kind of relished that story and how his shoulders were bleeding, and I always thought, 'Why?' Why would somebody think that was a good thing? If you don't have, within yourself, the desire, the need, the energy, the conviction, the perseverance for this practice, why do you think that being hit is gonna develop that in you, is gonna rouse that? It won't! It will temporarily, maybe, because you don't have a choice. But this is not natural. This is not healthy."

"Why did you stay?"

"There was no place to go. What else could I do? It wasn't that I was critical of it at the time. That was all I knew. That was what was going on. So what else? And I was so grateful to my teacher – and still am so grateful to him – that he was willing to put up with this immature, really, really selfish person. I don't think I could have put up with me, but he did. He must have seen something, for whatever reason. You know? I worked very closely with him. I became his disciple in 1969. I was always with him. I was his secretary and taking care of his needs. And there was nobody else."

There were other centers, of course, but stories were already circulating about the behaviors of certain teachers elsewhere.

"Rochester didn't have the same interpersonal problems that arose elsewhere?" I ask.

"Okay, I wouldn't say that entirely!" She laughs easily and frequently.

"Perhaps not the same kind of interpersonal problems?"

"There were lots of interpersonal problems, but they took the form more of…." She pauses. "Let me back up a little: As I said before, the atmosphere was highly competitive there. But it was competitive in terms of where you were in your practice, who got through their koan, who was working on this book. You weren't supposed to talk about this, but people inevitably found out about things. And people were really focused on that, advancing in wisdom – not so much in compassion, sadly – but in wisdom definitely. And so that was where a lot of our energy went. That and the fact that we were exhausted. I was so tired after years of getting up really early, going to sesshin all the time, and working all day, on my feet all day, that if I had ten minutes, I would fall sound asleep. I used to go back to my apartment, sleep, come home, come back to the center, work, work, work, work, go home for half an hour, sleep. And that was what it was. I don't think we had the energy for anything else other than the intensive practice we were involved in.

"And certainly our teacher was celibate. And there was never the slightest trace of his sexual involvement with…anyone! Even his wife, who was in Japan. They were divorced. And the precepts – from day one – were emphasized at the center. He spoke about them. We took the ceremony of jukai, taking the precepts, twice a year. We knew that they existed, and he didn't change the wording to make it sound like, 'Well, it's okay if you drink, but just don't get drunk too often.' No. Nothin' like that.

"And I'll tell you one other thing, and I think this is really important. He did not emphasize emptiness. And what I've seen, teachers who talk a lot about how empty they are – the importance of emptiness, being truly empty – are people who are not compassionate. Because they're stuck in this realm of" – in a sing-song voice – "'absolute freedom,' and they're 'one' with everything. But they've lost the whole side of the precepts. And this is critical. You can't really be enlightened if you're sitting there on top of that pole feeling just empty. You have to get down into the world and live a true life, and this means engaging with people. And that is just as much part of enlightenment as emptiness. Form and emptiness. Not two. So, anyway, my teacher did not emphasize that. He did talk about compassion. It's just that we chose not to hear it, I think."

"How did you become a teacher?" I ask.

"Roshi told me I should."

"And then you came here."

"Yeah, we moved to Vermont."

"We?"

"My husband and two children and I."

"Okay, so somewhere during those eighteen years in Rochester, you got married."

"Oh, I did! Yeah. My husband was a member of the center, and literally I walked into a room, and he was sitting on a couch, and I grabbed my friend who was nearest me and said, 'Who's that?' And that was that. I knew we were going to get married the minute – the instant – I laid eyes on him. For a guy, it took him a week or so."

"Guys can be slow."

"Some are real slow."

Sunyana and her husband, Jed, took turns serving on staff at the center. To earn the money needed to support their family, she became a baker. By 1985, her husband took a job at the Rochester Psychiatric Hospital, and she was able to return to being on staff at the Center.

"He's a psychologist?" I ask.

"He has a Ph.D. in psychology; he's not a clinical psychologist. He does psychological testing or something like that. Doing tests...testing things...I never am sure what he's doing!" she laughs. "The stuff that he does is very abstruse, and I don't quite understand it. But it's fine. He understands it. He's a good fellow."

I ask if he still practices Zen.

"Oh, yeah. Yeah, he's not my student, but he's the treasurer. I don't think I could have done this without him. I don't have a head for numbers. He does."

"So Roshi Kapleau told you you should start teaching. Why did you choose Vermont?"

"Because I had wanted to move to Vermont my whole life."

"Oh? Why?"

She shrugs and says, with a shy smile, "Because I love cows. I love cows, and I love green rolling hills, and I love mountains. And when I was young, we always drove though New England on family trips, and Vermont was just this magical, beautiful, wide-open space with no bill-boards, and not so many cars or people, and I just loved it, and had always thought, 'Someday I'm going to move to Vermont.'

"So, what happened was, Roshi said, 'So, you should start teaching. Why don't you and Bodhin teach together.'" Both she and Bodhin had been ordained at this point, and Bodhin was already teaching at the Rochester Center. "Well," she says, lowering her voice to a whisper, "that's not gonna happen. That's not a good idea. That's not gonna work out. Bodhin has to have his space, right? But Roshi really wanted that. So Bodhin and I talked about it, and it was clear that that was just not a good idea for either of us. Or for the Rochester Center either. Every teacher needs to spread their wings, find their own feet, go in whatever direction they need to go in. So then Jed said, 'Well, we've always wanted to move to Vermont. Why don't we do it?' So he was the one who suggested it, and I said, 'Well, okay. If you're ordained, you're not supposed to work. You're supposed to be supported by your community. There is no community. You don't have a job. We're gonna uproot the family. Do you really think this is a good idea?' And he said, 'We can do it.' So we searched around for a house. We finally found a house just down the road. A small house that had an upstairs that was maybe the size of this room." The room we are seated in is not much larger than fourteen by ten feet. "It was supposed to be the master bedroom. And, in fact, it had a bathroom off it, just like this. And so that became our zendo. It was up a little flight of stairs. And below that was this big room that was the living room. And on the other side of the house were two bedrooms; one for our girls – who were five and eight, at the time – and one for us. And a kitchen. That was our first zendo."

The space was just about adequate at first, because there were only two other practitioners. "Two members of the Rochester Center who lived in Vermont. So there were four of us. And that was it. Still it was really tight; it was really difficult."

The local community accepted them with New England nonchalance.

"When we moved in, Jed went over to introduce himself and talk to our next door neighbor, who was Mrs. Thomas – this is the Thomas Road – and she must have asked what I did, and he said, 'She's a Zen Buddhist Priest.' And she said, 'Well, we don't get too many of those in Chittenden County.'"

Still, the transition was difficult, especially for their daughters. "It was a wrench for all of us. I mean, here we were really at sea, not knowing anyone. Going from a place where you could not step out the door without seeing someone who was part of your community, and it had been a supportive community even though difficult. We had friends, and we knew Rochester, and we really liked living there. And we could easily have gone on living there had it not been for the fact it seemed like it was time for me to start doing this. But my husband was one hundred percent supportive, and it was not a question for him. It was just, 'This is the next step in our lives.' It all worked out. It was just a little bumpy at first."

Then they received a generous donation which allowed them to look for a place to establish a separate zendo. "We looked all over the place and found this one almost in our backyard. And we've just kept going from there."

"How did people find out about you?"

"Workshops, actually. Putting up posters. This was pre-internet days, right? So, just word of mouth."

"Students mostly? Young people?"

"No. No, it's the same demographic as came in the 1960s and '70s. So, they're my age, basically. So, back then, they were people in their forties. Now they're people in their fifties and sixties. We do get some young people. We do. But not enough. I wish there were more."

"What percentage of the people who attend workshops come back?"

"You know, that's a really interesting thing. I've found, in other places too, when a group starts up, very often the very first people to come are the people who are going to stay. For whatever reason, they're some of the most loyal people. It's as if there's that karmic bond that's like an electro-magnet – right? – and these are the people who stick. They have very deep roots in the Dharma."

One of her disciples, Dharman Rice, "came to our first or second workshop, and he's an ordained priest now, and he never misses a sitting, and he's just the pillar or our community. So there are those people. Then, as years go by, you might have a workshop with twenty-five people, of which you might get one member. So, you know? It doesn't really matter. I had one workshop which I would normally have cancelled because there were, like, three people! Ten had registered, but everybody cancelled but for these three. All three people became members. So, there's no way to know. Whenever I say, 'Maybe I should cancel' – I'll do anything to get out of having to give a talk – my husband will always say, 'No, you can't do that. You don't know. There might be one person there who's really ready.' And he's right. He's always right!" she chuckles.

"That can be off the record if you like."

"No!" she says, laughing louder. "No! Because it's true!"

Sunyana is the primary teacher of three centers which she considers a single sangha. The sister communities are in Costa Rica and Toronto. I ask which of those was established first, and it turns out that Costa Rica predates Vermont.

"Actually, they were my first students. In 1987, I gave a sesshin in Rochester. That was my first sesshin, and someone from Costa Rica came. And then I got this letter from Costa Rica saying, 'Would you please come and spend five months with us?' Well, ridiculous! My kids were very young, and there was no way that I was going to do that. So I talked to Bodhin. I said, 'Well, you know, here's this thing, and what should I do?' And he said, 'Go! Go!' And I said, 'Okay, I'll go down and do a sitting for a week or whatever.' So this was January or February of '88, before we moved here.

"And I went down there and met this ragtag group of people who had been practicing because my teacher had started that group in – I think – 1975. And they'd just been goin' along all that time without any support from anywhere. Fifteen people maybe. Maybe more. So I came, and all my love of South of the Border culture just…. I have such a strong karma, such a strong affinity with that. And these were just wonderful people.

"I don't know if you know the Tico culture. But they're very social people; very loving. Costa Rica is called the Switzerland of Central America because there's no standing army; there's national health-care. Higher literacy rate than in the US, at least at that time. Low infant mortality rate. So I really fell in love with them, even though there were aspects of that group that drove me crazy! They had no understanding of work. None! Because they were mostly middle class and upper middle class and everyone has maids. They didn't know how to lift a broom. They didn't know beans about putting away a chair. I mean, it was, like, jaw-droppingly astounding what these grown-ups just expected people to do for them. So that was a struggle that took me about fifteen years, and now they are about the hardest working group ever.

"Well, anyway, that's a long story. Yeah, so there are lots of stories; I could tell you lots of stories about that group. But at the end of that week, I just loved them, and they asked me to come and teach. So I put in a quick call to Rochester and talked to my teacher, who was still alive then, and said, 'What should I do?' And I talked to Bodhin, said, you know, 'What should I do?' Bodhin said, 'Well, I'm not goin' there!' Because his plate was full. He had Sweden, Germany, Mexico, and Poland out of the country, and in the country, there was Madison, there were just a lot of groups. So I said, 'Well, okay. They want to become my students, if that's okay with you.' He said, 'Absolutely.' And I talked to my teacher, and he said, 'Listen, they're going to drive you crazy. They're not easy. They're lovely people, but it's not going to be easy. Think hard about it.' What did I have to lose? I didn't have any students then. So I thought, 'Okay. Start with hard students and then it's going to get easier.' So, I did. And so the first year I think I went there once, and then I started going there twice, then I started to go three times, then four times, now I go six times a year. And they're wonderful, really wonderful."

"So, the same time I started teaching, one of my Dharma Brothers was given permission to teach, and he was in Toronto." This was Dane Zenson Gifford. "So he was the teacher there and in…." She pauses. "1994? That's right. We had just built our house. My parents decided we would pre-inherit, so they gave us money to build a house. And that was gonna make my life simpler. And that year, he – this teacher in Toronto – blew it. He was married, and he had an affair with a young woman. I don't think she was a member of the center, but I don't remember all the details. And this is Canada, and the Canadians were really clear: 'This is not okay. You have to leave.' So he was thrown out. And they wanted a teacher, and they decided they wanted a teacher who was in the Kapleau lineage. So there were only two or three people. Bodhin didn't feel he could do it; he was just completely filled up with his responsibilities. So they decided they wanted me to come. So I did. And I did for ten years, until my Dharma heir was ready to take over." Her Dharma heir is Ian Taigen Henderson.

"I love Canadians! I'll tell you something that happened on one of my early times there. It was around December, I guess, and for some reason I needed to go to the mall to get something. And the parking lot was really full, and Taigen offered to drive me. And so we're driving around, looking for a parking space. And he found one, except there's a car coming from the other way. And I said, 'Well, give up on that.' And Taigen says, 'No, no. He saw me.' And I said, 'Whaddya mean? He's just going to go in there.' Taigen goes, 'No he won't. He saw me.' And sure enough, the guy just passed through while Taigen manoeuvred his car into the spot. And I go, 'This is not Kansas anymore! Where are we?'"

I have been cut off more than once in a Canadian parking lot but agree that Canadians are often courteous about such things.

"There are so many differences between Canadians and Americans," she says, "and they're all wonderful differences. Each of the three sanghas complemented one another so beautifully. You know, Canadians don't promote themselves. They're much more quiet and laid back; very sincere and lovely. My husband, by the way, was at the University of Toronto; he taught at U of T for many years. We got married in Canada. We got married at the Toronto Zen Center, in fact, for various reasons. And Toronto and Rochester are so close, we would go there once a month, easily. So I had a very strong affinity for Toronto and Canada. I love Canada. So, yeah, very different and not so different. For my daughters it was wonderful. We'd go to the big city with lights and, you know, restaurants, and all different languages being spoken. It's such a multi-cultural city."

In all three locations, there are more people who attend sittings than there are formal students.

"We do have people who are my formal students, but I decided I did not want to take someone as a student just because they're here. They really have to want to do that. So normally what will happen is that a person will have gone to seven days of sesshin. That could be one seven day sesshin or a couple of three day sesshin or a three and a five. Whatever it works out to. A minimum of seven days' worth of sesshin. I feel that at the end of that amount of time, they know me as a teacher, and they should be able to make up their mind about whether or not they wish to make that commitment to work more closely. If they don't, that's perfectly fine, and they can continue on here. They just can't go to sesshin. Because in sesshin you're going to have to come into dokusan. And that means we have a relationship, and I don't want to hold somebody back. I'd rather they found a teacher that they do have an affinity with."

"You said that you came to that first sesshin in Rochester cold – no introduction, no support – and you were miserable."

She nods. "Yeah."

"Do you try to make it less miserable for first-timers here?"

"Nobody can make a sesshin less miserable for anyone. That's entirely up to them. But at least there won't be the anxiety that is generated by the atmosphere of sticks whacking and shouting and all that. Also we have a great variety of sesshin. We have the traditional seven day sesshin where you're up at 4:00 in the morning, you're sitting until 9:30 at night. Everybody's required to be at every activity. There's no leeway for personal expression including what you're wearing. It's very, very strict. No moving. Coming to dokusan three times a day. That's it. So that's a seven day sesshin, and those are three times a year.

"We have a Work Sesshin, which is very different. The emphasis is on outdoor work. Everybody works in the garden for about a minimum of four hours. Well, not everybody; there might be some people who are working in the kitchen. But the emphasis is really on working zazen, and there's less sitting zazen. So it's not easier, because it's strenuous activity, but it's different.

"And once a year there is this Vipassana-type retreat. No schedule. The only thing that's required is the work period which is an hour and a half long. There are no bells. People can get up when they want. If they want to sleep all day, that's up to them. I offer dokusan three times a day. I give a teisho once a day. We have chanting. Nobody's required to go to any of those. At first I thought this would be ideal for new people, because there's no pressure at all. But it turned out that the people who got the most from those retreats were the most senior people, who'd been to sesshin and who knew the benefits of sitting and who had some discipline and really relished that freedom of sitting as long as you want. You want to sit for an hour without moving? Fine. If you want to do kinhin for two hours. Fine. So, people love these retreats. And that's for five days. We don't do that for seven days.

"And then the fourth kind of sesshin is what we call a Jataka Sesshin. One of my dear friends who's now a Zen teacher in his own right is Rafe Martin who's a story teller. He comes, and he tells Jataka Tales and gives commentaries on them. We used to call these Working Person Sesshin because during the day there's nothing scheduled. It's just in the morning and the night. So the idea when I first started this,

I thought this would be great for anybody who has a job. They can just sit in the morning and the evening and then go off to work. What I didn't take into account is that not everyone works nine to five. Right? Professors – and there's a lot of them in sangha – they work at night or they have strange hours. Or doctors. So it didn't work out quite the way I wanted, but for some people it does work that way. So we do a full schedule on the weekend and then from Monday to Friday we just have formal hours in the morning and in the evening. And the day is completely open. People do whatever they want to do. And that's my favorite sesshin. Oh my gosh, it's wonderful! Rafe is an amazing story-teller. And the Jataka Tales are our life. They're not about anyone else. They're about us. And he makes them just come to life in a way that is unique. I've never heard anyone talk about them in the way that he does. So I just love that sesshin."

Throughout our conversation, Sunyana discusses some of the differences between her center and Rochester. "I have a much stronger emphasis on the Bodhisattva of Compassion, Kannon, because her presence in my life was so important, always has been since the day I met her. And so, Kannon is everywhere in the center. Another huge difference is the fact that we don't have staff. And that affects all aspects of life here, because everyone takes responsibility. So our practice is our life. Our life is our practice. And I hope I never hear from anyone, 'I don't know what this has to do with my life.' And I did hear that in Rochester. 'We're doin' this, but what effect does it have on my life?' And it doesn't. It takes a while for it to affect your life, but you need to make that connection from the beginning. So that's what I hope people see. That this is everything we do. It's the way we brush our teeth; it's the way we drive our car; it's the way we talk to our loved ones and strangers; it's the way we walk outdoors and smell the flowers. There's nothing that isn't practice. Nothing. So I hope people will get that. We didn't exactly get that in Rochester. That wasn't the focus that I knew about then."

"Where was the focus then?"

"Wisdom. Enlightenment. That was it."

"And here there's more focus on compassion?"

"I hope so. Well, not necessarily more but more evident? My teacher actually actively discouraged us from social outreach. And that's definitely not the case now in Rochester. But at that time, it was. And, of course, this was the '60s, the '70s, when there was so much activism going on, and he thought we needed to focus our attention within to develop ourselves. We were so immature and so scattered and so undisciplined and so drug-hazed that I think he was probably right about that. It's just that there were repercussions to that. And the repercussion was that we thought there was nothing more important in the world than enlightenment, and the more deeply enlightened you were, the better you were. Somehow you were more Buddha-ish or something. So that had its effect necessarily. It was not a good one. We were conceited as all get-out.

"So I began teaching Loving Kindness to my students. At every sesshin, there would be half an hour where we would do Loving Kindness, sending it to yourself, to a friend, so on and so forth. And then I started giving classes outside sesshin, and then I fobbed that off onto Dharman. And he's been the sole teacher of the Mettabhavana classes for many years now. And there are people who sign up for those classes and don't do anything else, but they often come back. And it's been a very important part of our community, teaching that. Teaching that way of loving acceptance."

Dharman Rice is a soft spoken man with an interesting history. As it turns out, he had been born in Egypt and grew up overseas before his family returned to the United States.

"I guess I came to Zen like most people," he says. "Out of suffering. My life was in a wreck. I was teaching philosophy at the University of Vermont, and I and a number of other people were fired in the Vietnam days for being militantly opposed to the war, or getting arrested, conduct unbecoming." He smiles at the memory. "And about that same time, my first marriage was falling apart. My life was in something of a shambles. And I gave myself six months to a year to get over all that. Well, a decade later I realized I was still a pretty angry, unhappy guy. Had a lot of therapy. Was fortunate enough to have therapy with a number of practitioners who had great sympathy for Buddhism; practiced themselves.

"Uh…I had actually – and I am very embarrassed to say so – taught Buddhism in a philosophy of religion class way back when before I had ever practiced. Knew nothing about it except what I'd read in books. But I had some kind of connection with it. And then coming here, it was sort of in a way like coming home. Felt like coming home.

"One thing I love about Roshi is that if you have a teacher, you have somebody who's going to tell you things that you don't want to hear sometimes. And the thing that I value about Roshi more than anything else is her integrity. I know that she doesn't ask anything of me that she doesn't ask of herself in spades all the time. And – over the course of twenty-five years – I have had to listen to a number of things that I didn't want to hear about myself but which were necessary for me to hear. And my being able to hear it was as a result of that faith in her integrity. She's a wonderful, compassionate person, who's a great baker and a great cook and all sorts of other things. But I think that at the end of the day it's the integrity piece. And when things are difficult, when I'm having trouble with my practice of one sort or another, it's that faith in her and in her practice and her integrity that I value the most."

Later he tells me, "I am so grateful that I've had a woman teacher rather than a man teacher. And I'm glad I haven't practiced 'Samurai Zen.' The Zen that we practice here is the practice of Kannon, the compassionate heart. And Roshi starting to do metta practice here is a function of that. And it's not that metta practice hasn't been a part of the history of Zen, but it's not been an explicit part of it, really. And it certainly hasn't been in the West until recently.

"I knew a lot of people who practiced at Rochester in the old days, and I'm not sure it would have suited me. I'm not sure I would have been happy there. I mean, it was too samurai. I don't know what else to say about it. But Roshi has gradually – but very deliberately – changed that here. I mean, we don't use the kyosaku. I don't know if you saw the kyosakus we use. They're sort of little mini-kyosakus which are just symbolic kyosakus that we use in the sweep at sesshin. And that's all. I usually monitor sesshins, and it's gotten to the place now where – other than the sweep before dokusan – we don't use the kyosaku at all. Roshi is of the opinion that Zen practice is very difficult, and, ultimately, if you don't find the energy to do it inside yourself, where are you going to find it? You know, you can't be beaten into enlightenment.

"The Mettabhavana practice was a course that Roshi asked me to teach. And one of the wonderful serendipitous things about that course was realizing that it goes hand-in-glove with our zazen, with our mindfulness practice. They're mutually reinforcing. There are many practices in Zen. Zazen is the main one, seated meditation, which is mindfulness or concentration meditation, usually involving a breath practice or a koan practice. Or it can involve chanting practice. The Metta practice is a practice of Loving Kindness, which is the six stages of sending metta to yourself, to a benefactor, to a dear friend, and so on.

"One of the things I learned about metta practice is that it's the Buddhist practice in which I think beginners can make the most progress. It's the quickest. And it's essentially learning how to be friends with ourselves and with others. And this practice of learning how to be happy and extend our feelings of loving kindness to others is one, as I said, that goes hand-in-glove with the concentration meditation. I mean, it's just a fact that the more we pay attention, the friendlier we feel. Paying attention is an act of love. It's something every teacher, every parent knows; we all know that. And it just is a fact, too, that the friendlier we are, the easier it is to pay attention. So in a way, our paying attention and our being friendly and happy and extending loving-kindness to others – opening our compassionate heart – are practices that go hand-in-glove.

"One of the things that happens, there are a number of people who come to the Center, take an introductory workshop, but they find sitting endless hours looking at walls daunting. And the metta practice is easier in that it's more something we can get in touch with in an everyday kind of way. And I do a continuing metta group, which means once you've taken the course you can come back once a month. We meet on the second Monday of every month for an hour in the evening. And I sort of bill it as a Lifetime Warranty for the Metta Class. If you're having problems with that practice, come back and we'll do it again. And there are people who will stay; this was sort of the idea to keep people in the orbit of the Center until they felt able to do, or willing to do, or desirous of doing the more intense kind of zazen practice. Some of them don't get to that place for all I can tell. And that's fine. That's just fine. To me, it's been a real eye-opener and something I love teaching over and over again, 'cause I love taking the course over and over again."

As I tour the property with Sunyana, we pass a group of men working on the roof, and she goes over to discuss something with them. As she does so, I admire the grounds and the statues unobtrusively displayed here and there. There is a Kannon, of course, and a statue of Jizo Bodhisattva under the magnolia tree in front. Behind the center, there is a field stone shelf with perhaps ten more Jizo figures adorned with red capes and hoods. Two have rakusus hanging from their necks.

I ask Sunyana if she still bakes.

A smile brightens her face. "Oh, I love to bake. I think baking is one of the most engrossing activities in the world. It makes me very happy to bake."

After she returns indoors, I spend a few more moments on the grounds before driving off. Jizo is – I remember – the protector of travellers as well as of women and children.

The pioneers who brought Zen to North America were all male. The very real difference in atmosphere between here and Rochester or Chapin Mill, it occurs to me, is at least partially due to the fact that Sunyana is a woman. The Vermont Zen Center is very much part of Philip Kapleau's legacy, but it is that legacy reflected from a feminine perspective. As Robert Aitken noted, one of the most important contributions North America has made to Zen is the inclusion of women in positions of leadership.

CHAPTER NINETEEN

Taigen Henderson

THE TORONTO ZEN CENTER IS ON HIGH PARK GARDENS IN WHAT IS NOW A well-to-do neighborhood on the west side of the city. I follow a stone path around the house to the back entrance, passing carefully cultivated and maintained flower beds. Downstairs, there is a zendo with about twenty-six places and a Buddha Hall opposite. A resident student takes me up to a sun-room on the second floor where I meet Taigen Henderson. In June 2013, when this interview takes place, his students still referred to him as Sensei, although since then he has been given the title "Roshi."

"It looks like the property taxes might be a bit steep here," I suggest.

"We were lucky," he admits. The center had previously been located in a neighborhood where property values sank because of fears that an expressway was going to be built alongside. When the expressway plans were withdrawn, housing prices jumped. The Center was able to sell their place for $400,000 and purchase their current property, a former nursing home, for $350,000. At the time, this was also considered a less desirable neighborhood because of the occasional stench drifting in from nearby stock yards. When the stock yards were closed, once again property values rose. "The property is now probably worth about $2,000,000," Taigen tells me.

The Toronto Zen Center is the first affiliate established by Rochester. It is also the first official practice center in Canada, and Taigen is the first Zen teacher whose training took place in Canada. "He wouldn't tell you that," one of his students informs me later, "because he's so humble." I am aware of that humility while we talk, but I am also aware of a quiet confidence in him. He's a man with a lot of life experience and seems very much at ease with where he is at the moment.

The same student also mentions that "He's a great story-teller." He is, and he has some pretty good stories to tell.

☸

"I was a member of the hippie generation, and I did a lot of travelling during high school in the summer months. I went back and forth across Canada a number of times. My first proper job was when I was 18; I was working for Inco in Sudbury as a 'hard rock miner.' Level 600 of the Frood mine. It was cold and wet, and the job was hard. There were three of us on the graveyard shift, and we were talking to each other and said, 'Let's go out west.' Sudbury was pretty bleak in those days so the idea of getting away sounded good. So we drove out to British Colombia and went into the bush, two hundred miles – as the crow flies – from the nearest road. We didn't see one other human being for two months.

"The plan initially was to do some prospecting. This fellow, Randy, who came up with the idea said that he knew a bit about prospecting. I didn't know anything about it but was interested in learning, and the third member of our crew was a German immigrant named Rainer, who seemed to be a good fit because he was a bit older and had some army experience. So the three of us bought equipment in Toronto and used our savings to get out to BC. However by the time we got there, we were short of funds. So we worked in a logging camp and then as forest fire fighters to get enough money to buy the rest of the supplies and hire a plane to take us into the area, at the headwaters of the Stikine River, which Randy said would be good for prospecting.

"Once that float plane landed on the lake and took off again, we were totally on our own, and it became evident pretty quickly that we needed to spend most of our time just surviving. It rained constantly, and we didn't even have a tent. We had to chop trees and make a cabin. It was also clear that Randy was not a prospector and pretty soon we ran out of food. We had to hunt to survive, and I was the one who knew how to hunt. There was a lot of wildlife. We saw moose, elk and bears; we also fished for speckled trout in the lake and Arctic grayling in the river." The experience would lead him eventually to become vegetarian.

"So after some six weeks, in late August, it started to snow, and the route we had initially chosen to leave by wasn't realistic. And the company that dropped us off had never once flown by since July, probably because of the weather. So when we decided to leave, the most direct route was down the Stikine River. There was a camp we'd stayed at during the forest fire fighting that wasn't too far away and there was this other place, Hyland Post, which we thought would be a good place to get some more supplies and or hitch a plane ride out."

They had a canoe, but it wasn't large enough for the three of them and their supplies, so they built a raft and set out down the river. "After a little while, the river got faster, and the raft went into a deadfall and was jammed there by the power of the river. Half our gear was underwater. So I straddled the logs half underwater and

place is deadly.' I brought it up in the union hall, but people didn't want to hear about that. So I decided, I'll just leave.

"It was mid-November. I got on a plane, left, came back here to Toronto, and it was really culture-shock when I got back here, which threw me into a little bit of a crisis. Then I found *The Three Pillars of Zen* in a bookstore in Yorkville and started to read it, and it was just like, 'That's it!' You know? I felt like, 'That's what I've been looking for.' Some kind of spiritual path."

He had just turned 20 years old.

"I read the book, and I saw that there was a Rochester Zen Center. So I asked some friends to take me to the border and then to Buffalo, where I got a bus to Rochester. It was quite an experience in 1970 in Buffalo, I'll tell you. Toronto boy. You can walk anywhere in Toronto. I'm walking down the street, and, all of a sudden, there's nobody around. I thought, 'Where is everybody?' And then I see people hanging back and in doorways. It was strange, and I didn't know what was going on."

Having spent the summer of 1969 in the deep bush of BC, Taigen was unaware of the racial tensions and riots that had marked the year.

When he got to the Zen Center in Rochester, he was told he would have to return for a workshop. "So, I came back in April, and they did the workshop, and Roshi Kapleau invited everybody who'd been to the workshop to come to the next day all-day sitting. So then we got to go to this all day sitting, and he said, 'Anyone who wants an interview.' So I came in for an interview. And he said, 'What would you like to do?' And I said, 'I would like to come here and train.' And he said, 'Well, what brought you to Zen?' And he had just given a talk on acid, pot, and Zen. And I had been aware of different mind-states through acid and pot, but I was really embarrassed about that so I said it was R. H. Blythe, which was half true because I was reading his commentary on the *Mumonkan*. And Roshi had this way. He was very perceptive. He just looked at me in this disinterested way, and my heart sank when I saw that look on his face. Then he brightened up. First he said, 'No.' Then he said, 'Well, maybe.' And so there was this carrot hanging there. 'But not right now. Go back to Toronto. Get settled. You can come back if you want.' So I did that. And when I called again, he said, 'Do you have any skills like carpentry?' 'No, I don't have any skills.' So I still couldn't stay, but I kept practicing, continued to count my breath on my own like they showed us in the workshop."

He went west again and took a two year course in Air Conditioning and Refrigeration at a community college in Calgary. "Because I thought I was too much in my head and needed to get some practical and down to earth type of training." He was receiving the Rochester newsletter – *Zen Bow* – and was re-reading *The Three Pillars* as well as the compendium of original texts published by Dwight Goddard as *A Buddhist Bible*. He also sat for half an hour before classes every morning.

Back in Toronto, after completing his course, he discovered a practice center affiliated with Rochester. "It was in a fairly low-rent district, but I went there, and there was somebody who seemed a little strange to me, and I didn't quite connect. So I went away.

"Then two things happened. I was listening to Ravi Shankar music.... Uh... actually, before this, the house next door burnt down. I was the one who caught it. It was winter time, and smoke is pouring out of the vent. And I must have been partly zonked by the smoke, because I was looking at it for – oh – at least a minute, going, 'What's wrong with this picture?' I couldn't figure it out. I was looking at the smoke, looking at the smoke, 'What's the matter with that? There's something wrong with that. I know that's not right.' And then it's like, 'Oh! Smoke! Fire!' And then I woke up everyone in the house, and the neighbor – who was a professor at York – woke him up, and he had his family in there. By the time the fire-trucks came, they broke the windows, the place went up like a match. Foof!

"So when I was listening to Ravi Shankar, I think there was a spiritual quality in that music that made me realize that life is impermanent. That was kind of the core part: that life is impermanent, and that if I don't do something now, I may not get a chance. This was kind of a wake-up call. And – lo and behold – there was a poster saying 'Workshop on Zen, Roshi Philip Kapleau at such-and-such a church.' It had been the day before! But it said, 'Afterwards, come back to 569 Christie Street.'"

Taigen walked over to Christie Street, rang the bell, and the door was answered by Hugh Curran, whom I would later meet in Surry, Maine. Curran was one of Kapleau's senior students at the time and had been sent from Rochester to act as the head of the zendo in Toronto. "He asked me to come in. I said that I wanted to start practicing, and that I'd like to move in, like, tomorrow. And he basically said, 'Yes. You can.'"

"So we were an affiliate Zen Center. And we'd go down to Rochester for sesshin and for ceremonies – Jukai and Vesak – which were actually quite wonderful. Hugh didn't stay long, then Pat Simons took over. Pat was the monitor when I went down to Rochester the first time, so I felt a real close affinity with him. He was a wonderful guy, a real character. An artist. Just a real spark. And there were about five residents at the time. That was the beginnings of the Toronto Zen Center."

"Did you ever spend time in the residential program in Rochester?"

"I never did. I wanted to move to Rochester, but Roshi Kapleau told me not to for some reason. But I would go to sesshin there when I could get away from work. And Roshi would sometimes come up. He held a few sesshin in Toronto."

"What kind of work were you doing?"

"I had gone into more of the construction field. I needed to find some kind of trade, some way of making a living. I had a Japanese friend, new to Canada, who started an aluminum business, so I went with him. I was an aluminum eaves trough guy. Went all over Toronto doing eaves trough and siding. Not so much siding. Mostly eaves trough."

"I did siding for a long time, in the days before vinyl."

"Wow! Good! So, you know what it's like. Up and down ladders and a lot of work like that. But it was hard for my friend to pay me what I needed, so I went on my own. Then I started to go into construction gradually from aluminum work." He pauses, then laughs. "I was watching *Sesame Street* with my son and saw something about aluminum siding, and it made me think I better move out of it. Anyway, so I started going into construction and started to do renovations. And that was a good fit because there was more variety, and Toronto is an old town. It was just when people started needing renovations. I was at the beginning of the rush. And there were no trades in Toronto. The skilled trades were pretty much construction stuff, the subways, the high-rises and so on. So it wasn't a regulated industry that way."

"Philip Kapleau was a lion. He was very stern. I had nothing but immense respect for the man. His presence was very powerful. But it was difficult to get into sesshin in those days, and it was difficult to get into dokusan. They always put the newcomers at the top end of the zendo, and then it was like blowing a whistle and fifty people trying to get into the dokusan line. And being Canadian and sort of polite, I wouldn't think you'd push people out of the way or anything. You know, just like, 'Okay, go ahead.' But I was in this three-day sesshin, and I couldn't get into dokusan. Three times a day. Missed every time. And then, I remember, like, losing it by the third day. I don't even remember.... Honestly, I don't remember. I think I probably pulled people down. I just ran like there's no tomorrow. Made sure my posture was easy to get out of, spun around, and just ran for the door and got the last spot. And then you get into dokusan, and he says, 'What's your practice?' And it's like you don't have anything in your mind at all." He is rocking with laughter as he tells the story. "You feel like a complete idiot!

"But, I wanted to say this about Roshi Kapleau, even though there were no words necessarily that were exchanged, I felt some power. Some inspiration was taking place in that interaction that was very helpful. Really helpful. And so it was quite interesting. It was like – I don't know – thirty seconds in the room and nothing happened.

"And his practice was always there. It was always available. He loved to go on walks. One time we were walking – I think it was Hugh Curran, Roshi, and myself – and we were just walking in Rochester. I guess I was visiting for a ceremony, and we were going somewhere. And Hugh or whoever was talking about this apartment he had to give up, how he loved this apartment. And Roshi piped up, 'Better to have loved and lost.' You know, a cliché, but when he said it somehow it wasn't a cliché. It had deeper meaning. It was really like, 'Oh, yeah!' It was like everything he said had that kind of quality which made you look more deeply into what it was. It wasn't just the words. There was a teaching there.

"One time he was here in Toronto. He was well-known by this time, and somebody said" – speaking in a gruffer voice – "'I wanna meet Roshi Kapleau.' It was on Christie Street. 'Where is he? Where 's Roshi Kapleau?' 'Upstairs.' So this guy came in, ran upstairs, took one look at Roshi, then turned around and ran out of the house!" Taigen spreads his hands and raises his eyebrows in amazement. "It was like he was a mirror. Whatever you brought, he showed you. And it was just like, 'Ha!' This guy saw something that scared him, and we never saw him again.

"Anyway, it was tough. And I have tremendous respect for the people in Rochester because a lot of them knew that this wasn't their…." He takes a moment to search for the proper way to express what he means. "That they're doing it for the Dharma. They're not doing it because that would be their choice. That was pretty clear to me. And I think Roshi told me not to come there because he knew I wasn't suited for that style. It was harsh. And the harshness didn't feel Buddhist to me, for some reason." He smiles and adds, "I failed to mention that I'd grown up in a Buddhist country when I was between five and eight. Sri Lanka. It was called Ceylon then."

"Well, okay, that's pretty significant. What were your parents doing in Ceylon?"

"My dad had been a pilot in the war, doing aerial reconnaissance, and he joined a firm in Toronto after the war that did aerial reconnaissance for maps. So we went to Sri Lanka, and they were mapping the country. And I had this feeling for Buddhism that I think came from that, because we were at the edge of Colombo at the time. And there was an adobe hut village and a temple near us. We used to go and visit the temple and harass the monks. You know? So we had a connection with the place. And more than that, it was like Ceylon was infused with it. It was like walking through a forest. You get wet. It got into you. It wasn't so much the Buddhist teachings – we weren't influenced by any teachings – but basically the feeling was everywhere."

"And you didn't find that same feeling in Rochester?"

"Not in those days. It was different."

For a while, Kapleau sent a number of senior students – like Hugh Curran and Pat Simons – from Rochester to supervise the Toronto center. "And basically they would do the all day sittings. We did a lot of all day sittings. We did two-day sittings as well with taped teisho and no dokusan. So it was fairly grueling to be sitting that many hours and not be able to get any personal instruction. It was just everybody sit, listen to a teisho from Rochester. So that was hard because, basically, the most difficult part of any sesshin is at the beginning, when your body is getting used to it. And then we would stop! So, it was not a good model to follow.

"Anyway, there was a period when Zenson Gifford came from Rochester. He was supposedly on his way to Japan. But he had a Polish wife, and they were having some passport troubles or problems with the documentation, and so they stayed in Toronto. And we asked him, 'Why don't you just stay and teach here?' And he said, well, he'd try it out for a year. So we nabbed him."

Gifford was responsible for moving the Zen Center to its current location, and he remained the resident teacher for five years. Then it came out that he had been in sexual relationships with students both in Canada and at an associate center in Poland.

"So the first thing we did was confront him, and he kind of hedged a little bit. But then after we had enough evidence, we said, 'No. No. You have to go.'"

"Who was 'we?'"

"Senior members. The board of directors. I was on the board. Probably some other members. So we said, 'We want you to go and consider taking some therapy, and we'll keep your position here. But we want you to take some therapy. And then come back, and you'd be on probation for a year.'

"It was hard for me, because I was very grateful to him. He had helped me a lot. My personal story is I'd gone bankrupt. I'd split up with my wife. I was taking care of a seniors' building as a kind of a caretaker. I had fallen on hard times. I started to drink. I was a mess. And he said to me, 'Why don't you come and help me renovate the house here?' I was looking for a way out, and that was the way out, and I started to come back to sesshin. I started practice again. I'd lost my practice. I hadn't lost my faith, but I'd lost my practice and ran into some really difficult personal times and issues. So basically, when I started renovating, it was like…. Building a zendo's like…. It's the love of your life. You know? It was something you just can't imagine. And he was very skillful, very sensitive. We had a lot of volunteer help, but he paid me. So we renovated the zendo, and it got me back on track. So I owed him a big debt of gratitude. So it was hard. It was very hard."

Gifford chose not to go into therapy, and the center began to look for a new teacher.

"And people were saying, 'We should not limit it to the Rochester lineage. Maybe we should look farther afield.' But a couple of us went down to talk to Roshi Kjolhede, and he said, 'Well, I can't do anything for you, but there are a couple of newer teachers in our lineage. You could ask them to come and do a sesshin.' So we asked Sunyana Roshi to come, and she did one retreat. I actually wasn't here for it. I was on holiday – I think it was in August – and I came back, and everyone said, 'She's going to be our teacher.'" He laughs. "It was like a *fait accompli*. So she agreed to take it up. Roshi Kjolhede's comment was, 'She'd be crazy to do that because she already has a center in Costa Rica plus a budding center in Vermont.' But she was very compassionate and said she would come a number of times a year. But she also said, 'I come with strings attached.' And we're like, 'A Zen teacher with strings attached?' She said you've got to get a new kitchen. Our kitchen used to be right in here in this little room. So there were a couple of stoves on that side. A couple of sinks on this side. And it was unbelievably difficult to run a sesshin and cook out of this room. So she said, 'You have to build a kitchen and build it in the basement.' So we said, 'Okay.'"

"What was she like?"

"A breath a fresh air. The first thing she said was, 'It's too dark in here. Why do you have all the windows covered up?' And it was like, 'Yeah. Why is it so dark in the Zen Center?' So she started peeling things off the windows. The windows of the zendo used to have screens so it was all artificial lighting, and it could be kept really dark. The Buddha Hall was dark; everything was dark. She just brought in the light. Literally and figuratively. Spiritually. And sort of expunged a lot of the negative feelings."

Center membership had fallen after the revelations about Gifford's behavior, but, with Sunyana's help, they began to rebuild. The Toronto members formed a close relationship with her students in Vermont. "We'd go there for ceremonies as well as them coming here. And she'd come here and whip up the sangha. I don't know how she did it. She just got us all working really hard and cleaning and turned it into a Buddhaland. She could transform the place for ceremonies. We had a Temple Night here. She would take these saris and a table and" – he makes a swishing noise and waves his hands – "she'd make an altar. She would just create it out of nothing. You know? So there's a very strong devotional element. Roshi Kapleau told us, 'When Sunyana comes, you'll see another aspect of Buddhism.' And he was absolutely right.

"I felt an affinity for her from the get-go. Actually, when she got married it was in Toronto. Jed Graef started practice at the Toronto Zen Center. And then when he went down to Rochester, that's where they met. So they wanted to have their marriage here. And I remember getting her a wedding gift and then getting a thank you note with the most exquisite script that I had ever seen. I couldn't believe it had been written by hand. Not only was the writing beautiful, but the message was beautiful. So that was 1975 or something. I can't remember the exact dates. So I felt a connection with her from way back."

"I was speaking with some of her senior students when I was in Shelburne, and one of them told me that he was glad to have had a woman teacher. That that made a difference to him. Did that have an impact on you as well?"

"Absolutely. Especially after what had happened with Zenson. And being able to open up in a different kind of way. Also the compassionate side was all of a sudden brought out. Whereas before that it had been very much the wisdom side. For instance, using the stick. We still used the stick quite a lot then. The monitors – I was one of the monitors – we would use it fairly vigorously in the zendo. And it did get people going; there's no doubt. But she started to cut back on it gradually. And we kind of resisted it a little bit because, 'What are we going to do? We're monitors! We need this stick! We gotta do something!' But that teaching – that it has to come from within – is absolutely true. You can push somebody into having an experience, but what are they going to do after that? You know? It needs to come from within. Might as well start having it come from within from the beginning."

"When Roshi came here, I was reconnecting. That's the way it felt to me. Reconnecting with deep feelings about Buddhism. It was kind of subtle, because it just kept on growing and growing. And then the concept of being ordained and everything grew and grew. And I think I felt like that when I was a kid. Actually, to my embarrassment, one of my high school friends showed me a yearbook where I claimed that I wanted to be a Buddha when I grew up. It was one of those smart-alecky replies you make in high school when people ask you questions like that. So what I'm trying to say is that it had been around a long time, but Roshi brought it out.

"And then something happened." He was contracted by the Homes First program to oversee a project in which homeless people were involved in building their own housing. "Homes First had a liaison person who helped, but I was the construction manager. Set up things. But also I had to communicate with the bigger trades, the electrical trades, plumbing trades. Organize the contracts. And I didn't have any experience in that. I wasn't that kind of contractor. I was a do-it-yourself kind of guy. But I knew how to run it, so I just ran it. But it was off the cuff, I've got to say, which was what they needed. Somebody who'd been trained properly to do it would never have done it. It just would not happen. You wouldn't get insurance.

You wouldn't have the protection. So basically it was sort of a once-in-a-lifetime kind of confluence of events. And it was a tremendous success. We got written up. It's in sociology textbooks now, and it was a lot of fun, and it felt like that's what I was meant to do. So I felt, at the time, 'This is what it's about.' This was going to be my life's work, and I was happy.

"But there'd been this one contract for windows and things like that that was not getting fulfilled. We'd signed kind of a rinky-dink contract form, and I kept on asking the guy, 'When are you going to turn up? When are you going to turn up?' The place was supposed to open in November. So he wasn't coming and wasn't coming. So I sent faxes to him, and I said, 'Listen, as of this date you're not on the contract. I'm getting somebody else to do it.' Date passed. Started somebody else doing it. They came in, did a good job, got it all done. Then the guy comes up and says, 'I'm going to sue you.' And he tries to sue the Homes First project. But, as I said, they were sort of an arm's reach away.

"So we had a discovery meeting coming up, and I thought, 'I better go home with all of the documents. Get them in order. I took them home, but I left them in the car, and somebody broke into the car and took my bag. And it was just like, 'Oh! That's the worst thing that can happen. This contract. We don't have any extra money.' It's like a thirty, forty thousand dollar contact. And I just felt sick. So I called up Homes First, and, all of a sudden, there was this coldness. Like, 'That's your job. Don't bring us into it.' And I realized, 'We really are on our own here.' And I just felt desperate. 'What the heck am I going to do?' So I went home, and I was sitting in this room, thinking, 'What can I do? What can I do?' And then that Zen spirit came back. Like, you just don't give up. You do anything. Just do something. So I thought, 'Well, okay, I'll make a poster. $1000 reward for bag.' I'll put it around the street. And I decided to put one up in the corner store. By this time it's getting towards night, and it'd been snowing a little bit. And as I'm going to the corner store, this little piece of paper comes blowing down the street at me, and I picked up. And, 'That's mine!' And then there's another one! So somebody wanted the bag, but they didn't want the contents. And they dumped them, and the papers had blown into a snow fence. I got just about everything back. So that really inspired me. This was meant to be my life's work.

"So it's a big success, and Homes First is going to do another one in a couple of years, and they want me in on the designing and everything. I wasn't being paid for it at this point, just basically came to some meetings and talked to them and talked to the architects. It was going to be on Strachan Avenue by the railway tracks. So we got the contract to clean the building. It was a big warehouse. And we had to take training to clean it, and we organized that. Got some hard-on-their-luck people – it was pretty dirty work – to clean all the pig shit out of this building and bleach everything. It was gross. So we're doing this, and at the same time we're designing this other thing. And I was having a hard time with the architect."

Taigen's concern was to keep costs down as much as possible. The architect, on the other hand, "seemed to want to make a statement. He felt his job was to make a really impressive place and do all kinds of things. So we were at loggerheads. And all of a sudden I found myself getting kicked off the project. And that was a big shock because I'd invested so much in it emotionally. So, I was pretty devastated.

"I had felt like everything I'd done in my life was starting to come together; I was going to do work that meant something. So I think I was looking for something else at that point. It wasn't a conscious thing. But it was kind of like, that was gone, something that had been meaningful and something I really wanted to do. Then I realized, 'Well, there is another area you find meaningful in your life.' It was like they were running on parallel paths, and then one wasn't available anymore. So it was natural to start looking at the other. I just wanted a deeper commitment and to be of service to people.

"Then one day Roshi sat down with a couple of us and was talking about, 'We really need somebody in Toronto.' And I thought she was talking to the guy beside me, and she kept on talking about somebody who would be committed, who had a sense of responsibility. And I'm, 'Yeah, yeah, yeah.' And then I realized she was talking to me, and I can remember the sweat dripping off the back of my neck. 'What?' And then – you know – she was looking at me like, 'Yes. I'm talking to you.' So she asked me to start taking on more of a leadership role here. That was before I was ordained; then, when I became ordained, she asked me to give some group instructions. Then she asked me to take on more duties gradually. Basically, 'You can give group instruction in such-and-such room. People can come and ask you questions during the all day sittings.' So we started doing that. Then she said, 'I want you to start thinking about teaching in a year.' And that was a bit of a shock. I hadn't expected it. Actually she ended up telling me, 'You've got to start teaching. You've got to give back.' So I trusted my teacher."

We talk about the programs currently offered at the Toronto Zen Center, and I express surprise that the center members still go to Vermont for sesshin.

"That's because I still wanted to keep training with Roshi Graef," he explains. "I felt…. Well, maybe I'll back up a bit. I had seen a lot of teachers move away from their teacher, I thought, too quickly. Zenson, for example. And I thought, 'You can always learn.' Although once I was sanctioned here, I was allowed to do whatever I wanted. Still it felt really valuable to keep training with a teacher, because the teacher has got twenty or thirty years experience teaching. So I decided right off the bat I was going to try to not cut the cord, as it were, but stay close to Roshi Graef and continue to nurture that relationship and go to Vermont with my students. And so that's what we do. Some of the sesshin we do here, and some we do in Vermont."

"You think it's important for a teacher to continue to deepen his or her own practice?"

"Absolutely. Absolutely. You know, people think teachers are on some kind of other level, that all of a sudden you've reach some level of enlightenment and that the same rules don't apply. And it's a misconception. A lot of people started their training young. They didn't get out in the world. They didn't have experience in the world. Then all of a sudden they're in the world again because you have to be in the world when you're teaching. You're not cloistered any more. Nobody is watching you, so you have to watch yourself. You know? Zuigan. 'Be awake. Be awake. Yes. Yes. Don't be fooled by others. No. No.'[68] So training with a teacher gives you that ability to communicate with somebody senior and to open up and to share problems with. Because – you know – there's all kinds of problems you just never had to deal with before."

"The way Chozen Bays put it to me was that she still felt the need for someone she trembled before, someone who held her accountable."

"For sure. For sure. Yeah. There's a phrase in the Metta Sutra: 'May I not do anything that the wise would later reprove.' And it's like Roshi Graef is the wise person that you wouldn't want to have to reprove you."

A little later I sit on the steps of the back porch of the Zen Center with two of Taigen's students. "What do you get out of it?" I ask them. "What do you get out of coming here and sitting and staring at a wall?"

"You get yourself," one tells me.

"What do you mean by that?"

"Well a lot of life is distracting. It distracts you from yourself. You get busy with things that really are none of your business, whatever it might be. And so what you get from sitting is you get to come back to yourself; you get to come back to your life and really value it. It's very precious."

"So why can't I do that on my own? Why do I have to come here?"

"Because it requires guidance. Meditation is tricky business. It can be dangerous. It's very important to have a teacher. It really helps...." She pauses, then starts again. "It's beyond helpful; it's essential. In my experience, it's been essential to have Sensei be a guide and an example of what honesty really looks like."

"How does he demonstrate honesty?"

"Everything about him demonstrates honesty. And integrity. He embodies the practice. He's completely there as a Zen practitioner. You can tell. What's so inspiring is not only is he there, you can see where you can go in thirty years or however long he's been practicing. So to know that one day we could be like Sensei and be that honest and be that courageous in every moment, that's extremely inspiring. I don't think I could figure that one out on my own. So it's very lucky to have a refuge to come back to yourself. And that's what the Zen Center is."

"I feel the same," the other says. English is not her mother-tongue, and she struggles slightly to express herself. "I feel we get more rid of the things than get something out of it. But in the same time we get everything, sort of. We get rid of all the concepts, all the pain that holds us back and tied into different darkness or different stages of confusion. And definitely you see beyond the way we were, the way we are. We constantly are reminded of the potential that we have. To see beyond the conditioning and the limitations that we constantly set on ourselves."

"We just finished a retreat," the first student says, "and Sensei quoted this poem that said, 'Act great.' You know? How potential is limitless and really to take that idea seriously. And it's so important to have a space where you can actually do that, take that idea seriously without cynicism or malice or being unrealistic or idealistic about it either. A place where you can be really clear about your potential."

"Basically," Taigen tells me, "the function of Zen is to bring people from a state where they're divided, scattered, thinking of the separateness of them and the world, standing apart from the world, to bring them from that into a place, first, where they've unified their minds, focused it, and then go beyond the discriminating intellect – go beyond their ego – and directly experience who and what they truly are. So basically, it's a spiritual path that takes people from one way of looking at the world to a totally different way of looking at the world.

"There are different kinds of practices Zen teachers employ, such as koans, shikantaza, breath practices, but basically they all bring the person's scattered mind – what we call the 'monkey mind' that jumps from here to there to there, always involved in thoughts – bringing it to a more one-pointed, concentrated calm. And then, if a person's working on a koan, and they're questioning deeply, their mind gets…not blank, but it's more like they just stop looking at things and associating them with the way they usually do. And at that point they're what we call 'ripe,' and there can be an insight into the nature of reality. It could be a sound. It could be a sight. It could be a whack maybe from a teacher, or just a word or something. And that will somehow, mysteriously, make them turn inwards and see something that's always been there, what we call the 'True Nature.'

"So it's basically just a practice, and it depends on people's affinity and how hard they practice. It doesn't really require any special abilities except perseverance."

CHAPTER TWENTY

Mitra Bishop

WINDING THROUGH THE SANGRE DE CRISTO MOUNTAINS AND A SECTION of the Kit Carson National Forest, the old High Road between Taos and Santa Fe is sharply curved and frequently marked by flower-decorated crosses memorializing fatal accidents. We keep our speed down. A secondary road branching off the High Road brings us to Mountain Gate – not the Mountain Gate Zen Center or the Mountain Gate Zendo, just Mountain Gate – located in Ojo Sarco, a community so small it isn't on our road map. "Sarco" is an archaic Spanish word meaning turquoise, so Turquoise Spring.

There is no sign marking the long drive that brings you to the main building. This is not a place one comes to by accident; there are no street drop-ins. People have to want to come here. And they do, from as far away as the Philippines, to study and work with a diminutive, energetic great-grandmother. Mitra Bishop Roshi is one of Philip Kapleau's Dharma heirs who, in spite of her age and experience, is also a continuing student of Shodo Harada.

My sister and brother-in-law, who live on the Colorado-New Mexico border, come with my wife and me for this interview, and as the five of us chat casually afterwards, I learn that Mitra went to grade school in Sault Ste. Marie, Ontario (where she learned Canadian spelling) and to high school in Crown Point, Indiana, less than an hour away from where my sister and I grew up. These loose connections – like the fact that Taigen and I both worked in aluminum home improvements – have no real significance, but they are fun to find.

The main structure is an adobe building surrounded by an arid landscape that looks, to me, like desert. My sister, however, suggests that's because I'm looking at it through the eyes of someone used to the Acadian Forest lands of Atlantic Canada. It is in fact, she tells me, an agricultural region, a transitional area between the piñon-juniper and ponderosa pine zones.

The zendo is located just within the entrance of the building; a calligraphy by Shodo Harada on its door states: "Great effort without fail will produce great light."

It has seating for fourteen, although another five places have been squeezed in for sesshin. There are large windows at one end, and sunlight warms the room. Mitra tells me that on moonlit nights they can sit without need for indoor lighting.

We meet in the single room – like a study – in which she lives and works. There is a statue of Kannon in a niche on one wall; another wall is filled with books. As in the zendo, the sun coming through the windows provides both light and warmth.

"For people willing to pick up the ball," she tells me, "Zen can lead to nothing short of total freedom, total liberation. And by total liberation, what I mean is liberation from your hang-ups, your conditioning, liberation from places where you're stuck. In other words, if you take it far enough, you're able to freely move in concert with life in effective, positive ways. We have the sixteen Bodhisattva Precepts in Japanese Zen. What 'total liberation' means is that your behaviour naturally accords with those precepts. And there is an incredible sense of freedom and joy that runs akin to a quiet river within. That is your potential. But it's not anything instantaneous. It takes a lot of hard work."

When I ask why, then, this doesn't seem to have been the case with certain American teachers, she tells me of Shodo Harada's answer to a similar question. Essentially, he'd said, people fail to complete their training.[69]

"People – pretty much everywhere – assume that there is a finish point in Zen practice. That they do their ten years, fifteen years, twenty years, and they're home free. This may or may not be the case. It's usually not the case. I think we need to take Joshu Jushin as a practice model; he trained for long decades before he ever began teaching and is known to have said, 'If a child of three can teach me, I will learn from that child.'

"Having a kensho experience allows one to see a bit more clearly. At the same time, it can take the lid off inhibitions. And unless we integrate what we experience through that kensho into our daily life we're quite liable to act in inappropriate ways; that's part of what's happened in these cases of abuse. Essentially, these people that we're seeing now receiving some karmic come-uppance haven't really trained sufficiently."

"I came to Zen through pain and suffering, which is kind of how everybody gets there sooner or later. But even as a child I had a sense that there was something beyond conscious awareness that I'd lost touch with and that it was important to reconnect with. As a result, many years later I thought about trying to do some meditation. Transcendental Meditation was really popular then. I was working at the time in the Washington DC area, and I thought about learning to do it. In fact, a friend of mine actually went to one of the introductory lectures and got a mantra and began practicing. I also called up a Tibetan Buddhist group and got information about where they were located and what their hours were, but I never followed up on it. So although meditation was of interest to me, I didn't follow up on those two leads. That was to come later.

"In 1973, when I was 32 years old, I was a commercial interior designer designing offices and banks and other commercial interiors. I was married to a diplomat, and we had two kids. Suddenly, with only three weeks' notice, my husband was assigned to the embassy in Turkey as a special assistant to the new American ambassador. I couldn't finish up the current jobs with my company soon enough to go with him so I stayed through the summer with the kids, and then in early September flew to Turkey. But by Christmas my life had crashed into pieces at my feet; everything I identified with, everything I counted on as 'me' had vanished."

"In what way?"

"My marriage disappeared. It was an odd situation. We'd been married thirteen years. He was the first boy I ever kissed. I met him at church camp, Presbyterian Church camp. I was thirteen, and he was fourteen. We hit it off, but we hit it off like brother and sister. We went ahead and got married when we were in college and then immediately had a child, my older son." She indicates a photograph on the wall. "He's a grandfather now!

"My husband was a wonderful – still is – a wonderful human being, and there was no reason to end the marriage. But after I had taken him to the airport to put him on the plane to Turkey, by the time I drove out of the parking lot, I couldn't remember what he looked like. It was shocking."

She completed her work in Washington, then turned her business over to someone else and flew with the children to join her husband. Soon after her arrival in Turkey, she attended an embassy welcoming party where she met an American professor who had spent some time at the Rochester Zen Center. He offered to teach her how to do zazen, but she declined. She may have had an interest, but she didn't yet feel any urgency about taking up practice.

One advantage of being in Ankara was that it provided her an opportunity to work on a degree in architecture. "The international university there – Middle East Technical University – accepted me into the architecture program. But then things started getting crazily mixed up. My classes were shifted around to where they were scheduled in conflict with one another, and, in my physics course where everybody else including the professor was Turkish, she started lecturing in Turkish; at the time, I didn't know that language."

Then, just before Christmas, she and her husband separated.

"There was nothing I could do about it. The marriage karma between us had just vanished. It was terrible because he didn't know what had happened; I didn't really know then, either. The kids were nine and eleven at the time. Everybody was in pain which was basically my fault. I bailed out of school because it was just impossible to keep up with what had happened along with the crazy schedule changes that had occurred there. And then I got into a relationship that was abusive, and I wanted to die. When I realized that I didn't have the courage to kill myself, it made me even more depressed.

"I'd created a huge amount of pain for the people I loved. In addition, my dream of finally becoming a licensed architect was thwarted. And it ended up that my kids weren't able to stay with me because the State Department wouldn't pay for their schooling if they weren't with my ex-husband. So I was failing at everything that mattered to me; my whole self-identity was being ripped away.

"My husband, in his pain, asked to be transferred, and at that time the only place Foreign Service Officers were being transferred was to the Embassy in Saigon. It was very close to the end of the war; I thought he would be killed, and one of our sons was living with him then, too and I thought he would not survive either. It was truly a Dark Night of the Soul."

Somewhere along the line, she was given a copy of Philip Kapleau's second book, *The Wheel of Death*. "I read it cover to cover in one sitting, and it left me with a question: 'What did the Zen Masters in this book know that allowed them to meet death with ease and tranquility, with utter lack of fear?'"

On New Year's day, she sought out the professor she'd met at the embassy party. "On January 1st, 1974, I found myself on his doorstep, and I sat down and crossed my legs for the first time."

She didn't find the practice easy. "But I was driven, and I knew without a doubt that there was no other way out of the anguish."

She was still living in Turkey. "I loved Turkey, loved the Turkish people. I felt so much at home there, so I wanted to stay." She had learned the language well enough to be able to find employment at Bogazici University as a bi-lingual secretary. But she returned to the US for a couple of months each year. "I'd borrow a car from my parents and drive to DC. Because of my previous design business there, all I had to do was pop into one of my former clients, and I could get as much work as I wanted. I'd go and work many, many hours and then return to supplementing my income in Turkey. In the summer of 1975 when I was back in the States, I was in a bookstore one evening after work, glancing through the extremely few books on Zen – there were maybe four or five of them on a small revolving rack – and one of them was the book *Zen Flesh, Zen Bones*. I picked it up, and something kind of jiggled in my mind. I started leafing through it, and the jiggle happened again. So I thought, 'All right, I'll buy this.' I took it home and opened it at random to the story about Hakuin being accused of being the father of a baby."

In the story, a young Japanese girl became pregnant and, when questioned by her parents, blamed Hakuin for her condition. After the baby was born, the girl's parents brought it to Hakuin, telling him: "This is your child. You look after it." His only comment was, "Is that so?" Although his reputation was in tatters, he looked after the child to the best of his abilities. A year later, however, the girl confessed to her parents that it was not Hakuin who had fathered the child; rather, it was a young man who worked at the market. Abashed, her parents rushed to Hakuin and apologized profusely for having discredited him. They explained that their daughter had agreed to marry the young man and asked Hakuin to return the child to her. Saying only, "Is that so?" he turned the child over.

"It turns out that story is not actually about Hakuin," Mitra points out. "It was probably Shido Munan who actually had that experience. So, I read the story and was suddenly plummeted into that mind state from which Shido Munan could simply say 'Is that so?' and leave it at that. Nothing to defend, nothing to uphold, no argument. The experience of freedom, the utter freedom and joy of that mind state was truly mind-blowing. I don't know how long I was in it. Eventually, I came to with tears of joy streaming down my face. And then, of course, the experience shut up like a book. After that it opened and closed and opened and closed and opened and closed. And I wondered, 'What on Earth is happening?'

"The only Zen connection I knew of was the Rochester Zen Center, and so I called it and said, 'I need to talk to somebody about something that's happened to me. Can I talk to the Roshi?' And they said, 'Well, you have to come to a workshop first, and then, after the workshop, you can talk to the Roshi.' So I dutifully extended my time in the States, went to the October 1975 workshop. I spoke with Roshi Kapleau afterward, absolutely petrified of him. All he said was, 'Well, that's not a very good book. If you want to read Hakuin, you should read Yampolsky's *Hakuin*.' So I bought the book, found it totally uninteresting, returned to Turkey, but kept on sitting."

Back in Ankara, she sat on her own, following the instruction she had received at the workshop but soon felt a need for more intensive practice.

"The next step was to go to a four day sesshin taught by senior students; it was what you had to do back then before you could go to a seven-day sesshin with the roshi. So I went to the March sesshin, caring only that I would survive the schedule; I've never been good with jetlag or insufficient sleep. But I did survive. Barely. Yet the Sunday morning after the sesshin, I was amazed to actually find myself wanting to go into the zendo, and I sat there, absorbed in practice, for two hours without realizing it. What I did realize during those two hours was that I had to get this monkey off my back, this background noise composed of constant judgment doing nothing but creating misery. I returned to Turkey and within a few months I realized what I really needed to do – because I couldn't bring myself to go into the room where my mat and cushion were for three weeks after that – was go to live at the Rochester Zen Center where I would be required to sit whether I felt like it or not. Trying to enter that room, much less sit, was like magnets resisting each other. So I applied to the November '76 sesshin – a seven day sesshin – was accepted, and moved to Rochester from Turkey."

Her description of the Rochester Zen Center in the '70s is much like those of others I had interviewed. When I mention the story of Sunyana and Bodhin colliding in the dokusan line, she remembers the incident. "And gentleman that he was, he helped her up, which allowed her to jump ahead of him, which she took full advantage of.

"During my first seven day sesshin, I fell on the floor and started to get up when I saw a pair of legs flying over me and decided it was safer to stay down." The chaos of the dokusan rush was too much for her, and after a few attempts, she chose to remain on her cushion when the bell rang. "But after a couple of days of that, I got pulled out of the kinhin line and sent into dokusan. I remember Sunyana was at the bell, and she looked at me kind of quizzically. I realize now, it was the dokusan line for people working on subsequent koans, and I was a rank beginner. But I went in, several feet off the floor, assuming I'd had kensho," she says with a laugh. "Kapleau Roshi said, 'Why haven't you been to dokusan?' And I said, 'I didn't have anything to say.' And he pulled himself up and roared at me, 'Don't you think I might have had something to say to you!' After that, I tried to get to dokusan. But I was hugely relieved when they started dividing the zendo up into sections, only one of which would go to dokusan at a time, because before that it was insanity."

She was on staff at the Rochester Center from 1976 until 1981, during which time her children came back to live with her. "Which was wonderful, though a little bit challenging, because in the interim they had become teenagers."

Then she joined the group that moved with Kapleau to New Mexico. "At the time," she explains, "I was married to a guy who had lived in Santa Fe."

"So somewhere along the line you got married again."

"Yes, I did. Actually, the guy whose legs flew over me in that first seven-day sesshin." They both took part in the expedition to New Mexico. "Whoever wanted to go could. We thought the center was moving out there more or less, and I wanted to continue training with Roshi."

Things didn't work out, however. "I picked Roshi up at the airport when he first moved here and took him directly to a picnic that the sangha had planned as a welcome for him. At the picnic, one of the local sangha members stood up and said, 'Roshi, we love having you here. We want to have you here. But we don't want you to tell us what to do.' He quietly took it in. He lived in Santa Fe for a year, almost next door to the center to see how things would work out. He came every Sunday to do sitting, teisho, and dokusan, and invited the sangha to his house for Sunday night movies. It was rare that anyone joined him for the movies and most of the sangha was interested in only minimal involvement, though there were a few of us who were more committed to practice. We sat at the Center a couple of other nights without him. And at the end of the year, partly because he'd fallen and broken his arm, partly because he hadn't realized it was so cold in New Mexico, but partly because the sangha, except a handful of us, just didn't seem to be very dedicated to practice, he decided to leave."

"I had wanted to be ordained when I first went to Rochester, but I knew it wasn't appropriate to ask because they would think I was asking for the wrong reasons. So I waited ten years. By then I was working for Barkmann Engineering in Santa Fe." The company encouraged her to get an engineering degree, and she also considered continuing her training in architecture but, in the end, decided her Zen training was more important. So in 1986, she requested ordination, and Kapleau readily agreed.

"Bodhin had been installed as abbot of the Rochester Zen Center by then, and Roshi was living in semi-retirement in Florida with increasing debilitation due to Parkinson's." Although Kapleau offered to authorize her to teach, Mitra didn't feel she was ready yet. "And it was at that point that somebody gave me – as a gift – a sesshin with Harada Roshi out in the Northwest."

She had met Harada Roshi when he'd paid a visit to Rochester and felt an "instant connection" with him. After the gift retreat, she decided to continue her training in Japan.

"There was no sense of conflict that you were going to work with other teachers?"

"No, because I'd already completed my formal training in Rochester, so it was okay for me to go elsewhere, or even to start teaching myself, which I didn't feel I was ready to do. In fact, when I came back to Rochester after living in Japan, Kapleau Roshi talked about my teacher being Harada Roshi. Kapleau Roshi took me through nineteen years of practice and through all of the koan curriculum that he taught, and to his credit – not all Zen teachers can be this free – he was very happy to see me continue, even under a different teacher. So I went to Japan in 1992.

"I spent two months at Sogenji, because of the connection with Harada Roshi, and a couple of weeks in Kyoto, sitting with Morinaga Soko Roshi. Then I did Rohatsu Sesshin with Tangen Roshi at Bukkokuji. Tangen Roshi had been what I call Kapleau's guardian angel at Hosshinji and was originally supposed to take over Hosshinji, but the Soto sect said, 'No way are you going to take over this temple! It's going to return to being straight Soto, no longer with any Rinzai influence.' Tangen Roshi's temple, Bukkokuji, was a one minute walk from Hosshinji. Very sweet little temple. I did Rohatsu sesshin with him, and it was very much like being in Rochester except in Japanese and with oryoki meals."

She returned briefly to Rochester then spent some time, at Kapleau's request, with the sangha in Mexico City. "I got hepatitis in Mexico, and a few months later came down with meningitis and encephalitis, and the combination flattened me. I was subsequently diagnosed with chronic fatigue; I could hardly move." In spite of her condition, however, she felt compelled to return to Sogenji in order to work with Harada Roshi for an indefinite period. "Everybody said, 'You're insane! Do you know what the winters are like in Japan?' I had been there in December, so I had a clue. I went, and it was exactly the right thing to do. I knew that as soon as I crossed the threshold of that main gate at Sogenji, after interminable delays and hours and hours on airplanes. Missed planes. Barely made the last train to Okayama from Osaka. Had a taxi driver who wasn't sure whether to let me out at the front gate or the back gate. And I didn't know, so he kept driving back and forth between them. Finally he let me out at the front gate, and I stepped over the threshold and felt totally, completely, finally home. It was well past midnight. Sesshin has already begun. Chisan had told me to head for the light; there was one light on – like a street light – at the temple. I set out for the light, feeling profoundly, deeply grateful, and finally home."

As we discuss Sogenji, I find another of those loose connections. One of the members of the sitting group I host had also been at Sogenji, and Mitra knew him. I mention that he described getting frostbite there.

"Yes, I got it every winter. In 1996, I went to a conference in India of Western ordained Buddhist women. It was in February, so I missed what they call the Dai Kan, the Great Cold, but it was cold enough that still I got frostbite before I left for

India, and when I arrived in India, where it was warm, chunks of skin fell off my hands. Yes, I know frostbite."

In spite of the frostbite, she describes her time at Sogenji as "one of the most incredible experiences of my life. Though the schedule in Rochester, by American Zen standards, was very intense, especially under Roshi Kapleau, at Sogenji it was even more intense. Ten minutes to four in the morning, you're in the hondo ready to start the morning chanting. There's an hour of morning chanting. Then you go to the zendo. Then there's sanzen; everybody's required to go to sanzen. Nowadays they can't fulfill that because there are more people, but back then there were few of us, and we would all get in. Most days you're in sanzen twice a day. There's no option to say, 'Sorry, Roshi, I didn't get a chance to memorize my koan' or 'I don't have an answer.' You simply dug down to bring forth the deepest response possible. Then, when you go in, you recite the koan and demonstrate your answer to it. No question about it! So you dig deep, and it's amazing what you can do under those circumstances."

"You said that when you first met Kapleau Roshi, he terrified you. What was your first response to Harada Roshi?"

"A deep, caring connection. Amazed by the palpable compassion that comes from him. He's very strict, and there are no hugs or touches, but the compassion is palpable. He doesn't talk a lot. I think he feels like time is short, and he wants to make every minute count. He'll speak to people at their level, but it's not generally small talk, and yet it doesn't seem like he's pontificating, either. He's totally human. The embrace of the man is amazing – not physical embrace, because he definitely doesn't do that – but the felt unconditional acceptance he radiates."

When she returned from Japan at the end of April 1996, Philip Kapleau sanctioned her as a teacher, after which she went back to New Mexico. There she stayed with Will and Lucie Brennan who had maintained the Mountain Cloud Center in Santa Fe and would eventually invite Henry Shukman to be their resident teacher.

Not long after resettling in New Mexico, "I got an email from some folks I knew in Missouri saying there was a group in California that was looking for a teacher on the internet. Was it okay if they sent my name? I said 'Okay' and then forgot about it. In the meantime this property [Mountain Gate] came up for sale again. I had had my eye on it earlier but had no money to buy it. But my father – who died while I was in India – willed me enough money to buy the property and so I did. Then those folks in California got in touch with me and asked me to come out and give them a sesshin. I said, 'I don't know you, so I don't feel it's appropriate to do sesshin with you, but I'll do an all-day sitting.' So I went. Their teacher was still alive, barely; she had emphysema. She had told the group to find another teacher. When I met her, she asked if I would take over the group. I learned later that one of the members of the group had asked Harada Roshi if he would come teach, and he'd said to get in touch with me."

"Who was the teacher?"

"Her name was Lola Lee. She wasn't an authorized Zen teacher. But she had a group, and they asked me if I would come back and teach them, and she also asked if I would do that. And then it was arranged that I would come back in January; it was October 1996 when I went there the first time, and then January 1997 I came back. Lola died the week before I returned."

The California community is known as the Hidden Valley Zen Center.

"A couple of years ago Harada Roshi asked me to take on one of his senior students and make her my successor. It took a lot of money and a lot of time, but we were able to get her a Religious Worker visa – she's German – and she's at Hidden Valley for now. She's not my successor yet; this is just the beginning of that possibility. We'll see if it works out. At the moment it's looking like it will."

"So you come here to the high country of New Mexico, and you build a zendo."

"That's where you start," she laughs. "I did the necessary architectural drawings to get a building permit for the zendo, and we built as far as we could – all of it volunteer labor – and then the winter weather closed in; it snowed before we got the beams up and the roof deck on. I had been given an ancient travel trailer and was living here on the land. We held our first sesshin in a very cold and snowing January. With the unheated travel trailer as the women's dorm, kitchen, and dining hall, we sandwiched ourselves in. The men slept in the unheated zendo which also had no electricity yet. After dark, we sat using kerosene lanterns and a kerosene heater. People were allowed to wear all the clothing they wanted – mittens, hats, blankets, parkas – and they did."

She searches for a photograph of the first sesshin. It was a small group, four participants and Mitra. Everyone is bundled in layers of clothing. The snow around the unfinished zendo looks deep.

"We can get a couple of feet of snow here. It was so nice to get the windows in! A young man I knew from Rochester took a quarter off from university and came out and stayed for three months. He helped a great deal and attended that first sesshin." She points him out in the photo. "And these are a couple of my students from Missouri. They were still in college and came out to Ojo Sarco every vacation to do zazen here. And after the sesshin, we continued construction."

The community is, as Mitra puts it, dispersed. "It's all over the map. People come for sesshin, and they also come – from time to time – for longer training. We do two almost back-to-back sesshin in March or April or somewhere spanning the two months. One is called an Elder Sesshin. It's a five day sesshin, and three or four or five days later we follow up with a seven day sesshin. Several people come and stay for both. One couple in South Dakota tells me they want to work two or three more years so they're eligible for decent retirement benefits, and then they want to move here so they can train full-time. They just bought a house here in the valley – within sight of Mountain Gate – so they're following through so far. And there are other people who come from different parts of the country and some from farther away than that. The biggest sesshin we've had was nineteen people. At this time, our facilities are really limited; before we got the Kannon-do they were even more so."

"Is that little cabin I saw a dormitory?"

"That's our old kitchen, which we built on the fly one November – as it started snowing – because the trailer was dying. Some years later we were able to buy the property next door. One day, the neighbor living there called me up and said, 'I haven't had a date in eight years. I'm out of here! You wanna buy it?' And I said, 'Yes.' Then I hung up the phone, and I thought, 'How are we going to do that?' We live on an extremely short shoestring. But Rochester was willing to give us a mortgage for the entire amount, and so we were able to buy it, and it's now paid off. We used that little shed – no running water but with electricity and a gas stove – as our only kitchen for years; now, finally, we have a kitchen with running water, and there's also extra sleeping space. We also have a Kannon Room, the Kannon-do we call it, for sitting whenever you feel like it and for doing metta meditation during sesshin, as long as there are few enough people in the sesshin so it doesn't need to be used as a dormitory."

The numbers are small but continue to grow. The fact that she is able to maintain the place without promotion is impressive. "I felt that if people needed to find it, they would."

"How do you get along with your neighbors?" I ask.

"Very well, actually. I wasn't sure in the beginning, because when I was living in Santa Fe I heard all kinds of stories about Anglos being burned out of old Spanish communities. Not in Ojo Sarco but there was a major series of incidents in Mora County. But my students and I have taken part in local community events. For example, when they were doing renovations on the tiny local church, one of my students and I went down and helped. I go to Las Posadas at Christmas-time which re-enacts the story of Mary and Joseph's search for room at an inn. With the dearth of Catholic priests in the area, it's about the only event that occurs in our local church. The first time I went, I went with my neighbor, Richard. There's a time in the mass when you turn around and say 'Peace be with you.' I turned, not expecting any welcome, and I found three hands extended to me. It was a beautiful experience.

"People here have been wonderful. They are quite generous. We built the zendo entirely by ourselves. With this part of the building, there was also a lot of volunteer labour but sometimes two or three local people were hired to help. That seems to have been appreciated by the community. One of the people we hired was a fellow who's a beautiful human being as well as experienced in building custom homes for a contractor. We hired him to do the interior framing in this part of the building, and I asked him also to do the porch framing, which he did. When the roofing came I asked him if he could do it also. He and his 11-year-old son and one of his brothers did the roof and wouldn't accept any money for it.

"We also had a very sweet old Mexican man working for us who couldn't read or write. It was November, and I was heading to California, and he was grouting the bathroom floor. I asked him not to wash the grouting tools inside because I knew the grout would clog up the pipes. By that time, we had hot water inside, and I'm sure he didn't realize the pipes would get clogged and naturally preferred putting his hands in warm water inside rather than the icy water at the hose outside. When I came back, the bathtub wasn't draining as fast as it had been. Then during our next sesshin, the toilet was backing up into the bathtub. So I called the plumber, and he came. I told him we were in retreat. He was absolutely silent. He pulled the toilet, snaked the pipes, put the toilet back on, and disappeared and never sent a bill. That's the kind of thing that happens to us up here."

Mitra had an opportunity to spend some time with Philip Kapleau just before his death in 2004.

"He was quite impacted by the Parkinson's, and he had tardive dyskinesia as a result of the medications. One of the side effects of the Parkinson's meds is that it can, in addition to letting you move, really make you move. And so he would constantly, involuntarily and uncontrollably wave his arms around to the point of even knocking his glasses off. And his voice was almost a whisper; you could hardly hear him talk. They were only allowing people to spend fifteen minutes at a time with him, and then his main caregiver would come in and say, 'Roshi, do you want to continue? Or is it time for so-and-so to leave?' She came in several times, and each time he said, 'No, it's not time yet.' We didn't speak. We just sat there in each other's company, with a deep and clear and tranquil, wordless communion between us. It was not necessary to have words. I treasure that time with him.

"He never quit practicing, never quit working on himself. He sat zazen daily without fail, and as soon as he could see where he was caught in some negative habit pattern, that was simply the end of it; I never saw it again in him. It was remarkable. There he was, growing older and older – a time in life when so many people get frozen in their negative habit patterns – and he continued to practice zazen; he continued to practice the Long Maturation; he continued to grow."

"Do you still work with Harada Roshi?"

"Yes. And I suppose I will till one or the other of us is dead. It seems kind of presumptive to assume you're done with your own training when you start teaching. That's part of the reason why we've had so many problems with the Japanese teachers. They came independently; Eido definitely came independently. Sasaki does not have a home temple in Japan, and I don't believe Eido does either. Neither seem to have been supervised by their headquarter temples. It's vital to continue your training. To assume you've gone as far as you can go just because you're authorized to teach is a pretty dangerous thing. If you look into the Jataka Tales you'll see that the Buddha was training for lifetimes before he became the Buddha. How can we think we're 'there' without having done a heck of a lot of training? I don't think twenty years, forty years – it's going to be my forty-first year of ongoing Zen practice in 2014 – I don't see that as necessarily sufficient. To me, to continue to open more and more through clear seeing and letting go of negative habit patterns is vital. And given how much I have seen in what opening I've done so far, I can only guess that I've got a lot more that's still hidden from me that I can open to and let go of and be clear on. There are times when I see where I can still be dysfunctional, and I don't want that. I want to continue training until everything is totally let go of and I can really live, moment to moment, that truly liberated mind state of Shido Munan."

In addition to the retreats for her Zen students in California and New Mexico, a month before my visit Mitra had initiated a Regaining Balance Retreat. "It's for women veterans with PTSD or women partners of veterans with PTSD, because the women partners of veterans with PTSD can actually have worse PTSD than their partners do. Six women were scheduled to come, but two of them ended up getting lost and getting frustrated and going back home. It turned out to be serendipitous because we originally had three people in each room, one room here and one up at the Kannon-do. But for women with PTSD, that's a bit too intense; it worked out much better with four total, so two in each room. So from now on – until we can expand our building – four is going to be our limit.

"It's not a Buddhist event. It's completely non-religious, non-sectarian. What we do is teach them the susokkan practice, the extended out-breath practice which is a Rinzai practice. And we take them hiking. We have a boundary with the National Forest here, so we just go out the driveway and across the road and walk. We also do a little yoga and teach some journaling and do a little art therapy. Basically that was it. It was only four days, but teaching them skills they can use to help themselves de-stress."

"Are you the facilitator?"

"I was the meditation teacher and taught the journaling, and one of my students and a friend of hers who's a therapist took them hiking; the therapist taught the yoga. We also had as part of our team a wonderful older woman who is a therapist who does a lot of work with veterans with PTSD, and she taught some of the art therapy and some poetry writing. So we had a team of four people, which was perfect for our veterans."

When my traveling companions return to pick me up, they join us as Mitra takes me to see the Kannon-do. "To open to our innate compassion is important," she explains. "Wisdom without compassion is not true wisdom. It's the same the other way around, too: compassion without wisdom is not real compassion, it's pity."

The walls of the Kannon-do are brown, and the white porcelain statue – on an old wooden cabinet – seems to glow in the dark-hued room.

"When we were going to buy this piece of property with this building on it, I knew that we wanted to dedicate one room to Kannon – Guanyin – and the practice of compassion; so we looked for a figure to grace the room. Santa Fe's famous for having all kinds of Buddhist figures, but they were quite expensive."

During a trip to New York state, someone suggested she try Toronto. So she and a friend drove to the city during a snow-storm which made the trip twice as long as it would have been otherwise. They arrived around noon. "We decided to have lunch first in a Vietnamese restaurant which I knew would have vegetarian food. The restaurant was on the second story, and at the first floor bottom of the stairway up to the restaurant there was a two-storey high painting of Guanyin with a stick of incense burning in an incense pot beneath it. That made it seem like we were in the right place." They asked the proprietor where they could find a Kannon figure. "He said, 'Well, there are about four places in town where you can find one; three of them sell junk, and the other's really expensive. So we wandered around and found the three places that had not very good figures. And then we also found the expensive one, where for $3000 we could get a gorgeous figure."

By chance, they noticed a basement shop filled with Asian statuary. "There were life-size bronze figures of Jizo, a standing Buddha, and a huge bronze Guanyin seated on a lotus base about three feet in diameter. It had a little tag that read '200' on it. We already had an altar, and I thought, 'Wow, we might have to get a different altar' because the figure was so large. So I asked the Chinese woman who seemed to work there, 'How much?' She said" – imitating her accent – "'Two hundred dollah.' And I thought, 'Wow, if it's $200, we'll buy it!'"

The woman didn't speak much English and phoned the store's owner, who came over and told the women, "'You want Buddha? Too much Buddha! Too many Buddha! See? See? Too many Buddha! Come! Come!' So following him, we zipped up the stairs and crossed a snow-covered alleyway, where he unlocked a door. We went in through a vestibule, and then through a kitchen, down into a basement. He was striding along at a brisk pace through this basement filled with figures, and I thought, 'Wait! Wait! Wait! I want to look!' He kept waving his hands around and repeating, 'See? Too many Buddha! Too many Buddha!' Around the basement, back up the stairs, back through the kitchen and foyer and back into the alley, across the alleyway he unlocks another door, and we repeat the same process. He went straight to the end of that basement, reached up, pulled down a long box, set it on a table, and there she was. And without asking the price I said, 'We'll take it!' Then I thought, 'Oh, my! What if it's $10,000?' But it turned out to be $500 Canadian – an incredible price.

"It's porcelain, and it's an individual piece. It's got a personal seal and another seal pressed into the back. So we put it on the credit card, and when we came out of the store, the sun was shining! The snow had melted! They carried it to the car for us, and we left for the border. The immigration officer asked, 'Have you got anything to declare?' 'Yes, we bought a statue.' 'What is it?' 'It's a Kannon Bodhisattva.' 'A what?' And he continued asking us questions and writing down stuff. Finally he asked, 'Well, is it old?' 'I don't think so.' Finally he said, 'Well, I should be charging you duty on this, but go ahead. Merry Christmas.' So we got back to Buffalo. I shipped it to Ojo Sarco, and...."

"There she is."

"There she is."

"And the long and the short of it is, you're telling me she's Canadian."

Mitra laughs. "Indeed!"

CHAPTER TWENTY-ONE

Three at the Springwater Center for Meditative Inquiry

TONI PACKER
WAYNE COGER
SANDRA GONZÁLEZ

1

Toni Packer's Springwater Center for Meditative Inquiry is located in an agricultural region about an hour south of Rochester. The Sitting Room, as it is called, is a large open space with windows that come nearly down to the polished hardwood floor. There is no altar. There is no religious iconography in this room – or any of the other rooms – although it is rimmed with the same square zabuton mats and zafu cushions one would expect to find in a zendo.

In 1981, Toni – as everyone called her – broke with the Rochester Zen Center in a schism which drew away half its membership. At the time of my visit, she was in her final illness, and I was unable to meet her. I formed, however, an impression of her not only from my conversations with those who knew her but from the Center itself. In retrospect, nothing is more emblematic of that impression than the windows of the Sitting Room. Instead of looking at a blank wall or seated in rows across from one another or facing an altar, the meditators at Springwater are free to turn their cushions to the windows and gaze out at vistas of agricultural fields and gently rolling wooded hills.

Toni was born in Berlin in 1927 and was six years old when the Nazis came to power. Her mother was Jewish, which put the family at risk; however, her father's stature as a scientist afforded them some protection. The children were baptized and raised Lutheran. Still, in spite of their father's position, it is likely that had the war continued much longer they would have been arrested and sent to the death camps. The terrors of the war – the memory of her father huddled in fright in an air raid shelter as bombs fell – as well as the later revelations about the Holocaust raised serious questions in the young girl's mind and heart. She was unable to reconcile the horrors of her youth with the concept of a caring God. Her experiences also left her with a profound suspicion of all forms of external authority.

After the war, her family moved to Switzerland. There she met and married an American university student who brought her to the United States. They settled in western New York. She enrolled at the University of Buffalo and acquired an interest in Zen from reading Alan Watts and D. T. Suzuki. When *The Three Pillars of Zen* was first released, she began a sitting practice based on the instructions provided in it. Later, when she learned that Philip Kapleau had opened a Zen Center only 75 miles from her home, she and her husband became members.

Toni was older and more mature than most of the members of the centre, and she was driven by more profound life experiences. She attended as many sesshin as she was able and progressed rapidly in koan work, quickly gaining Kapleau's notice and respect. By 1975, she was entrusted with leading sesshin at the center.

In 1981, confident that he had found in Toni someone to whom he could entrust the Rochester Center in his absence, Kapleau prepared to go to Santa Fe. What he was unaware of was that Toni had begun to question the necessity of certain forms at the Center such as the use of the kyosaku and the practice of prostrating before the teacher. In part, her questions came from reading the works of Jiddu Krishnamurti.[70] Toni brought her concerns to Kapleau just prior to his departure. He was surprised and disconcerted by her questions but, in the end, told her she could use whatever techniques she felt appropriate in dokusan as long as she retained the other structures he had established at the Center. He left for Santa Fe hopeful the situation was under control. Toni was less sanguine about the situation.

In an interview she gave to Lenore Friedman just a few years after these events, she explained how she was beginning to view things:

> I myself was doing all these prostrations, and lighting incense, and bowing, and gassho-ing and the whole thing. I realized that I was influencing people, just by the position I was in, the whole setup. I could see it, and I wasn't going to have any part in it anymore.

> Unless you are really set on discovering, if anybody supports you in not discovering, you won't do it. Which I find in Zen. The system is very supportive to not questioning some things. Even though it

claims to question everything. You question everything and you "burn the Buddha," but then you put him back up!

I examined it very carefully: did I have any division while I was bowing? It had always been said, "When you bow, you're not bowing to the Buddha, you're bowing to yourself. And when you're prostrating, everything disappears, you disappear, the Buddha disappears and there's nothing." I tried to look, and it wasn't completely clear. I could see there was often an image, of the bower, or of the person who "has nothing." Often there was a shadow of something, somebody there who was doing it. Or maybe the idea of being able to do it emptily![71]

Among other things, one's loyalties contribute to one's point of view. Throughout the interviews I conducted, I heard several accounts of what happened after Kapleau left for Santa Fe. There were also various interpretations regarding the degree of authority Kapleau had bestowed on Toni and whether or not he actually had viewed her as a successor. It is clear, however, that he intended her to be the principle teacher at the Zen Center in his absence, that he had authorized her to see students in dokusan, and to work with them on koans.

Toni tried to respect Kapleau's wishes about Zen Center forms, but, under her leadership, certain changes inevitably came about. She eschewed all outward manifestations of hierarchy and achievement – refusing, for example, to wear a rakusu – and relaxed the taut martial atmosphere for which the center was known.

Taigen Henderson attended a number of sesshin during this period and valued the changes. "Toni was very warm, very personal. Insightful. Deeply insightful. And she had a different style of teaching. Roshi's style was too harsh for a lot of people. Toni Packer had a much more gentle approach. She had the same kind of attention to insight but not so much kensho insight. More attention, awareness, to the moment in your daily life. It was exactly what I needed to hear at the time because I was a layman with a family. I didn't have that much time for hours and hours of zazen. For me, she offered a formula for daily life. She was wonderful."

Others did not welcome Toni's changes and wrote to Kapleau expressing concern that she was weakening the practice. Under pressure, Kapleau returned to Rochester the following June for a meeting of members who were unhappy with the way Toni was running things. The meeting reminded Toni of the kind of denouncements which had taken place in the Germany of her youth, and she found it hurtful.

By the end of the gathering, however, Kapleau expressed his support of her and gave her permission to bring about whatever changes she felt appropriate. But it was too late; Toni had already begun to wonder if she could continue to view or present herself as a Buddhist at all.

Instead of returning to Santa Fe that June, Kapleau went to Mexico, accompanied by Bodhin Kjolhede.

"I just had enormous admiration for Toni," Bodhin told me. "I think she's a magnificent model of enlightenment. I think she's deeply compassionate. Genuinely. Just flowing out of her. And it was a terrible shock to Roshi when she said she could no longer work in a Buddhist context.

"I can tell you the story: I was in Mexico with Roshi. He discovered I had some linguistic abilities, and he had been working on *Zen: Merging of East and West*, and had been floundering alone, so he decided he needed an assistant. And while we were down there, he got a call from Toni just two weeks before he was due to come up here for a trustees' meeting, and she said, 'I need to talk.' And he said, 'Okay. Good. I'll be there in two weeks.' And she said, 'It can't wait. I want to come down there.' And he said, 'Okay.' So she came down. They went out in the backyard and talked for maybe an hour. And he came in – to get a cup of tea or something – and he said, 'Toni says she can no longer work in a Buddhist context.' He was dumbfounded! Because she had never indicated that she had any problem with the Buddhist context. Anyway, that was it. And then he came up for that trustees' meeting and talked more with her, and that's where the big split happened. I was still in Mexico. So it just passed me by. I wasn't involved in the acrimony, all the discussions about whether she should stay or go and everything. And I guess because our mission statement says a 'Zen Buddhist context,' it was decided that she had to leave."

"It was decided? It wasn't her choice?" I asked.

"It may have been. I don't know. I think she was at least given a nudge. But I don't know."

"My memories of Toni are of this lovely, thin, very beautiful woman that you couldn't hug because her bones were so delicate," Sunyana Graef told me, smiling at the memory. "And Roshi respected her tremendously, but she wasn't his Dharma heir. He gave her the center, but there was never any ceremony of her becoming a Dharma heir. Bodhin was his first Dharma heir, and probably Zenson was his second, and I was his third. I think it went that way.

"So she was to take over, but then it became very clear that this wasn't going to work for her. And I respect her tremendously for being so clear with him. It was terribly painful for Roshi, but at the same time he completely understood that a person had to be true to themselves. Because he went through this with his own teacher. So there was that split. It happened."

"She took quite a number of students with her?"

"She did, and those were students who wanted to practice in that way. So I guess they were happier there. So that was fine."

Taigen remembers it as a painful period. "It was hard because I resonated with her way of teaching more than Roshi's at the time. But the center was started by Roshi, and a number of us who were, by that time, older members thought that really we should keep the center as part of his lineage."

Mitra Bishop remembered that about half of the membership left with Toni. "It was the people that didn't find an affinity with the intense way that Kapleau Roshi was teaching. To his credit, he changed his way of teaching after that and became much softer and much more himself."

I asked her what she meant by that.

"Back then it was very much Yasutani Roshi's voice that was coming out of Kapleau Roshi's mouth," she explained. "That became obvious to me when I went to live in Japan. That voice is still there in the flavor of *The Three Pillars of Zen*. There were a lot of rules back then that came out of the Japanese way of looking at things. Among other things, the people who had families and so didn't live at the Center – Roshi really wanted it to be a monastery – felt odd-man-out and less-than. There was a whole thing about who got to sit in the zendo and who had to go to the sub-zendo, which was the dining hall, or later the Buddha Hall. Nobody had rakusus until, at one point, Roshi had enough people who were working on subsequent koans in the *Mumonkan* that he gathered them all together and gave each of them rakusus. Because of this there started to be a 'have' and a 'have-not' group in addition to the local versus the staff people tensions. At one point, a rakusu was actually stolen."

More than 200 people joined Toni in establishing what she originally called the Genesee Valley Zen Center. She explained that the use of the term Zen was not intended to imply affiliation but was rather a descriptor of the method of seated meditation used. The new center was still located in Rochester. Then, in 1984, 284 acres of undeveloped farmland were purchased in Springwater.

A period of stripping down followed the establishment of the new center. At first, Toni continued to have students work with koans, then she gradually ceased to do so. The word Zen was dropped. Rules – even those governing retreats – became flexible. Participants were free to attend scheduled sittings or not as they chose. Nothing was mandatory except a daily work assignment and silence in certain places at certain times.

Toni encouraged her students to examine and question their assumptions about practice, about the roles of student and teacher, and to challenge any concept that came between themselves and the direct perception of self, others, and the external environment. She may have discarded the term Zen, but in a classic sense it was the approach expressed in the Linji koan John Tarrant had quoted me: "When something appears, don't believe it. Whatever confronts you, shine your light on it. Have confidence in the light that is always shining inside you."

There was, she pointed out, no "technique" for doing this. As a result, some people found the approach discouraging. They wanted direction, and she refused to define procedures. There were, she insisted, no "authorities" who could lead one to what she called "awareing" or the "work of the moment." One needed only to attend simply and directly to what was happening moment to moment.

Her teaching style, at least as it comes across on the printed page, was similar to the slow, reflective manner of Krishnamurti. When she spoke, her eyes often remained closed as if she were searching within for the precise way to express what she wished to get across. On one occasion, drawing attention to the sounds retreat participants could hear from both outside and within the sitting room, she is recorded as having said:

> In the midst of listening and chirping, humming and breathing, people want to know, "What meditation practice do you teach here? What should my practice be?" This is a frequent question asked by people interested in meditation, expecting to be taught a practice, wishing to become good at it. But where does the question itself come from? Is there an assumption that meditation must involve a practice? That a teacher is needed who knows what we have to do, what guidance we need, what path to follow, where to go? Is there a deep need to ask someone else, "What should I do? What is the right thing to do here?" Do we feel a need to be reassured in our persistent doubts: "Am I doing it right? Am I doing enough? Am I doing as well as the others?"

Each of us has a different motive for taking up spiritual practice. Yet a motive is there for all of us, isn't there? Maybe we are hearing an implied criticism in that question – that I shouldn't have any motive, because that is wrong. Whatever is being said here, no matter how critical it may sound, can these remain moments of simple listening? This heavily conditioned brain has difficulty in hearing anything innocently. Whatever is heard is fitted into a preexisting context laid down in the past. It hears criticism where there is none intended. It assumes that conditioned reactions that are pointed out in a talk are wrong and therefore the opposite – no conditioning – must be right. And that therefore I need to get rid of my conditioning, and please tell me what practice will do that for me. On and on. No criticism is implied, just watching the mind rattling on.[72]

She emphasized the questioning – the inquiry – rather than the answers, advising her listeners to maintain a "not knowing" mind. "Not knowing means putting aside what I already know and being curious to observe freshly, openly, what is actually taking place right now in the light of the question. Not knowing means putting up with the discomfort of no immediate answer."[73]

She went to say that the "essence of meditative inquiry is not obtaining answers but wondering patiently without knowing."[74]

Toni Packer had not named a successor, and the issue of what would become of the center when she died colored the atmosphere at Springwater throughout my visit. Toni herself had claimed she was unconcerned.

> – I'm not concerned about the future. I'm saying this completely honestly. From its very beginnings, which cannot even be remembered, this whole amazing unfolding of inquiry and discovery in silent space has completely taken care of itself in an unfathomable way. Shall we now worry about how it will continue? Even though I have been well acquainted with fear and worry about an uncertain future, or rather an uncertain present, since my early childhood days in Nazi Germany, I feel a total absence of this apprehension with regard to the work we do at Springwater.[75]

2

I arrive at the center shortly before lunch, and Wayne Coger, my contact here, invites me to join a handful of people for what turns out to be an excellent vegetarian lasagna. There is no particular program taking place at the moment, but there are people doing private retreats, including some who are here for extended stays. And there are scheduled activities one may take part in if one wishes.

Wayne tells me I would be welcome to attend a discussion circle to be led by Sandra González after lunch. It takes place in what had been Toni's apartment. Sandra is from Nicaragua and speaks with a charming Latin accent. Her English is excellent, but she retains some linguistic structures from the Spanish language such as occasionally dropping subject pronouns. In the print material I found in the entry way, she and Wayne are identified as "retreat leaders."

There are six of us in the discussion circle. People sit in silence until someone brings up a topic which others are free to respond to or alter as they wish. The topic that arises is "authority," the authority that teachers have or are given. Once the initial hesitations are overcome, the discussion becomes animated and moves freely.

After the others leave, Sandra and I remain behind. I begin the interview by referring to the discussion which has just taken place. "The impression one gets is that there isn't much structured authority here."

She doesn't respond immediately. Both she and Wayne have a habit of pausing and reflecting, often for quite a long time, before speaking. I timed one of Wayne's pauses at 41 seconds. Sandra's pauses are generally shorter than his.

"Yes," she says after a moment. "Even though there is a structure. Because – you know – in retreat we have a schedule. We have a functional guideline for different things that are required to put up a retreat. You know, like kitchen. Coordinating the retreat. Housekeeping. How we deal with details of cleaning up. So we have very specific and very clear instructions. You know? And this started in the Rochester Zen Center. So when I came in 1988, this was in place. At the same time, is a very organic kind of structure. There can be questions. And when a question comes either from the staff or the people that come for retreat then there is looking into that structure to check if that criticism is accurate. And then we are very democratic. I never saw Toni Packer saying, 'This has to be kept.' You know? Always open, and we have continued to do so, be open to criticism the same way we are questioning our own brain. So the same way, all this structure can be questioned. Is it functional still? Somebody comes by a new idea; it is put into a staff meeting. So we have change. When I came to this place was many things from the Zen Center still in place here."

Sandra had been engaged in Zen practice for seven years before she came to Springwater. She was 39 years old when she attended her first sesshin at Dai Bosatsu with Eido Shimano.

"What took you there?" I ask.

"An LSD trip. You don't need to write that down, but I have to be honest!" she says, laughing. "It was one thing, but not the only thing. There was – you know – a journey. A big journey inside. When I saw the contradiction in my life – you know – getting married with a guy very much like my father, and I say, 'What is this craziness?' With all the idea, 'I will never be like my mother, my father.' But there was repeating. You know? Repeating and repeating. So I studied psychology, and I did a lot of psychotherapy because in Nicaragua that was the only thing that was available, and I didn't resonate with Catholicism and Christianity. Then came the revolution in 1979. I came to the United States and here – you know – are more options. So I was, like, shopping around? Let's put it that way. I went to an ashram also in Florida. There was an amazing ex-monk, Dhiravamsa, and he mixed psychotherapy and spirituality. Coming from a psychological tradition, I say, 'This is great!' You know? Because it really helped to release energy and get in touch with so many issues that come from the past and the childhood."

Her "shopping around" brought her to Dai Bosatsu and, eventually, to Mount Baldy and Joshu Sasaki. She was studying with a female teacher in California who had been authorized to teach in the Vietnamese tradition when she came upon Lenore Friedman's book, *Meetings with Remarkable Women*.

"And I read about Toni Packer. And then it happened that I was very unsatisfied with the whole center issue with this woman teacher. She was really abusive of power, making preferences in students. I didn't like that. So my heart never connected. And I was listening to Krishnamurti in a video. I read his book before, but it never really make sense the way it did that precise moment. He spoke, and I could see the whole business of the authority and the guru. This is what I was seeing. You know? And then I remember reading about Toni Packer. At the Zen Center ten years, then she reads Krishnamurti and kind of leaving. So I said, 'I have to check it out, this woman.' Because what I love in the Zen tradition is the retreats. I just love retreats. Because it brings a lot of opportunity to just sit and break through – you know? – this cocoon we have. So that was, for me, amazing, that this woman had a center, still holding retreats but – as I read – in a new way! You know? So I came and I checked it out. And, Rick, I never left! I just fell in love with the whole thing. That was 1988."

"Can you remember what your first meeting with Toni Packer was like?"

"Well, I can tell you that my first retreat…." She stops a moment, then starts again. "I have to say this a little bit. When I drove from Tallahassee to here, I could feel the silence when I came. I could say – and I have written about this – it felt like coming home. True. So before seeing Toni physically, the whole place, everything kind of made sense. So when I start that retreat, here comes the authority again. You know, in those times she had these interviews, ten minutes, five minutes, a gong. Sitting on the cushion before her – you know – and there was this nervousness. So when I got up there, I was in shambles! And I told her, very briefly, that my whole work had been in koan study. And I said, 'What is your understanding?' She said, 'What is it that you came for?' And I say, 'I don't know, but all this feeling that I'm so inadequate and not knowing, this is what I really care about right now.' And she said, 'That's your koan.'" Sandra pauses to make the point and then repeats with emphasis, "'That is your koan.' And we kind of look, and I ask her, 'Well, how do you work with a koan here?' You know? Talking in those terms. And she said, 'You just wonder. You just wonder and be here. That's all. Even forget about the whole feeling and just watch. Just watch.' And, well, I took it to the heart. You know? All the energy that was available. So in the fifth day – and I have said this in talks – at the fifth day, when the mind was so anchored, right here with the birds, with the sound, with the breathing, not holding onto any koan specifically, she was giving a talk, and she mention the word 'images.' And was like a stopping of the thinking, whatever was there. It was like a beam of light, really, being shined into the moment when the brain feels itself as kind of stupid. Because I had often felt stupid, clumsy, and I used to make everybody laugh and feeling incompetent and all this. And it was dropped instantaneously, the whole problem. So what you see is that the energy happening was not me; what was clearly the intelligence was not mine or anybody's. Was free. The freedom of just being here. So, how could I not stay here after that revelation, and through the information that I was looking my entire life?

"When I came to her and said, 'Toni, this is happening. My entire life, I have been looking for some relief from this problem.' And she said, 'Well, you know, this is just the beginning. Many, many people when something happens, they decide they are a teacher, that they know.' And she said, 'This is the beginning because the tough part is to really understand in *minutiae* – you know – how this mind works.' And let me tell you, Rick, after that retreat and that unveiling, the mind became very humble for several years and more unfolding happened.

"But let me tell you, three years later I was having such a panic attack that I had to leave my house and come in residence here. Stay in a room. I can say it was a disease of the mind. There was a serious fear of dying, wanting to hold onto I don't know what. Five years in shambles. I have a photo of myself that you cannot recognize. Completely, completely in paranoia. Five years steady. And then I never left. I began to work in the center as the staff – in the beginning I was a guest paying – but I had Toni Packer, even though you can see that she can only do so much, because the looking and the understanding has to happen right here," she says, tapping her chest.

"What made Toni Packer a good teacher?"

handed the gear to the others who walked it to shore." His body temperature dropped dangerously, and he spent the night huddled by a fire fighting off hypothermia.

"The next day we divided up the gear, and Rainer and I took the two packs and walked though the bush while Randy took the canoe to the junction of two rivers. It took us about twelve hours of walking through the bush to get where he was, and it was well after dark. He said something about going ahead the next day, and we told him that we should stick together, but we were too exhausted to pay much attention. But he left us the next day without telling us because he thought he could walk up to Hyland Post in a couple of hours. It turned out that Hyland Post was no longer there, but we didn't know that. Rainer and I, on the other hand, had these heavy packs and a canoe, and we didn't think we could follow him through the bush on foot."

They loaded the canoe and went back into the river. "That paddle was pure freedom, like being an explorer. We never knew what was around the next bend. We just trusted in the Universe. A few times we almost didn't make it. There was a large whirlpool we couldn't avoid because, by the time we heard the rapids, we were in a canyon and there was no longer any banks. The whirlpool was after a hairpin turn in the river, and the waves were over our heads. The canoe was being pulled backwards into it, and I remember looking at the shoreline ahead and just putting the thought 'get to the shore' in my mind with complete and utter determination. Later in practice, I recalled the one-pointedness that we needed during this expedition and used it to inspire myself to apply the same energy and purpose to practice."

It took them six days to make it to a settlement where they informed the RCMP of their missing companion. "They probably thought we'd done him in and wanted to make sure we were in a place where they could find us."

The RCMP got them jobs in Cassiar, an asbestos mining town, then began a search for Randy. He was eventually found floating down the Stikine River on a couple of logs. Taigen and Ranier only learned that he had survived from an article in *The Vancouver Sun* which described his ordeal and reported that he had kept alive by eating frogs.

"Meanwhile, I was having trouble with my lungs, because I was breathing in asbestos dust. We packed forty tons. You just sew up the bags, put them on skids. There was dust everywhere. And I was getting this cough. So I talked to this guy who was into yoga, and he said, 'Well, do Lion's Breath.' 'Well, what the heck's Lion's Breath?' Hah!" He demonstrates, exhaling forcefully. "Hah! 'Like this.' So I would do that after shift. Then he said, 'There's something else you might be interested in. It's a book called *The Three Pillars of Zen.*' But he didn't want to lend his copy.

"It was about this time that my mother sent me an article about asbestosis. They were talking about it in the brake-linings of cars in New York City being dangerous, and I was sweeping up a half inch of asbestos dust every shift. So I thought, 'This

"Is not a teacher. You know? She is not invested in the role. That's it. That's what makes her, I would say, a natural teacher, because understanding, sharing – what you saw here in the discussion – looking together, that is it. One-on-one, groups, and talks. Because talks were an invitation to look. But not like putting out a tradition. No, just talking about images and things. One man, Stephan Bielfeldt, said, 'She never gave me what I wanted.' I think that really is the signature of Toni.

"It was like this for me. Everyone wants to have a certainty, a practice, an orientation, a checking-out by an authority – in this case, Toni Packer – to tell me how I was doing in my sittings, in my understanding. And she always answered with another question. 'Why do you want to know? What is it that is going on that brings that question?' Never drawing any conclusion. She said many times, 'Don't let the mind conclude with anything.' Because the whole world – you know? – the perception is closed. So keep it open. Keep it open, because life is an unfolding of meaning. So why conclude, 'This is it'?"

"The gentleman who was seated here," I say, referring to the discussion circle, "said that when he saw the two of you together, he saw there was love. That was the term he used, right? And she said to him?"

"She said to him, 'You are in it.'"

"It is love, and you're in it. What do you think she meant by that?"

"Well, she was pointing to the fact that we cannot recognize anything what we call 'outside' that is not already here in us. Because whatever we say is a projection of what is already here," she says, tapping her chest. "So love is not over there. Is right here. And that is true for anything. You know, sometime I can hear this brain judging somebody because was insensitive about something. And when the judgement happen and takes over is because I have lost touch. I cannot see the judgement that has happened here. So that brings humbleness and, I will say, true compassion. Because then I cannot divide myself from anybody. The more I see myself in others, the less I separate myself from anybody."

Wayne Coger grew up in Rochester and began practicing at Kapleau's Center when he was about 20. "I had been interested from an early age in the questions that, to me, were taken head-on in the Zen books that I encountered in my late teens." He speaks slowly and reflectively. "I don't know why that happened, why these questions were so important. I had a very comfortable life, a nice family, good friends, and so forth. One event that does stand out is the sudden and unexpected death of a close friend when we were both about twelve years old. I was shocked and confused and couldn't find anyone who would say anything that sounded authentic about what had happened. The adults in my life were as confused as I was but tried to offer palliatives, reassuring utterances that sounded flat and unconvincing. It was as if we had to find some way to explain something that was inexplicable. And so somehow I became more and more convinced that it was really important to meet difficult questions directly. And that became the over-riding interest, those troublesome and irritating questions."

He did not find the atmosphere at the Rochester Zen Center particularly welcoming. "There was something very forbidding – is that the right word? – something austere about the Zen Center. And I was also a very shy person. There was so much ritual. It was very strange. I hadn't grown up with that sort of thing. And part of me was saying, 'Well, if this is what it takes, that's what I'll do.' But then I became intrigued when Toni started talking and writing about a simpler and more direct approach to this work."

"Did you have much contact with Philip Kapleau?"

"Not a lot. I thought he was quite brilliant, and his talks were very erudite. He really illuminated the historic and contemporary manifestations of Zen Buddhism. And he brought out the vitality in the old Zen stories. He was very careful to always give the Japanese and Chinese names of the teachers and to give some context to the koans or whatever else he was reading. As a person, he was incredibly…." He pauses before he finds the term he wants. "'Finicky' I guess is the word I'd use. I don't know if it was a teaching device or if that was just the way he was or perhaps a little bit of both. He was an incredible organizer and had a great business sense, which most of us here lack," he adds, with a chuckle.

"How was Toni different?"

He doesn't answer immediately. "Maybe one thing I left out was that Roshi was somewhat remote. He had a lot of students. He was hard to get to at times. But even when you were talking directly with him, there was a testing quality. Toni was much more accessible, friendly, but at the same time, there was an incredible vitality. I first heard her speak at a conference in Providence, Rhode Island, and the sense was that she was speaking from direct experience, not speaking about something but speaking from a meditative listening. Those are probably not the words I would have used at that point, but there was just a sense of something different, something very immediate and authentic.

"That's the word that came to mind. Authenticity. Not a confessional kind of honesty, but the honesty of just being oneself in the moment and discovering what that is from moment to moment. So that was very intriguing, but she also talked about testing things for oneself; not taking what the speaker was saying as gospel. And she talked about looking and seeing, that we didn't have to aspire to some perfected state. We could look at ourselves as we are in the moment. And, again, that felt very different. And the words came as a real invitation to something very exciting."

Although Wayne wasn't living in Rochester during the period when Kapleau left Toni in charge, he came back for a Thanksgiving Celebration at the Center.

"I was met at the door by someone who immediately barked at me," – in a gruff voice – "'Go this way!' It was no big deal – it was kind of usual at the Rochester Center – but the person came back about five or ten minutes later and apologized. And that was quite unusual; I was totally taken aback. That had never happened to me there, that anybody had said, 'I was out of line. I'm sorry. That was over the top, and it wasn't necessary.' I can't remember exactly what the words were, but they conveyed warmth and friendliness, a humanness that had been missing from the carefully cultivated tough Zen exterior. So I did notice a change. I had forgotten about that. That whole weekend, that flow of warmth and friendliness was very evident."

"Why did Toni leave the Rochester Zen Center?"

"I'll give you my interpretation, but I must stress that this is only my interpretation. While she was at the Center, Toni was asked to be available to meet with students who were having emotional or relationship difficulties. This would free Roshi Kapleau to focus his energies specifically on Zen practice. So everything outside of practice was delegated to Toni. My sense is that she began to see that there was a disconnect. People were going to sesshin, having fantastic experiences, building up incredible energy, battling through koans or being frustrated by koans, and at the same time experiencing difficulties with their emotions, their partner, their roommates, and their ordinary life. There was sorrow and suffering evidenced around life situations, illnesses, break-ups, our everyday concerns. Toni began to question whether this division between life situations and practice was really necessary or actual, whether there really was a separation. So the question became (these are my words) 'Could there be a way of working that doesn't make that distinction? Could we take the everyday situation, the thing that's bugging us right now, and let that be the koan?' In this way we could question, meditatively look into our reactions, our fears and our everyday concerns.

"And I think a factor in Toni's unwillingness to remain in the Buddhist tradition came from her experience growing up in Nazi Germany during the Second World War. She became acutely aware of the difficulties, the real pain and suffering that came with identifying with one's country, one's religion, with this perceived need to belong. The 'me' may be felt to be diminished if I've subsumed myself in a group, but in fact the 'me' enlarges and takes on the group identity. We may feel stronger but only in relation to or in comparison with another individual or group. The group identity is sustaining and maintaining the conflict inherent in self-identification; it perpetuates division and discord. So, there was a wondering, a questioning about whether it would be possible to do what is essentially religious work without the trappings of religion, without identification, without needing to say, 'I'm a Quaker. I'm a Buddhist. I'm a Hindu or a Muslim.' And in this way we might begin to question the whole basis and structure of identity, begin to be free of all of this.

"There is a third thing that comes to mind, and that is the question of hierarchy, the idea that there's one person or some group of senior or elite persons who is or are in the know, and that there are the others below them – the seekers, the unenlightened or the ignorant – who are at the mercy of the people in the know. So we have asked if we can do this work without the trappings of traditional religion and now – now that Toni is ill – we are asking if it is also possible to proceed in this meditative inquiry without a teacher."

"How did the members of the Rochester Center feel when she left?"

"There was a lot of…." Again, he takes a moment to search for the word. "Animosity? Sadness. Like a divorce."

"So like a divorce, were people expected to choose sides?"

"Yeah. But some people didn't. Some people said, 'Okay, this is enough of this. I'm going on. Going back to graduate school or finding another tradition or center.' We were all fairly young at the time. But, by and large, people either stayed with the Rochester Zen Center or went with what was then called the Genesee Valley Zen Center."

In 1984, it was not immediately clear, however, what form the GVZC was going to take.

"There were lots of conversations and lots of meetings. People talked about starting a school or a kind of community. The discussions were very lively and very democratic. And one of the common themes – and one of the things that Toni was also very strong on – was the possibility of getting a place in the country. At that time we were thinking about having a place in both the country and the city. That didn't prove to be feasible in the long term, although we did maintain a presence in Rochester for several years.

"After identifying our desire to locate in a country setting, a Land Search Committee was formed. The search was difficult, and there were many tantalizing possibilities that didn't work out for one reason or another. But after about a year of looking, one of the members of the committee saw an ad for this property and made an exploratory visit. A group of us, including Toni, came down to see what was beginning to look like a strong possibility. To us it was just mind-boggling; it was just so beautiful. And it was also a blank canvas, a fresh tableau, a place to begin afresh. There wasn't a building here that needed a lot of work or that didn't quite suit our purposes. The landscape was pretty much as it is now, a mixture of fields and forest, but the fields were overgrown and the forests had been recently heavily logged. At one time it was a farm, from the early 20th century till the 1960s, and there were some out-buildings, a few of which are still standing."

"How did you afford it?"

"We conducted a fund-drive. At that time, a lot of the membership lived in Rochester so it was very easy to communicate with each other. People came down, took a look. We had a wide base of small donations. We only had a few donations and loans that were in the five to ten thousand dollar range; the rest were much smaller. We relied on ourselves, on volunteer labor and on our ability to be thrifty. A lot of us were in our early 30's and late 20's and didn't have a lot of construction experience but were eager and willing to learn and do. And we had a lot of fun!"

"Clearly a lot of thought went into the design of this building. It isn't the work of an amateur."

"We had a designer from the membership who had done smaller projects and saw this as a chance to really spread his wings and to do something that he really felt was worthwhile. He and his business partner worked up some drawings, and we selected one that we found appealing and thought we could afford. We hired a contractor who was a member of the Rochester Zen Center who worked for a very small salary. The rest of the crew was volunteer and a few of the volunteers were very good carpenters."

"Plumbers? Electricians?"

"It's amazing how well things are working considering how much was learned on the job."

I try to get a sense of the organizational structure of Springwater from Sandra, but it isn't easy. When I mention that she is on staff, she says, "Not really, you know."

"Oh, come on!" I object. 'Your photograph is in the pamphlet. It's on the website!"

"Okay." she concedes, laughing. "Well, you know, Toni never wanted to name anybody, and she said, 'I won't go into this kind of handing the tradition to somebody else.' But then her work – but don't take this literally, because I don't want to speak for Toni – but she felt that the place was so amazing. And is an organization, really. You know? We have by-laws, trustees, and everything like that. Board of

Trustees. And she felt that the circumstances – even though she didn't want it – was needing her to name some people that can carry on the work, the center. And that's when she asked me, Wayne, Richard Witteman, and another woman who died."

"So you do have authority. You are, in effect, a senior teacher."

"I know what you mean," she says with a sigh. "We can say a facilitator."

"Okay, facilitator. And you facilitate?"

"Retreats."

"Okay, so let's say I'm someone who's heard about this place, and I come knocking on the door. I've never done any kind of spiritual practice before, but I think I'd like to give it a try. So I come to the door. Who would be the first person who'd speak to me?"

"Reception."

"Okay," I say, laughing. "So I come to reception and say, 'Hi! I wanna try this out. Your sign says "meditative inquiry." I want to learn how to inquire meditatively.' What's the receptionist going to say?"

"'So you're interested in this work?'" Then in a deeper voice, gently making fun of me, "'Yes.' 'So there are some people here if you want to meet, if you are interested.'"

"And who are those people? Who would I be directed to?"

"Me or whoever is here. Wayne. She can choose."

"Let's say you're the person here today. So the receptionist directs me to you, and I tell you that I've read a little bit about meditation, maybe even tried it out. But basically I feel there's something missing in my life, and I'd like to see if there's something more I can get by coming here."

"Okay. So, let's look at this desire that you can get something from here. So we begin to explore. Let's look at the intention, motivation that brought you here. And that, factually, is meditative inquiry. Let's explore right now all these motivations that brought you here. What ideas are there? And let's put it all open. Let's air the whole thing out. So it's an inviting."

"So it comes back to what Toni Packer said to you, 'This is your koan.'"

"That's it," she says, almost in a whisper. "And can be through questioning if we have motives within. You know? Kind of, 'I came sometime with a confused mind and there is this….' You felt it here in the circle. You or anybody can ask a question that can bring some person to see that the mind is going zzzzoom! So – you know – this is a space for everything. There can be some wisdom that's not coming from you but coming from just the seeing what is going on."

"So, if I went to Mount Baldy, for example, or if I went to Dai Bosatsu, I would be taught a practice. Following the breath. Counting the breath. Maybe given a koan. But here, I would be told to inquire…."

"Invited to inquire what is happening right now. You know, Rick, we start where we are. Does that make sense? We start where we are. So, I even can say that in this kind of looking at what has been brought right now – the question, 'What is meditative inquiry?' and 'I want to change' – that is what is here. This is what is concrete and factual. So not coming from an idea of what Springwater is. So isn't that already directly coming from this moment? Invited to this moment?

"When we engage in practice there is an assumption that hasn't been looked at; there is a feeling a person has that he needs something. And that is false. So why start with something false? That 'If I do this, this, this, this and that – how many years – I am going to get some enlightenment, some release.' When the truth is that there is no problem. When the understanding is there, you don't feed that. You start with the reality that right here" – clapping her hands – "we are fine. When the mind is right here, not making a scene or making a problem, we're fine with what we are, really."

It is my question about the function of meditative inquiry that provokes the 41 second pause before Wayne replies. "I'm wondering about the word 'function,'" he says finally.

"What does it do?"

"The quick answer is that there's no doing in meditative inquiry, that meditative inquiry is an open listening without any doing and without a doer. In this open wondering there is no going forward and no accumulation, all of the things that we generally associate with doing or functioning. So to me it's somewhat like asking, 'What is the function of breathing or of the sun shining?' We could break it down, and we could look at the scientific changes that occur or our psychological reactions to a sunny day or a grey day or continual rainy days. But in the moment, this moment, there is sunshine, listening, breathing and a wondering that we can call meditative inquiry. What is the function? There's an alive, aware, breathing body – bodies – and the 'function' is not separate from the totality of life."

"How does it differ from zazen?"

"I really don't know; I haven't used that word in recent years. But what comes to mind is that zazen involves sitting quietly and motionlessly. I was about to say the practice of sitting quietly, but let's stay with the simplicity of quiet sitting. We don't have to add words. So sitting quietly is – in my experience – conducive to what we are calling meditative inquiry. And we call it meditative inquiry for lack of a better phrase; there's nothing frozen about the language. Sitting quietly is conducive to meditative inquiry, to awareness, but it's also an embodiment of meditative inquiry and awareness."

"Do you see a continuity between what you're doing here and the Zen tradition?"

"It's hard to get into that comparing mode, to see continuity without thinking about past, present, and future."

"Well, I'm not exactly asking you to compare the two. But there is a historical sequence. Toni Packer studied with Philip Kapleau, then she left and established this place. So there's at least that much of a connection."

"Let me approach this in a different way and see if I still answer your question. Reading and hearing words attributed to the Buddha, Bodhidharma, Huang Po or Hui Neng or Roshi Kapleau and Bodhin and others has been – and is – very helpful. Reading words, hearing talks that are alive with the energy of discovery, one is often struck by how vital, how clear the expression is. I don't think so much in terms of continuity but marvel at the aliveness of these words. And, yes, they were said, in some instances over 2000 years ago, but they are fresh and, to this reader, completely new, not as evidence of a lineage but as beautifully simple expressions of what is right before us.

"If there is a tradition, it is a timeless tradition, an untraditional, unconventional tradition. The texts, the words themselves and who said them is not important. What is felt to be vital is what the words point to, what is behind them, the spirit of inquiry. Then we're not using them as a kind of support or as a confirmation of what we think or believe but are really interested in what the person is saying and in exploring that for one's self. What we usually think of as continuity is a building, a moving from step to step to step. This movement of continuity requires thought, involves memory and keeps us from what is actually occurring in this moment. Isn't it wonderful to simply pause, to be here with the feel of the breath, the chair, the light in the room?

"If something is alive to us, it doesn't matter what triggers or fires that interest. And yet there is a beauty to this possibility that we actually are in conversation with what was spoken or written so many years ago. Then the words are alive for me, for people – for any of us – who are truly interested. In Zen and other meditative traditions, there is much that may very well sound incomprehensible but that nevertheless catches you in some way. You really wonder, 'What are they saying, why put something that way, in such an unusual expression?' It catches one's interest and lights a fire, and the vitality of that burning is present. And because we look for causes and explanations, we feel there must be precedent. This doesn't come out of thin air. But can we really know where interest, where insight comes from? Is it okay to not know, to not seek for continuity?

"This is a long answer to your short question: Is there continuity? In a moment of fresh seeing, of waking up, there is no continuity, there is no time. But we could also say yes, that the same energy – the same interest that's been driving human beings, that's been enlivening human beings for centuries – is present. One can sense that presence. Can we trust in that, stay with this presence, this being here?"

"Something I'm reminded of here," I say, "is a Trappist Monastery where I used to go for private retreats. They provide an environment but not much in the way of instruction about what to do with that environment. Is that a fair assessment of what happens here? An environment has been provided for people to undertake – with minimal direction – a personal inquiry?"

"I'll go along with that. But I'll add that there's also a sense that people find strength in working together. And then, again, that might speak to your question about continuity and possible similarities or dissimilarities from more tradition-al centers. The coming together of people in a retreat to sit together, to dialogue together and to question – one on one with the person giving the talks or with each other – facilitates this inquiry. The quiet presence of each other deepens and strengthens the energy of the sitting as well. Even if, in the sitting, something comes up that's disturbing, we may see that it's okay, that it's good that the disturbing stuff is exposed. And there is this possibility of working with each other, seeing what comes up, what kind of clashes may occur, even in a retreat environment. In the work period, in the kitchen or in housekeeping, one may get an unwanted criticism or instruction. It's a chance to see our reactions and our interactions, as they play out, in a silent community, in communion with each other, as well as in what you brought up, in a personal quest."

"But it would not be over-stating it to say there is a minimum of direction provided?"

"I would say, yes, there is a minimum of instruction and that it is purposefully minimal, although we do have guidelines for retreats."

"But those appear to be primarily matters of form. Don't talk during these hours and so on."

"Yeah."

"So let me try an analogy, because this intrigues me. Suppose I'm someone who loves guitar. Now there are some people who can just pick the instrument up and start playing riffs every bit as good as Mark Knopfler or Jimmy Page without any instruction at all. They're the type of people – like my son – who drive me crazy. But then there's somebody like me who plugs away but needs someone there to show me what to do. So I suspect there are people who come to meditative inquiry and are kind of naturals. But there also has to be a lot of plunkers like me who need someone to show them how to make a C chord. What do you do with them?"

"We learn together."

"But that's not going to work because somebody has to tell me, 'Put your finger there. Put that other finger here, and that one here.' I might watch you, and I might learn that way. 'Hey, that's how he's doing that!' But it would probably have gone faster if you'd actually told me what to do."

He pauses again before going on. "In this work, we're not making a C chord, but let's go with the analogy. And we're also not learning to high jump or dance the tango either. In those disciplines, there's a precedent, a standard that has been established. If you're going to dance ballet, you have to train and learn the postures and movements of ballet – I don't know any other way – or it won't be ballet. In meditative work we look at what is presenting itself in the moment: the breath, the sounds and sensations and the thoughts that come and go. We may see, as well, how we are with each other; how we listen or how we don't listen; how we strive and how dissatisfied we often are. We were talking about that yesterday, how sometimes we discover that we're tremendously dissatisfied most of the time. We're in the car, and we're driving down the road, and we're wondering how long it will be until we get to the rest stop or to where we're going to have lunch. And then we have lunch and we're wondering when we'll get back on the road. Or, back on the road, we're wondering when we'll get back home. At home, we wonder when there will be another trip. That's kind of a caricature, and yet when we observe from moment to moment, we begin to discover that there is a constant discontent, a restlessness or uneasiness. And the equivalent of learning the C chord in meditation would be learning a technique, a way to turn the restless mind off – assuming that that is possible – but I'm doubtful.

"We – I – do talk about quiet, about sitting meditation. Well, we don't really use the word 'meditation' so much as simply 'sitting.' And this kind of sitting is a stopping – a pausing and listening – but not as a means to an end. And I don't think this has to be incredibly abstruse or complicated even for somebody coming the first time. Actually it might be more difficult for somebody who has learned a lot of technique, who has trained in a traditional center. But really, we're not asking very much; we're not inviting someone to do some tremendous or heroic feat. We're saying simply, 'See if it's possible to sit quietly and listen.' And if it's boring, to listen to the boredom, to discover something about that. If it's an endless chain of confusing thoughts, to wonder about that. To look at that. As thought begins to quiet itself to listen and to be with that. And see if there's a pull to get thinking again, to get busy. If there's some fear of the quiet, it is wonderful to question into the fear, into the uneasiness. And when we get together in group or private meetings, we can talk about these things that are coming up; that becomes the material that we're working with, what's actually happening. So that's our C chord: What's actually going on, to look and touch the whole, to feel the shape and texture of what comes up. It may all be memory, but we're looking at memory freshly, in this moment. So if there is continuity, it is continuity of presence or stability of presence. In this looking we might begin to wonder if it is possible to stay here, to not always be moving towards or longing for some imagined state.

"And isn't it the same with what we call spiritual progress? We imagine we're going somewhere and that when we get there all our problems will be solved; we'll be sitting on a cloud. Somebody said in the group yesterday, 'There'll be no suffering.'" We both laugh gently. "Good luck. I'd like to look at the possibility that we are already here, that this present moment – even with whatever difficulty might be arising – is the destination, is wholly and totally complete.

"So maybe I never learn to play the guitar very well. But, in that realm – what in Buddhism is called the 'relative realm' – we've got lots of tools. You can go to a good guitar teacher or nowadays you can even study guitar on the internet."

"So that brings me back to my question," I say. "What's the function? What do I get out of doing this? Why bother?"

"Ah! Okay. I thought that's what you meant by your question, that's why I was hesitating. Why bother?" He falls back into one of his silences, then: "Well, what quickly comes up is that the involvement in this work is, for me, choiceless. There has been an itch or an urge for many years to explore this business of being human and all that comes with that including the questions that come up around the matters of birth and death and our life of conflict. What the Buddha called 'suffering,' our greed, anger and ignorance. It wasn't enough for me – or it wasn't satisfying – to merely read about or think about religious questions and concerns.

"The Buddha was reported to have gone to see sages and tried various practices. He did these things and at some point said, 'I'm just going to sit down. I'm really going to look directly and will not get up until this matter is resolved.' There is in that stopping, in that directness, a sense of 'Damn the consequences. I don't know where this is going to lead me, but I'm going to go all the way with this.' Like an explorer who feels certain that there is something. There is a way out; there is an answer.

"Maybe there isn't necessarily a way out, but can there be a resolution to this matter of suffering, to this 'being human' question? The Buddha points to a resolution that he calls right understanding. We might call this being here, presence, or awareness. The word doesn't really matter. This understanding is not the result of a cause, does not come from my scheming, desiring, trying, succeeding, failing, keeping-score mind. There is something – or no-thing – that is none of that. It can't be pinned down in words and yet the sense here is that it is not so far away. At some point, perhaps when we were very young, there was some realization that we're not just these superficial movements of self-pity and envy – this shifting from elation to utter despair – that there's some stability, some presence, and that this presence is very sure and reliable.

"Toni has said that this work is arduous. I would agree that it is hard to look at oneself, at the parts that don't fit one's images and beliefs about oneself. We may have simplified and opened the approach to meditation, but it still can be very difficult at times. For instance, if I like to tell what I consider harmless little jokes, I might, upon reflection, discover that there is anger and aggression in my 'humor.' This can be a really neat thing to discover, but it may also hurt as well. Or I might find that my desire to be helpful is often fueled by my desire to be liked or to be praised. This is not about putting oneself down but discovering how we are from moment to moment. What we sometimes call the 'me circuit' thrives on praise and reassurance and on a kind of intentional ignorance. The work of looking under the covers of this ignoring can be difficult at times.

"There is also a sense here that those who need to find a place like Springwater Center will do so. Coming to this work is choiceless. The 'why's' of meditative work are often the hardest thing to understand and express. Better to let it all be and to come to this with some innocence and humility."

By the time of my visit, Toni was no longer able to see students. I ask Sandra if Toni had any continuing input into the operations at Springwater.

"Not at all," she tells me.

"So already this center is operating independently of her."

"Totally. Always, of course, she's an inspiration, but, I know what you mean. More and more she didn't even want to hear about the daily running of the center. She didn't have the energy. So we just had to" – she claps her hands – "had to mature. You know? And look for ourselves. She is very conscious not to make people dependent on her. Even though we depend. You know? I discovered that I felt a lot of insecurity when I didn't see Toni in group meetings. I went through all that. We all did. But I will say, that now is running well."

"So if I understand you, Toni has identified people to carry on her work, but she hasn't named a successor."

"Yes."

"What about you and Wayne? Are you looking for people who might be able to carry this all into the future?"

"I haven't given one thought about that. Who knows where the whole thing can go. Who knows? I cannot talk to that. I do not know."

I put the question more bluntly to Wayne. "What will happen here when Toni dies?"

"We'll find out. Toni would frequently say something like – and again this is putting it in my own words – 'If you want to find out what's going to happen in the future, find out what's happening now. How are we living this moment, this day?'"

"You'd said earlier that at the coming AGM you're going to look at the role of the teachers."

"Yes. We need to revise the by-laws."

"But realistically, it isn't just a matter of revising by-laws. It's the sense of what's going to become of the community. She was the resident teacher. Whether you use the term or like the term or not, that's what she's been. And probably now one of the three of you, or the three of you together, will become that resident teacher. So in some way you must be preparing yourselves for continuity."

I've become used to his pauses by this time. "Well," he says after a bit, "I'll tell my own story, and it's very short. I came here in the summer of 1984 thinking that it would be wonderful to go to retreats and be on staff for a while, until I returned to the real world. Now I am close to 30 years of being on staff and in Springwater. At some point, when I was still in my early 30s, thoughts like, 'I really need to make a decision. I've got to find out what I'm going to do with my life. Am I going to go to graduate school? Or even, and more accurately, finish college?' I had shared with Toni my confusions and yearnings, but at some point something simply dropped away. I realized that I loved what I was doing and didn't need to think constantly about the future. What needed to happen would present itself. And I shared this with Toni as well. I remember saying that I was just letting the matter rest in the belly, listening and seeing what comes. And it wasn't said in a casual way. And I'm still here and still in that same place. I'm just going to listen, and we'll see what comes. I find that if there is less self-involvement and less worrying, there is more energy for a creative meeting of whatever might be. And I feel that this is the continuity of the Center. And perhaps we can keep on in this really odd way and see if it's possible to discover from moment to moment what we are. How we are. And that doesn't preclude making schedules and asking other people if they would be willing to participate in this work, to lead retreats. We can freely and easily do all of those things. And yet at the same time we can see if it's possible to do so without creating any more structure than is necessary, without creating a new hierarchy. It is the listening, the awareness and the love that flows from the silence and joy of awareness that sustain the Center, and that, for me, sustains a passionate interest in the work of the Center."

The October following my visit to Springwater, I was included in a list of recipients who were sent a group email from the Center:

> Dear Friends,
>
> Our beloved Toni Packer passed away August 23, 2013, in the presence of friends, at the Livingston County Center for Nursing in Mt. Morris, New York. Though she never considered herself to be either a teacher or the founder of a religious center, for many of us she was the embodiment of the possibility of both awareness and meditative inquiry. Her love for what she called the work of this moment was contagious and the clarity she evidenced was radiant.
>
> On October 12, a splendid day of autumn light, warmth and color, over 100 friends and family attended a memorial gathering for Toni at the Center. After a period of quiet meditation together, we listened to a talk by Toni from the July 2002 retreat. Many participants then stood, and gave moving tributes to her and expressed their appreciation of her life and work. Some music followed. Toni was fond of the Beatles "Let it Be," and we sang it together and then an impromptu "Nowhere Man." More music filled the air as the gathering had lunch and enjoyed some chocolate afterwards, remembering Toni's love for it. In the afternoon Toni's son Remo, together with family and friends, spread some of Toni's ashes on the Center land and waters.

On the revised website, Wayne and Sandra, along with Richard Witteman and Stephan Bielfeldt, are now identified as teachers.

CHAPTER TWENTY-TWO

Dosho Port

T HE PIONEERS WHO BROUGHT ZEN PRACTICE TO THIS CONTINENT IN THE 1960s and '70s generally established their centers either on the west coast or in New York state. The two exceptions were Walter Nowick who, somewhat reluctantly, taught in rural Maine, and Dainin Katagiri who inaugurated the Minnesota Zen Meditation Center in Minneapolis in 1976.

Katagiri had come to America thirteen years earlier to serve as an assistant priest at the Soto Temple, Zenshuji, in Los Angeles. The temple was both a spiritual and cultural center for the ethnic Japanese population of the city. It had a large congregation, and several priests, including Taizan Maezumi, were already engaged there. When he left Japan, Katagiri had pictured himself as a missionary bringing Buddhism and Zen to the west, but, when he arrived at Zenshuji, he was assigned to work with the English-speaking second and third generation members, few of whom, if any, had any interest in Zen practice.

During a trip to San Francisco, Katagiri visited Shunryu Suzuki, then the priest of a similar temple. Sokoji was not as large as Zenshuji, but there seemed to be a lot more going on, including a handful of non-Japanese students who showed up at the temple to practice zazen early each morning. When Suzuki invited Katagiri to join him in San Francisco, the younger man happily agreed.

Katagiri was intrigued by but not entirely comfortable with the young Western students. They struck him as undisciplined. They took little apparent care of their appearance or even their hygiene, and it seemed unlikely to him that they could be serious Buddhist practitioners. There were about fifteen when Katagiri started at Sokoji, but the number kept growing. Eventually, the zendo in which they practiced needed to be expanded. Soon after that, the congregation at Sokoji began to resent the time and attention claimed by the meditation students, and Suzuki separated the programs, establishing the San Francisco Zen Center on the corner of Page and Laguna Streets.

Katagiri was the Master of Training at the new center, and students addressed him as "roshi." Although younger than Suzuki, he was more traditional, and his inclination was to impose a stricter discipline; however, he did not dispute Suzuki's authority and deferred to the latter's vision for the center and its operations.

Katagiri's break with Suzuki occurred when it became clear that Richard Baker was being groomed as Suzuki's successor. Katagiri envisioned establishing a center for members of the mainstream society. When he received an invitation from a small group of Zen students in Minneapolis, it appeared he would have an opportunity to do just that. He believed that chilly Minnesota – populated with the hard-working descendants of Scandinavian and German immigrants – would be a more sober environment for Zen practice than San Francisco with its riotous youth population. Katagiri imagined a center where people would come to sit zazen on their way to and from work.

Things did not turn out that way.

Dosho Port has a wry smile and a self-deprecating sense of humor. When I first meet him, he is in mufti with a cap to conceal his shaved head. There is nothing about his appearance to indicate that he's a Zen teacher, but, as I learn later, he dresses up well.

"I was a young person in the '70s, and I was looking for something. I was raised Catholic, and I thought I might become a priest, although with puberty that went out the window. But when I was in elementary school, that was my vocational direction. Then I went to see this priest when I was fifteen or sixteen – you know, small town in Northern Minnesota, still very parochial in a sense – and asked him a number of questions. I don't remember what they were, but it seemed there were inconsistencies in what was being presented and even some hypocrisy. So, I just laid it all out like a teenager might, and he was like, 'Well, you just have it all wrong.' And I think he even used the line about, 'God's way is not for us to understand. It's not our job to understand God.' And it just didn't make sense. It just didn't seem like the right thing for me. So I stopped going to church."

"Was your family very devout?"

"Pretty much. My mom and her mom, particularly, were devout, and, when I was eventually ordained a Buddhist priest, my grandmother was mad at my mom for about a decade. She was completely fine with me because it wasn't my fault that my mother had let me go astray. They reconciled, but she was crabby with her for about a decade."

"She held the grudge that long?"

"Well," he shrugs, with a slight smile. "You'd have to ask her. But I'm telling the story.

"So in college, I tried drugs, sex, and rock-n-roll, and although fun for short periods of time, they weren't satisfying. And I had this friend who took part in many of these experiments with me. One summer, while I was working in a paper-mill in Northern Minnesota, he sent me a book. It came in a brown paper bag he'd duct-taped together, and I think he had written my address on it in black shoe polish. We were wannabe hippies – although it was after the hippie thing – and on the back of the package he'd written, 'I found it!' So I opened it up, and it was *The Three Pillars of Zen*. And when I opened the book, it was one of those 'Damn, maybe he did find it' moments. I started to read it, then sat zazen in my parents' basement with some old couch cushions, and it was a total disaster. The pictures were so militaristic in that version that I just couldn't do it. But it was a very powerful book for me, and I felt like I'd found my practice."

"How old were you?"

"Twenty. Then I came to Minneapolis and was hanging around in this guy's apartment while he was at work, and I started reading the phonebook backwards – I think other people were there and various intoxicants were involved – and I found 'Zen Center.'" He laughs, admitting, "I didn't have a very good attention span, so it was really lucky that it was backwards and it was Z. The Minnesota Zen Center had just started, and later I found out that the place I was living in when I was going to college was two blocks from where Katagiri had been living for several years, and yet I never ran into him or knew about him. So I went over there, and I was deeply impressed. I was impacted by his presence. Couldn't understand a lot of things he said. His English was never very fluent. Although later, traveling with him in Japan, I was amazed to discover that he actually had a hard time understanding Japanese also. I was a special ed teacher by then, and it was like I had diagnosed him as having an auditory learning issue, because often monks would come and say stuff to him, and he'd go, 'What? Oh?' And he did the same thing in English."

"The form of Zen he taught would have been very different from what you read about in Kapleau."

"Yeah. Yeah. And actually after I had zazen instruction from him, I took a pilgrimage to the east coast; hitchhiked out there in, like, November or something and tried to find the Rochester Zen Center. I showed up in Rochester with almost no money and in a snow storm, but I couldn't find the Zen Center. In retrospect, I don't know what happened, but I couldn't find it. It wasn't in the phone book. So I called my girlfriend and had her wire money to me via Greyhound and took the bus back to Minneapolis. Years later, when we were doing a Zen Teachers' meeting in Rochester, Kapleau was there but very old and sick. They kind of wheeled him out into the courtyard with blankets wrapped around him, and we all lined up and came to greet him. When I met him, I smiled and told him I'd read his book and how important it was and how it changed my life. And he kind of looked up and sized me up a little bit and then said" – in a croaking voice – "'For the better, I hope.'

"So I went back to Minnesota and studied with Katagiri. And, you're right, it's a very different style, although my present feeling is that the differences are kind of exaggerated. Everyone needs a foil. So the Soto uses the Rinzai 'gaining mind' as a foil, and the Rinzai uses the Soto 'passivity' and 'wallowing in quiet' as their foil."

After Katagiri and his family moved to Minnesota, the author, Robert Pirsig, donated money to purchase a property on Lake Calhoun. The building had been a half-way house for drug addicts and was in poor repair. Fortunately, instead of the mainstream Americans Katagiri had imagined, among the earliest people to come study with him were a handful of people from Stephen Gaskin's counter-culture commune, The Farm, and they brought with them the carpentry skills needed to renovate the new Zen Center.

"It was an old house," Dosho tells me. "The Katagiris lived upstairs. They had two boys at the time. Eventually we re-did the third floor. It was just two bedrooms. Mostly they lived on the second floor which was also used by the center. The doku-san room was up there and his study. And then downstairs a zendo with maybe twenty or so seats. More could be crowded in the middle. And a little Buddha Hall which had been the dining room of the house. There was a sun porch. So it was functional for us. Sesshin would be in the high teens to twenties. It was always a small group. And there were a lot of ex-hippies or present hippies. The women tended to be therapists, and the men tended to have masters' degrees or Ph.D.s but made their living being carpenters and things like that. It was kind of a wild gig. Katagiri had left San Francisco because he wanted to find 'real Americans.' I don't know if he did. I mean, they were as real as any Americans. There were maybe half a dozen or so people from Gaskin's Farm, so it was a significant group, but they didn't feel predominant to me. They were kind of doing their own thing. Like, when I first came, a guy from the Farm convinced himself that the true way to enlightenment was to do lots of zazen while smoking marijuana. And he was the ino, in charge of the zendo. I don't think Roshi knew what he was doing, but he would go out during breaks and smoke a joint and come back in. By that time, that didn't make any sense to me, but there was this little group that was like that.

"It wasn't a residential program, but – the way I think about it now – it was quasi-monastic because we had a couple of hours of practice in the morning and then everybody went off to work. Then evening zazen. And we had rounds of residential practice periods, which were pretty intense. Quasi-monastic. Then we started a monastery, or what we hoped would eventually become a monastery, in south-eastern Minnesota which is still functional. And we would have practice periods out there, though I don't know if we ever did a full ninety day practice period because the building and the weather just wouldn't accommodate it. But we'd have a sesshin every month, four seven-day sesshin a year. And we did a lot of sitting."

Members of the Minnesota Zen Center had to support themselves, and Dosho needed to find a job. "I had dropped out of college and was reading Gary Snyder and Kerouac and trying to do the Eric Hoffer thing – you know, revering the working man – so I got a job in a warehouse. But it was just so violent and crazy that I was like, 'I can't do it. I'm not one of these guys.' So it was, 'How can I earn a living and still do Zen practice?' That was my main care. So I went back to school and got a teacher's license in special ed."

He worked with students who were deemed to be "at risk."

"EBD – Emotional and Behavior Difficulties – mostly. Basically they were really good at getting adults to dislike them. The whole 'special ed' thing about them having some dysfunction or disability or whatever is just a fantasy. They're just kids, is all." He smiles and adds, "That perspective kind of limited my career mobility in the field.

"Somehow, just the way the way the karmic dice rolled, I ended up working with these 'throw away' kids. There's a lot of them. There's a significant population of African-Americans and Hispanic and various immigrant groups in Minneapolis, and it's a very segregated city. There's still a lot of poverty in the African-American community. So, especially after I came back from Japan, I wound up working in Minneapolis public schools with kids who didn't fit into the middle class white expectations of what they were supposed to be like. And you could see that in the United States it's like a throw-away system that ends with the death penalty. That's what I saw. It starts with getting sent out of class to the principal's office, especially if you're black and male, because you scare us, and you're doing something different, so you're out. And then there's all these grades in between. Prison. Probation. You could see the trajectory in Middle School. Corporate America. Prison America."

The job allowed him to continue practice at the Minnesota Zen Center, and the practice helped him with the job. "There's a stability that comes with practice, the capacity to let things go and move onto the next thing. I also think it develops the ability to empathise with other people without getting tangled up and co-dependent. And then because Zen was my main interest, I was kind of on the outside. So if a kid did something, I was more free to find out what really happened and didn't necessarily take sides with the kid versus the adult or the adult versus the kid."

I ask how he became a priest.

He chuckles before answering. "Yeah. One of the big things now – in Soto Zen in particular – is that priests are sort of like ministers. I certainly didn't see myself becoming a minister by being ordained. I just wanted to study with Katagiri. I heard Leonard Cohen say he studied with Sasaki, and if Sasaki had been a shoe-maker or something like that, he would have done that, become a shoe-maker, because he was connected. He just wanted to do what this guy was doing. And that's how it was for me. In my imagination anyway, I could think that if he was doing something else, that's what I would have wanted to do. And the forms – the robes, the bowls – were important to him, and, even though I didn't really fully or even partially get what that was all about at the time, I wanted to be in those clothes because he was. I wanted to see what it was like to be doing what he was doing and connect with him like that.

"So after studying with him for about three years, I told him during a dokusan that I wanted to be his disciple. He probably thought I was asking for Dharma transmission or something. It was, like, ten years later, after he died, that I looked back, and thought 'Oh!' But when I said I'd like to be his disciple, he sat there it seemed like forever. Maybe it was three minutes. And he had this frown, this inverted smile that was really a huge Bodhidharma face, and he looked up and said" – in a Japanese accent – "'It's not so easy.' Then he rang me out.

"Then about three years later, I'd kind of forgotten about it. I was board president of Zen Center at that time, and we were working on the calendar for the next year. I wanted to schedule something on some particular date, and he said, 'No, we can't do it that weekend because that Saturday is your ordination.' 'Oh yeah? That's interesting.' And he said, 'Yeah. So, have you sewn your robe?' 'No, I haven't sewn any robe. But I will, Roshi! I will sew my robe!'"

"What did ordination mean for him?"

"That's an interesting question. In the early days, we didn't really talk about it, and he was pretty evasive about it. It was a 'learn by doing' thing, so he wasn't into explaining. It was that Japanese style where you just had to put your body into it and just do it. And I don't think he was real clear about what it would be. A number of people wound up quitting about that time. A year or two before he got sick, he announced he wasn't going to ordain anybody anymore. He was going to take some time to figure this out."

"Well, for example, in the Kapleau tradition," I point out, "ordained persons are expected not to work outside the temple."

"The expectation was more that you'd be moving in that direction and do what you could to make the Dharma your life and kind of formalize your Dharma life eventually. Become kind of a spiritual professional. That was a phrase he enjoyed. He also emphasized that the point of the practice was to be able to continue the practice forever. He would say, 'No matter what conditions arose – whether you're without community, without teacher, without friends – continue the practice forever.' So that even if only one person did it, that was good."

In 1989, Dainin Katagiri was diagnosed with terminal cancer. Hoping to ensure the continuation of his work, he gave transmission to twelve of his students, including Dosho, but chose not to identify any one of them as his principal heir. It was his intention that they would remain peers, equally responsible for continuing the spread of the Dharma. It was, however, important to Katagiri that his heirs further their training in Japan.

"Katagiri Roshi wanted me to go to this training monastery in Japan – Zuioji – after he died," Dosho explains to me. "I had already planned to go on pilgrimage to Japan after receiving Dharma transmission. So during our last conversation, when he seemed to be doing pretty good – they thought he might be in remission – we had a debate for several hours about this monastery, which was kind of a monks' finishing school. It was very strong on etiquette, and, at the time, I didn't respect it. Finally he was like, 'Well, okay. Go to there for one month. And after one month, if you don't want to stay there, fine. You can leave.' And I said, 'Deal.' So after one month, right to the minute, I left. I'd happened to run into an old Zen friend on the plane going to Japan who had connected somehow with Tangen Harada at Bukkokuji.[76] So when I left the training monastery, I called Bukkokuji and said, 'Can I come?' And they said, 'No. Not really. We're not that interested in having you come here. If you aren't happy where you are, you probably won't be happy here either. So, no. Don't come.' So then, of course, I just went. And it was really an eye-opening experience to see the intensity of practice they actualized there."

After a year in Japan, Dosho returned to Minneapolis but didn't remain there long. He felt the atmosphere at the Minnesota Zen Center had become slack since Katagiri's death, and, because Katagiri had not appointed one, there was no formal teacher.

So in 1994, Dosho established his own group, Clouds in Water, which eventually relocated to Saint Paul.

"Why did I want to teach?" he repeats my question reflectively. "Well at the time, I think it was mostly because I felt obligated to. I had told Katagiri I would. I also thought I had something to share with people. But obligation, at first, was the biggest part of it."

To Dosho's surprise, his Minneapolis students showed some resistance to moving to Saint Paul. "The place we went to was just ten miles from where we had been meeting, and we went there because we were looking for the right place to meet, and it was a good place for us. But it was a bigger deal than I thought because a lot of people in Minneapolis didn't want to cross the bridge to Saint Paul. So at first the group dropped by about half, and then it really bloomed."

At its height, Clouds in Water had 150 members. Dosho remained the guiding teacher and executive director for ten years.

"Then, as my mother said, I had a mid-life crisis. I fell in love with a woman who was a student and the training coordinator. We left the center in 2004 and eventually settled in White Bear."

White Bear is a small community northeast of Minneapolis. Dosho's brother, who lived nearby, was going to Japan for six months and needed someone to house-sit. "And we just loved the area. It was really relaxing. One factor was my work in Minneapolis. By that time, I was working with some really intense kids, and I would run into them in grocery stores and on the streets when I was with my own kids, and that didn't feel right. I really didn't want to see these kids on the streets. So that was part of it. White Bear was a little removed from where I worked. I could leave work and have a different life out there."

I ask what he means by "intense kids."

"There were kids who committed murder, but also kids who were murdered. It was almost a weekly kind of thing, and it got to the point where my partner wouldn't want to watch the news with me because I was always saying, 'Oh, shit! I know that dude!'"

Both his own practice and his approach to teaching underwent some changes after his move to White Bear. He facilitated a much smaller zendo, called Wild Fox, which met in his basement family room. At the same time, he began koan study with the teachers of Boundless Way.

In his book, *Keep Me in Your Heart a While*, Dosho quotes Katagiri as saying: "In Rinzai Zen, they sit with many questions, many koans. In Soto Zen, we have just one big koan, so called shikantaza."⁷⁷ Through assiduous practice and adherence to the Four Vows, Katagiri's students sought to develop what he called "Selfishnessless." It was a challenging practice which promised, in Katagiri's words, "no sweet candy."

"I've come to think that the purpose of the koan system and the purpose of the Soto shikan taza system is the same," Dosho tells me. "As I see it, what Harada and Yasutani did was simplify the koan system so that it was portable. I don't think that was their intention, but, as a result of what they did, it was possible for Westerners to do their system without being Chinese classics scholars. So their system could sprout in the west. At the same time, Shunryu Suzuki and Katagiri and others here were trying to figure out how to help people, how to teach people to practice here, and so they simplified the monastic system, including zazen, in order to make it more portable. But without a monastic container, Soto Zen probably isn't complete as a system. I mean, people can be believers, but to actually taste the truth of Zen and open that up in their life without some kind of koan orientation is rare. It's possible, but it's rare.

"And also there's no system within Soto Zen – including the monastic system – that helps people move beyond the first opening. People in Soto Zen and the shikan taza system have kensho experiences, but, because there isn't the whole process of koan introspection following that, they don't have anything which makes it work in their lives. Integrates it. I think the koan system has that major advantage. Now, I think it's possible that if you to stay in a monastery for many years the difference isn't as big because then you have the forms you're coming up against constantly and there's the integration practice there."

"James Ford's teacher, John Tarrant," I mention, "calls koans a 'designed learning system.'"

"Yeah, I think that's true. I think the people that framed it, especially when you go back and work through the ranks with it, it's 'Damn! They really knew what they were doing.' They were really smart. I wasn't smart enough to get it while I was going through it, but it's like, 'Oh! They really structured this thing!' A lot of the questions seem arbitrary, but actually it's incredibly well thought through. So it's a very advanced kind of educational system. Discovery model. Outcome based. At least since Hakuin.

"I once asked Tangen Harada what the difference was between muji and shikan taza. He was sitting in dokusan with his little kyosaku, which he used to smack you with. Especially when you bowed and couldn't see it, he'd give you a crack on the back. He went" – speaking in a Japanese accent and making a sweeping motion with his hand – "'Muji – hhhoooo!' You know, like with a machete. Just missed me by a bit. Then he composed himself and went, 'Shikan taza!' and threw the kyosaku on the floor, and it kind of bounced. But, of course, people do get into it. Shikan taza's difficult. You really have to be grounded in breath. The koan system kind of tricks you into shikan taza. It's a very effective system like Tarrant told you. It's very sly. And on the Soto side, it's just open space, and that works too, in a way."

Because Dosho's work was in Minnesota and the Boundless Way teachers were in New England, it was difficult for him to meet with them as often as he would have liked, so he completed a large portion of his koan work by using Skype. When I express surprise, he tells me, "I agree that from the student's seat, at least, it's harder to do it that way for a lot of reasons. To make a koan presentation via Skype is more difficult. To try to connect with the teacher and enter that koan together is more difficult. But it can be done, especially since I've known James for years, and I've done sesshin with Melissa, David, and Josh. I think when you know each other beforehand, information is already present; you can kind of get the person in a different way. But I agree, and there's been some discussion about that on the teacher list-serves. Although some people are kind of fundamentalist about the on-line stuff being the wave of the future and that it has everything that meeting in person has, the preponderance of views is that it's kind of okay but has limitations. But almost everybody's doing on-line work, and probably most koan teachers are doing some koan work on-line."

In the spring of 2013, Dosho began his own on-line program, Vine of Obstacles. "I'm trying to find a way to use the technology without abusing Zen. The thing is that the number of people interested in going really deeply is a small group widely dispersed. So I tried to find some way to connect those people. And it's been very successful – much more successful than I expected – in terms of the practice people do."

During my second meeting with Dosho, I am introduced to one of his current students, Zenki, whose first contact with Dosho had been through the Vine of Obstacles website. Zenki had studied with Daido Loori at Zen Mountain Monastery but after that had been without a teacher for several years. "For me, the on-line practice was the only practice I had," he tells me. "I had been sitting by myself for a long time, which was kind of skeletal, and I missed sitting with a sangha and having a sangha. I really missed having a teacher. And so finding the on-line sangha was a lifeline to my practice, and it accelerated my practice."

Zenki had started koan study with Daido, and Dosho invited him to continue to work with koans while participating in the Vine of Obstacles program.

"But it must be a different dynamic than face to face work with a teacher," I suggest.

"A better dynamic than with Daido," Zenki tells me. "Because with Daido I didn't have as much access. I had much more access to Dosho than I did with Daido. The only time I had access to Daido was when I was at ZMM for sesshin."

"The other part of Vine of Obstacles that I think helps people is that they can see other peoples' practice," Dosho says. "The forums we have within the moodle allow for people to be aware of each other's practice more than they would in an in-person group. I think the course work is valuable, but I think getting a bead on what other people are actually doing both encourages people and humanizes the practice. They realize, 'I'm not the only one who's having trouble with this. I'm not the only one who isn't instantly in samadhi every time I sit.'"

He admits, however, that there are limitations. "Body practice – proper posture, how you hold yourself – is important in the Soto tradition, and it's hard to convey that on-line. You can't really see how people are sitting or whatever. And there isn't the sense of people being together and practicing together. So in that sense, it's two-dimensional. But people practice. Some maybe 20 or 30 minutes a day, and there are others who sit a couple of hours a day. People are doing serious practice this way. So I don't think of it as 'instead of'; I think it's a supplement to the in-person stuff. Because you can't do sesshin on-line; you can't do ordinations and things like that on-line."

There are a number of ways, besides the availability of on-line teaching, in which the current environment differs from that in which the American Zen pioneers operated.

"In the early days, Zen was very competitive," Dosho reflects. "Although we were in these little islands with no internet and really no connection to each other – there weren't any conferences or anything – once in a while, some runaway would straggle in from some place, and we'd pump him for information. But we were definitely our own planets. And we were competitive about what our schedules were and how much we sat and how intense it was, how difficult our place was. Today it seems like it's the opposite. Now it's competitive about whose center is the most accommodating. I was at this workshop and there was this young guy there – cute young guy – and he's like, 'Um…what is the minimum amount of asceticism necessary in order to practice Zen?' Now they're competitive that way!"

"One aspect of that earlier competitiveness," I start, "was that students competed with one another, each one wanted to become…."

"Yeah, the one true successor."

"On the other hand, there didn't seem to have been very many parishioners – people who took up Zen practice but kept their day jobs, raised families and did other things – the type of people that, from what I can tell, Katagiri Roshi seemed to have originally envisioned coming to the Minneapolis Zen Center."

"Yeah. People who come by once in a while and get the vibe and support it and stuff like that," Dosho says, nodding his head. "In takuhatsu in Japan – even though Zen is probably dying there – these little old ladies come out. They look like they're living in poverty, but they'll put $75, $100 in the bowl, and they'll just be crying, their faces flushed in gratitude at the opportunity to do it. You know? Americans aren't that way! We want it for us. And I understand it. I'm that way. So I think there has to be some broader connection, like you're saying. I think that's changing some. A lot of the centers are surviving now by becoming mini-churches and having children's practice and those kinds of things. And there's certainly some positive aspects to that, but the negative is that you can water down the practice. And because most places are so small, you can't be all things to all people so you have to pick and choose. And if you wind up being a church, you can't really train anymore."

Borrowing a term from James Ford, Dosho foresees a "coming great contraction" in North American Zen. There are centers which no longer have teachers and others where the teachers are aging. "So the trajectory's unclear. And a lot of them, like Springwater, were very centered on a personality. So what happens next?"

"There have been successful transitions," I point out. "In Rochester, for example, Bodhin might even be a little better teacher than Kapleau was. San Francisco – after they resolved all the craziness of the '80s – has had a number of successful transitions. What about Minneapolis?"

"No. I don't think it was successful. And I suppose it was Katagiri's responsibility that it wasn't. Basically he just – what's the term? – abdicated? He had cancer and was sick as hell for the last year of his life. So he just said, 'I gave Dharma transmission to these people. It's not my problem. Pick somebody.'"

"What do you think would be necessary to ensure that Zen remains viable in North America?" I ask.

"I don't think we've established that Dharma ecology yet you were talking about, where there are people engaged in the world who are practicing as well as people who are supported in some way to work with the Dharma in monastic-type settings so they can access the deeper level samadhi insights available when you cut away all the difficulties of daily-life. I think that's slowly starting to change. I don't know if it's enough to keep things going, but people are starting to specialize. And when there are specialists collaborating, then it gets healthier and healthier. So that's at least one piece of it.

"I also don't think we've had – maybe since Suzuki Roshi's *Zen Mind, Beginner's Mind* or Kapleau's *Three Pillars* – somebody who can articulate Zen for this culture the way the Dalai Lama and Thich Nhat Hanh can articulate their schools, present it in a way that people can understand what Zen has to offer. Maybe that'll happen, and maybe it won't."

I mention the devotion to Kannon and the metta practices I had encountered elsewhere in my travels.

"Yeah, that's a good idea," he says. "It's a big need in the culture too. There's a lot of Asian teachers who are surprised that so many North Americans hate themselves. You'd be considered psychotic if you hated yourself in Japan. Why would you do that? But for whatever reasons, a lot of Americans are really uncomfortable in their own skins. So we've developed an adaptation of metta practice as a psychological healing practice. I think it's effective. I got a little training in it and have encouraged some students to work with it. People who are really suffering and angry types particularly find it helpful."

Dosho mentions that among his students there are a Catholic priest and a Methodist minister, so he accepts that it isn't necessary to be Buddhist in order to practice Zen. "The question of the overlaps of Christianity or Judaism or whatever and Buddhism isn't something that's been all that important or interesting a question to me personally," he adds. "But I think those two men have come to the same point where instead of looking for overlaps they've concluded there is no overlap. Zen and Christianity are two different things. So they've maintained their Christian beliefs, especially their belief in God, but they're Zen practitioners."

"So is Zen necessarily a religious practice?"

"Probably. I mean, I don't know what you mean by religious, but there is – I think – the aspect of the Great Mystery that I think is really important. And if we lose that sense of the Great Mystery then, it isn't exactly…." He pauses. "I mean, you can secularize it, but it seems to me it's kind of dry at that point.

"But the idea of being a 'Buddhist' is really an American or a Western thing. In Japanese, there's no comparable word for 'Buddd-ist.' They don't '-ist' things like that. People would ask, 'What are you doing?' 'Oh, I'm doing Buddha study.' Or, 'I'm doing flower study.' Whatever there may be. It seems more open; you don't have to identify. I think because we spent centuries killing people because they didn't belong to the right outfit, we have this strong sense that you have to put your chips on the right group or you might get killed. But we don't have to follow that pattern because Buddhism is non-theistic, so you can be atheist or agnostic or Christian."

CHAPTER TWENTY-THREE

Two Teachers in the Kwan Um School of Zen

BARBARA RHODES
RICHARD SHROBE

CHINESE CHAN BUDDHISM SPREAD NOT ONLY TO JAPAN BUT TO KOREA AND Vietnam as well. The Koreans and Vietnamese have their own terms for the tradition – Soen and Thien – but have generally adopted the Japanese term, Zen, in America. The primary expression of Korean Zen on this continent is the Kwan Um School of Zen Master Seung Sahn, who was born, in 1927, to a Presbyterian family in what is now North Korea. He converted to Buddhism after the Second World War and came to the United States in 1972.

He was based in Providence, Rhode Island, and influenced many of the people who would form the second generation of Zen teachers on this continent. John Tarrant, for example, had his first opening experience during one of Seung Sahn's retreats. Before his death in 2004, he had given several students the same title he had: Soen Sa Nim. "Sa" means teacher, and "Nim" is an honorific; the title is generally translated as "Zen Master." Among these heirs are Richard Shrobe, who is now the North American Zen Master of the Kwan Um School, and Barbara (Bobby) Rhodes who is the International School Zen Master. Neither Bobby nor Richard are full-time teachers. Bobby works as a hospice nurse in California, and Richard is a psychotherapist in New York City.

I began my interview with Bobby Rhodes by asking how she pronounces her Dharma name – Soeng Hyang – and what it meant.

"It means 'Nature's Fragrance.' Like incense, kind of."

"And is the title 'Zen Master' roughly equivalent to the Japanese 'roshi'?"

"Well 'roshi' means 'teacher' in Japanese, right? So, yeah, that's basically what it means."

"But you're comfortable being addressed as 'Bobby'?"

"I am. I'm not comfortable with 'Zen Master,' so Bobby's fine. You know, you get in a tradition, and you follow the situation. That's what I did."

"How did you became involved in Zen? What brought you to practice?"

"Well, being born and suffering," she says, laughing. "As I think any child who comes into this world, you see a lot of pain and you have confusing situations. You observe hypocrisy and suffering."

"Hypocrisy?"

"Well, my family went to church regularly, and I didn't think the people there walked the talk. I always questioned why people weren't more pure or more forth-right in their actions, how they were saying a certain thing in church and not doing it in their daily life. I guess I started to notice this more when I was around twelve or so. Twelve or thirteen."

"What religious tradition did your family belong to?"

"Episcopal. And I stayed with it, but it just got more and more difficult. I started to faint in church. It was pretty dramatic. Every time we would come to the Apostle's Creed, I would faint, and I was really trying not to. I tried to sit near a window and get more comfortable and not kneel. But no matter what I was doing, I would just start to get dizzy. When I later told my teacher, Zen Master Seung Sahn, about this, he said" – mimicking his accent – "'Oh! Buddha was trying to get you out of the church!' He said it as a joke, but it was actually something that was pretty visceral with me.

"So I just started to teach Sunday School. Not really teach Sunday School but go and watch and color with the four and five year olds and watch them while every-body else was in church because I still felt kind of religious in the sense that I wanted to be part of things. Then one day this kid came up to me. He was four or five years old, I guess, and he asked, 'Where's Jesus?' And I said, 'God! I don't know.' That was my first koan, really. I swear, it hit me like a koan. He goes, 'Where's Jesus?' I said, 'I don't know.' And he said, 'Well, he was here last week.' And I said, 'He was?' Like that, talking to him as if he was an adult. He said, 'Yeah. You know, he was sitting over there with the black robe and reading us that book.' And what that was was somebody's father had worn a choir robe and was reading Bible stories to the kids. And I said, 'That wasn't Jesus. That was somebody's father.' And he goes, 'Oh!' And that was the end of my Christian experience in the sense of in a church."

"How old were you when this happened?"

"I was a sophomore in high school. I don't know. Sixteen or fifteen. But then I had to take my brother to his first communion. Nobody was around except for me that was willing to take him to church, because my parents were on vacation. So I walked him up to church, and I hadn't been in there for, like, two years. And of course, he was scared because he had to go up to the rail and take communion. So I went up with him. And then the Apostles' Creed started, and I had to leave the church because the same thing started to happen. And I was trying so hard, because my brother really wanted me to hang in there with him. But I had to walk out. And then I fell right on my face and cut my chin open. I had to go the hospital and get nine stitches in my chin, and my brother had to go to the rail by himself.

"So it was something that was hitting me strongly. Just as they said, 'on the third day he rose again and sat at the right hand of God,' that would just drive me nuts. I said, 'Well, where is God's right hand?' I think I was really ripe for koan practice, because I had that kind of mind. 'Where is God's right hand? Who sits by the left hand?' I don't know." There is a note of wonder in her voice even now. "It was really something. It was really my karma coming out where I needed to see it and touch it more intimately than those prayers I was repeating."

"Was it the act of reciting 'I believe' that you were reacting to?"

"Yes, because I didn't really believe it. And I was really trying not to react like that. I was not an hysterical person. I was popular in school. I had a sense of humor and was physically active. Just a pretty normal kid. Lots of friends. So I was really trying not to be weird and not to have that happen. I joined the choir and thought if I'm up in the choir it won't happen. But it was even worse up there. So I had to get out of the choir. And when I cut my chin when I fell flat on the cement, that's when I finally stopped."

"I went to three years of a diploma program at a nursing school and was thrown into a really acutely active hospital in Washington DC. That was really my first temple. We worked non-stop, and, back then, you only had two weeks of vacation a year. But I loved it. I loved medicine, so I was just thrown into the scene. There was a huge amount of physical suffering and psychic suffering in the hospital. And while I was there, Martin Luther King got killed and Washington burned; parts of the city were in flames. It was a really amazing time in my life to be in nursing school. I took care of somebody who tried to burn himself in front of the Capital Building. I spent a whole eight hour shift with him and watched him die. He had the most beautiful eyes. I couldn't talk to him. He was totally wrapped in bandages except his eyes and his mouth, and he was so sick. But just having things that intense happen, watching people come in with gunshot wounds, all those years of actively seeing so much suffering – and a lot of joy as well – that was my first Zen experience, I think. Being in that hospital for those three years.

"And when I got out, I still hadn't done psychedelics. I wasn't drinking or anything. I was just working. So for someone my age – I was seventeen when I went in and twenty-one when I left – when most people would be partying in college, I was working. But happy. I never went to a bar in my whole life until a couple of times on vacation when I got much older, in my forties. I remember sitting at a bar with someone and saying, 'This is the first time that I've sat at a bar!' You know? So it's not like I was a substance person. But after I graduated from nursing school, I worked in a free clinic for Mexican-American farm laborers in the San Joaquin Valley, and the doctor I worked for was into psychedelics. And he introduced me to marijuana and LSD, which was really good for me. I was out there for about two years in the desert. I never did drugs at a party or at a concert. I would just walk out and be with nature. And really it was a huge lift for me to do that. But after two years, I had had enough of it. I was tired; I wasn't learning new things from it. But I always bow to those things because they woke me up. I saw the potential that consciousness has. Then I started reading Krishnamurti."

"How did you find out about Krishnamurti?"

"Out there in California, everybody knew everything. So I just started talking to people about stuff, and somebody turned me onto him and D. T. Suzuki. I just loved that stuff. And I sort of leaned towards Zen because I thought it was so direct. You know? And I wanted to do koan practice. So I went to the San Francisco Zen Center, but they don't do koans. Actually, I didn't go to the Zen Center. I went to Tassajara, and I couldn't get in because they were having a sesshin. But I talked to a couple of the monks there, and they told me that they didn't do koan practice. So, right away, I said, 'Well, okay.' They were so sweet, but I just wasn't interested. Then I ended up coming out to the east coast and met my teacher."

I ask what had brought her East.

"I hadn't spoken to my parents for a while. They were living in Rhode Island, just outside of Providence. And I hadn't spoken to them for two years, because I just needed a break. So on an acid trip, this voice came to me: 'You've got to go make amends with your parents and go meet your teacher.' Some intuitive thing knew my teacher was out on the east coast. And they were both in the same state, that teeny little state of Rhode Island."

She looked for an apartment in Providence, and one of the places she looked at was above Seung Sahn's temple. She didn't take that apartment, but, after overcoming some anxiety about doing so, she did come back and knock at the temple door.

"At first, I was scared to go because I'd read all these Japanese books about getting hit. So I was afraid he'd be too severe. When I finally had the nerve to visit him, it was great. He was down on the floor doing calligraphy and was very sweet and friendly. And there was an American university student there who walked me around the apartment, showed me things, and introduced me to my teacher. And then, when I was leaving, he spoke hardly any English, but he said" – imitating his accent – "'Come back! Come back! We have a Dharma talk on Sunday.' He got up and walked me to the door and encouraged me to come back on Sunday to hear his talk. So I did that. And I liked him. I liked him very much. I liked how he taught."

The "temple" was actually a two bedroom apartment. Seung Sahn had one of the bedrooms; two of his students shared the other. Two weeks after meeting him, Bobby also moved in. "We had a big living room that we turned into a zendo and put up an altar. I slept in the Dharma room. I was a hippie, so I was fine. I was used to sleeping on the floor."

They lived in the apartment for two years, until the number of people who came to sit grew too large to be accommodated in the living room zendo.

"There were probably seven of us who were really steady students after two years. And he told us that we each had to give $1000 for a down payment on a house. And, you know, he never had anything. He was always very generous. So we all came up with the money. I had a job – I was nursing – so I gave him more than a thousand, and altogether we came up with about $8000. Back then, it was enough to put a down payment on a four-decker house in Providence. And that's where we moved and lived for about fifteen years before we bought another place."

She remained in residence for sixteen years, raising a child during that time. It wasn't until her daughter was ten that she moved out.

"We had retreats once a month. They were usually two or three days long. We did that consistently every month. And we had temples in Boston, New York, New Haven, so I would often go down and do those. Before I had my child, I was probably in two or three retreats a month. Actually, I worked every other weekend, so I would do the retreats the other weekends." She laughs gently. "I was very devoted. I loved doing the retreats. The meditation helped tremendously. I always found myself doing a retreat on a weekend and being totally refreshed Monday morning and really feeling how much the practice helped my job so beautifully."

"How so?"

"It was hand-in-hand. Like I said, I'd do a retreat on the weekend or we practiced every day; we practiced every morning and every night. And it helped me with the paramitas, with generosity and patience and gratitude. I always wanted to be a nurse, and I wanted to be a nurse even more as I practiced. It helped me to be a good nurse. And koan practice helped too, because I wouldn't know how to be with certain people and what they needed, and I would use it as a koan. I'd walk to their room; I'd focus on who I was going to see and how they were and try to be there, in the moment, with them. And I started to watch intuition kicking in much more than it had when I was younger. I felt like the whole practice was helping my intuition and my patience and my gratitude."

"In the mid-'60s," Richard Shrobe tells me, "I got involved in meditation practice and yoga with an Indian guru, Swami Satchidananda who founded an institution here in the United States called the Integral Yoga Institute. I was about 25 and had come to New York to be a jazz musician, and I was struggling, having a lot of issues trying to be a freelance musician around New York. I was also married and had one child. And someone gave me a book on yoga and meditation, which I read, and it seemed to speak to me. And that's how I initially got involved."

He was also a heroin user at the time. "It was part of the jazz culture," he explains. "I don't exactly know what made me go for it, but I did. And I struggled with that for a couple of years, and one of the ways out was practicing yoga and meditation."

"They helped?"

"Yes. I mean, when I read this initial book that I referred to, two things hit me. One is that we're always running after pleasure and creating pain. That's obvious to someone who has a drug problem," he says, laughing. "And second was that meditation practice is a way of attuning to something deeper and more fundamental in one's self, and I had had that experience – a little bit – through playing music occasionally, when you feel completely at one with the instrument, completely at one with what you were playing. So I understood what they were talking about."

"How long were you with Swami Satchidananda?"

"About four or five years. And I lived in a residential community here in New York. My wife, I, and my older daughter. We lived there for about four years."

"Were your wife and daughter practitioners as well?"

"Oh, yeah. My daughter was very young then, so her participation was limited."

"What about your family? Were you raised in a religious tradition?"

"I was raised Jewish."

"So how did your family react when you became a Hindu?"

"Well, I think the fact I wasn't using drugs anymore meant something. But also I remember periodically my father would ask me – both when I was practicing with

Swami Satchidananda and later when I was practicing with Seung Sahn – he would ask me things like, 'Is Zen a religion or a way of life?' And I remember one day asking him exactly how did he see the difference in those two? You know? And I would tell him it was more a way of life than an organized religion as such. But that's not totally true either, although I think it's true to a large degree. But he never had an answer when I put it back on him. He was still a practicing Jew."

"Was it an orthodox household?"

"No. It was one of those things where they would go to synagogue on the high holidays – Rosh Hashanah, Yom Kippur – and have a Passover Seder. But it wasn't like they were going to synagogue on a weekly basis. Although my father did start going almost every morning after my mother died. It helped him to calm down and feel a part of something."

"How did your involvement with the Yoga Institute come to an end?"

"It felt like it was time to be a little apart from this kind of residential community situation. And I wasn't as...enamoured with this Indian teacher as I had been in the beginning. I still respected him, but I felt I needed some distance. There were a number of reasons. One was I just felt I was, in a certain sense, not finding myself adequately, and the approach of Hindu yoga – if I were to contrast it with Zen practice – there's more of an emphasis on internalization and going inward and finding some quiet, still place within oneself. And I began to feel that that kind of meditation was not the greatest thing for me because I could be detached enough without that."

There were also internal problems in the community. "There was a sexual affair that occurred," he admits. "But I want to say that wasn't the sole or even the main motivator for us leaving. There were other reasons. We had other needs, I think."

He had read some books on Buddhism. "I remember reading *Zen Mind, Beginner's Mind.* I remember reading some books by Trungpa Rinpoche, *Meditation in Action* and *Cutting Through Spiritual Materialism.* I read Kapleau Roshi's book, *The Three Pillars of Zen.* And my approach to meditation was beginning to change in that direction. More emphasizing present-centeredness and awareness rather than internalization. Anyway, that summer we went to visit some friends of ours in Connecticut. In those days, we were pretty poor, and we used to visit our friends for a vacation – you know? – those who lived out in the country. So this couple said to me, 'We met this Korean Zen Master who has a center in Providence, Rhode Island, and Cambridge, Massachusetts.' And where they were living was up near the border of Connecticut and Massachusetts and Rhode Island, so it wasn't very far. Maybe an hour from there. So they said, 'He's leading a retreat this weekend in Cambridge. Would you be interested in going?' So I said, 'Okay, I'll go for one day.' Because my wife and kids were with me, and my wife didn't drive at that time, so I didn't want to leave them alone too long. But, anyway, I went for one day of this retreat, and I met Zen Master Seung Sahn and had two interviews with him. One the first morning, and then I stayed overnight and had another interview the second morning, and then I left. And he told me that he had a center in New York and that I could go and practice there. That's how I got involved."

"Do you remember your first impression of him?"

"Yeah. That he was quite vital and alive, and I liked this teaching phrase that he had: 'Don't know!' 'What am I?' 'Don't know!'" He chuckles. "Something like the story of Bodhidharma in front of the Emperor, where the Emperor asks him, 'Who are you?' And Bodhidharma says, 'Don't know.'"

"How was he different from your previous teacher?"

"There was less of a mystique around him than there had been around Swami Satchidananda. It's a matter of degree, and I don't want to make it sound like Swami Satchidananda was holding himself up as some other-worldly figure, but I felt Master Seung Sahn was more down to earth in certain ways and more direct."

"Hindu teachers have occasionally been accused of promoting 'guru worship,'" I note.

"Yeah."

"And there are stories of Master Seung Sahn's students affecting Korean accents after they'd been with him for a while."

Richard nods his head and laughs. "Yeah. Or using some phrases that became like slogans. And sometimes with the students affecting the Korean accent, there was a kind of humor. Soen Sa Nim's English was very limited and very unusual, just because of how much he knew and the phrases he would use to say something. And so sometimes there was a kind of tongue-in-cheekness about using those phrases. Kind of love and joking around at the same time."

"You said you started working with him in New York. He lived in Providence. Was there a resident teacher in New York?"

"No. He would come once a month – when he was on the east coast – to lead a three-day retreat. It would start on a Thursday evening and end on Sunday morning. And there were a couple of American students living there, holding down the fort. And there was also a Korean monk, because the American Zen Center and the Korean sangha were together in one facility. So they had their equivalent of Sunday-morning-go-to-church style Buddhism, and we had our Zen practice. And sometimes some of them would come and sit with us as well."

"But generally the Korean community kept separate from the American community?"

"Yeah."

"So, weekend retreats. Were there longer training periods?"

"There were, but I very rarely – if ever – participated in them because I had three children who were growing, and I had a profession that I was trying to get off the ground and make enough money to support my family."

"Were you still a musician?"

"Well, in the sense that I still play and practice the piano – which is my instrument – and I get together periodically with some other musicians to play. But I had gone to social work school and was working as a clinical social worker and went into private practice during those years."

"How did you get interested in that?"

"Initially, when I still lived in the Yoga Institute, a friend of mine was running a yoga component in a drug-rehab program, and he got burnt out and asked me if I was interested in taking over for him. That was just at the time where I had gotten my undergraduate degree, and initially I was considering getting education credits and teaching music in the public school system. But working in this drug program appealed to me, so I said, 'Okay. I'll try that.' So I started doing a mixture of teaching yoga classes and meditation, and then I got trained in running encounter groups. And after a few years of working there, it became clear that if you want to remain in the mental health profession, you had to get some sort of degree so you could be licensed. So I first explored getting a Ph.D. in clinical psych, but it was too long and drawn-out a process. The second option was to go to social work school. That's what I did. In fact, at the time when I met Zen Master Seung Sahn, I was in social work school."

I ask Bobby Rhodes how she became a teacher.

"Well, Soen Sa Nim made us start giving talks. I'd only been there six weeks or something, and he made me give a talk. He said he wanted us to all start helping him promote the Dharma. So the first talk I gave, I was so nervous. I had a copy of *Zen Mind, Beginner's Mind*, and I remember just going off and reading it in a park. I read my favorite passage or whatever and basically just regurgitated it." She laughs. "I was so nervous, I had diarrhoea before I had to give the talk. I really had performance anxiety. And he was just sitting there, nodding and smiling the whole time, and he didn't even understand half of what I was saying, because his English wasn't that good. And he told me it was a great talk. And it was a terrible talk. But it was like he wanted us to become comfortable sharing the Dharma as well as we could. So right away, he got us teaching, and before we moved out of that first temple – so within two years – he made three of us what he called 'Dharma teachers.' And we got longer robes, which – you know – is really not heard of. In Korea, they can't stand it that any of us got long robes. But that's what he wanted to do, and that's how he set up the organization. So I was called a Dharma Teacher by the time I'd only been there two years. And I think it did more good than harm. I think we just shared our enthusiasm for the practice and got to be better teachers as time went by."

"So you're pursuing a social work career and doing Zen at the same time," I say to Richard. "What was the process that led to you becoming a teacher?"

"That was his judgement call. I was never someone who did long retreats or went to Korea or any of those kinds of things that many people did in the course of their training. I was just very steady in my practice and very steady in showing up when he was around, having interviews with him, and he had a regular regimen of kong-ans[78] that he used as one indicator of a student's readiness to begin to teach. So if you had passed this regimen of kong-ans and he felt that your center was fairly strong and your everyday life was in order, then he felt he could make you a teacher."

"But not full-time. You still had a day job?"

"Yes. I made it clear to the rest of the teachers in the Kwan Um School that I was not going to let this totally consume my life, that I had a family and I had other things that I wanted and needed to do. So I kept a balance between these various things to the best of my ability."

"Zen helps us to be clear and compassionate and wise and move in the right direction," Bobby says.

"What does that mean?"

"It means be yourself, be your true self."

"How does it accomplish that?"

"By helping you drop your tethers, your karmic hindrances and waking up to your true self."

"Zen is a practice of becoming clear," Richard tells me, "returning to your original mind before concept and opinion and idea, and from that position being able to connect with circumstances and be helpful."

"Is there a difference between the way the Japanese Schools and the Korean School approach this practice?"

"Not fundamentally, I would say. The flavor might be a little different in terms of the cultural underpinnings. Also, the degree to which some particular center adheres to an Asian flavor as opposed to a modification of Asian flavor with American flavor. But essentially I think the bone of Japanese Zen and Korean Zen and Chinese Chan is all the same."

"Is there a methodology?" I ask Bobby. "A technique?"

"Well, pay attention to the moment. Over and over and over again."

"Is that more important than seated meditation?"

"Well, it's fluid. My teacher, Zen Master Seung Sahn, taught that lying down, sitting up, walking, eating, anything you're doing, brushing your teeth, to pay attention to that moment. So the sitting is not any more important than brushing the teeth as long as you're staying in the moment."

"Does the sitting have an impact on your ability to stay in the moment elsewhere?"

"I think it does. I think it helps train the mind. It's very difficult to do that in activity because you're already preconditioned. For example brushing the teeth, you're already preconditioned to be thinking about something else. What you're going to do next. Whereas sitting, you're supposed to be just being there. So I think the practice of sitting is very helpful."

"If I was someone who came to the temple for the first time and asked, 'What's meditation?' How would you explain it?"

"Meditation is understanding your true self, returning to the moment to see what's going on just now. So we do teach a certain technique. For your first visit, we have people sit for ten minutes, and we instruct them to breathe in on 'clear mind' and to breathe out 'don't know.' That's our beginner technique. Breathe in 'clear mind,' breathe out 'don't know.' It would probably take me ten minutes to explain this, and then we'd see if there were questions."

"What do you mean by 'don't know'? That's my question. What is it that I don't know?"

"You don't have to know what it is. Just say, quietly to yourself, 'don't know.'"

"Initially we teach everyone self-inquiry," Richard tells me. "'What am I?' We would teach them the formalities of sitting straight and how to hold their hands and all that, and initially have them watch their breath a little bit and watch their minds and keep an attitude of non-interference with whatever's going on in their mind. But then we will suggest that they raise up one fundamental question. 'What am I?' And if they ask that question sincerely a number of times, they'll come to a feeling like a question mark. That's what we call, 'Don't know.' And we'll encourage them to keep coming back to that feeling of 'Don't know.' And if they lose it, to, again, raise up the question and use that as an attunement devise to provoke what traditionally is called 'Great Doubt.'"

"So 'What am I?' is a kong-an?"

"Yes, but I would make a distinction between that kind of kong-an and the series of kong-ans that people are asked to work on in interviews. Because the 'What am I?' kind of kong-an is what's referred to in the Korean tradition as a hwadu, what the Japanese would call a wato. I forget what the Chinese pronunciation is; it's a little different. But essentially in the Korean tradition it means, 'one big question.' So one big question that students stay with pretty much throughout their practice careers. And then other kong-an are used as testing devices and as intuitive ways of teaching different aspects of Zen Mind."

"When we sit with 'What is this?' or 'What am I?'" Bobby elaborates, "that carries into your everyday life. So, when I'm nursing I'm doing 'what is this?' with how is it with this patient or how one of my co-workers or patients is acting, what they need, how it is just now, rather than having my agenda. To try to be fresh in that curiosity.

"My teacher never encouraged samadhi. He discouraged samadhi. So that's a little difference, I think, with some of the other traditions. He never wanted us to go into samadhi or to have what some people consider a deep meditation. He wanted us to be just sensitive to the wind and the sounds. Just that and not to lose perspective. Like if you had to leave the meditation room to walk to the bathroom, you wouldn't leave your meditation. He encouraged that. So 'How may I help you?' Always, 'How may I help you?'"

Compassion and wisdom, she tells me, arise together out of practice. "Once you have that openness, that human capacity to be completely open, compassion and wisdom are hand-in-hand." And with compassion and wisdom, one recognizes that the precepts are conditional. "You need to know when they're open and know when they're closed. So we use the example of if you saw someone about to pour poison into a reservoir, and the only way you could stop them was by shooting them, then you'd shoot them. We have a precept not to kill, but if you need to kill one person to save those 10,000 lives, you would kill him. So you have to know when those precepts were open or closed, and have a big well of questioning, 'How is it just now?' That's a big part of our practice, to ask, 'What is this?' or 'How is it just now?' And really ask it from our center. And pay attention."

She tells me that Seung Sahn had envisioned establishing a monastic community in the United States. "He tried very hard and really encouraged many of us to become monastics – including myself – but it just didn't work. I never did it, but a lot of people tried, mostly men, a few women. And it just didn't float somehow. We even had a monastery in Cumberland, Rhode Island, a separate building up on a hill, and he wanted it be developed and have some monks living there. It just never worked. There are monks in our tradition – I'd say we have at least thirty – but they all live in Korea."

"These are Western monks, you mean? Living in Korea?"

"Yeah, they're either from Europe or the United States."

I am curious about the structures that helped the Kwan Um School survive Seung Sahn's passing.

"We have a hierarchal situation with titles," Bobby explains. "The highest thing you can be in our school, of course, is a Zen Master. So we have about nine of those. Then we have people we call Ji Do Poeps, which means 'able to point the way.' 'Poep' means Dharma. 'Do' is path. 'Ji' is point. 'Point towards the path.' So there's that hierarchy. Then we have what we call Dharma teachers. So that's what we do. You do a lot of practice, you're doing well, you pass your koans, you get promoted. And I think we have a really great networking in Europe and Asia. All of us are connected. We all know each other and have conferences. Stay together that way."

Richard clarifies this. "In our school, we have a two-step process. First inka and then transmission. From Zen Master Seung Sahn's viewpoint – I don't know if every

Korean master would agree with this – but from his standpoint, inka was the initial making you a teacher, and then, some years later, transmission. So inka came first; transmission came second. It's the opposite of the way Maezumi Roshi's group has it."

"So inka is permission to be a teacher."

"Yeah, within the Kwan Um School. And transmission means you have the title 'Zen Master,' and you can be an independent entity if you want."

"So as a teacher with inka you'd be working under what? Guidance?"

"Initially yes. When someone first becomes a teacher in the Kwan Um School of Zen, we don't just plop them in the interview room on their own to work with students. We have them sit with a more experienced teacher. That's what I did with Zen Master Seung Sahn whenever he was in New York or if I followed him somewhere else. He would have me sit in the interview room with him, and he would ask the student some kung-an, and then he would tell me, 'Now you ask him some kung-an.'"

"Previously, as I understand it, he appointed all the teachers. What's the process now that he's dead?"

"Well, he had set up a process where he was not the sole person identifying the teachers towards the end. So anyone who has the title 'Zen Master' can say, 'I have a student who I feel is ready for inka.' And we have a process where the candidate has to go around and have kung-an interviews with five different teachers within the Kwan Um Zen School. And these five teachers – including the person's main guiding teacher – have to agree, 'Yes, this person seems to be right to be a candidate for inka.' And that system persists up to today."

"And transmission?"

"The same, except transmission's a little different. When Zen Master Seung Sahn was alive, he wanted us to go and sit with teachers outside of our school and lineage. So when I was in that process, I went and sat a retreat with Maezumi Roshi; I went and sat a sesshin with Aitken Roshi; I went and sat a sesshin with Sasaki Roshi and one with Eido Roshi here in New York. And then we had to report back to Zen Master Seung Sahn about how the interview process went with these teachers. And if he felt that what we reported was fairly clear, then we'd fulfilled part of the requirement for transmission. So even before he died, he set up a process. We have a committee of three Zen Masters within the Kwan Um Zen School, and when he was alive we would consult with him as well. But he got quite sick towards the end of his life, and he was just a figurehead in many respects. Anyway, the candidate for transmission is sent around to call on some teachers outside of our school, and they have to write up what went on in dokusan, then this small committee of three Zen Masters decides, 'Okay, we feel that you're ready.' Or, 'We think you should go back and call on this guy again.' Or, 'Go call on somebody else.' This process has some similarity with how it was in ancient China. Someone with transmission might travel around and call on many teachers."

"And is it that the candidate is having his degree of awakening attested to by these other teachers?"

"No. More that in the course of the interview – going back to when Zen Master Seung Sahn was alive – we would engage in some kind of Dharma Combat with the teacher we were visiting. So the Dharma Combat had to be reasonably clear. And the teachers we were going to call on knew what we were coming for, that we were Soen Sa Nim's students, and we were coming to sit retreat with them and have interviews."

"Whom might potential candidates go to now?"

"There are several people who have agreed to continue cooperating with us. Aitken Roshi's successor, Nelson Foster. Also Jan Chozen Bays, Sherry Chayat in Syracuse, and Shodo Harada Roshi when he comes here from Japan."

Then he adds, "Just to fill in the blank here. When Zen Master Seung Sahn died, we elected someone to take his place as the figurehead of the school internationally, and Bobby was the person who got elected. I think the term is four years, and she was elected a second time. It's coming to an end soon – her term."

This wasn't something she mentioned during her conversation with me.

Bobbie tells me this story about Seung Sahn: "This time we were driving from Boston to Providence, and it was in the evening, in the summer, and a bug hit the windshield. I was driving, and he was sitting in the passenger seat. And the bug looked like it was still alive. But I knew, by the impact, that it must have died. But it was moving from the wind, and he thought it was alive. I said, 'No, I think it's dead, Soen Sa Nim.' He said, 'No, I think it might be living.' I said, 'No, I think it's dead.' And he goes, 'Pull over!' He almost screamed with so much urgency. 'Pull over!' So I pulled over on 95, a major highway, and got out of the car. I lifted the bug off the windshield and showed it to him. It had died. But it was amazing how much he cared about that bug. That was his heart – you know – that was the kind of heart he had. Not to harm. That's what he always taught. Try to help. Try to relieve suffering."

CHAPTER TWENTY-FOUR

Three at Blue Cliff
BROTHER PHAP VU
BROTHER PHAP MAN (BROTHER FULFILLMENT)
SISTER DANG NGHIEM

BLUE CLIFF, OUTSIDE PINE BUSH, NEW YORK, IS A VIETNAMESE ZEN MONASTERY associated with Thich Nhat Hanh. Nhat Hanh lives at Plum Village in France but has three practice centers, including Blue Cliff, in the United States. They are monasteries in the traditional sense. There are over thirty celibate monks and nuns living at each. Here in Blue Cliff, there are thirty-three persons; slightly more women than men; slightly more Asians than Caucasians. Several of the Asian monks are refugees from the Bat Nha Monastery in Vietnam which the government of that country shut down in 2009.

Although Nhat Hanh's Plum Village Tradition is in the Linji lineage, there are some who question whether it is actually Zen. The focus is certainly less on seated meditation (there are only two 45 minute periods of sitting a day) than it is on the practice of mindfulness in daily activity. Clocks here ring the quarter hour, and, each time they do, both monastics and lay practitioners stop whatever they're engaged in and bring themselves back to attentiveness. There are about 60 short poems, called gathas, silently recited with various activities. Three are posted on the wall of the bathroom. The one by the light switch goes:

> Forgetfulness is the darkness
> Mindfulness is the light
> I bring awareness
> To shine upon my life.

Another is posted by the mirror, and a third is recited when turning on the water tap. There is also a gatha for the act of defecation.

The community is divided into two "hamlets," one on the west side of the road (Green Pine for the monks) and one on the east (White Crane for the nuns). It is simply a matter of crossing the road to reach the other, and throughout the day I see people moving back and forth. The administration building and dining hall are in the women's hamlet; the large meditation hall in the men's.

It is a decentralized community. There is an abbess at White Crane, but at the time of my visit there is no abbot at Green Pine. I am repeatedly told that decisions are not made by any single individual. Governance is the responsibility of the Bhikshu Council, and even its chair rotates. Brother Fulfillment tells me the abbot and abbess "don't play a major role of authority, but simply assist in maintaining harmony, peace, and happiness within the hamlet. Thay[79] has inspired us to create a 'leaderless community.' Everything should be decided by consensus among the community members. The Abbess and Abbott have more of a counseling and harmonizing role." They do, however, have the authority to make emergency decisions if there is no time for the community to meet.

It's easy to dismiss this all as slightly naïve, but it is also accessible and effective. Surprisingly, the majority of the people here are young, including two novices in their early 20s. Nor is it an easy path. Bhikshus – fully ordained monks – commit to abide by 250 precepts (novices start with ten); there are 100 additional precepts for the nuns. And yet none of this – including the apparent sexism – seems onerous to the people I interview. In fact, they all talk openly about how happy their lives are. There is also a playfulness in them that I had not expected.

It all seems to work much better than I think it should.

1

Brother Chan Phap Vu (Clifford Brown) organized my visit. It's clear he has some administrative responsibility at the monastery, so I begin by asking him what his role is.

"I don't know," he laughs. "We don't typically have formal positions. The best way I can put it is I'm an Older Brother. So that brings on quite a bit of responsibility, everything from – for example – organizing our teacher's tour in the US to training young monastics and aspirants. And I'm even a gardener, which I enjoy the most probably."

He grew up in Southern California "in the burbs. East of LA. Between LA and San Bernardino. I didn't enjoy it much, thought it was kind of a cultural wasteland. Wasn't much going on there except malls. In school, I studied Eastern Religions.

Took a class. I was interested in the teachings of Daoism, and I connected with that. Then I read more about Buddhism, and, eventually, it became a practice."

He was 38 when he began meditating by following the instructions he found in a book and timing himself with an alarm clock.

"Then I decided to look for a temple. At this time, I had moved to San Diego, and, of course, I looked in the yellow pages. How else are you going to find a Buddhist temple? And just a few blocks away was a Chinese Rinzai temple. So I went there. The teacher was a nun called the Venerable Yijhir, and it was an interesting place because Chinese temples served as community centers as well. So in the mornings, on Sundays, they would have chanting in the Pure Land style and the congregation was 99 percent Chinese. The one percent was the guy who was married to a Chinese woman. And in the afternoon, we had the sitting meditation practices, which was 99 percent western and maybe a couple of second or third generation Chinese. So Venerable Yijhir connected with the westerners. She liked to see us practice, and she knew that we liked meditation more than chanting. At least lo-ong chanting. So she started my training."

"How long were you with her?"

"I stayed there two years, and somewhere along the line – I don't know where – I thought, 'Hey! This monastic thing looks pretty cool.'"

"That isn't something that occurs to a lot of people."

"No. It doesn't. It's not like doctor, lawyer, monk. I liked the practice. I liked where it was taking me inside, and I think I just wanted more. And I saw her as an example. She had something. Not all monastics do, but she had it. And I thought, 'Wow! That's pretty incredible.' I think it made me aware of things about myself that I hadn't seen before. Eventually I was helping out with the services as a lay person in robes. And somewhere along the line, I thought, 'You know, this looks like an interesting life.'

"So I went to the main temple, which is a huge Chinese temple in Southern California, and I stayed there for a few months. But I was very much interested in not being Chinese. I wanted to see something Western. Western Buddhism. Western monasticism. And it didn't work out that way. They were terrific, and I love what they do. But they didn't seem to be quite ready for Western monastics and the flexibility that's needed. So I decided to look around a bit. And then someone said, 'Hey, there's going to be a monk at Balboa Park.' So I decided, 'Well, you know, I've seen a nun, but I really haven't seen a monk.' So I went down there, and it was Thay giving a day of mindfulness. And I saw these western monks going around in the brown robes. 'Wow! Never seen one of those before!' So it caught my eye. Thay has this way of taking the practice to a heart level which I didn't get so much in the other tradition. It seemed more mind stuff. Here Thay was talking about things of the heart. And these two are not unconnected. They're very connected. So that spoke to me on another level, you might say. I appreciated how he was as a monk."

"What do you mean by that?"

"Just the way he was. His presence was very touching. I thought, 'Wow! I'd like to be like that.' And his integrity as a monastic. Because you hear about so many things in the monastic community – issues and politics – and it kind of shakes your confidence. And here he was, in his 80s, led this incredible life, and always had this monk-integrity which I respect. It's not an easy path. So that's what caught my eye. And then seeing the other monastics and how his training came out in their lives. I decided, 'Well, I think I'll check this order out.' So I went to his community at Deer Park which was right up the road. This was in 2000, and they had just opened. I went up there, and it was in very shabby condition. So I got to help work on it. At first, I was intending to stay for a couple of weeks to see how it was, and then it really clicked so I decided to stay. And at that time, if you wanted to ordain you had to go to Plum Village in France. So I stayed at Deer Park as a lay person and then was sent over to Plum Village and spent two and a half years there."

There are stages of initiation in the Plum Village tradition. The first is called an "aspirancy"; this is followed by a three year novitiate, after which the individual may seek full ordination as a bhikshu or bhikshuni – the Sanskrit terms for monk and nun. After five years, a bhikshu or bhikshuni may also be deemed suitable to "receive the lamp," which is authorization to teach others. Brother Phap Vu completed his aspirancy at Plum Village and soon after was ordained a novice.

"Did ordination meet your expectations?" I ask.

"Yes and no. It was a mind-blower because here I was at this quiet little monastery in California, and then going to Plum Village where's there's sixty-plus monks. Four roommates in a room together. From different cultures. That was challenging for me. I've always said the hardest thing about being in the sangha is being in the sangha. So I really had to work with that. That was my koan, you might say. How to make this work and be sane and maybe find enlightenment as the saying goes."

"I was talking to a young woman at Zen Mountain Monastery not too far from here," I say, "and I asked her, 'What's it like living here?' And the first thing she said was, 'It's lonely.'"

He smiles and nods his head. "It can be that. It can be lonely. It can take you wherever the mind takes you. Really. All sorts of things. It's great training. Especially when things are done by committee. You learn the perfection of patience going in that direction. It's the training of Letting Go. Watching the mind. Letting go. And being okay with the stupidest decisions you've ever heard of in your entire life."

When he had completed the first two years of his novitiate, he was asked to return to the United States and assist the Maple Forest community in Vermont. It was a small group whose membership averaged about eight persons. It was there that he completed his novitiate and was ordained a bhikshu. In 2007, Maple Forest Monastery and the Green Mountain Dharma Center, also in Vermont, closed, and the monastics moved to the new Blue Cliff center.

"And you've remained here since," I remark. "So you've been engaged in Dharma practice continuously since 2000."

"Yes. I'm hoping it's working," he says, laughing.

"So say I'm a kid from the neighborhood, living in one of the houses I passed along the road on the way here. And I notice you guys out here, so I show up one day and ask, 'What's this all about?' What do you tell me?"

"If you were a local guy, I might say, 'Oh, we just practice mindfulness.'"

"And what does that mean?"

"Oh, that means being in the present. Enjoying it. Enjoying life more."

"Why?"

"Why? Why not?"

"No, I'm being serious. Let's say I just finished high school, and I don't know what I'm going to do. My parents want me to go to college, but I'm not sure that's my thing. So I come by here, and I really want to know: If I came here, what would I get out of it?"

"Okay. Well, this is where we would sit down and have what we call a consultation. That's when, one-on-one, we talk about issues in your life. So you're not sure what you want to do. That's an easy one. A lot of people go through 'I don't know.' And that's actually a good thing. But the important thing – in our tradition – is to practice to find some clarity. If you look at your mind right now, it's probably disturbed. It's probably running from here to there. Either running from something or to something. Or both. Well, of course you don't know what to do. So, we practice so that we can stop the running, stop the avoiding, stop chasing ideas."

"And how do you do that?"

"Finding your breath. Finding your center."

"And, of course, I probably wouldn't have any idea what you meant by that."

"You have to come sit with us, then you'll see."

"Okay, and maybe I'm open to that, but I'd also like to have a better sense of what I'm getting into. And maybe my parents think you're a cult out here."

"Okay. Go home. Go into your room. Sit cross-legged or on a chair. Relax your body. Follow your breath. That's all."

"And what's it going to do for me?"

"You'll find out," Phap Vu chuckles.

"Okay, let's change the scenario then. Suppose I'm somebody a little older, a little more mature. And say I spent some time at Zen Mountain, but it didn't work out. I don't get koans or whatever. What am I going find here? How would my experience be different?"

He's adept at dodging generalizations. "I don't know. I'm not you."

"Just keep to the nuts and bolts then. You're in the Linji lineage – the Rinzai lineage – and so is Dai Bosatsu on the other side of the mountains. They have a very distinctive Japanese flavor. Is there a flavor that would distinguish this tradition from other examples of Chan or Japanese Zen?"

He considers the question a moment. "Yeah, we have a very distinct flavor; it's almost unrecognizable in Zen. Some people don't call it Zen. I remember Thay was asked one time, 'What do we practice?' And he said, 'We practice Buddhism.'"

"When you described your experience at the Rinzai Temple in San Diego, you distinguished between the devotional Buddhists, who did the chants and the services, and the meditation practitioners. Which are you here?"

"Meditative rather than devotional, but we do have liturgy. We have prostrations; we call it 'touching the earth.' Reverence for the Buddhas and Bodhisattvas. But we believe that practice is everyday life. So, in that respect, we're a meditative school. When Thay was exiled in France, eventually he was confronted with all these students from the west. So his idea was to create or to foster a western form of Buddhism, a practice that spoke to westerners. That's the flavor. What we practice here is not what they practice in traditional Vietnamese temples. And you can say that we're not your traditional Zen school in that respect. But we have the understanding of emptiness, the understanding that Dharma is life. So we try to keep the practice fluid and not dogmatic."

"What do you mean by that?"

"What gets you to point B? You're at point A; how do you get to point B? One of our Fourteen Mindfulness Trainings is avoiding dogma, not creating dogma, not living by rules or teachings for the sake of rules or teachings. There needs to be context, relevancy, spirit behind the rules. Don't mistake the finger for the moon. That's our goal, and it works pretty well. It can get messy, but it's working."

The other thirteen Mindfulness Trainings are: openness; freedom of thought; awareness of suffering; compassionate healthy living; taking care of anger; dwelling happily in the present moment; true community and communication; truthful and loving speech; protecting and nourishing the sangha; right livelihood; reverence for life; generosity; and true love. For lay members, the last is a recognition that "sexual desire is not love and that sexual relations motivated by craving cannot dissipate the feeling of loneliness but will create more suffering, frustration, and isolation"; therefore, practitioners determine "not to engage in sexual relations without mutual understanding, love, and a deep long-term commitment made known to our family and friends." For the ordained, it is a commitment to chastity.

"In most of the forms of Zen which came here from Japan there's an emphasis on attaining awakening," I say. "Is that a factor here?"

"Not so much. Because…. How can I explain this? I try to inspire the young monastics to have great aspirations, because those get you through the difficult times; however, kill the Buddha. Don't get caught in anything. Don't get caught in Buddha or enlightenment. We don't use those terms very much here. You won't hear Thay talk very much about it because it's an idea. We don't know what that is. But if we practice, and we're diligent in our practice, that's the general direction."

By practice, he means mindfulness.

"In Thich Nhat Hanh's books," I say, "there's an emphasis on the gathas, those short poems. Is that something you use here? Is it an introductory practice? A continuous practice?"

"All of the above. The novices should learn their gathas and apply them. I'm very bad at gatha practice – I already have so much going on in my mind – and I'm lousy at rote repetition. But there are some very basic ones I use, especially when I have a very excited mind and I need something a little more concrete than just observing my breath."

"What would you use in that event?"

"Calm/Ease/Smile/Release. Even if I don't smile. Usually this is around some kind of relationship issue. Or in a meeting. You know: 'Calm.'" He grimaces humorously, clenching his teeth, and continues in a strained voice. "'Ease. Smile. Release!' And it takes me away from the angst and the outright anger…and sometimes it's got…." He's laughing so hard that he has trouble continuing. "Yeah, it takes your mind off all this crap the brain comes up with. Another time we use gathas is before we invite [ring] the bell, and we do that quite often here. And there's a gatha that I use in the morning when I wake up that's helpful."

"Meals?"

"We have a meal gatha that I use. We have the Five Contemplations that are read. That's different from a gatha, but it's contemplation as well. So there's different gathas for different kinds of activities, but they can become a hindrance if you use mindfulness to block people out and be unresponsive."

"Surely mindfulness is mindfulness of what's present."

"Ye-es and no. For example, this is a fairly common thing I see when we have a lot of practitioners come: So I'm in the kitchen. I'm washing my dishes. I'm doing 'washing dishes, washing dishes.' And then someone will say something in line. 'Sshh! Be quiet! I'm trying to be mindful!' I've seen that happen. That's not good mindfulness."

We're both laughing. "But a charming story," I say.

"A wonderful story. And following the breath can also hold you back. Because if you stay with it and it's time to let go and you don't, it becomes dogma. All practices can become dogma and be a hindrance."

When Nhat Hanh gives a retreat in the United States there can be as many as a thousand people in attendance. At Blue Cliff there are sleeping accommodations for 200 retreatants. The number of lay followers in the practice far outnumber the ordained. Brother Phap Vu tells me that parents even bring children to the retreats. There are more than twenty events and retreats scheduled in 2014.

"What draws people to the retreats?" I ask. "What brings them here? With their families."

"The monastics."

"I don't buy that," I object. "If I came here, it wouldn't be because there were a bunch of people in brown robes. There must be something about being in this environment and practicing here that they get."

"The monastics. We create the energy of any property we go to. We create a shelter where people feel comfortable, where they feel at home. They see that people care. That's what they want. That's what the world is missing. People who actually care. And that's our practice. We try to create that. That's my practice; I try to create that."

2

The current work coordinator at Blue Cliff is introduced to me both as Brother Phap Man and as Brother Fulfillment, the English translation of his name. I ask how he is normally addressed, and he tells me he is trying to retrain people to call him Brother Fulfillment. His birth name is Aaron Solomon. His father was Jewish but his mother Methodist, which was the primary religious influence in the household.

"My Mom's father was a preacher." Like Brother Phap Vu, Brother Fulfillment grew up in California.

When I ask what led him to the monastery, he says, "That question is always a question of looking back in time to see what the elements were. You know? But it's nice. It's good. I like looking back." He has a tendency to speak in brief, staccato, almost telegraphic phrases. "One thing was I went to a pre-school run by Catholic nuns. So that might have had something to do with it." He also laughs easily and often. "You never know. In fact, I was seriously considering becoming a Catholic monk until I found out how hard it was to enter the Catholic order."

"Jewish father; grandfather's a Methodist preacher; what led you to even think about becoming a Catholic monk?"

"Yeah. I don't know. I mean, that's one seed." (The concept of "seeds" is one which frequently arises in conversation here.) "Some of my earliest memories are there. But going forward, there's all kinds of other things. My parents were both very altruistic people. My dad's from New York. So he came to California with his family. Starting over. Old world Jewish people moving out to California. Doing something totally new. My mom from Kansas, moving out from the mid-west to California in the '60s. That kind of energy."

"Were they hippies?"

"You could say they both were in that movement, but they probably wouldn't have called themselves hippies. But, yeah, sure. They listened to Joan Baez. The whole program. There was a kind of altruism there they definitely transmitted to me. But it goes back. My grandfather was a minister, so I think, in many ways, I'm just continuing his lineage. That's the family business on that side. But on the other side a lot of teachers. Both of my parents were teachers."

Following the example of his father, Brother Fulfillment tried teaching math and science for a while, but it wasn't a good fit. Then he entered the Peace Corps and was sent to Nepal, where he taught in a primary school. It was there that he first encountered Buddhist culture.

"So besides the nuns, the next time I met someone who was a monk was in Nepal. He was a Buddhist monk who was eighteen but left a strong impression. I was very impressed by how much happiness there was. It's like, 'Most people are not that happy.' And it was very refreshing. But I didn't even consider, like, 'Oh, I could do that too' because of the cultural divide. You know? 'You gotta be like that to do that.'"

"You have to be Asian to do that?"

"Yeah, that was probably subconsciously my viewing of it. Then I had some difficulties, as always happens. Mostly with relationships with women. That was a big one for me. There was a woman I'd been dating at UC Berkeley who I thought I was going to marry. It was like the first real true love kind of set up. I was writing to her regularly from Nepal. And then she was going to come visit me, so I was very excited about that. And she showed up, but there was this big distance – I could feel that right away – and shortly after that I found out she had gotten back together with a previous boyfriend. So I was heart-broken. Went through that whole experience.

"She's my connection to this tradition though. Berkeley being Berkeley, she was a Peace and Conflicts Studies major. They had a major in that field, and they were using some of Thay's books. So, she was studying him and was very into it. And I could see something about that. I think that's what attracted me to her. I saw that kernel of Zen – that seed – in her. It was starting to grow. That sense of stability, confidence, not being pushed around so much. Just an aspiration to be a happy person. To be a free person. So that was kind of something that she was touching, and we talked a little bit about his teaching.

"But we split up. It was very painful. We went through the whole process, but she left me a book as part of that. 'Here, I'm leaving you, but read this book.' And you'll love the title of this book. It's our teacher's commentary on the four establishments of mindfulness, titled *Transformation and Healing*."

"So she had a sense of humor."

"Yeah. Well, to her credit, she's actually very sweet. I don't think she even intended it that way. It was purely, 'I want to help you.' I was like, 'Oh, that's great.' But I read it several times in Nepal. Didn't make a lot of sense. Sutra commentary with no reference point to any kind of practice. I was a confused young man at that time, I think." He laughs. "I'm less confused now. I was more confused then."

"Confused in what sense?"

"What am I supposed to do? How am I supposed to live my life? How do I deal with anxiety? Fear? Anger?"

"What were you anxious about?"

"Well, in Nepal, every day was anxiety producing because it's, like, 'How am I going to teach this class in a foreign language to these kids? How am I going to navigate this culture?' I mean, I still have anxiety, don't get me wrong. But now it's like, 'Okay. That's just anxiety. What are its roots? You're afraid of this. You're afraid of that. That's okay. There's a way. There's a practice to look at that, to hold that.' But at that time, I was being pushed around by emotions and didn't have much emotional intelligence, not growing up with that. My parents were divorced when I was ten. I've always been a very emotionally sensitive person, and I couldn't process that at the time.

"So I always tell people when they ask me, 'How did you become a monk?' – I usually bring up at some point that you gotta have enough suffering to want to do that. That's one of the key ingredients. So, looking back, there's also those relational elements."

"So your ex-girlfriend gives you this book in Nepal. You read it a couple of times. Did you start any kind of practice while in Nepal?"

"I didn't really know how to. No one had ever said, 'Okay, so this is how you follow your breathing. This is what it means to practice.' I was a very independent-minded person. Stubborn. So at the time, it was like, 'No. I don't want anyone to teach me anything. I'll figure everything out myself.' I did some experiments. I had another book on Tibetan Buddhism. It was a crazy book at that time for me to look at. *Time, Space and Knowledge* it was called. Tarthang Tulka. It had some meditations in there. Now I see it's very down to earth. At that time, I thought it was out in the outer space realm. I practiced some of those meditations in that book.

"Uh...I drank a lot of tea. Watched the sunset a lot. Sunrise and sunset. Nepal's very slow. I lived in a rural village about a day's walk from the nearest road, so it was way out there. Very primitive. No running water. No electricity. Beautiful people. In a way, that was my introduction to meditation. And it probably led me here in some way, because it was so community-oriented. What I recognized in Nepal was how valuable your neighbors are in a society where everyone depends on everyone else, and they're aware of it. Our connections are so fragmented in the west. We have our own everything. We don't share. We don't have community systems as such. That was very beautiful. So that's, I think, part of the attraction.

"So forwarding through that, all these traumatic experiences. More dating in the Peace Corps. More break ups. One more cycle. So I stopped doing that. Came back to California. And then the whole spiritual awakening process started for me at that time. I think it was a really heavy kind of despair coming from not knowing what to do with myself. Not feeling connected to people. Isolation. A lot of negative judgement about the culture that I lived in. It kind of looked meaningless – you know? – people are so busy in kind of a rat race. It got to a point where I was like, 'Well, I gotta do something about it.' And you're searching for something. So you look for it partly in relationships, partly in work. So trying to go back to my old job, computer work. 'Okay, maybe I should go back to school. Learn something.' I was still caught in that framework. 'Okay, I'll study computer science. I'm good at that.' You gotta do what you're good at. Right? Went back to Santa Cruz. A very special place, beautiful place. Coastal foothills. So, I went to graduate school. But obviously the problem was in here," he says, tapping his chest. "So I was still struggling. And... uh...."

He pauses then sighs. "What happened? Well, I started surfing. That was another kind of quote-unquote meditative thing for me. I always loved outdoor stuff. That's been a very healing thing. But I hurt myself. Things kind of getting out of control a bit. But what happened? A friend gave me a yoga tape! This is the whole story now! And I started doing yoga, even though I thought at the time, 'This stuff is weird!' But it had kind of this spiritual feel. Very soothing music, and people in white robes." He laughs. "The classic stuff! You know? And that was like so...."

He pauses again.

"My father's very skeptical of organized religion or anything like that, so I had that full-blown. It's a very Jewish thing. All religion, all spiritual stuff is just brain-washing and weak-minded. But when I started doing this yoga, actually it was quite pleasant. So at the end of the program, there's sitting meditation. Just five breaths. Right? Count 'em. Stay with it. One. Two. Three. Four. Five. It's amazing how hard that is when you've never done it before. But it was extremely pleasant. I thought, 'Wow! This is great!' So that was it. I started looking around from there. I saw one of Thay's books in the bookshop. I recognized his name from the other book. 'Oh, this is very interesting.' Picked up the book. *Heart of the Buddha's Teaching*. Blew me away. First page. Read the first page in the bookshop. Right there in the bookshop. It says something like, 'It's because you suffer – that's the good news – that's why you can find the path to healing and liberation. That's the good news. Suffering – what you're experiencing – is a good thing.' So for me, that was so honest, so real. Like, 'Yes, I've been through that.' He says, 'I grew up in a time of war. The French-Vietnamese War.' His whole life in war. Right? This poem about, 'My youth is like an unripe plum with the teeth marks still in it. I feel the wounds still vibrating in my body.' It was like, 'Wow!' This guy's been probably through worse things than I have, but here he is writing about the beauty of suffering as a good thing. Something you can use to heal yourself. So I said, 'Okay. This is good.' Looked through it some. Took it home and basically started practicing it. Very practical too. Do this. Do that. For example, don't abandon your spiritual roots. Very shocked to hear that. You have spiritual ancestors. Christian tradition. Jewish roots. He basically says, 'You have all these resources at your disposal. Why have you abandoned that? Why don't you look at your roots?'"

A friend in high school had given him a Bible with the words of Jesus printed in red ink. "So I started reading the red letters and ignored everything else to start. Because I flipped through things at random and like, 'Well, that doesn't make any sense at all. That can't be good!'"

"Smiting the Moabites? Stuff like that?"

"Exactly. That's can't be good. Let's see if there's anything good in here. And then I discovered the red letters. And actually I was blown away. I compared the two teachings side by side – the red letters and what Thay was writing. In *The Heart of the Buddha's Teaching*, he gives an overview of the core of Buddhism. And I was comparing them. And I could put myself – in my mind's eye – right in the place where the Buddha grew up, because where I lived in Nepal was a few hours away from where he lived. And the culture wasn't that much different. It was still mud and stone hut technology. So it was easy for me to imagine this guy wandering around in that environment, teaching these things. And then here's my Christian ancestry over here, and I'm looking at that, and I'm like, 'Wow! This is essentially the same thing.' And that was a big revelation. It was like, 'Wow! That's cool.'

"I started going to church. I didn't really want to, but there was a church across the street from my apartment in Santa Cruz, and one of the things Thay proposed was going back to your tradition and finding out what's going on. He said something like, 'You need a sangha. You need a community to practice with. You can't do this alone.' And this was all new to me, because I was a 'I-need-to-figure-this-out-by-my-self' kind of guy. So, like, 'Whoa! This is gonna be unpleasant!' But for some reason I really trusted this book. So I said, 'Okay. I can do that. I'll just be very non-biased. I'll just go to the church across the street. It's the closest sangha to me, so that's where I'm going.' Assembly of God. Pentecostal. Very interesting place. Good music! Heart! Real heart! You know? The teachings and everything. Interesting. Dogmatic. And kind of narrow and fearful. But not all of it. So it was a good lesson. 'Okay. This has some problems, but it has some good things.' Met a lot of wonderful people. Met another girl. Tried one more time. This time a spiritual relationship, right? And, yeah, the maturity wasn't there for either of us. And when that didn't work out, it was like, 'Yeah, well, so maybe being in a relationship's not such a good idea. Maybe I should become a monk.'" He has a great, unself-conscious laugh. "'Maybe I should be single the rest of my life. Abandon that whole thing.' I was like, 'Well, this is suffering. Just let that go, and I won't have to deal with that suffering anymore.' Of course, later I learned it is possible to have a very loving relationship with someone.

"And I had some good role models. Friends. Christian friends in high school. There was a close friend of mine – we're still very close – who grew up in a very strong Christian family, but sort of…. What would you say? They tried to be authentic. They weren't go-to-Church-on-Sunday kind of people. They were lifestyle people. They lived very simply in a cabin up in the mountains. That impressed me a lot. Partly that's what drew me back to the Christian thing. At first, I was, 'Wow! I want to be like this guy – Thay – but I don't want to be Buddhist.' Because Buddhism's kind of weird. Then I read about St. Francis. 'I want to be like this guy.' Thomas Merton. I'd read his work too. And I'd go through this whole phase. 'I want to be like that guy! I want to be like Gandhi!' You know? I think he was married. This kind of energy though. So, that's what I was consuming in terms of what I was reading, what I was studying."

Eventually, he left the Pentecostal church and joined a more mainstream congregation where someone introduced him to mantra meditation. "So I started doing that too. Plus the yoga. So I was getting more connected with meditation. Slowly these seeds were watered in me. There was this suffering with the relationships and with different things, and suddenly it was more like a realization, 'Wow! I could become a monk! That is something people do! People have done this.' But I felt very insecure about it. One half of me was saying, 'That's crazy. That just doesn't make any sense at all.' But there was this other thing that came up."

He found a Catholic monastery south of Santa Crux. "But Catholicism and the Christianity I grew up with are different worlds in many ways. So I had difficulties. I couldn't fit into it. And I asked one of the brothers what it takes to become a monk, and it sounded like at least ten or fifteen years of stuff between there and becoming a monk. And he said the first thing was, 'You should probably become Catholic.' Which to me didn't make a lot of sense. I was like, 'Well, I'll just become a monk, and then I'll become Catholic.' But that didn't really work for them. And I was very shy. Felt very awkward around all these people in robes and the whole ritual stuff. But the seed had grown, so it would push me."

Then he remembered that his interest had begun by reading Nhat Hanh. "That's what opened this up. This is the person I've trusted the most on the spiritual journey, and it's served me very well. So let's go for it. Let's go check this out. You gotta go and find out what these people are doing. Went down to Thay's monastery in San Diego – Deer Park Monastery. Showed up. Fell in love. There were some very strong monks and nuns there at that time. Westerners. One former Catholic priest. Very good energy. Came for a youth retreat. Met a lot of other young people. They didn't try to sell us anything. Just handed us a bunch of tools and said, 'Try this.' Very concrete. Down to earth. It all worked. It was very pleasant. Except for the sitting. A lot of pain in the legs even with my yoga practice. So the next day, I said, 'This is it. I want to be a monk in this tradition.'"

"And your skeptical father and the rest of your family, how did they react?"

"It's funny. My dad, after being very skeptical of religion, at that time had shifted himself because, when he remarried, the woman he married happened to be a recovering alcoholic in AA. And that's a spiritual tradition. And he was skeptical of that, but she brought him into it in a gentle way. And for him to support her and live with her, it was a necessity. So over my period of growing up, he was going on his own spiritual journey that I was unaware of. And so when it came time for me to tell him, he wasn't that surprised actually.

"My mother was my biggest supporter. The Methodist tradition she grew up in is very open. Her father was a civil rights activist and a Vietnam war protestor. A very progressive kind of guy. So she grew up with that. And my parents were, 'Whatever makes you happy.' The kind of line you get from parents who are somewhat liberal. Right? 'Whatever makes you happy.' They gave me a lot of space growing up. Very supportive. I think it was a shocker for them but not in the sense of, like, 'You can't do that!' More like, 'Wow! Okay, our son is going to do something else that's crazy.'

"But my mom's my biggest supporter because I did one intelligent thing. I recognized it would be hard to accept something like this without understanding it. So I took her with me to Plum Village, and I sold it to her because she loves France. So I said, 'We'll travel around Europe a little while, and then we'll go to this meditation center. Oh, and by the way, I think I might become a monk in that tradition.' She said" – in a cautious tone – "'Okay, that sounds good.' She liked the bargain. So we hung out in Europe for a little while – this is 2006 – then went to Plum Village. And she loved it. I think she enjoyed her stay more than I did because she didn't have any expectations. She didn't have an agenda or program. She didn't know what she was going to get. She just showed up. Which is sometimes – I think – the best way to go to a meditation center. And we stayed in different hamlets. She stayed with the nuns. I stayed with the monks. Which was great, so we couldn't get on each others' nerves. Yeah, she fell in love with it too. So I'm not surprised. None of this is very surprising. Like when you asked me all that, well in many ways I'm doing it for my parents. This is really what they want to do. My mom's coming in a couple of weeks. She'll probably spend the whole summer here. She likes it. My dad likes it too. He'll be here in the fall.

"My dad said something very interesting to me one time. The first time he came to visit Plum Village, he said, 'If I'd come here when I was young, I probably would have become a monk also.' So it wasn't that surprising that that's what I would want to do. Because, like I said, it was very quick. As soon as I came to the monastery, it was the first time, probably, in my life where I felt like, 'This is what I'm supposed to do.' I mentioned my anxiety. 'What was I supposed to do with myself?' That was probably the first time in my life when I felt, 'Okay. This is what I'm supposed to do.'"

Brother Fulfillment has been a monastic for seven years now. I ask if he still feels it's what he should be doing. He doesn't answer immediately.

"It's still very much what I want to do in my heart, but I gotta temper that with the fact that it's quite difficult at times. Which is probably why I like it. I really want to continue. That's my aspiration. I love so many things about this life. But it's very challenging. It's not that I'm questioning my aspiration. It's still very strong. What's different between now and when I was first in the monastery is that I'm not as naïve about what it means. I know that it's not like you become a monk and then everything's roses. That's not how it works. It's a path of transformation and practice. And, to be honest, you can do that as a monk or as a lay person. It's about taking the time in your life to do that. What it takes is the self commitment to do that. So, I'm very much still there. And I'd love to say, 'They're going bury me in this tradition.' That's really what I want."

"You said that what had struck you about that 18 year old monk in Nepal was how happy he was. Is this a happy place?"

"It's a very happy place. But it's a happy place not in a totally naïve sense. Which means it also has its suffering. But we recognize that. We try to practice in such a way that we can see there's no happiness without suffering. And we have the tools transmitted to us to know what to do with suffering so that we can create peace. That sounds like advertising, but that's our aspiration. That's what we're working with. For me, it's embodying that in my daily life so it's transmittable. If it's not embodied, if it's not alive in me, if it's just a bunch of ideas, it's useless. What really counts is that people come here, and they get in touch with it as I did when I showed up and said, 'Wow! This is it. Okay. There's something alive here.'

"But I have a more worldly view now because you gotta run a practice center. You've gotta deal with differences of opinion, conflict. You become an adult. You gotta grow up. You have responsibilities and stuff. So for me, the edge now is balancing the responsibility with the freedom of monastic life and the vows and the Zen tradition of nowhere to go, nothing to do. So, yeah, running this practice center, there's challenges and difficulties. But I've found it to be extremely rewarding. And having the time and the people to learn about things with, things that are not every day things. I think that's what I was always looking for in my life. Didn't want to learn about math, although I love the idea of how things are put together. I wanted to know the 'whys?' So where do you go to school to learn about how to just live? How to deal with your emotions or relationships with people? Then I discovered, 'Oh! There's a career for that!' And in the big sense too, like really waking up. Really getting to the bottom of it all. It's a long path, and that's plenty for a lifetime. Many lifetimes.

"So I think that my conviction was very strong when I entered the order. And I hold onto that as a vow. So it doesn't really matter what happens between here and someday I have to pass away. There's a thread here, or a rope, that I hold onto, and it can guide me through. This is just a journey. I don't really consider changing course, but I made a commitment to myself that if I have clear insight and peace and calm, then I can make a decision. I learned that partly from our teacher, because he said at one point he had to leave the monastery because of the war. He had to do something to help. He couldn't just stay hiding in the monastery, meditating. He had to go out and reach out and that brought him here, to the United States. But he said he didn't think about it. It wasn't an analytical decision. It was insight. And it was so clear. No question. So I'm not limiting myself. I just promised to do the decision making from clarity and insight. So I don't know what will happen in the future."

3

Sister Dang Nghiem tells me people call her Sister D. She is Vietnamese by birth, and there is a musical quality to her accent. Her voice is gentle and gives a false impression of shyness. As we walk to the meditation hall, she casually mentions, "I have written a book, too." That evening, I download it on my Kindle and learn further details about her life.[80] The story is both wrenching and inspiring.

"My mother passed away by the time I was twelve," she tells me, "and my grandmother raised me since I was a baby. Grandma often told me, 'When you grow up, first of all, you should raise your brother. Have him raised well and educated. Then you get a high education yourself. Then you should become a nun, and that will be the best way you can serve society.' My grandmother planted these seeds in me since I was seven or eight years old. I came to the US; I finished high school; I went to college in Tucson, Arizona; then I went to medical school at UC San Francisco. I finished medical school; I went to residency. I was able to realize my Grandmother's first two requests, raising my brother into a wonderful young man and obtaining a good education for myself, but becoming a nun was still a strange and haunting thought to me. I went to Thay's retreat when I was a resident. Even though I was raised as a Buddhist, I never really practiced it. My grandmother was a very deep practitioner, but I just went along with her, riding on the back of the bicycle to the temple when I was a child. In the US, as a teenager, I never went to the temple because I lived with foster parents who were Christian. In college and in medical school, I had no time for a spiritual life. While I was doing residency, one of the doctors said to me, 'You know, doctor, there is a Zen Master who's Vietnamese, and he's giving retreats all over the US. Maybe you'd like to attend one of his retreats.'"

She was born in Saigon during the Tet Offensive and named Huong, which means "fragrance." Her mother left the countryside as a teenager to work as a maid in Saigon. Sister D believes her mother suffered from verbal, physical, and sexual abuse during her time in the city. Eventually circumstances led her, as it did many young women at that time, to consort with US soldiers. Sister D is not certain whether her own father was American or Vietnamese, but it was clear from his light skin, facial features, and blond hair that her younger brother was of mixed heritage. This caused him grief both in Vietnam and the United States; in Vietnam he was taunted for his

American ancestry, and in North America he was bullied and called a communist because of his Asian ancestry.

For a while, the two children lived with their grandmother in the countryside.

> When I think of my grandmother, I think of somebody very peaceful. She would cook for us and take care of everything. When she had time, she would recite a Buddhist sutra. She would sit on her wooden plank bed, and, holding her beads, she would evoke the names of the Buddhas and the Bodhisattvas. She never wasted her time making small talk or gossiping about this or that person. She just sat very peacefully, and quietly prayed.[81]

When a patron maintained Huong's mother in a private house, she brought her children to the city to be with her, but it wasn't a healthy environment. Huong was conscious of and disturbed by the sexual demands made of her mother. Huong herself was sexually abused by an uncle when she was only nine and was sexually assaulted by a drunken policeman a year later. Rather than being a protector, her mother took out her own frustrations on her daughter.

> She pinched my thighs all the time, and made them constantly hurt with bruises that turned from red to seedling green then pale yellow. Every time, I sat still, gazing at my mother, and stubbornly kept from crying. Many times my mother screamed, kicked, and beat me as if I were a disgusting centipede. Afterwards, when I was sleeping, she would rub green oil on the bruises on my body and cry.[82]

When Huong was only twelve, her mother disappeared and was presumed to have been murdered. The children returned to the care of their grandmother. Fearful of the way her grandson was treated after the American withdrawal, the grandmother arranged for the children to emigrate to the United States under the auspices of the Amerasian Immigration Act which provided an opportunity for children of servicemen to be brought to the US. Huong was not yet 17; her brother was 13. She spoke no English when she arrived. They were placed with a succession of foster parents.

She did well in school, excelled in her language studies, and was eventually accepted into medical school. During her medical training, she did internships in India and Kenya but felt increasingly ill at ease with the impersonality of her chosen profession.

As a young physician, I was enthusiastic about helping people. Unfortunately, I often felt ineffective and helpless, because I saw that the deep problems were not really solved. I felt that in many ways, as medical doctors we were just putting Band-Aids on problems. We didn't get to the roots. If doctors rely only on science and technology, they may approach medical treatment for their patients as if they are waging a battle in a war. They may focus on the disease as the enemy. They may forget that patients are present and in great need of their comfort and support. There are many incurable diseases, and the compassion of a physician may be the only prescription that can help patients to live their remaining days with dignity and freedom. I wanted to be a doctor not only to treat illness, but also to help people to live meaningfully, and to die meaningfully.[83]

She had difficulties in romantic relationships because of her past but eventually found a loving partner in an audio engineer named John Seaver. Coincidentally, John introduced her to mindfulness practice shortly before she was informed about the retreats Thich Nhat Hanh was offering.

"While I was doing residency, one of the doctors said to me, 'You know, doctor, there is a Zen Master who's Vietnamese, and he's giving retreats all over the US. Maybe you'd like to attend one of his retreats.' I replied, 'Sure.' There was one in Santa Barbara, a month away or something. I thought to myself, I could go to this one, and so I asked permission from my residency program. They gave it to me right away, and so I went. On that retreat, I realized what we call the Four Noble Truths – the Buddha's essential teaching – about this deep suffering in myself and in my family. I mean, I always knew I suffered, but to have suffering as a noble teaching was something enlightening to me. What also moved me was that all these years, growing up, I thought of myself as a victim, but, in the retreat, I realized that I was the one perpetuating the suffering. I had become a perpetrator. I was no longer a victim but a perpetrator. Then I also learned that there's a way out. I saw that I could participate actively in the making of the suffering but also in the transformation of the suffering. This realization moved me so deeply. It also changed my views about religion, about Buddhism, because I had thought of religion as something like a superstition. However, in that retreat, I saw it was really a deep practice. A science. Something proactive. So that changed my attitude and view about Buddhism. After the retreat, I went back to residency, and I saw even more clearly how my suffering continued because of the daily pressure and stress as well as because of my ingrained habit energies. I had so little time to care for myself. Therefore, when difficulties of the past arose, I couldn't really take care of them. This awareness made me even more depressed than before. Then it happened that my partner died in an accident."

She was 30 years old; John was three years older. He went swimming in the ocean and didn't return. His body was never recovered. "His death woke me up. He lived a spiritual life, and, when he passed away, I didn't regret it for him, because he had lived a deeply joyful and meaningful life. His death woke me up because even though I had all the conditions of happiness, I was unhappy and even desperate at times. If not by the stress and pressure of the present moment, I would be suffering from nightmares about the past. I realized that if I were to die suddenly like him, I would not have peace in my heart. I could not have said that I had lived my life peacefully. I could not have said that I had truly lived my life so that I could just die then like my partner. This realization made me want to change the direction of my life. I wanted to live in such a way that if I were to die anytime in the midst of the day, it would be okay. That was why I left medicine and went to Plum Village to see Thay. I had just met him three weeks before that."

In her book, she states that within "three hours of learning of John's death, I knew it was time to become a nun."[84]

It took her three months to make the necessary arrangements, after which she abandoned her medical career and went to Plum Village. I ask if it met her expectations.

"To tell you the truth, I thought of Plum Village as only our teacher. I did not realize there was a whole community." She pauses a moment before continuing. "I had so much suffering, that I didn't have so many expectations about what it would be like. I just accepted it as it was, more or less, easily. What I needed was a teacher and a practice to help me take care of myself. It turned out that the sangha was there, and the sangha was crucial. My sisters were there, my brothers were there, our teacher was there, and they gave me that embracing environment like a cradle for me to care for my pain and suffering. So I discovered the sangha when I went to Plum Village."

She is more frank in the book. She was ordained only eight months after her partner's death, but found that being in a monastery with a hundred other nuns and no personal privacy (except in the toilet stall if one remembered to lock the latch) didn't resolve her difficulties. She still felt anger and resentment about her past and despair over her partner's death. She thought of suicide. Slowly, however, she developed the capacity to observe these feelings as they arose and allow them to pass.

One evening while I was listening to the sounds of a stream, I saw myself lying at its bottom, and the water filled my body. I followed my breath and listened. The next day I walked to the stream and saw that the water level was only up to my ankles! I had to chuckle at my thought from the previous night. It was not my time to die. I must live in order to become liberated from my own wrong perceptions and habit energies. I must live to know life for what it truly is.[85]

"In 2004, I went back to the US for a retreat for all of us monastics in the Plum Village tradition, and I have remained in the US since to help with the centers here. I was in Deer Park Monastery, California, for seven years, and then I was in Magnolia for one year." Magnolia Grove Practice Center in Mississippi is the most recent of Nhat Hanh's centers in the US. "I have been here in Blue Cliff for two and a half years. It was my anniversary a few days ago; I have been a nun for fourteen years now."

The Plum Village Tradition has more lay than monastic members, which – to Sister D's mind – is the way it should be. The laity, she stresses, is essential. "We have to have lay people. In the past and even now in some countries, lay peoples' main responsibility is to support the monastics. In our tradition, it is the opposite. Lay people's main responsibility is to practice. We transmit the teaching to lay people, and we only ask that they practice in their daily life. We don't even encourage them to convert to being Buddhists. Our teacher often says, 'If you practice mindfulness, you will find the jewel in your own tradition, and you will be able to help revive your own tradition.' Our teacher coined the term, Engaged Buddhism, in the 1960s. In the past ten years or so, Thay has started to talk about Applied Buddhism. Applied Buddhism means Buddhism in every aspect of life. So Thay said, 'When you stand with mindfulness, that's Buddhism. When you drive with mindfulness, that's Buddhism. When you eat with mindfulness, that's Buddhism. When you do things with awareness, that's Buddhism.' Thay has also said, 'If I have to choose between Buddhism and peace, I would choose peace.' So I can say that in our Plum Village tradition, if we have to choose between Buddhism and mindfulness, we would choose mindfulness. Why? Because while Buddhism may still be a concept or a philosophy, mindfulness in its true essence is a daily physical and mental training. Self-awareness is our innate human capacity, and we cultivate and strengthen it through concrete practices. Therefore, mindfulness can become a part of our life regardless of our religion, regardless of our profession, regardless of our culture. That's why when our lay friends come to our centers, we transmit the practices so they can apply them in everything they do in their daily lives. So they learn to do walking meditation, eating meditation, mindful breathing while listening to the telephone rings. They learn to practice deep relaxation, sitting meditation, and driving meditation. They practice loving speech and deep listening to themselves and to others. We also encourage them to join local communities so that they can continue their practice. There are now over a thousand local sanghas in the Plum Village tradition all over the world."

"If I went to a local sangha, how would they introduce me to practice?"

"In local sanghas, there are sometimes members who have practiced with us for years. Or sometimes a local sangha can be very new; there may be some young adults who go to the retreat and like it so much that they start their own group. So the level of experience depends, but they all know about the basic practices. A local sangha may meet once a week or twice a month, and they usually start with a sitting meditation session. It can be silent sitting or guided sitting. They may have Dharma sharing, in which they take turns to share about their lives and how they use the practice to transform difficulties and cultivate harmony. Some local sanghas watch Thay's Dharma talks on video before they have Dharma sharing. They may practice eating meditation in silence or walking meditation afterwards. Local sanghas organize Days of Mindfulness or a few hours of practice every week, every other week, or once a month, and their activities vary depending on how much time they have together."

"What kind of sitting practice would I be taught?"

"Probably a guided meditation. Our teacher wrote a book, *The Blooming of a Lotus*, and there are many clearly guided exercises. Meditation is a bird with two wings; one wing is stopping, and the other is deep looking. Stopping here means stopping the mind from wandering habitually to the past, the future, or getting caught in projects and anxiety of the present. So we always start a meditation with stopping, by bringing the mind back to the breath and then to the body. The Buddha taught this in the 'Discourse on the Full Awareness of Breathing.' As a result, we always start with breathing: 'Breathing in, I am aware that this is an in-breath. Breathing out, I am aware that this is an out-breath. In. Out. Breathing in, I follow the in-breath all the way through. Breathing out, I follow the out-breath all the way through. Follow in-breath. Follow out-breath.' As the mind becomes mindful and focused in the breath, we continue with the awareness of the rest of the body: 'Breathing in, I am aware that I have a body. Breathing out, I relax the tension in my body.' Then as we continue to anchor our mind in our breath and in our body, we proceed to the second part of meditation which is Deep Looking. There are guided topics such as looking into the four elements that make up our body, or looking into the five year old child in us, the five year old child in our father or in our mother."

"Our practices are very modern," she tells me. "They're based on the teachings of the Buddha – like I say about stopping and contemplation – but we modernize and upgrade them. For example, when you hear the sound of the telephone, you stop and breathe. The Buddha emphasized the importance of mindful breathing, but at the time of the Buddha there was no telephone. Now we use the phone rings to practice mindful breathing. This is Applied Buddhism. We breathe with the temple bell and the church bell. We breathe with the phone, the stop light, and the ambulance siren. The practice is pragmatic. The practice can be creative, fun and effective. People nowadays are developing anxiety disorder, depression, and many other mental illnesses because of stress. Many physical and mental illnesses are lifestyle-related, and stress is a big factor of our lifestyle. So when people apply the practice of breathing with the phone, they feel more relaxed, calm and stable. Most people don't have time to sit eight hours in meditation. Who can afford that? People cannot even afford twenty minutes a day to do sitting meditation. Our practice is to live every moment of our life in awareness. When you walk, it can be walking meditation. When you eat, it can be eating meditation. When the phone rings, it can be the phone meditation. When you drive, it can be driving meditation."

An element of play is also deliberately cultivated.

"Young people who come to our centers do not find themselves burdened or caught in rituals and in some kind of archaic teachings. They do not feel like suddenly they have to become solemn and all silent in order to become monks and nuns. For example, you will see our young Brother Bodhi skating around the monastery in the late afternoons, or he'll be playing his special instrument that sounds like screeching funeral music to most of us. We play the guitar. We write songs. The emphasis on play, practice, work, and study helps make it easier for young people to cultivate their spiritual life as lay practitioners or monastic practitioners."

"Many people ask me, 'Sister D, you must be very happy because you smile all the time!' I tell them, 'I am happy some of the time. Most of the time, I am smiling to my crooked thoughts.' The happiness that we taste in this practice is not that of chocolate. When you eat a chocolate bar, you get high. That kind of rush of happiness can make you edgy, restless, and then afterwards you hit the bottom, the sugar-low. The happiness that we touch here is like eating carrots and broccoli." She isn't speaking solemnly. We're both laughing throughout this analysis. "You feel calm while you're eating it. You feel good afterwards. You also know it's going to nourish you for time to come. So that's the happiness I touch more and more. As I walk from here to the meditation hall, I listen to the birds singing. I enjoy looking at the flowers on the sidewalk. I enjoy the steps that I'm taking. I touch stability. There's no sorrow in me; there's no planning or sadness. I can be with the present moment. It is so wonderful. Being aware of the good conditions available to us is a deep happiness. If sadness arises, I'm also able to recognize it right away. I'm able to breathe with it, smile with it, and keep it contained and manageable. Thus, I can be with what was, what is, what will be, and this is a deep happiness and a great power.

"As a doctor, you can have a lot of power. You can make important decisions about peoples' lives. But – you know – when you're angry, you're just angry. When you're sad, you're just sad. You cannot do much about it. You feel helpless. As a practitioner, I can manage my strong emotions. I can take care of my perceptions. I may not be able to change the past, but I can practice stopping and deep looking in order to transform my views and attitudes about the past so that it doesn't harm me and others anymore. I can learn from it, cherish it, and say, 'I am because I was, because of what I went through in my life.' I can smile to my pain with affection instead of trying to reject it or to suppress it. That, to me, is a great power and a great happiness. That, to me, is true happiness. So the happiness that we touch as monastic practitioners is from being able to be aware of and grateful for the simple conditions in our daily life. It is also from being able to embrace, transform and heal the pain of our lives. It also comes from the capacity to help so many people.

"As a doctor, I also helped many people but realized very soon in my career that my service was so limited. For example, I took care of a young man with an abscess in his arm because he had injected drugs into it. It was contaminated, so his arm got infected. We removed most of his biceps and even scraped his bone. He stayed in the hospital for two months, and we would check on his wound and dress it daily. Then he was discharged. Three months later he came back with another abscess on his abdomen. Why? Because we can dress his superficial wound, but we cannot address his deep wound – his past. When he goes out there, his sadness, his anger, his hatred for society, for his family, for himself will overwhelm him again, and he turns to drugs again. I saw how helpless that was, to not be able to address the deeper wounds. As monastic practitioners, we help many people – from children to teenagers to adults – to listen to their own suffering, to discover its roots, and to care for the wounded five year-old child in themselves. To see the transformation in each other and in our lay friends is our great reward. That is also our source of happiness."

"What's the hardest thing about being here?"

"The hardest thing? Well, to me the hardest thing changes. Sometimes the hardest thing is when I have a conflict with a sister, or we are not in harmony with each other. You have nineteen other sisters, but this one sister still sticks out in your mind. Sometimes that's hard, but we work on it. I learn to open my own heart, and to be more skillful, humble and patient. In some cases, I realize that it's not my problem. It's from their own background. It's their own baggage. If it was not me, it would be somebody else. Then I learn not to take it too personally but to give time and space and respect to that person to transform slowly, while I work on myself.

"Sometimes it's hard because you want to be with somebody. We are all very young. We still have desire. We still have attraction. We have loneliness. We have yearning. It is so poignantly alive. So we breathe with these waves again and again. I come to the realization again and again, 'I've been in relationships before, but they did not solve my problems. If I lose my monastic life, I would not have this spaciousness, freedom, and peace. I would not be happy, and then I would not be able to offer happiness to the person I love. Our love can turn into hate and resentment!' And so I come back to my own breathing, to be there for myself, and to live my daily life as mindfully and deeply as possible for true love to be possible.

"So the hardest thing changes from time to time. Yet, I have never doubted the Buddha and the Dharma although I have doubted the sangha sometimes," she says, laughing gently, "We are all human beings, and all too human. Deep inside, I've always been grateful to the sangha, and I know the sangha is essential to the practice. When the Buddha was about to pass away, the Buddha did not choose an heir. Even the Venerable Mahakasyapa was not the heir of the Buddha. He was not the next Buddha. That's very clear.

"The Buddha always took refuge in the sangha. Our teacher does exactly the same thing. Thay takes refuge in the sangha. The sangha makes decisions. As monastic brothers and sisters we train to be a community and to make decisions together. Even an abbess or an abbot, in our tradition, is only another member of the community."

"There is only the one teacher in the Plum Village tradition as I understand it."

"Our teacher is the one teacher that we have."

"And now he is approaching 90 years of age and doesn't have an heir."

"We are his heir. The sangha is his continuation."

"Okay. Again, as I understand it, he is the one who ordains anyone seeking to become a monk or a nun. So when he is no longer able to conduct those ordinations, who will take over that responsibility?"

"The sangha will. We now have many centers all over the world. Sometimes Thay cannot physically go there to perform the ordination. So while Thay is conducting an ordination in Plum Village, we also have the on-line transmission in the distant centers, and brothers and sisters there go through the whole ceremony by listening to our teacher's voice and following his instructions. At some point if the internet line is cut off, the appointed elder brothers and sisters would carry on the ordination ceremony, because we already have the text with us ready. We have been doing this since 2006, but thankfully, because our teacher is still alive, he gives the lineage names to the new monastic brothers and sisters. I envision we will continue to do that when Thay passes away. The new brothers and sisters would be disciples and children of the sangha. Of course, as elder brothers and sisters we teach them, mentor them, and take care of them, but they would not belong to any one of us in particular. Maybe in twenty years or thirty years, when we are much older, we will see. But I can say that most of us would prefer to have our brothers and sisters to be children of the sangha and not belonging to any one of us.

"We rely on the Sangha Eye – the collective wisdom of the community. All the decisions are made by the Bhikshuni Sangha, the Bhikshu Sangha, or the Dharma Teachers' Council. When our teacher passes away, for us to be able to continue the practice, we have to hold onto the sangha. If we go out there and try to have our individual centers – one temple with one monk or one nun – most of us would not last long. I certainly would not make it!"

"You're confident this will continue after Thay's death?"

"Yes. The sangha will continue our teacher."

Blue Cliff is an attractive community. Is it, however, a Zen community? Is this Zen Buddhism?

The fact that that question keeps arising bewilders Brother Fulfillment, as he writes to me several months after I interviewed him:

> Why is there a question about whether the Plum Village tradition is Zen? There seems to be an implication that we don't focus on sitting meditation as much or don't adhere to some of the form of others traditions. Personally, I think there is a misperception that Zen means sitting meditation or ritual practice. That's a kind of narrow lens that weakens the tradition. I think it's time to make the teaching relevant to real people with real lives. To me, that's the spirit of Zen. With Thay's guidance, we're attempting to go back to the core

of what Linji actually taught, as well as the core of what the Buddha taught, and to find our own insights and adapt the teaching and the practice to our insight and to the real situation of ourselves and the world. The Buddha didn't just teach sitting meditation; he taught the transformation of suffering in everyday life, for everyone, by a vast array of means, not just for monks and nuns. And we have a responsibility to keep adding to that body of practice. Our practice is meditation all day, every day, every moment, every action. To me, that's Zen. Sitting is only a small part of life. Linji taught that to walk as a free person on the Earth is the greatest miracle. When we sit down at our computers, do we sit as a free person? Do we return to our breath? This moment is the only important moment to wake up, to practice meditation.

Two Zendos in Maine

GREAT TIDES ZEN, PORTLAND
MORGAN BAY ZENDO, SURRY

1

THERE IS A SIGN OUTSIDE OUR HOTEL IN PORTLAND, MAINE, ANNOUNCING an Enlightenment Expo being held today and tomorrow. The promotional material in the lobby informs us that this is "Greater Portland's largest gathering of spiritual and holistic practitioners, products, and services." There are booths and workshops for psychic readings, animal communication, reiki, crystals, and chair massage. One of the headliners is a sea shell reader.

This type of thing tends to strike me as a little sad and desperate, but it's also evidence of a genuine hunger people have for a spiritual dimension in their lives. There seems to be, however, a sense that it should be easy; that it shouldn't require effort.

Of course, those attending this Expo could be equally suspicious of Zen with its agnosticism and taut discipline. "Why," they might well ask, "does it have to be that hard?"

Zen practitioners – along with other Buddhists – regularly chant the Three Refuges:

> I take refuge in the Buddha;
> I take refuge in the Dharma;
> I take refuge in the Sangha.

The Buddha, in this formula, is understood to be not just the historical figure, Siddhartha Gautama, but also the lineage (fictional and yet not, as Josh Bartok noted) of those who proceeded from him down to the specific sanctioned teacher with whom one works. To recognize one's teacher as an embodiment of this tradition is an important aspect of Zen. One of the earliest and most difficult lessons that American Zen had to learn, however, was that it can't be done uncritically. The community and the individual student must be ready to challenge the teacher when necessary, and teachers need to have the humility to recognize that their area of expertise is limited, that awakening is not awakening across the board. A teacher can be spiritually enlightened and yet, as John Tarrant put it, remain "pretty clueless about a lot of other things."

The Dharma is the teaching. Zen is the meditation school of Buddhism, and meditation is central to Zen practice. But, as James Ford pointed out, Zen teachers need to be more than meditation instructors. Zen is a practical way of doing Buddhism. It was a Catholic priest – Robert Kennedy – who expressed it to me that way. And, as Sunyana Graef and many others have insisted, it has to manifest in both prajna and karuna, in the development of both wisdom and compassion. The way Father Kennedy expressed it – no doubt influenced by Bernie Glassman – is that it should lead to a life of enlightened service to others. There is a growing sense throughout American Zen that the quest for prajna alone is selfish. As Mel Weitsman told me during the first interview I conducted, practice has to be undertaken for the benefit of others. And even while Bodhin Kjolhede warned that to become too engaged, socially or politically, runs the risk of diminishing the root of Zen practice, he also said that one's responsibility in Zen is to "respond to what needs to be done," and he, himself, has taken a leadership role in examining how that applies to environmental awareness and responsibility.

The Sangha is the community of those who pursue this path and support one another in doing so. As Brother Fulfillment at Blue Cliff learned, "You need a community to practice with. You can't do this alone." But in North America, Dosho Port pointed out, that community remains small and dispersed. Dosho and Eshu Martin have sought to address this situation by providing opportunities for people to belong to a electronic sangha. The reality is, after all, that the world in which Zen is practiced today is not only different from the cultural contexts of Tang Dynasty China or Medieval Japan, it is also different from the environment in which the pioneers who brought Zen to North American lived and taught. It is reasonable to assume that sanghas will evolve in a variety of new manners appropriate to contemporary conditions.

2

I'm in Portland for the first public workshop to be offered at Great Tides Zen, newly established here by Dosho and his partner, Tetsugan Zummach. The zendo rents space from the Stillwater Yoga Studio, and its first regular morning sit took place only six days prior.

When I first interviewed Dosho, a year earlier, he had still been living in Minnesota. Since then, he has relocated to the East Coast. "I knew for years that after my kids were grown and I was able to retire from the schools that I wanted to do something different. After looking around, I settled on Portland, in part because there aren't a lot of other Zen teachers in the neighborhood, and yet it's close to our friends in Boundless Way."

The workshop takes place on a warm Sunday afternoon in early September. The space is a bright second storey room with hardwood floors and large windows in a gentrified warehouse on one of the harbor wharves. Expectations are modest. Dosho and Tetsugan set out fourteen zabutons and zafus; when a fifteenth participant shows up, another zabuton is improvised with blankets. A couple of people have obviously sat formally before; they bow to their cushions and then to the other participants before taking their places. Most have done some form of meditation. One is an Episcopalian priest who had studied with Robert Kennedy and at Boundless Way. Another of the participants had begun working with Dosho's on-line program, Vine of Obstacles, and then moved to Portland from Florida when he learned Dosho was coming here.

Fifteen is a respectable showing for an introductory workshop. The question, however, is how many will return?

I ask Tetsugan if they have found the area welcoming.

"Overwhelmingly," she tells me. "We came here on a couple of occasions before we moved, and we've checked out several of the sitting groups both within the Portland city limits and then up around West Bath and Brunswick, and people have been very welcoming and willing to talk with us about the experience here. And at the same time, the message that we've gotten is, 'People aren't really into teacher-student relationships here. People in Maine like to do their own thing, and so you might have a hard time getting a group together. They're not joiners.'"

When, later, I describe my interview with Tetsugan to Hugh Curran, he remarks, "That's fairly accurate."

People in Maine value their independence.

3

One of my favorite zendos in the United States is located 140 miles northeast of Portland in the small coastal community of Surry. The Morgan Bay Zendo is well-hidden. There is a small parking area on the road. It's marked, but one still has to be alert to notice it. I find something pleasing about the idea of little zendos hidden in out of the way places such as this – Yoshin Radin's on the Lieb Road south of Ithaca, Mitra Bishop's in Ojo Sarco – delighting in the thought of something vaguely subversive taking place in these isolated areas. A rough path leads from the parking area through the woods. At its end is a statue of a head with a finger raised to its lips, inviting one to silence. There is a moss garden to the left of the path and a little further on, to the right, a statue of Kannon.

Both sculptures are the work of Lenore Straus, who attained kensho in the early '60s during a sesshin with Hakuun Yasutani at Pendle Hill, Pennsylvania. Her enlightenment story is one of those included in Philip Kapleau's *Three Pillars of Zen*. The Kannon statue marks the way to what is called the Roshi stone, a large glacial boulder bearing a plaque which proclaims:

> Here lie some of the ashes of the Japanese Zen Master Goto Zuigan, my teacher. They were placed here in October 1968, with hope that his teaching will continue.

The ashes had been placed there by Walter Nowick who died in February of 2013, just one month before I began this pilgrimage. The following November, a portion of Walter's ashes were buried here as well. Another portion was flown to Japan and scattered near the plot where the remainder of Zuigan Goto's ashes had been interred.

The zendo is a rustic but elegant wood structure situated by a small pond. It was designed by one of Walter's students who'd had experience working on movie sets. The sides of the sloped roof are in two sections, the upper section more sharply angled than the lower, suggesting the curved roofs of Asian temples. The lumber for this – and other buildings on site – was harvested from Walter's land and milled here. Inside, two rows of tatami-covered tans face one another, each with twelve zabutons. Once the bell is rung in the zendo, there is almost perfect silence. There are no electric hums. There is no sound of traffic. All one hears is the chirping of birds and the peeps of the frogs in the pond.

Walter Nowick was a Julliard trained musician and the first American to receive authorization to teach in the Rinzai School. He had studied with Zuigan Goto at Daitokuji for sixteen years, then, when Goto died in 1965, returned to America and to this farm on the Morgan Bay Road. He had no intention of teaching Zen, but people found out about him and started turning up. Nowick did not make it easy for them.

Hugh Curran, who was my host during my first visit to Morgan Bay, had been Philip Kapleau's attendant at the Rochester Zen Center for several years before coming to Maine. That didn't carry much weight as far as Nowick was concerned. The practice for prospective students, Hugh tells me, was "to come to the tree in the front yard and stand there for a little while." In spite of living in North America for decades, Hugh still speaks with an Irish lilt. "I came here in 1975, and I asked what I should do and was told by a student, 'You'll have to stand in front of the tree. And sometime Walter may come out and say, "All right, come in." Or he may keep you standing there.' So, I did that for two or three days. He came out and said, 'What do you want?' And I said, 'Well, I'd like to be a student.' And he said, 'No. No, I've got too many.'"

Hugh had to come back twice more before being accepted. In this way, a small community gathered around what was then called Moonspring Hermitage. Walter allowed students to build cabins in which they lived without electricity or running water and under training conditions which, although not as harsh as those in Japan, were rigorous by American standards.

In the mid-1980s, while the Cold War was still simmering, Walter – whose heritage was Russian – sought a way to promote greater understanding and tolerance between the United States and the Soviet Union. Because his expertise was in music, he launched the Surry Opera Company which performed in both countries and raised funds to promote intercultural understanding.

While several Moonspring students became members of the chorus, others felt Walter was spending too much time with music and not enough time teaching. They wrote him a letter in which they expressed their concerns. He responded with a brief hand-written reply:

> It has become distinctly clear to me that I have fully involved myself in music and that it has taken me from my work with you as a teacher. Because of this situation, I wish to inform you without further delay of my decision to resign from Moonspring as teacher. I will help in any way I can to support its growth. I hope you will accept this decision along with me as the wisest one for all of us concerned.

A handful of former students (including Hugh Curran and his wife Susan) set up a board in order to maintain the zendo, and Walter turned it over to them in 1985 with the request that the original name – which had been derived from his Dharma name – be changed. They reincorporated as the Morgan Bay Zendo, which evolved into a center for meditation practice unaffiliated with any particular school of Buddhism.

The day after the Great Tides workshop, I have tea with Susan Guilford and Nancy Hathaway on the verandah of the multi-purpose building opposite the zendo. This is my second visit to Surry.

Susan and Nancy – along with Hugh – are current members of the board of directors of the Morgan Bay Zendo. Nancy is also a Senior Dharma Teacher in the Kwan Um School of Zen. "Bobby Rhodes and I lived together at the Providence Zen Center," she tells me. "We raised our babies together." She also interned with Jon Kabat-Zinn and makes a living by teaching mindfulness-based stress reduction. Another board member, Tom Poole, is a student at the Dharma Drum Center not far from Blue Cliff Monastery. Dharma Drum is in the Chinese Chan tradition. Hugh Curran had also studied with the Dharma Drum teacher, Shi Fu Sheng Yen, and in the past has invited him to lead retreats at Morgan Bay.

Susan brings up the mission statement of the Morgan Bay Zendo on her laptop and reads it to me. The statement declares that the purpose of the zendo is "to establish, maintain, and support a religious and philosophical community center or centers dedicated to the study, precepts, and practice of Buddhism."

"It does not say Zen Buddhism," Susan point outs.

For nine months of the year, there is Sunday morning zazen in the zendo. In the summer, there is also a Wednesday night sitting, and this past year Nancy began holding Kwan Um-style sits on Tuesday nights. In addition to the regularly scheduled sitting periods, the zendo offers a slate of workshops and retreats over the summer, although this past year some of these had to be cancelled for lack of enrollment. Participation is never large; the best attended retreat during the past summer – Cultivating Loving Kindness – had fifteen people. During a later conversation with Hugh Curran, he argues that the Zen and Yoga day-retreats, which he conducted twice a year with the aid of two yoga instructors, have been well-attended in the past. But as Shishin Wick might have asked, what is well attended? Hugh tells me they averaged between 12 and 18 participants.

This is a beautiful place, but the reality remains that it is underutilized.

Susan informs me that, shortly after my first visit, the board decided to seek "the advice of an advisory committee to look at our situation and give us some strategic advice. We looked at every aspect of the zendo, the practice, the physical plant, all of that. And we're really taking to heart what they recommended. I think it's safe to say that their recommendations and the push that's given the board is going to inform what we're going to do from now on. And we're clear as a board at this point that we're not looking for another teacher. The advisory board mentioned that as a possibility. But they were working under the assumption that we're not planning to do that right now, and they don't really recommend it."

"I think there is, in fact, a little resistance to having a teacher," Nancy adds. "There has been in the past. There's been resistance to the word 'teacher' and having a teacher. My guess is that people here have just sort of had it with teachers."

"The board as currently constituted," Susan agrees, "doesn't presently want to have a teacher come. And if we did, the teacher that I might find would be different from the one that anyone else would want."

A few weeks later, Hugh makes a similar point. The situation in Surry, he tells me, is very different from that in larger population centers, such as Santa Fe where Henry Shukman had been recruited by the Mountain Cloud Zen Center. Morgan Bay, according to Hugh, needs to remain eclectic in order to remain viable. "You have to suit the people that come here. And if they say, 'Oh, well, you guys are into a particular form of Japanese Zen. We'd prefer to go someplace else.' Or, 'You're just a Chinese group, so we won't get involved.' Or just a Korean group or this or that. So we try to cover the whole gamut. If you got someone with transmission, transmission from what? From a particular group in a Korean tradition or a particular group in a Japanese tradition? That might be quite suitable for Portland or down in Boston, where people could decide, 'I'm not so great about that. I think I'll go to the Tibetan Center over here or to this group over there.' But we don't have ten different options. We have to be the ten for everybody."

Both Hugh and Nancy offer retreats at Morgan Bay, although Hugh admitted to me during our first meeting that he does not have official transmission in any of the Zen traditions. It can be a touchy point.

To have "transmission" or "inka" amounts to having a license within the Zen establishment to teach or, especially in the Soto tradition, to be the abbot of a temple. This can matter a great deal to students who want to be certain of the credentials of their teachers, especially if they hope to be similarly licensed at some point.

The "license" analogy comes from a friend of Hugh's, Brian Victoria.[86]

As we know, it is quite possible for someone to be a very good and safe car driver even though they are, formally speaking, "unlicensed" and vice-versa. In general, however, being "licensed" is some indication of skill level while being "unlicensed" suggests, but does not prove, they are not.

Victoria develops the analogy further to shed light on the inappropriate behavior of certain teachers.

If Zen students would simply treat inka and Dharma Transmission as licenses, they could readily understand that there is such a thing as "reckless drivers" let alone "drivers driving under the influence of alcohol," etc. Zen students should, as "pedestrians," always exercise the utmost precaution in crossing the street and even more precaution when riding in a car driven by one of these folks. Seat belts, air bags, plus as much "common sense" as can be mustered, are all of the utmost importance!

Both Nancy and Hugh eschew the term "teacher." Ruben Habito – a former Jesuit priest who received Dharma transmission from Koun Yamada Roshi in the Sanbo Zen tradition – called Hugh a "facilitator." "I like that term," Hugh tells me. "I facilitate."

But while the board – and they themselves – might not consider them teachers, I wonder if it isn't likely that retreat participants do. Nancy admits that it's probable.

"But I don't think of Nancy or her role here as 'teacher' with a capital 'T,'" Susan insists. "Or Hugh. I think of it as a lower case 't.' I mean, Hugh has no credentials, but he offers wisdom, as we all do, and he's sharing that here. And I think of Nancy's role in this context as a person who has tremendous wisdom and experience."

"People in this community, like Susan, who have studied for a long time wouldn't be interested in having me be their teacher," Nancy says.

I concede the point. "But given your mission statement," I say, "the purpose of the Morgan Bay Zendo is to maintain a Buddhist presence in the region. Right?"

Susan frowns. "For me, it's not that Down East Maine needs to have a Buddhist presence. It's more like, this place is here and has provided – and is providing – a place for people to practice Buddhism, therefore we should nurture that."

"Zen is a practice," Nancy reminds me, "and we're a practice center, and it's to encourage, to cultivate the mind that's before thinking and to open to what we call, in the Kwan Um School, 'not knowing.'"

"And you believe that people coming to the retreats offered here can encounter that?"

"Of course."

Given the nature and interest of the students who come to Morgan Bay, perhaps the matter of licensing is beside the point.

Morgan Bay provides a beautiful environment conducive to practice; there are people here with extensive experience in several traditions but not a resident teacher. Guest teachers have led retreats and workshops not only in Zen but in yoga, mindfulness, and even Burmese Theravada Buddhism. Hugh points out that, especially in the '90s, they had significant attendance at retreats led by teachers like Shi Fu Sheng Yen. But that was then and this is now, and the immediate issue is solvency, which means continuing to attract people to come for retreats or extended stays.

Susan refers to Hugh's Zen and Yoga retreats, noting that those who attend "always felt that the day has been extraordinary. We are accustomed – and you are accustomed – to silence, to slowing down, looking at things, that whole mindfulness quality. But a lot of people out in the world are not. So just to come to a place that's quiet and beautiful and where you have to slow down is a gift for a lot of people."

Following the recommendations of the Advisory Committee, the board is considering developing the site so that it can be rented to other groups and used as a location for private, non-guided, retreats.

"I asked the board this question," Nancy says. "'What would you like to see down here?' So off the top of my head, what I would like to see? I'd like to see people living here for the summer who want to practice and train in Zen. I would like to see those people be involved in raising vegetables and preparing food. I was going to say, I would like to see more people here, but I'm very protective. Not too many. A few. But definitely I would like to see more people coming. And retreats."

Susan's vision is similar. "I love the idea of there being places for people to be able to come for short or even longer periods of time to work on themselves. And so to provide a place for them to do that and a structure for them to do that. Encouraging retreats from different traditions so that people can find what speaks to them. And having a lot of younger people involved so that it's evolving. Because I feel it has a future that isn't knowable at this point. I see it evolving, and we – the people who are on the board right now – are caretakers of it. Whatever its future is is not clear, because we're not part of a tradition. If you're part of the Catholic Church, you know where that Church is going to be, potentially, a hundred years from now. We don't know that.

"Walter didn't intend to start this, but he allowed it to flower at that particular moment in time in his own way. And here it is. People have picked it up, not because he asked them to pick it up, but because it's here. And I think it has a purpose in our culture that we don't even know yet. And so right now, we need to keep it going and take small steps so that it can survive and so that we can encourage that growth."

4

Dosho and Tetsugan are in full Soto robes during the workshop in Portland, rakusus tucked under their belts. "Keeping this way alive is hugely important for the future," Dosho tells me. It is what Chozen Bays had called "the prime directive," making sure the way does not die out. For Dosho, the "way" is both the practice and the tradition which maintains it.

The workshop starts with a review of the purpose and path of Zen, then covers correct posture, focussing the attention in meditation, kinhin (walking meditation), prostrations, liturgy, and even a brief overview of the precepts.

"Zen doesn't do anything," Tetsugan tells me. "You do Zen. So it's really about what you bring to it and what you put into it. If you're just interested in a little stress reduction, if you just want a little community, that's fine. You come and you engage to that extent. But I think the emphasis shifts if you decide you want to enter training. Daido Loori had this saying that in practice you decide what you want to do; when you enter training, it's decided for you."

And training requires some kind of formal environment, a relationship with a teacher, and a commitment of time and energy. I suspect the idea of practice appeals to a larger number of people than the idea of training and all that it involves.

Toni Packer, who removed herself from the formal atmosphere of the Buddhist tradition, said that she wasn't worried about the future of the practice of meditative inquiry:

> I'm not concerned about the future. I'm saying this completely honestly. From its very beginnings, which cannot even be remembered, this whole amazing unfolding of inquiry and discovery in silent space has completely taken care of itself in an unfathomable way. Shall we now worry about how it will continue?[87]

If Zen were not available, no doubt some other form would evolve to take its place for those few Dosho had spoken of who may be widely dispersed yet still want "to go deeply." Zen isn't, of course, the only route, but it is a route, and, for me, it remains a valid one in spite of the difficulties it has faced being established on this side of the Pacific.

But it is not, and has never been, an easy route.

"People, Americans especially, do seem to be interested in the fast and easy way," Dosho tells me as we sit in a park before the workshop. "And even though Zen is the 'sudden school,' a lot of times it's not so fast and not so easy. When I met Joseph, one of the teachers at the yoga center, I said, 'We're going to start at 5:30 in the morning.' He said, 'Wow. That's kind of inconvenient.' And I said, 'Yeah – you know – Zen is inconvenient, uncomfortable, repetitive, and uncompromising. Do you want to try it?' And he said, 'Yeah. I think so.'"

Postscript

Zui Jiao was a disciple of Zhaozhou. After his master's death, Zui Jiao visited the Zen teacher Fayan Wenyi. Fayan commented, "Your teacher was a remarkable man. I understand that once a cypress tree was the subject of his talk. Is that so?"

"There was no such talk," Zui Jiao asserted.

"There wasn't? That's odd. All of the monks I've met who studied with Zhaozhou speak of his reference to a cypress tree in answer to the question, 'Why did Bodhidharma come from west?' How can you claim otherwise?"

Zui Jiao roared, "My master said no such thing! Please don't disrespect him by saying so!"

Acknowledgments

Many people generously assisted in the preparation of this book. I am grateful to each of them:

- Hadrian Abbot (Tahoma Sogenji)
- David Anderson (Springwater Center)
- Geoffrey Shugen Arnold (Zen Mountain Monastery)
- Josh Bartok (Greater Boston Zen Center)
- Jan Chozen Bays (Great Vow Zen Monastery)
- Sarah Bender (Springs Mountain Sangha)
- Mitra Bishop (Mountain Gate, New Mexico, and Hidden Valley Zen Center, California)
- Melissa Myozen Blacker (Boundless Way Zen Temple). Special thanks to Melissa who, along with David Dae An Rynick, provided me a home base on my way to and from conducting interviews in New York state.
- Louis Bricault (Montreal Zen Center)
- Roger Brouillette (Montreal Zen Center)
- Ti'an Callery (Vermont Zen Center)
- Shinge Roko Sherry Chayat (Dai Bosatsu Zendo)
- Wayne Coger (Springwater Center)
- Brother Contemplation [Quan Chieu/Taylor Rentz] (Blue Cliff Monastery)
- Hugh and Susan Curran (Morgan Bay Zendo). Special thanks to Hugh and Susan for providing me a room in Surry.
- Dr. Ann Cutcher (Enso House). Special thanks to Ann for "flushing" my ears.
- Sister Dang Nghiem [Huong Huynh] (Blue Cliff Monastery). I am also grateful to Sister D for permission to quote material from her book, *Healing: A Woman's Journey from Doctor to Nun*. Berkeley: Parallax Press, 2010.
- Lodru Dawa (Great Vow Zen Monastery)

- Roch Denis (Montreal Zen Center)
- Joan Yushin Derrick (Zen Mountain Monastery)
- Monique Dumont (Montreal Zen Center)
- Bonnie Durland (Springwater Center)
- Garrett Evans (Great Vow Zen Monastery)
- Christopher Ezzell (Puget Sound Zen Center)
- Carole Ferrari (Toronto Zen Center)
- Katherine Foo (Boundless Way Zen Temple)
- James Ford (Boundless Way Zen)
- Brother Fulfillment [Phap Man/Aaron Solomon] (Blue Cliff Monastery)
- Patrick Gallagher (A Toronto Zendo of Sanbo Zen)
- Bernie Glassman (Zen Peacemakers)
- Sandra González (Springwater Center)
- Sunyana Graef (Vermont Zen Center)
- Jodo Tina Grant (Dai Bosatsu Zendo)
- Kelly Anne Graves (Great Vow Zen Monastery)
- Malcolm Griffin (Montreal Zen Center)
- Susan and Charles Guilford (Morgan Bay Zendo)
- Zenshin Michael Haederle (North Valley Sitting Group)
- Blanche Hartman (San Francisco Zen Center)
- Nancy Hathaway (Morgan Bay Zendo)
- Taigen Henderson (Toronto Zen Center)
- Special thanks to my sister-in-law, Ging, and her husband, Richard Hudson who drove me to the various locations for the west coast interviews.
- Father Kevin Hunt (Day Star Zendo)
- Father Robert Kennedy (Morning Star Zendo)
- Jody Hojin Kimmel (Zen Mountain Monastery)
- Bodhin Kjolhede (Rochester Zen Center)
- MyoO Renate Krämer (Enso House)
- Dairin Larry Larrick (Tahoma Sogenji)
- Myo On Susan Linnell (Albuquerque Zero Zen Center)
- Albert Low (Montreal Zen Center)
- Sister Elaine MacInnes (Freeing the Human Spirit). I am also grateful to Sister Elaine for permission to quote material from her book, *Zen Contemplation: A Bridge of Living Water*. Toronto: Novalis, 2001.
- Special thanks to Mary Main and David Wiggins, who provided me a home-base while I conducted interviews in Toronto.
- Seiju Bob Mammoser (Albuquerque Zen Center)
- Konrad Ryushin Marchaj (Zen Mountain Monastery)

- Genjo Marinello (Chobo-ji)
- Eshu Martin (Zenwest Buddhist Society)
- Special thanks to my sister, Anita McDaniel, and her husband, Gene Ramsey, for their hospitality in Colorado.
- Special thanks to my wife, Joan McDaniel, who accompanied me on most of these trips and who read and re-read the drafts of each chapter.
- Levi McGovern (Great Vow Zen Monastery)
- Gary Morgan (Great Vow Zen Monastery)
- Zengetsu Myokyo (Enpuku-ji)
- Tenney Nathanson (Desert Rain Zen)
- Special thanks to John Negru for taking in an orphan.
- Jeffrey Onjin Plant (Zen Mountain Monastery). Special thanks to Onjin for asking me the question.
- Mihaela Poca (Toronto Zen Center)
- Dosho Port (Great Tides Zen)
- John Pulleyn (Rochester Zen Center)
- David Yoshin Radin (Ithaca Zen Center)
- Marcia Khadija Radin (Body Mind Restoration Retreats)
- Special thanks to Jim and Jackie Reither for their hospitality in Albuquerque.
- Bobby Rhodes (Kwan Um School of Zen)
- Robert Moshin Ricci (Zen Mountain Monastery)
- Dharman Rice (Vermont Zen Center)
- Kaijo Matthew Russell (Dai Bosatsu Zendo)
- David Dae An Rynick (Boundless Way Zen Temple)
- Stephen Zenki Salad
- Shea Ikusei Settimi (Zen Mountain Monastery)
- Richard Shrobe (Kwan Um School of Zen)
- Henry Shukman (Mountain Cloud Zen Center)
- Myoki Stewart (San Francisco Zen Center)
- Myogen Steve Stucky (San Francisco Zen Center)
- Joan Sutherland (Cloud Dragon: The Joan Sutherland Dharma Works)
- John Tarrant (Pacific Zen Institute)
- Peter Torma (Enso House)
- Cynthia Trowbridge (Enso House)
- Edie Tsong (Cloud Dragon: The Joan Sutherland Dharma Works)
- Cheryl Vanderburg (Freeing the Human Spirit)
- Brian Daizen Victoria (International Research Center for Japanese Studies, Kyoto)
- Brother Phap Vu [Clifford Brown] (Blue Cliff Monastery)

- Michael Waldron (Mountain Cloud Zen Center)
- David Weinstein (Pacific Zen Institute)
- Mel Weitsman (San Francisco Zen Center)
- Jean Ann Wertz (Zen Mountain Monastery)
- Gerry Shishin Wick (Great Mountain Zen Center at Maitreya Abbey)
- Tetsugan Zummach (Great Tides Zen)

Notes

1. Mark Oppenheimer, *The Zen Predator of the Upper East Side* (The Atlantic Books, 2013).

2. http://sweepingzen.com/everybody-knows-by-eshu-martin/ - November 2012.

3. Letter from Myo On Susan Linnell to the Witnessing Council, January 19, 2011.

4. The full text of the poem by Chizuko Karen Joy Tasaka can be found on the website http://sasakiarchive.com maintained by Kabutso Malone. Kabutso also maintains a much longer archive of primary sources on Eido Shimano at http://www.shimanoarchive.com.

5. From the statement posted by Ryushin Marchaj on the ZMM website, January 26, 2015.

6. SFZC is a Soto Zen Center; Dai Bosatsu, in the Catskills, is the first Rinzai Zen monastery in America.

7. Michael Downing, *Shoes Outside the Door* (Washington, DC: Counterpoint, 2001), p. 75.

8. Ibid., p. 145.

9. Shunryu Suzuki, *Zen Mind, Beginner's Mind* (New York: Weatherhill, 1994), p. 21.

10. http://www.sfzc.org/zc/display.asp?catid=1,5,157&pageid=520.

11. The other was Robert Aitken's heir, Nelson Foster.

12. http://www.sfzc.org/zc/display.asp?catid=1,10&pageid=3977.

13. Although "osho" is a traditional term, it is not in common use at other centers. Joshu Sasaki and Rinzai-ji use a vocabulary which often differs from that of other American Zen centers.

14. http://sasakiarchive.com/PDFs/20121201_Kogan_Seiju.pdf.

15. http://www.nytimes.com/2013/02/12/world/asia/zen-buddhists-roiled-by-accusations-against-teacher.html?_r=0.

16. See page 19 above.

17. Email dated Dec 11, 2012.

18. Letter to Joshu Sasaki and Board of Directors of Rinzai-ji dated July 6, 1992. http://www.sasakiarchive.com/PDFs/1992_Resignation_letter.pdf.

19. http://www.bodymindretreats.com.

20. November 30, 2013. http://sasakiarchive.com/PDFs/20131130_ZCV_Eshin. pdf.

21. Letter dated December 13, 2016. http://www.sasakiarchive.com/PDFs/20131213_Gang_of_18_Hosen_Demand.pdf.

22. One of "breakthrough" koans most frequently given to beginning students: A student of the way asked Zhaozhou in all seriousness, "Does a dog have Buddha nature?" Zhaozhou replied, "Mu!" ["No" or "nothing."]

23. Soen Nakagawa was Eido Shimano's teacher and the first abbot at Dai Bosatsu. See Richard Bryan McDaniel, *The Third Step East: Zen Masters of America* (Richmond Hill, ON: Sumeru, 2015), Chapter Eight.

24. http://www.shimanoarchive.com/PDFs/20100816_Takabayashi.pdf.

25. http://northwestdharma.org/2013/06/takagone.

26. http://www.shimanoarchive.com/PDFs/20131213_Lewis_Sweep.pdf.

27. When the database was restored a few months later, access was limited to AZTA members. In an email to me, James Ford explained that this was because AZTA views itself as a mutual support group and not "as a credentialing body, and the list has been seen by some to imply a kind of endorsement."

28. Zen Master Rama (Frederick Lenz) was a self-proclaimed spiritual teacher generally considered to have been a cult leader.

29. Dosho Port, *Keep Me in Your Heart a While* (Somerville, MA: Wisdom Publications, 2008), p. 29.

30. Shodo Harada, *How to Do Zazen* (Kyoto: The Institute for Zen Studies, 2010), pp. 4-5.

31. Ibid., p. 7.

32. Ibid., p. 24.

33. Ibid.

34. Ibid., p. 35.

35. Ibid., p. 25.

36. David Daiku Trowbridge, *Enso House* (Greenbank, WA: Abiding Nowhere Press, 2013), p. 66.

37. Ibid., p. 69.

38. Sanbo Zen does not recognize Philip Kapleau as an authorized teacher and questions his right to claim authorship of *The Three Pillars of Zen*. They insist that the book was the work of three people, Kapleau and two others

he identifies as his "collaborators" in the Editor's Preface – Koun Yamada and Akira Kubota – but whose names do not appear on the title page. The actual wording on the title page states that the book is "compiled and edited, with translations, introductions and notes, by Philip Kapleau."

39. Elaine MacInnes, *Zen Contemplation: A Bridge of Living Water* (Ottawa: Novalis, 2001), p. 22.

40. Ibid., p. 25.

41. Ibid., p. 28.

42. Ibid., p. 46.

43. Ibid., p. 52.

44. Ibid., p. 106.

45. Michael Danan Henry received Dharma transmission from Philip Kapleau and, later, from Robert Aitken. He is considered a member of Aitken's Diamond Sangha lineage.

46. Lin Yutang, *The Wisdom of Laotse* (New York: The Modern Library, 1948), p. 41.

47. John Tarrant, *The Light Inside the Dark* (New York: Harper, 1998), p. 19.

48. Ibid., p. 5.

49. Nyogen Senzaki was a Rinzai monk who lived in the United States from 1905 until his death in 1958. Before WWII broke out, he entered into a long distance correspondence with Soen Nakagawa which eventually brought Nakagawa to America. See Richard Bryan McDaniel, *The Third Step East: Zen Masters of America* (Richmond Hill, ON: Sumeru, 2015), Chapter Two.

50. Albert Low is the director of the Montreal Zen Center.

51. After Tarrant left Hawaii, Aitken's principle heir was Nelson Foster. Foster was one of the two teachers – along with Richard Baker – who declined to be interviewed for this book.

52. See fnt. 22.

53. Shasta Abbey in California.

54. Traditionally, students seeking to be accepted by a teacher make a gift of incense.

55. Tarrant, op. cit., p. 13.

56. An essay by Dogen that begins: "Because all things are Buddhadharma, there are delusion, realization, practice, birth and death, Buddhas and sentient beings. Because myriad things are without an abiding self, there is no delusion, no realization, no Buddha, no sentient being, no birth and death. The Buddha way, thus, is leaping clear of abundance and lack; therefore, there are birth and death, delusion and realization, sentient beings and Buddhas."

57. Some variation of the question "Who am I?" ("Who am I before thought arises?" or "Who is aware?") can be used as an initial, or "breakthrough," koan.

58. Helen Tworkov, *Zen in America* (San Francisco: North Point Press, 1989), p. 143.

59. Chogyam Trungpa was a Tibetan born lama believed to be the eleventh incarnation of the traditional abbots of the Surmang Monastery. After the Chinese invasion of Tibet, Trungpa came first to Britain, then to the United States where he founded the Shambhala school of Buddhism.

60. John Daido Loori, *The Eight Gates of Zen* (Boston: Shambhala, 2002), pp. 6-8.

61. G. I. Gurdjieff was an Armenian spiritual teacher who sought to help students achieve what he called a "higher state of consciousness."

62. Dennis Genpo Merzel is, along with Bernie Glassman and John Loori, one of Taizan Maezumi's Dharma heirs.

63. Konrad Ryushin Marchaj and Kay Senyu Larson, "How to Start a Monastery" http://www.mro.org/mr/archive/18-3/articles/monastery.htm.

64. Acharya Rajneesh (or Osho) was a cult leader known as the "Sex Guru" because of his promotion of sexual freedom. He established a community in Oregon, which, in 1985, engaged in the largest bio-terrorism act to be carried out in the United States when his followers tried to poison the residents of a nearby community with salmonella.

65. The Jesus Prayer is a Christian meditation practice in which the prayer is silently repeated, like a mantra, in conjunction with one's breath. Breathing in, one recites, "Lord Jesus Christ," and breathing out, "have mercy on me."

66. James Ishmael Ford, *Zen Master Who?* (Boston: Wisdom Publications, 2006), pp. 153-54.

67. http://www.rzc.org/wp-content/uploads/2012/01/Roshi-and-His-Teachers. pdf.

68. Case twelve in the *Mumonkan*.

69. See page 117 above.

70. As a child in 1929, Krishnamurti had been identified by the Theosophical movement as the incarnation of Maitreya, the Buddha of the future, and they groomed him to become the "World Teacher." When he reached the age of 34, however, he dissolved his association with the Theosophists, denied their claims for him, and advised would-be disciples and followers to question all forms of authority or religious formulae.

71. Lenore Friedman, *Meetings with Remarkable Women* (Boston: Shambhala, 2000), pp. 52-53.

72. Toni Packer, *The Wonder of Presence* (Boston: Shambhala, 2002), pp. 5-6.

73. Ibid., p. 12.

74. Ibid., p. 13.

75. Ibid., p. 33.

76. Tangen Harada had been trained as a kamikaze pilot during the war and had committed himself to die in the defence of his country. The war ended, however, before he was called upon to make that sacrifice. Driven by what now seemed the pointless deaths of so many of his companions, he became a student and later the heir of Daiun Harada Roshi, with whom both Yasutani Roshi and Philip Kapleau later studied.

77. Port, op. cit., p. 21.

78. Kong-an is the Korean term for koan.

79. Nhat Hanh's students refer to him as "Thay," which means "teacher."

80. Sister Dang Nghiem, *Healing: A Woman's Journey from Doctor to Nun* (Berkeley: Parallax Press, 2010), E-edition.

81. Ibid., Location 91.

82. Ibid., Location 151.

83. Ibid., location 484.

84. Ibid., location 587.

85. Ibid., location 1004.

86. See pages 84-85 above. The Brian Victoria quotations come from an email sent to Hugh Curran on October 25, 2014.

87. Toni Packer, op. cit., p. 33.

Glossary

Abhidharma – A collection of sutra commentaries, probably dating back to the 3rd Century BCE. The Abhidharma is part of the *Tripitaka* (Three Baskets) which make up the canonical scriptures of Buddhism. The other two parts are the Sutras (the recorded teachings of the Buddha) and the Vinaya (the rules that govern monastic life).

Ahimsa – To do no injury.

Ango – 90 day intensive training period.

Angya – "To go on foot." The term refers to the traditional pilgrimage undertaken by Zen monks in the later phase of their training.

Awakening – One of several terms referring to achieving insight into the basic interconnectedness of all of Being.

AZTA – American Zen Teachers Association.

Bhakti – Devotional practice.

Bhikshu – Sanskrit term for a monk.

Bhikshuni – Sanskrit term for a nun.

Blue Cliff Record – See *Hekiganroku*.

Blue Tara – see Tara.

Bodhidharma – Legendary Indian figure who brought Zen to China. Bodhidharma is considered the 28th patriarch of India Buddhism and the first patriarch of Chinese Zen.

Bodhisattva – An enlightened (Bodhi) being (sattva). Certain historical or legendary Bodhisattvas function much the same as Saints in the Christian tradition.

Bodhisattva Precepts or Vows – A moral code for monks and nuns common in Mahayana Buddhism.

Book of Serenity – A classic koan collection, also known as the *Shoyo Roku*.

Buddha – Literally, "The Awakened One." When used with a capital B, it usually refers to the historic Buddha, Siddhartha Gautama. With a lower-case b, it refers to any enlightened being.

Buddha Hall – In temples, the hall where devotional activities such as chanting are carried out. The hall normally contains an image of the Buddha. Cf. Hondo.

Buddhahood – The state of being fully awakened.

Chan – Chinese term which the Japanese pronounced as "Zen," meaning meditation.

Dahui – Dahui Zonggao, a 12th century Chinese Chan master who revitalized koan practice.

Dai- – A prefix meaning "great," as in Dai-kensho.

Daisan – Private meeting between teacher and student, similar to dokusan or sanzen.

Dao – Formerly "Tao." The "way." The term originates in Daoism (Taoism) and refers to the fundamental nature of reality.

Daoism – The teaching regarding the nature of the Dao.

Daodejing – Formerly *Tao Te Ching*. The basic text of Daoism. It is a collection of 81 verse chapters attributed to the legendary Laozi.

Denkai denbo – In some schools of Rinzai Zen, the first of two stages in the transmission process, followed by inka shomei.

Dharma – A term with multiple meanings but generally referring to the teachings of Buddhism.

Dharma Heir – The heir of a Zen teacher whose understanding of the Dharma qualifies him/her to be a teacher as well.

Dharma Holder – An initial stage in the formation of a teacher, comes before receiving full transmission. Cf. Denkai denbo.

Dharmakaya – In Mahayana Buddhism, one of the "three bodies [kaya]" of the Buddha. It is the realm of Emptiness from which all being arises and to which all being returns.

Dharma Transmission – see Transmission

-do – A suffix referring to a room or space dedicated to a specific activity or purpose. A zendo, for example, is a space in which Zen (meditation) is practiced.

Dogen Kigen – 13th century Japanese Buddhist credited with bringing Soto Zen to Japan.

Dokusan – Private interview between student and teacher. Cf. Sanzen.

Emptiness – A basic and easily misunderstood Buddhist concept about the nature of Reality. Essentially, emptiness refers to an intuition (rather than an intellectual understanding) of the fact that all things are empty of self-nature, i.e., are composed of a variety of elements which are in a constant state of flux and are interdependent with all other elements. The term may also refer to the formless – and yet creative – Void from which all things arise and to which they return.

Five Defilements – See Klesas.

Five Desires – The five senses.

Four Noble Truths – 1) All of existence is characterized by suffering; 2) Suffering is caused by craving; 3) Suffering can be ameliorated by overcoming craving; 4) Craving can be overcome by following the Noble Eightfold path, which consists of right view, right intention, right speech, right action, right livelihood, right effort, right mindfulness, and right meditation.

Four Vows – 1) To save [liberate] all beings; 2) to eliminate endless blind passions; 3) to pass innumerable Dharma Gates; 4) to achieve the great way of Buddha.

Fusu – A temple official in charge of administrative and financial matters.

Gassho – To bring the palms of the hands together, often accompanied by a bow. It is a sign of respect and reverence.

The Gateless Gateway – see *Mumonkan*.

Genjokoan – A work by Dogen Kigen. See fnt. 56.

Go – A two person board game which originated in China about the 5th century BCE.

Green Tara – See Tara.

Guanyin – See Kannon

Hakuin – Hakuin Ekaku, 18th century Japanese Zen monk and reformer of the koan tradition.

Han – A suspended wooden block struck with a mallet to signal events at a temple.

Hanshan – Semi-legendary 9th century Chinese Zen poet.

Hara – The abdomen, especially when understood as a person's center.

Heart Sutra – A short sutra on "emptiness" frequently chanted in Zen monasteries and temples.

Hekiganroku – A classic koan collection, also known as the *Blue Cliff Record*.

Hinayana – "The Lesser Vehicle." A term used in Mahayana Buddhism to refer to earlier schools of Buddhism. Those schools prefer the term Theravada, The Way of the Elders.

Hondo – The main hall of a Japanese Temple. Cf. Buddha Hall.

Hosan – The period between training periods in a Zen temple.

Hungry Ghosts – "Pretas." Hungry Ghosts are images of the unquenchable appetites to which all persons are subject.

Hwadu – Korean term for Wato, which see.

Ikebana – Flower arranging.

Inji – The attendant to an abbot or teacher.

Inka (inka shomei) – "Authorized seal proving attainment." Official transmission, especially in the Rinzai School. It is the recognition by a teacher that the student has completed training and is ready to teach independently.

Jataka Tales – Popular folk tales about the previous lives of the Buddha in various animal and human forms.

-ji – A suffix meaning "temple."

Ji Do Poep – In Korean Zen, the rank before that of a Zen Master (Soen Sa Nim). The term means "Able to point the way."

Jihatsu – A set of nested bowls used for meals. Cf. Oryoki.

Jikijitsu – The monitor in charge of a zendo.

Jizo Bodhisattva – A Bodhisattva sometimes portrayed as a child, sometimes as a pilgrim. Jizo is the protector of children, women, and travellers.

Joshu Jushin – See Zhaozhou Congshen.

Joriki – Energy derived from meditation.

Jukai – Formally accepting the Precepts and becoming a Buddhist.

Kado – Ritual tea ceremony

Kagyu – A Tibetan school of Buddhism known as the "Oral Lineage."

Kanji – Japanese adaptation of Chinese ideograms.

Kannon – "Guanyin" in Chinese. The female Bodhisattva of Compassion.

Kao – A formal signature in kanji.

Karma – Literally, "action." The concept in Asian thought that actions have consequences. Popularly viewed as one's past actions, in this or previous lives, resulting in one's current situation.

Karuna – Compassion.

Keisu – A bowl-like bell.

Kenshukai – A teacher-training retreat in the Sanbo Zen tradition.

Kessei – A formal training period in the Rinzai tradition.

Kensho – Seeing into one's True Nature. Enlightenment.

Kinhin – Walking meditation.

Klesas – The Five Defilements or Poisons: Ignorance, Attachment, Anger, Pride, and Envy.

Koan – (The plural of "koan" is "koan.") Usually an anecdote from the lives of the Zen masters of the past – primarily those in Tang Dynasty China – often expressed in the form of a question. The question or situation described becomes the focus of a Zen student's meditative practice and helps the student attain insight. While koan cannot be resolved through reasoning, an understanding of them can be achieved through intuition. Individual koan are referred to as "Cases," in the sense of legal precedences in jurisprudence.

Kotsu – Staff of office carried by Zen teachers.

Kwan Um – The Korean School of Zen established by Seung Sahn.

Kyosaku – "The Encouragement Stick." A long stick flattened at one end, used by monitors during zazen to encourage (or wake up) meditators.

Linji – The Chinese name of Rinzai.

Maha Prajna Paramita – The great wisdom that carries one to the other side.

Mahayana – "The Greater Vehicle." The Buddhist schools which evolved from the earlier Theravada tradition, much as Protestantism evolved from Catholicism. Zen is a form of Mahayana Buddhism.

Maitreya – The Buddha of the future.

Mala – An rosary of 108 beads.

Mantra – A word, phrase, or short prayer which is repeated as a focus of meditation.

Metta – Loving-kindness.

Mettabhavana – Meditation on loving-kindness.

Mondo – A Zen dialogue.

Mu – "Wu" in Chinese. Meaning, "No, not, nothing." Usually refers to the opening koan in the *Mumonkan*: A student of the way asked Joshu in all seriousness, "Does a dog have Buddha-nature?" Joshu replied, "Mu!"

Muji – The koan "mu." See above.

Mumonkan – A classic koan collection, also known as *The Gateless Gateway*.

Nirmanakaya – The body (kaya) of the Buddha as a physical individual who lived at a particular time in a particular place. See also "Dharmakaya."

Oryoki – A formal way of eating using three nested bowls. Cf. Jihatsu.

O-sesshin - Some Rinzai schools distinguish between o-sesshin, which is always seven days, and other sesshin which may be for shorter periods.

Osho – Priest.

Ox-Herding Pictures – A series of ten illustrations portraying the stages of growth in Zen practice. The illustrations show a young man seeking, finding, and taming an ox.

Paramitas – The Six Perfections: generosity, ethical behavior, tolerance, diligence, concentration, and insight.

Parinirvana – Usually refers to the death of the Buddha.

Prajna – Wisdom.

Precepts – Ethical teachings Buddhists commit to abide by.

Rakusu – A bib-like garment representing the robe of the Buddha.

Realization – Realization of one's True Nature, and therefore realization of the True Nature of all of Being. Awakening.

Rinpoche – A spiritual teacher within Tibetan Buddhism.

Rinzai – The School of Zen practice derived from Linji Yixuan.

Rinzai-ji – "Rinzai Temple." Joshu Sasaki's primary temple located in Los Angeles.

Rohatsu – The anniversary of the Buddha's enlightenment in December. The sesshin associated with this anniversary is considered the most daunting of the year.

Roshi – Literally, "Old Teacher." In North American Zen it has come to mean a fully qualified Zen teacher.

Samadhi – The state of concentration or absorption.

Samsara – The repeated cycle of rebirth, life, and death.

Samu – Work period.

Samugi – Work clothes. Informal clothing worn by Zen monks.

-san – A Japanese suffix roughly equivalent to "Mr." or "Ms." It can also refer to a mountain, as in Tahoma-san.

Sangha – The community.

San matsu documents – Official documents of transmission, particularly in the Soto School of Zen.

Sanzen - Private interview between student and teacher. Cf. Dokusan.

Satori – Awakening, enlightenment.

Satsang – A formal talk by a Hindu teacher.

Skhanda – The five aggregates or elements which make up a person. As enumerated in the Heart Sutra, these are: physical form, sensation, thought, impulse (choice), and consciousness.

Seichu – Particularly in the Rinzai-ji School, a three month intensive training period.

Seiza – Traditional manner of sitting on one's heels in Japan.

Sensei – Teacher. In American Zen, usually implying less authority than a Roshi would have.

Sesshin – (The plural of "sesshin" is "sesshin.") A Zen retreat, traditionally seven days long.

Shika – In the Rinzai-ji system, the temple administrator. In other temple systems, the Guest Master.

Shikan Taza – Simple awareness as a meditation practice. In shikan taza, the meditator does not have a particular focus, such as the breath or a koan.

Shingon – A Buddhist sect brought to Japan from China by Kobo Daishi.

Shodo – Calligraphy.

Shoji – In Japanese architecture, a window or door made of translucent paper stretched over a wooden frame.

Shoken – In Boundless Way Zen, taking individual vows with a single teacher.

Shuso – Senior Priest.

Soen Sa Nim – In Korean Zen, a term meaning "Zen Master." In Kwan Um Zen, it generally refers to Seung Sahn.

Soto – The School of Zen descending from Sozan Honjaku and Tozan Ryokai.

Soto-shu – The administrative headquarters of the Soto Zen in Japan.

Stupa – A memorial mound.

Susokkan – Breath meditation.

Sutra – In Buddhism, scriptural writings usually, but not always, attributed to the Buddha.

SZBA – Soto Zen Buddhist Association.

Takuhatsu – Ritual begging.

Tan – A platform in a zendo on which meditators sit.

Tao – see Dao.

Taoism – see Daoism.

Tao Te Ching - see *Daodejing*.

Tara – A female devotional figure and bodhisattva particularly in Tibetan Buddhism. There are several manifestations of Tara associated with specific colors. The "Green Tara," seen as a manifestation of the Bodhisattva of Compassion, is considered the earliest of these. The "Blue Tara" represents the removal of hindrances to awakening.

Tatami – A mat traditionally made of rice straw, twice as long as wide.

Tathagata – A title attributed to the Buddha meaning "The One Who Has Attained."

Teisho – A formal talk given by a Zen teacher.

Ten Ox-herding Pictures – see Ox-herding Pictures.

Tenzo – The temple cook.

Thay – In Vietnamese Zen, "teacher." Usually refers to Thich Nhat Hanh.

Three Characteristics of Existence – Annica (impermanence), dukkha (suffering), anatta (no permanent self).

Three Gems – see Three Refuges

Three Refuges – Buddhists take "refuge" in the Buddha, the Dharma, and the Sangha.

Three Treasures – see Three Refuges.

Toya – A day in Zen temples when discipline is relaxed and rules may be broken with impunity.

Transmission – Formal recognition that an individual has completed their training and may become a teacher.

Unsui – A postulant.

Upaya – Skillful means. The variety of techniques used by a teacher to assist a student to come to awakening.

Vedanta – Hindu philosophy.

Vesak – Anniversary of the Buddha's birth.

Vipassana – Meditation techniques associated with Theravada Buddhism.

Wato – A single word or image taken from a koan and used as a focus in meditation. "Mu" is a wato.

Yong Maeng Jong Jin – Term for "sesshin" in Korean Zen.

Zabuton – The mat on which a meditation cushion (zafu) is placed.

Zafu – "Buddha" (fu) "seat" (za). A meditation cushion.

Zazen – Seated (za) meditation (zen).

Zazenkai – A longer period dedicated to meditation practice, usually lasting one day.

Zen – Literally, "meditation." Zen Buddhism is the meditation school of Buddhism.

Zenji – A teacher of the Dharma.

Zhaozhou Congshen – Ninth century Chan master. His "mu" (cf.) is one of the most commonly assigned initial koan. Once when asked the significance of Chan (Zen), he replied, "The cypress tree in the garden."

Zori – Thonged Japanese sandals.

About the Author

Richard Bryan McDaniel taught at the University of New Brunswick and Saint Thomas University before starting a 27 year career in International Development and Fair Trade. He is the creator of the YMCA Peace Medallion.

A long time Zen practitioner, he is the author of *Zen Masters of China: The First Step East*, *Zen Masters of Japan: The Second Step East* and *The Third Step East: Zen Masters of America*.

He can be reached at rickmcdaniel@bellaliant.net.

CPSIA information can be obtained at www.ICGtesting.com
Printed in the USA
BVOW05s2258041115

425623BV00004B/125/P